DAYDREAMS IN THE WIND

Other Books by Floyd M. Orr

The Tiddler Invasion: *Small Motorcycles of the Sixties* (2013)

Paradigm Shift: The Palin Matrix: *The Progressive Left Strikes Back!* (2011)

Ker-Splash 2: *The High Performance Powerboat Book* (2010)

Timeline of America: *Sound Bytes from the Consumer Culture* (2006)

The Last Horizon: *Feminine Sexuality &The Class System* (2002)

Ker-Splash! *Recreational Power Boaters Guide* (2002)

Plastic Ozone Daydream: *The Corvette Chronicles* (2000)

Also by Floyd M. Orr

"Stangworld" & "Magical Days", featured only in
Mustang Legends: *The Power, the Performance, the Passion*
(Voyageur Press, 2004)

"Vetteworld", reprinted from *Daydream* in
This Old Corvette: *The Ultimate Tribute to America's Sports Car*
(Voyageur Press, 2003)

Daydreams in the Wind

Collectible Open Sports Cars of the Sixties

Floyd M. Orr

NIAFS Press

Nonfiction in a Fictional Style
Austin, Texas

All Rights Reserved. Copyright ©2016 Floyd M. Orr

No part of this book may be reproduced or transmitted in any form or by any means, graphic, electronic, or mechanical, including photocopying, recording, taping or by any information storage or retrieval system, without the permission in writing from the publisher.

Ride of the Vampires ©1989, 1992, 2000, 2016 Floyd M. Orr

Quote from *A Tale of Two Cities*, Charles Dickens, 1859

This book is a work of nonfiction. Any and all facts and figures presented herein are accurate to the best of our knowledge. The publisher and author disclaim responsibility for any misprints, math errors, or other inaccuracies presented. Any and all celebrity, corporate and trademark names are mentioned for identification purposes only. This is not an official publication.

Cover Design by Author.
Digital Photo Processing at Paladin Studio, HSB

Front Cover: 1961 Jaguar XK-E in Opalescent Silver Blue with Dark Blue Interior and Top - ©Greg Gjerdingen from Willmar, USA - (CC)
Back Cover (top): 1961 Mercedes-Benz 190 SL - ©ProfReader - (CC)
Back Cover (bottom): 1965 Corvette Sting Ray 396 at an NCRS event in New Braunfels, TX - ©1986 Floyd M. Orr Collection

Published by NIAFS Press

ISBN-10: 069267974X   ISBN-13: 978-0692679746

Printed in the United States of America

"Is everybody in? The ceremony is about to begin."
Jim Morrison of The Doors, 1970, introducing *The Celebration of the Lizard*

Dedication

This book is dedicated to my wife and muse Miss Pamela, who tolerated me while I read and talked of nothing but cars and car books for four years. This extensive project is a homage to some of the most proficient and dedicated authors and auto journalists of my generation who have been gone for years. May they spend their time in heaven driving their favorite cars.

Figure 1 - 1961 Jaguar E-Type Series I 3.8 Roadster in Red. ©Alf van Beem (PD)

Acknowledgements

I want to thank Danielle Carey, Customer Relationship Center Representative at Jaguar Land Rover North America, LLC, for her help with photos from the Jaguar Media Pages.

Numerous excellent books on the various enthusiast automobiles of our youth have now been out of print for decades. My hope is that this book will provide informative assistance to enthusiasts and collectors for many years to come.

Figure 2 - 1966 Shelby 427 Cobra in Black on Display at Bonhams in Paris. ©2012 The Supermat (CC)

Introduction

Daydreams in the Wind is a book of facts, production figures, specifications, history and nostalgia. Its numerous charts represent its backbone chassis. Its many photos display its nostalgic heart and you can feel its pulse from its extensive bibliography. Its engine has been driven by extensive research and its brain is a labor of love.

Many hobbyist automobile publications produced during the 1960-1990 period have long been out of print. These books represented volumes of data on collector cars. Most dealt with individual brands and some with very specific models. They were written by experts within the marques; some were racers, some were journalists, and some were actual ex-employees of the factories that built our beloved four-wheeled toys. Almost as many of these writers have passed on as have the availabilities of their products. We are left with the Internet, a wild and crazy frontier upon which any gunslinger with a keyboard can spread opinions, misconceptions and misstated *facts* that are endlessly repeated like the echoes in a deep canyon.

The purpose of *Daydreams in the Wind* is to preserve this massive quantity of data before it is blown into the wind of the Internet madness, forever lost to those few who may wish to read the truth and revel in its beauty. The prose is just literary enough to distinguish a flair for nostalgia, separating the extensive data into memorable increments. It is the author's hope that *Daydreams in the Wind* will have a shelf life for generations of convertible sports car enthusiasts to come.

Figure 3 - Ferrari 275 GTS in an elegant metallic blue. With 300 produced, a case could be made for calling this the first mass-produced Ferrari touring spyder. ©Rex Gray, Southern California (CC)

List of Cars Covered

Alfa Romeo Spider, Duetto Spider, 1750 Spider & 2000 Spider
Aston Martin DB Mark III / 5 / 6 / V-8 Volante
Austin-Healey Sprite, 100, 100S, 100M, 100-6, & 3000
Chevrolet Camaro, Corvair & Corvette Convertibles
Datsun 1500, 1600 Sports & 2000 Sports
Dodge Challenger Convertible
Excalibur Series I, II & III
Ferrari 250 Cabriolet, California, 275 GTS & NART, 330 GTS & Daytona Spyder
Ferrari Dino 246 GTS & 308 GTS
Fiat Cabriolet 1200, 1500, 1600, 1500S & 1600S
Fiat 850 Spider, 124 Spider & Dino Spider
Ford Mustang Convertible & Thunderbird Convertible
Intermeccanica Apollo GT, Italia Spyder & Indra Spyder
Jaguar XK 120, XK-140, XK-150 & E-Type
Jensen-Healey
Lotus Elan
Maserati 3500 Spyder, Mistral Spyder & Ghibli Spyder
Mercedes-Benz SL 190, SL 300, SL 230, SL 250 & SL 280
MG Midget, MG A, MG A Twin Cam, MG B & MG C
Monteverdi 375S
Morgan 4/4, Plus 4 & Plus 8
Plymouth Barracuda Convertible
Pontiac Firebird Convertible
Porsche 356, 912 Targa, 911 Targa, 914 & 914/6
Shelby Cobra 260, 289 & 427 and Shelby Mustang Convertible
Sunbeam Alpine & Tiger
Triumph Spitfire, TR Series & Stag
TVR Tuscan & 3000S
Volkswagen Karmann-Ghia Cabriolet

Table of Contents Overview

Front Matter: iii

Chapter 1: Timelines, Acquisition and Ownership   1
Chapter 2: The Big Three Affordable English Antiques   43
Chapter 3: English Aberrations, Eccentricity, and Elegance   109
Chapter 4: German Engineering Comes to America   179
Chapter 5: Affordable Italian Brio from Fiat & Alfa Romeo   223
Chapter 6: Topless Italian Exotics   249
Chapter 7: Flirtations with Comfort and Convenience   289
Chapter 8: Hybrid Hotrods - The Essence of Speed & Style   319
Chapter 9: The Early Pony Convertibles   359
Chapter 10: Corvettes Take Us to 1990   411

Appendix: 483

Figure 4 - This 1962 Corvette in Sateen Silver with a white top and red interior is on display at an NCRS event in San Diego. Cars that compete in events sponsored by the National Corvette Restorer's Society have to meet the highest standards of authenticity. Note the correct narrow-band whitewall tires, spinner wheel covers, painted headlamp rims, mesh grille, and body-colored side cove. The 1962 models received the new 327 V-8 with a minimum of 250 gross horsepower. ©2012 Kowtoonese (CC)

Table of Contents

Front Matter:
Dedication   iii
Acknowledgements   iv
Introduction   v
List of Cars Covered   vi
Contents Overview   vii

***Chapter 1:* Timelines, Acquisition and Ownership**   1
    From a '50 Chevy to the Trans Am That Got Away   2
    Introducing the Daydreams: Who Made the Cut and Who Didn't?   15
    Collectible Open Sports Cars of the Sixties Chart   21
    Timeline of Sports Car Features and Details   22
    Timeline of Model Year Introductions   23
    Pop the Top: The Cool, the Acceptable, and the Infuriating   23
    Engines: From Peddling Hamsters to Roaring Lions   35
    Wheels: Rolling Through Transitions of Wheels, Tires & Steering Wheels   36

***Chapter 2:* The Big Three Affordable English Antiques**   43
    Ubiquity Squared: MG B to Triumph Spitfire   44
    Spridget / Spitfire Timeline   50
    Austin-Healey Sprite   51
    Austin-Healey Sprite Production Chart   54
    Austin-Healey Sprite Color Chart   56
    The Big Healeys   58
    Big Healey Comparison Chart   63
    Big Austin-Healey Color Chart   64
    Big Austin-Healey Production Chart   66
    MG - Octagonian Dominance   67
    MG B Roadster Model Year Timeline   72
    MG B Roadster Production by Model Year Chart   73
    MG Midget Mark I, II & III Color Chart   74
    MG Midget Mark IV & 1500 Color Chart   75
    MG Midget Production Chart   77
    Sprite / Midget / Spitfire Chart   78
    MG A / B / C Production Chart   82
    MG B Mark I Color Chart   83
    MG B Mark II Exterior Color Chart   84
    MG B Mark III Exterior Color Chart   85
    MG C Color Chart   85
    MG A / B / C Chart   86
    Looking Through British Racing Green Granny Glasses   88
    Triumph Spitfire Production Chart   94
    Triumph Spitfire Color Chart   94

  Triumph TR-3A Color Chart 95
  Triumph TR-4A & TR-250 Color Chart 97
  Triumph TR-6 Color Chart 97
  Triumph TR Production Chart 98
  Triumph TR Comparison Chart 99
  Conveniences Added to Austin-Healey, MG, & Triumph Sports Cars 100
  Six-Cylinder Shootout 101
  A-H 3000 / TR-250 / MG C Comparison Chart 104
  Classic English Sports Car Test Results Chart 105
  Selected Affordable English Antiques Ratings Chart 106

Chapter 3: English Aberrations, Eccentricity, and Elegance 109
  Triumph Stag 110
  The Legendary Morgan Eccentricity 114
  Morgan Production Chart 117
  Jensen-Healey 119
  Jensen-Healey Color Chart 124
  Breaking the Rules: TVR Tuscan & 3000S 125
  Tuscan / 3000S Production Chart 130
  Eccentric English Sports Car Comparison Chart 132
  The Classic Lotus Elan Convertible 133
  Lotus Elan Color Chart 140
  Lotus Elan Comparison Chart 142
  1968 Sprite / 1968 850 Spider / 1968 Elan / 1990 Miata Comparison Chart 143
  A Different Breed of Cat 144
  Jaguar XK-120 / XK-140 / XK-150 Chart 157
  Jaguar XK Roadster / Convertible Production Breakdown Chart 158
  Jaguar XK-E Color Chart 160
  Jaguar XK-E Convertible Chart 161
  Jaguar Comparison Chart 162
  Aston Martin 163
  Aston Martin Engine Chart 170
  Aston Martin Production Chart 172
  Aston Martin Comparison Chart 174
  Elegant English Sports Car Test Results Chart 176
  Selected Elegant English Ratings Chart 177

Chapter 4: German Engineering Comes to America 179
  Volkswagen Karmann-Ghia Cabriolet 180
  Karmann-Ghia Cabriolet Production Chart 182
  Karmann-Ghia Cabriolet Chart 184
  Porsche 356 Cabriolet 185
  Porsche 356 Cabriolet Production Chart 188
  Porsche 911 & 912 Targa 190
  1967-75 Porsche 911 & 912 Targa Engine Chart 196
  Porsche Targa 911 & 912 Production Chart 197

Porsche 914   199
Porsche 914 Production by Model Year Chart   203
Porsche 914 Production by Calendar Year & Engine Chart   204
Porsche Performance Chart   204
Porsche Targa Comparison Chart   207
Mercedes-Benz SL Series Roadsters: 190, 300, 230, 250 & 280   209
Mercedes-Benz SL Comparison Chart   216
Mercedes-Benz SL Roadster Production Chart   219
Selected German Sports Car Ratings Chart   220

Chapter 5: **Affordable Italian Brio from Fiat & Alfa Romeo**   223
Fiat Cabriolets   224
Fiat Cabriolet Chart   225
Fiat 850 Spider   226
Fiat 850 Spider Chart   232
Fiat 124 Sport Spider   232
Fiat Spider Production Chart   235
Alfa Romeo Spiders   236
Alfa Romeo Spider Series Chart   243
Alfa Romeo Spider Series Production Chart   244
Fiat / Alfa Spider Comparison Chart   245
Affordable Italian Sports Car Test Results Chart   247
Selected Affordable Italian Ratings Chart   248

Chapter 6: **Topless Italian Exotics**   249
Fiat Dino Spider 2.0 & 2.4   250
Fiat Dino Spider Color Chart   254
Ferrari Dino 246 GTS   254
Ferrari 308 GTS   258
Ferrari V-12 Cabriolets & Spyders   261
NART Spyder Chart   269
Ferrari V-12 Cabriolet & Spyder Comparison Chart   272
Ferrari V-12 Cabriolet & Spyder Production Chart   273
Classic Ferrari Tests Chart   275
Maserati Spyders   277
Maserati Spyders Chart   283
Ferrari / Maserati Spyders Comparison Chart   284
Elegant Italian Sports Car Test Results Chart   285
Selected Exotic Italian Ratings Chart   286

Chapter 7: **Flirtations with Comfort and Convenience**   289
Sunbeam Alpine   290
Sunbeam Alpine Comparison Chart   294
The Land of the Rising Sun   295
Datsun Sports Chart   300
Chevrolet Corvair Convertible   301

Corvair Convertible Production Chart   306
Corvair Convertible Engine Chart   306
Alpine / Datsun Sports / Corvair Comparison Chart   307
The T-bird Phenomenon   308
Thunderbird Convertible Specifications Chart   315
Classic Ford Thunderbird Convertible Production Chart   316
Selected Comfortable Sports Car Ratings Chart   317

Chapter 8: **Hybrid Hotrods - The Essence of Speed & Style**   319
Sunbeam Tiger, Shelby's Stepchild   320
Sunbeam Tiger Color Chart   323
Sunbeam Tiger Production Chart   323
Snake Charmer   324
Shelby Cobra Specifications Chart   328
Shelby Mustang Convertible   330
1966 Shelby Mustang Convertible Chart   335
Shelby Mustang Engine Chart   336
The Confusing Street Shelby Mustang Production Chart   337
Shelby Comparison Chart   339
Shelby's Snakes Performance Chart   340
The Intermeccanica Connection   341
Monteverdi 375 Spyder   347
Excalibur Series I, II & III   349
Excalibur Production Chart   354
Excalibur Series I-II-III Chart   355
Selected Hybrid Hotrods Ratings Chart   357

Chapter 9: **The Early Pony Convertibles**   359
Ride the Ponies   360
Pony Car Convertible Production Chart   363
1964 - 1973 Mustang Convertible   365
Mustang Convertible Production Chart   368
Sixties Mustang Base Convertible Chart   374
Sixties Mustang Sports Convertible Chart   375
1967 - 1969 Camaro Convertible   377
Camaro Convertible Production Chart   382
Sixties Camaro Base Convertible Chart   383
Sixties Camaro Super Sports Convertible Chart   384
1967 - 1969 Firebird Convertible   385
Firebird Options Production Chart   390
Sixties Firebird Base Convertible Chart   391
Sixties Firebird Sports Convertible Chart   392
1967 - 1971 Barracuda Convertible   393
Barracuda Base Convertible Chart   398
1970 - 1971 Challenger Convertible   399
Barracuda & Challenger Convertible Production Chart   402

Challenger Base Convertible Chart   403
Sixties Chrysler Pony Car Sports Convertible Chart   404
Pony Car Features Introduction Year Chart   405
Pony Car Performance Coupe & Convertible Production Chart   406
Mustang Test Results Chart   407
Other Pony Car Test Results Chart   408
Selected Early Pony Convertibles Ratings Chart   409

Chapter 10: **Corvettes Take Us to 1990**   411
Rose Colored Goggles from the Mists of Time   412
Corvette Generation Quick Chart   416
Impressions of America's Sports Car   417
Production by Model Year, Body Style and Series Chart   432
Corvette Convertible Production Chart   433
First Standards & Options   435
C1 Corvette Engine Chart   436
C1 Corvette Performance Chart   438
C2 Corvette Engine Chart   440
C2 Corvette Performance Chart   441
The Coveted Sting Rays and Exciting Stingrays   443
C3 Corvette Engine Chart   453
Ride of the Vampires   455
C3 Corvette Performance Chart   463
Bargains of the Current Era   467
Yuppies in the Wind Tunnel   472
C4 Corvette Engine Chart   476
C4 Corvette Performance Chart   477
Selected 1953-90 Corvette Ratings Chart   480
The Future May be Ludicrous and Ridiculous.. but It Still Might be Fun!   481

APPENDIX   483

Glossary   483
Bibliography   487
Internet Bibliography   503
Photo Credits   506
Photo Index   515
Chart Index   517
About the Author   519

Chapter 1: *Timelines, Acquisition & Ownership*

Figure A1 - The elegant simplicity of the interior design of this 1963 Jaguar XK-E Series I 3.8 is clearly displayed. This red E-Type has a tan leather interior and a similarly toned vinyl top boot that does not quite match in shade. You can see the thin seatbacks and aluminum trim on the console and center dash panel. The pointy, old-fashioned toggle switchgear is aligned below the minor instruments. Just below, a metal E-Type emblem is attached to the console panel where an optional radio could be installed. ©Emmanuel Didier (PD)

This chapter will give you a basic feel for the author's personal history and perspective. You will drive through a circuitous maze of unexpected trails that meander through the past and take roads that abruptly reach dead ends. The most difficult bridge you will have to cross is to accept the fact that the normal rules followed by most enthusiast car books have been stretched into a new shape. All fixed roof models have been banished, regardless of their affinity with topless models described herein. Far too many of the previously available books on the subject have been European. The first thing this book does is offer as American an approach as possible. The USA was in a special place between 1950 and 1975, particularly with regard to cars. In the beginning, the world needed a few years to recover from World War II. By the end of this stated period, U.S. safety and emissions regulations had all but strangled the life out of sports cars sold in the USA. This is the story of those many fruitful years between, when exciting driving experiences proliferated. These are the cars of our daydreams.

From a '50 Chevy to the Trans Am That Got Away

Figure A2 - 1950 Chevrolet Deluxe 2-Dr. Sedan. My dad bought it in 1960 for $100. He gave it to me as my first car in 1965. My 1950 Chevy had the Thrift-Master Six of 216 c.i. with 92 hp and a 4.11 axle. The top speed was approximately 100 mph. A new option for 1950 was the Blue Flame 235-inch engine with 105 horsepower paired with a two-speed automatic called the Powerflite Automatic and a 3.55 axle. I changed its original black to bright blue and "updated" the interior with black vinyl door panels, walnut contact paper on the dash, a genuine walnut steering wheel from J.C. Whitney, bright blue carpet, and black buckets from a GTO. The car remained in the family through a total of <u>three</u> rebuilt engines and a zillion miles. *The Bomb*, as my cousin named it, was finally sold for $200 in Austin, Texas, in 1979. ©1974 Floyd M. Orr Collection

You don't have to have muscles to drive things, so I became fascinated with motorized transportation so early in life that I cannot even remember the origin. When the Sears catalog arrived, I eagerly snatched it up to check out the ubiquitous Allstate motorcycles, scooters, and mopeds, immediately after a look at the latest bras and panties, of course. This was a time before everything. There were no Honda 50's yet, and the Puch Twingles were a lot more serious looking than the Cushman Eagle and Highlander. This was that narrow era between the Whizzer and Simplex motorbikes and the Japanese Tiddler Invasion that would arrive just a few years later. This was a rosy fantasy period when the red and cream $159.95 Allstate Moped was the entry-level ride that every pedal-pushing twelve-year-old lusted after. We also lusted after Marilyn and Bridgitte, but that's another story.

    The earliest images of four-wheelers I have are of my parents' drab beige '49 Chevy fastback and the two-tone green '53 Buick that replaced it. Soon thereafter I could identify any car by its tail lights, and my favorite became those of the legendary 1959 Cadillac. Within another five years my fascination would turn to Corvettes, Porsches, Lotus Elans, and Austin-Healeys, not to ignore Mustangs and Firebirds. *Daydreams in the Wind* is a book about a love affair with cars. The appeal should be to anyone of the Baby Boomer Generation who has grown up fascinated with cars. Although the legends of the distant past may be mentioned in the book, the details are strongly focused on the legends of more recent history. The premise is that America reached a wonderful peak within the development of its own culture in the year 1970. The availability of exciting cars that were actually affordable to the masses was at its zenith in 1969. After that time, it was mostly a downhill ride into a brave new world of safety modifications and emission controls.

Figure A3 - This white 1957 Oldsmobile Super 88 Sedan is very similar to the one in which I learned to drive. Our family car at the time was a white Super 88 Holiday Sedan. That was Olds lingo for what we usually refer to as a Four-Door Hardtop. According to the brochure, Olds called the interior fabric Airweave Trilok and leather. Ours had a red, black, and white combination that could only have been designed in the Fifties. The T-400 V-8 produced 277 gross horsepower and 400 pounds of torque from 371 cubic inches through a Jetaway Hydra-Matic three-speed automatic transmission. ©John Lloyd, Concrete, WA (CC)

My fascination with large American cars with large V-8 engines, loads of chrome, and of course, fins up the wazoo, would continue unabated until one fine spring evening in 1962. My best friend was a member in good standing of a traditional Pontiac family. His dad drove a Star Chief to work. I think it was a dark blue 1959 model. The Star Chief was the series with middle-grade trim between the Bonneville and Catalina. They stopped making them many years ago, although the other two series continued for some time. His mom drove some Pontiac sedan that I cannot recall. After all, this was more than fifty years ago, so don't go claiming I have

Alzheimer's or something! Anyway, his mom surprised us all by trading in her sedan for a 1962 Bonneville Convertible! It was a lovely sky blue with white top and an interior design I shall never forget. The bench seats were soft, leather-like vinyl in a blue/white/silver pattern. Surprisingly, I cannot tell you if that car had a 389 or 421 or what the gross horsepower rating was, but it probably had a four-barrel carburetor and air conditioning. My friend took me for a leisurely nighttime cruise around town in that convertible, inadvertently creating a special nostalgic moment in my life.

Although I would like to describe for you how the wind blew my hair into my face, like all classic convertibles did back then before sophisticated wind management was invented, but I'm afraid I cannot. You see, back then I had what was called a *flattop*. The hair on my head was hardly over an inch long. If you have read my previous book, insert plug here for *The Tiddler Invasion*, you know that by 1971 my blond hair would slop over my shoulders. That was the style in 1962 and that was the style in 1971. Blame The Beatles if you want, but that's what transpired back in those special days of The Sixties. We went from a culture of surf music by The Surfaris in 1963 to Mark Farmer of Grand Funk Railroad dressing like a blond Indian with shoulder length hair in 1970.

That '62 Bonnie floated over the smooth roads of the good old days. Looking up above from the passenger's seat into that starlit sky punctuated with street lamps ruined me forever. I mean *forever*! I would never again lust after a coupe or sedan, no matter how much exterior chrome or gross horsepower it had. I am a nature kind of guy. I like the suburbs. With the exception of the inherent narrow mindedness, I adore small towns. I particularly like small towns just outside the realm of suburbia, which is where I live now. I love the exurbs. I love resort towns. I love Cabot Cove, but that's another story. That big Bonnie floated over the smooth streets of that sleepy Delta town. The Southern air was warm on that spring evening, commingling the low sounds of the night with the breeze of the topless car. To this day, I savor the convertible experience more at night than in the day, particularly when the summer sun is bearing down from above and driving the eyes into a squint. The experience is similar to that of a quiet house in the country. It is a visceral and emotional experience of the head and the heart. Life does not get any better.

This was not the end of the story. My friend's mom traded in her '62 for a black 1965 with white interior and top. Even if the 1962 model described had a 389, this one had a 421. Both cars had a three-speed automatic, power steering, power brakes, air conditioning, whitewall tires, and soft vinyl bench seats. Although the classy but complex multi-toned interior had been replaced by a simpler version of all white with black carpet and other components, there was still a distinct aura of luxury. The monaural AM radio in both cars had rear speakers and the *reverb* option. The rear speaker was set into the rear seat at the top center position. (Remember, there is no rear deck or parcel shelf in a conventional American convertible.) You could turn a knob to set the preferred level of reverberation delay. As you maximized the reverb effect, it sounded like an overzealous deejay introducing an early Sixties rock act in a huge auditorium. My pal's mom had basically purchased this car so that he could take it to college while it was still quite new, so the small town cruises continued well into the Sixties.

Flashing ahead a few decades, I now cruise the lake in a Bayliner Capri bowrider from 1989. Although my wife and I have discussed either selling or trading in this boat countless times over the years, one emotional issue always drives me to change the subject. This boat has an elegant interior of soft, leather-like vinyl that has been exquisitely designed using multiple colors. The boat's hull is blue and white, as many Bayliner Capris still are today, but the interior is trimmed in navy, royal blue, sky blue, and light gray with red piping. More modern Capris have bland interiors of light gray or tan with a navy carpet for contrast. How blah can you get? (Stay tuned for an unexpected commercial. Check out my book, *Ker-Splash 2: High Performance Power Boats* for a read in the same style as this one, except the only wheels are on the trailers.) The convoluted point to this story is that I am *still* obsessed with elegant interior design in multiple shades of color. Hint: I think the 1982 Collector Edition Corvette is *gorgeous*, and quite desirable as a current collectible, to boot.

I have another color obsession, too, dark exterior colors with white interiors and matching white tops. If a white interior and/or top is not offered on a particular car, my favorite choice is *always* a matching black top and interior. In a few rare cases, I like a black exterior with tan interior and top. For the record, the most common color combination for Ferraris, red exterior with tan interior and top, makes be barf! So you see, as you read through this book you will stumble over one clue after another that I am a certified nut, but in a good way, just like you. When it comes to convertibles, it was the first two I had intimate contact with that warped me forever. So much for the color department....

Figure A4 - This happens to be the most appropriate photo I could locate to accompany this part of the story. This 1965 Bonneville Convertible is white with a solid blue vinyl interior and white top and boot. You can probably assume that its engine is the venerable 421 with a four barrel and three speed automatic. The likelihood that it also *reverberates* is less so. I wouldn't throw this one out of my garage, but I would still prefer a darker exterior with a white interior to match the top. ©Sicnag (CC)

As the Monty Python boys would say, "and now for something completely different". Wait a minute. Something must have happened soon after 1965 to drive me away from the two-ton Bonneville land yachts, and that *something* will certainly surprise you. Hold onto your big T-bone steak and potatoes because the tea and crumpets are coming! Before that fateful year was out, my family had moved into a new location only a half mile away on the other side of campus, where I would begin riding to school with a new associate who drove a car I had never before heard of or seen. It was a ratty old Morris Minor Convertible, of all things! It was either

Timelines, Acquisistion & Ownership

dull, ugly grey or dull ugly tan, I don't even remember which it was. The well-worn interior was red leather and the window frames remained fixed when the top was down, like my later heartthrob, the Lotus Elan S/E. The ugly grey/tan canvas top folded back in a stack like its nemesis, the VW Beetle Cabriolet. The most distinguishing thing about my new neighborhood was its steep hills and sharp curves, most of which were combined into a series of slaps of a two-ton Bonnie's grille. The little Morris took to those hills and curves like Donald Duck on acid! The suspension was compliant, the seats were plush, the comfort factor was high, but the g-forces were a new experience! My new addiction soon led to similar experiences with a Beetle Cabriolet or two, and you can guess where the story went from there. Is it any mystery now why my lust factor for topless sports cars soon began to rival that of my *Playboy* collection?

Figure A5 - This Morris Minor 1000 Cabriolet is cream with a bright red interior. Although this is a right hand drive model, I chose this photograph because the color is so similar to the car in the story. This is a slightly newer model with aluminum window frames. The car I had a close encounter with had body-colored painted steel frames. Yes, Martha, the 1000 stands for the engine displacement and that does not mean it is more than twice that of a Pontiac 421, either! ©Brian Snelson, Hockley, Essex, England (CC)

I would not know a 1953-55 Corvette from memory if it ran over my foot because they were produced before my time in sports cars. I was a maniac for Cadillacs and Packards back in those days, but what did I know? I was only seven, but you can bet your booties that those of a slightly older ilk can react to their memories of 1955 the way I can remember Todd and Buzz driving their black-and-white Corvette into my living room a few years later. For a measly $3817 in 1958 you could buy a Corvette "fully equipped" (as salesmen like to say) with Powerslide, Parking Brake Alarm, Windshield Washer, and the Snowcrest White painted cove. With this hot option package and enough chrome to sink a Buick, the color of preference just had to be Regal Turquoise! Although the '58 is arguably the tackiest of all Corvettes in its exterior Buick imitation, 1970 offered the tackiest color combo with the Daytona Yellow exterior, white soft-top and green interior. Any eyewitnesses to this abomination raise your hands! I'll go get the Pepto-Bismal.

Picture this: I have only about $5000 in my pocket when I approach the order form, but in 1965 this is enough. Beginning with the Convertible at $4106, I add $130 worth of 115 hp, side pipes for $135, 4-speed $188, a genuine Teakwood steering wheel for a silly $48, power brakes and steering $140, $43 for the Positraction and $16 for the tinted glass. Hey, Vern, I got $194 change here: wanna fill her up for me, and clean my tinted windshield, too, please. They were called *service* stations back in '65, remember? Hold the tacky in this fantasy, Vern. This little baby is Nassau Blue with white top and interior. It's too bad that $5000 might as well have been five million dollars to a high school kid in 1965.

Figure A6 - This Roman Red 1959 Corvette closely matches my nostalgic mental image from the TV show, *Route 66*. Technically, the first car owned by Todd was a 1960 model that looked very much like this car, only a model year newer. Todd and Buzz visited a crazy little Mississippi town in their first adventure in our living rooms on October 7, 1960. ©Lebubu 93 (CC)

I have been fascinated with car interiors as long as I can remember. Why not concern yourself with the inner beauty that surrounds you every time you drive a car? There has always been a fascination for the shapes and colors of exterior steel, aluminum, and fiberglass, but whenever you are behind the wheel, the only thing in your line of sight is the hood line.

There have been many exquisite interior designs over the years, but a certain clever few from The Sixties stand out. The '64-'66 T-bird's rounded rear seat with its barroom-corner styling was distinctive. Although the 1965 Sting Ray had sumptuously broad panels in its seating surfaces, the '66 model returned to more traditional pleats because the wide panels tore their seams too easily. Entering through a door that curved into the roofline furthered the elegance of what may have been the most visually perfect interior in an American car. The 1967 Austin-Healey 3000 featured an unforgettable Olde English look of wood and leather in a tiny four-seat format. Of course the inside of an XK-E presented the same flavor in a larger, more upscale style with a lot more panache.

Figure A7 - This red Jaguar XK-E 4.2-liter Series 2 Roadster carries its red exterior color onto the face of its dashboard. The wood steering wheel has five holes in the spokes. The Series 3 V-12 model has a leather-covered steering wheel with only four holes. This car has red piping around the seats and console that may not be factory original. The instruments have chrome trim rings. Later models have black rings. I have not been able to positively verify this, but this example is likely a 1968 or '69 model. The 1970 models had the black trim rings. ©Dawid 783 (GNU)

The Interior Decor Group was an option on late-1965 and all 1966 Mustangs. The incredibly low price of about $100 bought you a lot of classy trim, and over 100,000 Mustangs of these two years were built with this option package. Popularly called the *Pony Interior* due to the embossed running ponies on the front surfaces of the seatbacks, the IDG was offered in a large selection of single and two-tone colors. The light blue and white combination has always been my personal favorite. A measly $107 bought you the gauge cluster from the GT, a fake-wood steering wheel with matching trim on the dash, a more elegant upholstery pattern, chrome pedal trim, and fancier door panels with integral armrests if your Mustang was built after February 1965. The '66 version of all Mustangs got the GT's instrument panel, so the Pony Interior cost only $94 throughout that whole production year. The Decor Group did not include the console in the option price, but if you ordered the console, too, it featured additional plastic wood trim to match the dash and steering wheel. As you might imagine, the rarest and most delectable combination is a convertible with the console, air conditioning, and a manual four-speed!

Figure A8 - The '65-66 Mustang's Interior Decor Group option has become known as the Pony Interior. The embossed Mustangs stampede across the upper front side of the seatbacks. Although the package was available in many colors, solid or two-tone, this silver blue and white combination has always been my favorite. You can see that the white vinyl boot never presented smooth lines over the recessed top. At least the top was covered and the boot color-coordinated. ©Herr Anders Svensson (GNU)

The Mustang Pony Interior was special because it brought such a high level of pseudo-elegance to the masses. With the exception of the Thunderbird, the 109,693 built dwarfed the production numbers of the other notable interiors mentioned. Have you seen the option price of leather seating surfaces on the front-buckets-only for a modern Mustang? The phrase *choke a horse* might come to mind. Pony interiors were offered in twelve color combinations in '65 and thirteen in '66. *Bland* is the buzzword for modern Mustang interior grays and tans. A few models feature slap-you-awake red, but the natural elegance of blue and white with wood accents is long gone.

Back in the middle 1960's, I often dreamed of buying my first new car, an Austin-Healey Sprite Mk. IV. I was especially fond of models with black interior and matching top and the optional wire wheels. Its simplicity and affordability were qualities I highly admired back then, and I still do. The main thing that has always kept one of these little squirts from moving into my garage is their legendary ornery British behavior and unreliability. Although I love the simplicity, the top design could have been slicker. The exact reason that the Mark IV model started my motor was because the Sprite *finally* received a proper convertible top that was actually attached to the car body and folded down underneath a vinyl boot! The Mk. III had received genuine roll-up windows, but the attached top did not arrive until the Mk. IV.

Figure A9 - This red 1968 Sprite MK. IV is a facsimile of my youthful lust. The 1968 model year is identified by its side marker lamps and lack of headrests. You can see how the attached black top is neatly stored beneath the boot. The antenna suggests that this car had an optional radio. The only thing it needs to push my buttons are wire wheels and a coat of British Racing Green paint. ©MiataSprite (GNU)

One morning in the early summer of 1968, I was literally on my way to the local Austin-Healey dealer in Memphis to pick out a new '68 Sprite Mk. IV that could have been blue or white, but my heart was set on a British Racing Green version. On the way to the dealership, I stopped by the Fiat dealership for one more look at the 850 Spider. I never made it to the Sprite Department and I have never regretted my decision. A top that snaps down under a vinyl boot is one thing, but a top that drops under a body-colored panel like a Sting Ray or Mercedes SL is quite another! The dealer didn't have any British Racing Green Spiders in stock, but since the little 817cc, rear-engine sports car was neither British nor a racer, white worked out just fine. The dealer had one with mag wheels, but since it was red, I settled for the standard steel ones.

Back in the good old days of 1966-68, when I was drooling in my shorts to acquire a new sports car, the Triumph TR series was one of my favorites within the $3500-$4000 range. Yes, we are talking about *new* car prices here, Maybelle. In those wonderful, heady days, $2000-2500 would buy you a Fiat 850 Spider, an Austin-Healey Sprite, or an MG Midget. Easing up the price scale, you approached the Triumph Spitfire, the Sunbeam Alpine, and the MG-B. The TR-250 was priced almost exactly at the same level as a Fiat 124 Spider, about $3750. Although still below the $4000+ of Sting Rays, this seemingly humble price put the TR-250 solidly in competition with a plethora of more powerful, luxurious, and of course more reliable, machines from the American pony stables.

Figure A10 - 1968 Triumph TR-250 in British Racing Green. The reflective silver tape attached to the edges of the black top was a real eyesore in the daytime. ©Mr. Choppers (GNU)

The TR-250 was a model Triumph built for only one year. The 1967 TR-4A had the old four-cylinder engine combined with the new independent rear suspension. The 1969 TR-6 featured the new for '68, 2.5-litre, six-cylinder engine surrounded by a new, sleeker body. The 1968 TR-250 was a transition model with the new six installed in the old body. All the TR's would sport an independent rear suspension from '68 onward. You can always identify a TR-250 by its unusual racing stripe across its nose. Although this model was sold in England as the TR-5, for some strange reason, the company decided to put this stripe over the nose of all the TR-5's sent to the U.S., its strongest market, and call them TR-250's.

I really wanted one of these when they were new in 1968. About the only reason I never bought one was that I didn't have $3750. There was another reason, but I didn't fully understand its power until much later, when I was considerably more mature. That reason is the legendary unreliability of the British sports cars of The Sixties. I could have been a lot happier in the long run with a nice Mustang or Firebird. Maybe I would have realized this back then, at the last minute before signing on the dotted line, but I'll never know. What I do know is that when I could only afford a sports car in the $2000 price range, I did choose a Fiat 850 Spider instead of an Austin-Healey Sprite. I actually did this on the day I had planned to sign on the dotted line for a British Racing Green Sprite. The more I learned why Lucas electrics were called the Prince of Darkness, the happier I became with my little Fiat. These little low-priced Italians proved to have a few foibles of their own and not last very well, but at least when they were relatively fresh and maintained, they were far less likely to make you cuss on a dark road in the middle of the night on a regular basis.

In the summer of 1977, I was in the market for my first new car since '68. I was driving what I called *The Inconspicuous Mobile* at the time, a 1969 Impala four-door sedan with a 350 and Turbo-Hydramatic. It was light brown with a white top and an equally bland fawn interior. When it needed a $600 AC repair, I decided I needed something closer to my roots. My roots vary quite widely in some circles, from high economy to high performance. All that I ask of any car is that it have somewhat clean, timeless styling and drive with the precision of quality engineering in the handling and interior ergonomics departments.

A friend of mine who was the son of a Pontiac dealer had a new Trans Am in 1970 when they came in only one color, white with blue stripes, so I was very familiar with the breed. I remember going with my mom to a Pontiac dealer and seeing a T/A 6.6 in brown on the showroom floor. Mom commented that she could certainly envision me in that car! I replied that I could, too, except mine would be white inside and out with the Special Equipment package and a four-speed manual transmission. Of course it would have the T-top and *Screaming Chicken* options, just like the brown one in the showroom.

There are three main drawbacks to any T/A of this vintage, particularly one with the SE package and Screaming Chicken decal on the hood. (1) You must wear gold chains around your neck with your shirt unbuttoned when you frequent the local disco. (2) You cannot carry squat on a long trip. (3) The CEO of Exxon will love you! If you can make it over these three hurdles, it's all downhill from there. The T/A looks, drives and acts like a car should, and the price is reasonable. Since I have never been one to give a rat's ass what other people think, #1 didn't bother me much, but #2 and #3 did. Both my mom and sister drove new Toyota Celicas. I bought a 1977 Toyota Corolla Liftback SR-5 instead. It had a *five-speed* transmission, styled steel wheels, stiff suspension, a good interior design, and it carried lots of stuff in its pseudo-station wagon motif. The problem was that it got 27 mpg at its very best on the highway and 17 mpg around town was downright common! This meager result from only 75 horsepower haunted me every day I owned that car!

Figure A11 - The only options on this 1977 Toyota Corolla SR-5 Liftback were the chrome roof rack with fake wood trim and the rear windshield wiper, neither of which were ever utilized, although they added an air of elegance. The best attribute of this model was its long list of standard sports car features. These included styled steel wheels, anti-roll bar, full instrumentation, console, and as the name denotes, a five-speed floor shift. The downside was that this rear wheel drive model was not particularly efficient with fuel, even though its 75 net horsepower always felt as if mice were frantically peddling in the engine bay. ©1977 Floyd M. Orr Collection

Little did I know in the summer of 1977 that less than one year later I would land a traveling job that would provide me with an included new lease car for each of the next twelve years. It wasn't long before I realized that I had nothing to lose by thumbing my nose at both Exxon and luggage capacity in my personal car. I sold the SR-5 with low mileage in 1980 to an old friend and I bought Max, named after Mad Max, but later referred to as simply *Baby*. She was a 1970 454 four-speed Stingray that inspired the publication of *Plastic Ozone Daydream*, my first book. I owned this beautiful beast for eighteen years. You see, the traveling job did not allow for the development of many long-term relationships. I wanted the old Corvette as much for the companionship of a local Corvette Club as anything else, and Max/Baby did a fine job of delivering on that promise. Baby could get 17 mpg on the highway, and that was quite good enough when she was only a secondary vehicle of transportation.

The 1970 Stingray had a removable rear window, chrome bumpers, high-compression engine, and a Kamm tail, all things I valued highly at the time. The 1977 Corvette was quite a turkey with its plastic-coated, sloped rear bumper, fixed glass rear window, and low-performance, small-block engine. I was actually unaware at the time how much I would later appreciate the 1980 Corvette, another one of my favorite model years, but that's another story, as told in *Plastic Ozone Daydream*. The '77 T/A 6.6, on the other hand, was the last of a proud breed. It already had the fastback rear with more luggage space in both the rear seat and trunk. The T-tops were a popular option, and the 400-cubic-inch engine was still available. I even liked the wheels and color choices better on the T/A than the Corvette in 1977, not to mention that it was $2000 cheaper.

I left out a detail just to build the suspense. Surprisingly, the Corvette club in Dallas has never been a national powerhouse, but the ones in Fort Worth and Austin were two of the largest and strongest in the country, and I assume they still are today. I was getting a little weary of the sheer massive size of The Metroplex, and due to the job and old friends in Austin, I was actually spending more time there than in my own city of Dallas! I moved to Austin in early 1980 and bought Max and joined the club before the year was out. Twenty years later I would re-publish all my stories from the Corvette Club Newsletter in an edited book format. I would do this from my home in Austin that I shared with the wonderful native Austinite I married in 1997. She finally got me interested in computers after I had avoided them like the plague for decades. We are now retired and live happily and quietly out in the Texas Hill Country in a house I designed on my computer, and this is my eighth book. None of this would have happened if I had simply bought a white 1977 T/A 6.6.

I have generally always been a Chevy man, but the company lost a lot of my respect throughout the '90's. I still drive my '90 Z24 as a routine set of wheels. It only has 100,000 miles on it, and it was the last version of the Cavalier built in Ohio, where anything named Cavalier or Z24 ought to be built. Our entertaining car for special occasions is a 2000 Mustang Convertible with only 7000 miles on it. Let's put the top down and go for a cruise!

Introducing the Daydreams: Who Made the Cut and Who Didn't?

Figure A12 - This example of a first series Mazda Miata is too new to be included within the parameters of this book. Although Corvettes and Aston Martins up through 1990 have been included, those models represent a direct continuation of earlier models. The MX-5 Miata was an all-new model for 1990. The Austin-Healey Sprite Mark IV is most certainly one of the stars of this book. Production for the U.S. halted after the 1969 model year. This example is a 1967 or '68 model without the headrests mandated for 1969. The attached top is folded neatly underneath its boot. Both cars are red with black interior and top. ©MiataSprite (GNU)

The Open Cars Rule: Repeat after me: *Americans love their open cars*. Convertibles, phaetons, roadsters, spyders, Targas, T-tops are *always* the most desirable as sports cars, particularly as nostalgic, *collectible* cars. Like automatic transmissions, fixed roofs are good for nothing outside the realm of utilitarian transportation. This is a book about *fun cars*, cars to enjoy driving, cars to be seen in, cars to light the fires of your imagination. The first thing we are going to do is to eliminate cars with fixed roofs. I don't care how exciting, beautiful or collectible they are: Ferrari GTO's, Lamborghini Countaches, Sting Ray Split-window Coupes, Mercedes Gullwings, and Ford GT-40's have been covered in many other books. This is a book for the enthusiast who wants the wind in his hair, regardless of how it gets there.

The Parameters: All included models must be topless versions of sports or sporty cars designed, built, and/or sold primarily in the U.S. market in the 1960's. The principal model year period covered is 1955 through 1975, allowing for sort of a power up and cool down period around the actual '60's. Many models began their development as early as 1948, but few were fully in production and exported to the USA before 1955. We are all familiar with how devastating the 1970's were for most cars due to new emission and safety rules, making the post-1975 models generally slow and boring. An exception to the 1955-75 period is the Corvette, which is covered in detail up through the 1990 model. Why? At this point in time, the 1990 model has just reached the twenty-five-year point to be officially designated as an antique by most U.S. state laws. In addition, for domestic collectors at least, the 1976-90 Corvettes have reached a trough in the price scale and are therefore excellent bargains. The Aston Martins and a few others are continued up through part or all of the 1976-90 period, too. All must be either two-seaters or at most, 2+2's, eliminating the plethora of interesting midsize muscle cars of the period. The removable tops can be of all types except for sunroofs or optional T-tops on any pony car coupes. The 1984-85 Corvette Coupes are nominally included because their roofs are removable and they fill the gap between the Stingrays and the 1986-90 Convertibles. The '86-'90 Coupes are also nominally included for obvious reasons. The only T-tops included in this book are the standard removable tops of the 1968-82 Stingrays. Horsepower ratings in the charts should be SAE Gross to be consistent with ratings as they were stated prior to 1972. Any stated ratings for 1972-90 are of course *net*, measured with the standard exhaust system and all engine accessories connected.

Figure A13 - 1978 Corvette Stingray Pace Car. ©Greg Gjerdingen, Willmar, USA (CC)

Considerations: There were plenty of Karmann Ghias built at over 80,000, and they made Bugeyes and 850 Spiders look like speed demons! The 0-60 time of the *fastest* one in 1970 was 21 seconds. The 850 Spider's time was 17 seconds. In spite of their low levels of straight-line performance, these models certainly deserve to be included. These were extremely popular in the USA, particularly as first sports cars. The Ghias offered practical levels of durability and practicality. The 850 Spider lacked both those qualities to some degree, but its styling, handling, and pedigree of Weber carbs, Bertone construction, and modern engineering were exceptional for the price. The Bugeye Sprite introduced ultimate simplicity to sports car buyers, racers and tinkerers. The Honda S-600 and S-800 were never officially imported, eliminating them from this book, although with great reluctance, since they represented the true introduction to four-wheel Hondas. A few small convertible models, such as the VW Beetle and Renault Caravelle, have not been included simply because they are officially closer to sedans than sports cars. One of the most difficult decisions to consider was the inclusion of all the American musclecars that were produced as convertibles with exactly the same drivetrains as their pony car little brothers. As was the case with the Beetle Cabriolet, these were all sporty, topless versions of what were officially called Intermediate Sedans. Yes, they handled better and were more fun to drive than most any other types of American cars of the period, but the fact remains that they were at their essence hopped up standard-issue sedans with lots of style and entertaining accoutrements added. The final consideration, of course, is why were the massive numbers of equivalent coupes not included? The answer is quite simple: their massive numbers would have expanded the size and cost of this book beyond the intended realm. If I may plug one of my earlier books, *Ker-Splash 2: The High Performance Powerboat Book*, all fishing boats were discarded from the production of that book for precisely the same reason.

Four-speed Manual Transmission: A four-speed manual transmission should be considered the most important delineating asset of all these cars, next to their wind in the hair capabilities. However, most of the imports included these as standard, and a few even had five-speeds, but most of the American models listed base prices without them. All of the Base Pony Cars and some of the Muscle Pony Cars came standard with three-speed manuals, a few even disgustingly mounted on the column. The reason the four-speed option has not been integrated into the prices listed for these models is that exact production figures for four-speed convertibles are not available. Rather than confuse the production totals listed for each model, I have chosen to mention the additional cost of the four-speed option in the notes below the appropriate chart of these car types. Of course the 4+3 and six-speed manuals in the C4 Corvettes are more than acceptable. A few models, such as a handful of the Corvette model years and most of the T-birds, were produced only with automatic transmissions.

The Outliers: Although the Ford Thunderbird has never been an actual sports car, I feel it would be a travesty to not include it. The T-bird was conceived as Ford's personal luxury attack on the Corvette. Although only the first three production years were two-seaters, convertibles continued to be produced through 1966. These models are therefore some of the heaviest and least sporty models covered in this book. At the other end of the spectrum, we have the crude little Austin-Healey Sprite roadster and its utilitarian opposition from Germany, the Karmann-Ghia. The VW needs to be included for the sheer number sent to the U.S. over a long production run, although you could argue that the Ghia was never the *purebred sports car* the Sprite so proudly pronounced. The early pony convertibles deserve inclusion because they have been so relentlessly popular in the USA. You can have anything from a putt-putt driver to a quarter-mile stomper in essentially the same body and chassis. Lastly, many very low production sports models have been included for completeness, as well as the readers' fantasies. Some of these are, and have always been, very expensive, such as the Aston-Martins and V-12 Ferraris. Some were built at a reasonable price, but their current costs can only be described as explosive, like a 427 Cobra launched off the line. Some have even remained consistently (somewhat) affordable, such as the less powerful and popular Shelby Mustangs. You may be surprised to discover the Apollo GT, Monteverdi, and Excalibur rolling through these pages, too.

Timelines, Acquisistion & Ownership

Figure A14 - As disgusting as it sounds, more than 48,000 Camaros were shoved out the dealership doors with three-speed manual transmissions in 1967. There is no accurate record available as to how many of these were convertibles, but we do know that less than 13,000 had the shifter on the floor where it belongs. This white with red interior six-cylinder convertible more than likely has a two-speed Powerslide, but if not, a low-option example such as this one is a prime candidate for that despicable three-on-the-tree! ©Mr. Choppers (GNU)

The Photos: *Daydreams in the Wind* was never intended to be a picture book. There are countless coffee-table volumes with beautiful photos printed on thick paper. These have always been readily available and they still are, albeit printed in China, of course. There are even books printed in the USA with the best photos *and* information available on particular marques and models. The catch is that these books are inevitably expensive, two to three times the retail price of this one. The photos in *Daydreams in the Wind* are included mostly to provide visual aids to the captions. Few are rare and all are in glorious black and white. Significant time and effort has been expended to select the best photos and make them as presentable as possible with the technology available. Modern publishing can reproduce a digital photo with ease, while the quality reproduction of one taken with a film camera in 1965 is much more difficult. For that reason alone, most of the photos selected have been of restored cars photographed relatively recently. The obvious place to find such cars is at a car show. Outdoor shots are generally superior to any originating from museums with fluorescent lighting, therefore the outdoor versions have been heavily favored. A stylistic factor in this publication is that most of the photos are full-car shots stretching from margin to margin and all have been closely cropped to best show off the car, not the scenery. The exceptions to this full-car view are the interior shots displayed on each chapter page. These are all shown from the perspective of the driver's seat, the best place to enjoy any of these nostalgic rides.

Figure A15 - 1965 Intermeccanica Apollo 5000 GT Coupe in Red. ©Rex Gray, Southern California (CC)

Inspirations: *Daydreams in the Wind* was inspired not by either the affordable picture books or the expert analysis marque books. This one was specifically intended to complement and carry forward into the future the type of information that used to be readily available from four specific sources. The first is the *Illustrated Buyer's Guide* Series in which American and English authors have compiled data on a particular brand or series within a brand. The second is the hardback *Collector's Guide* Series published in England by English writers and journalists. These wonderful little books have only two negative issues. One, they were always composed from an English, not American, perspective, and two, practically all of these have been out of print for some time. The third group is composed of the *Corvette Black Books* and their copycat equivalents published for a few other brands. Although chocked full of facts and data, the problem is that the Corvette is the only car that has been consistently covered and updated. Most of the rest have become quite difficult (or expensive) to acquire. The only current exception is the Porsche 911, for which a new edition has recently been released. The fourth source is of course *Road &Track* and *Car and Driver*. The only information you are going to find in these two now is the occasional article compiled on the subject of classic collectibles.

The Charts: The charts represent the true heart and soul of this book. While researching and compiling the massive amount of data to be included, if a paragraph would certainly lead the reader through an interminable maze of facts and number crunching, then a chart was born. The entire purpose of each and every chart is to clarify the data for the reader, to help him more easily remember the information that fascinates him. Aside from this basic parameter, selecting the particular information that deserved inclusion in the book was a very difficult task.

Color charts have been included seemingly at random, but there is a method to my madness. This sort of information is very easy to find for Corvettes, Mustangs, Camaros, and many others; colors for the high-production English roadsters, not so much. Ditto for option availabilities, comparing the same American and English brands. When available information seems sketchy, fallible or downright invisible for certain years or models, then tough judgment calls are necessary. From the several years of research and compilation this book required, a significant portion was spent trying to fill in *NA* (Not Available) boxes within charts. Colors were one of two tough subjects.

Another tough subject, and one I personally treasure far above all the rest of the data in the book, is that of accurate production figures. I was not seeking only total figures by model, but as many breakdowns by year, body types, power trains, and options as possible. What you see is what you get. There are possibilities for incorrect information to have sneaked in throughout the book. That is why every reader should pay careful attention to the *Notes* included below every chart. If there is not one questionable issue, it is another. Remember, you are reading information first made public as many as sixty or so years ago! These numbers had to have been calculated, recorded and preserved by many individuals who are no longer alive. Let us honor their demise by retaining the integrity of their legendary efforts.

Figure A16 - This view of a lovely Old English White Jaguar XK-140 Drophead Coupe shows off its neatly stacked tan top and chrome window frames and wire wheels. ©Nightflyer (GNU)

Collectible Open Sports Cars of the Sixties Chart

Model	Years Built	Production
Alfa Romeo Spider	1966 - 1994	127,643
Aston-Martin Convertible	1950 - 1989	1578
Austin-Healey 100	1953 - 1959	29,103
Austin-Healey 3000	1959 - 1967	42,917
Austin-Healey Sprite	1958 - 1969	129,362
Chevrolet Camaro Convertible	1967 - 1969	63,154
Chevrolet Corvair Convertible	1962 - 1969	148,862
Chevrolet Corvette C1	1953 - 1962	69,015
Corvette Sting Ray Coupe & Convertible	1963 - 1967	117,964
Corvette Stingray Coupe & Convertible	1968 - 1982	542,861
Corvette Coupe & Convertible	1984 - 1990	229,864
Datsun Sports Convertible	1963 - 1970	56,924
Dodge Challenger Convertible	1970 - 1971	5741
Excalibur Series I-II-III	1965 - 1979	1842
Ferrari Dino 246/308 GTS	1972 - 1985	9284
Ferrari V-12 Spyders	1957 - 1974	809
Fiat 850 Spider	1967 - 1973	124,660
Fiat 124 Spider (USA)	1968 - 1982	170,720
Fiat Dino Spider	1966 - 1973	1587
Ford Thunderbird Convertible	1955 - 1966	125,282
Ford Mustang Convertible	1965 - 1973	290,762
Intermeccanica Coupes & Spyders	1961 - 1974	658
Jaguar XK-120/140/150	1950 - 1961	30,357
Jaguar XK-E Coupes & Convertibles	1961 - 1975	72,520
Jensen-Healey	1972 - 1976	10,498
Karmann-Ghia Cabriolet	1958 - 1974	80,837
Lotus Elan Coupes & Convertibles	1962 - 1973	12,224
Maserati Spyders	1960 - 1972	495
Mercedes-Benz SL	1955 - 1971	76,651
MG A	1955 - 1962	101,081
MG B Roadster	1962 - 1980	399.070
MG C Roadster	1967 - 1969	4550
MG Midget	1961 - 1980	226,526
Morgan Plus 4	1954 - 1969	4754

Plymouth Barracuda Convertible	1967 - 1971	11,511
Pontiac Firebird Convertible	1967 - 1969	44,144
Porsche 356 Convertibles	1950 - 1965	22,723
Porsche 914	1970 - 1976	118,978
Porsche Targa	1967 - 1975	35,527
Shelby Cobra	1962 - 1968	975
Shelby Mustang Convertible	1966 - 1970	1659
Sunbeam Alpine	1959 - 1968	69,251
Sunbeam Tiger	1964 - 1967	7083
Triumph Spitfire	1963 - 1980	314,332
Triumph Stag	1970 - 1977	25,877
Triumph TR2 - TR6	1953 - 1976	255,393

Collectible Open Sports Cars of the Sixties Chart Notes:
The production figures displayed in this capsule chart include a few discrepancies due to the variations in source material and parameters included. This chart is intended as an overall comparison. For more accurate details and an in-depth breakdown of the numbers, see the charts under each car type.

Timeline of Sports Car Features and Details

1948 - First fifty Porsche 356's built
1952 - The first Austin-Healey. the Healey 100, appears at the London Motor Show
1953 - The lift-up fiberglass boot panel introduced on the Corvette
1954 - First lift-off hardtop on a production car optional on the Triumph TR-2
1955 - T-bird becomes the first Personal Luxury Car / Fuel injection on Mercedes SL
1956 - Triumph TR-3 gets front disc brakes
1957 - Mechanical fuel injection mass produced for the Corvette
1958 - Twin cam engine in MG A
1961 - Jaguar XK-E with aluminum engine and disc brakes
1962 - Ferrari GTO is introduced as a definitive *homologation special*
1963 - FM radio and air conditioning in Sting Ray
1964 - Ford Mustang launches the pony car trend
1965 - Mustang GT and Pony Interior packages / Sting Ray 396
1966 - Porsche Targa concept first shown in Germany
1967 - OHC inline six & hood tach on Pontiac Firebird / Big-block engines in pony cars
1968 - FM Stereo & headlamp washers on Stingray / Triumph six-cylinder engine
1969 - Safety headrests
1970 - Porsche 914, the first affordable mid-engine sports car
1971 - Compression ratios reduced to run on unleaded fuel
1972 - Net horsepower ratings introduced
1973 - Energy-absorbing front bumper introduced on the Corvette Stingray
1974 - Energy-absorbing rear bumper added to the Corvette Stingray

1975 - Catalytic converter added to Corvette Stingray single exhaust system

Timeline of Model Year Introductions

1949 - Jaguar XK-120
1951 - Morgan Plus 4 / Porsche 356 Cabriolet
1953 - Austin-Healey 100 / Chevrolet Corvette / Triumph TR-2
1954 - Porsche 1500 Speedster
1955 - Ford Thunderbird / Jaguar XK-140
1956 - Alfa Romeo Giulietta Spider / MG A / Porsche 356A Cabriolet / Triumph TR-3
1957 - A-H 100/6 / Alfa Giulietta Veloce Super Spider / Ferrari 250 GT California LWB
1958 - A-H Sprite / Jaguar XK-150 / Triumph TR-3A /VW Karmann-Ghia Cabriolet
1959 - Austin-Healey 3000 / Fiat 1500S OSCA Spider / MG A Twin Cam
1960 - Ferrari 250 GT Spyder Californa SWB / 356B Cabriolet / Sunbeam Alpine
1961 - Jaguar 3.8 XK-E
1962 - Cobra / Fiat 1600S Spider / Lotus Elan / MG Midget / TR-3B, TR-4 & Spitfire
1963 - Corvette Sting Ray / Datsun 1500 / Fiat 1500 Spider / MG B / 356C Cabriolet
1964 - Alfa Giulia Spider / Barracuda / Ferrari 275 GTS / Maserati Mistral Spider / Tiger
1965 - Ford Mustang / Jaguar 4.2 XK-E / Triumph TR-4A
1966 - Datsun 1600 / Ferrari 330 GTS
1967 - Camaro / Datsun 2000 / Excalibur / 850 & Dino / Intermeccanica Italia / Firebird
1968 - Morgan Plus 8 / Porsche Targa / Shelby Mustang Convertible / TR-250
1969 - Ferrari 365GTS/4 / Maserati Ghibli Spider / MG C / Monteverdi 375C / TR-6
1970 - Excalibur Series II / Porsche 914 & 914/6
1971 - Jaguar 5.3 XK-E V-12 / Triumph Stag
1972 - Jensen-Healey
1975 - Excalibur Series III
1976 - Alfa Romeo Spider Veloce

Pop the Top
The Cool, the Acceptable, and the Infuriating

This book is about two-seater, 2+2, sports and sporty cars with removable tops. The only T-tops that count are the ones on the 1968-82 Stingrays. These were the first of the T-tops. The open space is much larger than on the later T-topped pony cars. The Corvette T-tops were standard equipment on all Coupes, and on the '68-'72 models the rear windows were also removable. The Porsche Targas and GTS Ferraris with their full-sized removable roof panels are also included, but no sunroof options on coupes have been allowed in this story. All topless two-seaters, including the luxurious, yet barely sporty 1955-57 Thunderbird, are included. No American compacts or mid-sized muscle cars are represented, as they are essentially five-seater sedans, no matter how sporty or powerful they may be. The result of these parameters is that most, but not all, of the 2+2 convertibles in this book are first-generation American pony cars and most, but not all, of the two-seaters are true-blue sports cars. Some of these removable tops are wonderfully efficient designs, some are good designs with a few caveats here and there, and some are a total pain in the butt to use, and even then they do very little to protect you from the elements or your stuff from petty thieves. This is their story.

Let's start at the beginning, a time likely before you, this author, or most Baby Boomers were born. Many of the 1955-75 cars in this book were descendants of earlier designs. If you have read many car books, you already know that most authors refer to these as *postwar* models, the cars produced during the Baby Boom immediately following World War II. The short version is that these were generally English or German marques. Ferrari and Maserati had been around a while, but it would be years before either would produce a Spider in any sizable production number for the American market. Very few Alfas or Fiats were exported to the U.S. and America's Corvette would not appear until 1953. The Japanese would not even enter the game until the '60's. Porsche would lead the export pack with its 356 Cabriolet and the pack would be a whole herd of Limeys. From the get-go, the Porsche had a decently designed convertible top: point one goes to the Krauts. The pack that followed included many designs that were the descendants of prewar models. The spindly, legendary MG TC and the Jaguar SS 100 defined this category. Their postwar soul mates would have envelope bodies riding on wider wheels and tires, but their roadster roofs and side curtains would still be stuck in the prewar department.

Figure A17 - British Racing Green Austin-Healey 3000. ©Allen Watkin, London, England (CC)

The early English roadsters employed thin, single-layer fabric tops that had to be attached to the metal framework of the roof structure and the car body by the driver and/or passenger of the car. In most cases, *and* was a lot easier than *or*. The occupants had to step out of the car, open the trunk and pull out the top fabric and metal top bows (usually stowed separately). The metal structure was then affixed to the car's body. Then the fabric (vinyl, canvas, or whatever) had to be attached to the framework. Okay, that takes care of the sun, but what if it's raining? The occupants have to also remove from the trunk a set of side curtains. In the earlier models these were generally made of flexible clear plastic, a smaller version of what you might see on a runabout boat. Later versions were composed of two panels of plexiglass on each side. What? There were no door handles? That's right; on most of these cars you pushed an arm inside the side curtains to reach the interior door handle. That meant that on the flexible type, you unsnapped a couple of snaps or slid down a zipper to open the door from the outside. With the plexiglass type, one panel slid forward and back so you could reach inside. As mentioned previously, petty thieves had to be *really stupid* not to figure this out!

Figure A18 - This little red Spitfire is likely the way most of us remember the model. This one is a Mark 2 with the optional overdrive and painted wire wheels. The wire wheels were true knock-offs on these early Spitfires and the overdrive was a very desirable option. Both add to the desirability of a Spitfire today. All Spitfires had roll-up windows. The single-layer, black vinyl top is a three-window design with only two top bows for structure. The top and frame on the Mark 2 are not permanently attached to the body, but they will be on the Mark 3 model. The early Spitfires are still sought for their more attractive chrome bumpers, wire wheels, and unencumbered engines. ©Akela NDE (CC)

Once you got the top erected and the side curtains installed, you and your usually wet, disgusted passenger could reenter the warm, dry environment of a properly British sports car. Of course the interior was neither of these things. Nor was it quiet once you started the engine and began roaring down the road underneath that primitive, airy, leaky top design. The rear edge of the top was snapped down in the manner of a proper top boot. The tight, heavy-duty clamps of an American convertible were anathema to proper English motoring. Although you may have broken a fingernail or two and cursed like a sailor in the Royal Navy while trying to hurriedly snap down the top fabric in a downpour, your reward was not the dryness of an Arabian desert or the quiet of a mid-Seventies Ford LTD sedan. The transmission still rattles and/or whines, the wind sears through the corners of the windscreen and the water drips in like a leaky faucet. Once you get up to a decent cruising speed, the single layer top will add its flap-dance to the party, too. Are we having fun yet? Can the sun pleeeeease come back out now?

Thank goodness the roadster top was not the final word from the builders of English sports cars. The English produced a body type they call a *drop head coupe*, essentially what we Americans call a convertible, with a top permanently attached at the rear and roll-up or electric windows. Generally speaking, many of the British cars covered in this book began as *roadsters* and slowly over the model years were developed into *drop head coupes*. This was true of the Jaguar XK Series, the MG B and Midget, the Austin-Healeys, and the Triumphs. The XK roadster was the first released, the DHC was later added, and by the time of the E-Type roll-up windows and attached tops were standard. The MG B began with roll-up windows, following its MG A model predecessor in its roadster configuration only, but the top was not attached on the B until its later model years. This was also true of the Triumph Spitfire and TR-4. The TR-2 and TR-3 had remained true roadsters until the end of their production. The MG Midget and all the Healeys began production as true roadsters and ended as convertibles, DHC in English lingo.

Some of the lower production English brands should be mentioned here. When was the last time you saw the top erected on a Cobra? That's because Carroll Shelby left the drafty antique AC design mostly alone. All the Cobras were true roadsters, side curtains and all. You know what that means. Who would take a Cobra out of its locked and security protected garage on any day that it just might possibly be a 20-percent chance of rain, anyway? Of course all the Morgans were roadsters with side curtains, many of the sliding plexiglass variety. Sunbeam tried to design its Alpine and Tiger models with a top that was a cut above those of its three higher-volume competitors, the Healeys, MG's, and Triumphs. Sunbeam generally succeeded in this endeavor. All of these were true convertibles with attached tops and roll-up windows. Don't forget, though, they are still from the land of leaky erector sets, even though Chrysler and Shelby stuck their fingers in the pie. All those cute later model Lotus Elans had electric windows because there was not enough elbow room in the interior to operate windup window mechanisms. The Elan top was attached, but it was still very British. Translation: it was a barrel of monkeys to erect in a rainstorm. The little-lamented Jensen-Healey gave it its best experienced English try and it is likely the electrical system or boring styling will bug you before you throw a tantrum over the quality of its soft top. Another low-volume beastie, the Triumph Stag, combined a T-top (like a Stingray) with a large zip-out rear window (like a Targa). With its problematic engine, the Stag is even less lamented than the Jensen-Healey. The Aston Martins did indeed have high-class, multi-layered tops, as if they were the first cousins of the Rolls Royce Corniche or something. The catch is that their retail prices and low production numbers were breathing that same stratospheric air as the Corniches.

This evolution from roadster to true convertible has positive and negative points. If you want normal, logical convenience and comfort, there is no advantage to a roadster. If you want the ultimate wind in your hair, bugs in your teeth, devil may care concept mixed with your holier than thou, early-production original, then there is some logic in your willingness to erect an ineffective, cantankerous top and side curtains. These were the *original* designs, of course, usually featuring lighter vehicle weight and sprightly performance. Although the later attached tops were more completely professionally engineered and installed, therefore more easily erected and more water and wind tight, for the most part these tops are still of only a single layer. Wind flapping at speed and noise intrusion are still major concerns. In several models, these attached tops take up some of the previously available luggage space behind the seats when lowered. On some models, you must still step out of the car after lowering the top to snap down the vinyl boot or tonneau cover. Generally speaking, the early versions of these cars may offer tons of happy go lucky enthusiasm in both driving and style, while the later versions offer more convenience and comfort. In many cases complementary accoutrements such as more luxurious seating, dash, carpeting and equipment contribute additional comfort to the later models. Most enthusiasts of a particular brand, especially in this later day and age, are already fully aware whether they are fans of early or late production cars. It just so happens that in the world of topless cars, the top design can be wonderfully satisfying or woefully aggravating.

Figure A19 - Volkswagen Karmann-Ghia Cabriolet in green, showing off one of the best tops in the business.
©Infrogmation (GNU)

Those Krauts, you know the type, they loooove engineering and bragging about it. The lowly VW Beetle Cabriolet has always had one of the best convertible tops ever designed. Multi-layered, water tight, wind tight, and quiet, about the only thing you can fuss about is the way it stacks up into your rear vision when folded. Although the Beetle Cabriolet does not qualify for inclusion here -- it's derived from a four-seater sedan -- the Karmann-Ghia does barely make the cut as its sports car equivalent. Although the Karmann-Ghia's top is not the vision-blocking stack of the Beetle, it still looks a bit bulky when folded. There is still little doubt that these German designed tops are far superior to anything from England in this period, particularly from within the affordable class. The Porsche 356 Cabriolet top is of course similar in design and quality; however, the low-profile Speedster version is less comfortably convenient. As with the Brits, the later models of the 356 and K-G are going to be the most perfectly built top-wise.

Figure A20 - Metallic Green Porsche 911T Targa. No, the T does not stand for Targa. The T series comprised the lower-priced 911 models, both Coupes and Targas, for a number of years. The earliest T models had carburetors, but the later ones sent to the U.S. were fuel injected. ©Nakhon 100 (CC)

In 1966 Porsche introduced a wonderful new idea the company named the Targa, after the legendary Targa Florio race in Italy. The new Targa top design was first introduced on the 911, then on the 912, and finally the 914. For some reason it took two years for the company to export the first Targas to the lucrative U.S. market where we *love* convertibles. The 911 Targa and 912 Targa arrived here as 1967 models, and all the 914's were Targas from the beginning of their production. The USA received both the four-cylinder model and the 914/6 as 1970 models. Like its 1968 Stingray competitor, the first Targa had a removable rear window -- in this case a zip out plastic one like many traditional convertibles have had at times. Unlike the Stingray, the removable roof panel was relatively lightweight plastic. As an option you could even order an accordion style roof panel that was particularly convenient to store when removed from the stainless roll bar. Later 911 and 912 Targas had a fixed fastback glass rear window. Long-term endurance of the large format plastic rear window and wind buffeting when removed were the reasons stated for its discontinuation. The roll bar of the 914 was regular steel covered in black vinyl and the only top choice was the standard hard plastic panel. Although large in area, this panel stored easily in the car. Like that of the 1973-77 Stingray, the 914's rear window was small, simple, flat, vertical, and permanently installed. As you may surmise, the 912 with a zip out rear window or a 914/6 with its Porsche engine and standard removable roof panel are highly sought as collectibles. An early 911, especially the first 911S Targa with a plastic rear window, is also quite collectible today, although it took decades to reach its current desirability status.

The Mercedes SL series was one of the pioneers of quality convertible top design and operation. The first series, the 190 and 300 SL's of 1955-63 had traditional vinyl boots over their vinyl tops. The new series 230 SL introduced in 1963 brought the exquisite aluminum boot, which continued through the production of the 250 SL and 280 SL in later years. All the 190/300/230/250/280 SL's also offered an optional bolt-on hardtop. The later series (after the initial 190/300) sported the unusual nickname of *Pagoda* for their unusual, concave-shaped hardtops.

The Italian brands have properly been with the topless program for a long time. Even the earliest Fiat Spiders imported into the USA had convenient top designs, permanently attached with roll-up windows. Most of the models sold in the USA were actually built by either Bertone or Pininfarina. All the Ferrari Cabriolets and the Fiat 124 Spider were Pininfarina designs and products. You easily see in the exterior lines that the same man designed the 124 Spider and the Ferrari 275 GTS. The Fiat 850 Spider was built by Bertone, the same company that built most of the Lamborghinis. The top designs of all these models were slick, convenient, and effective, easy to erect with good wind and water sealing. The cheap little 850 (of all models!) offered the bonus of a hinged metal boot lid like the one on a Mercedes SL of the period. Of course all the Corvette Convertibles have had this feature since the beginning. You do not even have to get out of the car to clamp down the boot! Most of the Italian soft tops lie squarely between the British single-ply rags and the thick, multi-layered Germanic stacks in design and effectiveness. Some later Ferrari GTS models applied the Targa principle with small vertical glass fixed rear windows and large plastic removable roof panels. Like the Porsches and later C4 Corvettes, these large panels fit into niches designed into the storage areas of their respective models. They were generally lighter and a bit less difficult to handle than those of the C4, however.

The Japanese produced only a few Datsun models that fit within the scope of this book. The attached black vinyl soft top folded neatly under a boot and all models had roll-up windows. The Datsun tops were roughly equivalent in convenience and quality to the Italian soft tops of the period.

The Corvairs, later Thunderbird Convertibles and all the American pony cars utilized basically the same top design. Since these cars were all 2+2 models, the top was necessarily longer and heavier than that of any of the two-seat sports cars. That meant that you either had a power top, as many of them offered this option, or you had to stand beside the car to push the heavy top down into its well behind the rear seat or to pull it up to the windshield header. Most of these tops may not have been up to the multi-layered quality of fabric as some of those by VW, Porsche, and Aston Martin, but they were above all the rest of the soft tops described in this book. Wide, strong (and heavy) top bows were used and most had at least one inner layer of fabric. Most of the exteriors were in standard vinyl, but unlike most of the British and all of the Italian, German, and Japanese brands, the tops were often available in several colors other than black or tan. Standard windows were always of the roll-up variety, with electric windows on some option lists.

Timelines, Acquisistion & Ownership

Figure A21 - The black vinyl top on this late model red Corvair was quite typical of the breed. Unlike many of the removable tops on the English roadsters, the bows hold the fabric tightly sealed over the side windows.
©Christopher Ziemnowicz (CC)

The power top option was included on 9956 1965 Corvairs, 4350 '66 models, and only 743 1967 models. The decreasing numbers reflect more on the decreasing production of Corvair convertibles in general than they do on the popularity of the power top. Power windows were never an option on Corvairs of these three model years. The Mustang had a power top option from 1964-onward, but power windows were not available until 1971. The Camaro and Firebird had power top and windows options in 1967. The Barracuda had only a manual top and roll-up windows in 1967-69 and received both power options in 1970. The Challenger had both power top and power window options in 1970.

This brings us to the multi-talented Corvette, top-wise. Chevrolet started a wonderful trend in 1953 with the simple, lift-up hinged cover for the top instead of a vinyl boot. Not only does this provide a very clean look, as if the car were a roadster with the top stored in the trunk, but it is quick and easy to use. There is no vinyl boot that has to be stretched taut and snapped down over the top. Just unclamp the top from the windshield header, fold it back and drop the hinged cover back down over it. The 1953-55 Corvette was a roadster with side curtains, but the 1956-on had roll-up windows with power windows as an option. The soft top was of a pretty consistent quality, comparable to the larger convertible tops on other American cars. The early roadster models still had a few bugs to be worked out, but from the 1958 models to date, the Corvette has always sported an exemplary soft top. A bolt-on hardtop was an option on Corvettes from 1956 through 1975 (convertibles were not produced in 1976-85) and again in 1989-90. Although the hardtop could be ordered alone (in some model years) or with the soft top, two people were required to attach or remove it so this was generally intended as a winter/summer arrangement. There have been more ways to let the sun and wind into a Corvette other than simply removing the entire top. The Corvette has traditionally been one of the few sports cars that offer additional options within the same model years.

Figure A22 - This is a rear shot of the Stingray I owned for eighteen years. This machine is a 1970 Stingray Coupe with the 390-hp LS-5 454, wide-ratio four-speed, 3.08 Positraction, AC, and power steering and brakes. The black exterior was not a standard color in 1970. The green interior made for a Lamborghini-like color combination. The T-tops and rear window have been removed in this photo.

©1983 Floyd M. Orr Collection

The 1953 Corvette was not the first convertible with a flip-up boot panel covering the retracted top. The 1929 Duesenberg Model J Disappearing-Top had a rigid panel hiding the convertible top in the 1930's. The chassis and drivetrains for this Duesie were built in 1929 and 1930. Models were bodied by various coachbuilders for the entire J Series up through 1937. It took that long to sell all the pre-manufactured chassis during the height of The Depression. Generally, the model years between 1929 and 1937 were determined by the coachbuilder. The most famous of these was the Walter M. Murphy Company of Pasadena, California, although other constructors may have produced Disappearing-Top J models. J Series production included about 200 cars, but only a small percentage of these were convertibles with the Disappearing Top feature. Most of the J Series production had a 420-inch, DOHC, 32-valve straight 8-cylinder making 265 horsepower. Less than fifty of the total J Series were equipped with 320-hp supercharged engines of the same design. The wheelbase was 142 inches! Four side pipes exiting on the right side only were standard on the SJ (supercharged models) and optional on the others. The DT models were constructed in two body styles: Torpedo Roadster and Convertible

Timelines, Acquisistion & Ownership

Coupe. The TR had a slim boattail ending in a sharp V at the rear bumper line. The CC had a more conventional rear deck that curved downward in parallel with the rear fenders. At least some of the Torpedo Roadsters, and maybe all, had aluminum trim covering the entire rear deck. The Convertible Coupes had only thin trim strips along the sides following the curve of the rear fenders. Some of the Convertible Coupes were also distinguished by suicide doors. Only four Torpedo Roadster Disappearing-Top J models are known to still exist with their original bodywork. One of these four, an early-production red Torpedo Roadster with saddle leather interior, sold for $3 million at auction 1/29/16. It was not even in its original color scheme, silver with blue fenders. It is unknown how many Disappearing-Top Convertible Coupes are still as original from the factory and in the hands of lucky collectors.

Figure A23 - A closer shot of the same car open to the breeze. ©1983 Floyd M. Orr Collection

Chevrolet introduced the T-top concept with the Stingray Coupe in 1968. Although this choice would continue through 1982, the concept did not remain static. The 1968-72 models had removable glass rear windows. The 1973-77 models had the same small vertical rear windows, but they were not removable. The 1978-82 models had large glass fastback rear windows that were not removable and see-through glass T-tops (in place of body-colored fiberglass) were optional. The T-tops were replaced by a single large, body-colored removable panel on the C4. In 1984 and 1985 this was the only roof choice in a Corvette, but even then you could order an optional transparent plastic roof panel instead. The 1986-90 models offered the same body-colored fiberglass roof panel as the earlier C4's, but now there were several additional top choices. The convertible body style with soft top had returned, although there would not be an optional hardtop for the convertible until 1989. A removable see-through plastic panel was optional for the coupe in either a bronze or blue tint and you could even order both tinted and opaque top panels. (Some of these top choices would continue into the C5's, well beyond the scope of this book.)

A few words of opinion are in order at this point. The comments pertaining to the antiquities of the English soft tops should probably be taken with a grain of salt in the case of selecting a car as a present collectible. The concepts presented here are intended to bring all the details of your choices together in one volume. Considering the ages of all these vehicles in this book, they can all be officially registered as antiques and I doubt that anyone would choose one of these fun beasties as transportation. With that consideration, it would behoove you to compare the concept of owning an early original design with all the emotional flair that might entail. Practicality and convenience be damned!

At the opposite end of the scale, you might find a lovely Corvette C4, or one of the later, more boring and less collectible C3's, that you could drive somewhat more than occasionally. In that case, take note of the convenience, or lack thereof, of using a particular Corvette's topless features. The 1968 model is famously the sloppiest built of all Corvette years, and the '69 model is only a bit better. Production was slowed and quality control emphasized more and more from 1970-onward. The body structure of any Corvette Coupe is going to be more solid than that of any comparable Corvette Convertible. What may not be so obvious is that the higher performance engines are going to stress the structure more and the Convertible will be more susceptible to showing signs of this stress, particularly with an older model. Not only that, but the higher the performance, the more likely the car has been driven hard, drag raced, or autocrossed at some time in its illustrious past. The sheer torque of some of the big-block engines can put a slight twisting stress on the body structure. The wide tires and stiff suspension transmit every bump into the body structure, too. Be sure to look for stress cracks in the fiberglass, a *very* common issue with old Corvettes. Rust may be the bane of most of the imported cars in this book, but stress cracks haunt the Corvette. Here is where a choice of selecting an old Corvette in Coupe or Convertible mode gets tough. The Convertible will nearly always be worth more as a collectible. Coupes have been outselling Convertibles as new cars since 1969. The Coupes offer such a delicious way to let the sun and wind in occasionally while keeping all your stuff locked up conveniently or the air conditioning on the remainder of the time.

You may not have thought about this, but the standard T-tops on a 1968-82 Corvette are quite bulky and heavy and you will not want to scratch the paint on the exterior panels. The T-tops are intended to be strapped down in the luggage area behind the seats when not in use and this is more unwieldy that it sounds. The only luggage space you have is that shelf behind the seats. There is no trunk in any 1963-96 Corvette! If you simply lay the T-top panels side by side, they will hog your entire space. The built-in, color-coded straps are used to tie each top panel against the left and right side of the luggage area at an inconvenient angle. This is better than laying them flat, but it is no fun to do. You have to sit in the seat holding the heavy panel, twist your upper body around facing rearward and tie each panel into position. The rear window stores on top of a horizontal panel that drops down from inside the top portion of the luggage area. The reason you may have read that the 1973-77 model has increased luggage space is this drop down panel is absent, slightly increasing the vertical luggage space. It is true that removing the rear window increases the wind turbulence, but personally I like looking back there and seeing nothing but air. I am obviously a convertible maniac and you probably are, too! The optional glass T-top panels of the 1978-82 models are nice to look through in cold weather, but they let in a little more heat in the summer. Most of all, they are *heavy*, but the good news is that strapping them down into the larger luggage area of these fastback models is considerably easier. Note that the only hatchback Stingray is the 1982 Collector Edition.

For you enthusiasts looking for a classic of the future that offers modern comforts while easily choking down crummy fuel with ease, I have included the 1984-90 C4 models. Your choice is simple here, a conventional soft top that can be lowered or erected with minimal drama or one big plastic panel that can be lifted off and placed in the luggage area. In this case removing and storing the transparent top is little different from the opaque one. As stated earlier, the removable hardtop was not available for the Convertible in 1986-88. Here are two final notes concerning the one-piece removable roof panel of a C4 Coupe. It is heavy and bulky enough to be a delicate operation for one person to remove or attach, particularly on a windy day. Secondly, much more than with the C3 T-tops, the single roof panel is a structural component. You will notice the difference while driving with it removed. In the C3, you are more likely to hear increased creaks and groans only as you traverse uneven surfaces at low speeds. At cruising speeds in a '68-'72 Stingray Coupe with the tops and rear window removed, you will hear the wind... just like in a real convertible!

Figure A24 - This little OHV four-cylinder in this Bronze Yellow 1972 MG Midget represents the *hamster* side of the equation. This is the venerable 1275cc version of which Spridget fans are aptly proud, although most would greatly prefer the pre-emissions 1967 version. ©Dave 7, Lethbridge, Canada (CC)

Engines
From Peddling Hamsters to Roaring Lions

The cars in this book utilize a wide range of powerplants. The only issues they have in common is that they are all gasoline powered and there are no front-wheel-drive units. Some have rear-engine, rear-wheel-drive with air cooling. These include the Corvair, Karmann-Ghia and many of the Porsches. The Fiat 850 Spider is the same except it is water cooled. The Porsche 914's and Ferrari 246 and 308 GTS are mid-engine with water or air (Porsche) cooling. All the rest have front engines, water cooling, and rear-wheel-drive. The engine similarities end there.

The common, low-priced English roadsters all have relatively simple, overhead valve four-cylinder engines, some with two or three carburetors, usually SU brand. None of these engines had overhead cams or fuel injection and most were derived from lowly sedan variants. Models included the Spridgets, Spitfire, MG A and B, TR-2/3/4, Sunbeam Alpine, and Morgan Plus 4.

Figure A25 - Close to the top of the motorized food chain is this 427 Cobra engine. This photo was listed as belonging to a 1965 model, but with Cobras, who knows? The origin of this powerplant could be most anything, but whatever it is, it is most certainly not small, weak, quiet or slow! ©Joe Mabel (GNU)

The upper models of these same brands used larger inline six-cylinder engines of similar types and specifications. These include the A-H 100-6 and 3000, MG C, and Triumph TR-250, TR-6, and Stag. Jaguar designed its own SOHC inline six-cylinder aluminum engine to use in all the

Timelines, Acquisistion & Ownership

XK roadsters and drop head coupes prior to the 5.3-liter V-12 of the XK-E Series III. Aston Martin utilized variants of a DOHC Six in its early models and a DOHC V-8 in the later ones.

Wheels
Rolling Through Transitions of Wheels, Tires & Steering Wheels

Figure A26 - This book is crammed to the axles with chrome knock-off wire wheels, but this is the only set you will see on a 1969 427 Corvette! ©1980 Floyd M. Orr Collection

As with the removable top designs discussed earlier in this chapter, these three components of a sports car have their own little niche in the story. Whatever top your sports car came with is pretty much what you are stuck with, for better or worse. In contrast, the wheels, tires, and steering wheel are the three items most likely to have been changed by the original selling dealer, a previous owner, or the new owner, you. Let's assume that in general, a car should have its original engine and its original paint color and type to be what we refer to as a collectible. This is also true of its wheels, steering wheel, and tires, but the similarity ends there. These three components can easily be offered as factory original standards or options, dealer-installed accessories, or aftermarket products. The obvious observation is that they so often *were* available within these various contexts. To complicate matters further, these issues varied all over the spectrum among brands, models, and years. A few of these replaceable items sometimes increase the collector value of a car, or at least make it easier to resell. Some of them make the car a whole lot more livable as a driver. Some are much cheaper and more available on today's market than are the correct, original items. A few of these items, such as modern radial tires, are not only cheaper, but much safer to use in modern traffic and road conditions.

First of all, I want to state that this article is *not* about the ridiculously oversized diameter of modern wheels that some people put on cars of the '60's and call them *Resto Mods*. I personally think those things are stupid in concept, silly, and look ridiculous. If you want to put eighteen-inch wheels on your restored 1967 Camaro, you are reading the wrong book. Practically every original car in this book came equipped with 13, 14, 15, or 16 inch wheels. The modern-style 16's apply to the C4 Corvettes only.

The discussion here is not about wheel diameter at all. It is about wheel *type*. We take for granted our lightweight, reliable aluminum alloy wheels today. Many bread and butter sedans even have them now, at least as a factory option. This was a totally different story during the timeline of this book, 1955-75. The English cars had wire wheels that were near the end of their production heyday and most sports cars were getting their first alloy wheels near the end of this production period. Many of both the wire and alloy wheels were optional, not standard. Some wheel types were impractical and some were highly desirable. The plot thickens when you realize sometimes these two characteristics were shared by the same wheel option.

Let's begin with the wire wheels. Many English sports cars were responsible for the popularity of wire wheels. Of course these derived from the spindly ones from the prewar era, but for purposes of this book we are including those models after World War II. These were the models with envelope bodies and steel disc or wire wheels, such as the Austin-Healeys, MG A/B, TR-2/3/4, all the XK Jags and many more. The important points to keep in mind are that many of these models came standard with disc wheels and wires were never a factory option, some offered the wires as standard and the disc wheels were optional, and some offered wires in some model years but not in others. The great majority of these wire wheels were painted silver; few were chromed from the factory. Wire wheels produced for the U.S. market prior to 1968 generally were of the knock-off variety, a favorite of racers. From 1968 onward, no auto wheels had knock-off *ears* (spinners). Some models were of a knock-off type, but you inserted a special tool in the hub to hit with a hammer to loosen the wheel and then removed the tool. The general idea of the ban on the spinners involved unnecessary danger to pedestrians, or to the car's occupants in case of a serious crash. Mustangs and Corvettes even lost their spinner wheel cover designs for the 1967 model year.

You do know that real wire wheels are heavy steel and require a lot of maintenance, don't you? Cleaning, painting or polishing them is no picnic and the spokes loosen over time from hitting potholes and such. The weight is *unsprung* weight, the worst kind for handling. Contrasting these indisputable engineering facts are the equally indisputable financial and emotional facts. Many classic British cars, and even a few early Ferraris, are worth a lot more money today with wire wheels. Then there is the emotional factor. If you lusted after a particular wire-wheeled English roadster that the captain of the football team drove in high school while you piloted the family Plymouth.... You know where your heart lies.

Ford introduced and popularized what the company called Styled Steel Wheels on the 1965 Mustang. The GTO got sort of a styled steel wheel in 1965. An updated version would be referred to as Rally I Wheels in 1967 when the much more popular Rally II wheels became an option on both the GTO and Firebird. The spoked Rally II model is always a bonus to have on an early Firebird. The Camaro got a styled steel wheel similar to the Pontiac Rally I in 1968.

Unlike the British wire wheels, there is no downside to the ownership of styled steel wheels on any pony car model.

Contrary to the obvious, there was never a magnesium wheel option for the Corvette at any time within the purview of this book. All models had wheel covers from 1953 through 1962. Knock-off aluminum wheels were shown in the brochure in 1963, but technical problems prevented the option from being produced. The 1964-66 models did have the option and for 1967 only, they were offered in a bolt-on design. A new bolt-on aluminum wheel design debuted in 1976. From then on, most Corvette models have had aluminum wheels of one design or another up through the scope of this book, 1990, and beyond.

This wheel discussion basically revolves around whether or not to change the wheels on a prospective purchase. Obviously I personally run the other way from any vehicle that has had any sort of non-factory wheel flares added in order to allow oversized wheels. We are talking only about wheels that fit within the stock wheel wells. Some of the middle period Spridgets came stock with disc wheels, but the factory optional wires were wider, allowing larger tires and adding to their appeal. Some of the later optional aluminum Corvette wheels were also wider, but optional wheels were often the same size. Some of the low-production hybrids such as the Cobras and Tigers, as well as the later Ferraris and Maseratis, were not mentioned above. These models were usually delivered with some sort of alloy wheel design indigenous to the brand. It is always a high priority on these models to have the original type of wheels as far as collectible values go. However, this is much more true of the Italians than the hybrids. Aftermarket mags on a Cobra or Tiger may not be much of a detriment, but try to stay with stock sizes and popular styles.

Let's roll on to tires. Although the French tire company Michelin launched the ground breaking Michelin X Radial tire in 1946, it would be years before the cars in this book came from the factory with radial tires. The Corvette would not get radials until 1973 and none of the pony cars in this book had them. We're talking nylon or rayon cord wide oval bias plies here, folks. Simply go onto the Tire Rack website and you will find countless reasons to put modern radials on your old sports car! They are more available, more appropriate for modern driving conditions, safer (particularly at high speeds) and cheaper than specialty retro tires. The only positive attribute they lack is the essence of being *original*. My advice is unless you are housing a *trailer queen* that only takes an occasional free ride to a car show, study the huge Tire Rack selection and go for it. Now I say this mostly in relation to the American models. The imports can be a little different.

Surprisingly some little squirts like the Spridgets had radial tire options years before the American models. Radials were a factory option on Sprites and Midgets in 1968. First of all, we are talking about *little* tires here, sports fans. Most of these will be thirteen-inchers and some will be skinny fifteen-inchers, and both types the opposite of the low-profile American styles. Getting the maximum amount of rubber on the road is not nearly as important when you have hamsters frantically peddling in the engine room. When I replaced the tires on my 1968 Fiat 850 Spider, I used (the new style for the time) Wide Ovals. The little squirt did, indeed, corner like nobody's business, but it felt a little squishy, as opposed to firm, when in that hard cornering mode. It also gave up a little in gas mileage and acceleration. The 39-cent premium fuel of the day sneered at the economy loss, but the little 52-horsepower engine struggled a little more to keep up with traffic. There will be few choices of tires of types and brands these days that will fit these classics, so your decision may well be made for you.

The standard steering wheel rim in the 1963 Sting Ray was color-coded to the interior, as with previous Corvettes. A new wood-grained plastic wheel was a $16 option, but only 130 cars had it. The 1964-67 Sting Ray had a wood-grained plastic steering wheel rim as standard equipment. In the 1965 and 1966 model years only, you could order an optional teakwood steering wheel, a rare and coveted option today among Corvette aficionados. The 1968 model had a plastic wood-grained steering wheel sixteen inches in diameter. The 1969-72 steering wheel rims were black vinyl and fifteen inches in diameter. The 1976 Corvette is somewhat infamous for its four-spoke, color-keyed vinyl steering wheel borrowed from the lowly Vega. You could change it, but should you?

Figure A27 - **This bright red classic interior design belongs to a 1962 Austin-Healey 3000 Mark II. Even the carpet in this example is bright red . The black plastic steering wheel with spring spokes virtually screams vintage English. The chrome passenger grab bar and wood shift knob add touches of elegance.** ©Valder 137 (CC)

Many of the wire-spoke, plastic-rimmed wheels of the early English roadsters have long ago developed problems and been replaced. These are generally difficult to restore if cracks have appeared in the rims and these early style wheels are expensive to replace. You may find used cars of these sorts with the popular real wood or leather rims and chrome, stainless, or black painted spokes. These were very popular in the middle to late Sixties as modern replacements for the more quaint original designs. This falls under the category of a *driver* vs. a *trailer queen*. Generally speaking, the older the English roadster, as in prior to 1966, the more out of place one of these wood wheels appears. Consider, too, that there is little moisture protection for whatever steering wheel is present in an early roadster. The bottom line is that so many of these little English roadsters are hardly valuable collectibles in the first place. From the Jaguars on up, it probably pays to restore the steering wheel to whatever was original equipment, whether it is your favorite or not.

Figure A28 - This elegant interior of light tan leather and rich polished wood belongs to a Jaguar XK-140 Drophead Coupe, the same car pictured earlier in this chapter. The interior of the XK-140 Roadster was similar in layout, but without the wood dash and vent windows. The Roadster also had a chrome grab handle in place of the glove box. You cannot see it in this small photo, but the tachometer needle spins counter-clockwise and a small clock is inset into the bottom portion of the tach. Other than facing the passenger, the speedometer is normal in design. The XK-140 had an unusual, large-diameter steering wheel with no dish and four flat spokes. ©Frodo Inge, Holland (GNU)

  The Germans and Japanese tended to stick to basic plastic steering wheels in the first place. You will rarely see anything else on most of the Karmann-Ghia, Porsche, or Datsun Sports models. Unfortunately, the relentless emphasis on engineering excellence in these models generally precludes the wood or leather rim fascinations that fans of American and British cars enjoy. Stick with the plastic.

The Italian cars generally had modern looking steering wheels from the beginning. Many of them were either real wood or plastic wood, down to the lowly Fiat 850 Spider. Of course the ones on Ferraris and Maseratis were real wood. I am not sure about Alfa Spider steering wheels.

All the steering wheels on the pony cars were plastic. As far as I know, there were a lot of wood-grained wheels on the ponies, but they were all plastic, whether standard or optional. The more modern styling of these wheels usually negated a desire to *update* the look. They were also a little more impervious to the cracking apart that inflicted the early English designs.

Timelines, Acquisistion & Ownership

Chapter 2: *The Big Three Affordable English Antiques*

Figure B1 - The Triumph TR-4A dash was very attractive with its white on black instruments with chrome rims set in a dark polished wood veneer. The later TR-250 changed the chrome bezels to flat black and the polished wood to a matte finish. I prefer the less distracting layout, but many TR purists especially like this one. This car still has its steering wheel with spring spokes, a rare find today. ©Arnaud 25 (PD)

Back when many of us were in college, or at least of approximate college age, that special time when we so deeply want to own our first real topless sports cars, three English brands dominated the U.S. market. Austin-Healey, MG, and Triumph sent hundreds of thousands to the USA. Each produced a standard series and an entry level series, few of which are particularly collectible today, yet they are dripping with nostalgia for our youth and an especially enlightening time in the history of American culture. Still desirable are special performance models constructed in small numbers. You may have wanted one of these when you were nineteen, but you drove a battered model of the more common series. The current lust in your heart is for a pristine example of the one the snotty frat boy's dad bought for him, or maybe the one your older brother brought back from Europe.

Ubiquity Squared: MG B to Triumph Spitfire

Figure B2 - A basic Triumph Spitfire Mark 1 in red with a black top and standard disc wheels. ©Sicnag (CC)

As you are well aware by now, this book is not going to regurgitate the well worn path of sports car history. The subject has been covered in great detail in countless books. Servicemen returning from Europe after World War II brought their spindly MG's home with them and America will never be the same. Blah, blah, blah. What this book will do is to describe the physical and emotional reasons why American sports car history developed in the precise manner it did. Let's begin with those quaint little English roadsters. Put on your stringback driving gloves and get out your raincoat because we rarely bother with that ornery, leaky contraption the Brits call a hood.

Most of the relevant history began after the war in the late '40's. The seed for the Corvette's birth had been sown by 1952. The English ringleaders were the MG's at the bottom of the price range and the Jaguars at the top. The Corvette would launch itself smack between these two in the U.S. market and remain there long past the eventual demise of the MG brand. The MG's would always offer affordability at the bottom of the market while Jaguar rolled along the edge of the luxury car market. Although the MG TC and TD are the models most often credited with sparking the sports car revolution in the USA, it was the later MGA model with its steel disc wheels, envelope body, and high production figures that really brought sports cars to the masses. There were only about 10,000 TC's and 30,000 TD's produced, but MG A production topped 100,000. Jaguar offered its XK-120, XK-140, and XK-150 models throughout the Fifties. By the end of the decade, Austin-Healey and Triumph would expand the competition.

The one key feature these cars had that sparked the revolution was a removable top. It is my humble opinion that if the Brits had been exporting only fixed roof cars to the U.S. in about 1946 to 1976, their success here would have been minimal. There had always been American-built convertibles, but they were always large, bulbous, tanks by comparison. Most of them drove like a ship and handled like a waterbed on wheels. The second feature the little Brits offered was nimble, fun-to-drive, sports car handling. Before the birth of the Corvette, named appropriately after a small ship, the fun to drive concept was foreign only.

Figure B3 - This early black MG B is typical of the breed. This is probably a 1968 model with its bolt-on wire wheels and lack of headrests. No, that is not a dent in the hood. It's just a reflection of sunlight. However, the little raised square portion of the hood next to it, directly behind the MG emblem, does appear a little battered on this example. ©Bull-Doser (PD)

Affordability, removable tops, and sprightly handling abounded in these little English roadsters, but modern convenience and practicality for American driving conditions, not so much. Let's begin with the top, in most cases a separate frame and fabric covering that was removed completely from the rear deck and stored in the trunk. These were not convertibles, but true roadsters, as only the first three production years of Corvettes were. The fit of these tops left a lot to be desired. Wind and water found its way in no matter how carefully the top was erected. The erection itself was not a quick affair, either, more akin to an old man in the pre-Viagra days than a teenager. On the earliest models, even outside door handles and roll-up windows were features of the future. The heaters were notoriously inefficient and air conditioning was an option only when you left the cantankerous top in the trunk. The trunk itself was rarely carpeted, or even covered in fancy cardboard, and the spare tire not only hogged most of the trunk space but added its own flavor of road and rubber dirt to whatever luggage you could squeeze in there. The small square footage behind the seats of any 1968-77 Stingray is a luxury ride for your luggage by comparison. Another favorite component the English companies loved to leave back on the factory floor was a fully synchromesh transmission. They were good at producing shifters that snick-snicked from gear to gear, but downshifting into first was an art to them when it should have been an artifact.

Figure B4 - This red Austin-Healey 100 is on display here at a British car show in Austin, Texas. You cannot miss the sporty laid down windshield or chrome knock-off wire wheels on this beauty!

©1985 Floyd M. Orr Collection

MG released its ubiquitous B model in 1962. Its klunky pushrod four produced a little less than 100 gross horsepower, and as with the MG A model noted above, its first gear was still unsynchronized and its top was still stored in the trunk. It did offer a nice, tight unibody construction, short-throw shifter, taut suspension, and nimble (but a bit heavy) steering and brakes quite adequate for its modest performance potential. At least the windows rolled up! The B's junior first cousin, the austere but superbly simple Austin-Healey Sprite had debuted in 1958 with its bugged out frog headlamps and full bonnet hinged like the later XK-E Jaguar and the much later Corvette C4. The now legendary *bugeye* look came about because A-H decided that hidden headlights, as a number of future legends would have, were too expensive a development for such a minimally engineered and priced car. Since MG and Austin-Healey had merged under the BMC (British Motor Corporation) banner by the era of the new MG B, the company decided to carry on the vaunted Midget name on a badge-engineered Sprite. The Midget was introduced about four months prior to the MG B. Unlike the higher priced B, the Midget would have Plexiglass side curtains until 1964. The differences between a Sprite and the B's little brother were absolutely minimal. The most distinguishing were a *waterfall* grille instead of the Sprite *egg crate* and chrome "blonk strips" down the body sides of the Midget. The seat upholstery piping inside was also slightly different.

The Austin-Healey story roughly parallels that of MG. The company released its first A-H 100 model at a London car show in 1952 and began production of the four-cylinder model the next year. The first model had a three-speed transmission that was actually a four-speed with an ultra-low first gear blocked off. This BN1 model was soon replaced with the BN2 with an actual four-speed. Less than 15,000 of these four-cylinder big Healeys were built through the '56 model year, when a new six-cylinder version was introduced. The 2660cc four was supplanted by a 2639cc six and a small 2+2 configuration was squeezed into the interior. The new 100 Six produced 102 gross horsepower at its introduction in 1956. The engine was increased to 117 horsepower in 1957 and production had been moved to the Abingdon MG plant by the end of the year. Over 14,000 100 Six's were built through the end of the Fifties. The six-cylinder model is identifiable by its 92-inch wheelbase, over the 90-inch version of the BN1 and BN2. The later models also sported somewhat sleeker styling and a little higher level appointments, although two-seaters and cars lacking the desirable overdrive transmission were produced until the end.

Figure B5 - This 1961 Austin-Healey 3000 Mk. II shows off several popular options of the day. The two-tone red and black paint complements the black top and interior. The silver-painted knock-off wire wheels, driving lights and luggage rack complete the package. ©Mick, Northamptonshire, England (CC)

Austin-Healey released its final six-cylinder model in late 1959 with the 3000 model. There was an obvious new larger engine of 2912cc and all models had front disc brakes and were assembled at the MG factory. Although the 3000 was basically very similar to its predecessor in its body and drivetrain, the new model would be slowly developed as the most deluxe Austin-Healey ever. Nearly 43,000 would be manufactured until its demise in 1967, forced by the new U.S. regulations that took effect on January 1, 1968. Like most of the other affordable, topless English sports cars of the Sixties, the USA was by far the largest market for the big Healeys, with the majority built with left hand drive and shipped over here. The deluxe developments began with the similar design as the 100 Six, with two-seater and 2+2 models and those with and without overdrive all produced simultaneously. This pattern would evolve toward the final Mark III models with feature-laden 2+2's shipped to the USA with overdrive, heater, roll-up windows, attached top, walnut dash, and adjustable steering column, with attractive two-tone paint, wire wheels, and removable hardtop as options. The thing to keep in mind about the Austin-Healey 3000 is that since production was halted before the performance, looks, or drivability were lessened by regulations, the later models are the ones generally most sought by enthusiasts.

Although *Daydreams in the Wind* covers the far reaches of the topless sports cars of The Sixties, from the uber-powerful Shelby Cobra to the ultra-rare Ferrari NART Spyder, the heart and soul of this book belongs to these two ubiquitous little sports cars, the MG B and Triumph Spitfire. Neither one is my personal favorite. If I was given unlimited cash and ordered to buy one of each of the cars discussed in this book, probably the only one that would enter my garage *after* the Spitfire and B would be the Karmann Ghia! Not only would that premise be true, but so would a much more likely scenario in which I could choose to spend my hard-earned cash on a sports car, either then or now. The B and Spitfire would finish close to last in my choices, no matter what the circumstances. Then how can I dare refer to these as representing the very soul of my book? They may not be my personal favorites, but these two, and their close familial associates, represent what most of this nostalgic quest for sports car nirvana is all about for the largest number of enthusiasts. Both were built from 1962 to 1980 in humongous numbers, most of which were immediately shipped to the USA, no matter which production year of this nearly two-decade lifespan we are talking about. The ubiquity of these two models is clearly reflected in the Bibliography by numerous road tests, comparison tests, and books published about them. Of course we are all familiar with the B's little brothers and the Spitfire's bigger ones that served to expand the influence of this family of MG's and Triumphs much further than might be noticed at first glance. The Fiat Spiders may have challenged the British models in the late '60's, but by that time the Brits had already had a decade's head start.

That last statement is true in one sense, but quite incorrect in another. This particular anomaly can be construed as the defining nature of this book. My central purpose has been to capture this special era called The Sixties and to define all of these cars within the context of the whole picture. Keep in mind that although many models of sports cars began to be imported into the U.S. in small numbers years prior to the 1960's, it was that glorious decade that brought the boom in their numbers, whether we are talking about Sprites or Ferraris. Although the importation of certain models was occurring, how many Fiat 1500's have you seen? How many MG A's? Do you see the difference? Sandwiched between the big Healeys and the Sprite in the consumer price range, the MG B did not really see much competition in the U.S. from anything without a Triumph badge until the Fiat 124 Spider of 1968.

Figure B6 - You can identify this red 1963 MG Midget as a Mark I model by its windshield and bare rear deck. The flat windshield has no vent windows and the top has been completely removed and placed in the trunk. Note the standard disc wheels. ©Hugh Llewelyn, Bristol, UK (CC)

Figure B7 - This is the little British Racing Green Bugeye that everybody loves! Note the sliding Plexiglass side curtains. ©TTTNIS (CC)

Spridget / Spitfire Timeline

3/31/58 - Bugeye Sprite production begins.
5/20/58 - The Austin-Healey Sprite is announced as a new upcoming production model.
5/61 - The Austin-Healey Sprite Mark II is announced.
6/61 - The MG Midget Mark I, companion model to the Sprite, is announced.
1962 - The Triumph Spitfire is introduced for the 1962 model year.
10/62 - The 1100cc engine is announced for the Sprite Mark II and Midget Mark I. Front disc brakes are included with the larger engine.
1964 - Wire wheels and metal hardtop become optional on the Spitfire Mark 2.
3/64 - The Sprite Mark III and Midget Mark II are announced with roll-up windows.
10/66 - The Sprite Mark IV and Midget Mark III are announced with a new 1275cc engine and an attached convertible top with an American-style snap-on vinyl boot.
1967 - The Spitfire Mark 3 is introduced with a walnut dash and attached top.
10/69 - The Sprite Mark V is announced for Europe only; discontinued from export. The Midget Mark IV is announced to continue export to the USA.
1973 - Spitfire Mark 4's exported to the USA receive the 1500cc engine.
1974 - Spitfire 1500 model finally has instruments directly in front of the driver.
10/74 - The Midget Mark IV 1500 is announced with the 1500cc Spitfire engine.

Figure B8 - Most of us agree that the early Spitfires are much more attractive with the optional wire wheels. This red Mark 2 has the correct optional knock-off wheels in painted silver, not chrome. ©Akela NDE (CC)

Austin-Healey Sprite

Figure B9 - Here is a red one with chrome wire wheels, just for you! ©Hajotthu (GNU)

Austin-Healey introduced the world's most famous *squirtabout* in 1958 with the *frogeye* or *bugeye* Sprite, whichever term of endearment you prefer. To this day, this super-primitive little car is worth a lot more than its faster, more comfortable descendants. The original Sprite was a *roadster*, to say the least! There were no door handles. There was no trunk. The top literally defined what we now refer to as an *erector set* design. The car was so tiny that you needed the open interior door panels just for a place to put your elbows. You need to get out? Just pull that little wire dangling by your elbow. The endearing Bugeye was replaced by an all-new body in 1961 that I happen to like, although most people prefer the previous frog look. The Mark II Sprite was still a full roadster with side curtains, but there was now a more conventional body design with a trunk. The Sprite would receive roll-up windows and a few other comforts a couple of years later, but it would be 1967 before the top was finally attached. The engine grew from 948cc to 1098cc halfway through the Mark II roadster production. You would think that the larger the engine the better, but some sources are not too keen on the 1098cc engine. They claim the crankshaft was a bit overstressed in this model; however, many of these have been running for decades. Disc front brakes and optional wire wheels were also introduced with the 1100 engine. The 1100 model continued from the last roadsters through the Mark III with roll-up windows. Everybody seems to love the 1275cc engine introduced with the attached convertible top package on the 1967 Mark IV. They like it even better than the 1500cc Spitfire engine that would be given to the later surviving Midget. Unfortunately the Sprite would never see a fully synchronized transmission, as included with the Midget 1500. The Spridgets did receive alternators and negative ground electrical systems on the 1968 models. This allowed the fitting of updated radios without the hassle of the previous models.

The Sprite will never be a particularly expensive collector car. You will generally pay twice as much for a Mark I Bugeye than for a Mark II-IV, given equivalent condition, of course. Probably the most common non-original issue will be the engine. Great numbers of the original 948cc type have been worn out or destroyed in amateur racing events. The 1275cc engine will generally be the most likely substitute when this happens. Although the 1100cc and the late Midget 1500cc types will fit, the 1275cc is far the most popular. The later engine may not even devalue a Mark II or Mark III that much, unless the car represents a concours level restoration. Second to the Bugeye, the Mark IV is distinctly the most desirable Sprite, mainly due to its better top and engine. The only downside to the Mark IV is that the interior and luggage space may feel a bit more cramped than in the earlier models. This is because the top drops down into the well behind the seats, taking up interior luggage space, and the more padded seats, door panels and dash encroach just a bit on elbow room.

Figure B10 - This red 1963 Austin-Healey Sprite Mk. II has the standard disc wheels with optional whitewalls.
©Carolyn Williams (CC)

The Mark II Sprite was joined by its companion Mark I Midget in 1961. The Mark II and III Midget joined the Mark III and IV Sprite, respectively in '64 and '67. This development was consistently a most blatant example of badge engineering. Whereas the Sprite had a simpler egg-crate grille, the Midget sported a version of the MG waterfall grille. The Midget had chrome anti-blonk strips down each side and contrasting color piping on the seats that was just a teensy bit more elegant. Some steering wheels varied slightly and of course the brand name emblems were different. The steering wheel of the early Midgets was gold plastic instead of black. The instruments and floor covering were styled just a bit differently. Early Sprites had a black rubber mat floor covering while that of the Midget had a speckled pattern. The interior of both models was carpeted from the advent of the 1100 engine to the end of production. Everything else about a Sprite and Midget of the same model year was for all practical purposes identical. They built a few more Sprites than Midgets in each of the early years, but the Midget numbers overtook those of the Sprite in the later years. The only model year in which the production of the Midget far outnumbered that of the Sprite was in 1969, the Sprite's last year in the USA. Minimal differences in collector prices between the two brands have persisted for decades, although when new the Midget was always priced a little above the Sprite.

Figure B11 - This classic blue Midget is showing off its optional wire wheels and tonneau cover. ©Nightflyer (GNU)

As with most of the cars in this book, when you are looking for a nice collectible, rust is always the biggest booger. On a Sprite it can attack most anywhere, from the base of the windshield to the trunk floor. Check out the suspension attachment points, door sills, and floor pan. Even those little holes in the side panels for the jacking points can be a problem. The little round rubber seals for these holes may have rotted decades ago and the holes left exposed to water for years. Rubber seals around the gas cap and at the base of the windshield are also suspect. Never forget that in that long ago and far away dealership once sat a brand new Sprite for less than $2500 that any wild and crazy young man could afford.

Although obviously troublesome, wire wheels are certainly the most collectible asset of a Sprite, probably even on the early models before wires were a factory option. Keep in mind that these were never chrome except from the aftermarket. All factory wires were silver painted. Leather upholstery for the seats was a factory option in 1961. This choice may or may not have been continued on later models. To the best of my knowledge, I have personally seen only vinyl in any Spridget. Dealer-installed options were common on all the Sprite models. A tonneau cover was a popular option and some cars may have radios, particularly the later models. As shown on the accessory order form displayed elsewhere in this chapter, a walnut shift knob and chrome luggage rack were popular dress-up options.

Figure B12 - Pale sky blue Bugeye on a cloudy day... ©Supermac 1961, Chafford Hundred, England (CC)

Austin-Healey Sprite Production Chart

Year	Model	Production	Year	Model	Production
1958	Mark I	8729	1966	Mark III	7024
1959	Mark I	21,566	1967	Mark IV	6895
1960	Mark I	18,665	1968	Mark IV	7049
1961	Mark II	10,059	1969	Mark IV	6129
1962	Mark II	12,041	1970	Mark V	1292
1963	Mark II	8852	1971	Mark V	1022
1964	Mark III	11,157			
1965	Mark III	8882	Total	Mk. I - V	129,362

Austin-Healey Sprite Production Chart Notes:

The numbers in the chart were sourced from *The Sprites and Midgets: A Collector's Guide* and the *Illustrated Austin-Healey Buyer's Guide*. Although the listed figures represent total Sprite production, a very high, but unknown, percentage of these came to the U.S., although none of the 2314 Mark V's produced in 1970-71 were imported into the USA. The production totals and the years listed do not exactly match what we know as the Mark I through Mark V models. The figures themselves are accurate, but there is some overlap among the model years and Mark Series. According to *A-Z of Cars 1945-1970*, the series totals were: Mark I 48,987, Mark II 31,665, Mark III 25,905, and Mark IV 22,790. This total of 129,347 is slightly different than that shown by the year breakdown in the chart.

Figure B13 - 1965 Sprite Mk. III in Red. The '65 model had 61 horsepower and a base price of $1965. ©Sicnag (CC)

Austin-Healey Sprite Color Chart

Year	Model	Exterior Color	Interior	Top
1958	Sprite Mk. I	Speedwell Blue	Blue	Black
1958	Sprite Mk. I	Pale Primrose Yellow	Black	Black
1958	Sprite Mk. I	Dark Green	Suede Green	Black
1958-59	Sprite Mk. I	Cherry Red	Matador Red	Black
1958-60	Sprite Mk. I	Old English White	Matador Red	Black
1959	Sprite Mk. I	Old English White	Black	White
1959	Sprite Mk. I	Old English White	Matador Red	White
1959	Sprite Mk. I	Cherry Red	Matador Red	White
1959	Sprite Mk. I	Iris Blue	Blue	White
1959	Sprite Mk. I	Leaf Green	Suede Green	White
1959	Sprite Mk. I	Nevada Beige	Matador Red	White
1959-60	Sprite Mk. I	Nevada Beige	Matador Red	Black
1959-60	Sprite Mk. I	Leaf Green	Suede Green	Black
1959-60	Sprite Mk. I	Iris Blue	Blue	Black
1959-60	Sprite Mk. I	Old English White	Black	Black
1961	Sprite Mk. II	Speedwell Blue	Cornflower Blue	Blue
1961	Sprite Mk. II	Signal Red	Black	Black
1961-62	Sprite Mk. II	Highway Yellow	Black	Black
1961-62	Sprite Mk. II	Deep Pink	Black	Black
1961-62	Sprite Mk. II	Old English White	Black	Grey
1961-62	Sprite Mk. II	Black	Cherry Red	Grey
1961-63	Sprite Mk. II	Black	Red	Black
1961-63	Sprite Mk. II	Dove Grey	Red	Grey
1961-63	Sprite Mk. II	Old English White	Red	Grey
1962	Sprite Mk. II	Iris Blue	Cornflower Blue	Blue
1962	Sprite Mk. II	Signal Red	Red	Black
1963	Sprite Mk. II	Signal Red	Black	Red
1963	Sprite Mk. II	Signal Red	Red	Red
1963	Sprite Mk. II	Old English White	Hazelnut	Hazelnut
1963	Sprite Mk. II	Black	Hazelnut	Hazelnut
1963	Sprite Mk. II	Iris Blue	Blue	Dark Blue
1963	Sprite Mk. II	Fiesta Yellow	Black	Black
1963	Sprite Mk. II	British Racing Green	Black	Black

Year	Model	Body Color	Trim	Top
1964	Sprite Mk. III	Old English White	Hazelnut	Hazelnut
1964	Sprite Mk. III	Black	Hazelnut	Hazelnut
1964	Sprite Mk. III	Iris Blue	Blue	Dark Blue
1964	Sprite Mk. III	Signal Red	Red	Red
1964	Sprite Mk. III	Signal Red	Black	Red
1964-65	Sprite Mk. III	Fiesta Yellow	Black	Black
1964-66	Sprite Mk. III	British Racing Green	Black	Black
1964-66	Sprite Mk. III	Old English White	Black	Black
1964-66	Sprite Mk. III	Old English White	Red	Grey
1964-66	Sprite Mk. III	Dove Grey	Red	Grey
1964-66	Sprite Mk. III	Black	Red	Black
1965-66	Sprite Mk. III	Tartan Red	Red	Red
1965-66	Sprite Mk. III	Tartan Red	Black	Red
1965-66	Sprite Mk. III	Riviera Blue	Light Blue	Light Blue
1966	Sprite Mk. III	Pale Primrose Yellow	Black	Black
1967-68	Sprite Mk. IV	Old English White	Black	Black
1967-68	Sprite Mk. IV	Old English White	Red	Black
1967-68	Sprite Mk. IV	Tartan Red	Black	Red
1967-68	Sprite Mk. IV	Black	Red	Black
1967-69	Sprite Mk. IV	Black	Black	Black
1967-69	Sprite Mk. IV	Basilica Blue	Black	Black
1967-69	Sprite Mk. IV	British Racing Green	Black	Black
1967-69	Sprite Mk. IV	Pale Primrose	Black	Black
1969	Sprite Mk. IV	Tartan Red	Black	Black
1969	Sprite Mk. IV	Snowberry White	Black	Black

Austin-Healey Sprite Color Chart Notes:

This list of color combinations may not be absolutely correct. Additional choices may have been available in certain years. Some color combinations may not have been available in the U.S. market.

The Big Healeys

Figure B14 - Ladies and gentlemen... presenting the Holy Grail of Austin-Healeys, the 100S! ©Rama (CC)

Five years prior to the release of the ultimate minimalist sports car, Austin-Healey began production of its legendary 100 model, the beginning of what enthusiasts of the future would refer to as *The Big Healeys*. In its short lifespan of fifteen years, Austin-Healey would become famous for its diminutive Sprite and its larger brother, considered the big gun of the British Motor Corporation group. Within the specific production period of each model, the Austin-Healey 100 Four, 100 Six, and 3000 were marketed as the largest, most powerful of the BMC sports car lineup. BMC threw in the towel in the face of the new U.S. regulations facing the company for 1968. This should not be surprising since the basic design originated way back in 1953. Legal updates to the 3000 at that time would have been prohibitively expensive and surely difficult to accomplish as the future regulations increased, so A-H chose to allow the vaunted Big Healey to honorably slide into a quiet demise. Unfortunately, BMC's attempt to replace the 3000 in the market with the new six-cylinder MG C flopped miserably. The company managed to shove only 4550 of the MG B look-alike roadsters out the dealer doors over a three year period.

    The Austin-Healey 100 was born the same year as the Corvette. Primitive was the correct description for sports cars in 1953. The 100 had an OHV four-cylinder producing ninety horsepower. The first gear in its four-speed sourced from a completely different model was so low that the factory chose to block it off in the Healey application. It was an actual four-speed that was applied as a three-speed in the new sports car! Is that strange or what? After constructing over 10,000 of the BN1 model this way, a new BN2 model was introduced two years later with a proper four-speed shift. It would be another decade before the Austin-Healey 3000 received a properly attached convertible top with roll-up side windows. Part of the charm of the early models was that the windshield could be folded down for that extra-sporty look. The windshield became a standard type fixed in place for the 100 Six and 3000 models, leaving this little asset to the four-cylinder models only.

Figure B15 - Austin-Healey 100 Six BN4 in red and cream with a black tonneau. ©Adrian Pingstone (PD)

Two special four-cylinder big Healeys were produced in small numbers. The fifty-five 100S models represented the race package. You are not likely to find one of these for sale outside an auction. Even a ratty one of these currently could set you back $700,000. We're talking about a million for a nice one. The aluminum Westlake head and other special tuning features pushed the horsepower up to 132. With the weight cut to less than a ton, the 100 S could do 0-60 in less than eight seconds. The 100S was the only Austin-Healey produced with four-wheel disc brakes, too. Watch out for counterfeiters of this especially valuable Healey. The 100M was far more available and affordable, even back in 1955. With a little diligence, you can likely locate a nice one of these for about $100,000. The 100M was an optional high-performance kit costing $290 added to cars pulled from the assembly line by the factory. Dealers could install the kits, too, but all the components may not have been changed by these kits and cars with dealer-installed kits are far less valuable today. You are likely to discover a fair number of BN2 models out in the marketplace currently sporting 100M accoutrements. These may have been dealer-kitted when new or recently modified with available parts. Just keep in mind that these cars are worth little more than ordinary BN2 models. The distinctive louvered hood with leather retaining strap is easily added. The matching serial numbers stamped into the edge of the hood and the chassis plate most precisely identify a genuine factory 100M.

Figure B16 - Austin-Healey 100M BN2 in black. ©Sicnag (CC)

The Austin-Healey 100 Six is generally the least loved of the line. The six-cylinder engine brought more smoothness in the firing sequence at the expense of more weight. The horsepower increased from 90 to 102 while the weight went from 2150 to 2480. Strangely enough, the six-cylinder is ever so slightly *smaller* in displacement than the four! The company did not change the engine out of stupidity. The original four-cylinder engine was taken out of production by BMC after 1955. The head design of the early six-cylinder models was problematic, but improvements were soon made. You can spot one of these early head designs externally by the distinctly vertically mounted SU carburetors. The later, improved heads have the carbs mounted at a thirty degree angle. Even with the six-cylinder engine, a BN4 could not beat a twelve-second 0-60 mph time. You can see from the chart that the 2+2 BN4 models outnumbered the two-seater BN6's by more than two to one. Due to their smaller numbers and sportier looks, the two-seaters are still the more collectible. At today's auction prices, you might pay about $40,000 for a nice BN6, but you can add the rear seats and drop that figure by as much as $5000. As with many of the other English cars in this book, wire wheels will always add to the value. The second most desirable option would be the removable hardtop.

Figure B17 - Here is a 100M in a light metallic green with its windshield laid down. ©Dave 7, Lethbridge, Canada (CC)

Austin-Healey produced its crown jewel of big-six power in 1959-67 with the 2912cc, aptly named 3000. These were built in three series, with each succeeding group offering more power and luxury at the minor expense of quick, responsive handling and bugs in your teeth fun. Series I began with 124 horsepower pushing 2460 pounds. Series III ended with 150 horsepower pushing two-hundred additional pounds. By the time production began, the two-seater big Healeys were losing ground to the 2+2 models. The sportier type was outnumbered four to one, even in the first series. Unlike the earlier big Healeys, though, the 2+2 gradually gained favor with buyers who enjoyed the comfort and luxury features of the later models.

The Series I 3000 could break the ten-second 0-60 barrier and stop considerably quicker than the 100 Six due to its new Girling disc front brakes. As with all the Healeys, rust was still the ultimate booger. Plexiglass side curtains continued on the Series I models, as did the choice of two or four seats. The plastic steering wheel of these models is difficult to restore. You might see a lot of aftermarket wood wheels on these cars today. The Mark II model was introduced in 1961 with three SU carbs. This was done solely to homologate for racing. The triple carb setup brought synchronizing issues without doing much to increase performance, in spite of a claim of 132 horsepower instead of 124. Another little anomaly is that the Mark II name continued on a model released in early '62 that reverted back to the twin SU carbs, but now produced 136 horsepower. This was also the first Healey with both roll-up windows and a fully attached convertible top. Power brakes were optional for the first time on this second edition of the Mark II. You can spot one of these cars by its bare steel dash and interior layout that are generally identical to the earlier cars, except with roll-up windows. The gearshift will also be in the center of the transmission tunnel. It was offset on the earlier cars. The removable hardtop became an extremely rare option because now the attached soft top assembly had to be removed from the car before the hardtop could be set in place.

Figure B18 - Maroon and white 1964 Austin-Healey 3000. The Mark II model weighed 2370 pounds and had a base price of $3699 in 1965. ©Bull-Doser (PD)

The 1964-67 Austin-Healey 3000 Mark III is the car most enthusiasts are enthused about. By this time the power rating had reached either 148 or 150 horsepower, depending upon the quoted source. The brochure stated 150. The interior design is a beautiful classic with its real wood veneer dash, new electric tachometer, console, and fold-down rear seat. Models sent to the USA had included overdrive, heater, adjustable steering column, power front disc brakes and wire wheels. A radio was still optional at extra cost, as was the popular and attractive two-tone paint job. The Mark III received standard power brakes and a revised exhaust system that finally increased the miserably low ground clearance of the earlier cars. The final improvements arrived later in 1964 with an improved frame and rear suspension that raised ground clearance even further. The way to tell a Phase Two car from a Phase One is by the later car's separate parking lights and turn signals and the greater fender clearance over the rear wheels.

Unlike some cars covered in this book, the A-H 3000 has generally increased in value as the model years and luxury features have progressed forward. This is still true today. A Mark III is likely to cost you tens of thousands more than a Mark I. A '59 model might be $50,000 for a nice drivable example. A '67 Mark III could easily be $60,000 and the price escalates from that point. Enthusiasts love that classic wood dash combined with roll-up windows and a fully attached convertible top, and I don't blame them a bit!

Figure B19 - 1967 Austin-Healey 3000 Mk. III in all black. The Mark III model weighed 2650 pounds and had a base price of $3699 in 1965. ©Mick, Northamptonshire, England (CC)

Big Healey Comparison Chart

Model	Type	CI / CC	HP	Wt.	Brakes
1953-56 Austin-Healey 100 BN1	I-4	162 / 2660	90	2015	Drum
1953-56 Austin-Healey 100 BN2	I-4	162 / 2660	90	2150	Drum
1955 Austin-Healey 100S	I-4	162 / 2660	132	1925	Disc
1956-57 Austin-Healey 100-6	I-6	161 / 2639	102	2435	Drum
1957-59 Austin-Healey 100-6	I-6	161 / 2639	117	2480	Drum
1959-60 Austin-Healey 3000 Mk. I	I-6	178 / 2912	124	2460	Disc
1961-62 Austin-Healey 3000 Mk. II	I-6	178 / 2912	132	2530	Disc
1963-66 A-H 3000 Mk. III	I-6	178 / 2912	136	2650	Disc
1967 Austin-Healey 3000 Mk. III	I-6	178 / 2912	150	2650	Disc

Big Healey Comparison Chart Notes:
All Austin-Healey 3000's had a 92-inch wheelbase. The original base retail price of an early 3000 Mark III was $3565. The 100S model had four-wheel disc brakes. All others had discs on the front wheels only.

Figure B20 - Silver and Old English White 3000 Mark III. ©©Allen Watkin, London, England (CC)

Big Austin-Healey Color Chart

Model	Exterior Color	Model	Exterior Color
1955-56 100 BN2	Black	1955-56 100 BN2	*Optional Two-Tones*
1955-56 100 BN2	Old English White		
1955-56 100 BN2	Healey Blue	1955-56 100 BN2	Black w/Red
1955-56 100 BN2	Spruce Green	1955-56 100 BN2	Red w/Black
1955-56 100 BN2	Florida Green	1955-56 100 BN2	White w/Black
1955-56 100 BN2	Reno Red	1955-56 100 BN2	Blue w/White
1955-56 100 BN2	Gunmetal Grey	1955-56 100 BN2	Green w/White
1959-60 Mk. I	Old English White	1959-60 Mk. I	Black
1959-60 Mk. I	Colorado Red	1959-60 Mk. I	Metallic Ice Blue
1959-60 Mk. I	Pacific Green	1959-60 Mk. I	Florida Green
1959-60 Mk. I	Primrose		
1961 - 1967 3000	Old English White	1961 - 1967 3000	Black
1961 - 1967 3000	Colorado Red	1961 - 1967 3000	Florida Green

1961 - 1967 3000	Metallic Ice Blue	1961 - 1967 3000	British Racing Green
1965 3000	Black	1965 3000	Ivory White
1965 3000	Healey Blue	1965 3000	Colorado Red
1965 3000	British Racing Green		

Big Austin-Healey Color Chart Notes:

The 1965 model had roll-up windows, attached top, and wire wheels as standard. Whitewalls, radio, and tonneau were optional. The *H* brochure we have is for the USA and it is slightly different than the *A* one from online listed as 1963. The U.S. model had more standard equipment, including an adjustable steering column, heater, windshield washers, wire wheels, overdrive, and power brakes. Radio, tonneau cover, and luggage rack were options.

Figure B21 - Here is a parting shot of a restored 1955 British Racing Green 100M. The leather hood strap and chrome knock-off wires are clearly visible. ©Chris 73 (GNU)

Big Austin-Healey Production Chart

A-H 100 Models	Built	A-H 3000 Models	Built
1953-55 100 BN1 3-speed	10,688	1959-61 3000 Mk. I BN7 2S	2825
1955-56 100 BN2 4-speed	2765	1959-61 3000 Mk I BT7 2+2	10,825
1955 100S Racer	55		
1955-56 100M	1159	1959-61 3000 Mk. I	13,650
1953-56 Four-Cylinder	14,667	1961-63 3000 Mk. II BN7	355
		1961-62 3000 Mk. II BT7 2+2	5095
1956-59 100-6 BN4 2+2	10,286	1962-63 3000 Mk. II BJ7	6113
1958-59 100-6 BN6 2S	4150		
		1961-63 3000 Mk. II	11,563
1956-59 Six-Cylinder	14,436		
		1964 BJ8 Mk. III Phase 1	1390
1953-59 A-H 100	29,103	1964-67 BJ8 Mk. III Phase 2	16,314
Total A-H 100	29,103	1963-67 3000 Mk. III BJ8	17,704
Total A-H 3000	42,917		
Total Big Healey Production	72,020	1959-67 3000 Mk. I/II/III	42,917

Big Austin-Healey Production Chart Notes:

All the figures in the chart represent the total production for all markets. The Austin-Healeys were designed for the American market from the outset and about ninety-percent of production was sent to the USA. The figures are sourced from the *Illustrated Austin-Healey Buyer's Guide*. The production number stated includes only the factory 100M's. The BN4 was a 2+2 and the BN6 was a two-seater. The A-H 3000 was built in seven types without clear delineations between the model years. The final production year for the big Healey was 1967, when 3051 were produced. All Austin-Healeys had a four-speed transmission with an unsynchronized first gear. Clausager's *Original Austin-Healey* quotes slightly different figures of 10,030 BN1's and 4604 BN2's, including the special models.

MG - Octagonian Dominance

Morris Garages launched the low-priced topless sports car craze in America with its TC model. The company built 10,002 between 1945 and 1949, but only 2001 were officially imported to the U.S.; however, an unknown number were personally brought here by American servicemen. Production of the 1950-53 TD model nearly tripled with 29,664 built. The TF model was a bit less popular with only 13,000 produced in 1953-55.

The first MG with a modern envelope body was the A model released in 1955 and produced until the new B model was released in mid-1962. The A model had fifteen-inch wheels, as would its descendant the C. All the B models had fourteen-inch wheels. The A and B models used a pair of six-volt batteries in a positive-ground electrical system, a definite deterrent to upgrading the radio system in one of these cars. The twin six-volt batteries would not be replaced with a single twelve-volt until 1975. The most collectible MG A is clearly the Twin Cam hot rod model built in small numbers in a brief period in 1959-60. The Twin Cam also had disc brakes and these were carried over into a 1600 DeLuxe model with a more reliable OHV engine in the same time period. There was no lockable secure compartment on any of the MG A Roadsters. There were no outside door or trunk handles, either. You had to reach underneath the side curtain to open the door from the inside with the top erect. The trunk release was inside the passenger compartment. Rear visibility was improved in 1957 with the addition of rear corner windows in the soft top of the Roadster.

Figure B22 - This MG A has a number of options from both the factory and the aftermarket that were typically popular when this car was new. The black exterior with red interior was a common color for the era. The radio. chrome luggage rack, and fender mirrors could have been factory installed, but the wood steering wheel and the wider, chrome knock-off wires and exhaust tip likely were not. ©Robotriot (GNU)

At first glance you might expect the new MG look and envelope body design to evolve from the A model into the B, with the Midget following later as the entry-level MG with similar design and styling. Regardless of how it all began behind closed doors at the company, the new Midget preceded the B by one model year. The 1962 MG B would look very much within the family style, with just enough additional space, power and panache to upstage the Midget. The body was much the same, although a little wider and flatter. The wheels were fourteen inch instead of thirteen and the OHV 1798cc four-cylinder became MG's standard powerplant for decades to come. The engine produced 95 gross horsepower with twin SU carbs. The only early alteration to the engine was a change from a three-main-bearing crankshaft to a smoother, more reliable one with five bearings in October 1964. The new crank and a standard oil cooler improved the 1965 model. The result would be that the most desirable B's are usually the 1965-67 models with the five-bearing crank and no emission controls or safety bumpers. You also get the added bonus of standard leather seats on the early models. The MG B did not get an all-synchro transmission until 1968. The 1968 Mark II model also received an updated electrical system with negative ground and an alternator, as did the Spridgets at about the same time, as mentioned earlier. An official, much-improved convertible top arrived in 1970, although an optional, but more primitive, attached version had been available since the mid-Sixties. The shame of it is that these improvements appeared only after the engine began to be slowly strangled by emission controls. Like some other cars in this book, if I were seeking an MG B, I would compare and contrast the 1965-67 models very carefully with the 1968-70 alternative. For me, the sacrifice of a little horsepower might be worth having the better top and transmission.

Figure B23 - Here is a typical MG A in Old English White with red interior and black top that has the correct silver-painted knock-off wire wheels. ©Charles01 (GNU)

The 1971-80 B's are another box of English chocolates. In parallel, I'm sure that Forrest Gump would say much the same thing about the 1971-79 Midget. The EPA did cause the horsepower of the B to slowly erode down to a snail-slow 62 net horsepower by the mid-Seventies, but all the candies in that box are not sour. Interior furnishings gradually improved to the end. The seats were covered in vinyl instead of leather in 1970, but they were redesigned for more comfort and adjustable for rake. Sixty-spoke painted wire wheels or chrome wires were optional. You could get an optional factory AM/FM stereo radio with 8-track or cassette in 1975. For the record, AM/FM mono was the only thing that fit in a '75 Midget. The interior vinyls and carpet were of a higher grade than in the early days, when a three-year-old B that had been parked in the sun and rain could appear positively ancient. Fancier wheels and exterior stripes jazzed up the exterior and drew your eyes away from the massive black bumpers. To meet new headlight and bumper height laws, the B was raised up on its suspension, which did nothing for its flat cornering capability.

Figure B24 - The massive black bumpers mandated for the U.S. market were not only heavy and ugly, but their raised height negatively affected the handling of the delicate little MG B. This red 1975 model shows off the attractive mag-style wheels of the later MG's. These are known as the Rostyle wheels. ©Mr. Choppers (GNU)

MG constructed 4550 six-cylinder MG C Roadsters from 1967-69. The C models had either a fully synchronized four-speed or an automatic transmission. It is unknown how many were exported to the USA. The C had a 145-hp, 2912cc inline six that added 209 pounds to the car. The *Illustrated MG Buyer's Guide* states this weight increase as 340 pounds. No matter which weight is correct, the MG C suffered from understeer that made the car less fun to drive than the B. While the top speed was increased from the B's 105 mph at best to an easily reached 120 with the C, the tall gearing of the C made the six-cylinder model *slower* around town. The C was a much better highway cruiser, but the slower, ponderous handling really hurt the car's reputation.

The bottom line for the current time is that with its extremely high production numbers, the MG B is barely considered a collectible car. With less than 5000 MG C Roadsters built, you might pay twice as much for one today as an equivalent model B. That isn't saying much, however. The nice example of a B might cost you $10,000 while the equivalent C might be $20,000. You risk the project not being cost effective if you choose to restore an example of either model, although the C clearly has the edge. On the other hand, your chances of locating the B you want of the right year in your original color preference and in fine condition is *much* greater. All things considered, the B has become the ultimate ubiquitous English sports car. The C has that Rodney Dangerfield problem of never achieving the respect of the somewhat fickle enthusiast market. Maybe what you really need is one of each. You can enjoy driving the B while you polish the C for car shows.

Figure B25 - This white MG C sports the popular chrome wire wheel option. ©Alf van Beem (CC)

Figure B26 - This Inca Yellow 1979 MG Midget 1500 represents the final year of production. This photo shows the Rostyle wheels with chrome trim rings and the massive rear safety bumper. The 1500 designation refers to the 1493cc Spitfire engine utilized in the Midget after the parent corporation absorbed Triumph. ©ChiemseeMan (PD)

The 1961-79 Midget deserves a few footnotes here. We know the Midget was for all practical purposes identical to the Sprite in the Sprite's Mark II through Mark IV iterations. As with the Sprite, the Midget got a fully attached convertible top in 1967. Unlike the B, which offered a choice of top designs for many production years, the top on the Spridgets was either removable through 1966 or attached from 1967-onward. The 1970-79 Midget continued as the B's little brother and the Sprite's direct descendant. The differences between the Sprite and Midget were covered in the Sprite section. The Midget continued alone throughout the Seventies as the Spitfire's leading competitor. The 1970-73 models carried on with the same 1275cc OHV four-cylinder as before, with the power weakening a little each year. The Midget received much the same interior style and comfort features as the B. By the middle of the decade, the Midget was the slowest of its kind, with the cumbersome handling brought by its big, high, safety bumpers. Since Triumph had become a part of the same conglomerate, the 1975 Midget was given the Spitfire's larger 1493cc engine to help offset the EPA power losses. The 1967 Midget had shared 65 horsepower with its Sprite stablemate. This number had diminished to 54 by the 1972 model. By the end of production, the most the Midget could muster was 50 net horsepower from its 1500 engine with a single Zenith-Stromberg carburetor. The Midget still had only an AM radio in 1970 as its best entertainment option. By 1975, either the AM or AM/FM option was available in a Midget, still in glorious monaural sound only.

Someone had a bad idea without consulting with the engineering department and changed the straight rear wheel arches to curved ones to stylishly match the front arches in 1972. The straight rear arches had been a structural element of the Sprites and Midgets, protecting this weak area of the body from bending or collapsing. Examine this area thoroughly for signs of stress if you are considering a 1972-74 Midget. Late in the 1974 production year, MG introduced what it referred to as the AN-6 Midget. Changes included safety bumpers, the

1493cc Spitfire engine, and finally a fully synchronized gearbox from the Austin Marina. The figure for 1974 shown in the MG Midget Production Chart represents only the models constructed prior to the upcoming major changes for 1975. These changes also included a return to the straight rear wheel arches for proper rear body structure support. The company quietly hoped this last change would go unnoticed by consumers.

MG B Roadster Model Year Timeline

1962 - 95 hp - Three main bearings - non-synchro first - leather seats - positive ground
1963 - 95 hp - As '62 with twin SU carbs - Optional overdrive and fiberglass hardtop
1964 - 95 hp - Electric tachometer standard
1965 - 95 hp - Five-bearing crankshaft & oil cooler standard
1966 - 95 hp - Leather seats - Attached top & painted wire wheels optional
1967 - 98 hp - Front anti-roll bar standard - Air conditioning optional
1968 - 92 hp - Synchronized first gear - Negative ground with alternator
1969 - 92 hp - Negative ground - AM/FM mono, console, clock & chrome wires optional
1970 - 92 hp - Rake adjustable vinyl seats & Rostyle wheels standard
1971 - 89 hp - Improved folding top design & black aluminum grille
1972 - 78 hp - Rostyle wheels - Glove box & face-level air vents - Side stripes optional
1973 - 78 hp - New grille design - Armrests standard
1974 - 78 hp - Radial tires & bumper guards - Safety bumpers with raised bumper height
1975 - 62 hp - Single Zenith-Stromberg carb - Single 12V battery - Power brakes
1976 - 62 hp - Improved suspension tuning to match the high-mounted, heavy bumpers
1977 - 62 hp - Larger anti-roll bars - Improved dash - Electric clock standard
1978 - Twin thermostatically controlled engine fans & sealed cooling system
1979 - Black Limited Edition w/silver stripes, luggage rack and leather steering wheel
1980 - 80-mph speedometer

Figure B27 - This 1972 MG B has the classic look in British Racing Green, black top, chrome luggage rack and the correct silver-painted, bolt-on wire wheels. ©Oxfordian Kissuth (CC)

MG B Roadster Production by Model Year Chart

Series	Year	Built	Series	Year	Built
Mark I Roadster	1962	4518	Mark III Roadster	1972	26,222
Mark I Roadster	1963	23,308	Mark III Roadster	1973	19,546
Mark I Roadster	1964	26,542	Mark III Roadster	1974	19,713
Mark I Roadster	1965	24,179	Mark III Roadster	1975	19,967
Mark I Roadster	1966	22,675	Mark III Roadster	1976	25,860
Mark I Roadster	1967	15,128	Mark III Roadster	1977	24,482
Mark II Roadster	1968	17,355	Mark III Roadster	1978	21,703
Mark II Roadster	1969	18,896	Mark III Roadster	1979	23,221
Mark II Roadster	1970	23,866	Mark III LE (USA)	1979	6682
Mark II Roadster	1971	22,511	Mark III Roadster	1980	10,891
			Total B Roadsters	1962-80	397,265

MG B Roadster Production by Model Year Chart Notes:

As with the Austin-Healeys and the MG Midget, the above figures are roughly correct in total. In actuality, there were many cases of each Mark Series designation overlapping model years. There may be some confusion as to what figure represents a model year and what represents a calendar year. The year-by-year MG B production figures were sourced from the website mg-cars.org.uk. Note that no two sources seem to agree as to the exact production number of MG B Roadsters. This source states 397,265. Clausager's *Original MGB* quotes 386,961. Some online sources state 399,070; however, this figure cannot be verified by a reputable print source. Wherever 399,070 is quoted, the math is incorrect when figures stated by the same source for the GT coupe are added to a quoted total.

Figure B28 - Old English White 1965 MG Midget Mark II with optional painted knock-off wires. ©Sicnag (CC)

MG Midget Mark I, II & III Color Chart

Year	Model	Exterior Color	Interior	Top
1961	Midget Mk. I	Clipper Blue	Black	Black
1961-62	Midget Mk. I	Almond Green	Black	Black
1961-62	Midget Mk. I	Farina Grey	Black	Grey
1961-62	Midget Mk. I	Farina Grey	Matador Red	Grey *
1961-63	Midget Mk. I	Black	Black	Black
1961-63	Midget Mk. I	Black	Matador Red	Grey *
1961-63	Midget Mk. I	Old English White	Black	Black
1961-63	Midget Mk. I	Old English White	Black	Grey *
1961-63	Midget Mk. I	Old English White	Matador Red	Grey *
1961-63	Midget Mk. I	Tartan Red	Black	Red *
1962	Midget Mk. I	Tartan Red	Matador Red	Red *
1962	Midget Mk. I	Clipper Blue	Dark Blue	Dark Blue *
1962-63	Midget Mk. I	Ice Blue	Black	Black

1964	Midget Mk. II	Black	Red	Black
1964-65	Midget Mk. II	Dove Grey	Red	Grey
1964-66	Midget Mk. II	British Racing Green	Black	Black
1964-66	Midget Mk. II	Old English White	Red	Grey
1964-66	Midget Mk. II	Old English White	Black	Black
1964-66	Midget Mk. II	Riviera Blue	Light Blue	Light Blue
1964-66	Midget Mk. II	Tartan Red	Red	Red
1964-66	Midget Mk. II	Tartan Red	Black	Red
1965-66	Midget Mk. II	Black	Black	Black
1967	Midget Mk. III	Old English White	Black	Black
1967	Midget Mk. III	Tartan Red	Red	Black
1967-68	Midget Mk. III	Riviera Blue	Light Blue	Black
1967-68	Midget Mk. III	Basilica Blue (dark)	Blue	Black
1967-69	Midget Mk. III	Mineral Blue (dark)	Black	Black
1967-69	Midget Mk. III	Pale Primrose	Black	Black
1967-69	Midget Mk. III	Black	Black	Black
1967-69	Midget Mk. III	British Racing Green	Black	Black
1968-69	Midget Mk. III	Snowberry White	Black	Black
1968-69	Midget Mk. III	Tartan Red	Black	Black

MG Midget Mark I, II & III Color Chart Notes:

Color combinations followed by an asterisk were confirmed by the *Standard Guide to British Sports Cars*. A few of the color combinations without asterisks are questionable. As noted in the Mark III section, Basilica Blue and Mineral Blue are dark and similar. I doubt that both these shades were ever offered simultaneously in the same market.

MG Midget Mark IV & 1500 Color Chart

Model	*Exterior*	*Interior*	*Exterior*	*Interior*
1970	Blue Royale	Black	Flame Red	Black
1970	British R. Green	Black	Glacier White	Black
1970	Bronze Yellow	Black	Pale Primrose	Black
1971	Blaze	Black	Bedouin	Autumn Leaf
1971	Bronze Yellow	Black	British Racing Green	Autumn Leaf
1971	Flame Red	Black	Teal Blue	Autumn Leaf

Year	Exterior	Interior	Exterior	Interior
1971	Glacier White	Black		
1972	Aqua	Navy	Glacier White	Navy
1972	Blaze	Navy	Harvest Gold	Navy
1972	Bronze Yellow	Navy	Mallard Green	Autumn Leaf
1972	Flame Red	Navy	Teal Blue	Autumn Leaf
1973	Glacier White	Navy	Blaze	Navy
1973	Bronze Yellow	Navy	Black Tulip	Ochre
1973	Harvest Gold	Navy	Mallard Green	Ochre
1973	Limeflower	Navy	Teal Blue	Ochre
1973	Damask Red	Navy		
1974	Mirage	Black / Navy	Teal Blue	Autumn Leaf
1974-75	Bracken	Black / Navy	Tundra	Autumn Leaf
1974-75	Glacier White	Black / Navy	Aconite	Autumn Leaf
1974-75	Citron	Black / Navy	Harvest Gold	Autumn Leaf
1974-75	Blaze Red	Black / Navy	Bronze Yellow	Black / Navy
1974-75	Damask Red	Black / Navy		
1975	Flamenco	Black	Tahiti Blue	Black
1976-77	Damask Red	Black	Tahiti Blue	Autumn Leaf
1976-77	Chartreuse	Black	Sandglow	Autumn Leaf
1976-77	Flamenco	Black	Brooklands Green	Autumn Leaf
1976-77	Glacier White	Black		
1978-79	Leyland White	Black	Russet Brown	Beige
1978-79	Inca Yellow	Black	Brooklands Green	Beige
1978-79	Vermillion Red	Black	Pageant Blue	Beige
1978-79	Carmine Red	Beige	Chartreuse	Black

MG Midget Mark IV & 1500 Color Chart Notes:

Some of the color combinations in this chart have not been confirmed by multiple sources. In fact, several sources disagree concerning the details. Additional colors, as well as other color combinations, were likely available in some model years. It is not known how many of these color combinations were exported to the USA, but it is likely that most were produced for our market, at least in certain years. Ochre was an interior color used only on the 1973 models. Although the exact interior colors of the 1974 models are officially unknown, it is highly likely that they consisted of Autumn Leaf and Black or Navy. In other words, the Navy interior shade may have been phased out at the end of production for either the

1973 or 1974 model year. All 1975 interiors were either Black or Autumn Leaf. Any 1980 Midgets were simply titled as such when they were sold in 1980. The last Midget left the factory in 1979.

Figure B29 - A red Midget Mark I with chrome wire knock-offs on display in Italy. ©Luc106 (PD)

MG Midget Production Chart

Year	Series	Production	Year	Series	Production
1961	Mark I	7656	1971	Mark IV	16,410
1962	Mark I	9906	1972	Mark IV	16,158
1963	Mark I	7625	1973	Mark IV	14,130
1964	Mark II	11,450	1974	Mark IV	9690
1965	Mark II	9162	1975	1500	17,261
1966	Mark II	6842	1976	1500	17,121
1967	Mark III	8330	1977	1500	14,340
1968	Mark III	7372	1978	1500	15,400
1969	Mark III	13,085	1979	1500	9777
1970	Mark III	14,811			
			Total	1961 - 1979	226,526

MG Midget Production Chart Notes:

All the figures in the chart were sourced from *The Sprites and Midgets: A Collectors Guide*. The 1961-62 Mark I models had the 948cc four-cylinder. This was updated to 1098cc for the 1963 model year. As with the Austin-Healey Sprite series, the production totals and the years listed do not exactly match what we know as the Mark I through 1500 models. The figures themselves are accurate, but there is some overlap among the model years and Mark Series. All the following production breakdowns came from other sources. There were 16,080 '61-'62 Midgets produced with the 948cc engine. The Mk. II Midget with 59 hp included 26,601 cars. The Mk. III included 22,415 models with chrome bumpers and original styling.

Sprite / Midget / Spitfire Chart

Model	Type	CI / CC	HP	Wt.	Price
1959-60 Austin-Healey Sprite Mk. I	I-4	58 / 948	43	1480	$1795
1961-62 A-H Sprite Mk. II	I-4	58 / 948	46	1540	$1985
1963 Austin-Healey Sprite Mk. II	I-4	67 / 1098	56	1560	NA
1964-66 A-H Sprite Mk. III	I-4	67 / 1098	59	1566	$2000
1967-69 A-H Sprite Mk. IV	I-4	78 / 1275	65	1650	$2200
1961-62 MG Midget Mk. I	I-4	58 / 948	46	1620	NA
1963 MG Midget Mk. I	I-4	67 / 1098	56	1620	NA
1964-66 MG Midget Mk. II	I-4	67 / 1098	59	NA	NA
1967-68 MG Midget Mk. III	I-4	78 / 1275	65	1560	$2255
1969-70 MG Midget Mk. III	I-4	78 / 1275	62	NA	$2279
1972-74 MG Midget Mk. IV	I-4	78 / 1275	54	1636	NA
1975-78 MG Midget 1500	I-4	91 / 1493	56	1775	$3949
1979 MG Midget 1500	I-4	91 / 1493	50	1820	$5395
1962-64 Triumph Spitfire Mk. 1	I-4	70 / 1147	63	1568	$2199
1965-66 Triumph Spitfire Mk. 2	I-4	70 / 1147	67	1630	$2249
1967 Triumph Spitfire Mk. 3	I-4	79 / 1296	75	1680	$2373
1968-69 Triumph Spitfire Mk. 3	I-4	79 / 1296	68	1652	$2295
1971 Triumph Spitfire Mk. 4	I-4	79 / 1296	58	1717	NA
1972 Triumph Spitfire Mk. 4	I-4	79 / 1296	48	1717	NA
1973-75 Triumph Spitfire Mk. 4	I-4	91 / 1493	57	1735	$2895
1976 Triumph Spitfire 1500	I-4	91 / 1493	57	1735	$4295
1980 Triumph Spitfire 1500	I-4	91 / 1493	57	1735	$7365

Austin-Healey, MG, Triumph

Sprite / Midget / Spitfire Chart Notes:
All Austin-Healey Sprites and MG Midgets had an 80-inch wheelbase. All Triumph Spitfires had an 83-inch wheelbase. The original base retail prices quoted in some cases may not be exactly accurate for the model year or years listed. Note the change to net horsepower ratings in 1972.

Figure B30 - This driver's view of a Seventies MG Midget displays a black interior in its final, most comfortable design. The fat steering wheel is an aftermarket item. ©Klugschnacker (CC)

Next Two Pages:

Figure B31 - 1966 MG Accessories Order Form. ©1966 Floyd M. Orr Collection

Figure B32 - Radio and Air Conditioning options descriptions for the 1966 MG models.
©1966 Floyd M. Orr Collection

ACCESSORY ORDER FORM

GROUP	NO.	ITEM	MODEL	PART NO.	SELLING PRICE	TOTAL
A	1	RADIO	ALL	HAC700 ☐	51.00	
	2	INSTALLATION	MGB	HAC701 ☐	11.00	
	3	KIT	MG 1100	HAC708 ☐	14.00	
	4		SPRITE/MIDGET	HAC703 ☐	14.00	
	5		3000	HAC704 ☐	11.00	
B	1	AIR	MGB & MGB/GT	HAC1000 ☐	360.00	
	2	CONDITIONER	MG 1100	HAC1001 ☐	335.00	
	3		3000	HAC1002 ☐	385.00	
C	1	LUGGAGE	MGB	5303 ☐	39.95	
	2	RACK	SPRITE/MIDGET	5306 ☐	39.95	
	3	(PERMANENT)	3000	5306 ☐	39.95	
	4	(DEMOUNTABLE)	ALL	5318 ☐	26.95	
	5	(DETACHABLE)	ALL	5313 ☐	22.95	
D	1	SKI RACK	ALL	5315 ☐	22.95	
E	1	GRILLE	MGB	5522 ☐	17.95	
	2	GUARD	MG 1100	5520 ☐	17.95	
	3		SPRITE/MIDGET	5513-2 ☐	17.95	
	4	*Also fits rear	3000	*5506 ☐	12.95	
F	1	EMBLEM	MGB	*6816- ☐	12.95	
	2	RUBBER	SPRITE	*6821- ☐	12.95	
	3	MATS	MIDGET	*6822- ☐	12.95	
	4	(SET)	MG 1100	*6823- ☐	9.95	
	5		3000	*6817- ☐	9.95	
		*Use appropriate suffix number for color: 2 (black); 3 (white); 4 (red)				
G	1	WALNUT	MGB	*8228- ☐	3.75	
	2	SHIFT	MG 1100	*8226- ☐	3.75	
	3	KNOB	SPRITE/MIDGET	*8226- ☐	3.75	
	4		3000	*8223- ☐	3.75	
		*Consult AMCO catalog for type desired using correct suffix number				
H	1	CUSTOM	MGB	7222 ☐	49.95	
	2	CONSOLE	MGB/GT	7228 ☐	49.95	
	3	(BLACK	SPRITE/MIDGET	7232 ☐	49.95	
	4	ONLY)	SPRITE/MIDGET	*7238 ☐	49.95	
		*For cars fitted with B.M.C. approved radio and kit				
I	1	SUN	MGB	5117 ☐	7.95	
	2	VISOR	SPRITE/MIDGET	5108 ☐	6.95	
	3		3000	5105 ☐	6.95	
J	1	SCUFF PLATE	MGB	6528 ☐	3.95	
	2	(SET)	3000	6510 ☐	3.95	
K	1	THRESHOLD PLATE	MGB	6527 ☐	4.95	
	2	(SET)	SPRITE/MIDGET	6509 ☐	4.95	
L	1	4-WAY WARNING FLASHER	ALL	HAC901 ☐	7.33	
M	1	THROTTLE	MGB	6526 ☐	2.95	
	2	PLATE	SPRITE/MIDGET	6500 ☐	2.25	
	3		3000	6507 ☐	2.95	
					TOTAL ▶	

Purchaser_____Make_____Model_____

Dealer/Distributor_____Date_____Salesman_____

Austin-Healey, MG, Triumph

– A –
PUSH-BUTTON ALL-TRANSISTOR RADIO

Shown: Model HAC-703 designed for Sprite-Midget cars. See page 5 for other model numbers.

ESPECIALLY DESIGNED BY MOTOROLA FOR MG-AUSTIN HEALEY CARS

- 12-month warranty
- Completely transistorized
- Pre-wired for your car's electrical system—no adapter plugs or switches needed
- Plays the instant you turn it on—no warm-up needed
- Five push-buttons can be pre-set to your favorite stations
- Duplicates interior finish of your car

Easily and rapidly installed—one basic chassis fits all vehicles

– B –
AIR CONDITIONING
CUSTOM DESIGNED BY COOLAIRE FOR MG-AUSTIN HEALEY CARS

Quiet, draft-free cooling in city traffic and on the open road.

- 12-month warranty
- Automatically-controlled traffic condenser fan
- Dual blower motors
- Dashboard mounted controls
- Full-range temperature settings
- Three-speed blower control
- Completely enclosed evaporator case
- All-aluminum evaporator coil
- Rust-resistant cases
- Borg-Warner compressor
- Chrome louvers and discharge grills
- Instant controlled toe-board cooling

You save on installation, too. Components slip right in with few changes necessary to car.

Shown: Model HAC-1000 for MGB/-GT. See page 5 for model numbers for other MG-Austin Healey cars.

Figure B33 - Note the knock-off disc wheels and modern wood steering wheel on this MG A Twin Cam. The wheels are correct for the model; the steering wheel is not. The unusual color combination of a British Racing Green body and light grey dash may be non-standard, too. Not shown from this angle, but from another photo of the same car, the seats are a darker grey than the dash and trim. The wind wings that are barely visible were another popular option on these true roadsters. ©Mr. Choppers (GNU)

MG A / B / C Production Chart

Model	Years	Built	Model	Years	Built
MG A 1500	1955 - 59	58,750 *	MG B Mk. I	1962-67	116,350
A 1600 Mk. I	1959 - 62	31,431 *	MG B Mk. II	1968-71	82,628
Mk. I DeLuxe	1959 - 61	70	MG B Mk. III	1972-80	198,287
A 1600 Mk. II	1961 - 62	8429 *			
Twin Cam Road.	1959 - 60	1723	MG B Roadster	1962-80	397,265
Twin Cam Coupe	1959 - 60	388			
Mk. II DeLuxe	1962	290	RHD B Roadsters	1962-80	64,233
			LHD B Roadsters	1962-80	322,728
Total MG A	1955 - 62	101,081	Total B Roadsters	1962-80	386,961
			MG C Roadster	1967-69	4550

MG A / B / C Production Chart Notes:
Of the more than 100,000 MG A Roadsters and Coupes built, over 80,000 were imported into the USA. It would be a good guess to say that within the combined figures in the chart of Coupes and

Roadsters that the Roadsters comprised at least 80% of the production sent to the USA. *Wikipedia* states that 8198 MG A Mark II Roadsters were built, but that exact figure may be suspect, although it is surely close. MG A figures with an asterisk include Coupes.

According to the *Illustrated M. G. Buyer's Guide*, total MG B production was 512,733, including approximately 150,000 GT coupes. A total of 399,070 MG-B's were produced between 1962 and 1980. The MGB Register of Australia website quotes MG B Roadster production as 386,961 + 125,282 GT's = 512,243. These numbers were obviously sourced from *Original MGB* by Clausager, who also writes that 64,233 of the 386,961 were right-hand-drive. That leaves 322,728 LHD Roadsters built.

Representing the last hurrah of the MG B were the 6682 Limited Edition black MG B roadsters produced for the U.S. market in 1979. The highest production year for the MG B may have been 1979 with 29,903 Roadsters built, assuming that no serial numbers were skipped in the sequence. For some reason, production for the 1979 model year began early, in May 1978, explaining the high production number. The 1979 production figure for the MG B Roadster may not be precisely correct.

MG B Mark I Color Chart

Year	Model	Exterior Color	Interior	Top
1962 - 1965	Mk. I	Chelsea Grey	Red	Grey
1962 - 1965	Mk. I	Iris Blue	Black	Blue
1962 - 1965	Mk. I	Iris Blue	Blue	Blue
1962 - 1967	Mk. I	Old English White	Black	Grey
1962 - 1967	Mk. I	Old English White	Red	Grey
1962 - 1967	Mk. I	Black	Black	Grey
1962 - 1967	Mk. I	Black	Red	Grey
1962 - 1967	Mk. I	Tartan Red	Black	Red
1962 - 1967	Mk. I	Tartan Red	Red	Red
1962 - 1967	Mk. I	British Racing Green	Black	Grey
1964	Mk. I	Chelsea Grey	Red	Black
1964 - 1965	Mk. I	Iris Blue	Black	Black
1964 - 1965	Mk. I	Iris Blue	Blue	Black
1964 - 1967	Mk. I	Old English White	Black	Black
1964 - 1967	Mk. I	Old English White	Red	Black
1964 - 1967	Mk. I	Black	Black	Black
1964 - 1967	Mk. I	Black	Red	Black
1964 - 1967	Mk. I	Tartan Red	Black	Black
1964 - 1967	Mk. I	Tartan Red	Red	Black
1964 - 1967	Mk. I	British Racing Green	Black	Black
1966 - 1967	Mark I	Mineral Blue	Blue	Blue
1966 - 1967	Mark I	Mineral Blue	Black	Black
1966 - 1967	Mark I	Mineral Blue	Blue	Black
1966 - 1967	Mark I	Mineral Blue	Black	Blue

1967	Mark I	Pale Primrose	Black	Black

MG B Mark I Color Chart Notes:
Most of these color combinations were verified by U.S. brochures.

Figure B34 - This beautiful gold MG B is the way we would like to remember this model, with chrome wire knock-offs, chrome bumpers, attached top and headrests. This combination applies to the 1969-72 models, although many B fans would prefer an even earlier model with no emission controls. ©Spanish Coches (CC)

MG B Mark II Exterior Color Chart

Years	Colors	Years	Colors
1968 - 1969	Black	1970 - 1971	Bronze Yellow
1968 - 1969	Snowberry White	1970 - 1971	Flame Red
1968 - 1969	Mineral Blue	1970 - 1971	Glacier White
1968 - 1971	British Racing Green	1971	Bedouin
1968 - 1969	Tartan Red	1971	Midnight Blue
1968 - 1969	Chelsea Grey	1971	Teal Blue
1968 - 1970	Pale Primrose	1971	Blaze
1970	Blue Royale	1971	Mallard Green
1970 - 1971	Black (Special Order)		

MG B Mark II Exterior Color Chart Notes:

These colors were sourced from the MGB Stuff UK website and verified by Clausager's *Original MGB* and other sources. The 1968-69 tops may have all been black. All the 1970-71 tops were black.

MG B Mark III Exterior Color Chart

Years	Colors	Years	Colors
1972	Aqua	1974 - 1976	Citron
1972	Flame Red	1975	Tahiti Blue
1972 - 1973	Mallard Green	1975 - 1977	Flamenco
1972 - 1973	Bronze Yellow	1976 - 1977	Sandglow
1972 - 1974	Teal Blue	1976 - 1977	Tahiti Blue
1972 - 1975	Blaze	1976 - 1977	Chartreuse
1972 - 1976	Harvest Gold	1976 - 1980	Brooklands Green
1972 - 1976	Black (Special Order)	1977 - 1980	Carmine Red
1972 - 1977	Glacier White	1977 - 1980	Triumph White
1973	Black Tulip	1978 - 1979	Inca Yellow
1973	Limeflower	1978 - 1980	Leyland White
1973 - 1977	Damask Red	1978 - 1980	Pageant Blue
1974	Mirage	1978 - 1980	Russet Brown
1974 - 1975	Aconite	1978 - 1980	Vermillion Red
1974 - 1976	Bracken	1978 - 1980	Black (Special Order)
1974 - 1976	Tundra	1980	Snapdragon

MG B Mark III Exterior Color Chart Notes:

These colors were sourced from the MGB Stuff UK website and verified by Clausager's *Original MGB* and other sources. All the 1972 tops were black. In 1972, Mallard Green and Teal Blue had Autumn Leaf interiors. All other 1972 exterior colors had Navy interiors. Some of the 1978 exterior colors were available with Beige interiors. All other 1978 exterior colors had black interiors.

MG C Color Chart

Year	Exterior Color	Year	Exterior Color
1967-69	Snowberry White	1967-69	Pale Primrose Yellow
1967-69	Black	1967-69	Tartan Red
1967-69	Grampian Grey	1967-69	British Racing Green

1967-69	Sandy Beige	1967-69	Mineral Blue
1968	Golden Beige Metallic	1968	Riviera Silver Blue Metallic

MG C Color Chart Notes:

The Golden Beige Metallic and Riviera Silver Blue Metallic paint were $300 options in 1968 only. All tops were black and all interiors were black leather. Total MG C production was 8999, with 4550 being Roadsters.

Figure B35 - This Pale Primrose 1968 RHD English model MG C is equipped with optional chrome, knock-off wire wheels. Painted wires were standard in both Britain and the USA. At a glance the C looked just like the B. Although the C had fifteen-inch wheels and other detailed differences, the casual observer would see jut a B with a hood bulge. This lack of distinguishing visuals from the much lower priced, and far more common, four-cylinder model depressed U.S. sales considerably. ©Allen Watkin, London, UK (CC)

MG A / B / C Chart

Model	Type	CI / CC	HP	Wt.	Price
1955-59 MG A 1500 Mk. I	I-4	89 / 1489	68	2020	$2195
1955-60 MG A 1600 Mk. I	I-4	97 / 1588	78	1988	$2445

1959-60 MG A Twin Cam	I-4	97 / 1588	108	2185	$3345
1961-62 MG A Mk. II	I-4	99 / 1622	93	2050	$2450
1962-67 MG B Mk. I	I-4	110 / 1798	95	2128	$2658
1968-71 MG B Mk. II	I-4	110 / 1798	95	2220	$2885
1972-79 MG B Mk. III	I-4	110 / 1798	62	2286	$4795
1980 MG B Mk. III	I-4	110 / 1798	60	2600	$8000
1967 MG C	I-6	178 / 2912	145	2460	$3355
1968 MG C	I-6	178 / 2912	145	2500	$3355
1969 MG C	I-6	178 / 2912	145	2500	$3700

MG A / B / C Chart Notes:
All MG A models had a 94-inch wheelbase and all MG B models had a 91-inch wheelbase. The original base retail prices quoted in some cases may not be exactly accurate for the model year or years listed. The specifications shown for the 1972-79 Mark III MG B directly represent the 1976 model.

Figure B36 - Here is a final look at a classic MG A. This example features painted bolt-on wire wheels, chrome luggage rack, radio, wind wings, and a black tonneau cover. ©Tvabutzku1234 (CC)

Looking Through British Racing Green Granny Glasses

Figure B37 - British Racing Green Triumph TR-6. ©Sicnag (CC)

The reason you have never seen or heard of a Triumph TR-1 is that only one prototype was built in 1952. Although little changed at the time of its release to the public in 1953, the new TR was denoted as the TR-2. Its 2-liter, 90-hp four-cylinder was placed in a ladder-type chassis with a separate body, like a Sting Ray, except with a steel body and a tiny engine. The company produced over 8500 TR-2's through 1955, most going to the USA. All were of course true roadsters with side curtains. What else could they have been with those sporty cut-down doors? A twelve-second 0-60 time felt a lot faster when you could practically reach out the window and file your fingernails on the pavement!

The TR-3 would continue through three iterations: TR-3, TR-3A, and TR-3B. All of the last type would be sent to the American market. This is the model that truly established the brand in the U.S. during its 1955-62 production span. The little roadster began little changed from its TR-2 predecessor. Another five horsepower from larger carbs and a new grille were the distinguishing marks of the early TR-3. An anti-roll bar and electrical overdrive on the top three gears were options from the beginning and front disc brakes were made standard in 1956. The darling of the USA was, generally speaking, the TR-3A model with its wider grille, external door handles and lockable trunk moving it a little closer to being a civilized roadster. Over 58,000 were built, and of course most of these arrived on our shores. Power was still around 100 gross horsepower producing a twelve-second 0-60.

Figure B38 - Red TR-4 at the Hudson British Car Show. The TR-4 was the first TR with an envelope body and roll-up windows. This example has the standard, but not particularly popular, silver disc wheels with chrome wheel covers. ©Bull-Doser (PD)

A strange affliction occurred in 1961 when the TR-4 was introduced with its new envelope body (no more fingernail filing on the go). U.S. dealers were concerned that the rabid customer base of the TR-3A would balk at the modernization of their favorite manicure assisted design. The Triumph factory still had some TR-3 body parts to disperse, so they continued building TR-3's for American customers who were not pleased with the new body style. (Can you imagine what might have happened if Chevrolet had pulled this little trick with the Sting Ray in 1968?) They began pushing the remaining fingernail filers out the door as TR-3B's, simultaneously with the new 1962 TR-4's. About 530 of these TR-3B's were just A's with the new fully synchronized four-speed from the TR-4. The remaining TR-3B's, numbering 2804, were also produced simultaneously with the other TR-3B's and the new TR-4's. These hybrids had not only the new transmission, but the new 2138cc engine of the TR-4, too.

Figure B39 - Red TR-3B. ©Taymoss (GNU)

    The TR-4 would be the first of several envelope body on frame TR designs, many thousands of which would be sent to the USA. The top was completely removable, but the roll-up windows were present from the beginning. With the exception of a handful produced with the old 1991cc engine for two liter restricted competition, the TR-4 series all had the 2138cc engine and fully synchronized gearbox. The body was designed by Michelotti, who also created the Triumph Spitfire and the Maserati Mistral discussed elsewhere in this book. More than 40,000 TR-4's were produced in 1961-65. The TR-4A model with a new chassis and independent rear suspension was released in 1965; however, about 25% of production was built with the old live axle rear suspension adapted to the new-style chassis. The A model also got a new attached convertible top. Only the top frame had been permanently attached in the earlier TR-4. Both models had polished walnut dashes and leather seats as standard equipment. The instruments had bright chrome bezels. Wire wheels with forty-eight spokes were optional, either painted or chromed. The TR-4A in both iterations continued in production well into 1967, when the TR-5 (with fuel injection) was introduced in Britain and the TR-250 (with carburetors) was designed to meet the new U.S. regulations.

    The TR-250 was a special one-year model produced in 1968 for the American market only. It featured the new 2.5-liter six-cylinder that would continue for many years in the TR-6, but its body was the same Michelotti design as the TR-4A. The TR-250 is easily identified by its matte finish walnut dash with flat black instrument bezels, vinyl upholstery (leather seats were no longer available) and a Camaro SS-like GT stripe that droops across the nose (instead of encircling it as on the SS). The TR-250 also had the new side marker lights required in the USA and a somewhat unattractive reflective tape stripe sewn into the convertible top. The latter was so ugly you might find a car for sale now on which the owner has spared it the embarrassment. New mag-style chrome wheel covers were standard and wires were still a popular option. Many fans do not like the mag covers, but I think they are decently attractive, and certainly a lot lower maintenance. Although the Europeans got a 150-hp engine, the strangled carbs on the U.S. version produced only 111 horsepower (104 according to some sources). This still improved the TR-250's acceleration to 10.6 seconds 0-60 mph. One of the most unusual considerations concerning the TR-250 is that you could even buy air conditioning as a $395 option. Few other

English sports car below a Jaguar ever offered this comfort to American buyers. The U.S. market received 8484 TR-250's, more than twice the total number of TR-5's produced for all of Europe.

In 1969-76, 86,249 TR-6's were exported outside England, most of them to the USA. In the beginning at least, for the U.S. market, this was the same TR-250 drivetrain wrapped in a new, sleeker body not designed by Michelotti. Consulting on the new body was done by Karmann of Karmann-Ghia fame. U.S. models actually *lost* seven horsepower from the previous TR-250. The somewhat unpopular wheel covers of the TR-250 were replaced with mildly styled steel disc wheels with trim rings after the first batch of TR-6's was produced. Wire wheels were always an option up through the '71 models. The TR-6 has been included in this book as a continuation of the original body-on-frame TR series. As we move deeper into the '70's, we all are aware that all cars became *really boring* with their much higher prices for far less performance. The TR-6 slowly became an artifact from an earlier time that managed to survive in the U.S. market far longer than some of its English contemporaries. The model years became gradually more sophisticated in the realm of convenience and meeting regulations, while its performance and satisfaction as a modern sports car dwindled. Although its TR-7 successor would sell like hardtop hotcakes upon its release, the TR-7 in hindsight has become the Mustang II of Triumphs. The TR-6 will always be a more collectible sports car, particularly the early model years.

Figure B40 - This black 1965 Spitfire Mark 2 has the standard disc wheels painted body color with chrome hubcaps. Even with their smaller engines, the early models are still more attractive with their simple chrome

bumpers. Note the chrome strips on the fenders and the round parking lamps. The right side external latch for the clamshell hood is visible here. To open the hood, you had to unlatch it on each side. ©Bull-Doser (PD)

There are a few simple reasons why the Spitfire is not one of my personal favorites, and I shall get to those in a moment. The focus of this story is that the Spitfire *does* profoundly represent the ultimate beginner sports car for a virtual horde of buyers. Realize, of course, that we are actually speaking in the past tense here, because the point revolves around what the Spitfire was at the time of its actual production in the '62-'80 time period. The car was initially offered as a competitive alternative to the Sprite and Midget. At that time, British Leyland was marketing the twins against the Triumph in the American market. You might envision Austin-Healey as Chevrolet, MG as Pontiac, and Triumph as Oldsmobile during those heady days. The Spitfire was conceived to be ever so slightly up-market from the Spridgets, with all three marketed through separate dealerships; however, as with the three American brands, these British brands were often sold in pairs through the same dealerships, although as with the GM brands, rarely would all three be offered at the same location.

We all have our reasons for making the personal selections that we do, and here is my choice concerning the Spitfire. First of all, the precise way an instrument panel looks and operates is of supreme importance to me, and the placement of the speedometer and tachometer in the center of the dash on Sixties Spitfires was totally unacceptable to me. You may not be aware that the company did this to keep manufacturing costs down with the construction of both left and right hand drive cars. This does make perfect sense, but that does not mean that Leyland could ever sell me one. I would have bought a Sprite or one of the larger TR's instead. My second problem with the Spitfire is the same thing discussed in a negative manner in all the numerous road tests of early Spitfires: the cornering behavior of the primitive swing-axle independent rear suspension. My third complaint would have been the separate body on frame design that made the Spitfire always seem *looser* than the Spridgets, and the engines were generally a bit rougher, too. Although all three models received a properly attached top in 1967, the Spitfire still had its instruments mounted in the center of the dash. The instruments would finally be placed in front of the driver on the Mark 3 in 1969.

This brings us to the reason that 1970 was sort of a watershed year, even though Spitfire production would continue for another decade, with higher build numbers than in The Sixties! As with many models, both foreign and domestic, 1970 would be the last year of total high-performance. The horsepower of the Spitfire would drop to 63, even as the dash and rear suspension were greatly improved. Like so many other adult toys marketed in the U.S. in The Seventies, the sales success would grow as the desirability of the product actually diminished. Examples of this pattern were the original Honda 750 Four motorcycle of 1969, the Fiat 124 Spider, and the Corvette Stingrays. The performance slid downward as the prices and sales numbers rushed upward.

I personally harbor a strange emotional attitude toward the Spitfire. Even I like the improved dash, top, interior, and independent rear suspension of the later models. The seats are more luxurious and the fender lines are cleaned up without the chrome strips covering seams. A proper wood dash with instruments directly in front of the driver were what I always wanted in the first place, but.... The bloom was already off the rose for this type of primitive sports car by the mid-Seventies. The Spitfire may have once offered a realistic alternative to a 124 Spider or

MG B, but against a backdrop of X1/9's and 914's, it began to look more like an antique from Aunt Millie's garage.

Normally I am a big fan of low, wide cars as opposed to tall, narrow cars. There has always been a pertinent exception to this preference. I have absolutely zero lust in my heart for an MG B. I would take the equivalent Triumph instead: TR-4A, TR-250, or TR-6, depending on the model year being considered. The TR-4A and later have independent rear suspension. The TR-250 and TR-6 have six-cylinder engines like the MG C, which was famously slower in acceleration than the B! It had a higher top speed and smoother firing pulses, but its everyday superiority to the B was minimal at a higher initial price. The wheels, instrument panels, and top designs of the Triumphs also influenced my preference for the TR series. MG was particularly hard-headed in its reluctance to develop fully synchronized transmissions and attached, convertiblE-Type tops.

Taken from the evidence of high production numbers, low list prices, and inclusion in numerous sports car comparison tests in magazines spanning nearly two full decades, the MG B was the Spitfire's only true competition as the ultimately ubiquitous topless sports car of our youth. This book includes a corral full of topless pony cars with equally representative low prices and high production numbers, but those are not true sports cars. It is of little consequence that the author of this book never seriously considered the purchase of a Triumph Spitfire because a large percentage of you readers did. With that, I leave you to your fond memories of assembling a cantankerous, and not particularly effective, soft top to the surprising lift of an inside rear wheel on a tight corner or racetrack, even if the track really was only a mall parking lot.

Figure B41 - Compare this blue Mark 4 to the black Mark 2 above. Note the different wheels and lighting details. The seams are gone from the tops of the front fenders. The new Kamm tail with large tail lights is not visible from this angle, but the severely protruding black bumper guards cannot be missed! ©Hunt Triumph 1500 (PD)

Triumph Spitfire Production Chart

Model	Years	Production	Model	Years	Production
Mark 1	1962 - 1964	45,753	Mark 4	1971 - 1974	70,021
Mark 2	1965 - 1966	37,409	1500	1975 - 1980	95,829
Mark 3	1967 - 1970	65,320	Total	1962 - 1980	314,332

Triumph Spitfire Production Chart Notes:
All stated production figures are from *Wikipedia*. From *Road & Track* November 1986: Early Spitfires had overheating problems in warm weather and only the late models had synchromesh on first gear.

Triumph Spitfire Color Chart

Color	Series	Years	Color	Series	Years
Spa White	1	1962-6/63	Emerald Green	4	1/72 - 1974
Lichfield Green	1	1962-6/63	Mallard Green	4	9/72 - 1974
Powder Blue	1	1962-6/63	Magenta	4	2/73 - 1974
Pale Yellow	1	1962-6/63	Pimento Red	4-1500	1/72 - 3/77
Phantom Grey	1	1962-6/63	Carmine Red	4-1500	1/72 - 1980
Jonquil Yellow	1	6/63-8/64	French Blue	4-1500	9/72 - 3/77
Black	1 - 2	1962-10/65	Mimosa Yellow	4-1500	2/73 - 3/77
Signal Red	1 - 4	1962 - 1/72	Maple Brown	1500	1975 - 3/77
Conifer Green	1 - 3	6/63 - 9/69	Java Green	1500	1975 - 3/77
Wedgwood Blue	1 - 4	6/63 - 1/72	B. R. Green	1500	1975 - 3/77
White	All	6/63 - 3/77	Delft Blue	1500	1975 - 3/77
Royal Blue	1 - 3	10/64-1970	Topaz Orange	1500	1975 - 3/77
Jasmine Yellow	3	9/68 - 5/70	Leyland White	1500	3/77 - 1980
Valencia Blue	3 - 4	9/68 - 1/72	Vermilion Red	1500	3/77 - 1980
Damson Red	3 - 4	9/68 - 9/72	Inca Yellow	1500	3/77 - 1980
Laurel Green	3 - 4	9/69 - 1/72	Russet Brown	1500	3/77 - 1980
Sienna Brown	3 - 4	9/69 - 1974	Brooklands Green	1500	3/77 - 1980
Saffron Yellow	3 - 4	5/70 - 9/72	Pageant Blue	1500	3/77 - 1980
Sapphire Blue	4	1971 - 74	Tahiti Blue	1500	3/77 - 1980

Triumph Spitfire Color Chart Notes:
Unlike the other color charts, this Spitfire Color Chart has been organized into a left column, then right column model order. There was too much overlap of many exterior colors by series and model year to break the chart up into appropriate groupings of models.

Figure B42 - This black TR-3A represents one of the most popular Triumphs both then and now. This example has disc wheels, whitewalls, and a cream interior. You can easily discern a TR-2 from a TR-3 by the latter's much wider grille opening. ©Bull-Doser (PD)

Triumph TR-3A Color Chart

Exterior	Interior
Black	Black, Blue, Silverstone Grey, Purple, or Red
Sebring White	Black, Blue, Silverstone Grey, Purple, or Red
Signal Red	Black, Red, or Silverstone Grey
Powder Blue	Blue or Black
Pale Yellow	Black or Silverstone Grey
Silverstone Grey	Silverstone Grey, Red, or Purple

British Racing Green	Silverstone Grey or Red

Triumph TR-3 Color Chart Notes:

Interiors were offered in vinyl or optional leather in Red, Black, Blue, and Silverstone Grey for several model years. Tops and side curtains were either black or white. Specific color combinations within certain production periods only, of course, were available in these hues. The specific combinations shown in the chart were sourced directly from a 1960 brochure for the TR-3A. There were likely more color combinations applicable to certain other years of TR-3 and TR-3A production.

Figure B43 - This screaming yellow zonker 1955 TR-2 has a black interior, top and tonneau. The Minilite wheels, bumper guards, wind wings, fender mirrors, hood tie-downs and driving light were popular aftermarket additions to this first Triumph TR model. Restorers often polish the trim strips on the fenders, as on this car, but they should be painted body color. Of course this is the far more common *short door* model TR-2. The earliest production models had doors that opened to the bottom of the rocker panels. The *long door* TR-2 is a rare collectible today. ©Charles01 (CC)

Triumph TR-4A & TR-250 Color Chart

Models	Years	Exterior Color	Interior Color
TR-4A	1965	Black	Black / Matador Red
TR-4A / TR-250	1965-68	New White	Black / Matador Red / Tan
TR-4A / TR-250	1965-68	Signal Red	Black / Matador Red / Tan
TR-4A / TR-250	1965-68	Racing Green	Black / Light Tan
TR-4A / TR-250	1965-68	Wedgewood Blue	Midnight Blue
TR-4A / TR-250	1965-68	Valencia Blue	Black / Light Tan
TR-4A / TR-250	1965-68	Royal Blue	Black / Midnight Blue
TR-4A / TR-250	1965-68	Royal Blue	Shadow Blue / Tan
TR-250	1968	Jasmine Yellow	Black / Light Tan
TR-250	1968	Damson	Black / Tan

Triumph TR-4A, TR-250 & TR-6 Color Chart Notes:
All tops were probably black. Minilite wheels may have been a factory option during the TR-4 through TR-250 production years. This may or may not have applied to Spitfires, too.

Triumph TR-6 Color Chart

Model	Exterior	Model	Exterior	Model	Exterior
1969	Conifer Green	1971-73	Sienna Brown	1974-75	Maple Brown
1969-71	Royal Blue	1972-74	Sapphire Blue	1975-76	Topaz Orange
1969-71	Signal Red	1972-74	Emerald Green	1975-76	Java Green
1969-72	Jasmine Yellow	1972-76	Pimento Red	1975-76	Racing Green
1969-72	Damson Red	1973-74	Mallard Blue	1975-76	Delft Blue
1969-76	White	1973-74	Magenta	1976	Inca Yellow
1969-76	Black	1973-75	Mimosa Yellow	1976	Tahiti Blue
1970-72	Laurel Green	1973-76	Carmen Red	1976	Russet Brown
1971-72	Saffron Yellow	1973-76	French Blue		

Triumph TR-6 Color Chart Notes:
Most, or possibly all, TR-6 models had black vinyl tops. All interiors were black vinyl except three exterior colors that were available with either Black or Matador Red vinyl: Signal Red in 1969-71 and Black and White in all years, 1969-76.

Figure B44 - The front turn signal lamp housed in the front end of the chrome strip that continues down the side of the car is the key visual mark of the Triumph TR-4A. This model was built on a new chassis both with or without IRS and there were many detail improvements over the previous TR-4, but the two models appeared almost identical. This example has the correct optional chrome bolt-on wire wheels. ©Martini-IansV (GNU)

Triumph TR Production Chart

Model	*Years*	*Production*	*Model*	*Years*	*Production*
TR-2	1953 - 1955	5805	TR-4	1961 - 1964	37,661
TR-3	1955 - 1957	12,091	TR-4A	1965 - 1967	25,390
TR-3A	1958 - 1962	56,340	TR-250	1968	8484
TR-3B	1962 - 1963	3331	TR-6	1969 - 1976	86,249
Side Curtains		77,567	Roll-up Windows		157,784
			Total TR	Export	235,531

Triumph TR Production Chart Notes:

The numbers in this chart were sourced from *The Triumph TRs: A Collector's Guide*. Triumph produced 255,393 TR-2 through TR-6 models worldwide in 1953-76. The figures above include only export models, most of which were LHD and sent to the USA. Distinguishing characteristics of the TR-2 included the lack of door handles, trunk handle, and radiator grille. The TR-3 had the same body with a proper grille, a little more horsepower and front disc brakes. The TR-3A added more comfortable interior accoutrements with door and trunk handles. The B was a transition model produced in small numbers for U.S. buyers who wanted the TR-3 body. Later B models had the TR-4's larger engine and synchronized first gear. The TR-4 brought an Italian-styled body with roll-up windows, synchromesh four-speed, and a 2138cc engine. The TR-4A brought a properly attached convertible top and optional independent rear suspension that required a new chassis design. The TR-250 had a new 2498cc, OHV Six producing 111 horsepower for $3395. Options included AC $395, overdrive $175, and wire wheels $118. The TR-6 sported a sleeker new body.

Triumph TR Comparison Chart

Model	Type	CI / CC	HP	Wt.	Price
1953-55 Triumph TR-2	I-4	121 / 1991	90	1848	$2499
1956-58 Triumph TR-3	I-4	121 / 1991	98	1988	$2625
1959-61 Triumph TR-3A	I-4	121 / 1991	95	2050	$2675
1962 Triumph TR-3B	I-4	121 / 1991	95	2050	$2365
1962 Triumph TR-3B	I-4	130 / 2138	100	2138	NA
1961-64 Triumph TR-4	I-4	130 / 2138	100	2130	NA
1965-67 Triumph TR-4A	I-4	130 / 2138	104	2240	$2840
1966 Triumph TR-4A IRS	I-4	130 / 2138	104	2310	$3624
1968 Triumph TR-250	I-6	152 / 2498	111	2350	$3395
1969-71 Triumph TR-6	I-6	152 / 2498	106	2360	$3425
1972-73 Triumph TR-6	I-6	152 / 2498	106	2390	NA
1974-76 Triumph TR-6	I-6	152 / 2498	106	2428	$6050

Triumph TR Comparison Chart Notes:

All the Triumph TR Series models had an 88-inch wheelbase. The original base retail prices quoted in some cases may not be exactly accurate for the model year or years listed. The listing for the 1966 TR-4A IRS represents an *as tested* price.

The Big Three Affordable English Antiques

Figure B45 - This 1968 Valencia Blue TR-250 has the very rare Surrey Top option. The rigid rear window turns this model into a Porsche Targa sort of experience. This photo shows the standard white nose stripes and redline tires of the TR-250. This car has the standard black interior with white piping on the seats. The painted bolt-on wire wheels and chrome luggage rack were popular options. ©Simon Clay (GNU)

Conveniences Added to Austin-Healey, MG, & Triumph Sports Cars

Disc Brakes	All-Synchromesh	Roll-Up Windows	Attached Top
Sprite Mk. II	Never (in U.S.)	Sprite Mk. III	1967 Sprite Mk. IV
A-H 100S	Never	A-H 3000 Mk. II	A-H 3000 Mk. III
Midget Mk. I	1975 Midget 1500	Midget Mk. II	1967 Midget Mk. III
MG A 1600	1968 MG B Mk. II	1962 MG B Mk. I	1965 MG B Mk. I
Spitfire Mk. 1	Spitfire Mk. 4	1962 Spitfire Mk. 1	Spitfire Mk. 3
1957 TR-3	1961 TR-3B	1961 TR-4	1965 TR-4A

Six-Cylinder Shootout

Figure B46 - This Austin-Healey 3000 Mark III looks quite elegant in Black with optional Old English White side panels. The 3000's broad rear quarter blind spot with the top up is quite prominent from this angle. ©Mutari (PD)

Before we depart this chapter about The Big Affordable Three brands, I want to present a direct comparison of their respective six-cylinder swansongs of the era. Austin-Healey chose not to attempt an update of its aging Mark III 3000 when the new U.S. rules kicked in at the beginning of 1968. We shall be examining details of the final 1967 model here. Triumph could no longer find a feasible way to increase the performance level of its four-cylinder TR Series in the face of these same new regulations. The body and chassis of the TR4A had been born in 1965, twelve years later than that of the Austin-Healey. Triumph found a way to update for the new regulations while keeping the power at least up to the level of the 1967 TR-4A. England and the rest of Europe got a new fuel-injected TR-5 producing 150 gross horsepower, but the USA had to make do with the one-year-only TR-250 model with performance generally still at TR-4A levels. In the initial concept, BMC wanted a new six-cylinder model to replace the Austin-Healey 3000. Their answer was the MG C. This turned out to be a somewhat flawed reply at best. Whereas the TR-250 benefited from its wood veneer dash, independent rear suspension, and smooth six-cylinder engine, the MG C suffered from its increased weight over the front wheels and nearly identical body to the ubiquitous MG B at a substantial price premium.

While you are staring at the current-day sticker shock listed at the bottom of the chart below, keep in mind that all three of these sweethearts retailed at about $4000 or a little less back in the good old days of 1967-68. In the USA at least, their leading showroom competition were the new pony convertibles. A potential buyer could choose ultimate sports car pedigree and handling quality from the list below or comfort, reliability, and honking straight-line performance from the ponies. America will never go home again to such affordable choices of heaven on wheels.

Figure B47 - **This photo of a British Racing Green MG C was taken in Montreal, apparently on a somewhat foggy day. You can see the hood bulge with its chrome strip across the front. The new hood was necessary to clear the taller six-cylinder engine. The optional top has been folded down into the boot on this example. A removable type was standard on the C. This example has the standard painted wire wheels.** ©Bull-Doser (PD)

Figure B48 - This is the final dash design for the Triumph Spitfire. The instruments were finally placed directly in front of the driver. The steering wheel and seats were comfortable, attractive, and modern in styling.... ©Akela NDE (CC)

Figure B49 (previous page) - It's just a crying shame that the dash and interior design of the previous photo had to be paired with this face! This is a British Racing Green 1980 Triumph Spitfire 1500 with tan interior, the final year of Spitfire production. Some enthusiasts would say it was a mercy killing. ©Bull-Doser (PD)

A-H 3000 / TR-250 / MG C Comparison Chart

1967 Austin-Healey 3000	1968 Triumph TR-250	1968 MG C Roadster
OHV 2912cc - 150 hp	OHV 2498cc - 104 hp	OHV 2912cc - 145 hp
83mm bore x 89mm stroke	75 bore x 95mm stroke	83mm bore x 89mm stroke
Twin SU Carbs	Twin 1-bbl. Stromberg	Twin 1-bbl. SU
4-Speed + Overdrive	4-Speed Manual	4-Speed + Overdrive
Non-synchro First	Synchronized Gearbox	Synchronized Gearbox
No Optional Transmission	Overdrive Optional	3S Automatic Optional
Body on Frame	Body on Frame	Unibody Construction
Cam & Peg Steering	Rack & Pinion Steering	Rack & Pinion Steering
Live Rear Axle	Independent Rear	Live Rear Axle
Front Disc - Rear Drum	Front Disc - Rear Drum	Front Disc - Rear Drum
Painted Wire Wheels	Rostyle Wheel Covers	72-spoke Painted Wires
No Optional Wheels	Painted Wires Optional	Chrome Wires Optional
Dunlop Road Speed	Redline Radials	Radial Tires
2650 pounds	2350 pounds	2420 pounds
0-60 mph: 9.8 seconds	0-60 mph: 10.6 seconds	0-60 mph: 10.0 seconds
Top Speed: 116 mph	Top Speed: 107 mph	Top Speed: 120 mph
Vinyl Seats	Vinyl Seats	Leather Seats
Attached Top Standard	Attached Top Standard	Attached Top Optional
Silver Blue w/White Cove	BRG w/Black & Black	BRG w/Black & Black
Production: 3051	Production: 8484	Production: 4550
Hagerty: $62,318	Hagerty: $23,964	Hagerty: $18,746
Range: $40,000 - $140,000	Range: $13,000 - $53,000	Range: $10,000 - $50,000

A-H 3000 / TR-250 / MG C Comparison Chart Notes:
   Although they have identical dimensions, the six-cylinder engines of the Austin-Healey 3000 and MG C are different in many respects. The colors listed represent my favorite fantasies. The 3000 would be in Silver Blue with the special white two-tone option and the other two would be in British Racing Green. All tops and interiors would be black. The quoted production figures are for one year only, however, the TR-250 and MG C build period included a few extra months. All the TR-250's and most of the 3000's and MG C's were exported to the USA. The Hagerty auction prices shown were the averages at the time of publication. The ranges cover the widest condition span, from daily drivers to perfectly restored examples.

Classic English Sports Car Test Results Chart

Model & Details	HP	Weight	0-60	1/4	TS
1953-55 A-H 100 2660cc Four 3SM (*IAHBG*)	90	2176	10.3	NA	111
1958-60 A-H Bugeye Sprite (*IAHBG*)	43	1480	23.7	NA	79
1965 Austin-Healey 3000 Mk. III (*R&T*)	148	2650	9.8	17.4	116
1967 Austin-Healey Sprite Mk. IV (*R&T*)	65	1560	14.7	19.9	93
1961 MG A 1600 Mk. II (*R&T*)	90	2050	12.8	18.7	NA
1962 MG B 1798cc (*R&T*)	94	2080	12.5	18.5	NA
1967-69 MG C 2912cc (*IMGBG*)	145	2420	NA	NA	120
1967 MG Midget Mark III 1275cc (*R&T*)	65	1560	14.7	19.9	93
1976 MG Midget Mk. IV 1493cc (*R&T*)	56	1775	15.5	20.1	83
1979 MG Midget 1493cc (*C/D*)	50	1820	16.3	20.7	86
1956 Triumph TR-3 1991cc (*R&T*)	100	2090	12.0	18.4	NA
1962 Triumph TR-4 2138cc (*R&T*)	105	2200	10.5	17.8	NA
1963 Triumph Spitfire 1147cc (*R&T*)	63	1555	15.5	20.8	NA
1965 Triumph Spitfire Mark 2 (*R&T*)	67	1630	15.0	20.4	92
1965 Triumph TR-4A (*R&T*)	105	2330	10.5	17.5	107
1967 Triumph Spitfire Mk. III 1296cc (*C/D*)	75	1650	16.5	20.5	91
1967 Triumph Spitfire Mk. 3 1296cc (*R&T*)	75	1680	13.6	19.3	100
1968 Triumph TR-250 2498cc (*R&T*)	111	2350	10.6	17.8	107
1969 Triumph TR-6 2498cc (*R&T*)	106	2360	11.6	18.2	NA
1974 Triumph Spitfire Mk. IV 1493cc (*R&T*)	57	1735	15.4	20.2	94
1979 Triumph TR-7 Convertible (*R&T*)	89	2470	11.5	18.5	109
1980 Triumph TR-8 Convertible (*MT*)	137	2662	8.5	16.6	NA
1980 Triumph TR-8 Convertible (*C/D*)	148	2620	8.1	16.2	117

Classic English Sports Car Test Results Chart Notes:
The base price of the 1966 MG Midget Mark II was $2125. The MG B in the same year was $2725. The Triumph Spitfire was $2249. The base price of the Spitfire would climb to $2345 by 1969. (Oh, the horror!) The '69 TR-4A was $2895. By 1976 base prices had risen to $3949 for the MG Midget, $4295 for the Triumph Spitfire, and $4795 for the MG B. Popular options on each were still wire wheels ($135), AM/FM ($150), and tonneau cover ($50). *C/D = Car and Driver. IAHBG = Illustrated Austin-Healey Buyer's Guide. IMGBG = Illustrated M.G. Buyer's Guide. MT = Motor Trend. R&T = Road & Track.*

Selected Affordable English Antiques Ratings Chart

Years	Model	Collect	Drive	Desire
1958 - 1960	Austin-Healey Bugeye Sprite	B	B	B
1961 - 1969	Austin-Healey Sprite Mk. II-IV	D	C	C
1953 - 1956	Austin-Healey 100	B	C	C
1955 - 1956	Austin-Healey 100 M & 100 S	A	D	A
1956 - 1959	Austin-Healey 100 Six	B	C	D
1959 - 1967	Austin-Healey 3000	B	B	B
1961 - 1973	MG Midget Mk. I-III	D	C	C
1974 - 1979	MG Midget 1500	D	C	D
1955 - 1962	MG A	B	C	C
1959 - 1960	MG A Twin Cam	A	D	B
1959 - 1962	MG A DeLuxe	B	C	C
1962 - 1967	MG B Mark I	C	C	C
1968 - 1971	MG B Mark II	D	C	C
1972 - 1980	MG B Mark III	D	B	D
1967 - 1969	MG C	B	C	C
1953 - 1955	Triumph TR-2	B	D	D
1956 - 1958	Triumph TR-3	B	D	C
1959 - 1961	Triumph TR-3A	A	C	B
1962	Triumph TR-3B	A	C	B
1961 - 1965	Triumph TR-4	B	C	C
1965 - 1967	Triumph TR-4A	B	B	B
1968	Triumph TR-250	B	B	B
1969 - 1976	Triumph TR-6	C	A	C

Models Ratings Chart Definitions:

Years: In most cases, the years listed include the total production years for a particular model series. Some model years within a series may be considerably more desirable than other years.

Models: In some cases many variations are included in this category and in others the models included are very homogeneous. This is generally self explanatory.

Collectibility: This is what most of you want to know, the bottom line on how likely the model or series is likely to climb in value over the coming years.

Drivability: This is an indicator of how adaptable the machine can be to drive for transportation or pleasure in the modern world, considering collector value, parts availability, fuel quality, comfort, performance and miscellaneous other factors.

Desirability: This defines the nostalgic, emotional wow factor, without regard for collector values or everyday usage.

General: No machine is given a failing grade. If it made it into a rating chart, at least a few hobbyists find that model interesting.

Figure B50 - We leave this long chapter of the classic sports car era with an all-black 1973 MG B. Although the power strangling had already begun, the 1973 model offered the standard Rostyle wheels, headrests, comfortable seats and last delicate chrome bumpers. It's just too bad that that convertible top was still an infernal contraption that was tricky to handle without the top frame slicing holes into the vinyl. ©Paste (GNU)

The Big Three Affordable English Antiques

Chapter 3: *English Aberrations, Eccentricity, and Elegance*

Figure C1 - **This familiar, luxuriously inviting interior belongs to a 1968 Jaguar E-Type Roadster. Its vintage is easily identified by its combination of flat safety switches on the dash and the lack of headrests on the seats. The steering wheel with brushed aluminum spokes is real wood. The dash has a black crinkle finish. The seats, console and door panels are cream. The carpet is just a shade or two darker.** ©Jaguar Media Pages

The British sent us a lot more than mass-produced affordable sports cars from The Big Three. Most were positioned upmarket from the MG's, Austin-Healeys and Triumphs. A few were disastrous mistakes, a few were screaming successes, and many were just plain eccentric. You may desire one of the first group, although by now you certainly are aware of the monetary pitfalls. Your taste may fall in line with most everyone else's, meaning that you will pay dearly for a sexpot like that on the cover of this book. The eccentric group falls somewhere in the middle. You have to join a club to locate parts and service, but you will certainly be surrounded by compatriots.

Triumph Stag

Figure C2 - You can clearly see the unusual top design of the Stag in this photo of a pretty blue 1974 model. The shade of blue looks much like the Grabber Blue on a 1970 Mustang Boss 302. The T-bar is fixed in place, no matter what top configuration is present. The soft top folds neatly underneath a metal boot. Note the unusual wheel design unique to the Stag. ©The Car Spy (CC)

Only 2871 Triumph Stags were exported to the USA, a little more than ten-percent of the total production, of which most remained in Europe. This number for U.S. Stags comes from Wikipedia. The *Illustrated Triumph Buyer's Guide* states 6780 came to America. This could mean *literally* America, not only the USA. Wikipedia claims the 6780 number includes all export models. The same source states that 25,877 Stags were sold in total over seven years of production. The Stag is probably the only English car in this book that was more popular in England than in the U.S. Although imported here only in 1972-73, the model continued in England through 1977. The Stag's Achilles' heel was clearly its Triumph 3.0-liter, SOHC V-8, an all-new engine design by Triumph for the Stag. This engine was utilized only in the Stag and it had reliability problems out the grandest wazoo. Its single-row cam chain needed to be replaced every 25,000 miles, but the big bugaboo was overheating. The Stag had lots of methods for accomplishing this feat. Coolant starvation from the positioning of the water pump over the engine, water pump failure itself, blown head gaskets, and corroding cooling systems were the leading culprits. Once the engine had severely overheated, the alloy heads warped and cemented themselves to the iron block. Separating these and making the necessary repairs could be very expensive. Some would say not cost effective. Main bearing and timing chain failures were also common. Large numbers of these engines in Europe have long ago been replaced with engines of more reliable design. As we all know, whenever this is done to make the car livable, resale cost effectiveness as a collectible flies out the window.

This may be the car that leads the pack in not being a viable collectible or restoration project among all the cars covered in *Daydreams in the Wind*. The top design is totally unique to itself. Considering the focus of this book on topless European sports cars of the 1955-75 period, the Stag certainly earns its due. It was designed to be a flagship Triumph to soar even above the TR-6. It is really quite a shame that the Rover/Buick aluminum V-8 was not used instead. Elsewhere in this book you will see mention of this wonderful engine. It was in my own family's 1962 Buick Special and it *was* a sweetheart: lightweight, spunky and reliable. Several opinions have been written as to why Triumph did not use this engine. Some sources say that Rover claimed they could not supply enough engines. Others say that Triumph management was determined to show off their new V-8 design. Whatever the case, from a U.S. export standpoint at least, this turned out to be a horrible mistake. Triumph in the USA probably spent a fortune in warranty repairs. Any way you crunch the numbers, cost effective, it was not!

Figure C3 - This yellow 1973 Stag is one of those few sent to the USA. The front turn signal lenses are solid amber and of course it has left hand drive. ©Dave 7, Lethbridge, Canada (CC)

The Stag offered a luxurious leather and wood interior, a nice dash full of TR-6 instruments, and a comfy rear seat. All of this was underneath a padded roll bar with a T-connector to the windshield. Early models could be purchased with a soft top only, hardtop only, or both, like a 1963-67 Sting Ray Convertible. All later models supposedly came with a soft top with the hard top optional. Later models may have all come with both tops as standard. Since "later" in this case can mean up until 1977, I am not sure what top configuration most or all of the '72 and '73 U.S. models had. U.S. models may also have had vinyl roof coverings on their hardtops. Most of the total production used Borg-Warner three-speed automatic transmissions. The TR-6 four-speed manual, with or without the Laycock overdrive on third and fourth, was also available. It is unknown exactly how many of the U.S. cars were equipped with which transmission. Power steering, brakes, and windows were standard. The 1972 and early '73 cars were designated Mark I and the later 1973 cars were Mark II's. The 1974-77 cars in Britain were called "late" Mark II's. I would guess that Triumph bailed the slow-selling Stag out of the U.S. market before the big bumpers and catalysts kicked in for the '74 model year. This was probably a wise move.

Figure C4 - This red 1972 Stag displays its soft top up over the T-bar framework. Notice the wide, brushed silver pillars that show outside the roll bar when the top is erect. The amber over white front lamp lenses identify this as a European model. This car does not have the alloy wheel design more common to Stags. This design appears similar to the mag-style wheel covers of the 1968 TR-250. It is difficult to discern from this angle if these are wheels or wheel covers. A very attractive optional hardtop featuring large rear side windows was available. The rear quarter blind spot was significant with the soft top up. Although either type of top covered the T-bar, the hardtop offered a cleaner, slicker look for the ill-fated Stag. ©TR001 (CC)

Stags seem to be stuck in *Stagflation* mode at Hagerty's auction price scale. The *Illustrated Triumph Buyer's Guide* long ago stated that prices would never go down from the area around the original list price, but that is not saying much when you consider the cost and hassle of replacement parts for such a famous *Edsel*. Hagerty's currently indicates that Stags range from about $6000 up to $32,000, but that is not the whole story. The $32,000 was back before the Big Bust of '08 and the price curve has been a flat pancake since 2009. There does not seem to be a lot of hope for a Stag fan, although the model is obviously quite rare today, particularly in this country.

If you are considering the purchase of a Stag, the experts all agree that the engine in general, and the overheating issue in particular, should be your leading consideration. If an engine has been replaced with another type other than a Triumph SOHC 3.0 V-8, walk away. If the engine in the car cannot withstand scrutiny of all the common overheating issues, at least look for those that could have already caused permanent, severe damage, such as the heads welded to the block. I would hazard a guess that all the little trim pieces and other doodads indigenous to the model are very rare and very expensive today. Any car with both tops, the optional alloy wheels, and the optional air conditioning will certainly be more desirable. Keep in mind that the early 1973 cars in particular might have elements of both Mark I and Mark II versions. Parts were applied at the manufacturer until supplies were depleted. Sources have stated that not only was there a continuous flow of minor changes throughout the life of the Stag, but there were also some particular additions and changes indigenous to U.S. export models. I am sure you can guess that some of these were to meet regulations and some were made to satisfy consumer preferences for more fully equipped cars. Even Bond, James Bond, drove an early model Stag in the 1971 film *Diamonds Are Forever*. How cool is that?

The Legendary Morgan Eccentricity

Figure C5 - 1957 Morgan 4/4. ©Sicnag (CC)

The Morgan has remained England's *new old* sports car since before most of us were born. The company's tradition has always been tradition. The lewd, crude Morgan is about as modern as a dial telephone. The earlier models are more akin to the all-black, two-piece phone Sheriff Andy Taylor used to call somebody through Sarah the operator! The 1955 and later models covered here all had running boards, flat windshields, bulging headlamps, and erector-set roadster tops. The frames were constructed of wood, and of course rot and deterioration has consistently been a bone of contention for hobbyists and collectors. The engines sourced from Ford, Triumph, and Rover have always been straightforward transplants from mass-produced models. None of the manual transmissions had a synchronized first gear until just in time for the big horsepower drop of 1972. Disc brakes at least stopped the front wheels since the beginning of the '60's, but nothing, I mean *nothing*, has ever been done to alter the famous rock-hard ride of a Morgan. All Morgans are air conditioned if you stow the primitive top where it belongs. If you want comfort and convenience buy something else. If want to see all the other drivers on the road stare at your grinning face, drive a Morgan.

Morgan launched an updated version of its 4/4 model with a 92-inch wheelbase in 1950, later referred to as the Series I. To fit within the parameters of this book, the first Morgan to be discussed here is the 4/4 Series II introduced in 1955 with a new chassis design with the Plus 4's 96-inch wheelbase. The Series II came with either a standard 36-hp Ford 1.2-liter Four or a hopped up 40-hp option with twin carbs. The only transmission available was a manual three-speed. The Series III offered modern hydraulic shock absorbers and a 39-hp, one-liter Ford engine coupled to a four-speed manual transmission. The Series IV brought 62 horsepower and disc brakes. The 1600 used an English Ford 1.6-liter Four producing 70-95 horsepower. All models had a four-speed manual with synchromesh on the top three gears. All the Series II and later Morgan 4/4's were two-seat roadsters with primitive tops and side curtains.

Figure C6 - Pretty light metallic green Morgan Plus 4 with its beige top up. ©Alf van Beem (CC)

The Morgan Plus 4 had a longer chassis with a 96-inch wheelbase and hydraulic drum brakes. The original model, introduced in 1950, used a Standard Vanguard 2088cc Four, but most of the Plus 4's of this period used Triumph engines. The '53-'61 models had the 1991cc TR-3 engine and the '62-'68 models utilized the 2138cc Triumph TR-4 powerplant. The Triumph engines brought the 1850-pound Morgan into the modern world of performance for the period with 0-60 times under ten seconds and top speeds of about 100 mph. Front disc brakes were optional in 1959 and standard equipment from 1960-onward. The Plus 4 models included two-seat Roadsters, 2+2 Roadsters, and Drop-Head Coupes with better tops and fixed side window frames.

The company launched its long-lived Plus Eight powered by the legendary Buick Rover aluminum V-8 in 1968. Although this model has continued for decades to be produced for various markets, only the early 1968-75 models fit within the parameters of this book. The plain steel wheels with hubcaps of the Plus 4 were replaced with fancier alloy wheels without hubcaps on the new Plus Eight. All these early models used a four-speed manual transmission. Due to the lightness of its aluminum V-8, the 98-inch wheelbase Plus 8 weighed only slightly more than its slower Triumph-powered ancestors. The four-speed was not synchronized in first gear, but a limited-slip differential was standard. The '68-'73 models were gasoline powered in the normal manner, but the 1974-75 models sent to the USA had to be converted to propane propulsion by U.S. dealers to comply with emission regulations. Power decreased from 184 horsepower down to about 150 in 1972 as the compression ratio had to be lowered to run on U.S. pump unleaded. The catalytic-converter era finished off the normal pump-gas Morgan for the U.S. market. A fully-synchronized four-speed had finally arrived in 1972.

Figure C7 - Morgan Plus 8 in bright red with bolt-on chrome wire wheels and its top erect. Note the eccentric design of the continental kit and luggage rack. ©Amaud 25 (CC)

Morgans have been produced in small numbers steadily for a long time. Most of their auction values have remained pretty stable in the $25,000 to $40,000 range for a nice example of most models. The only exception is the rare Plus 4 Supersport model. With only 101 produced over many production years, you may have been surprised to discover prices still flat and stable as late as 2014, but this little jewel has been discovered in 2015. A recent price spike has taken the Supersport up to $70,000 to $100,000.

Figure C8 - This lovely two-tone beige 1968 Morgan Plus 4 is a prime example of how we like to reminisce about Morgans. The top is down and the leather strap is prominently displayed across the long hood. ©Bull-Doser (PD)

Morgan Production Chart

Model	Years	Production	Model	Years	Production
4/4 Series II	1955 - 60	386	Plus 4	1950 - 52	893
4/4 Series III	1961	58	Plus 4	1953 - 61	2237
4/4 Series IV	1962 - 63	114	Plus 4	1962 - 69	1523
4/4 Series V	1963 - 68	639	Plus 4 SS		101
Total 4/4	1955 - 68	1197			
			Total Plus 4	1950 - 69	4754
4/4	1955 - 68	1291			
4/4 1600	1968 - 82	3513	Plus 4	1950 - 69	4584

Morgan Production Chart Notes:

The 4/4 designation refers to four wheels and four cylinders. The 1291 Morgan 4/4's of 1955-68 listed above were constructed on a lengthened chassis. The base price of the 4/4 in 1966 was $2685. The 1966 Plus 4 was $3175. The *Complete Book of Collectible Cars 1940-1980* lists the 4/4 Series II-V as 387 + 59 + 206 + 639 = 1291. These figures represent 94 more cars than the numbers listed by Graham

Robson's *A-Z British Cars 1945-1980* (2006). *Hemmings* and *Wikipedia* state 4584 Plus 4's built in 1950-69, and this number includes 26 Plus Four Plus coupes. The Plus 4 listings by engine came from the *Complete Book of Collectible Cars 1940-1980*. The rare Supersport models were constructed with light alloy body panels and used Triumph TR Fours slightly souped up to 115 horsepower by a specialty tuning firm.

Jensen-Healey

Figure C9 - You can tell from the smaller chrome front bumper that this pretty yellow Jensen-Healey is a 1972 or '73 Series 1 model. This example has aftermarket wheels. ©Dave 7, Lethbridge, Canada (CC)

One could say the Jensen-Healey was one of those footnotes to English roadster history. As with the MG C that preceded it, the parent company planned a successor to the Austin-Healey 3000 made obsolete by the new 1968 EPA and NHTSA regulations on auto emissions and safety, respectively. The 3000 had been the final iteration of a 1956 design and it would have been quite insurmountable to update it to the new U.S. rules without embarrassingly ruining the model's looks and performance. Another unsuccessful attempt had already been made by the Triumph Stag, making the Jensen-Healey the final, and most successful attempt. The third time was the charm in this case. A modern new body driven by a very modern DOHC, sixteen-valve Lotus four-cylinder certainly was a better idea than the unreliable Stag or the boring MG C that could not even outrun the company's own much cheaper B version. For the record, about 9000 MG C's were produced, almost reaching the 10,000 number of Jensen-Healeys. The Stag may be best not remembered.

The Lotus two-liter four produced 140 horses from its 121 cubic inches to propel about 2100 rear-wheel-drive pounds. The transmission was a Chrysler four-speed built in the UK. The suspension was distinctly not harsh, and you can suppose they learned this from Lotus. Even without independent rear suspension, the J-H stuck to the pavement pretty well. One of the car's best features was its front/mid-engine design with a true 50/50 weight distribution with a driver. This probably contributed to its adept handling, even with rear drum brakes and no stabilizer bars. The only handling complaint from the period was the cowl shake over rough surfaces. Maybe the car was just trying to prove that it was a real Healey. The overall sports car driving quality of the Jensen-Healey was quite high. So was the interior comfort, at least in nice weather with the top down.

Figure C10 - The wrinkly fit of the tan vinyl top is quite visible on this dark metallic Jensen-Healey. The exact color of this car is not clear from the original photo. It could be a brown, maroon, or even a very dark red. The brown interior color seems to be another shade, darker than the tan top. Note the chrome luggage rack and non-stock Minilite mag wheels, too. ©Dave 7, Lethbridge, Canada (CC)

In typical English fashion, the Jensen-Healey's Achilles' heel was its top. Geez, Louise, what is *wrong* with you Limey blokes? Would it have embarrassed you too much to buy a Fiat 124 Spider and just copy the top design? The production of your erector set tops was one thing in 1963, but this new model hit American streets in *1973*! What part don't you understand about your #1 market? The U.S. magazines noticed this very British abomination right off the bat. I won't repeat what they said, but I will tell you that I laughed when I read it. Come on, guys! You get some of those flat-black-painted flat pieces of steel and you attach them to the car and arrange them in such a way that when you reach behind you and grab the little vinyl handle at the front inside edge of the thick vinyl top, you can pull it up and over your head. What do you know?! There are a couple of little snap-down clamps here that you can mash downward toward the top edge of the windshield. They each go *ka-whamp* and ta-daaa... it's raining only outside, not inside, too. Why was that so stinking difficult?

Beyond my little rant about an unnecessarily recalcitrant top design, most likely the truly unfortunate issue of the Jensen-Healey simply was the bad timing of its introduction. The trough of the combined effects of safety regulations, emissions rules, monetary inflation and the fuel crisis occurred right there in 1973-75. The auto industry slowly began to crawl back out of its politically forced nosedive after that period, but by then it was way too late to save Jensen or any of its products. At more than 10,000, the Jensen-Healey was actually the highest production car the Jensen company ever produced. However, the Jensen-Healey was designed from the beginning as an affordable, relatively high production sports car to compete with the Fiat 124 Spider, MG B, and Triumph TR-6. All three of these were much older designs. The J-H had a hot little Lotus engine, modern styling, and good handling. Unfortunately that modern styling with its rather simple face and Triumph Spitfire look in the rear was less inspired than that of the curvaceous Austin-Healey 3000 and many potential buyers were distinctly not impressed. The Jensen factory executives at the time blamed mostly the workers' unions for the company's demise, but I tend to think that was only a small part of the picture. I cannot help but think the Jensen-Healey would have sold considerably better in the lucrative U.S. market with a sexier, less angular body and a more modern convertible top. But maybe that's just me.

The Jensen-Healey was first shown in Europe in March 1972, but it would be March 1973 before the U.S. magazines actually received a car to test. Wikipedia and other sources list the production figures for the early cars as 3347 called Mark I's and sold up through May 1973. The same sources state that 2501 Jensen-Healeys were sold in the USA and Canada in 1973. It is unknown exactly to what degree these two figures overlap to define actual sales of the Mark I model in the U.S. The Mark II model introduced in August 1973 had an upgraded interior with lots of wood trim and other accoutrements and optional, dealer-installed air conditioning. The 1975 model had a true close-ratio, five-speed gearbox sourced from the BMW 2002. The fifth gear was not an overdrive, as is often the case. Production would end in August 1975 with only 7142 cars built. This number included the final batch of Jensen-Healey convertibles labeled as JH 5 models on their fender badges. The JH 5's had catalytic converters and a few other changes (most likely few of them good). The total of these three variants equals 10,489 production models. Slightly higher total figures quoted elsewhere include a few prototypes. The company closed its doors in May 1976. It has not been verified exactly how many of the Jensen-Healey production came to the USA. Sources do not agree whether or not the convertible Jensens continued in production until the factory closed or only through August 1975, with production ceasing as production of the GT 2+2 began.

Figure C11 - This DOHC Lotus engine in a Jensen-Healey is not stock, as you can tell from the open element air filters on what might be twin two-barrel Weber carbs. ©Colin MB (CC)

In retrospect the Jensen-Healey represented the good, the bad and the ugly. The closest to ugly was probably the boring styling with its simplified lines and busy body panels. Both of these elements were intentionally designed to make the J-H cost effective to manufacture and affordable to repair; however, as with most English roadsters of the classic period, rust was still a huge issue. The early interior design was quite plain; most were all black, with a small unknown number produced in tan. European models were built with Dell'Orto carbs, but American versions used smog-resistant Strombergs. Probably the ugliest components of all were the huge black safety bumpers of the 1974-76 models. Unfortunately a U.S. customer could not get the BMW 5-speed without the ugly bumpers. The bad element certainly encompassed the erector set top, but unfortunately there were the usual British reliability gremlins along for the ride, too. Worst of all, the DOHC Lotus engine had a problem throwing its timing belt and sending the engine to its costly demise. This has been an issue with other early, high-revving OHC designs with toothed timing belts, such as the Fiat 124 Spider and 308 Ferraris, too, so Lotus has not been alone in this regard. The Lotus, however, came to demand timing belt changes at no more than 18,000 miles, an especially low figure for a volume-priced model. In contrast, the recommendation for the 124 Spider was 25,000 miles. Rampant inflation from the period caused the price of an American version to enter our market at about $5000 and leave it only three years later at about $9000! For starters, the good news is that now the Jensen-Healey is currently one of the cheapest cars in this book! It is unlikely you will have to pay much more than the final original price, and that's not so bad in new millennium dollars. Released at the time it was, all the Jensen-Healeys exported to the U.S. had a low compression ratio that ran on regular fuel of the day. Of course finding one that has survived the rust and timing belt issue may not be easy. When you do get your paws on one, though, you will have a classic sports car with a real 50/50 weight distribution, a high-performance engine producing more than one gross horsepower per cubic inch, and a sports car that is probably less common than Ferraris in your hometown!

Figure C12 - This is the more luxurious interior of the Series 2 models, featuring contrasting piping on its white seats and wood veneer on the dash and console. ©Akela NDE (CC)

Jensen-Healey Color Chart

Exterior	Exterior	Exterior	Exterior	Exterior
Black	Yellow	Pacific Blue	Oakland Green	Sebring Silver
Red	Mustard	Malaga Blue	Pine Green	Silver Grey
White	Tangerine			

Jensen-Healey Color Chat Notes:

As far as I know, practically all J-H convertibles had black interiors and tops. The convertibles were built in two series: The first 3356 produced in 1972-73 are referred to as Series 1 or Mark I cars. The 1974-75 cars, Series 2 or Mark II, had more luxurious interiors, optional AC, and different bumpers. There were 7142 of these produced for a total of 10,498 cars.

Figure C13 - This red 1975 Jensen-Healey is one of that last batch of JH 5 models. Note the special badge on the lower front fender. You can spot a Series 2 a mile away by its big black bumpers. The wheels are stock, but I don't know about those Hercules H/P 4000 tires. According to *Road Test Magazine*, these final five-speed models retailed in the U.S. for $8445 with a few options and dealer prep. Performance results included 0-60 in 8.3, the quarter in 16.6, and a 121-mph top speed. ©Ozza Davies (CC)

Breaking the Rules: TVR Tuscan & 3000S

Sometimes you just have to admit that rules are meant to be broken. These two TVR models break the prescribed parameters of this book, just as the legendary brand has been an exception to the general consensus since the company was founded in 1947. The Tuscan we are discussing here is the original TVR model with that name produced in tiny numbers in 1967-70. The top was not removable. The 3000S sold in the USA in 1978-79 was a full-blown roadster, side curtains and all, and it was the first topless TVR. So one breaks the topless rule and the other the timeframe rule, what's the big deal? What does either model have to do with the subject of this book?

A man named Trevor Wilkinson founded the company and named it after himself. Many small specialty manufacturers have existed within an endless tumult of shoestring success, bankruptcies and varied ownership. When it comes to tumultuous history, TVR has been one of the most prolific. The reason these two models deserve a place in this book is due to the efforts of Arthur Lilley and his son Martin Lilley, who purchased the company in 1966, and an American named Gerry Sagerman, who imported the cars into New York from the time of the Lilley takeover until the Eighties. Martin and Gerry ran the operation of designing, constructing, and marketing the cars until the two had a falling out that they both could likely regret. The creative team were the honored celebrities at a reunion of TVR enthusiasts in New Jersey in 2005. Many pleasant memories of an earlier time were shared by all.

Figure C14 - This beautiful blue 3000S shows off its chrome bumpers and optional chrome Wolfrace alloy wheels. ©Colin MB (CC)

In TVR nomenclature, the Lilley-Sagerman team created the M-series models. Named after Martin, these were sandwiched between the Granturas and the Wedges. The Grantura models had fiberglass bodies constructed by the Grantura Engineering company. The Wedges were a group of TVR models from the Triumph TR-7 Doorstop School of Car Design. The Granturas, and their Ford V-8 cousins, the Griffiths, were somewhat half-baked. The Wedges quickly became the answer to a question few enthusiasts asked. The M models represent the broad field of successful, desirable, classic TVR's. Martin and Gerry's work together was sandwiched by the Tuscan and the Taimar Roadster. The first Tuscan was just a rebadged Griffith and the Taimar Roadster was the name *Road & Track* titled its road test of The Convertible, the name of the car from its birth parents. The Convertible and the Taimar Roadster were the same car sold officially as the 3000S. The funny part about that is that (a) the car is a roadster, not a convertible; (b) the S cannot stand for Spyder because it's English, not Italian; and (c) it is a direct equivalent to the Taimar coupe. Personally, I think it should be called the Taimar Roadster.

In spite of many eccentricities, particularly shortcomings in the comfort and convenience department, the TVR brand has always had my number. For me it all began when I discovered the existence of the original 1967 Tuscan. This was a tight little fiberglass coupe fitted with a Mustang drivetrain. It went like stink on a skunk and stuck to swirling ribbons of pavement like a Superglue sandwich with Elmer's Glue-All. A brochure we have from 1967 states the base price with the 271-hp V-8 as $5445 FOB New York. Available exterior colors were Ermine White, Regal Red, Signal Red, Riviera Blue, Diamond Blue, Sherwood Green, Metal Light Green, April Yellow, Malibu Gold, and Silver Grey. The interior with all colors was black vinyl with wood veneer trim. The brochure lists the dry weight as 2128 pounds. The axle was a 3.07 with a 2.36 first gear. Brakes were disc front and drum rear. Other standards were rack and pinion steering and wire wheels. The brochure photo shows knock-off wires, but the accompanying spec sheet simply says *wire wheels* without denoting *bolt-on* or *knock-off*.

Approximately 280 Griffith 200 and 400 models were sent to the U.S. in 1963-65. These were shipped to the U.S. without drivetrains that would be installed at the Griffith facility in New York. After the Lilley family took over the company and began keeping more accurate records, exactly ten more Griffith 400's were produced in 1966, six with left hand drive. The Griffith weighed 1905 pounds. The 195-hp 289 was standard and the 271-hp was optional. The short wheelbase of the early TVR's was 85 inches. The long wheelbase was 90 inches. All Griffiths and Tuscans had 72-spoke, knock-off wire wheels. The Special Equipment (SE) model had the solid-lifter 289. The Griffiths and SWB Tuscan had five-inch width wheels. The LWB Tuscan models had six-inch wheels. The road test of the Tuscan 302 in July 1970 had 5.5 x 15-inch alloy wheels and drum rear brakes. *R&T* claimed the test car was the first LWB Widebody, yet it had to be near the end of production. This final Tuscan model may not have actually reached the U.S. in 1968, and maybe not even in 1969. Another issue is the knock-off wires. Would these have not been bolt-on by 1967? Did all the Widebody models have a 302?

Figure C15 - This green 1969 Tuscan is in the paddock at Mallala Motor Sport Park in Australia. The owner of this particular car is Laurie Burton. This car has a full roll cage and oversize wheels and tires. ©GTHO (CC)

The Ford small-block V-8's in TVR's were installed in New York, including all the 1963-66 Griffiths and 1967-70 Tuscans, although not in the same shop. The Griffiths received their final assembly from Jack Griffith, the man who originally had the idea for a Cobra copycat. Minimal development was done to the little coupes when the big bad 289 Windsors were stuffed into them. Minimal engine cooling and differential strength brought a disgusting taste to the mouths of American buyers. The first thing Martin Lilley did was to address these issues when he transformed the Griffith into a Tuscan. The real Tuscans began with what became known as the short wheelbase model in 1967. The Tuscan was transformed two more times. The LWB version got a five-inch longer wheelbase and minor body modifications. The final version was nicknamed the Widebody model with smoother contours and more interior room. In general there is little mistake in identifying a Tuscan. They all look very much alike, even though the body trim, dash design and other interior details varied over the four-year production period. Oh, I almost forgot the punch line: less than 75 Tuscans were built!

The first 28 Tuscan V-8 models were the short wheelbase type, similar to the model's Griffith predecessor. The next 24 were the long wheelbase type with a slightly altered body on a TVR Vixen chassis, and the last 21 were the LWB type with SE trim. The final batch produced were nicknamed as the *Widebody* type and they were probably all powered by Mustang 302 engines. The question of the decade is whether or not any production models were actually constructed with the screaming 290-horsepower Boss 302 powerplant and whether or not any Boss 302 model is still around, terrorizing the neighbors. *Road & Track* tested a Widebody base 302 model in 1970. This car was not noted as an SE model and it had the standard two-barrel

302. This is in conflict with other sources that considered all the Widebody models as the SE type.

The Tuscans were custom-built by hand in such small numbers over a four-year period that it is difficult to track the precise changes in the design as production continued. This issue was greatly compounded by the fact that the engines and transmissions were installed in New York after the body, frame, and running gear of the machines had been constructed in Blackpool. Most of the information available today concerns the earliest Tuscans of 1967 and the last ones of 1970. Quite a lot of specific information from the middle of the production period is missing in action. The first models had knock-off wire wheels that would have been illegal in the U.S. by the start of 1968. The last models rolled on alloys. All the Tuscans had fifteen-inch wheels. Did the middle group have bolt-on wires? We do not know for sure. Were a choice of bolt-on wires or alloys offered on some models? Maybe. Of course there are many issues surrounding the utilization of the Ford small-block V-8's. There seem to have been no records kept of how many Tuscans were produced with each engine. I have personally found no information on the 250-hp 4-bbl. option mentioned by *Road & Track*. Were any cars actually produced with this engine? Did they have single or dual exhausts? Note that the 250-hp 302 was available in the Cougar, but never the Mustang, which utilized a 250-hp 351 instead. If you consider the direct availability by model year of the engines, the 271-hp K-code 289 should not have been available after 1967. The three 302's with 2-bbl., 4-bbl., and solid lifters should have applied to all the 1969-70 models. Only the '68's should have been open to any ambiguity in the powerplant department. The Special Equipment designation was originally chosen by Jack Griffith to denote the solid lifter models, but the SE seems to have later been applied to all the LWB Widebody models except the one tested by *Road & Track* for its July 1970 issue. Finally, what's up with *R&T* referring to the test car as the prototype or first in the series when production of the whole Tuscan line *ceased* at Blackpool at about that time?

The Tuscan name continued on a similar, but much slower, model powered by an English Ford V-6 in 1969 through 1971. The Tuscan V-6 was never certified for sale in the USA. The regular M series went into full production in 1972. Since the Ford V-6 was never adapted to EPA standards, TVR chose to utilize the Triumph 2498cc inline six-cylinder for the U.S. market. TVR just piggybacked onto the certification process already cleared for takeoff in the TR-6. Things would come full circle when the Taimar Roadster nee 3000S was released in 1978 for the U.S. market with the Ford Capri V-6.

My personal obsession for the original Tuscan series never waned. The concept to a large degree was what I always wanted: a three-quarter-sized and powered Corvette. You could also envision a much smaller, sportier Mustang GT Convertible. Whatever the fantasy, it has been with me for a very long time. The newly introduced 1964 Mustang was far too plain, yet simultaneously too large and heavy. At the opposite end of the spectrum, the 1968 Corvette was extravagantly space inefficient. I loved the Corvette's front-mid-engine design. I loved the Mustang's practicality. The problem is that never the twain shall meet. I love many of the traditional English dash designs with genuine wood veneer trim around an understated instrument layout. If only the gauges and electrics in the Triumph TR-250 were as reliable as those in an American product! Luggage had to be loaded behind the seats of a Tuscan, as in a Corvette. I would have much preferred a convertible model with proper trunk access.

Figure C16 - This white 1978 3000S is precisely stock for a U.S. model with its black bumpers, amber side marker and turn signal lamps, and front air dam. ©Dave 7, Lethbridge, Canada (CC)

TVR brought at least part of my fantasy to America eight years after the last Tuscan. The Taimar Roadster (can I call it that?) had my number! A shapely, sexy body covered a tube frame. A Ford Capri V-6 producing 142 horsepower with a Weber two-barrel carb propelled the sporty roadster at a respectable pace. I am not sure exactly how Sagerman and TVR managed to certify a combination of catalytic converter and Weber carburetor, but they did. I shall always remember being in Denver at the time the Taimar Roadster was released. I was occupied with business during the day, so I had to locate the TVR dealer after hours to see the new Convertible live in the fiberglass. I stood in the chill of that autumn evening with my fingers gripping the chain link fence while my eyes carefully absorbed every detail of the latest TVR. The company had finally built a topless TVR just for me.

Ruh-roh. The top is attached to the body, but those are *side curtains*! I have spent years disparaging the Triumph Spitfire for its center-focused dash design, and now TVR has to have one, too. Triumph had finally ditched theirs. Why did TVR have to copy it? We know the whys and wherefores of both these disgusting components. Triumph was trying to keep the retail price of the early Spitfires down with minimal differences between left hand and right hand drive models. The Convertible 3000S *was* a topless Taimar, the moniker of the latest hatchback M-series coupe that was the immediate predecessor of the new roadster. The change in windshield design left insufficient room between the top of the dash and the steering column for the normal placement of instruments directly in front of the driver. The requisite design of the doors left insufficient space for retractable roll-down or electric windows. The windows had been electric on the Tuscan, by the way. At least the test reports of the day gave the convertible top design decent ratings. It was a copy of that designed for the Jensen-Healey. Unfortunately, the same road testers scoffed at the specific ergonomics of the Roadster's driving environment, as their predecessors had done in tests of the Tuscan.

Tuscan / 3000S Production Chart

Model	Year	Built	Model	Year	Built
Griffith 200 & 400	1963-65	300	3000S RHD	1978-79	191
Griffith 400 LHD	1966-67	6	3000S LHD	1978-79	67
Griffith 400 RHD	1966-67	4			
			Total 3000S Production	1978-79	258
Total Griffiths	1963-67	310			
			3000S LHD U.S.	1978-79	49
Tuscan V-8 LHD	1967	24			
Tuscan V-8 RHD	1967	4	3000S Turbo RHD	1978	7
Tuscan LWB LHD	1967-68	12	3000S Turbo RHD	1979	5
Tuscan LWB RHD	1967-68	12	3000S Turbo SE RHD	1979	1
Tuscan Widebody LHD	1968-70	19			
Tuscan Widebody RHD	1968-70	2	Total Griffith LHD	1963-67	286
			Total Tuscan LHD	1967-70	55
Total V-8 Tuscans	1967-70	73	Total 3000S LHD	1978-79	67

Tuscan / 3000S Production Chart Notes:

The production figures in this chart were sourced from *The TVRs, Grantura to Tasmin: A Collector's Guide*, and verified in part by *Wikipedia* and Motorbase.com. The Griffith 200 had a sloped tail and few were constructed. The Griffith 400 debuted in April 1964, the same time as the Mustang and Sunbeam Tiger. The 400 model with the signature TVR Manx tail was produced in much higher numbers, although no accurate production records are available. Approximately 280 of the original 300 Griffiths built remained in the USA. The ten cars listed as Griffith 400's produced in 1966-67 were built by the new Lilley organization as a brief continuation of the original Griffith 400.

Wikipedia states that a total of 258 3000S models were built. This coincides with *The TVRs, Grantura to Tasmin: A Collector's Guide*, which lists 129 1978 models and 129 1979 models ordered by the factory. *Wiki* goes on to say that 67 of the 258 were left hand drive, and of these, 49 were U.S. models. *Wiki* states that thirteen 3000S Turbos were constructed, one of which was Martin Lilley's personal car. Lilley's specially built 3000S Turbo was the only Special Equipment convertible built. The SE model, the single convertible and a handful of coupes, had a limited slip differential, leather interior, and larger wheels and tires with flared fenders to accommodate them. None of the M-series Turbo models were certified for sale in the U.S., including the 3000S. All the reported 49 sent here were standard models and all were more or less identical with the exception of colors.

Figure C17 - 1979 TVR 3000S Convertible. This U.S. example is in a deep blue with black interior and top. Note the look of the wheels. This design was standard equipment on all 3000S models. Standard size wheels were six inches wide on fourteen-inch rims. ©Colin MB (PD)

Eccentric English Sports Car Comparison Chart

Model	Type	CI / CC	HP	Wt.	Price
1959-61 Morgan Plus 4	I-4	121 / 1991	90	1915	$2700
1962-64 Morgan Plus 4	I-4	130 / 2138	100	1915	$2960
1965 Morgan Plus 4	I-4	130 / 2138	100	1915	$2965
1966 Morgan Plus 4	I-4	130 / 2138	100	1915	$3350
1967 Morgan Plus 4	I-4	130 / 2138	100	1915	$3890
1968-70 Morgan Plus 8	V-8	215 / 3529	160	1876	NA
(1970-77) 1973 Triumph Stag	V-8	183 / 2997	145	2800	$7000
1973 Jensen-Healey	I-4	121 / 1973	140	2155	$4795
1976 Jensen-Healey	I-4	121 / 1973	140	2155	$8689
1967 TVR Tuscan SE U.S.	V-8	289 / 4727	271	2274	$5445
1970 Tuscan U.S.	V-8	302 / 4949	220	2240	$6250
1978 TVR Taimar Roadster OHV	V-6	183 / 2994	142	2335	$15,900
1979 TVR 3000S Roadster OHV	V-6	183 / 2994	135	2335	$16,900
1979 TVR 3000S Turbo (UK)	V-6	183 / 2994	230	2436	NA

Eccentric English Sports Car Comparison Chart Notes:
The Morgan Plus 8 had a 98-inch wheelbase. The original base retail prices quoted in some cases may not be exactly accurate for the model year or years listed. The Tuscan road test in the July 1970 *Road & Track* listed a base price of $6250. The car tested had the optional AM/FM for $150, but it did not have other options available at the time. These included the Boss 302 engine for $700, a 250-hp four-barrel 302 for $300, and air conditioning at $500.

The Classic Lotus Elan Convertible

The Lotus Elan holds a special place in the legendary history of sports cars. Of course the convertible model is the one everyone cares about, particularly in America. The difference between an Elan and an XK-E is that the Elan is small and light. The difference between an Elan and an Austin-Healey Sprite is that the Elan was not designed to a low price point and has all the right stuff. The difference between an Elan and a Corvette is cubic inches, a *lot* of cubic inches. The difference between an Elan and a Mustang can be measured in the wheelbase. The difference between an Elan and a Duetto is a lot of zippity-doo-dah. The Elan could not have been more appropriately named.

The Lotus Elan and Europa: A Collector's Guide states that 12,224 Elans were built in 1962-73. This number includes the 22, or 25, depending on which number you believe, early models produced between October 1962 and May 1963 with a 1498cc engine that was later recalled and replaced with the regular 1558cc unit at no charge to the customers. This twelve-thousand figure includes the two-seater coupes and convertibles produced for all markets. There were an additional 3300 2+2 models built. The production figures officially break down into 7895 S1-S3 models. All the S1 series of 1962-64 were convertibles. The numbers were split with coupes in 1965-73. No coupe/convertible breakdown of the numbers is available. Neither is a statement of the number exported to the USA. The S4 model released in early 1968 complied with all the new U.S. regulations. There were 2976 S4's built for all markets. The final Big Valve Sprint model of 1971-73, the one most experts claim is the best of all Elans, numbered only 1353. Ferrari generally sold about a third of its production in the U.S. Austin-Healey and Jaguar sold at least 80% of their production to us Yanks. I suspect that Lotus ranked somewhere between these extremes.

Figure C18 - This red 1964 S1 Elan does not have the distinctive fixed chrome window frames of the later models. It does have the standard wheels and silver painted bumpers common to most Elans. ©TTTNIS (CC)

After the engines were switched in the first 22-25 models, all Elans shared the same drivetrain. The original standard specifications included chain-driven double overhead cams, twin Weber carbs, four-speed transmission, 3.90 axle, four-wheel solid disc brakes, independent rear suspension featuring Chapman struts, and knock-off styled steel wheels. The axle ratio was tightened up to 3.77 on later models, and a 3.55 was an option in some years. The Special Equipment package introduced in 1966 added a slightly higher state of tune for the DOHC Four, closer-ratio gears in the four-speed, power disc brakes, and center-lock wheels. The standard engine made 105 gross horsepower and the SE version 115. The final Sprint version developed 130 horsepower with Webers for the European market, but the U.S. models had Zenith-Stromberg carburetors and only 113 net horsepower. Although it was a bit heavier, the Sprint was the fastest of all Elans, and probably the most reliable, too. Comparing horsepower from the same perspective, the Sprint was quoted as producing 126 horses. Although a few Elans were built at the end of production with five-speed transmissions, none of these were sent to the U.S. At the time of publication in 1986, the author of the *Illustrated Lotus Buyer's Guide* estimated that 3-4000 Elans were still feasible for collectors and restorers. This figure of course includes coupes and convertibles that were never shipped to the U.S.

Figure C19 - This red 1963 1600 S1 has the rare optional hardtop. ©Dave 7, Lethbridge, Canada (CC)

The S1 model can be identified by its simple one-piece, curved windshield without vent windows or side window frames and a cluster of small, round tail lamps in the rear. The side windows were glass and were operated manually. The dashboard was bare metal and the steering wheel had slotted spokes. The floor was covered in rubber mat. The battery was in a compartment behind the driver's seat. A removable hardtop was offered beginning in mid-63, but it was not a popular option. All Elans had vinyl upholstery on seats with acceptable fore-aft adjustment for long or short legs. The S1 continued through the 1964 model year.

An elegant wood veneer dash was the most identifiable change to the S2 model. The slotted-spoke steering wheel was the same as on the S1. The tail lamps were gathered into a slender, rounded, horizontal frame. Most of the remaining changes were less visible, but they made the car more drivable and dependable. These included a lockable glove box, quick-release gas cap, and larger front brake calipers. Knock-off wheels became a popular option. All S1 and S2 models had a 3.90 axle ratio. An optional 3.55 axle and a close-ratio gearbox became available in late 1965. It is not clear if any or how many S2 Elan Convertibles were built with either or both of these separate options.

Figure C20 - This white 1969 S4 SE Elan is easily identified by its rectangular tail lights, headrests, and fixed window frames. Note the bolt-on wheels on this U.S. model. ©1977 Floyd M. Orr Collection

All Elans had retracting headlamps. Early models were raised by vacuum and closed by a spring. These surely included all S1 and S2 models, and at least most of the S3's, but it is unclear exactly when the change was made to raise the lights with springs and close them with the vacuum. If you will recall, the lights on Emma Peel's Elan in *The Avengers* closed with a quick thump by spring power. Since Diana Rigg's appearances as Mrs. Peel aired from September 1, 1966 through March 20, 1968, one can surmise that her Elan was probably of the Series 3 type. The change to spring-up and vacuum-down headlights probably coincided with the other regulations met with the introduction of the Series 4 in March of '68. Sometimes the vacuum effect would slowly leak in a parked car over a matter of hours, allowing the lights to slowly rise. If you park your late-model Elan overnight, you may find it winking at you the next morning!

The Special Equipment option package was made available at the beginning of 1966. Obviously this makes Series 2 S/E models somewhat rare, since the S3 would be introduced in

June of that year. The package included detail changes to the engine output and combined three previously separate options: power brakes, knock-off wheels, and the close-ratio transmission. Did some of these have the 3.55 axle, too? Were any sent to the U.S.? What we do know is that once we reached June of '66, most or all of the Elans imported here were S3 and later models with what was originally known as S/E equipment. They all had power windows, power brakes, previously optional styled steel wheels, close ratio four-speeds, and DOHC Fours producing 115 or more horsepower.

There were many updates made with the S3 in June 1966. The distinctive fixed chrome side window frames on the Elan Convertible came with the standard electric windows of the S3 model introduced in 1966. The long slots in the steering wheel spokes were changed to four round holes in each spoke. Carpeting was added to the interior floor. The trunk lid was enlarged to overlap the rear edge of the body, rather than being a rectangular opening in the top of the rear deck. The standard axle ratio was changed from 3.90 to 3.77 during the S3 production period.

Lotus responded to the new U.S. federal regulations with the S4 released in early '68. Flat toggle switches arrived on the dash, as they had on the Jaguar XK-E. A ventilation flap was added at each end of the dash, but these were too small to be very effective. The vinyl upholstery on the seats and door panels was now perforated for ventilation. The horizontal, rounded tail light cluster was increased in size to a larger rectangle. The wheel arches were squared off and flared to cover larger tires.

In November 1968, essentially for 1969 models for the U.S. market, the Weber carburetors were replaced with Zenith-Strombergs. The carburetor change was made for all markets at that time. You could easily spot a U.S. model by its crossover pipes extending over the engine head from the carburetors to the exhaust system. The Stromberg carbs and connector pipes would continue on the Sprint models sent to the USA until the end of production. A small hood bulge offset to the right was necessary to cover the taller Zenith-Stromberg carburetors. The bulge remained on the hood, even after the European model went back to the higher-performance Weber carbs in late '69. (Some European models were equipped with Dell'Orto carbs instead of Webers.)

Lotus produced its best Elan in the Big Valve Sprint in 1971-73. Detail changes to the valve system and other components brought a 10-20% power increase, depending upon the figures you are comparing. Throughout its decade of production, Lotus claimed 105, 115, 120, 126, and 130 horsepower for the Elan. The last three numbers apply to the Sprint, a model easily identified by its gold painted bumpers and two-tone paint with thin stripes down each side, separating the contrasting colors. Another Sprint identifier is that the hood bulge of the S4 had been removed. Driveline components were strengthened a bit to handle the additional power. Generally speaking, in most of its details the Sprint was a continuation of the Series 4, but with more power and a little additional style added. The Sprint was produced for approximately two and a half years until the last one was constructed in August 1973.

Figure C21 - The smooth hood is quite visible in this shot of a blue and white Sprint. This is the English model with right hand drive and knock-off wheels. ©Brian Snelson, Hockley, Essex, England (CC)

Although the Elan always looked as cute as a petite blonde cheerleader sitting on the showroom floor, there were, and still are, a number of negative issues that seemingly will never go away. The convertible top on the Elan may not have been the worst design ever, but it was still very bloody English! Unlike its cheaper MG, Triumph, and Austin-Healey brothers, the convertible top frame was always attached to the car body of the Elan; however, the vinyl fabric still had to be fastened down to the frame at many points. *Car and Driver* said in a test that you could not erect the top in less than fifteen minutes, even with two people on the job! That comment was in a test of a Big Valve Sprint model, no less, not an S1. What is with these Englishmen and their infuriating convertible top designs? The Elan's convertible top fared above average in keeping the weather out, but it did not do much to squelch the noise level inside the cockpit when erected. If you plan to listen to the radio, keep in mind that the fiberglass body does not keep ignition noise out of the system or provide a good reflecting surface for antenna reception. Corvettes have always had these problems, too, but the designers long ago figured out how to suppress the ignition noise. Lotus never did solve this problem in the Elan. The interior is so noisy with the top up, anyway, so maybe this is a moot point.

The Elan is a legend in its own time for its handling. Keep in mind, though, that this means diving into tight curves with elan, not sailing across Oklahoma on I-40 in a side wind! The short wheelbase, narrow track, and light weight were not the hot ticket for freeway travel. Air conditioning was never an option, and even the later models with ventilation ducts on the dash did not provide much cooling air to the interior. The engine cooling system on the Elan was marginal from the beginning and only a little improved on the later models. The little handling jewel was very sensitive to misalignment of wheels or frame damage from a minor accident.

Either could easily turn the jewel into a lumpy piece of coal. Fiberglass body repair on the Elan is easy, but frame repair is much trickier and expensive. Back in the '80's, whole new frames and whole new bodies were still being produced in England for Elan restorations. I do not know if these are still available, and if they ever were in the U.S.

The DOHC Ford with an iron block and special Lotus head is generally a reliable little bugger. A timely replacement of the timing chain is always paramount to its lifespan, of course. Keep in mind, too, that most any Lotus is going to have been revved to its redline countless times by any previous owner, so overall longevity is not that great in the first place. Some of the ancillary components are particularly short-lived. Rust is not often a big factor in a fiberglass-bodied Lotus, but moisture can become trapped in certain inconvenient locations such as the suspension components and the portion of the frame that contains the air-tight suction for the headlamp operation. The Ford transmissions were rarely a problem, but the rear drivetrain area might require close inspection. In the inside, upholstery and related components are generally durable. Like most English cars, the instruments could prove to be a nuisance.

Figure C22 - This is an unusual 1970 S4 SE with the bumpers painted the red body color instead of silver. The wheels are bolt-on gold with chrome trim rings. This example is left hand drive with the tiny, mid-mounted side marker lamps of a European model. My best guess is that this car was built for Canada or the Continent and the trim colors were the discretion of the owner. ©Akela NDE (CC)

The driving experience of the Elan was also not as perfect as we would like to remember. The gas pedal was way too stiff and the rubber doughnuts in the driveline were a legendary aggravation, particularly in the early models. Quick handling was its obvious forte. You would think this might be a wonderful advantage in everyday traffic, and it was, but the Elan's low visibility from sleepy drivers of ponderous sedans could be a hazard in itself. The dedicated Lotus faithful hold a strong contingent, even in the U.S., and this can be a blessing when seeking parts, service, or just solid advice spoken from experience. However, these owners may be your only hope. Lotus has a sporadic history as a U.S. operation rivaled only by Lamborghini. The company has changed parents, distributors, and dealers as often as Charlie Harper has gone through girlfriends.

The Lotus Elan holds a very special place in my heart and in *Daydreams in the Wind*. Probably more than any model discussed here, it fits the title like a stringback driving glove. It was such a *perfect looking* car. It was not an out-of-date antique a few years after its introduction like many MG's and Triumphs of the day. It was a truly modern car with an overhead cam engine, four-wheel disc brakes, and a fully synchronized transmission. Its straight-line acceleration was closer to a '60's muscle car than an imported roadster. Its body lines were simple, elegant, and virtually timeless. Like many Ferraris of its day, it still looks good! The Elan stands today as a shining example of a classic sports car that was always a wonderful experience to *dream* of owning. Real day-to-day ownership proved to be somewhat more like a slap in the face. The last word is that at the time the Lotus Elan was produced, many of us desperately wanted a Miata. It would be decades before Mazda had the perfect insight to take a classic Elan to Japan, disassemble it, study it, and reproduce it with all its infuriating flaws and unreliability left where they belonged in the first place, in England.

Figure C23 - Yellow Lotus Elan Sprint. ©Tony Hisgett, Birmingham, England (CC)

Lotus Elan Color Chart

Model	Exterior Color	Model	Exterior Color
1963 S1	Carmen Red	1963 S1	British Racing Green
1963 S1	Medici Blue	1963 S1	Cirrus White
1963 S1	Sunburst Yellow	1963 S1	Fiesta Yellow
1964 S1	British Racing Green	1964 S1	Cirrus White
1964 S1	Carmen Red	1964 S1	Medici Blue
1965 S2	Monaco Red	1965 S2	British Racing Green
1965 S2	Cirrus White		
1966 S3	Monaco Red	1966 S3	British Racing Green
1966 S3	Cirrus White		
1967 S3	French Blue	1967 S3	Wedgewood Blue
1967 S3	Carnival Red	1967 S3	Burnt Sand
1967 S3	Lotus Yellow	1967 S3	British Racing Green
1967 S3	Cirrus White		
1968 S4	Wedgewood Blue	1968 S4	Royal Blue
1968 S4	French Blue	1968 S4	Cirrus White
1968 S4	British Racing Green	1968 S4	Lotus Yellow
1968 S4	Carnival Red	1968 S4	Bahama Yellow
1968 S4	Burnt Sand		
1969 S4	Royal Blue	1969 S4	French Blue
1969 S4	Cirrus White	1969 S4	Carnival Red
1969 S4	Bahama Yellow	1969 S4	Lotus Yellow
1969 S4	British Racing Green	1969 S4	Burnt Sand
1970 S4	Royal Blue	1970 S4	French Blue
1970 S4	Regency Red	1970 S4	Carnival Red
1970 S4	Bahama Yellow	1970 S4	Lotus Yellow
1970 S4	British Racing Green	1970 S4	Burnt Sand
1970 S4	Cirrus White	1970 S4	Metallic Lagoon Blue
1970 S4	Colorado Orange	1970 S4	Pistachio Lime Green

1971 Sprint	Cirrus White	1971 Sprint	Carnival Red
1971 Sprint	Lotus Yellow	1971 Sprint	Metallic Lagoon Blue
1971 Sprint	Colorado Orange	1971 Sprint	Pistachio Lime Green
1972 Sprint	Cirrus White	1972 Sprint	Carnival Red
1972 Sprint	Lotus Yellow	1972 Sprint	Metallic Lagoon Blue
1972 Sprint	Metallic Tawny Brown	1972 Sprint	Indigo Blue
1972 Sprint	Sable	1972 Sprint	Black Gloss
1972 Sprint	Colorado Orange	1972 Sprint	Pistachio Lime Green
1973 Sprint	Firecracker	1973 Sprint	Carnival Red
1973 Sprint	Metallic Tawny Brown	1973 Sprint	Metallic Lagoon Blue
1973 Sprint	Metallic Glacier Blue	1973 Sprint	Metallic Mid Green
1973 Sprint	Metallic Purple	1973 Sprint	Monaco White
1973 Sprint	Olympic Blue	1973 Sprint	Indigo Blue
1973 Sprint	Sepia Brown	1973 Sprint	Bitter Green
1973 Sprint	Lotus Yellow	1973 Sprint	Cirrus White
1973 Sprint	Sable	1973 Sprint	Pistachio Lime Green

Lotus Elan Color Chart Notes:

As far we can surmise, all original-type Elan convertibles had black vinyl tops and interiors. The S/E (Special Equipment) model became an option in 1966. The S/E models had 115 horsepower. The option package also included power brakes, close-ratio four-speed, and center-lock wheels. Most, if not all, of the Elans shipped to the U.S. between 1966 and 1970 were S/E models. The Sprint continued with the same equipment and a more powerful Big Valve engine making 126 horsepower. Most of the Sprints produced had two-tone paint jobs and all had gold, instead of silver, painted bumpers.

Figure C24 - Interior of a 1969-model white Elan SE. ©1977 Floyd M. Orr Collection

Lotus Elan Comparison Chart

Model	Type	CI / CC	HP	Wt.	Price
1963 Lotus Elan	I-4	91 / 1498	100	1500	NA
1963-64 Lotus Elan	I-4	95 / 1558	105	1500	$3922
1965-66 Lotus Elan S2	I-4	95 / 1558	105	1534	$4330
1966 Lotus Elan S2 SE	I-4	95 / 1558	115	1534	$4995
1967-69 Lotus Elan S3 SE	I-4	95 / 1558	115	1515	$5600
1970 Lotus Elan S4 Sprint SE	I-4	95 / 1558	126	1630	$5133
1973 Lotus Elan S4 Sprint SE	I-4	95 / 1558	120	1640	$5693

Lotus Elan Comparison Chart Notes:
The Lotus Elan had an 84-inch wheelbase. The original base retail prices quoted in some cases may not be exactly accurate for the model year or years listed.

Figure C25 - The neat top boot, fixed windows frames, two-tone paint divided by gold striping, and flat hood are visible on this red and cream Sprint. The bumpers were also painted gold on the Sprints. You can identify it as a European model by its knock-off wheels and lack of side marker lamps front and rear. ©Alf van Beem (CC)

1968 Sprite / 1968 850 Spider / 1968 Elan / 1990 Miata Comparison Chart

Spec	1968 Sprite	1968 Spider	1968 Elan	1990 Miata
Drivetrain	Front / Rear	Rear / Rear	Front / Rear	Front / Rear
Displacement	1275cc / 78	817cc / 50	1588cc / 98	1600cc / 98
Engine	OHV	OHV	DOHC	DOHC
Horsepower	65 hp	52 hp	115 hp	115 hp
Transmission	4-speed	4-speed	4-speed	5-speed
Weight	1560	1640	1580	2100 lbs.
Top Boot	Vinyl	Metal Lid	Vinyl	Vinyl
Top Speed	100	90 mph	119	126 mph
0 - 60	14.7	20.0	8.0	8.1

A Different Breed of Cat

Figure C26 - Jaguar XK-120 Roadster in British Racing Green. Note the flat two-piece windshield, rear fender skirts and wide whitewalls. These early Jags generally came with the skirts on cars with disc wheels. Wire wheels were never covered by skirts. ©P Lawrence 99cx (CC)

We are all well aware by now that the top of this British Racing Green heap of English topless tin purrs like a big puddytat. Jaguar unleashed its growling XK-120 as its first postwar attack cat on the lucrative U.S. market. The sleek envelope body and high performance from its DOHC 3.4 liter inline six immediately endeared the new Jaguar sports car to enthusiasts worldwide. From its introduction in 1948 to the final production XK-150 in 1961, Jaguar slowly built its presence and reputation in the U.S. market. Actual series production did not begin until October, 1949, and one of the earliest production models went to Clark Gable. The earliest XK-120's were roadsters with aluminum bodies. These were changed to steel bodies with aluminum hoods, doors and trunk lids early in 1950. A coupe joined the line in 1951 and a proper convertible, a drophead coupe in English lingo, was added in 1953. The DHC had a fixed windshield, door handles, wind-up windows and a top that folded behind the seats. The roadster, in the English tradition of course, had none of these amenities. The 120's came standard with steel disc wheels and rear fender skirts. There was an optional Special Equipment package that included wire wheels and dual exhausts. The wires were body-colored for the most part, but some late models had chrome wires as a factory option. None of the wires were covered by fender skirts.

Figure C27 - This red 1953 XK-120 Drophead Coupe is showing off its tan top. Note the body-colored windshield frame and vent windows of the DHC model. Like the XK-120 Roadster pictured, this DHC also has the disc wheels with rear fender skirts. ©Lothar Spurzem (CC)

Figure C28 - This black 1954 XK-140 Roadster appears similar to the XK-120 Roadster. Note the bumper guards and two-piece windshield in a silver metal frame. This example has the popular chrome knock-off wire wheels. This one also sports blackwall tires and a red tonneau. ©Ekki01 (GNU)

The 1955 XK-140 brought rack and pinion steering and the same engine as in the 120, but moved forward three inches in the chassis. This brought more nose heaviness to the handling, but allowed the battery behind the seats to be moved up front with the engine. This cleared space for either more luggage capacity in the Roadster or a small rear seat in the DHC. The weakness of drum brakes began to show up through less fade resistance in the heavier 140. Engine power was increased a little in the 140 with 190-210 horsepower, as opposed to 160-180 in the XK-120. Road tests of the day showed about 8.5-9.0-second 0-60 times. Far the most common 140's in the U.S. were the DHC models and nearly all of them had wire wheels.

English Aberrations, Eccentricity, & Elegance

The 1957 XK-150 lost a bit of the charm of the 140's cut-down doors and slinky shape. The new DHC made up for the charm loss with four-wheel power disc brakes and other mechanical improvements. You can easily spot a 150 with its one-piece, curved windshield and roll-up windows. In the interior, the 150 had a leather-covered dash and the 140 used burled walnut, at least on the DHC and Coupe. The 140 Roadster's dash was uncovered. The XK-150 Roadster also had exterior door handles. Early models came only with the original 3446cc engine, but the 3.8 from the sedan was made an option in 1959. The two undersquare engines shared the same long stroke, but the 3.8 had a larger bore. Late model '59-'61 150's could be equipped with a choice of two displacements, two heads, and three compression ratios. Check out these details carefully if you are considering the purchase of an XK-150! A Roadster model was introduced in 1959 with the same two-seater specifications as the earlier 140 in its relationship to the DHC and Coupe models. Prior to the release of the S and 3.8 options, early XK-150's were the slowest of the Jaguar XK series due to slightly higher weight over the comparable 120's and 140's. Practically all the XK-150's built had the standard wire wheels and left hand drive. S models were distinguished by their triple SU carbs and hotter states of tune, available in either 3.4 or 3.8 displacement.

Figure C29 - This black beauty is a coveted Jaguar, an XK-150S. That little silver spot at the base of the one-piece windshield is the *S* emblem. This car has the prerequisite chrome knock-off wires and black tonneau, but the white shoulder belts over the red seats were not standard equipment. ©Herr Anders Svensson (GNU)

The focus of *Daydreams in the Wind* lies squarely in the Sixties. The three XK models that preceded the XK-E should be considered the preamble of the story. The history of these models is of course important to our complete understanding of the Jaguar legend. In America particularly, the Jaguar E-Type *is* the legend.

Some enthusiasts would name the 1961 Jaguar E-Type, called the XK-E in America, as the most beautiful sports car in history. There is quite a bit of both agreement and argument for this premise. Personally, I am not sure that the XK-E is ahead of the Lamborghini Miura or the Ferrari 308 GTB or GTS, but this is just my opinion. Your mileage may differ. Irregardless, how else would you explain the relentless popularity over the past fifty years of a car so infamously troublesome and demanding to properly maintain? The only car that inherently *demands* inclusion in *Daydreams in the Wind* as much as the Jaguar XK-E is the Sting Ray. In typical fashion, the E-Type utilized the same 265-hp, 3.8-liter DOHC Six as the XK-150S upon its introduction. The E-Type would continue with this same powerplant at the same horsepower rating through 1964. First gear was never synchronized and the gearbox was famously recalcitrant, at least compared to its successor. The shape of the E-Type was all-new, yet strangely familiar to fans of the previous XK models. Although sometimes referred to as a roadster, all the topless E-Types were true convertibles. The tops were never of Volkswagen quality, but they were far superior to those of every English brand, except maybe the Astons. All XK-E's had roll-up windows and four-wheel disc brakes. The line began with the 3.8-liter Series I of 1961 and ended with the 5.3-liter Series III of 1975.

As mentioned in performance chart notes elsewhere in this book, the E-Type was introduced with a bit more fanfare from the magazine testers than it deserved. The earliest cars tested were *ringers* especially prepared by Jaguar and presented to the magazines. The company really wanted to show that the new E-Type could reach 150 mph and it did! The only catch is that the production models would be somewhat less adept in the high-performance arena. Nevertheless, the Jaguar XK-E stormed into America like a whirlwind dervish. The first batch of cars were shipped here a few months before any Englishman could even buy one! The Jaguar executives knew their market was us from day one.

Figure C30 - This red 1961 XK-E on display at Bonhams has silver painted knock-off wire wheels. ©The Supermat (CC)

English Aberrations, Eccentricity, & Elegance

Figure C31 - **This 1963 E-Type Roadster has the optional chrome wire wheels and its black vinyl boot is neatly snapped down. The turn signals are above the bumper, as on all the early models. This is a clear view of the covered headlights that are so popular with collectors. The base price of this beauty will be only $5585 in 1966, even with the larger engine, synchronized transmission, and many more improvements.** ©Dan Smith in Indianapolis (CC)

The original XK-E had several distinguishing characteristics. The DOHC six-cylinder, 3.8-liter engine had triple carburetors, a manual choke, and separate pushbutton starting. The three SU carburetors could be difficult to keep in synch, so some American owners switched to a later twin-carb manifold for easier tuning. The electrics were powered by a generator in a positive ground system. The seats were quite thin and minimalist in design. The seatbacks had distinctive rounded tops and were not adjustable for rake. All were upholstered in leather, however, all the materials and patterns were not identical and some of these are very difficult to replace as perfect originals today. There were three windshield wipers and the headlights were covered by glass that, although stylish, tended to disperse the light in a disturbing manner on a dark country road. All the Series I cars through 1964 had knock-off wire wheels.

Figure C32 - This unusual bronze 1968 XK-E Roadster is shown in Canada. This is interesting because this left hand drive car shows the new uncovered headlights, but it has knock-off chrome wire wheels. These knock-offs may or may not have been legal in Canada for the '68 model year, and of course they may have been added later. The headlights are set back in the fenders with delicate chrome trim. ©Bull-Doser (PD)

The 1965 4.2-liter engine brought with it a new alternator charging a negative ground electrical system. The generator in the old positive-ground 3.8 struggled to keep from discharging the battery in heavy traffic with the lights on, a severe inconvenience at the least! The new 4.2 was rated at the same 265 gross horsepower as the old 3.8. All the cars built in 1961-64 were designated as Series I, even with many changes brought by the larger bore 4.2 engine. A 4.2 S1, model years 1965 through 1967, can be visually identified by its combination of covered headlights and thicker, more luxurious seats with more conventionally shaped seatbacks. Late '67 models lost their knock-off "ears" on the wire wheels. Along with the uncovered headlights that appeared a couple of months later, these changes became the key external alterations heading into the Series 1.5 period. Driving-wise, the 4.2 was much improved with a new transmission. The old 3.8 four-speed, sometimes referred to as the Moss transmission, lacked a synchronized first gear and was something of a recalcitrant beast to shift. The 4.2 with all-synchromesh gears was a new delight. Most U.S.-bound E-Types of the period had 3.54 rear axle ratios. European models had 3.07 or 3.31 ratios. The dashboards were black and silver and the steering wheels were real wood on all the 3.8 and 4.2 E-Types, but the glove box would not have a door and lock until the Series 2 model.

Figure C33 - This 1969-70 E-Type in British Racing Green has the correct bolt-on chrome wire wheels and the headlights have been brought slightly forward in the fenders and a wide chrome trim piece covers them. Compare this to the 1968 model above. ©Stahlkocher (GNU)

The U.S. regulations were about to kick in on 1/1/68, so Jaguar chose to gradually change over to the new parts beginning in the summer of 1967. This would later cause Jaguar fans to unofficially designate a Series 1.5 when the factory never employed this as an official model designation. As far as Jaguar is concerned, there was a Series I 4.2 liter model in 1965-68 and a Series II 4.2 liter in 1969-70. The unofficial Series 1.5 has become the way car people discuss the transition period that was generally applied to the 1968 U.S. export models before the company began building all XK-E's much the same for all markets. A good comparison would be the carbureted Triumph TR-250 for the 1968 U.S. market and the 1968 fuel injected TR-5 for the European market. The lack of traditional knock-off wheels, the unobstructed headlamps, and the crash-safe rocker switches were specifically mandated by 1968 U.S. regulations. The size, presence and positioning of tail lamps and side marker lamps were further results. On a more disturbing note, the change to two carburetors from three may have made the synchronization job easier, but the change was made directly for emissions reasons, translated as a loss of power. Keep in mind that Jaguar was well aware from the beginning where their sales were coming from and therefore did not try to drag their feet in meeting U.S. regulations, as many other European manufacturers did. Note in the chart below that the horsepower loss advertised by the factory has always been just a bit mysterious. The company stated 245 gross horsepower in brochures, while in other sources quoted 171 DIN horsepower a year or so before the USA required figures stated in SAE net, which are very similar to DIN figures. Was there a gradual power loss between 1968 and 1970? I am not sure. Only the factory knows precisely what they did when changing the details of the engine in the XK-E for various markets.

Figure C34 - You can get a good look at an XK-E top in this shot of a silver blue 1968 model. The wheels are bolt-on and the tail lights are above the bumper. ©Rudolf Stricker (PD)

The Series 2 XK-E would be constructed for all markets in 1969 and '70. The model would gradually become more comfortable and luxurious as it gained weight. Continual changes would be made to build a better product, however the writing was on the wall. The E-Type has always been sandwiched in the market by the Corvette and the Porsche 911, both of which changed rapidly between 1965 and 1970. Jaguar had to do something to catch up, but for the time being, the company was stuck with a design from 1961, older than that of their close rivals. Jaguar's answer to this dilemma was a twelve-cylinder engine in a quiet, refined, SOHC, oversquare design. Air conditioning had been made an option on the 4.2 Series I of 1965 and optional power steering had first been offered on the Series 2 2+2 only. Power steering would be made standard with AC still optional on all Series III V-12's, including coupes and convertibles. However, AC was available only on left hand drive versions with the 4.2 engine. Keep in mind that, like the Sting Rays and Stingrays of the era, the XK-E allows a lot of heat into the interior from its powertrain, so don't expect the AC to feel like that of your Impala in Texas traffic in July. As with the Corvettes, the later the model, the more likely the effectiveness of the air conditioning system due to improvements in insulation, among others. As for the power steering, some drivers complained of its loss in feel over the standard Jaguar steering. The leading other difference would be that the 96-inch-wheelbase chassis would be discontinued and the V-12 convertible would share the longer wheelbase of the original 2+2 coupe. This change also allowed engine accessories and emission equipment to more easily fit within the engine compartment. Even though the 5.3-liter V-12 was an aluminum alloy design, the larger engine and chassis and the additional luxury and convenience accessories necessitated the standard power steering. The V-12 generally allowed the power to weight ratio of the XK-E to return to Series 1 level.

Figure C35 - Here is the familiar 4.2-liter DOHC Six in a 1968 Series 1 E-Type. Note the triple carburetors.
©TTNIS (CC)

A little comment about wheels is appropriate here. As with several of the less haughty English roadsters discussed in this book, chrome wire wheels were not standard equipment on the Jaguar XK's. They were *optional at extra cost*, unlike some of the lesser brands, from the factory. The standard wire wheels were painted. In some cases the standard wheels were steel disc, not wires. This was the case with the early XK-120 and all the Series III V-12 cars. All the models in between had the painted wires as standard. Wire wheels were standard on the XK-140 and XK-150 while the steel disc wheels were optional. All the Series I and 1968 XK-E's had wire wheels, but at least one source states the steel discs returned as an option on the Series II models. (The disc wheels are not mentioned in the 1969 brochure I have. Maybe the disc wheels were offered outside the U.S.?) Another anomaly appears with the Series III when the wires may have been standard in some markets, but they were extra cost in the U.S. where the steel discs were the base wheel. These were silver painted with chrome trim. All-chrome versions of the same disc style were an option in at least some V-12 model years. There is a special lesson to take away here. As with the aforementioned four-cylinder roadster peasants, chrome wire wheels in the U.S. market are practically always a financial asset with these cars. This is particularly true of the Jaguars, on which the chrome wires were always a factory option. Who knows exactly how many, but a *very* high percentage of XK Jags were sent to the U.S. shod with wires in the first place. The pertinent question might be how many of these were of the chrome variety? If you want chrome wires on your XK, this is surely the one item least likely to dent your car's value, no matter what it had when it left the factory.

Figure C36 - 1972 Series III V-12 E-Type in all-black on display at Bonhams. ©The Supermat (CC)

The problem was that Jaguar was still stuck with a 1961 design. This demerit manifested itself mostly in the complexity of the inner body design, which collected and hid rust like a cat hiding its kill from other predators. This rust issue is probably the leading cause of the high restoration and retail costs of XK-E today. The second issue is probably the result of Jaguar's unique marketing concept for the E-Type from its inception. The XK-E has always been marketed above the cost-effective reliability of the Corvette, just below or at the same level as the engineering oriented Porsche, and well below the competing V-12's of Ferrari. Add in the legendary antiquity of most of the English brands and you arrive at an obvious reliability/maintenance problem. Although the Jaguar DOHC Six and the SOHC Twelve have always been long-wearing engine designs, you cannot say the same for Lucas electrics, other English component suppliers, relentless British antiquity or designs built to a price point. Ferrari could charge whatever it wanted for its V-12 hotrods, which required far more maintenance than the more pedestrian Jaguar design intended for everyday use. The catch is that the XK-E was obviously built to a price point, but the Ferrari was not. You got what you paid for in 1972 and you still get what you pay for today. The Jaguar is locked into a zone all its own between the high cost and high value of a V-12 Ferrari and the much more cost effectiveness of a Porsche or Corvette. When considering the purchase of an XK-E of any vintage, you must add another bit of insult to injury. We have to accept the fact that many previous E-Type owners may have purchased the cars back when they seemed to be cheap buys and then failed to put the cash into their purchases to keep the maintenance done properly. Refer back to the initial problem with any E-Type, rust, and you can begin to consider the broad scope of this problem. It has always been relatively easy to put a band-aid fix on a particular visible body panel without addressing the much more complex rust problem underneath. When you see that high asking price for a really nice E-Jag these days, you may be looking at one that has had its rust and other issues repaired properly... or maybe not. It is your responsibility as a buyer to uncover the truth before handing over your cash.

Figure C37 - This is the cockpit of a 1965-67 XK-E 4.2 liter Series I. The black leather seatbacks are the second design for the E-Type. There are no headrests. There is no glove box door, only a cubbyhole. The switches on the dash are protruding toggles. The ignition key hole is in the dash, there is no clock and the windshield has three wipers. ©Nightflyer (GNU)

To honestly cover the Jaguar XK-E phenomenon for this book, we need to enumerate some of the issues inherent in the ownership of such a demanding mistress. The XK-E has always been unique to itself since its birth and immediate popularity in the U.S. market. There is a wide gap in price and production numbers between the Aston Martins and the E-Type. A similar gap has always existed between Ferraris and Alfa Romeos. The difference between these two comparisons is that the Jaguar has specifications closer to the Aston than the Alfa has to the Ferrari. Jaguar has always attempted to market a sports car that could actually be utilized for touring the USA, as opposed to the garage queen Ferrari V-12 that might see the light of day only on special occasions. This situation would have been different if the XK-E was not British, but it simply is an English car with Porsche production numbers and Ferrari complexity.

Triumph, Morgan, Jensen-Healey, TVR, Lotus, Jaguar, A M

Figure C38 - This silver blue XK-140 Roadster really captures the simplicity and innocence of the era for us, does it not? ©Spartan 7W (CC)

Unlike practically every Ferrari, Sting Ray, and even muscular pony car of the Sixties, the XK-E has not radically increased in value over the past thirty years. However, parts and service costs have increased dramatically. The electrical system of the Jaguar is English; i.e., unreliable. The early Series III cars had a *quad fantail* tailpipe design that looked cool with its upward slant, but allowed water to enter easily and rust out the system within a few months. Replacement exhaust may not cost that much, but keep it out of the rain if you want this system to remain stock and original. The company changed to a better twin outlet system midyear in 1973. The clutches have been a problem in many cars. A mechanic has to remove the engine to replace the clutch. The rear suspension sub-frame unit must be dropped out of the car and disassembled in order to do a brake job on the rear discs. Rust can be so prevalent on the E that even the elegant but huge front hood must be replaced, at an exorbitant price. You can buy a fiberglass replacement, but your resale value will suffer considerably. The interior of Connelly hides and luxurious wool carpet will cost a lot more to replace than the interior package of a Corvette. You might be able to buy a new go-to-work car for the price of a complete engine rebuild. It might be a little squirtabout of Asian heritage with all the panache of macaroni and cheese, but it *will* deliver you to your destination. Overheating has always been something of a relentless problem for Jaguar owners, particularly in the warmer parts of the USA. The company slowly improved the cooling of the E-Type from the first 3.8 to the last 5.3, but don't hold your breath that you will never be stranded in an awkward location by your XK-E, no matter the vintage. Never trust the odometer on a car you are considering because the likelihood that the instrument has been out to lunch for some considerable time during the car's life is about as likely that your tomcat will get into fights. The bottom line is that many people see the Jaguar XK-E Roadster as the epitome of sports touring cars. When you drop down into one, smell the leather and feel the controls, the emotional tug is unavoidable. There is no tacky, overly styled plastic as in most Corvettes. There is a lot more warmth and luxury than found in the cold, functional interior of most 911's. This cat growls and purrs with the best of them. Just keep in mind that he is also a tomcat who sprays the furniture.

Figure C39 - This deep maroon 1955 XK-140 Drophead Coupe shows off its tan top, chrome wires, and wide whitewalls of the day. Notice the chrome strip down the trunk lid with the locking handle smoothly aligned with it. The chrome trim widens into a backup lamp. ©LA2 (GNU)

If you are reading this book, you are automatically aware that open cars are nearly always more valuable than closed coupes, and that has always been true of E-Types in the USA in particular, no matter what the vintage of the car or the year in which the discussion is taking place. When it comes to Jaguars, there has never been another car quite like it in this regard. When the E-Type was born, all Corvettes were convertibles and Porsches were available as either coupes or convertibles. By the end of the E's era, all Corvettes were still built as either convertibles or coupes with T-top panels and all Porsche 911's were either coupes or Targas. Neither of these competing brands had adapted such a radical engine design change in the middle. This leaves the Jaguar in a specific market all its own. You can pay more for the topless model or not. It does not matter which engine it has or whether it was the first model or the last. When you start with a 3.8, you will get a rare, crude, wild and crazy ride. If you begin with a 5.3, you will get a quiet, mellow, luxurious cruiser that has about the same ultimate performance level as that early 3.8. In between lie all sorts of compromises. Make your choice and growl or purr, whichever is the cat's meow to you.

Triumph, Morgan, Jensen-Healey, TVR, Lotus, Jaguar, A M

Figure C40 - This black beauty is obviously on display at Bonhams. This is a 1972 Series III in all-black with optional chrome knockoffs. Of course this type of wheel was not legally sold in the U.S. in 1972. Contrast the bumper overriders of this model to those of the 1974 in the next photo. If you were to compare the bumpers of a 1972 and 1974 Corvette, you would see a similar contrast. The bumpers on the '74 Stingray required more money and effort to develop than the simple overriders applied to the 1974 Jaguar. The Corvette Stingray continued through 1982. The final production year for the E-Jag was 1974. ©The Supermat (CC)

Jaguar XK-120 / XK-140 / XK-150 Chart

Details	XK-120	XK-140	XK-150	XK-150S
Model Years	1950 - 1954	1955 - 1957	1958 - 1961	1959 - 1961
Production	12,078	8884	7929	1466
Body	Low-cut Doors	Low-cut Doors	High Doors	High Doors
Windshield	Flat Two Piece	Flat Two Piece	Curved	Curved
Dashboard	Walnut	Walnut	Leather	Leather
Body Styles	RD/FHC/DHC	RD/FHC/DHC	FHC/DHC/RD	FHC/DHC/RD
Displacement	3.4 - 3442cc	3.4 - 3442cc	3.4 / 3.8	3.8 - 3781cc
Horsepower	160 / 180	190 / 210	190 / 210	250 / 265
Carbs	Dual SU	Dual SU	Dual SU	Triple SU
Brakes	Lockheed Drum	Lockheed Drum	Dunlop Disc	Dunlop Disc
Wheels	Disc / Wire	Disc / Wire	Wire	Wire

157

English Aberrations, Eccentricity, & Elegance

Jaguar XK-120 / XK-140 / XK-150 Chart Notes:
Some sources state only 12,055 XK-120's were built. All the production numbers listed in the chart and below came from the *Complete Book of Collectible Cars 1940-1980*. A small unknown number of XK-150's were produced with steel disc wheels instead of wires. XK-150 production included 2265 Roadsters, 2672 Drophead Coupes, and 4445 Fixed Head Coupes. These figures differ slightly from those in the chart. Only 361 XK-150S models were open cars with left hand drive.

Figure C41 - This front view of a 1974 Series III E-Type shows off its protruding black bumper guards added for this model year to meet federal standards. Notice the forward set headlights and their wide chrome trim. You can also see the two windshield wipers of the later models. The change to a raked back windshield did not allow space for the third wiper drive motor. Unlike the earlier models, most of the Series III production had disc wheels instead of wires. The hood ornament is not standard fare for any E-Type, only the Jaguar sedans. The finish on the hood vents does not appear stock, either, but this anomaly may just be the result of reflection sunlight. ©Bull-Doser (PD)

Jaguar XK Roadster / Convertible Production Breakdown Chart

Years	*Model*	*Details*	*Production*
1949 - 1954	XK-120 Roadsters	All Markets	7631
1953 - 1954	XK-120 DHC	All Markets	1769
1954 - 1957	XK-140 Roadsters	All Markets	3347
1954 - 1957	XK-140 DHC	All Markets	2740

1957 - 1961	XK-150 3.4 Roadsters	All Markets	1297
1957 - 1961	XK-150 3.8 Roadsters	All Markets	42
1957 - 1961	XK-150 3.4 DHC	All Markets	1903
1957 - 1961	XK-150 3.8 DHC	All Markets	586
1957 - 1961	XK-150S 3.4 Roadsters	All Markets	888
1957 - 1961	XK-150S 3.8 Roadsters	All Markets	36
1957 - 1961	XK-150S 3.4 DHC	All Markets	104
1957 - 1961	XK-150S 3.8 DHC	All Markets	89
		Total	20,432
1961 - 1964	XK-E S1 3.8 Roadsters	Left Hand Drive	6885
1965 - 1967	XK-E S1 4.2 Roadsters	Left Hand Drive	8366
1968	XK-E S1.5 Roadsters	All Markets	1994
1969 - 1970	XK-E S2 Roadsters	All Markets	8627
1971 - 1975	XK-E V-12 Roadsters	Left Hand Drive	6119
		Total	31,991

Jaguar XK Production Breakdown Chart Notes:

The figures listed in this chart were those available from the *Illustrated Jaguar Buyer's Guide* and various other sources at the time of publication. The totals are not meant to directly correspond to anything other than an estimate of the number of topless, left-hand-drive Jaguar XK models originally available to U.S. buyers. Remember that most of the production listed as All Markets and practically all the numbers listed under Left Hand Drive were exported to the USA.

English Aberrations, Eccentricity, & Elegance

Figure C42 - This lovely red E-Type Series 1 on display at Pebble Beach is the visual aid most Jaguar sports car enthusiasts dream of when an XK-E comes to mind. This one has chrome knock-off wires and luggage rack. The top is snuggled underneath its black boot on this left hand drive model. The turn signals above the bumper and covered headlights are clearly visible. ©Jaguar Media Pages

Jaguar XK-E Color Chart

Years	Exterior Color	Interior Choices
1961-62	Claret	Beige
1961-62	Imperial Maroon	Tan
1961-62	Indigo	Light Blue / Red
1961-64	Bronze	Beige / Tan / Red
1961-64	Pearl	Dark Blue / Red
1961-64	Mist Grey	Red
1961-64	Cotswold Blue	Dark Blue
1961-64	Opalescent Gunmetal	Beige / Light Blue / Dark Blue / Red
1961-64	Opalescent Dark Blue	Dark Blue / Red
1961-67	Opalescent Dark Green	Light Tan / Tan / Beige / Suede Green
1961-67	Sherwood Green	Suede Green / Light Tan / Tan
1961-68	Carmen Red	Biscuit / Beige / Red / Black
1961-68	Opalescent Silver Grey	Dark Blue / Light Blue / Grey / Red
1961-68	Opalescent Silver Blue	Dark Blue / Grey
1961-69	Cream	Cream / Red / Black
1961-74	Black	Light Tan / Tan / Grey / Red / Cinnamon

1961-74	British Racing Green	Biscuit / Light Tan / Tan / Beige / Suede Green / Moss Green / Cinnamon
1963-64	Sand	Beige / Black
1963-68	Opalescent Maroon	Beige / Maroon
1963-74	Pale Primrose	Biscuit / Beige / Red / Black
1965-68	Golden Sand	Light Tan / Red
1965-72	Warwick Grey	Light Tan / Dark Blue / Red / Cinnamon
1965-74	Dark Blue	Lt Blue / French Blue / Grey / Red / Russet Red
1968	Beige	Light Tan / Tan / Red / Suede Green
1968-72	Willow Green	Beige / Tan / Grey / Suede Green / Cinnamon
1969-72	Ascot Fawn	Beige / Cinnamon / Red
1969-72	Light Blue	Light Blue / Dark Blue / Grey
1969-74	Sable	Biscuit / Beige / Grey / Cinnamon / Moss Green
1969-74	Signal Red	Biscuit / Beige / Dark Blue / Red / Black
1969-74	Regency Red	Biscuit / Beige / Grey / Cinnamon / Russet Red
1970-74	Old English White	Lt. Blue / French Blue / Dk. Blue / Red / Black
1972-74	Lavender Blue	Biscuit / French Blue / Dark Blue
1973-74	Fern Grey	Tan / Olive / Moss Green
1973-74	Silver Grey	NA
1973-74	Heather	Antelope / Cerise / Maroon
1973-74	Azure Blue	Biscuit / Dark Blue / Cinnamon
1973-74	Green Sand	Tan / Olive / Cinnamon

Jaguar XK-E Color Chart Notes:

The 1961-71 3.8 and 4.2 tops came in black, blue, and tan. The 1971-74 V-12 tops came in black, blue, and buckskin.

Jaguar XK-E Convertible Chart

Details	Series 1 3.8	Series 1 4.2	Series 1.5	Series 2	Series 3
Model Years	1961-1964	1965-1967	1968	1969 - 1970	1971-1975
Production	6887	5888	2479	7853	6120
Wheelbase	96 inches	96 inches	96 inches	96 inches	105 inches
Displacement	3781cc	4235cc	4235cc	4235cc	5343cc
Carburetors	3 SU	3 SU	2 Zenith	2 Stromberg	4 Stromberg
Horsepower	265	265	265	245	250
Transmission	No Synch	Synchro	Synchro	Synchro	Synchro
Windshield	Upright	Upright	Upright	Upright	Sloped

Wipers	Triple	Triple	Triple	Triple	Twin
Headlights	Covered	Covered	Exposed	Exposed	Exposed
Small Lights	Above	Above	Above	Below	Below
Dash Knobs	Toggle	Toggle	Rocker	Rocker	Rocker
Wire Wheels	Knock-off	Knock-off	Bolt-on	Bolt-on	Bolt-on
Wheel Width	5 inches	5 inches	5 inches	5 inches	6 inches
Weight - RT	2720 lbs.	2815 lbs.	NA	2867 lbs.	3380 lbs.
Weight - CG	2688 lbs.	2744 lbs.	NA	2800 lbs.	3220 lbs.

Jaguar XK-E Convertible Chart Notes:

The production numbers listed include left hand drive convertibles only. Total V-12 production was 9382 in 1972-75. The USA received 43,765 of the total production of 72,520 E-Types. Sources do not agree, but Wikipedia states 26,003 E-Type Convertibles for 1961-71.

Several elements were phased in gradually on Series 1.5 cars. The verification of the exact time of the phase-in of the twin Zenith-Stromberg carburetors on U.S. models, rocker dash switches, and bolt-on wire wheels is difficult to discern. The Small Lights designation refers to the tail lights and/or side marker lights as located above or below the bumpers. The Bolt-on Wire Wheels actually utilized a special nut on the center hub. A tool supplied with the car allowed a knock-off hammer to be used.

When the 3.8-liter XK-E was released in 1961, Jaguar was determined to have magazine testers declare the model a 150-mph sports car. The company sent specially prepared cars with blueprinted engines to several British publications. The actual top speed of production models was about 145 mph. The claimed horsepower for the production 3.8's and 4.2's was 265. but 220 was closer to the truth. The federalized 1969-70 4.2-liter S2's produced only about 171 DIN (net) horsepower, but 245 gross horsepower was quoted in some sources, including the 1969 brochure. Federal regulations did not officially require the stating of net horsepower until the 1972 model year.

Weight - CG is the dry weight as stated in *The Jaguar E-Type: A Collector's Guide*. Weight - RT is the weight stated in *Road & Track* and *Car and Driver* road tests. Note that there were several discrepancies involved in these stated figures. One source listed the weight of the 4.2 Series I Roadster as 2465 pounds and another listed 2515 pounds. Considering the comparative weights of the others listed, 2815 seems as if it should be the correct figure. The claimed dry weight of the 1966 Roadster in the brochure is 2464 pounds. No specific figures were available for the 1968 model, but it is easy to surmise this figure as falling directly between that of the Series I and Series II models.

Jaguar Comparison Chart

Model	Type	CI / CC	HP	Wt.	Price
1951 Jaguar XK-120 DOHC	I-6	210 / 3442	180	3080	$3500
1955 Jaguar XK-140 DOHC	I-6	210 / 3442	190	3250	$3600
1957 Jaguar XK-150 DOHC	I-6	210 / 3442	210	3220	$4500
1960 Jaguar XK-150 DOHC	I-6	231 / 3781	220	3520	$5200
1959 Jaguar XK-150S	I-6	210 / 3442	250	3220	$5600
1960 Jaguar XK-150S	I-6	231 / 3781	265	2968	NA

1961-64 Jaguar XK-E Series I 3.8	I-6	231 / 3781	265	2721	$5595
1965-67 Jaguar XK-E Series I 4.2	I-6	258 / 4235	265	2750	$5384
1968 Jaguar XK-E Series 1.5	I-6	258 / 4235	245	2750	$5352
1969 Jaguar XK-E Series II	I-6	258 / 4235	245	2800	NA
1970 Jaguar XK-E Series II	I-6	258 / 4235	245	3018	$5675
1971 Jaguar XK-E Series II	I-6	258 / 4235	245	3018	$6500
1972-73 Jaguar XK-E Series III	V-12	326 / 5343	250	3380	$7599
1974-75 Jaguar XK-E Series III	V-12	326 / 5343	244	3450	$9200

Jaguar Comparison Chart Notes:
The Jaguar 150S had a 102-inch wheelbase. The Jaguar XK-E Series I & II had a 96-inch wheelbase. The original base retail prices quoted in some cases may not be exactly accurate for the model year or years listed.

Aston Martin

Figure C43 - 1959 Aston Martin DB2-4 Mark III Drophead Coupe. This example is black with saddle interior and top. ©Mr. Choppers (GNU)

Bond, James Bond. If Sean Connery had not driven a silver DB5 Coupe into the American popular consciousness in 1965, most of us would never have even heard of Aston Martin. The third Bond film was first released in late '64, but *Goldfinger* first appeared in U.S. theaters in January 1965. By the numbers, Aston Martin barely made it into this book. Accurate production figures by year, body style, and export market are difficult to come by, but as the chart below shows, there has not been an average of more than 100 Aston Martin convertibles built per year throughout the entire 1950-1990 time period. This means worldwide, not for the USA, where the numbers have been relentlessly miniscule. For the special parameters within this book, we are going to cover the topless Astons from the first six-cylinder convertible of 1953 through the V-8 convertible of 1989, which coincides with the end of a series. Due to the small numbers imported, particularly in the early years, these later Volante V-8's are the most likely models that you as an American might have seen, and they are the most available in the current collector market.

Aston Martin long ago carved out its special niche between Ferrari and Rolls Royce. The cars are large, fast sporting road cars, more akin to the high-line Ferrari touring coupes than the more mass-market Dino derivatives. The company employs time-consuming assembly techniques such as hand crafted aluminum bodies. Inside of every Aston you will find sumptuous Connolly hides and luxurious carpet trimmed with loving care. The engines produce ample horsepower and torque without the high stress of a comparable race-inspired Ferrari powerplant. Aston Martin's use of inline six-cylinder engines began with the DB2. Previous models utilized a four-cylinder design. All engines were of double-overhead-cam type, hand-built mostly of aluminum alloy.

Aston Martin nomenclature can be a bit confusing. Up until the AM Vantage model of 1972, available only as a coupe, the Vantage title referred to the high-performance package. The Vantage name was briefly applied to all the V-8 coupes produced in the early Seventies, a period when no AM convertibles were built. The topless Volante returned to the lineup in 1978. The Volante name has been applied to all Aston Martin convertibles from the DB-6 through the Series 2 of 1986-89. The Vantage name returned in 1977 for the specially tuned models sold in Europe. Due to the obvious emissions rules, the USA received only engines in standard tune from that point onward. Note of course that this means all Volantes sent to the U.S. since have standard V-8 engines, even if the Vantage label has been applied. This chapter basically covers three sets of Aston Martin convertibles: the 2.6 and 2.9 liter Sixes of the '50's, of which relatively few were imported, the 3.7 and 4-liter Sixes of the '60's, representing somewhat higher numbers in the U.S., and the V-8's of 1978-89, which became popular here, even with their detuned engines.

The original DB2 was a compact two-seater. The engines on these early models can be problematic due to low oil pressure, overheating, and head gaskets with exceptionally low tolerances. The wheels were sixteen-inch, painted knock-off wires and the instruments were clustered in the center of the dash. The DB2/4 of 1953-57 was a 2+2 of the DB2. Its inline six was enlarged to 2.9 liters. The bumpers were of a more protective two-piece design and the windshield was a more modern, curved one-piece type. A 1954 A-M DB-2/4 Mk. I convertible was used in *The Birds*. The Mark II convertibles had Tickford bodies and the coupes were bodied by Mulliner. Most of the changes from the earlier cars were small running alterations that made the cars more comfortable and convenient. The Mark III model brought many engine improvements that increased the power dramatically. Zero-to-sixty times dropped to 8.5-10 seconds. Girling disc brakes were optional on the front wheels of the early Mark III's and standard on the later ones. Instruments were properly clustered directly in the driver's line of sight. The Mark III would continue in production past the intro of the DB4 Coupe in 1958. The DB4 brought a 3.7-liter aluminum inline six, four-wheel disc brakes, and rack and pinion steering, but only coupes would be produced in the first three series.

The new convertible arrived in late '61 for the 1962 model year. Only seventy of these beauties would be produced. It is unknown how many came here. In addition, a confusing array of SS or Vantage engine combinations with four-speed and automatic transmissions were offered on the DB4 models. There was even a GT engine of up to 302 gross horsepower. The base engine had 240 horses. The final Series 5 DB4's were three inches longer with fifteen-inch wire wheels. For even more confusion, consider that the Vantage bodies were trimmed more like the upcoming DB5. With all these variations, only small clusters of DB4 cars were essentially identical. Touring of Milan designed the styling of all the DB4's and the sleek convertibles are highly sought today. The Achilles' heel of the DB4 is its delicate aluminum engine with extremely close tolerances and numerous running changes. Overheating, body corrosion, and clutch and transmission issues have also plagued restorers. With proper restoration these cars are durable, but an engine rebuild of one of these is particularly expensive for an inline six.

Figure C44 - This light grey 1965 DB5 with red leather interior is a left hand drive model with chrome knock-off wire wheels. Notice the one-piece bumpers; these would be changed to two-piece on the DB6, as shown in the next photo. A backup lamp would be positioned between the two rear bumper halves on the DB6. This is as close to a *Goldfinger* Convertible as you are going to get! ©Shane D. Mattaway (GNU)

Coinciding with the mood of this book, the DB5 launched the legendary reputation of the Aston Martins in 1963. The DB5 and DB6 compose the heart of the sporty convertible Astons. The inline six was bored out to four liters and the body was sleek enough for James Bond. As you will read later, when the Volantes returned as V-8 models in 1978 after a seven-plus year absence, they had moved much closer to the Rolls Royce Corniche in weight, style, performance, and wealthy American consumer appeal. If you squint your eyes real tight, you can still see the pony car sportiness in the DB5 and DB6. The returning Vantage Volantes belong on Rodeo Drive with the 450 SL's and Beemer Cabriolets. Only nineteen of the DB5 Convertibles had left hand drive. These few are real cherries for today's auction marketplace!

The Vantage models produced 314 horsepower with three Weber carbs instead of 282 with the standard SU carburetors. An alternator replaced the generator. An overdrive five-speed became optional, possibly only on Vantage models. A three-on-the-tree automatic was coupled with the standard engine on six cars. It is unknown if any of these were convertibles. The five-speed was made standard equipment soon after production began. All the DB5 models can by identified by their covered headlights, but a few late DB4's had these, too. Since you are probably dying to know, four early production DB5 Coupes were purchased for the making of *Goldfinger*, two originals with a few variations between them and two identical copies to be used as backup vehicles if needed. As of 1986, these four were in the hands of collectors, three in the USA and the fourth in Canada.

The 123 DB5 Convertibles built were not called Volantes. That name would not be applied until the DB6, even though the earliest of those would actually be DB6's built on DB5 chassis. A metal, not fiberglass, removable hardtop was offered as an option on the DB5 Convertible, but few were produced. It is not known if any of the precious nineteen had the hardtop option. A DB5 can be identified by its sloping tail with vertical tail lamp array. The DB6 would have a Kamm tail and more modern, larger tail lamps in a horizontal pattern. A fine DB5 Convertible can cost $1.3-1.8 million today. Add a couple hundred thousand for a Vantage Convertible. One of the 37 short chassis DB6 Volantes takes that up to $2-3 million. A base engine DB6 Volante drops the price down to about a half to one million. Even though these models are rare, they are far more available than one of those 37. A 1970 Vantage Volante from the last production year currently hovers around $1,500,000. The 1970 Vantage was rated at 325 horsepower. You can save about $200,000 by going with the 282-hp engine. Here we go again with those stinking automatics: a '66 base engine DB6 Volante is worth *$100,000 less* if it has an automatic transmission. Factory air adds $40,000 to a half to one million dollar car.

Figure C45 - This is a Metallic Grey 1967 Aston Martin DB6 Vantage Volante Convertible. This right hand drive model has a black leather interior, wood steering wheel, and chrome knock-off wires, all standard on the DB6. The Vantage designation means this example has the optional engine. This of course is a DOHC Six with

three Weber carbs producing 325 gross horsepower. Power steering and air conditioning were new options available on the DB6. The 1966 Coupe retailed for $15,495. The Volante would have been a little higher. ©Mr. Choppers (GNU)

Before we continue describing the DB6, I want to once again repeat the mantra of this book. The Sixties in the USA were truly a blessed era. Practically every element of our economy and consumer culture was booming. The early '60's were a time of awakening and the later '60's represented a period of refinement. I suspect that the readers of this book are stronger fans of one or the other period and this feeling permeates every attitude you possess about classic cars. If you cherish the awakening, you most lust after those premiere, historic models that launched a trend. For example, when it comes to Aston Martins in America, you can divide the brand's culture into pre-*Goldfinger* and post-*Goldfinger* time frames. For you whippersnappers, the DB5 was built from July 1963 through September 1965. The movie was released in England in 1964, but did not reach our shores until January 1965. This book is mostly about the post-*Goldfinger* era for all the cars contained herein. Then that period divides again into the early Sixties versus the late Sixties and very early Seventies. I fall into that latter group. There is not a car in this book from before 1966 that I would prefer over its later '60's direct descendant. Your mileage and opinion may vary, of course. The point of this Aston Martin story interruption is that most of us reading this lust after one or the other, the DB5 Convertible or the DB6 Volante. We love them deeply, far more than the later Vantage Volantes that we have far more likely drooled over as they passed by us on the streets of the USA.

Bring on the Kamm tails! I *wuv 'em*! The DB6 was a somewhat larger, heavier car. The optional Vantage engine was increased from 314 to 325 gross horsepower. Air conditioning was still an option and so was that stinking automatic transmission. A limited slip differential and power steering joined the option list on a car with a four-inch longer wheelbase. A power top was standard equipment. Here is a little point to remember: all AM Convertibles have manual tops and all Volantes have power tops. The rear seats in the 2+2 seating were a little roomier in the longer DB6. Although the weight increase over the DB5 was not that great, handling did become somewhat more ponderous. There is no doubt that comfort and convenience items increased with the DB6. If you compare the 1965 and '69 models of most of the cars in this book, you will find much the same parallel. Higher production and less emphasis on the sports car driving experience diminished the collector value of a DB6, but I would *never* evict one from my garage, even if it *is* British.

The 1970 DB6 Mark II Volante was the swan song of the Aston Martin six-cylinder convertibles. Only 38 of this final version were constructed, bringing up the obvious parallel to the short chassis DB6 Volantes of a few years earlier. The obvious identifiers of the Mark II model are the flared wheel wells covering wider fifteen-inch wheels and tires. The wheels were still knock-off wires, but chrome wheels may have become standard by this time. A new electronic fuel injection system was optional, but its pre-production engineering proved to be half-baked and only forty-six cars had this option. It is not known how many of these were Volantes. The troublesome system was often replaced by Webers. Aside from the problems with the early cars with AE Brico fuel injection, these final six-cylinder Astons were highly developed in the reliability department. Clutches, transmissions, head gaskets and cooling systems had been sorted out. There were still a few electrical gremlins and corrosion problems to deal with, as with any Sixties English car, but the drivetrain had become quite durable.

After a hiatus similar to that of many brands of the day, Aston Martin convertibles returned to production in the summer of 1978. Series 1 models can be identified by their wide, flat hood bulge, as on the 1981 green car pictured. Earlier Coupes had a scoop at the forward edge of the bulge, but this had been deleted by the time of the Volante introduction in June '78. The 1970-73 Coupes had utilized Bosch fuel injection. Weber carburetors returned to Coupe production in August 1973, necessitating a somewhat obvious raised hood bulge. A confusing issue is that the first V-8 Coupes were released in 1970. The Series 2 Coupes were introduced in 1972 with single headlights instead of duals, a different grille, and a few other distinguishing marks. The Series 3 Coupes were sold from 1973 until a few months after the introduction of the new Volante, called Series 1 with four two-barrel Webers. The Series 1 Volantes coincided with Coupes known as Series 4. Cruise control became an option for the first time later in the production of what were called the Series 4 Coupes and Series 1 Volantes. The final series covered in this book are the Series 2 Volantes of 1986-89 that coincide with their companion Series 5 Coupes. The dark blue 1986-89 S2 Volante pictured later has a flat hood because the bulge was not necessary to cover the Weber-Marelli electronic fuel injection, as it had been with the carb setup. Emission controls strangled the power of all the U.S. models throughout the long production period. Most models imported here had higher numerical axle ratios to keep the acceleration times low at the expense of top speeds. We are generally talking about 0-60 mph times as low as six seconds. Some European Vantage Coupes could reach 160 mph, but 130 was close to the limits of the American versions. I suspect this lower number is particularly true for the Volante models.

Figure C46 - This 1979 Metallic Brown Series I Volante shows off its tan convertible top with broad rear quarter blind spots when the top is erect. The alloy wheels are the correct design, but those delicate chrome bumpers would never have been allowed to enter the USA in 1979, although this example has left hand drive.
©Mr. Choppers (GNU)

Most models retailed for $13,000-15,000 in the Sixties. With the infamous inflation in the USA in the Seventies, the original price of a 1978 V-8 model had risen to $47,500! Of course some of this price gain was due to AM pricing the V-8 model far above that of the previous six-cylinder models. Aston Martins have been fitted with four-speed and five-speed manuals and three-speed automatics over the years, according to model. All models had the standard four-speed until an overdrive and automatic options were added with the Mark III of 1957. Chrome wire wheels and whitewall tires were standard on all the DB6 models sent to the USA. Power steering and AC were optional. Either the ZF five-speed manual or the Borg-Warner three-speed automatic were available at no extra cost. The DBS V-8 was introduced in 1969 with alloy wheels instead of wires. The ZF manual five-speed or a Chrysler TorqueFlite three-speed automatic were available on all V-8 models at no extra cost. Twenty-six special 1987-89 Prince of Wales Volantes were built to special order without the ground effects package. These are considered the most valuable and desirable of all the V-8 Volantes. However, it is unknown if any of these cars were U.S. spec cars or not.

Figure C47 - This metallic green 1981 V8 Volante has the correct alloy wheel design, but its bumpers would never pass U.S. inspection by the Bumper Police. ©Martin Pettitt, Bury St. Edmonds, UK (CC)

The classic Aston Martin Convertibles currently start at about $100,000 and prices rapidly climb skyward. One thing that pushes the prices upward is that there were no Volantes built as DBS models, currently as coupes only, the cheapest of the bunch. Most of these were sent to the USA with the troublesome Bosch mechanical fuel injection system. Reportedly, this system gave headaches to both the factory and the early owners. Of course the factory had to develop a better idea to meet our EPA regulations, but the much-improved Weber-Marelli electronic fuel injection would not arrive until 1986. Although Hagerty's does not currently value the Bosch fuel injected models any lower than the models with Weber carburetors, that might just be an anomaly of only a few cars that have recently passed the auction block. Hagerty's even favors the fuelies with higher prices, but I question the consistency of this pricing. I would expect that modern owners would still prefer the Weber carbs. As with most cars in this book, the middle to late Seventies models are usually the turkeys. At the other end of the scale, we have the DB5 and DB6 Convertibles that are trending well over $1,000,000 with especially rare models surpassing $2 million. Look for one of the rare ones with AC and five-speed. According to Hagerty's, the cool air will add $40,000 to the value and the manual shifter will add an astounding $100,000!

Yes, the special six-cylinder cars are currently in steep ascension. Yes, these are the models the bidding billionaires are seeking. But let's get back to those turkeys. Like the 1976-90 Corvettes, I have made an exception to the parameters of this book. If you happen to have $100,000-200,000 burning a hole in your floorboard, the 1978-89 Aston Martin Volantes are currently some of the best high-level bargains in this book! The V-8 models were much more expensive and better equipped cars than their six-cylinder ancestors when they both were new. Now the V-8's are rolling down the trough of the collector car price index. The manual transmission can add $10,000 to the price of even these low-baller Astons. Your biggest decision might be whether or not you want a low-powered EPA-strangled model and/or if the Bosch fuel injection on the car you have found has all its parts and has been sorted out by the previous owner. The final word on the Aston Martins is that these are very expensive cars to restore. DOHC aluminum V-8's, aluminum body panels, and Connelly hides don't come cheap. Neither does the specialized labor necessary to rebuild these components correctly. Weigh heavily the idea of a recent restoration or a finely caressed example. You might save a wad of cash and numerous headaches in the long run.

Aston Martin Engine Chart

Years	*Model*	*Size*	*HP*	*Induction*
1950-53	DB2	2580cc I6	105	2 1-bbl. SU
1950-53	DB2 Vantage	2580cc I6	125	2 1-bbl. SU
1953-54	DB2/4	2580cc I6	125	2 1-bbl. SU
1954-57	DB2/4	2922cc I6	140	2 1-bbl. SU
1955-57	DB2/4 Mark II	2922cc I6	165	2 1-bbl. SU
1957-59	DB Mark III	2922cc I6	162	2 1-bbl. SU - S.E.
1957-59	DB Mark III	2922cc I6	178	2 1-bbl. SU - D.E.
1957-59	DB Mark III	2922cc I6	180	3 1-bbl. SU - D.E.
1957-59	DB Mark III	2922cc I6	195	3 2-bbl. Weber D.E.
1958-63	DB4	3670cc I6	240	2 1-bbl. SU
1961-63	DB4 Vantage	3670cc I6	266	3 1-bbl. SU
1959-61	DB4GT & Zagato	3670cc I6	302	3 2-bbl. Weber
1959-61	DB4GT & Zagato	3750cc I6	314	3 2-bbl. Weber
1963-65	DB5	3995cc I6	282	3 1-bbl. SU
1964-65	DB5 Vantage	3995cc I6	314	3 2-bbl. Weber

1965-71	DB6	3995cc I6	282	3 1-bbl. SU
1965-71	DB6 Vantage	3995cc I6	325	3 2-bbl. Weber
1969-71	DB6 Mk. II Vantage	3995cc I6	325	Fuel injection
1967-73	DBS	3995cc I6	280	3 1-bbl. SU
1967-73	DBS Vantage	3995cc I6	325	3 2-bbl. Weber
1969-73	DBS V-8	5340cc V-8	320	Bosch F. I.
1973-81	AM V-8 (Europe)	5340cc V-8	432	4 2-bbl. Weber
1973-78	AM V-8	5340cc V-8	310	4 2-bbl. Weber
1976	AM V-8 (U.S. market)	5340cc V-8	288	Bosch F. I.
1977	AM V-8 Stage 1 (U.S.)	5340cc V-8	305	Bosch F. I.
1978-85	AM V-8 (U.S. market)	5340cc V-8	245	Bosch F. I.
1977-90	AM V-8 Vantage	5340cc V-8	380	4 2-bbl. Weber
1986-90	V-8 Vantage X-Pack	5340cc V-8	403	4 2-bbl. Weber
1986-90	AM V-8 Vantage (U.S.)	5340cc V-8	309	Weber-Marelli F. I.

Aston Martin Engine Chart Notes:
Forty-seven DB Mark III's were built with the 180-horsepower engine and only ten with the 195-hp Weber version with higher compression and hotter cams. The 1986-90 Volantes had a flashy ground effects package. The European version had a high-performance X-pack engine with Weber carbs. U.S. models had to make do with a fuel-injected version producing an approximate 300 net horsepower never officially stated by the factory. S.E. = Single Exhaust. D.E. = Dual Exhaust.

Figure C48 - 1986-89 Deep Blue Aston Martin V-8 Volante S2. The seats are cream leather with navy piping. Although this example has left hand drive, this car could never have passed U.S. regulations with those trim chrome bumpers. The BBS wheel design was introduced in 1983. Note the low hood line denoting a Series 2 with fuel injection. The domed hood was no longer necessary to cover Weber carburetors. ©Mr. Choppers (GNU)

Figure C49 - 1986 Aston Martin Vantage Volante in U.S. trim. This white car has a tan leather interior with chocolate piping on the seats. Its alloy wheels are the standard BBS design introduced in 1983. Note the electric antenna on the right rear fender and the big black safety bumpers. In the fuel-injected 1986-89 Series 2 Volantes, the Vantage was just part of the name. Not only did this title not denote a higher tuned V-8, but the power output was stifled considerably for the American market. ©Mr. Choppers (GNU)

Aston Martin Production Chart

Model	Built	Model	Built
1950-53 DB2 Coupes & Conv.	410	1950-53 DB2 Convertible	102
1953-55 DB2/4 2+2 CP & CV	565	1953-55 DB2/4 Mk. I Conv.	73
1955-57 DB2/4 Mk. II CP & CV	199	1956-57 DB2/4 Mk. II Conv.	26
1957-59 DB Mk. III CP & CV	552	1959 DB Mk. III Convertible	84
1958-63 DB4 CP & CV	1110	1962-63 DB4 Convertible	38
1959-63 DB4 GT CP & CV	76	1962-63 DB4 Vantage Conv.	32
1960-62 DB4GT Zagato Coupe	19	1964-65 DB5 Convertible	123
1963-65 DB5 Coupe & Conv.	1059	1965-66 DB6 Volante Conv.	37
1965-70 DB6 Coupe & Conv.	1788	1967-70 DB6 Volante Conv.	111
1967-72 DBS Coupe	788	1967-70 DB6 Vantage Volante	29
1969-72 DBS V-8 Coupe	405	1969-70 DB6 Mk. 2 Volante	38
1972-89 V-8 Coupe & Conv.	2360	1978-85 V-8 Volante Series 1	352
1974-90 Lagonda Sedan	645	1986-89 V-8 Volante Series 2	208

1977-90 AM V-8 Vantage Coupe	458	1986-89 V-8 Vantage Zagato	37
Total C & C 1950-1990	10,434	Total 1950-1989 Convertible	1290

Aston Martin Production Chart Notes:

The left column represents figures directly from Aston Martin and these include the worldwide production of both coupes and convertibles. Notice that the V-8 total covers production way beyond the normal parameter of this book and several coupe-only models from this period have not been included here. The *Illustrated Aston Martin Buyer's Guide* significantly differs from the figures in this left column only regarding the total production of the DB5 model. The *IAMBG* claims only 1021 DB-5's and 1504 DB-6's were produced. There are additional small discrepancies in the totals listed by these sources, probably accounted for by pre-production or special bodied examples manufactured.

The right column represents figures from *Wikipedia* and other sources, such as the *Complete Book of Collectible Cars 1940-1980*, and includes the worldwide production of convertibles only, both right and left hand drive. By comparing the two columns, you can see that at least a few convertibles were built for which specific numbers were not available to include in the right column. The 37 early DB6 Volantes had a shorter chassis and construction elements of both the DB5 and DB6. These elements included the four-inch shorter wheelbase of the DB5, the interior of the DB6, and several minor visual cues from the DB6 exterior. Sixty-eight of the 1967-70 DB6 Volantes had automatic transmissions. The V-8 Coupes were built throughout most of The Seventies without Volante equivalents.

No Aston Martin convertibles were produced for the 1971-77 model years. When the convertibles returned, they would be exported to the USA in small numbers with emission-strangled engines of lower power than their European counterparts. The Series 1 cars had carburetors and the total production of 352 cars has been verified by the *IAMBG* published in 1986. The Series 2 fuel-injected Volante totals from *Wikipedia*, as stated in the chart, are questionable. *Wikipedia* itself lists the Series 2 figure as 192, 208, 216, or 245, depending on the counting method and source. In my opinion, the 208 plus the 37 Zagatos is the most likely to be the truth. The Series 2 Volantes had a ground effects package deleted from the 27 Prince of Wales editions. Fifty-six V-8 Vantage Volantes were sent to the U.S. with Vantage body trim and de-smog engines, but the model years were not specified at Wikipedia. These fifty-six were of course the opposite of the Prince of Wales cars. According to Supercars.net and the Gooding Auction in Scottsdale, fifty-eight were sent to the USA, eleven of these with manual transmissions.

Aston Martin Comparison Chart

Model	Type	C. I. / CC	HP	Wt.	Price
1953-67 Aston Martin DB2/4	I-6	157 / 2580	125	2730	NA
1953-67 Aston Martin DB2/4	I-6	178 / 2922	140	2730	NA
1959 Aston Martin DB Mark III	I-6	178 / 2922	195	3000	$7450
1962 Aston Martin DB4 Coupe	I-6	224 / 3670	240	2885	$10,000
1963 Aston Martin DB4	I-6	224 / 3670	266	2885	NA
1964 Aston Martin DB5 Coupe	I-6	244 / 3995	282	3310	$13,200
1965 Aston Martin DB5 Vantage	I-6	244 / 3995	325	3310	NA
1965 DB6 Volante Mark I	I-6	244 / 3995	282	3310	$11,578
1966 DB6 Coupe	I-6	244 / 3995	282	3310	$15,495
1966-70 Aston Martin Volante	I-6	244 / 3995	282	3250	$15,400
1966-70 A M Vantage Volante	I-6	244 / 3995	335	3760	NA
1970 Volante DB6 Mark II	I-6	244 / 3995	282	3310	$13,053
1970 DBS V-8 Automatic Coupe	V-8	326 / 5340	282	3501	$20,000
1969-73 A M DBS V-8 Vantage	V-8	326 / 5340	400	3850	NA
1977 A M V-8 5-S Coupe U.S.	V-8	326 / 5340	282	3873	$33,950
1977 A M V-8 Stage 1 Bosch FI	V-8	326 / 5340	305	3850	NA
1978 A M V-8 DOHC Coupe	V-8	326 / 5340	245	3850	$47,500
1978 A M Volante Series 1	V-8	326 / 5340	245	3850	$69,000
1979 A M Volante 5-speed	V-8	326 / 5340	245	3950	$71,835
1980 AM Volante Automatic	V-8	326 / 5340	275	3951	$79,650
1980 AM Volante Five-Speed	V-8	326 / 5340	275	3924	$81,500
1983 A M V-8 Coupe	V-8	326 / 5340	200	4101	$96,000
1983 A M Vantage Volante	V-8	326 / 5340	200	4167	$115,000
1985 A M Automatic Coupe	V-8	326 / 5340	200	4101	$100,000
1985 A M Vantage Coupe	V-8	326 / 5340	200	4101	$110,000
1985 A M Vantage Volante	V-8	326 / 5340	200	4167	$125,000
1986-90 A M Vantage US FI	V-8	326 / 5340	309	4190	$125,000

Aston Martin Comparison Chart Notes:
The Aston Martin DB Mark III had a 99-inch wheelbase. The 1966-70 Volantes had a 102-inch wheelbase. The original base retail prices quoted in some cases may not be exactly accurate for the model year or years listed. The $69,860 listed from an unknown source for the Volante is for the 1979 model.

This may or may not be a Vantage price. The low net horsepower and high weight figures quoted are for the U.S. models.

Figure C50 - This final look at a Vantage Volante is a 1989 model in red with white top and interior. The seat piping is red and so is the center section of each of the highly collectible Ronal sixteen-inch alloy wheels. These wheels are no longer available, but copies have been produced. The ones on this car could very well be copies if the originals had developed cracks, as porous alloys can do. Note the ground effects package combined with the black U.S. bumpers. This combination defines this particular model as one of those built for the U.S. market with the European style of the X-Pack Sports Package, but it has the same detuned powerplant as the white car in the previous photo. ©Mr. Choppers (GNU)

Elegant English Sports Car Test Results Chart

Model & Details	HP	Weight	0-60	1/4	TS
1973 Jensen-Healey 2.0 (*R&T*)	140	2155	9.7	17.3	125
1967 TVR Tuscan SE U.S. (*Motor*)	271	2274	5.7	14.1	155
1970 TVR Tuscan SE U.S. (*R&T*)	220	2240	7.2	15.4	119
1978 TVR 3000S fuel injection (*R&T*)	142	2335	7.7	16.6	121
1979 TVR 3000S Turbo 2-bbl. Weber (*Wikipedia*)	230	2436	5.8	14.5	139
1964 Lotus Elan 1600 (*R&T*)	105	1500	8.5	16.9	107
1967 Lotus Elan S/E 3.55 axle (*R&T*)	115	1580	8.0	16.4	119
1969 Lotus Elan S4 SE CP 3.77 axle (*R&T*)	110	1630	9.4	16.8	110
1972 Lotus Elan Sprint 1558cc (*R&T*)	113	1640	8.4	16.0	112
1973 Lotus Elan Sprint 1558cc (*C/D*)	120	1590	6.8	15.4	100
1970 Lotus Europa S2 1470cc (*R&T*)	82	1460	11.2	18.2	109
1971 Lotus Europa S3 1565cc (*R&T*)	82	NA	9.4	17.0	116
1972 Lotus Europa Twin Cam (*R&T*)	113	1555	8.3	15.5	114
1973 Lotus Europa Special 5-Speed (*R&T*)	113	1665	9.6	17.0	117
Jaguar E-Type 4.2 3.54 axle CV (*Collectors Guide*)	265	2867	7.2	15.5	126
1965 Jaguar E-Type 4.2 Convertible (*R&T*)	265	2800	7.0	14.9	NA
1965 Jaguar E-Type 4.2 Convertible (*C/D*)	265	2515	6.5	15.0	NA
1966 Jaguar E-Type 4.2 Coupe (*C/D*)	265	2860	7.1	15.4	116
1969 Jaguar E-Type 4.2 Coupe (*R&T*)	245	3020	8.0	15.7	NA
1972 Jaguar E-Type 5.3 3.54 axle CV (*R&T*)	250	3380	7.4	15.4	135
1974 Jaguar E-Type 5.3 Convertible 3.31 (*RT*)	241	3432	7.4	16.4	NA

Elegant English Sports Car Test Results Chart Notes:
   The 271-hp Tuscan SE tested by *Motor Magazine* had a fuel consumption rate of 16 mpg. The wheelbase was listed as 90 inches, so we can assume this was an early production LWB model. The 1965 E-Type Convertible *Road & Track* test has not been verified. This could have been a test of a Coupe instead. *C/D* = Car and Driver. *RT* = Road Test. *R&T* = Road & Track.

Selected Elegant English Ratings Chart

Years	Model	Collect	Drive	Desire
1972 - 1973	Triumph Stag	C	D	D
1955 - 1968	Morgan 4/4	C	C	C
1953 - 1969	Morgan Plus 4	C	C	B
1968 - 1973	Morgan Plus 8 (U.S., gasoline)	B	B	B
1973 - 1975	Jensen-Healey	D	B	D
1978 - 1979	TVR 3000S	B	B	A
1962 - 1965	Lotus Elan S1/S2	C	D	B
1966 - 1973	Lotus Elan SE & Sprint	B	C	A
1961 - 1968	Jaguar E-Type Series I 3.8 & 4.2	A	D	B
1969 - 1970	Jaguar E-Type Series II 4.2	A	C	A
1971 - 1974	Jaguar E-Type Series III V-12	A	C	A
1953 - 1962	Aston Martin DB2, DB2-4, & Mk. III	B	D	B
1963 - 1965	Aston Martin DB5	A	C	A
1966 - 1970	Aston Martin DB6 Mark I & II	A	C	A
1978 - 1985	Aston Martin Vantage Volante Series 1	B	B	B
1986 - 1989	Aston Martin Vantage Volante Series 2	B	B	B

Models Ratings Chart Definitions:

Years: In most cases, the years listed include the total production years for a particular model series. Some model years within a series may be considerably more desirable than other years.

Models: In some cases many variations are included in this category and in others the models included are very homogeneous. This is generally self explanatory.

Collectibility: This is what most of you want to know, the bottom line on how likely the model or series is likely to climb in value over the coming years.

Drivability: This is an indicator of how adaptable the machine can be to drive for transportation or pleasure in the modern world, considering collector value, parts availability, fuel quality, comfort, performance and miscellaneous other factors.

Desirability: This defines the nostalgic, emotional wow factor, without regard for collector values or everyday usage.

General: No machine is given a failing grade. If it made it into a rating chart, at least a few hobbyists find that model interesting.

Chapter 4: *German Engineering Comes to America*

Figure D1 - This interior shot is of a 1968 Porsche 912 Targa. Note the full set of instruments. As described in this chapter, even the 912 Targas had the sportier dash layout. Indigenous to the breed, the seat panels are breathable black vinyl and the floor mats are that distinctly Germanic type. Note the familiar Porsche design of the polished spokes of the wood steering wheel. The brushed dash panel displays the 912 emblem on the far right. The optional radio with its mechanical push buttons is of the correct vintage. ©Valder 137 (CC)

Three brands sent topless sports models to the USA in respectable quantities during The Sixties. Volkswagen produced the Karmann-Ghia, Porsche became the centerpiece of the German sports car industry, and Mercedes-Benz built high-end luxury models for the elite. The Ghia fought its way through the sea of Brits and Italians to be the affordable sports car with engineering as its guidepost. Sprouting from the ashes of WWII and the Beetle, Porsche launched its 356 series to American adulation. Many more models, as well as engineering styles and technologies, would land on our shores over the coming decades. Mercedes originally constructed a very special and expensive Gullwing destined to become an American collector car auction darling, then added a convertible version. The long-lived SL Series would become the flaunted symbols of Rodeo Drive.

Volkswagen Karmann-Ghia Cabriolet

Figure D2 - The VW sports car was the opening bid for a German convertible back in the good old days. This creamy gray '61 model displays a typical K-G look with its moon hubcaps and whitewall tires, although I suspect most Ghias left the factory with blackwalls. Karmann-Ghia Cabriolets would be built for more than a decade until the company finally replaced their entry-level sports convertible with something completely different, the Porsche 914. ©Martin V. (GNU)

This car bores me to tears, but I have to include it in *Daydreams in the Wind*. It is a significant part of our history as sports car nuts. The way I relish the Fiat 850 Spider with its 817cc rear engine and body by Bertone, there are many of you out there who feel the same way about the Karmann-Ghia. Porsches have always been overpriced, particularly the service and maintenance costs, if not the original purchase price. We all know that VW engineered one of the absolute best convertible top designs with its Beetle Cabriolet that has ever been developed. We know those Beetle Cabriolets have always been built in the same Karmann factory as the Karmann-Ghias, even when the VW Beetle sedans have been built in the normal VW factory. Do you see the Fiat/Bertone resemblance? Volkswagen built Beetle Convertibles from 1953-79 with horsepower ratings beginning at 36 and ending at 60. The company produced Karmann-Ghias from 1956 through 1974 with the same horsepower ratings. Convertibles of the sports car variant did not appear until 1958. There were about 6-10 times as many Beetle Convertibles produced each year than Karmann-Ghia Convertibles, with topless K-G production peaking at 5873 in 1970. There were 331,847 Beetle Cabriolets built in 1949-1979 and 80,837 Karmann Ghia Cabriolets built 1957-74. Some sources state the number as 80,897.

Like the 850 Spider, the Karmann-Ghia remained a very civilized, low-powered sports car for the American masses built upon the company's ubiquitous sedan chassis. Throughout its exceptionally long production run, the K-G remained a thoroughly reliable machine that could be trusted to reach the driver's destination, unlike its many English contemporaries. The Ghia Cabriolet brought quality German engineering to sports car fans lacking Porsche budgets. Like the Fiat Spiders, its top design was superior to most anything else built at the time. Its relatively soft suspension and nimble handling brought more similarity to the Fiats, but its air-cooled flat four in the *trunk* offered a noisy, windy experience for the sports car driver. There was one other very significant difference between the Fiats and the Ghia. The latter's larger displacement producing low power ratings was the source of the Ghia's long-term reliability. Most Fiat sports cars were tuned to the wing speed of a hummingbird, exciting to drive but an Achilles' heel for long engine life.

Figure D3 - This light blue K-G Cabriolet is showing off its front trunk. If you squint really hard, you can spot the spare tire standing upright in its well in the forward edge of the trunk. This car has its top boot neatly snapped down over its low stack. The top on its Beetle sister stacks up twice as high! ©Rudolf Stricker (GNU)

When the Cabriolet was introduced in 1958, the thirty-something horsepower over the rear wheels was less than awesome. For 1961, horsepower jumped to 40 at 4900 rpm and the final-drive ratio changed from 4.43:1 to 4.37:1 to slow engine speed, though the ratios of first and fourth gears were tightened in an effort to preserve *acceleration*. Engine size increased to 1.3 liters for 1966 and horsepower rose to 50 at 4600 rpm. There was another bump to 1.5 liters and 53 horsepower for 1967, and a step up to 1.6 liters and 57 horsepower for 1970, and finally, to 60 horsepower in 1971. The 1600's were the quickest Karmann-Ghias, capable of 0-60 mph in about 21 seconds and a top speed of around 82 mph. A switch in final drive for manual-transmission models in 1972 increased top speed to 90 mph. The 1600's also had better stopping power, thanks to their standard front disc brakes. When VW revamped its power ratings for 1973, switching from gross to net figures, the Karmann Ghia was re-rated to 46 horsepower.

Figure D4 - It is not clear from this B&W photo, but this late model Karmann-Ghia has a real wood veneer dash and at least a few more instruments and controls than that of a Beetle Cabriolet. ©Masur (PD)

Karmann-Ghia Cabriolet Production Chart

Model	Production	Model	Production	Model	Production
1958	1325	1964	3691	1970	5873
1959	1770	1965	4003	1971	5567
1960	2044	1966	4827	1972	3076
1961	1891	1967	3174	1973	2650
1962	2723	1968	4157	1974	1926
1963	3387	1969	4584		
				Total	56,668

Karmann-Ghia Cabriolet Production Chart Notes:
All production figures above are from the *Complete Book of Collectible Cars 1940-1980*. The figures represent USA sales only and some may be estimates. Other sources list 80,837 or 80,897 for the worldwide Karmann-Ghia Cabriolet production. Total Ghia production from Germany including coupes was more than 445,000. The Karmann-Ghia received a fully synchronized gearbox in 1960. The 1961 Cabriolet price was $2495. Compression was dropped from 7.7 to 7.3 in 1971, so the higher hp for '71

cannot be correct. An 8-track with AM radio was an option in 1974, when the base price of the Cabriolet was $3935.

Aside from the excellent convertible top, the Cabriolet offered many positive attributes, most of which are still applicable today. The fit and finish of the cars was far above average for Sixties imports. Best of all, Beetles and Karmann-Ghias have the fanaticism of Trekkies supporting their favorite classics. You may be able to locate parts and service on these antiques easier than any other imports in this book. The Cabriolet is a Beetle underneath the body and of course the engines and transmissions are extremely similar. Probably the Ghia's biggest negatives are the ways in which it does not look or sound like a proper sports car. The dash layout, shift mechanism, and wheezy engine are little sportier than that of the lowly Beetle. In spite of these shortcomings, the Karmann-Ghia has more than its share of fans who enjoy waving at their English sports car compatriots sitting on the roadside with fuming, overheated engines or dead electrical systems.

Figure D5 - This yellow Karmann-Ghia is a 1960 (or slightly newer) model. The chrome grilles over the front air intakes were new for 1960. Note the solid painted steel wheels without brake vents and the typical for the period white steering wheel. The chrome hubcaps have a distinctive shape. ©Michael Spiller, Bradford, UK (CC)

Karmann-Ghia Cabriolet Chart

Year	CI / CC	HP	Year	CI / CC	HP
1959 - 1965	73 / 1192	36	1970	97 / 1584	57
1966	78 / 1289	50	1971	97 / 1584	60
1967 - 1969	91 / 1493	53	1974	97 / 1584	48

Karmann-Ghia Cabriolet Chart Notes:

All Karmann-Ghia's had a 94-inch wheelbase. All models had air-cooled, opposed four-cylinder OHV, carbureted engines. The 1959-65 version weighed 1750 pounds. The original base retail prices quoted in some cases may not be exactly accurate for the model year or years listed. The quote for the 1959-65 model is $2725 and $3935 for the 1974 edition.

Figure D6 - This is a front view of the green Cabriolet pictured earlier in this section. Compare this 1968-70 model to the early '60's model above. The most visible changes are the more angular lines of the door mirrors and the smoother hubcaps over silver painted, vented steel wheels. ©Masur (PD)

Porsche 356 Cabriolet

The first line of Porsche convertibles was launched in 1950 and continued into the 1965 production year, even after the introduction of the 911 Series. When you consider that it would be several years before the Targa appeared on U.S. shores, this makes perfect sense by extending the availability of a topless Porsche. You can see from the chart below that the production numbers of the early cars were quite small, not even reaching four digits until the introduction of the unexpectedly popular Speedster introduced in 1955 as an economy model. Several varieties of the 356 Series were developed and marketed, from the original model to the 356A of '56, the short-lived D model of 1958-59, the B of '60, and the C introduced in 1964.

From the very beginning, Porsche has always designed a model with a particular body and chassis design, then proceeded to manufacture that design for a considerable number of years, while constantly updating the powerplant. This usually meant many small increases in the displacement and power ratings accumulated over the years of production. The 356 Series was no exception. The engine was taken directly from the VW Beetle and modified with a different crank, hotter cam, better-breathing heads and manifolds, and dual carbs. The earliest models had a 1.1-liter, four-cylinder, OHV engine producing only 40 horsepower. This was increased to 1.3, 1.5, 1.6, and two liters over the production span. Horsepower went all the way up to 130 with a racy DOHC model. These figures may sound tiny today, but the 356 was never a large, heavy car. It had an 83-inch wheelbase and the weight remained relatively close to one ton, ranging at its widest span from 1700 to 2300 pounds. These figures made for a consistently nimble, fun to drive sports car.

Figure D7 - This rich blue 1957 Porsche 356 Speedster has a tan interior. The Speedster was designed as an economy model Porsche, but it is in high demand by collectors today. ©Mr. Choppers (GNU)

Distinctive features define each type within the 356 range. The early cars up through 1952 had flat, two-piece windshields. The '53-'55 models had an unusual windshield comprised of two flat panels connected and creased in the center. The 1956-69 356A model introduced a modern curved windshield and the DOHC Carrera engine was an option. The B model was an interim affair. Some of the Coupes were actually built by welding the optional hardtop onto a Cabriolet. The C model was the first with disc brakes at all four wheels. Previous models had all drum brakes. You might expect, as I had previous to beginning the research for this book, that the 356 continued in production alongside the new 911 mostly because of the Cabriolet model. The sales figures show otherwise. According to *Wikipedia*, Porsche built 14,151 356 models in 1964, but you can see from the chart that only 1764 of these were Cabriolets.

Figure D8 - This steel blue Porsche 356 Cabriolet is a very early model. Take note of the light tan interior with very neatly fitting top boot, the tiny parking lamps, minimal bumpers and baby moon hubcaps. You can easily discern this early 356 from the later 356A by its two-piece windshield. The front nose emblem states simply PORSCHE. ©Nakhon 100 (CC)

From 1955 through 1962, Porsche built three series of 356 roadsters. The term *roadster* as used here is not completely accurate, but I am trying to avoid the word *stripper*, which was in truth the more accurate description. The first series, the Speedster of 1955-59 had a simplified, single-layer top and a cut-down, curved windshield. The top was permanently attached but there were no roll-up windows. The Convertible D was the Speedster's replacement. The windshield height was increased and roll-up windows were added, but the top and accoutrements remained cheaper than those of the regular 356 Cabriolet. Ironically, the model called the Roadster was not a roadster at all, but a continuation of the Convertible D as a lower-priced 356B.

What began as a high-falootin' Beetle Cabriolet, or a pedigreed Karmann-Ghia Cabriolet beginning in 1958, if you will, has become a highly prized collector car. Just in recent years, as in 2013, right in the middle of a recession for the 99%, the 356 convertibles, particularly what were the bargain-basement models originally requested by Max Hoffman for the U.S. market, and those with the Super 90 (90 hp) or Carrera engines (105-130 hp), have exploded in value. These have become like the L-88's and L-89's of big-block Corvettes. The lesser models of lower performance, higher production and more practical street application have consistently moved upward in collector values, but the very rare pseudo-race models have exploded. I guess there is no substitute for the expansive disposable incomes of the 1%. Most of the 356 models have begun a climb upward since about 2010 and some of these paths have been very steep indeed. A 1600 Super Speedster from 1959 is currently in the $200,000 to $400,000 range. Even a regular 356 Cabriolet now starts at about $150,000. Prices for a Carrera Speedster have been exploding upward since 2013, with $1.5 million not an uncommon auction price. *Wikipedia* claims only about 140 Carrera Speedsters were built over five years of production.

Figure D9 - Red Porsche Speedster. Notice the distinctive chrome strip on the side and the bumper guards and rail not on the early 356 pictured above. ©Motohide Miwa (CC)

Porsche 356 Cabriolet Production Chart

Model	Year	Production	Model	Year	Production
356 Cabriolet	1950	65	Speedster	1955	1334
356 Cabriolet	1951	350	Speedster	1956	1056
356 Cabriolet	1952	217	Speedster	1957	1170
356 Cabriolet	1953	615	Speedster	1958	552
356 Cabriolet	1954	144	Speedster	1959	32
356 Cabriolet	1955	299			
356A Cabriolet	1956	430	Speedster	1955 - 59	4144
356A Cabriolet	1957	542			
356A Cabriolet	1958	1382	Convertible D	1958	386
356A Cabriolet	1959	944	Convertible D	1959	944
356B Cabriolet	1960	468			
356B Cabriolet	1961	1617	Convertible D	1958 - 59	1330
356B Cabriolet	1962	1609			
356B Cabriolet	1963	1568	356B Roadster	1960	561
356B Cabriolet	1964	932	356B Roadster	1961	1529
356C Cabriolet	1964	832	356B Roadster	1962	812
356C Cabriolet	1965	2333			
			356B Roadster	1960 - 62	2902
356 Cabriolet	1950 - 55	1690			
356A Cabriolet	1956 - 59	3298	Total Roadsters	1955 - 62	8376
356B Cabriolet	1960 - 64	6194			
356C Cabriolet	1964 - 65	3165			
			Total 356	1950 - 65	22,723
Cabriolets	1950 - 65	14,347			

Porsche 356 Cabriolet Production Chart Notes:

According to Brian Long's *Porsche 356* books and other sources, a total of 76,313 Coupes and Cabriolets were produced between 1948 and 1965. It is not known exactly how many of these were sent to the USA.

Figure D10 - This gorgeous silver 1959 Porsche 356A Cabriolet shows off its red interior and black boot snapped down over the stacked top. Note the white plastic steering wheel indigenous to the model. You can identify this as a late '59 by examining the top rail. This rail was raised an inch or two higher above the bumper mid-year to offer more body protection. ©Rex Gray, Southern California (CC)

Porsche 911 & 912 Targa

Back in 1966, I picked up a brochure from underneath a table at a Porsche dealership. This would come to be one of my most prized brochures. It was a brochure printed in September 1965, mostly in German, but with some English text, of the new Porsche Targa. The cars used in the photos were Irish Green and Polo Red, two of the official standard Porsche colors offered at that time. The brochure introduced both 911 and 912 Targas, although neither would roll onto U.S. soil until 1967. Of course the photos showed the cars in every combination with tops on and off, windows raised and lowered, and the plastic rear window zipped up and zipped down. For a convertible fan like me, this new idea was a revelation!

Figure D11 - This is a prerelease brochure photo of a very early Porsche Targa. It would take nearly two years after the release of this brochure for Targas to actually reach our shores. The side windows are raised and the rear window is zipped out in this shot. These steel disc wheels were the only choice initially available. The popular mag-style of the 1967 911S would later spread to the other models as an option. ©1966 Floyd M. Orr Collection

A little historical background is needed here to see how stunning the new Targas were. There were no T-tops or convertible roll bars back then. Everything was either a closed coupe that could possibly have an optional sunroof, or a true convertible, no matter what the nationality or nomenclature. Even with the final U.S. introduction in '67, the Targas beat everyone else to the U.S. market by at least a model year. The Corvette T-top would not arrive until 1968, nor would the Shelby Mustang Convertible with a stylish sort of roll bar. Unlike the Shelby, the Targa's bar was a genuine roll bar. Although the Corvette's T-top strengthened the coupe's body structure, it was never certified as an actual roll bar, either. Later T-top designs outside the Corvette realm would mostly constitute a pair of big holes cut into production coupes. The 914 would not appear until 1970 and the Dino GTS, although stunningly gorgeous, would bring up the rear in 1972. Although the Stingray's rear window was made of glass and was removable, the convertible effect was still less than that offered by the original Targa. Within two model years, the Targa would predate by a full decade the Corvette fastback design with a large fixed rear window and removable roof panels.

Figure D12 - This British Racing Green 1968 Targa 912 is showing off its completely open-air mode, including its engine cover. ©Valder 137 (CC)

Production of the new 911 Coupe began in September 1964, but it would be February '65 before a 911 reached the U.S. market. The first topless 911, the Targa, would not arrive for a couple more years after that. The 356 Cabriolet continued in production after the six-cylinder 911 Coupe was introduced. This allowed continual sales of a four-cylinder engine and a topless model almost up until the 912 Targa was introduced. Porsche built 2562 912 Targas in the 1967-69 model years. This amounted to less than 8% of total 912 production: the company underestimated the demand for the Targa body style. (Well, duh!) Actual Targa production began in December 1966 for the European market, but the first Targa would not arrive in the U.S. until the summer of '67. It was a 912 Targa. There are only 140 912 Targas with a zip-out rear window currently accounted for in the USA and only about twenty of these are '69 models. Targas built after 1/1/68 with the zip-out rear window were not 2+2's: their rear seats were replaced with additional storage areas. The Targas with fixed glass rear windows still had 2+2 seating. The Targas with glass rear windows could be ordered with the two-seater configuration, but it is unknown if this applied to U.S. imports, since the glass window version was very popular in the export markets.

The attractive five-spoke Fuchs alloy wheels were introduced in 1967. These lighter, mag-style wheels will always be a desirable option. The wheelbase was increased more than two inches in '69, decreasing the susceptibility of the early 911's legendary oversteer. Both the 911 and 912 received twelve-volt electrical systems instead of the six volts of the 356 Series. Since the 911's instrument panel was made standard on the 912 in '67, all Targas have the five-dial instrument cluster. Porsche began with a 1991cc SOHC Six for its 911 Series and gradually increased the displacement over the years. The engine was increased to 2195cc in 1970, 2341cc in 1972, and 2687cc in 1974. The company continually improved the rear-weight-bias handling with increased rear tire sizes and the juggling of several design components such as the battery and oil tank. All five-speed 911's were changed from the racing shift pattern to the ubiquitous street pattern in 1972.

Figure D13 - This is a 2.4-liter 911T Targa with the optional Fuchs alloy wheels introduced on the S model in 1967. ©The Supermat (CC)

Transmission choices in the Targas comprise a very short story. Three transmission types were offered in the 1967-75 period. A standard four-speed manual was basic equipment on all the U.S. imports. An optional five-speed manual was much more common then, and of course it is much more desirable now. The five-speed was standard in most markets on many models, but optional in the U.S. market. Fortunately a large portion of the inventory shipped here had the optional transmission. Even most of the lowly 912's had the five-speed. A pseudo-automatic called the Sportomatic was introduced for the 1968 model year. This four-speed, clutch-less shift system was available on most models through the '75 model year, and later as a three-speed unit, but it was never popular. When looking for a collectible Porsche, the five-speed will always be the best choice, regardless of model. A close-ratio gearset was offered on the 1967 911S (and probably the regular 911, too). Certainly a car with this option is now highly desirable as a collectible. Check carefully for worn out synchros on any car you are considering. All the Porsche transmissions were fully synchronized, but the rebuilding of a 911 or 912 transmission can be very expensive, since the engine must be removed to service the transmission.

Figure D14 - This dark red Targa is one of the rare 912 models with the zip-out rear window. This example shows the plastic window closed. I believe the chrome disc wheels were a factory option, although not nearly as popular as the Fuchs alloys. ©Cjp24 (GNU)

On the other hand, the selections in standard and optional paint colors and standard and optional interior colors and fabrics have been astoundingly complex. No charts are included here because most of this specific information is currently available elsewhere online and in books. Porsche always offered at least half a dozen standard exterior colors plus a spate of optional colors for each model year. The option prices were never cheap and the metallic paints were always the most costly, although in my opinion the most appropriately attractive for the car. The Irish Green and Polo Red cars shown in that pre-release Targa brochure were two of the nine standard colors offered in that first year of the Targa. This would also be the first year of many to come in which a large number of special color choices at extra cost would be offered. In 1966, there had been only four of these; in 1967 there were thirty!

The interior design of the 911 and 912 has always been more about ergonomic efficiency than style or luxury; however, from the beginning of production of these models Porsche has offered numerous choices of colors and fabrics. Beginning with four basic colors in '67, all the base interiors in the 1967-75 years were vinyl with cloth or leather optional. The leather option was available for either the seats only or the whole interior. Breathable vinyl in various patterns was generally offered on the seating surfaces in lieu of smooth vinyl. Probably the most memorable of seating choices were the madras or houndstooth cloth seating surfaces available in several color patterns.

Porsches have always offered a substantial option list, at substantial prices, too, of course. The mag-style Fuchs alloy wheels initially available only on the '67 911S would remain a popular option on all models for many years to come. Air conditioning was first made available in 1969, but it would be a sweltering mistake to expect that high-priced German AC to cool with the reliable effectiveness of that of a '69 Stingray or Mustang. A tonneau cover for the Targa was also first offered in 1969. The big option news for 1970 was a new ZF limited slip differential available with either a 40% or 80% lockup mode. This was also the first year power windows were available. All models had optional Blaupunkt or Becker radios and sound systems. Despite the high prices of these units, most any Japanese brand of the period could produce higher quality sound and/or better long-distance radio reception. Many road testers of the period lamented this unfortunate blight upon sports cars that drove and handled so well.

The top design of the Targa models varied a bit over time. The original, pre-production brochure discusses a hardtop that matches the body color, but if these were ever produced, I have never seen one. All the Targa hardtops I have seen are the matte black ones, as pictured in that same brochure. They are made of rigid fiberglass with a black vinyl covering. Also mentioned is a soft top that can be *rolled* up. I do not know of any Targa top that could actually be rolled up, but an accordion type was definitely produced. I am not certain of this fact, but I think the accordion type, folding fabric top was standard on all 1967-73 Targas. Beginning in 1974, this type was an option at extra cost, with the solid black fiberglass model as standard. The option price was $235 in 1974 and was required with air conditioning because the rigid top would not fit in the front luggage compartment with the AC components taking up space. According to the *Road & Track* test of the period, the fixed rear window created quite a bit of wind buffeting at speed that did not even diminish with the side windows up.

You may find this a strange comparison, but I think a discussion of the 1968-75 Corvette is relevant to the overall concept of this book. As mentioned earlier, when Chevrolet engineers developed the T-top design, part of its purpose was to give the topless Corvette a stiffer structure. Unlike the Targa of a year earlier, the T-top was not such a direct reaction to whatever was feared the NHTSA might legislate in the future. The Corvette Convertible continued in production from 1968 through 1975. Traffic noise, the rise of FM Stereo rock stations, and the refinement of air conditioning systems were the variables that affected the increasing Corvette Coupe sales at the direct expense of Corvette Convertible sales during this period. Looking at the Targa Production Chart below, it does not appear that Targa sales declined in the '69-'75 period as readily as sales of the Corvette Convertible. Keep in mind, though, that the Porsche brand was not established in the USA to the degree of the Corvette at this time. Pardon my impertinence, but the rise of the Wall Street Cocaine Cowboys of the Eighties had not yet exploded. Nouveau riche Americans were not yet enamored of the Porsche brand. Enthusiasts still pronounced the name correctly, with two syllables. This pattern was ever so slowly developing throughout the Seventies, so the apparently stable Targa production figures through the period simply reflect the growing trend of 911 Coupe sales in the USA. Proportionally, the sales of both Corvette Convertibles and Porsche Targas were slowly declining in the 1968-75 era. Full convertibles from all brands, including Corvette and Porsche, would come roaring back in the second half of the Eighties.

You may find the production chart below to be more than a little confusing. Welcome to the club. The reason for this is simple, yet complex, and I hope to clarify the situation with this explanation. The production period of 1967 through 1975 happens to be the transitional slide down the pit of performance oblivion due to the new EPA regulations. Porsche held a quite unique position among sports cars at that time, and basically still mines the same market. Porsches are the most expensive sports cars that American drivers might buy to actually drive somewhere. Porsches have always excelled in engineering and drivability, leaving the noise, discomfort, and inconvenience to the mostly Italian exotics. Porsches have simultaneously never been apple pie conveyances like Corvettes. The company has never been as retail price cost conscious as Chevrolet, nor as elegantly frivolous as Lamborghini. Porsche did not whine about the cost of fuel injection in the EPA era as Chevrolet most certainly did, not returning the real thing to the Corvette until 1985! Porsche executives and engineers never threw up their hands in disbelief at the EPA demands, as did Ferrari when they released the Boxer or Lamborghini with their Countach. Porsche did not import their 911S in 1968 or their latest Carrera in 1973, but otherwise the company efficiently worked to comply with the new EPA regulations from 1968 onward.

Figure D15 - This gold Porsche Targa has what appears to be an *electric* finish on it. The interior is black on this fixed-window Targa. I am not sure if the stereo speakers installed on the rear shelf are a factory option or not. ©Toni V (CC)

Some of the production figures in the chart are taken from published company records. It is quite unfortunate, but the factory did not delineate Targa from Coupe production numbers for the U.S. market until 1974. The 1967 figures represent total production, not just U.S. imports. All the 1967-69 912 figures represent all markets. It is unknown if any of the 268 regular 911's of 1968 were imported. The 911L of 1968 was the first 911 specifically modified for the American market. All 1969-1970 figures represent all markets, as do the 1971-73 E and S figures. The 1971 T US figure of 3476 includes all 911T Coupes and Targas constructed for the USA. The 911T had Weber carbs in 1969, but like several other brands in this book, the Webers were changed to Zenith carburetors in 1970 to meet EPA requirements. The U.S. import figures for the 911T in 1972 and '73 represent models fuel injected specifically to meet EPA regulations. The European T models were still carbureted. All the 1972 U.S. T models used mechanical fuel injection. This was updated to Bosch K-Jetronic CIS (Continuous Injection System) in January 1973 after 781 early 1973 models had been produced with the old mechanical system. All 911's received the Bosch Continuous Injection System in 1974. The 1974 model of the Carrera used a 175-hp six-cylinder with CIS for the USA only. These are the 246 models in the chart. Other markets got a 210-hp Carrera with mechanical fuel injection. In 1975 the USA received only special variants of the S and Carrera.

A very desirable collectible Targa is the special Silver Anniversary model of 1975. The SA option package was offered on 911 and 911S Coupes and Targas in all markets. Only 249 of the 911S Targas sent to the U.S. had this Option Code M426. The package included Silver Metallic paint with blackout trim, five-speed, Blaupunkt Bamberg AM/FM/cassette with power antenna, silver alloy wheels, rear anti-roll bar, sport steering wheel, heated rear window, headlamp washers, and a special dash plaque.

1967-75 Porsche 911 & 912 Targa Engine Chart

Model	Years	Size	HP	Bore / Stroke	Induction
912	1967 - 1969	1582cc	90	82.5 mm x 74 mm	2 2-bbl. Solex
911 / L	1967 - 1968	1991cc	130	80 mm x 66 mm	2 3-bbl. Weber
911S	1967	1991cc	160	80 mm x 66 mm	2 3-bbl. Weber
911T	1969	1991cc	110	80 mm x 66 mm	2 3-bbl. Weber
911E	1969	1991cc	140	80 mm x 66 mm	Bosch MFI
911S	1969	1991cc	170	80 mm x 66 mm	Bosch MFI
911T	1970 - 1971	2195cc	125	84 mm x 66 mm	2 3-bbl. Zenith
911E	1970 - 1971	2195cc	155	84 mm x 66 mm	Bosch MFI
911S	1970 - 1971	2195cc	180	84 mm x 66 mm	Bosch MFI
911T	1972	2341cc	140	84 mm x 70.4 mm	Bosch MFI
911T	1973	2341cc	140	84 mm x 70.4 mm	MFI / K-Jetronic
911E	1972 - 1973	2341cc	165	84 mm x 70.4 mm	Bosch MFI
911S	1972 - 1973	2341cc	190	84 mm x 70.4 mm	Bosch MFI
911	1974	2687cc	150	90 mm x 70.4 mm	K-Jetronic CIS
911S	1974	2687cc	175	90 mm x 70.4 mm	K-Jetronic CIS
Carrera	1974	2687cc	175	90 mm x 70.4 mm	K-Jetronic CIS
911S	1975	2687cc	165	90 mm x 70.4 mm	K-Jetronic CIS
Carrera	1975	2687cc	165	90 mm x 70.4 mm	K-Jetronic CIS
911S CA	1975	2687cc	160	90 mm x 70.4 mm	K-Jetronic CIS
Carr. CA	1975	2687cc	160	90 mm x 70.4 mm	K-Jetronic CIS

1967-75 Porsche 911 & 912 Targa Engine Chart Notes:
The 912 had an OHV four-cylinder and all 911's had SOHC six-cylinder powerplants. Some sources stated the horsepower of the 912 as 102. Some sources indicate that some 1969 911T models had Zenith carburetors. It is unclear if all the U.S. T models had Webers or not. The dry weight of the base 912 Coupe was 2095 pounds. All the Targas weighed a little more. The dry weight of a 1967 911S Coupe was 2272, with the Targa respectively a little heavier. All the other 1967-75 Targas weighed about 2400-2500 pounds dry. Some sources show the 1969 model as hitting the scales at about 2250-2300 pounds, but I am not sure why this model would be lighter than a '67. It had a longer wheelbase, larger wheels and twin batteries, and the Targa had a new, large glass rear window. MFI = Mechanical Fuel Injection.

Porsche Targa 911 & 912 Production Chart

Model	Production	Model	Production	Model	Production
1967 911	718	1970 T	2545	1973 T US	2083
1967 911S	483	1970 E	933	1973 911E	1055
1967 912	544	1970 S	729	1973 911S	925
1967 Targa	1745	1970 Targa	4207	1973 Targa	4063
1968 911	268	1971 T US	3476	1974 911	3110
'68 911L US	5134	1971 E	935	1974 911S	898
1968 912	1217	1971 S	788	'74 Carr. US	246
1968 Targa	6619	1971 Targa	5199	1974 Targa	4254
1969 T	282	1972 T US	1821	1975 S US	1517
1969 E	858	1972 911E	861	'75 Carr. US	174
1969 S	614	1972 911S	989		
1969 912	801			1975 Targa	1691
		1972 Targa	3671		
1969 Targa	2555			911 Targa	32,965
912 Targa	2562			912 Targa	2562
912 Zip-Out	140	All Targas		1967 - 75	35,527

Porsche Targa 911 & 912 Production Chart Notes:
The 912 Targa with zip-out rear window was produced alongside its 911 companion in 1967 and 1968 only. The 140 produced are included within the total 912 Targa figure of 2562. Depending upon the source, approximately 30,300 912 Coupes were sold worldwide in 1967-69. The 1968 figures include 268 *regular* 911 Targas. It is not known if any of these base Targas came to the USA, although less than 500

base Coupes were imported. Most, if not all, the production figures by model year stated above have been verified by the *Porsche 911 Red Book 1965-1999*, the *912 Registry*, and published factory records, as well as various other sources.

Porsche 914

Was this car destined to be the ultimate stepchild? Many would say so. Designed and built by Porsche, Volkswagen, and Karmann, the 914 was never a full-blooded Porsche, a truly affordable VW sports car, or a replacement for the ancient Karmann-Ghia. There is little doubt that it was some of all these things, and its bastardly heritage haunted the car from its inception. Let's go back in time for a moment to absorb the full picture.

Figure D16 - Note the black GT stripes and unusual wheel design on this orange Porsche 914. ©Pujanak (PD)

The VW Beetle Cabriolet had always been a four-seater non-sports car with lovable cache, a pathetically underpowered engine, and legendary build quality. All the topless Beetles were built in the Karmann factory, no matter where the Beetle sedans may have been manufactured at the time. VW began production of its official topless sports car, the Karmann-Ghia, in 1958 with the same three qualities. As a Fifties design at least, the K-G Cabriolet had a much sportier, sexier body than the Beetle Cabriolet, but underneath the steel bodies, the cars were much the same. Although the Beetle Convertible, as we Americans called it, would continue in production for decades as the affordable darling of Beverly Hills, the lower-production Karmann-Ghia was losing its sporting image to many competitors from England and Italy. By the end of the Sixties, an American sports car buyer had a boatload of choices and any of them could leave the roly-poly Karmann-Ghia for dead in most types of spirited motoring. Of course the weak little K-G could have the last laugh when it came to top design, practicality, reliability and longevity, but the die had been cast. Fifties styling with a final horsepower rating of sixty was hardly still a sports car by American standards in the Seventies.

Porsche had produced their up-market version of the Karmann-Ghia up through 1965, but the long-lived 356 Series was then replaced by the 912 with the all-new 911 body and chassis. The 912 would be discontinued as the affordable Porsche after 1969, clearing the path for the brand-new 914. The new design would eventually replace the Karmann-Ghia and the 912 as both the VW sports car and the affordable Porsche. So far, so good, but few are ever truly happy with compromise, sealing the fate of the 914's reputation before it even began.

Figure D17 - This 1970 Porsche 914/6 also happens to be orange, a popular color for the early models at least, if not for the later ones, too. ©Michael Barera (GNU)

The 914 has several strong pluses in its favor. All 914's have Targa tops that store easily in the rear trunk. Yes, Dumbkopt, there is a second trunk up front with the spare tire carried within its own compartment below the front trunk floor. The plastic top panel fastens to the windshield and roll bar with four clamps and attaches inside the rear trunk area when removed. The rear window is flat, vertical, and fixed in place, like that of a 1973-77 Corvette Coupe. As in the Corvette and the 914's bigger 911 Targa brothers, cockpit turbulence is minimal with the fixed rear window. All the 914 four-cylinder models ran originally on what was then *regular* gas. Note that the change to unleaded fuel at the pumps across America occurred smack in the middle of the 914 production run. I would guess that modern gasoline would be less of a problem than with most of the other cars in this book. All the four-cylinder 914's sent to the USA were fuel-injected. The 914 got terrific mileage, which meant a 400-mile range under average conditions and a 500-mile range on a trip! Although some servicing issues are best handled by a Porsche specialist, there is an obvious cost and hassle advantage in having at least a partial VW powertrain. The 914 may have had a few reliability issues, but they were still less prevalent than those of any English car of the period, and probably less than those of many Italian cars, too, particularly those of the longevity nature. The VW-type engines were all very low-stress designs and rust in a 914 was never as big a problem as it is with English and Italian cars. The 914 benefited from being an all-new modern design in 1970. The interior was roomy and wide with lots of elbow room. The top design was slick and sealed well, although the air-cooled engine right behind the occupants' heads was quite noisy in the VW tradition. All 914's had five-speed manual transmissions and the four-cylinder models had Bosch electronic fuel injection. The 914/6 had twin Weber carburetors.

I want to interject a little personal note. The four-cylinder 914 is probably the most likely German car that I would have ever considered buying. You can tell by the content of *Daydreams in the Wind* that I have always been partial to American and Italian sports cars. I would never buy a Mercedes because they are not sporty enough and too expensive to maintain. The VW and Karmann-Ghia models are too slow and boring to drive. I like the 911 and 912 Targas quite well, but not so much that I would choose either over some other competitor of the same vintage and price range. The 914 is a different story, though. I like its affordability in both initial cost and servicing. I *love* its long cruising range on regular gas with a low-revving, low-stress engine. It lacks the fragility from rust and engine component wear that plagues Fiats, yet functions as an affordable alternative. Would I love the 914 so much if its top was not removable? No. Would I ever buy a 914 if it had a fixed roof? Hell, no.

At the time of its release, the 914 shared the spotlight with the 914/6, a model built more by Porsche than VW with a price to match. These models were produced and sold only from the earliest 1970 production through the first part of the 1972 model year. With their thoroughbred Porsche engines and less than 3500 built, all the 914/6's have been collector's items for decades now, with prices to match. A 914/6 is likely to cost you three times that of a four-cylinder model on the current market. The figure is likely to be just a little less than what you will pay for a 911T Targa of the same vintage with the same Porsche engine. Keep in mind, too, that the Porsche servicing on these models is of course going to be much more expensive. Although any 914 owner should be wary of utilizing any old VW mechanic to maintain his 914 four-cylinder, this issue becomes critical with the 914/6. As far as the bodies go, the ones for the six-cylinder models were assembled in the Porsche factory, but they have equivalent assembly quality reputations as the ones assembled by Karmann. The main differences between the 914/6 and the lesser, more common models are the engine, brakes, and components of the suspension and other mechanical systems. The five-speed transmissions were all the same. The 914/6 had a slightly more upscale interior and instrument layout and a higher level of exterior trim as standard equipment. However, the deluxe exterior package was an option on the four-cylinder models and many cars had it. I can certainly imagine that dealers in California and other hot Porsche markets probably ordered much of their stock somewhat loaded with various options. The 914/6 used a lower variant of the 911 engine. Induction was via a pair of three-barrel Weber carbs, even on the U.S. models. A comparable new 911 Targa cost about $1000 more than a 914/6 in 1970-72. This is most likely the leading variable that determined the low sales volume of the 914/6. The 914/6 did not scream *Porsche* from its exterior appearance, although its exhaust sound did. If you did not hear one running, you would have to squint to know that it was not one of those ordinary Karmann 914 Fours. Chevrolet learned much the same lesson twenty years later when its ZR-1 Corvette looked pretty much like a regular Corvette whose engine had not been to Stillwater, Oklahoma, and back! ZR-1 sales never did much, either.

The 914 was not perfect. Surprisingly, one of its leading foibles was a reluctance to restart after a long trip, doing one of the things this model did best! The cause was a starter solenoid that would fail when hot. Only a small percentage of cars had this problem, but it could be *really* annoying! Other problems with the 914 were less obtrusive and for the most part were corrected by the factory as the model years progressed. Of course this was a time of constant price inflation, so the later cars cost considerably more than the early models. Early transmissions were quite recalcitrant to shift and all models had the racing configuration with first gear outside the H-pattern, a general nuisance in stop and go traffic. Interior assembly left something to be desired, particularly with vinyl panels that tended to prematurely come unglued. Instrument failures were not uncommon, either. Of course Porsche service costs deserve a second mention here, too.

Figure D18 - Another popular color for the 914 was bright yellow. I am not certain if these pseudo-Ferrari-looking, star design alloy wheels were a factory option or not. I do not recall ever seeing a 914 with these wheels on the streets of the USA. ©N914 (PD)

The Porsche 914 was the first rear-mid-engine street car produced for the masses. Of course the Fiat X1/9 would soon follow and the Boxster would carry the torch decades later, albeit in a more common Porsche price range. The *rear* designation here refers to what we normally call a mid-engine. Corvettes, TVR's, and even the Jensen-Healey have had a *front* mid-engine design for decades. When the engine weight is behind the front axle, the price is usually paid with cramped space efficiency and heat billowing up from the driveline into the cockpit. When the engine is in front of the rear axle line, the concern is violent oversteer when the driver dives into a corner. Of all the classic sports cars with the engine in either the rear or mid-rear, you are less likely to tear up your favorite toy by overcooking a corner in a four-cylinder 914 than in any other model. The engineering principles determining this situation are straightforward. The Beetle and Karmann Ghia have rear engines and low power and 911's have rear engines with high power, but the 914 is in the sweet spot in this regard with a mid-engine of moderate power.

A final note concerning the 914's removable top details why the Porsche 914 deserves special attention in *Daydreams in the Wind*. The later X1/9 offered the same efficient top design and on-board storage, but on a car with a more fragile reputation. There was no doubt which one was more fun on a long freeway trip, either. Many 911 and 912 Targas had the same top design, but the former is expensive, both to purchase and maintain, and the latter are quite rare, and sort of expensive. The 914 will always have the advantage of its VW connection, but with a more modern, and somewhat safer, top design than that of the Beetle Cabriolet or Karmann Ghia Cabriolet. Many more modern models have copied the 914's top, such as the Ferrari 308's, etc., but at much higher purchase and maintenance costs. In its own charming way, the somewhat maligned VW/Karmann/Porsche 914 was and is a little sweetheart of a classic topless sports car.

Porsche 914 Production by Model Year Chart

Year	Model	Production	Year	Model	Production
1970	914	13,312	1970 - 1976	Total 914	115,621
1971	914	16,231			
1972	914	21,580	1970	914/6	2668
1973	914	27,660	1971	914/6	443
1974	914	21,370	1972	914/6	260
1975	914	11,368			
1976	914	4100	1970 - 1972	Total 914/6	3371

Porsche 914 Production by Model Year Chart Notes:

All the figures in this chart were sourced from a Chassis Production Chart at *Wikipedia* that was not originally sourced from Werner Oswald's book, *Deutsche Autos 1945-90, Bd. 3*. Another source, *Porsche 914 & 914/6: The Definitive History of the Road & Competition Cars* by Brian Long, states 4075 as the number of 914's sold as early '76 models. Mr. Long also lists the number of 1975 models as 11,369. His numbers for the 914/6 are 2657, 432, and 229, totaling 3318. His book lists the total production as 115,597 + 3318 = 118,915. Altogether, Mr. Long's numbers are a little lower than those quoted by other sources. The total number of six-cylinder 914's constructed may have been only 3332, as the chart below shows. Most sources quote one or the other of these figures. The model year production figures for the four-cylinder 914 have been confirmed in *The Porsche Family Tree*, however only the 1971 figure for the 914/6 is confirmed by this source. In that pamphlet produced by the factory, no official totals are stated for 1970 or 1972.

Porsche 914 Production by Calendar Year & Engine Chart

Year	Engine	Production	Year	Engine	Production
1969	1.7 liter	1543	1972	2.0 liter	4817
1970	1.7 liter	20,241	1973	2.0 liter	16,639
1971	1.7 liter	15,993	1974	2.0 liter	5597
1972	1.7 liter	19,713	1975	2.0 liter	5469
1973	1.7 liter	7861			
			Total	2.0 liter	32,522
Total	1.7 liter	65,351			
			1969	914/6	29
1973	1.8 liter	3903	1970	914/6	2760
1974	1.8 liter	11,415	1971	914/6	306
1975	1.8 liter	2455	1972	914/6	237
Total	1.8 liter	17,773	Total	914/6	3332
Total	1.7/1.8/2.0	115,646		Total 914	118,978

Porsche 914 Production by Calendar Year & Engine Chart Notes:

All the figures in this chart were sourced from the *914 World* website. The total figures (only) for the four and six cylinder model in this chart were confirmed by *Wikipedia* as sourced from *Deutsche Autos 1945-90, Bd. 3*, by Werner Oswald, 2001. The *Complete Book of Collectible Cars 1940-1980* states that 78,643 four-cylinder 914's were built in the 1969-75 period; this number may represent the actual number sent to the USA, but the book does not clearly make this point. No other estimate of U.S. imports has been confirmed.

Porsche Performance Chart

Details	HP	Weight	0-60	1/4	TS
1965 Porsche 911 Coupe 1991cc (*R&T*)	145	2360	9.0	16.5	132
1966 Porsche 912 1582cc (*R&T*)	90	2140	11.6	18.1	NA
1967 Porsche 911S 1991cc Coupe	160	2380	8.1	15.7	141
1969 Porsche 911E 1991cc (*R&T*)	140	NA	8.4	16.0	NA
1970 Porsche 914 1679cc (*R&T*)	85	2085	13.9	19.2	109
1970 Porsche 914/6 1991cc (*R&T*)	125	2195	8.7	16.3	123
1970 Porsche 911S 2.2 Coupe 2195cc (*R&T*)	200	2390	7.3	14.9	144

1972 Porsche 911T 2341cc (*C/D*)	140	NA	6.9	15.1	NA
1972 Porsche 911S 2341cc (*C/D*)	190	NA	6.0	14.4	NA
1974 Porsche 911 2687cc (*R&T*)	150	NA	7.9	15.5	130
1975 Porsche Carrera CA 2687cc (*R&T*)	160	NA	8.2	16.5	134
2000 Porsche Boxster S 3179cc 6SM (*R&T*)	250	2855	5.5	14.0	162
2002 Porsche 911 Carrera 3596cc (*R&T*)	320	3215	4.9	13.4	177

Porsche Performance Chart Notes:
C/D = Car and Driver. R&T = Road & Track.

Figure D19 - Here is a last look at an early red 911 Targa with the popular Fuchs alloy wheels. ©Nakhon 100 (CC)

German Engineering Comes to America

Figure D20 - These two black beauties are two of the hottest varieties of Porsche 356. The car on the left is a 1960 Super 90. Notice the leather tie-down straps on the trunk lid. This example has a red interior and black top. The car on the right is a 1965 SC. If you squint, you can see its flat hubcaps indigenous to the 356C models, which had four-wheel disc brakes. Both cars sport one of those strange looking, almost vertical chrome **luggage racks.** ©Greg Gjerdingen, Willmar, USA (CC)

Figure D21 - This cream with black interior and top Porsche 356 Cabriolet 1600 is a 1964 model, one of the last of the breed before the 911 series took over. The transition between the drum-braked 356B and the disc-braked 356C occurred during this model year. I cannot discern the type of this model from this angle because the shape of the hubcaps is not clearly visible. ©Mr. Choppers (GNU)

Porsche Targa Comparison Chart

Model	Type	CI / CC	HP	Wt.	Price
1967 Porsche 912 Targa	OP-4	96 / 1582	102	2130	$5190
1968 Porsche 912 Targa	OP-4	96 / 1582	102	2135	$5350
1969 Porsche 912 Targa	OP-4	96 / 1582	90	2140	NA
1967 Porsche 911 Targa	OP-6	121 / 1991	148	2380	$6390
1967 Porsche 911S Targa	OP-6	121 / 1991	180	NA	$7390
1968 Porsche 911L Targa	OP-6	121 / 1991	148	2430	$6900
1969 Porsche 911T Targa	OP-6	121 / 1991	125	NA	$6415
1969 Porsche 911E Targa	OP-6	121 / 1991	140	NA	$7615
1969 Porsche 911S Targa	OP-6	121 / 1991	190	NA	$8315
1970 Porsche 911T Targa	OP-6	134 / 2195	142	2390	$7205

1970 Porsche 911S Targa	OP-6	134 / 2195	200	NA	$9250
1971 Porsche 911E Targa	OP-6	134 / 2195	155	2485	$9078
1972 Porsche 911T Targa	OP-6	143 / 2341	140	NA	$7985
1972 Porsche 911S Targa	OP-6	143 / 2341	190	NA	$10,230
1973 Porsche 911E Targa	OP-6	143 / 2341	165	NA	$9760
1973 Porsche 911S Targa	OP-6	143 / 2341	190	NA	$10,860
1974 911 Targa	OP-6	164 / 2687	150	2470	$10,800
1974 911 Carrera Targa (U.S.)	OP-6	164 / 2687	175	2470	$14,425
1970 Porsche 914	OP-4	102 / 1679	85	2085	$3695
1973 Porsche 914	OP-4	120 / 1971	100	2195	$5299
1970 Porsche 914/6	OP-6	122 / 1991	125	2070	$6099

Porsche Targa Comparison Chart Notes:

The 1967-68 Porsche Targas had an 87-inch wheelbase. The 1969-70 models had an 89-inch wheelbase. All Porsche 914's had a 96-inch wheelbase. The original base retail prices quoted in some cases may not be exactly accurate for the model year or years listed. The Mercedes SL was nearly twice the price of a 911 in the mid-Sixties.

Mercedes-Benz SL Series Roadsters: 190, 300, 230, 250 & 280

Figure D22 - I have carefully selected this photo of a light gray 1958 Mercedes-Benz SL 190 with red interior and black soft top to introduce the SL Series. Its wide whitewalls and erect top give it a special antique look from this angle. Note the prominent *eyebrows* over the wheel wells and white plastic steering wheel that distinguish the series. ©Sicnag (CC)

The Mercedes Roadster line launched in 1955 were never true roadsters, although this is the official moniker applied by the company. The convertible tops were from the very beginning of production a sophisticated design that sealed well and dropped underneath either a vinyl or rigid boot. The tops were always attached to the body at the rear and the side windows were either roll-up or electric, making all the SL's true convertibles. Most likely Mercedes chose the Roadster moniker because these models were not four-seater Cabriolets. The original 300 SL and 190 SL utilized a conventional snap-on vinyl boot to conceal the lowered soft top. The original 190SL is the only carbureted SL with its twin two-barrel Solex carbs. All the remaining SL's were fuel-injected from the beginning. The 190 was a four-cylinder and all the models through 1971 were sixes. Aside from the startling gullwing doors of the 300SL Coupe, the induction system was one of the key innovative features of the series. As with the Porsche 911 and 912, the Mercedes 300SL and 190SL Roadsters were very similar in body, with the engine as the chief difference between the two models. Also like the Porsches, there were a number of minor differences in trim and features. The 190SL used a sedan-derived chassis that was much cheaper to manufacture than the special tubular spaceframe of the 300. The mass-produced 190 used a 2.0-liter, SOHC four-cylinder producing 104 gross horsepower from an iron block and aluminum head. The 300 had a 3-liter six making about 215 gross horsepower. Both models had a 94-inch wheelbase and a four-speed manual transmission. The 190SL had drum brakes and thirteen-inch wheels and weighed about 2600 pounds with its hardtop in place. The drum brakes on the earliest 190's were not power assisted. Power brakes were offered as an option after the first three months of production and made standard on all models in mid-year 1956. The four-speed was fully synchronized. The 190 had an approximate thirteen-second 0-60 time. The 300 Roadster weighed about 3200 pounds with its optional hardtop. Its top speed was 40-50 mph above that of the 190 four-cylinder. It had brakes of a similar design as the 190, but its wheels were fifteen-inch.

Figure D23 - **This 1957 300 SL Roadster was the expensive, low-production big brother to the 190 SL. The bright red paint on the body is matched on the wheel covers. This example has a tan interior and top. Note that the panel covering the top on this model is a matching tan piece, probably not made of steel. It may be a steel panel covered in textured vinyl or leather. You cannot miss the distinctive 300 SL side panel design behind the front wheel wells. The steering wheel is white, of course.** ©Christopher Ziemnowicz (PD)

Figure D24 - This 1963 Mercedes 300 SL Roadster is golden brown in color with a matching interior, including the steering wheel. The components of obvious note are the wide whitewalls, rapidly falling out of favor by 1963, and the black removable hardtop. ©Rex Gray, Southern California (CC)

The 300 SL has been a collectible car practically since the beginning, but the 190 has only recently entered the realm of high-priced auctions. Most likely its four-cylinder performance level has held it back, since many thousands of the 230/250/280 SL's have been built in the interim. All the SL models are quite complex machines with the inherent restoration costs rising exponentially over the years. Fans have generally preferred to spend their money on the later cars despite their high production figures.

Figure D25 - You can barely discern the body-colored metal top panel on this red Mercedes 230 SL. This example has color coordinated hubcaps and amber turn signals and side marker lights. ©Alf van Beem (PD)

Unibody construction has allowed rust to creep into invisible places, such as within double-walled panels. The wheel wells and floorpan are common culprit areas. Today repairs on even the *el cheapo* 190 can cause restoration costs to soar into the stratosphere. That may not be such a deterrent in a Gullwing, but the 190 SL was designed as a plebeian model to be produced for the masses. It was not until recently that 190 prices began to really climb. Make a note in the back of your mind how likely a cheap or badly executed body repair completed decades ago might have denigrated an SL's value. Watch out particularly for cars that look beautiful with sparkling chrome, shiny paint and soft leather, but a bad body repair from years past effectively masks the true cost of any future restoration.

Figure D26 - This view of the 1967 M-B 250 SL shows off its delicate chrome bumpers and chrome dual exhaust tips. This model still has the color coordinated hubcaps and amber lamps. Note that the white top panel fits almost flush with the steel body, but does not quite match the car's white exterior paint. ©Mr. Choppers (GNU)

The 230 SL was introduced for the 1963 model year. The 230 was a natural continuation of the 190 with a more modern, boxier body and a more powerful SOHC inline six-cylinder powerplant producing 150 gross horsepower propelling the car's approximate 2800 pounds. Mercedes would copy the Corvette's permanently attached, rigid boot panel to cover the top on all models from the 230 SL onward. The panel would be aluminum instead of fiberglass, of course, and painted body color. The doors, hood and trunk lid were also aluminum. The wheelbase was kept at 94 inches and as on the previous models, the rear suspension was independent, and a bit on the complex side. The new 230 SL was the first sports car designed with the passenger compartment as a *crush proof box*, a safety feature of most sedans that we take for granted today. All these new M-B sports models had standard radial tires and power brakes with discs in front. The 230 was also the first of the SL series to offer power steering and a four-speed automatic transmission as options, along with the requisite hardtop. An optional five-speed manual was introduced in mid-1966, an option popular in Europe, but not the U.S., making it very desirable as a collectible 230 SL today.

Figure D27 - This white 1968 250 SL is on display with its removable hardtop in place. Look closely at the roofline and you can see why these cars have been nicknamed *Pagodas* or Pagoda Roofs. Its distinctive concave shape is like that of no other car, Mercedes-Benz or otherwise. This car has thin whitewall tires, correct for the year, but not very common on European Mercedes models, which were usually shod with expensive blackwall Michelin radials. ©The Supermat (CC)

The short-production 250 SL had a longer stroke in its engine, producing more torque with no increase in the horsepower rating. The 250 was a more drivable machine with a pleasant demeanor. Its claims to fame were four-wheel power disc brakes, a 21-gallon fuel tank, and an optional limited slip differential. The larger engine had seven main bearings and an improved cooling system. The body and chassis remained the same as on the 230. The last of the 250 SL models sent to the USA had the new interior safety features required for 1968, and of course all the 280 production had them. You could say the 250 SL was the last of the SL Series sold in the USA as true sports cars. The luxury and convenience equipment would slowly permeate the soul of the 280 SL more and more as production continued toward the advent of the V-8 models.

Figure D28 - This dark green 1971 280 SL appears to be much like its predecessor. This was the last year for this body style. European 280's made 170 horsepower, twenty more than the 250 SL, but U.S. models like this one had about 160 gross horsepower. If you squint, you see the distinctive shape of Mercedes-Benz headrests in tan. ©Bull-Doser (PD)

Figure D29 - This navy blue 280 SL is showing off its tan soft top matching its tan interior. This is a U.S. model with European-style alloy wheels. Notice the huge blind spot of the soft top that is negated by the rear windows of the removable hardtop. ©Spanish Coches (CC)

VW, Porsche, Mercedes-Benz

Figure D30 - This photo of a light green Euro-spec 280 SL shows off the later, more stylish version of the *Pagoda*-style hardtop attached to the later model sold as the 280 SL in Europe. America did not receive this new body series until 1973 and all U.S. models from that point forward had V-8 engines. This one has a new DOHC variant of the Mercedes Six. Compare this hardtop design to the one on the 1968 250 SL shown above. Not only are the windows of a different shape, but a chrome trim strip has been added to each side of the *sunken* roof. The front of this car is similar to the 450 SL shown below. ©M 93 (PD)

The 280 SL represented an inevitable change. A larger bore increased the power to 170, another one of those natural improvements for the era. The U.S. regulations were on the way to make the cars' emissions cleaner, but the obvious result would be heavier and slower sports cars. The 280 would be the last of SOHC inline sixes, replaced by a V-8 in 1972. As you may have guessed, along with the four-speed automatic made available with the 230 SL came other comfort items such as air conditioning and power windows. These items became more prevalent with each passing production year, particularly on the U.S. models. The 280 SL had a standard oil cooler and color-coordinated wheel covers instead of the hubcaps of the previous models. The '69 models received transistor ignition systems midyear and Fuchs alloy wheels were optional in the final year of production.

As you may have surmised, most of the SL's sent to the U.S. had automatic transmissions. The 230 SL came standard with a four-speed manual, but most Americans preferred the four-speed automatic. A manual five-speed option was made available during the last year of production and this option is, of course, much in demand on the collector market today. More than 12,000 280SL's were sent to our shores, practically all equipped with four-speed automatic and air conditioning. Only 882 280SL models worldwide had the ZF five-speed manual.

After remaining stable for nearly a decade, auction prices of the SL's have shot upward quite recently. Even a relatively common 230SL with a four-speed automatic and in nice condition is now priced well north of $50,000. The prices of the later 280SL are currently about $80,000 and up. The 190SL has benefited from its early production status with prices commonly well over $100,00. Of course the most costly SL today is not a convertible; it's an aluminum gullwing coupe built only in 1954-55 in exceptionally small numbers, as in only 29 constructed in total for both model years. You will have to cough up $4-7 million for one of these closed cars with the funny doors. According to Hagerty's, the optional wheels and fitted luggage of the day will add $70,000 to the price! A more common steel Gullwing or Roadster will cost only about $1.5 million. A dealer in Sarasota, Florida, of all places, was at one time offering a 1965 230 SL with right hand drive and other European features for the ground breaking price of $495,000. This blue with tan interior and automatic transmission car had been purchased new in London by John Lennon.

Figure D31 - This is probably the Mercedes SL look we are all more familiar with, since this body style replaced the models covered in this book and has been produced in far higher numbers, particularly for the USA. The photo of this light golden green 450 SL was taken in Australia, so this car has right hand drive. The centers of the full wheel covers, as opposed to the earlier hubcaps, are still color coordinated to the body. The biggest change visually from the older models is in the headlight area. ©Jeremy G 3030 (CC)

Mercedes-Benz SL Comparison Chart

Model	Type	C. I. / CC	HP	Wt.	Price
1959-62 Mercedes-Benz 190 SL	I-4	116 / 1897	120	2552	$3998
1957-63 M-B 300 SL Roadster	I-6	183 / 2996	215	3000	$11,400
1963-66 Mercedes-Benz 230 SL	I-6	141 / 2308	150	2855	$6587
1967 Mercedes-Benz 250 SL	I-6	152 / 2496	150	2870	$6897
1968-71 Mercedes-Benz 280 SL	I-6	170 / 2778	195	2900	NA

Mercedes-Benz SL Comparison Chart Notes:
All the Mercedes SL models had a 94-inch wheelbase. The original base retail prices quoted in some cases may not be exactly accurate for the model year or years listed. The 300 SL was at one point priced at $10,950 plus $178 for the optional hardtop.

Figure D32 - This rear view of the same car displays the familiar M-B headrest shape in a dark gray interior. The top boot now matches the color and texture of the steel body instead of the interior. ©Jeremy G 3030 (CC)

The 450 SL that would be produced in large numbers and shipped to the USA, commonly with luxury features such as automatic transmission, air conditioning, and whitewall tires, replaced the sportier SL's discussed in this book. The rear end was very squared off with large, rectangular tail lights dominating the look, as shown in the photo of a European 280 SL above. The 2.8 liter Six was available with the new body in some model years in the rest of the world, but this was a new DOHC design. The U.S. received only the larger V-8 variation. The first of these new V-8 models reached the U.S. in 1973 and they would soon have protruding safety bumpers to match their low net horsepower ratings. These were hardly better than those of the previous six-cylinder models. For the USA the 4.5-liter V-8 was installed even in the 1973 cars labeled as 350 SL's. The 4520cc SOHC V-8 reached its peak net horsepower rating at 190. Even the much later (and short-lived, low production) 5549cc 560 SL of 1986-89 made only 227 net horsepower. By then the base weight had reached 3650 pounds. When you factor in the automatic transmissions and additional weight of these federalized cars, you will see why these later SL's have become anything but sports cars.

Figure D33 - Here is the big money shot: one of the few coupes that are worth as much or more today than the equivalent convertible. This car is metallic silver with red interior, a popular color for the model. ©Axion 23 (CC)

Figure D34 - This steel blue M-B 280 SL with tan interior and black top is an unusual example of the later bodied 280. The main point of its inclusion here is to show the newer top design with rear quarter windows in place of wide blind spots. The unusual part is that this car has U.S. safety bumpers, European alloy wheels, and no side marker lamps. It has U.S. plates and the car was spotted in East Hampton, New York. I smell a gray market car, popular here in the early days of federal regulations. ©Vetatur Fumare (CC)

Mercedes-Benz SL Roadster Production Chart

Model	Years	Production		Model	Years	Production
190 SL	1955	1727	830	230 SL	1963	1465
190 SL	1956	4032	1849	230 SL	1964	6911
190 SL	1957	3332	1806	230 SL	1965	6325
190 SL	1958	2722	628	230 SL	1966	4945
190 SL	1959	3949	1650	230 SL	1967	185
190 SL	1960	3977	1264			
190 SL	1961	3792	1509	230 SL	1963 - 67	19,831
190 SL	1962	2246	772			
190 SL	1963	104	54			
				250 SL	1967 - 68	5196
190 SL USA	1955 - 63	10,362				
All 190 SL	1955 - 63	25,881				
				280 SL	1967	143
300 SL	1957	554		280 SL	1968	6930
300 SL	1958	324		280 SL	1969	8047
300 SL	1959	211		280 SL	1970	7935
300 SL	1960	249		280 SL	1971	830
300 SL	1961	250				
300 SL	1962	244		280 SL	1968 - 71	23,885
300 SL	1963	26				
				230/250/280	1963 - 71	48,912
300 SL	1957 - 63	1858		All SL	1955 - 71	76,651

Mercedes SL Production Chart Notes:

Some of the production figures in this chart were referenced from *Deutsche Autos 1945-90, Bd. 3*, by Werner Oswald, 2001, via *Wikipedia*. The left column of the 190 SL production represents worldwide production; the right column represents U. S. sales. The U.S. sales figures for the 190 SL were sourced from the work of Bruce L. Adams, the USA's foremost authority on these models. There is a six-unit discrepancy in Mr. Adams' totals: either the 10,362 figure is too low or the 25,881 is too high by six cars. U.S. sales of the six-cylinder 230, 250, and 280 SL models in 1963-71 totaled 19,440. Exports to the U.S. included 4752 230SL's, 1761 250SL's, and 12,927 280SL models. The 250 SL was produced for less than fourteen months.

Selected German Sports Car Ratings Chart

Years	Model	Collect	Drive	Desire
1958 - 1974	Karmann-Ghia Cabriolet	D	B	D
1950 - 1965	Porsche 356	B	B	C
1955 - 1959	Porsche Speedster	A	C	B
1967 - 1969	Porsche 912 Targa	B	B	B
1967 - 1975	Porsche 911 Targa	B	B	B
1970 - 1976	Porsche 914	D	B	D
1970 - 1972	Porsche 914/6	B	C	C
1957 - 1963	Mercedes-Benz 300 SL	A	D	A
1959 - 1962	Mercedes- Benz 190 SL	B	C	B
1963 - 1966	Mercedes- Benz 230 SL	B	C	B
1967	Mercedes- Benz 250 SL	B	C	B
1968 - 1971	Mercedes- Benz 280 SL	B	B	B

Models Ratings Chart Definitions:

Years: In most cases, the years listed include the total production years for a particular model series. Some model years within a series may be considerably more desirable than other years.

Models: In some cases many variations are included in this category and in others the models included are very homogeneous. This is generally self explanatory.

Collectibility: This is what most of you want to know, the bottom line on how likely the model or series is likely to climb in value over the coming years.

Drivability: This is an indicator of how adaptable the machine can be to drive for transportation or pleasure in the modern world, considering collector value, parts availability, fuel quality, comfort, performance and miscellaneous other factors.

Desirability: This defines the nostalgic, emotional wow factor, without regard for collector values or everyday usage.

General: No machine is given a failing grade. If it made it into a rating chart, at least a few hobbyists find that model interesting.

Figure D35 - Here is a final look at an elegantly restored 190 SL in brown with a light tan interior and top. The conventional snap-on vinyl boot and unconventional white plastic steering wheel are clearly visible. ©Rudolf Stricker (PD)

German Engineering Comes to America

Chapter 5: *Affordable Italian Brio from Fiat & Alfa Romeo*

Figure E1 - This elegant interior with wood steering wheel and dash belongs to one of the lowest priced cars covered in this book, the Fiat 850 Spider. This red example has the requisite black vinyl interior. The wood dash covering is actually cost-effective vinyl, but it looks good nonetheless. The flat shape of the black plastic shift knob is correct. I am not sure about the wooden steering wheel with polished spokes, however. This may be an aftermarket wheel of genuine wood. This is the only shot I have seen of an 850 Spider wood steering wheel with polished spokes. The black rubber floor covering dates this as a 1967-69 model. An unusual feature of the 850 Spider is the glove box. Note that a grab bar is attached to the door and the lock is set near the bottom center. The trick is that the vinyl wood panel you see is not actually a door. When you push the lock button, a plastic tray drops down from underneath. ©Alexxsandro (CC)

The English may have tried to corner the affordable convertible sports car market in the U.S., but a pair of Italian brands produced models for our market, too. The cars from the island nation may have dominated by sheer numbers, but Fiat and Alfa Romeo outflanked the British in the areas of modern style and engineering development. The spearhead of this concept was the superior convertible top designs created by the Italians. They were also with the program on synchromesh transmissions, overhead cam engines, and roll-up windows. The icing on these tasty cakes was styled by Bertone and Pininfarina, and many models were even constructed by these legends.

Fiat Cabriolets

Figure E2 - This black Fiat 1500S Spider has always been a rarity in the U.S. Although sold here prior to the release of its descendant the 124 Sport Spider, numbers imported were always limited. This example is a European model with left hand drive. ©Berthold Werner (GNU)

Like the many English companies exporting small sports cars to America in the '50's and early '60's, Fiat started small and slowly expanded their Yankee operations. Fiat was close to a decade behind the English and Germans in the quest to establish a fruitful beachhead in the expansive U.S. market. The company's earliest attempts at producing a small, cost-effective sports car flopped. It would be 1960 before the diminutive 1.2-liter 1200 Cabriolet landed on our shores. The minimal dealer network did not begin to expand significantly until the introduction of the 850 Spider in 1967. Many would say, and you know I agree, that the late '60's were the really special time for the little convertible sports cars of both English and Italian ancestry.

Fiat introduced its 1200 Cabriolet in Italy in 1959. The body designed by Pininfarina for the Cabriolet was pleasant rather than stunning. Some might call it a smaller version of the Ferrari 250 Cabriolet and they would not be wrong. This parallel was the direct ancestor of the later Ferrari 275 GTS and the Fiat 124 Spider. The link between the earlier models may not be obvious simply because so few Americans have ever seen either brand's entry into the U.S. market. These were the first two mass produced touring cabriolets by their respective Italian parents. Within three years, the 1200's tiny engine would be increased to 1.5 liters and Fiat began to become recognized in the USA. Fiat sent the 1500 and its later 1600 variant to the U.S. in 1962-66 in relatively small numbers and these are still rare today, although not particularly interesting or collectible. It is uncertain how many 1200, 1500, and 1600 Cabriolets were sent to the USA. *The Complete Book of Collectible Cars 1940-1980* states that approximately 43,000 of these models were built, but I would be surprised if more than twenty percent of those came here. Less than ten percent might be more accurate.

Included in that 43,000 production were a few very special 1500S and 1600S models. These were DOHC hotrod variants produced alongside their more common cousins. The back story is that The Maserati Brothers were running a sort of Carroll Shelby style operation known as O.S.C.A. The English translation would be Official Special Construction Automobiles for this builder of race cars and special sports models for the street. The OSCA 1.5 and 1.6 liter powerplants were not the same as the equivalent Fiat OHV engines, even though all the cars were built by Pininfarina. These special engines were designed originally by OSCA, not Fiat. As noted in the chart below, the exact displacement of the Fiat OHV 1600 is not known. I would venture a guess that few of the Fiat 1600 models were exported to America. *Car and Driver* tested the 1500 OHV model as late as December 1966. By that time, the 850 Spider was already in production for the Italian market. *Car and Driver* had one word for the top design: *perfect*. The testers also liked the ergonomics and high comfort level. Complaints included the small displacement engine, brakes that locked unevenly, and a recalcitrant five-speed shift design. The OSCA models are of course somewhat more collectible today than are the basic versions. Although the bodies were generally identical with the base models, the S versions can be identified by their high-performance DOHC engines and four-wheel disc brakes.

Fiat Cabriolet Chart

1200	*1500*	*O.S.C.A. 1500S*	*1600*	*O.S.C.A. 1600S*
1959 - 1963	1963 - 1966	1959 - 1963	1962 - 1966	1963 - 1966
1221cc OHV	1481cc OHV	1491cc DOHC	OHV 1.6-liter	1568cc DOHC
53 hp	83 hp	90 hp	NA	100 hp
Hood Scoop	No Hood Scoop	Hood Scoop	No Hood Scoop	No Hood Scoop
92 inches	92 inches	92 inches	92 inches	92 inches
1995 lb.	2103 lb.	2000 lbs.	2315 lb.	2194 lb.
Drum / Drum	Disc / Drum	Disc / Disc	Disc / Drum	Disc / Disc
$2595	$2639	NA	NA	$2830

Fiat Cabriolet Chart Notes:
The 1964-66 1600S can be identified by its quad headlights and lack of a hood scoop. The 1500 tested by *Car and Driver* in 1966 had a smooth hood and a single headlight on each side. The 1500 Cabriolet received a five-speed transmission in 1965. *Road Test* gave high marks for the modern comfort and convenience features of the 1966 Spider 1500 with its 83-hp engine and five-speed for $2585. *Car and Driver* praised the same features, but said the shifter was a bit ornery. The hood scoop notations are not precisely correct. Early models had a wide, functional scoop and later cars had a flat hood. However, I have seen at least one photo with a smaller scoop on a later model. It is unknown if the smaller scoop was functional and how many cars or models had it.

Affordable Italian Brio

In their usual format, Fiat produced many thousands of sedans in house for the European and other markets. In a manner reflecting a similar pattern among European motorcycle manufacturers, only the top-of-the-line sportiest models were very successful in the USA. Americans have always considered small affordable sports cars as either recreational toys or transportation for youngsters of college or high school age. These sportier models were generally assembled by the more exotic Italian carrozzeria, more often than not Bertone or Pininfarina. This pattern held true from the beginning of the '60's, through the '70's, and into the '80's with the X1/9 and Spider 2000, the last Fiat sports cars sent to the U.S.

Fiat 850 Spider

Figure E3 - 1968 Fiat 850 Spider in Red. You can identify the year by the lack of headlight lens covers and headrests. ©Lothar Spurzem (CC)

My 1968 Fiat 850 Spider had to have a partial engine rebuild after it was hardly past two years old. I don't know the exact date or mileage on the car at the time because I had been financially forced to sell the car before this calamity happened. With the maturity and experience of age, I now understand why it happened. I ran the stink out of that helpless little fifty-cubic-inch engine. Most owners of the day sent the tach needle flying with every launch from a stoplight, but that was because you had to somehow keep up with traffic, and it made you feel like a race car driver to boot. But I did more than that with my little 850. The model had an unusual feature:

a hand throttle that could be treated like a crude cruise control. Back in those good old days, freeway speed limits were 70-75, but you had to top about 85 mph out in the open before anyone seemed to care! This was long before radar guns became common as revenue collectors in a world of way too low speed limits. The official top speed of an 850 Spider was about 85-90 depending on which source you believed. Let's just say that mine often registered about 90, which most likely indicated an actual 85. As a naive twenty-year-old, I obviously thought my 850 Spider was a VW Beetle, a little rear-engine car that could cruise all day at or near its top speed. It was white with black top and interior and cute as a bug (no pun intended). One of my friends called it a frog due to its uncovered 1968 headlights. It was my first sports car and my first new car and I loved it to death (obviously literally). I wish I had one now in perfectly new condition, waiting for a retiree to drive it with a little more mature passion.

Figure E4 - Bright yellow 850 Spider with its top up. ©Robotriot (GNU)

The first 850 Spiders came to the U.S. as 1967 models, the only year imported with 843cc engines and glass-covered headlights. The 1968 model lost the covered headlights for good and the head was shaved for an 817cc engine with slightly higher compression. Depending upon the source, the horsepower rating was generally 54 horsepower for the 843cc engine of 1967 and 52-hp for the 1968 817cc model. The headlights were required to meet new U.S. regulations that took effect January 1, 1968, and emission restrictions from the EPA took effect on the same date. The high-compression head reduced the engine displacement to just below a fifty-cubic-inch cutoff point for the emission equipment. This concept was tossed away by Fiat for the 1969 model year when the engine displacement was increased to 903cc with the proper emission equipment. The 1969 model also received distinguishing headrests in the form of taller seatbacks. While the seats and headlamps continued along with the 903cc engine through 1973, the 850 Spider's final production year, the horsepower most likely slowly decayed each year as the emission rules tightened. Most sources claim the 1967 model is the most collectible due to its unfettered 843cc engine and sleek covered headlights. Personally I prefer the uncovered lights for both exterior appearance and better night vision. My favorite year would be the 1970 with the highest horsepower rating of all and the headrests. As stated above, depending upon the source, the 1970 903cc produced as much as 58 gross horsepower. According to *R&T*, the U.S. model did not get the larger engine until the 1970 model year due to bugs in the emission control equipment. The 1972 model had a 9.5:1 compression ratio, lowered to 8.5:1 in 1973. The 1970 model weighed 1555 pounds.

The color patterns offered for the bodies of the 850 Spider have been elusive. Paint colors were acrylic enamel solid colors, never metallic. A red, medium blue, pale blue, white, a sort of taxi cab golden yellow, British Racing Green, lime green, bright green, and bright yellow were probably the most common colors. Black has been listed as an exterior color in some sources, but I have never seen one. Official 1970 colors were: French Blue, Racing Red, Canguro Orange, Positano Yellow, and Veridian Green. All of the early years and most of the later models had black tops and interiors. A few of the later colors such as BRG and bright green were available with tan interiors, but as far as I know, all the tops were still black. Bright green was available with black or tan interior in 1972-73.

Figure E5 - Fiat 850 Sport Spider in Red. ©Tvabutzku1234 (PD)

The shift knob of the 1968 model was black plastic in a tall, oblong shape. This changed to a round shape in 1970. The 1967-71 models had a walnut-grained contact-paper type dash covering and the 1972-73 models had brushed aluminum panels. The steering wheel had two brushed aluminum spokes with four drilled holes in each spoke in 1967-69. These were changed to flat-black painted spokes in 1970. The rims were black plastic in 1967-68 and wood, simulated wood or black leather in the later models. The 1971 model continued the wood-rimmed steering wheel with two black spokes from 1970. The 1972-73 models had a black leather rim with black spokes. According to an early *R&T* test, there were no sun visors on the 1967 model, but the '68 got padded ones as standard. Full interior carpeting was added in 1970. A minimal plastic console was probably added in 1970 with the carpet, but it might have appeared earlier in 1969. The Racer model with its fixed roof got the console, a black vinyl dash panel, and a real wood steering wheel with black spokes in 1970. The 1972-73 models also had a console, in tan if the car had a tan interior, but the carpet was still black.

On the exterior, the 1968 model also received rear bumper guards and a backup light. Three wheel types were available: the standard silver painted disc wheels, Rader Chapparal-style diamond spoke type with bright finish for $195, and four-spoke mags in a natural light bronze finish. The 1972-73 models were distinguished by a chrome upper rail connecting the bumper guards at both the front and rear to meet the new for '73 five-mph bumper standard. One source states that the 1971 model had the 1972-73 bumpers, cost $2294 new, and weighed 1590 pounds. According to Wikipedia, the Sport Spider name arrived in 1970 with the 903cc engine. The question is still how did the little front bumper rail in 1973 meet the NHTSA regulation?

The Austin-Healey Sprite and MG Midget had finally received a properly attached convertible top for the 1967 model year when the Fiat 850 Spider was introduced to the USA. The Sprite and Midget had the advantage of a front engine about 1.5 times the displacement of the 843cc Spider and the directly attached shifter was famous for its short snick-snick action. Everything else was clearly in the Fiat's favor. The little Spider that actually undercut the retail price of the Sprite was loaded with modern features. These included: a body by Bertone, independent rear suspension, a fully synchronized four-speed, aluminum head, progressive Weber two-barrel, headers, an efficient heater, reliable electrics, a top that neither leaked in the rain nor flapped in the breeze, and a lift-up/snap down top panel like those on the Sting Ray Convertible and the Mercedes SL. Convenience details included a clean, vinyl padded and lighted luggage compartment with the battery and spare tire neatly covered. The rear engine was easily accessed for routine maintenance and there was a convenience lamp in the engine compartment, too. The floor covering was black rubber mat. That may sound drab, but if the 850 was ever caught in a rainstorm, there was no carpet to rot or stink. My memory is vague on this point, but I believe there were even a couple of easily accessed water drain holes under the driver and passenger side mats.

Affordable Italian Brio

Figure E6 - This photo of my own white 1968 850 Spider was taken by an amateurish photographer with a Kodak Instamatic in a shady area. This print was made from a scanned slide. ©1968 Floyd M. Orr Collection

With that progressive two-barrel Weber, you could not *make* the little beastie get less than 30 mpg, no matter how hard you wound it out all over town. It would easily cruise at 80 mph on the freeway, but unfortunately that particular ability may have been the downfall of its engine longevity. Cornering on rails was something it could do all day long. The suspension was just stiff enough to allow very sticky road holding and the steering was delightfully light with nothing up front but the battery and spare tire. In case you are wondering about the rear weight imbalance, I never found it to be any sort of problem at all. The rear-mounted, water-cooled engine in the 850 is small, light, and has minimal torque. The one and only time I ever managed to break the rear end loose on a curve was one late night blasting through a curvaceous inner-city freeway route. The rear stepped out in a high-speed, four-wheel drift that was easily controllable. The slide was quite reasonable, considering that I was going about 70 mph in an area posted at 30!

The 850 Spider had its weak points in the longevity department. These did not include its appearance, which to this day ranks as one of the most stylish small, cheap, topless sports cars of all time. The weakest link, of course, was the tiny engine that had to be revved to the max practically all the time. Mine needed a valve job after only about two years. The cheap little thirteen-inch tires wore out quickly and I replaced them with wider ones. I cannot remember if that was before or after my famous slide, but to be honest, I think it was after. The vinyl covering on the driver's seat cushion began to split at one seam after less than two years. No, I am not some sort of lardbutt. I weighed about 120 pounds soaking wet in 1968! Unfortunately, that is no longer the case. *Road & Track*'s reports on the 850 Spider mention several foibles I never experienced with mine. These included the electrical system, instruments, starting problems, carburetor issues, oil leaks, cooling problems, brake problems, water leaks into the interior, shift linkage difficulty, and a problem with the clutch. The upholstery could have been tougher and the original tires of longer lasting quality, but the engine wear was at least partially the result of my own naiveté. These were the good old days before 55-mph and radar guns and I drove my little 850 as if it had been born in St. Louis with an engine constructed in Tonawanda, New York! Of course this describes my next sports car, one I would not purchase until 1980, a car that had actually been produced while I still owned my Spider. It was built in 1970 with *Stingray* script on its fender and its engine relentlessly loafed along, no matter how high the speedometer registered.

Figure E7 - **This little red car is not your ordinary 850 Spider. This is a Fiat-Abarth 1000 Spider. Its engine has been enlarged and tuned to within an inch of its life by the legendary aftermarket Fiat tuner, Carlo Abarth. Like Shelby Mustangs, the Fiat-Abarth hotrods had a lot more than just an Abarth exhaust system added. Unlike the Shelby Mustangs, though, the 1000 Spider was and still is extremely rare in the USA. I happened to have been in the right place at the right time at a dealership in Memphis in 1967 to ask my best friend and little sister to pose in this rare little beastie. If I recall, the sticker on this new car was about $3500 or a bit more, about one and a half times the cost of a regular 850 Spider.** ©1967 Floyd M. Orr Collection

Fiat 850 Spider Chart

Model	Engine	Dash	Steering Wheel	Floor	Bumpers
1967	843cc	Woodgrain	Plastic / Brushed Spokes	Rubber	Single Line
1968	817cc	Woodgrain	Plastic / Brushed Spokes	Rubber	Two Guards
1969	817cc	Woodgrain	Wood / Brushed Spokes	Rubber	Two Guards
1970	903cc	Woodgrain	Wood / Black Spokes	Carpet	Two Guards
1971	903cc	Woodgrain	Wood / Black Spokes	Carpet	Two Guards
1972	903cc	Brushed	Leather / Black Spokes	Carpet	Twin w/Rail
1973	903cc	Brushed	Leather / Black Spokes	Carpet	Twin w/Rail

Fiat 850 Spider Chart Notes:
The total production figure quoted in *Italian Sports Cars* for the 850 Spider is 124,660, approximately 90% of which were sent to the USA. The Fiat-Abarth OT-1000 Spider was built with a highly modified 1000cc engine in 1967-69. It is not known exactly how many of these were produced. According to the brochures, some 1969 steering wheels may have had black spokes.

Fiat 124 Sport Spider

Figure E8 - This pretty blue Fiat 124 Spider is a typical example of the early models. As you can tell from the combination of headrests and delicate chrome bumpers, this one falls somewhere in the 1969-72 range. This

example has standard wheels and an optional chrome luggage rack. Note the neatness of the vinyl top boot, too. ©Pujanak (PD)

The most likely Italian Spider that you have had a close encounter with was a Fiat 124 Spider. There were at least 130,000 produced and most of these came to America in the 1968-1985 period. Aside from its far lower production predecessors and its rear-engine go-kart little brother, the 124 Spider became *the* ubiquitous affordable Italian Spider for most American sports car enthusiasts. Many of these guys discount the 850 as not having enough horsepower to even be called a proper sports car. Many others have never even seen any of the 124's ancestors on our shores. Of course some of these were imported, but it was the 124 and 850 Spiders that really opened the U.S. market for Fiats. While many considered the 850 to be an around-town scootabout for girls, the 124 Spider was clearly a full-blown sports car. The DOHC front engine, five-speed transmission, and four-wheel disc brakes placed it a full stage above the 850. At one-and-a-half times the price, so did its retail cost from the time of its introduction to the USA one year after the 850 Spider. Probably due to the better longevity of the 124, creating far more usable examples still available today, the current prices of the two Fiat Spiders are not far apart, although the 124 will still cost you more, particularly for the later models.

Let's cover the foibles of the 124 right now while the issues of the previously described 850 are fresh in your mind. According to *Road & Track*, some of the 1968 124 Spiders developed premature valve failures, just like their little OHV brothers. The problem was apparently solved with the '69 models. Since I have not had sufficient contact with any later 850 Spiders, I cannot say if the problem was exactly the same and solved concurrently with the larger engine or not, but I suspect it was. The 124 also had problems with weak upholstery seams, instruments, electrical system, tire wear, and the clutch. The 124 added disc brake squeal to its list of annoyances, but of course noisy brakes never stranded anyone in the middle of the night. If you want to test fate, buy an English roadster.

Of course this is the point at which the story comes together. The 124 Spider was not only the pipsqueak 850's *real sports car* big brother; it was the MG B's nemesis. The 124 brought affordable comfort, convenience, and reliability to the sports car masses of America. There were several of British origin that attempted to do the same thing, the ringleader of this gang being the Sunbeam Alpine. It was the only convertible within the 124's price range that tried to offer comfort to the masses. The other Brits were higher priced. The Datsun Sports brought even more Japanese reliability to the table, but their styling and handling were not up to even the level of the MG B. As covered in a later chapter, the USA produced its Corvair and Germany brought us a few affordable models. The problem was that the Corvair was hardly a sports car and the Karmann-Ghia barely was one. The Porsche 914 gave it a good try, but at a price considerably above that of a 124 Spider. Only the 124 brought Italian styling, handling, and overall panache to the affordable sports car field. What better cake icing could you wish for than a car that looked very similar to a Ferrari 275 GTS because it was styled and built by the same people?

The 124 Spider is that *invisible* sports car that does not come readily to mind in a fantasy, but it is the one you or I might actually purchase. It was and is considerably cheaper to buy and maintain than an Alfa, and it does not punish the driver with a simian driving position. For most Americans, this last point is much more significant than it may seem. The driver of the Fiat 124 Spider enjoys all the comforts offered by many much larger and more expensive sports cars. A real wood steering wheel sits in front of a real wood dash full of an excellent array of white-on-black gauges set within flat black surrounds. The seats are just plush enough to be really comfortable while still being supportive enough for fast cornering. There is adequate space for an adult passenger to sit sideways on the contoured, upholstered bench behind the front bucket seats. All the controls are quite light. The steering doesn't have or need a power steering pump. None of the pedals are too stiff or have travel that is excessive. Of course the convertible top is a model of simplicity and snug fit, although unlike the 124's little brother, you do have to snap down a conventional vinyl boot to get the neat top-down look.

The twin cam four of the 124 Sport Spider was designed by Aurelio Lampredi, who had earlier created a V-12 engine for Ferrari. The original engine was a 1438cc producing 96 horsepower. Sold only in Europe in 1967, this model reached our shores for the 1968 model year. The original design had an 80mm bore with a 71mm stroke. The latter was increased to 80mm also for the '71 model, bringing the displacement up to 1608cc and the horsepower up to 104. In 1973 the stroke was reduced slightly to produce 1592cc. The displacement was increased to 1756cc in 1974 and finally to 1995cc in 1979. All models had Weber carbs until fuel injection was instituted in 1980. The injection was Bosch L-Jetronic, rated at 102 horsepower for the U.S. models. In all states except California, the carbureted and injected models were sold in 1980. From 1981-onward, only injected models were sent to the USA. Seven-hundred turbocharged models were sold in the U.S. in 1980-81. Practically all the Sport Spiders sold in the U.S. had five-speed manual transmissions. The GM three-speed Turbo-Hydramatic was optional in 1979-85, but thankfully, due to the minimal torque of the high-revving DOHC two-liter four, this was not a popular choice for proper sports car buyers.

Figure E9 - This bright red 124 Sport Spider is showing off its smooth top and fancy wheels. ©Bidinson (CC)

Fiat Spider Production Chart

Model	Years	Production	Model	Years	Production
1200 Spider	1959 - 1963	11,851	124 Spider	1967	5618
1500 Spider	1960 - 1966	20,420	124 Spider	1968	4935
1600S Spider	1960 - 1966	2275	124 Spider	1969	11,307
			124 Spider	1970	12,089
1200/1500/1600S	1959 - 1966	34,546			
			124 Spider	1970	14,288
850 Spider	1966 - 1973	124,660	124 Spider	1971	13,412
			124 Spider	1972	12,362
Dino 2000 Spider	1965 - 1969	1163	124 Spider	1973	12,783
Dino 2400 Spider	1969 - 1973	420	124 Spider	1974	15,754
			124 Spider	1975	14,143
Dino Spider	1965 - 1973	1583	124 Spider	1976	11,862
			124 Spider	1977	14,012
124 US 1438cc	1968 - 1970	20,246	124 Spider	1978	16,105
124 US 1608cc	1971 - 1972	21,222	124 Spider	1979	18,943
124 US 1592cc	1973	8728	124 Spider	1980	14,435
124 US 1756cc	1974 - 1978	68,430	124 Spider	1981	4747
124 US 1995cc	1979	16,926	124 Spider	1982	3456
124 US 1995cc	1980 - 1982	31,358	124 Spider	1983	2480
124 US Turbo	1980 - 1981	700	124 Spider	1984	2577
124 US 1995cc	1982 - 1985	3110	124 Spider	1985	1504
124 Spider US	1968 - 1985	170,720	Pininfarina	1970-85	172,863

Fiat Spider Production Chart Notes:

Figures in the first column were sourced from the *Italian Sports Cars*. The production years for the pre-124 models are quoted from the same source. Some sources refer to these early models as Spiders and others as Cabriolets. Considering the Ferrari 250 GT connection with these cars, Cabriolet is more likely the correct title. Figures in the second column for 1970-85 were sourced from Pininfarina production records. The second group probably represents calendar year, not model year, production. Note that the repeated 1970 figures do not match. The four 1967-70 figures at the top of the last column are of unknown origin and unsubstantiated. The figures in the left column for U.S. exports of the 124 Spider were sourced from the Spider Web site in Great Britain. *Wikipedia* states that about 75% of 124 Sport Spider production was exported to the USA. The Spider Web total represents about 86% of worldwide production. The book *Essential Fiat 124 Spider and Coupe* by Martin Buckley states that 209,346 124 Spiders were produced in 1966-85.

Alfa Romeo Spiders

Figure E10 - This delicate little red 1300cc Alfa Romeo Giulietta Spider has always been something of a rarity in the U.S. ©Marvin Raaijmakers (CC)

Alfa Romeo has a racing history that began long before the development of the models discussed in this book. As with a few other cars included in *Daydreams in the Wind*, the actual history of the Alfalfa Spiders began about 1955, but continued into the Nineties. May I call you *Alfalfa*, as a term of endearment, I mean? Sometimes I just cannot resist it. There are three perspectives we might have taken on this particular Alfalfa story: the deep racing history, the story that began in the USA when Benjamin Braddock got a Duetto Spider for graduation, or a somewhat comprehensive story of the Alfa Spider bloodline. We are choosing this third path, one that aligns the topless Alfalfas with the other cars in the book. This means we shall at least provide a bit of background on the delicate little 1300cc Giulietta Spider, its 1600cc Giulia Spider successor, the up-market, low-production 2000 Spider, its six-cylinder 2600 Spider successor, and of course what we Americans commonly know as the Alfa Spider of 1966-1994.

This story was particularly difficult to research. There seems to be a lot of confusion over precisely what quantity of what models were actually, officially imported into the USA and when. The production figures in the charts that follow required considerable number crunching to arrive at these figures. Unfortunately, I shall probably never know which ones are accurate and which are not. Statements of production by model year and by calendar year are sometimes quoted. As with all the other charts in this book, I have tried to present the data by model year as often as possible. The Alfa figures should be by model year, but I can never be certain, especially considering the many discrepancies I uncovered among various sources in my research. Where possible, I have noted specific quantities that were exported to the U.S., but you can assume that most of the quoted production figures include total production of that particular model for all markets. We're not done yet. There are two additional caveats to be kept in mind. First, we know that Alfa produced many smaller-engine companion models over the years, such as later versions of the 1300cc type, that were never officially exported to the USA. Some of these could be included in the figures stated. Secondly, there were of course companion coupes for most models that could also have been included within the quoted figures. Just bear in mind that Alfa has always resided in that no-car's-land between the massive Fiat corporation and the exclusive Ferrari organization. Alfa has likely been trapped between these two extremes of lots of facilities and personnel to keep extensive records and a tiny production facility that has always had countless worshipful journalists and fans keeping track of facts and figures for them.

Figure E11 - With its 1600cc four-cylinder, this red Giulia Spider represented a step up from the tiny engine of the Giulietta. ©Brian Snelson, Hockley, Essex, England (CC)

Alfa released its little Giulietta Spider in 1956. More than 17,000 were built through 1962. It is likely that only a small percentage of this sizable production made its way to the USA. How many? I do not have a clue. This first little Spider was powered by a 1.3-liter DOHC four-cylinder derived from the sedan with somewhat less power. This was an alloy block and heads producing about eighty gross horsepower propelling a lightweight aluminum body. A Veloce model was added later and 2796 of the 17,000 total had this higher performance engine. It is doubtful that many Giulietta Veloce Spiders made it to the USA. Although these models were produced in the period ending in 1962, prior to any complications presented by U.S. regulatory agencies, their reliability and longevity were little suited to American conditions. Their alloy bodies resisted rust better than comparable all-steel models, but their bodies were a bit fragile and replacement parts scarce. These small, high-strung drivelines were not noted for longevity, either. The Giulietta Spiders were noted for being the first of the touring spider series from Alfa. Their production period and numbers were quite significant, especially from a European standpoint, and they were designed and constructed by Pininfarina, just like their direct descendants.

From 1962 through 1965, Alfa produced an updated version of the Giulietta Spider with a 1.6-liter engine. This model was given the Giulia name, along with its coupe and sedan counterparts. The new model had a five-speed transmission instead of the Giulietta's four-speed. You could spot a Giulia Spider by its added hood bulge to cover the larger engine. Otherwise, the Guilia Spider was, and looked pretty much like, an updated Giulietta Spider. The Giulia's DOHC alloy four-cylinder displaced 1570cc and hence began the drivetrain bloodline Americans would later recognize as the Duetto. The Giulia Spider engine had dual Weber carbs and produced about 105 gross horsepower, about the same as its future body replacement, the Duetto. Approximately 9000 Giulia Spiders were built, plus another 1000 Veloce models, introduced in 1964. The 2116-pound Giulia had a claimed top speed of 107 mph. Its 0-60 time was 9.5 and its quarter-mile was 17.2. The Veloce had a little more horsepower and produced slightly higher performance. Although both the standard Giulia and the Veloce came to America in some small numbers, it is not known exactly how many or the exact state of tune of each type imported. There may have been a gap in time between the importation of the Giulia Spider and its replacement Duetto.

Figure E12 - The 2000 Touring Spider was Alfa's up-market convertible. Like the other Alfa models prior to the Duetto, sales of this one in the USA were minimal. ©CHK 46 (GNU)

Before we get to the Alfa Spiders we all know and love, the company's two larger touring models need at least a small mention. Alfa sold a little less than 3500 examples of a model the company called the Spider 2000 in 1958-62. These were designed as more expensive and luxurious entrants in the convertible marketplace, much like the Ferrari Cabriolet models. At least some of these did come to the USA, but it is unknown how many. These were designed and built by Touring instead of Pininfarina. The Spider 2000 was strictly a two-seater originally, but a 2+2 version was added in 1961. The 1975cc DOHC four-cylinder produced 131 gross horsepower through a five-speed transmission. Power drum brakes, solid axle rear, and a claimed top speed of 110 mph defined the Spider 2000. Unlike its sportier brothers, this model used twin Solex carburetors instead of Webers. The 2600-pound luxury convertible was no speed bunny with 0-60 in about eleven seconds and the quarter in eighteen. You can see by the production numbers that the luxury Alfa was not particularly popular and is probably quite rare in the U.S. Sources have stated that this model's success was mostly limited by its premium price at the time, as well as sufficient competition within its price bracket.

Figure E13 - This silver 1961 Touring Spider 2600 displays its taut black convertible top and bolt-on wire wheels. Note the hood scoop change from the 2000 Spider. ©Genossegerd (GNU)

Alfa updated the Spider 2000 with a six-cylinder model appropriately named the Spider 2600 in 1962. Alfa produced about 2200 of these DOHC Sixes with five-speeds and 2+2 seating. As with its predecessor, the sedans and coupes were of a different design and not built by Touring, as the Spiders were. The 2584cc engine produced 162 gross horsepower and the factory claimed a top speed of 124. The 2600 was considerably quicker than its four-cylinder ancestor with a 9.2 0-60 and the quarter-mile in 16.9. The engine was alloy, whereas the Spider 2000 Four had had a cast iron block. The 2600 also had triple Solex carburetors and weighed about 200 pounds more than its predecessor. The weight of the six-cylinder slowed down the handling of the big 2+2 Alfa. Most fans of the time much preferred the more nimble Giulia and Giulietta. The dated design, ponderous handling, and uncompetitive retail price kept the sales of the 2600 even lower than those of the 2000, in spite of its smooth six-cylinder engine. This fact left the Spider 2600 one of the truly rare Alfa Romeo convertibles in the U.S. today.

Figure E14 - The Duetto Spider has always been easily defined by its covered headlights in the front and its smooth boattail in the rear. This red example was photographed in its home country. ©E. Peiffer (GNU)

Now let's get down to the Al-FAL-fas, baby, the fun part, the cars everyone knows and loves, the 1600/1750/2000 Spiders that came to America from the time of *The Graduate* all the way up to 1994! First of all, let's get the timeline straight. Charles Webb first published the novel starring Benjamin Braddock and his new girlfriend, Elaine Robinson, in 1963. Being the nerd that I am, I was one of the relative few who read the book before I saw the movie, which had its official release in New York City only on December 22, 1967. Most every other American would learn Benjamin Braddock's name and see his hot little Italian job for the first time in 1968. Of course I knew that Ben was driving a 1967 Duetto Spider with its covered headlights. What I would not learn until much later was that no 1968 or 1970 Duettos had been imported into the U.S., although it was obvious at the time that for some reason the Duetto name had been dropped. As you can see in the chart, there were three model years of the Duetto

Spider built, but only 1967 models were fully imported into the USA. Any '66 models brought here are probably quite rare.

Let me be candid concerning my personal attitude toward the Alfa Romeo Spider. I would never buy one and I have never desired one. This is not a condemnation of the Spider, but a market comparison issue. I probably like the exterior appearance of all the Spider models as much as anyone. The original boat tail Duetto is probably my favorite, but I like the later ducktail models, too. I like the way the car drives. It definitely fills a specific, necessary niche in the market. The car magazines have always *loved* the Spider. It has won many of their comparison tests. The one and only reason I have never lusted after an Alfalfa Spider is that I like its competition within the relative price range a little more. The competing choices vary with the model year and timeframe. These begin with the Sting Ray and end with the Miata. In between, I favor the Stingray, Firebird, Mustang, 124 Spider, X1/9, and even the Porsche 914. I absolutely mean no disrespect to those who love their Alfas!

Figure E15 - This white 1969 shows off its smooth boattail. The alloy wheels and wood steering wheel may not be correct for this model. Although this example has California plates and was labeled as a 1969 model, note the lack of headrests on the red seats. This is probably a '67. If only we could see the headlights from this angle.... ©Pat Durkin, Tustin, CA (CC)

The first impression I had when driving a Duetto was of its famous arms out with knees bent driving position. Although I am only 5'10", I am exceptionally long-legged. This should be your first big clue why the Spider loses my lust to those competitors mentioned above. The second thing I noticed was the stark dash and interior layout with rubber mats and the shift lever poking out from underneath the dash. The last item I wish to discuss is probably the most distinctive of the Alfa Spider. At least this is what caught my attention and held it. The slightly undersquare

DOHC four-cylinder was a torquey little engine! It reminded me not of a Fiat 124 Spider, but of a mid-Seventies Toyota Celica. Coincidentally I would have opportunities to drive a couple of Celicas back in those days, so I guess you could say the Celica drove like the Spider, not the reverse. Since I have been a fan of Toyota Corollas and Fiat Spiders for a long time, it is obvious that I enjoy their screaming little engines that race up the tachometer with every shift. The Celica and Alfa Spider operate from an alternative philosophy, one that splits the difference between a Fiat and an American V-8. Of course the Duetto runs circles around the larger, heavier models in twisty, top-down driving, but it does not rapidly wear out its engine like a Fiat Spider, either.

Figure E16 - Here is the familiar Series 2 Alfa Romeo Spider with its larger engine, uncovered headlights, alloy wheels and Kamm tail. This example is what is probably the most common color for the Spider, red with black interior and top. ©Rudolf Stricker (CC)

Some people find the boat tail Duetto to be more attractive than the later ducktail model. I agree with that assessment, but only to a small degree. However, the rarity of the original design will always keep its price at least a little above that of the long-production later one. The Graduate model was produced for the U.S. market in 1985-90. Like the original Porsche Speedster, the Graduate model was actually a "stripper" version introduced to make the Spider more affordable. This was, of course, after the inclusion of luxury conveniences and general inflation had increased the retail price of the stock Spider considerably above the $3950 of the original Duetto. As has often been the case with other brands, the U.S. models had featured increasingly more standard equipment as the '70's and '80's progressed. The base price had more than doubled to $8895 by 1977. When a current prospective buyer is considering an Alfa Spider, he has three displacements to choose from, at least once he decides the later body trim is acceptable. Looking at the chart, you can see three distinct induction choices: Weber carburetors in the Duetto, SPICA mechanical fuel injection on either the 1779cc or 1962cc engines, or Bosch electronic fuel injection on the 1962cc.

The top design of the Alfa Spider is probably the direct equivalent of that of the Fiat 124 Spider. Magazine testers of the day praised both cars equally for the efficiency and effectiveness of their convertible tops.

Alfa Romeo Spider Chart

Year	Model	Engine	Induction	Details	Production
1966	Duetto	1570cc	2 Weber 2-bbl.	Boat Tail	NA *
1967	Duetto	1570cc	2 Weber 2-bbl.	6325 *	6325 *
1968	Duetto	1570cc	2 Weber 2-bbl.	Boat Tail	NA *
1969	Spider Veloce	1779cc	SPICA	Kamm Tail	NA
1970	Spider Veloce	1779cc	SPICA	Kamm Tail	2539
1971	Spider Veloce	1779cc	SPICA	Kamm Tail	3735
1972	Spider Veloce	1962cc	SPICA	Kamm Tail	4121
1973	Spider Veloce	1962cc	SPICA	Kamm Tail	4848
1974	Spider Veloce	1962cc	SPICA	Kamm Tail	5107
1975	Spider Veloce	1962cc	SPICA	Kamm Tail	5189
1976	Spider Veloce	1962cc	SPICA	Kamm Tail	4338
1977	Spider Veloce	1962cc	SPICA	3814	4183
1978	Spider Veloce	1962cc	SPICA	3918	3868
1979	Spider Veloce	1962cc	SPICA	Kamm Tail	4129
1980	Spider Veloce	1962cc	SPICA	Kamm Tail	5584
1981	Spider Veloce	1962cc	SPICA	1436	1653
1982	Spider Veloce	1962cc	Bosch Electronic	2274	1923
1983	Spider Veloce	1962cc	Bosch Electronic	5430	5365
1984	Spider Veloce	1962cc	Bosch Electronic	6177	6587
1985	Spider Veloce	1962cc	Bosch Electronic	5939	5590
1986	Spider Veloce	1962cc	Bosch Electronic	7015	7215
1987	Spider Veloce	1962cc	Bosch Electronic	4647	4339
1988	Spider Veloce	1962cc	Bosch Electronic	4171	4090
1989	Spider Veloce	1962cc	Bosch Electronic	3995	3950
1990	Spider Veloce	1962cc	Bosch Electronic	7106	7106
1991	Spider Veloce	1962cc	Bosch Electronic	8994	9073
1992	Spider Veloce	1962cc	Bosch Electronic	3564	3640
1993	Spider Veloce	1962cc	Bosch Electronic	1923	1956
			Total	1966 - 1993	116,453

Alfa Romeo Spider Chart Notes:
The numbers in this chart were sourced from Pininfarina's build records. These include 20,436 smaller engine models produced only for European markets during various periods. The engine specifications listed apply only to the U.S. models. It has not been confirmed if any Duettos were sent to the USA in 1966. A total of 6325(*) Duettos were manufactured; it is unknown exactly how many were sent to the USA, but we do know that no 1968 or 1970 models were imported. The 1993 build total from Pininfarina includes 190 cars sold as 1994 models in the U.S.

Slightly different production figures for some model years are listed in the *Details* column. These were sourced from the CarsfromItaly.net website. These numbers total 62,671. The same site lists approximate build figures of 8723 1750 Spiders, and 88,240 2000 Spiders.

The SPICA fuel injection was a mechanical type; the later Bosch system was electronic and much more complex, although more reliable. Carpeting and interior colors other than black were made standard in 1978.

Alfa Romeo Spider Series Production Chart

Model	Years	Engine	HP	Production
Alfa Romeo Giulietta Spider	1955-62	1290cc	65	14,300
Alfa Romeo Giulietta Veloce	1956-62	1290cc	80	2796
Alfa Romeo 2000 Spider	1958-62	1975cc	115	3459
Alfa Romeo 2600 Spider	1962-65	2584cc	145	2257
Alfa Romeo Giulia Spider	1962-65	1570cc	90	9256
Giulietta / Giulia / 2000 / 2600	1955 - 1965	All	All	33,160
1600 Duetto Spider (Boat Tail)	1966 - 1967	1570cc	109	6325
1750 Spider Veloce Series 1 (US)	1969	1779cc	118	2215
1750 Veloce Series 1 (Boat Tail)	1968 - 1969	1779cc	118	4674
1750 Veloce Series 2 (Kamm Tail)	1970 - 1972	1779cc	118	4027
2000 Spider Veloce Series 2 (US)	1971 - 1982	1962cc	132	22,059
2000 Spider Veloce Series 3 (US)	1982 - 1989	1962cc	128	19,040
2000 Series 3 Quadrifoglio Verde	1986 - 1989	1962cc	128	2598
2000 Spider Graduate (US)	1985 - 1990	1962cc	128	NA
2000 Spider Veloce Series 4	1990 - 1993	1962cc	126	18,456
2000 Spider Veloce	1971 - 1993	1962cc	132	98,463
2000 Spider Veloce (*Wikipedia*)	1971 - 1993	1962cc	126	88,643

Alfa Romeo Spider Series Production Chart Notes:

With the exception of the DOHC inline six-cylinder of the short-lived 2600 Spider, all engines were DOHC four-cylinders, mostly constructed of aluminum alloy. Alfa began offering the 1570cc option in 1962 and referred to dual-carb models of either displacement as Veloces. The Giulia Spider was a 1.6-liter version of the earlier, 1.3-liter Giulietta Spider. The Spider 2000 was a two-seater designed and built by Touring. Its 2600 successor had 2+2 seating. The Alfa 2600 Spider has front quarter windows that may or may not open as vent windows. The previous 2000 model has only side windows. Touring designed and built the bodies of the 2600 model. All the 1955-65 pre-Duetto numbers represent totals for all markets. The 1969-71 (4674) and 1971-93 (98,463) production numbers are from the Appendix of *Italian Sports Cars*. Note that 4674 is listed in the chart as including 1968-69 Boat Tails only. The production for 1969 Boat Tails for the U.S. was stated by the Duetto Register website. Any variance in these listed numbers from other sources is minimal, although in many cases the stated figures are not identical. The onset of 1968 U.S. regulations and the lack of specific bookkeeping made accurate production numbers for the 1967-71 period, particularly for U.S. imports, very difficult to ascertain.

Fiat / Alfa Spider Comparison Chart

Model	Type	CI / CC	HP	Wt.	Price
1967 Fiat 850 Spider	I-4	51 / 843	54	1620	$2110
1968 Fiat 850 Spider	I-4	50 / 817	52	1640	$2109
1970-73 Fiat 850 Spider	I-4	55 / 903	58	1640	$2500
1959 Fiat 1200 Cabriolet	I-4	74 / 1221	55	1940	NA
1964-66 Fiat 1500 Spider	I-4	91 / 1480	83	2128	$2585
1962 Fiat 1500S Cabriolet DOHC	I-4	91 / 1480	90	2000	NA
1966 Fiat 1600S Cabriolet DOHC	I-4	96 / 1568	100	2000	NA
1968-69 Fiat 124 Spider	I-4	88 / 1438	96	2086	$3694
1970-72 Fiat 124 Spider	I-4	98 / 1608	104	2142	$3752
1973 Fiat 124 Spider	I-4	97 / 1592	107	2116	NA
1974-78 Fiat 124 Spider	I-4	107 / 1756	88	2116	$5759
1979-80 Fiat 2000 Spider	I-4	122 / 1995	82	2315	NA
1981-85 Fiat 2000 Spider FI	I-4	122 / 1995	101	2291	NA
1980-81 Fiat 2000 Turbo Spider	I-4	122 / 1995	120	2315	NA
1959-61 Alfa Giulietta Spider	I-4	79 / 1290	65	1896	NA
1965 Alfa Giulia Spider Veloce	I-4	96 / 1570	112	2180	NA
1966-67 Alfa Romeo Duetto Spider	I-4	96 / 1570	125	2195	$3950
1970 Alfa Romeo 1750 Veloce	I-4	109 / 1779	132	2346	$4298
1977 Alfa 2000 Spider Veloce	I-4	120 / 1962	111	2430	$8895

1967-68 Fiat Dino Spider 2000	V-6	121 / 1987	160	2535	NA
1969-70 Fiat Dino Spider 2400	V-6	145 / 2418	180	2733	NA

Fiat / Alfa Spider Comparison Chart Notes:
   All Fiat 850 Spiders had an 80-inch wheelbase. The Fiat 1200/1500/1600 Series Cabriolet had a 92-inch wheelbase. The Fiat 124 Spider had a 90-inch wheelbase. All Alfa Romeo Spiders had an 89-inch wheelbase. The Fiat Dino Spider had a 90-inch wheelbase. The original base retail prices quoted in some cases may not be exactly accurate for the model year or years listed. The $3752 listed for the 1970-72 124 is for a 1971 model tested by *Car and Driver* with a base price of $3482 with alloy wheels ($135) and radio ($85) plus dealer preparation charges.

Figure E17 - This 2600 Touring Spider in red shows off its standard steel wheels with chrome hubcaps and its slick top boot that snaps flat to the rear deck. ©Luc106 (PD)

Fiat, Alfa Romeo

Figure E18 - This is the Kamm tail of the Series 2 Spider pictured earlier in this chapter. Note the chrome exhaust tip exiting in the center and the 2000 emblem on the left rear. ©Rudolf Stricker (CC)

Affordable Italian Sports Car Test Results Chart

Model & Details	HP	Weight	0-60	1/4	TS
1965 Alfa Giulia Spider Veloce (*R&T*)	129	2150	10.5	17.4	109
1966 Alfa Romeo Duetto Spider (*R&T*)	109	2195	11.3	18.5	NA
1971 Alfa Romeo 1750 Spider (*R&T*)	115	2315	9.9	17.5	NA
1977 Alfa Romeo Spider 2000 (*R&T*)	111	2430	10.0	17.6	104
1982 Alfa Romeo Spider 2000 (*R&T*)	115	2495	11.7	18.3	NA
1965 Fiat 1500 Spider (*R&T*)	80	2120	17.0	20.2	94
1967 Fiat-Abarth OT-1000 Spider (982cc)	62	1598	12.4	18.8	99
1967 Fiat Dino Spider 1987cc (*R&T*)	166	2530	8.0	NA	NA
1968 Fiat 850 Spider 817cc (*R&T*)	52	1640	20.0	21.7	90
1968 Fiat 124 Spider 1438cc (*R&T*)	96	2090	11.9	18.3	NA
1970 Fiat 850 Racer 903cc (*R&T*)	58	1690	17.9	21.0	84
1970 Fiat 850 Racer 903cc (*C/D*)	58	1705	15.0	19.8	85
1974 Fiat X1/9 1290cc (*R&T*)	66	1995	15.3	20.1	NA
1981 Fiat X1/9 1498cc (*R&T*)	75	2160	12.4	18.6	NA

Affordable Italian Sports Car Test Results Chart Notes:

Affordable Italian Brio

The 1965 Fiat 1500 Spider had an as tested price of $2707. The 1965 Alfa Giulia Spider Veloce had an as tested price of $3670. Fiat increased the 124 Spider's engine displacement to 1608cc for the 1971 model. The Fiat-Abarth OT 1000 Spider sold in 1967 for $1000 more than the regular Spider. There were a total of 124,660 850 Spiders built from 1967-74, but we do not have a breakdown by model year; however, about 90% of these came to the USA. Fiat produced at least 130,000 124 Spiders over a much longer time period, 1968-86. Some sources quote a much higher figure. Dino Spider production included 1163 two-liter models and 420 with the later 2.4 liter engine.

Selected Affordable Italian Ratings Chart

Years	Model	Collect	Drive	Desire
1959 - 1966	Fiat 1200 / 1500 / 1600 Spider	D	D	D
1962 - 1966	Fiat O.S.C.A. 1500S & 1600S	C	D	C
1967	Fiat Abarth OT-1000 Spider	C	D	B
1967 - 1973	Fiat 850 Spider	D	C	C
1968 - 1985	Fiat 124/2000 Spider	D	A	C
1980 - 1981	Fiat 2000 Spider Turbo	C	B	C
1955 - 1965	Alfa Romeo Giulietta & Giulia Spiders	B	D	C
1958 - 1965	Alfa Romeo 2000 & 2600 Spiders	C	D	C
1967	Alfa Romeo Duetto Spider	B	C	A
1969	Alfa Romeo 1750 Boat Tail Spider	B	C	A
1971	Alfa Romeo 1750 Spider Series 2	B	C	B
1971 - 1993	Alfa Romeo 2000 Spider	C	B	C
1985 - 1990	Alfa Romeo 2000 Spider Graduate	C	B	C
1986 - 1989	Alfa 2000 Spider Quadrifoglio Verde	B	B	B

Models Ratings Chart Definitions:

Years: In most cases, the years listed include the total production years for a particular model series. Some model years within a series may be considerably more desirable than other years.

Models: In some cases many variations are included in this category and in others the models included are very homogeneous. This is generally self explanatory.

Collectibility: This is what most of you want to know, the bottom line on how likely the model or series is likely to climb in value over the coming years.

Drivability: This is an indicator of how adaptable the machine can be to drive for transportation or pleasure in the modern world, considering collector value, parts availability, fuel quality, comfort, performance and miscellaneous other factors.

Desirability: This defines the nostalgic, emotional wow factor, without regard for collector values or everyday usage.

General: No machine is given a failing grade. If it made it into a rating chart, at least a few hobbyists find that model interesting.

Chapter 6: *Topless Italian Exotics*

Figure F1 - **This stunning red interior belongs to a 1958 Ferrari LWB California Spyder. Notice the beautifully polished wood steering wheel and gauge array in a distinctly straight line. The glove box has an unusual shape with the key lock facing upward. The mirror is attached to the top of the dash and there are no vent windows. It is too small to see in this photo, but even the chrome ashtray lid behind the shift lever is adorned with a tiny prancing horse logo.** ©Rex Gray, Southern California (CC)

The brands covered in this chapter need no introduction. They represent the epitome of style, performance, price, collectibility and what we might call the lust factor. The only areas in which these cars are not the ne plus ultra are cost effectiveness, space efficiency, and low-maintenance reliability. The step up into the clouds begins with the Fiat Dino Spider and continues with the Ferrari Dino models. The V-12 Ferrari stratosphere is joined by the more mundane, yet less common, Maseratis. The Lamborghini brand is absent only because the company did not build and send a topless model to the USA until the Jalpa of the '80's. Ferrari decidedly dominates this chapter with its long succession of open models. Some were extremely low production, resulting in ridiculous auction prices today, but many have flaunted with affordability and availability in the U.S. This latter group have generally been designed especially for our market and Americans have always loved them. Enzo's son Dino would have been proud to see his name shrieking across the USA with the sound of ripping silk.

Fiat Dino Spider 2.0 & 2.4

Figure F2 - This red Fiat Dino Spider has a black top and interior and knock-off alloy wheels. ©Allen Watkin, London, England (CC)

There were 1163 Fiat Dino 2000 Spider and 420 Fiat Dino 2400 Spiders produced in 1966-73. At least one source claims a total of only 1557, but the book *Italian Sports Cars*, *Wikipedia* and most other sources substantiate the 1583 production figure. Most of the production remained in Italy, so compared to the Cobra and Shelby Mustang Convertible that could be barely considered production models, there are probably far less Dino Spiders in the U.S. The Fiat Dinos were never officially imported into the USA, however, a half-hearted effort to export the 2400 model was made and some were sent here, but the exact number is unknown. The Fiat Dino Spider 2000 was designed and built by Pininfarina with final assembly in Fiat's Rivalta plant. Final assembly of the 2400 model was carried out by Ferrari in its Maranello plant. Note that the *Dino Collector's Guide* states that practically all the 2-liter Spiders stayed in Italy.

All the 2000 engines were constructed of alloy by Fiat. All the 2400 engines had iron blocks with alloy heads and were built by Ferrari. The 1987cc cars had solid axles and the 2418cc cars had independent rear suspension. All models had four-wheel power disc brakes, but the Girling type utilized for the 2400 Dinos were the same ones as used on the Miura and Pantera. The five-speed manual of the 2000 model was a Fiat design. The 2400 used an improved ZF type. The 2-liter Fiat Dino Spider had performance practically identical to that of the 1990 Cavalier Z-24 Coupe: 0-60 in 8.1, the quarter in 16.0, and a top speed of 127, a little more than the 121 of the Z-24, per *Road & Track*'s contemporary test. The 2000 model weighed 2535 and the 2400 came in at 2733 pounds, per Wikipedia.

Figure F3 - This British Racing Green (or close Italian proximity) Fiat Dino 2000 is an early production model on display in Italy. Note the separate chrome exhaust tips, delicate chrome bumpers, alloy wheels with knock-off spinners, and the lack of headrests on the seats. ©Luc106 (PD)

Like the Maseratis discussed later, the Fiat Dino Spider deserves inclusion because its tiny presence in the U.S. is offset by its general significance as a classic Italian sports convertible. Its close relationship to Ferrari and its status as a collectible long ago cemented its place in sports car history. You are not likely to ever see a 2000 Spider model here, but the 2400 you are more likely to come across happens to be the one with an engine actually built by Ferrari, as well as the model with independent rear suspension. No road Ferrari of the day except the Dino 246 had IRS. No Ferrari even remotely in the Fiat Dino's price bracket offered a front engine design with ample trunk space in the rear for touring. The Fiat Dino Spider split the marketplace difference between an Alfa Spider and a Dino 246 GTS. What makes it so special is that it was the only model of the day that even attempted to fill this particular niche. Like the Maserati Mistral and Ghibli, the Fiat Dino Spider was a true convertible, which has added immensely to its long-term appeal as a collectible. Still today, any Spider will cost you more than twice the price of a comparable Coupe. The biggest question you might need to ask concerning the Fiat Dino Spider is how many are actually available in the USA and how many of those might have a legality issue concerning the federal regulations for its particular model year.

Here is the dilemma. The 2000 model would not face any of the federal issues in 1967, its first year of production. The 1968-70 models would face increasingly stringent requirements. The problem for Americans is that so few of these were ever imported in any capacity. The later 2400 models were far more likely to be brought here, but by then they were facing 1971-72 requirements for exhaust emissions, unleaded fuel, and numerous NHTSA components. All the Spiders were built with triple two-barrel Weber carbs. The factory quoted figures were 160 horsepower for the 1987cc engine and 180 horsepower for the 2418cc model. Other than engine placement and exhaust design, these Spiders used the same engines as the Ferrari Dino equivalents with higher claimed power ratings. Some sources have implied that there is probably little power difference between the two brands. These power ratings could be *gross* or *net* and they could really be the same or not. Compare this scenario to that of most every other car in this book, including the Ferrari Dinos and you will see that all the others lost power as they were federalized over the extended 1968-72 period. Most of these models lost their Webers to Zenith-Strombergs for the U.S. market. Obviously these carburetors could pass emissions testing at the cost of the ultimate performance provided by the Webers. The question remains as to the situation a particular Fiat Dino Spider you may wish to purchase now faces at your local DMV.

Figure F4 - This red 2400 Dino is posing in Germany. Notice its saddle tan interior with headrests and wood steering wheel, bolt-on alloy wheels and horizontal grille bars. The turn signal lamps are red. Compare this to the first Dino Spider photo. That car has knock-offs, white lamp lenses, and an egg crate grille. ©Hubert Berberich (PD)

If you like the styling and design of the Ferrari 275 GTS, Fiat 124 Spider, Maserati Mistral Spider, and the various iterations of the Alfa Spider, the Fiat Dino Spider will probably be pleasing to your eyes. It has a similar sort of curvaceous appeal with somewhat conservative lines. The engine provides a nice compromise of torque and racy power, the transmission shifts better than its mid-engine counterpart from Ferrari, and its interior layout is refreshingly classic, as well as ergonomic. The bodies were steel, but the quality of the steel used in Italian cars of that period was not the best and rust-resistant technology was in its infancy. You might want to inspect closely for the dreaded Fiat tinworm epidemic in any example you are considering. The convertible top design is a model of how to do it right, much like the vinyl tops of the Dino's Italian contemporaries. The brakes and handling are commensurate with what you would expect, shining above those of most of the English cars, and even of the American ones of the same period. You can generally spot a 2000 with its knock-off wheels and lack of headrests. The 2400 has headrests and bolt-on wheels. The interior was adequately designed, but not particularly stylish. Windows were of the roll-up type with a typically Italian well-designed, black vinyl convertible top. Unlike many of its Italian contemporaries, there was no wood on the dash, steering wheel or shift knob, at least on some models. However, a wood steering wheel and dash trim have been seen in at least one interior photo. The steering wheel itself was distinctive with three flashy chrome slotted spokes and black rim. The seats were vinyl with breathable vinyl center seating surfaces and available in several colors with black probably being the most common.

Any American who adopts a Fiat Dino Spider should be concerned with legal registration issues and parts and servicing issues more than anything else. Officially imported cars of the 1970-72 period needed to have side marker lights, bolt-on wheels, rocker switches on the dash, head restraints, and a lockable, collapsible steering column. In the engine department, minimal emission rules were just beginning. Air pumps were common, but the big bugaboo of strict regulation and enforcement involving catalytic converters was a couple of years away. By 1972, American cars were running on low-lead fuel or unleaded with lower compression ratios and net horsepower claims were the order of the day. Production of the Fiat Dino Spider ceased in June 1972. These cars were always more Ferrari than Fiat, and this was especially true of all the 2.4-liter cars, the ones far more likely to be discovered today in the USA. Even in their original time, the Fiat Dinos were not treated as regular Fiats by the Italian giant. The bad news is that chasing down certain model-specific or cosmetic hardware is likely to be about as challenging as trying to win a scavenger hunt at midnight on the wrong side of town. The good news is the Fiat Dino Spider is one hell of a clever design, a beautiful Italian mistress for sunny afternoon daydreams.

Figure F5 - This is a rear shot of the same red Dino 2400 in Germany. From this angle, you can see the taut fit of the black top, the design of the bolt-on alloy wheels, and the rough finish of the muffler and tailpipe.
©Hubert Berberich (PD)

Fiat Dino Spider Color Chart

Exterior	Interior	Exterior	Interior	Exterior	Interior
Silver	Maroon	Green	Beige	White	Red
Silver Blue	Black	Green	Bronze	White	Black
Metallic Blue	Beige	Dark Green	NA	Red	Black
Metallic Blue	Black	Yellow	Bronze	Red	Beige
French Blue	Beige	Yellow	Black	Bright Red	NA
Medium Blue	Black	Gunmetal	Black	Dark Red	NA
Medium Blue	Beige	Gunmetal	Beige	Black	Beige
Orange	Black	Dark Grey	NA	Black	Green

Fiat Dino Spider Color Chart Notes:
At least one additional color, another shade of red with an unknown interior combination, was probably offered. It is unknown if any of the colors in this chart were restricted to either the 2000 or 2400 models. It is also unknown which of these colors might have been exported to the U.S. NA = Not Available.

Ferrari Dino 246 GTS

Figure F6 - Red 1973 Ferrari Dino 246 GTS. ©Mr. Choppers (GNU)

Ferrari first introduced the Dino name to a road machine with a production of 152 aluminum Dino 206 GT's, and few if any were exported to the U.S. These baby Ferrari coupes did not have a Ferrari label or prancing horse logo anywhere on the vehicles. The all-alloy two-liter V-6 engines were built by Fiat. These were the same engines installed in the Fiat Dino models, too.

This first mid-engine Ferrari road machine would evolve through the 246 GT Coupe in 1969 and a GTS targa would join the lineup in 1972. Very few Ferrari Dinos were exported to the USA prior to the 246 GT in late 1969. The factory phased out knock-off wheels on the Dino in early 1970, so the question of their legality in the U.S. might have been moot by that point. The 2.4-liter models would have an engine built by Ferrari with a cast iron block. The bodies were designed by Pininfarina and constructed by Scaglietti. Sources do not seem to agree as to the exact total number of 246 GTS's produced in 1972-74. Some say 1180 and others 1274. There were 235 right hand drive cars accounted for that went to the UK, but there are no records of how many 246 GTS models were sent to the USA.

The Dino 246 GT tested by *Road & Track* cost $14,740 with optional electric windows, had 175 horsepower, top speed was 141, 0-60 in 7.9 and the quarter in 15.9. It weighed 2770 pounds and got 12.7 mpg. Leather interior was a $275 option and cloth seat inserts were $65. This test was done on a 1973 model. A 1974 *Road & Track* test of a 246 GTS produced performance figures of 0-60 in 8.0, quarter-mile in 16.2, a top speed of 141, and 15.5 mpg fuel consumption. Pricing of this loaded topless model was considerably higher than that of the Berlinetta tested only a few months prior. The base price was $15,225 and the price with options was $18,195. These included metallic paint, wider wheels and fender flares, air conditioning, leather upholstery with something called *Daytona seat panels*, power windows, and radio with electric antenna.

Figure F7 - Metallic Baby Blue Dino 246 GTS. This is a European model with the covered headlights similar to those on the Alfa Romeo Duetto Spider. ©Allen Watkin, London, England (CC)

Here is a timeline that might give you a little perspective on the 246 GTS. All the prior model Ferraris for the road were front-engine V-12's. The last topless production model was the Daytona Spyder and the company had not produced even 125 of these at the top price range level for sports cars of the day. Lamborghini had released the first mid-engine for the street, the Miura, in 1966 as a transverse V-12 coupe. Lotus had been building its tiny little Renault OHV-powered mid-engine Europa when the company released its much improved Twin Cam model in 1972 at approximately the same time as Ferrari released the 246 GTS. The Ferrari's price was more than twice that of the Europa Twin Cam. The Lotus had a 1.6-liter DOHC Four while the Ferrari was powered by a DOHC V-6 of 2.4 liters. The Ferrari was made of steel and weighed considerably more than the fiberglass Europa. The 246 GTS was a little quicker with a considerably higher top speed. About four times as many Europa Twin Cams as 246 GTS's were constructed. There are no official U.S. export statistics available for either car. Unlike the Lotus, the Ferrari utilized the Targa top design popularized earlier by the Porsche Targa and high-volume 914. The Europa proudly displayed its constructor's name and logo. The Dino GTS did not. When you open your checkbook today to buy a classic Europa Twin Cam, your checkbook will only whimper. When you whip it out for a 246 GTS, it will scream like a Ferrari, because everybody knows that's what a Dino 246 GTS is, not only a genuine Ferrari, but one of the company's most attractive, successful models.

The Dino 206, of which only 152 coupes were produced, began a new era at Ferrari in 1968. This was the beginning of the line of smaller, less expensive, less powerful road cars built by the company. In actuality the beginning of the road Dinos reflected Ferrari's increasing alliance with Fiat, the obvious mega-manufacturer of Italian cars. Beginning in this time with this model, Ferrari would increasingly over the next several years become in essence the exotic sports car division of Fiat. The two companies would cooperate and complement each other in the development and production of many future models to come. This action would particularly serve to expand Ferrari's American market. Not coincidentally, this expansion period coincided with the new U.S. regulations and having the support of Fiat probably saved Ferrari from a tumultuous financial history like that that has plagued Lamborghini for decades. The 246 GTS constructed of steel with a larger iron-block engine and a targa top would follow four years after the Dino 206 GT began production. The rest of the story comprises American consumer history. Since the advent of the Dino, amid federal regulations at approximately the same time, several of the larger Ferraris, such as the Boxer, were never officially imported. The Dino bloodline has defined most of the Ferraris cruising Main Street, USA, since the Sixties.

Figure F8 - This is an unusual 246 GTS in black, a very rare color for a 246 GTS. Note the wider alloy wheels, rear electric antenna and the lack of a rear bumper on this California car. ©Rex Gray, Southern California (CC)

Figure F9 - This red Dino 246 GTS is a U.S. model with standard wheels, uncovered headlights, amber turn signals, and black interior. For some unknown reason, this example is being shown with its bumpers removed. Metallic paint for $270 and leather seats for $450 were popular options in the U.S. market, along with a radio and power windows. ©Dan Smith (CC)

The culmination of what I call *poured over the wheels* styling began with the Dino 246 GTS. You can see its obvious trail from the NART Spyder, through the 206 GT, through the 1968 Corvette, the 246 GTS, the 308 GTS, 328 GTS, and beyond. Whenever I compare the 246 GT and NART to the first Stingray, I cannot help but think of the chicken or the egg? Whatever the case, I love it! This look has always had my number. The best view is from the left rear quarter, at human eye level above the low sports car with the roof removed. With less than 1300 built in those precious two years of 1972-74, no wonder the 246 GTS remains one of the most coveted Ferraris, particularly in the good old USA!

There is of course an up and a down side to 246 GT ownership. On the upswing, you get outstanding looks, performance, handling, snob appeal, and general driving quality. On the downside lies an expensive mistress that will forever require expensive attention. The two leading boogers are the timing chains and rust in crevices of the steel body. (Isn't this always the case?) As a serviceable transportation device, the GTS offers decent comfort for two occupants, but the noise level is high and no suitcases of any decent size are allowed along for the ride. The spare tire is carried in the front compartment and a trunk of just under seven cubic feet is located behind the engine. The targa top can quickly and easily be removed and stored behind the seats or in the trunk by one person, allowing the DOHC V-6 to sing to your ears. (Taller drivers might find compromised leg room with the top stored behind the seats.) The singing is sweet, but the gated shift lever connected remotely to a transmission in the rear is not so much fun. About the only interior adjustment for comfort is the fore and aft setting of the driver's seat. Although the GTS is in some ways the perfect California cruiser, the state's ex-governor Arnold would be a tight squeeze into its small driver's seat. Routine maintenance is not for the backyard mechanic. The transverse placement of the engine closely behind the bulkhead ensures accessibility issues to go along with the superb mid-engine handling. Although there are no Ferrari names or logos on the Dino, you better believe the cashier at the repair shop is fully aware that this is a F-E-R-R-A-R-I.

Ferrari 308 GTS

Figure F10 - Gunmetal Gray Ferrari 308 GTS. ©1983 Floyd M. Orr Collection

Along with the 1984-90 Corvette C4 and the Aston-Martins, we are making an exception of the 1977-85 308GTS by including it in *Daydreams in the Wind*. This book is intended to expound upon sports cars in the American market and the 308 GTS certainly brought an all-new ballgame to the USA from Ferrari. All the Ferrari V-12 Spyders barely broke the 800 barrier in the *total* number produced of *all* models. Only a small percentage of these ever made it to the USA! The 246 GTS probably broke this record in U.S. imports in its little three-year lifespan, but this was only the prelude to the U.S. popularity of the 308 GTS. By November 1978, Ferrari had produced 767 308 GTS models. By the time the model was replaced by the 328 GTS, about 8000 had been built and distributed worldwide. Although sources have generally stated that only about 35% of Ferrari production normally comes to the U.S., I bet that percentage has become much greater since the launch of the 308 GTS. I doubt the launch of *Magnum, P. I.* in 1980 hurt sales much, either!

Road & Track tested a fiberglass 308 GTB in U.S. trim. It had 240 horsepower instead of the 255 of the European model. The European model also enjoyed a few advantages from its dry-sump design. For some reason, the U.S. models changed to a regular wet sump. Maybe it had something to do with emissions equipment or the standard air conditioning? Leather seats and power windows were standard, too. Both these items and AC may have been optional on the

European cars. Wheels were 7.5-inch alloy with four-wheel power disc brakes. The price was $29,990 with optional $315 metallic paint and $150 dealer prep. Weight was 3085 pounds. Gas mileage was 13 mpg from a 21-gallon tank. The performance was down considerably from the 246 GT tested by *R&T*, as noted above: 0-60 in 9.4, quarter in 16.7, and top speed 132. A later test of the new, at the time, 1978 GTS explained that the earlier stated numbers for the GTB had been somewhat incorrect. The testers had experienced clutch problems with that first example, causing a delayed launch from stop and expanding the acceleration figures. However, the horsepower listed should have been 205 net, as listed with the '78 GTS. The 205 was a true net figure derived from the original European model's 255. According to *Road & Track*, both cars should have been listed as having 205 net horsepower, no matter how divergent the performance figures. The '78 GTS ran the quarter in 15.8 and did 0-60 in 7.3. The top speed was 145, a suitable velocity for a Ferrari.

The 246 brought the first targa-topped Ferrari to the USA. The 308 expanded the popularity of this design and the 328 would continue the trend far beyond the scope of this book. The top on all these models was made of lightweight plastic that could be removed or replaced by a single handler. The top stored conveniently in a vertical angle behind the seatbacks. Unlike the Corvette C4 Coupes or some of the Mercedes SL's, you did not need a special tool to unlatch the top panel. All the Ferrari targas used small, vertical, fixed rear windows that allowed little turbulence into the cockpit at speed with the top removed. Much of the noise you heard emanated from cams and induction roar, with the whirring cams being more audible with the 246's separate cam chains.

All the V-8 models employed a single quieter toothed belt. Nevertheless, either the cam chains of the 246, particularly on the forward cylinder bank, or the single belt on the V-8's should be considered the #1 Bugaboo (with a *bullet!*) when choosing one of these cars. This goes for the Fiat 124 Spider, Fiat Dino Spider, and the Alfa Spider models, too! Consider how much all these cars are really similar. They are all Italian spiders either built by Fiat, or falling under the corporate umbrella of Fiat, and they all have DOHC engines. It has always been a costly proposition to pay an experienced mechanic to adjust and/or replace the cam chains or belt on these exotic little engines in tight engine compartments. How many Americans over the decades do you think may have been nonchalant in heeding the call to pay for such service?

The 308 GTS may not be the ultimate price-expanding collectible Ferrari. It might not have mind-bending acceleration or a phenomenal top speed. It *is* (insert expletive here) GORGEOUS! Few cars can rival its exterior appearance for sheer perfection of how the mind's eye, particularly that of an American, perceives the visual concept of what a Ferrari should be. This may not be so true of its interior design, but even that is not bad-- all functional, with just the right amount of style and luxury added. When it comes to removable tops, the 308 has one of the best designs. The 308 truly represents the beginning of a new era at Ferrari, one in which the factory really tries its best to build a Ferrari that Americans in large numbers want to buy. Every time one rolls by, the eyes of everyone within visual distance follow the beautiful rolling dart shape and their tongues feel prickly as if Brigitte Bardot herself had been driving the lovely apparition.

Figure F11 - 1979 Ferrari 308 GTS in classic Ferrari Red. ©TTNIS (CC)

Ferrari V-12 Cabriolets & Spyders

Figure F12 - The bright red Ferrari 250 GT Cabriolet represents the beginning of the road-going 250 convertibles. The Cabriolet name indicates that it was designed and constructed by Pininfarina. Notice the hood scoop, chrome knock-off wires, bumper guards, and large diameter wood steering wheel, characteristics of this Series II V-12 touring convertible. ©Mr. Choppers (GNU)

There is a paired group of cars in *Daydreams in the Wind* that deserves special descriptions in relation to the other cars covered in this book. This pairing consists of all the V-12 Spyders that Ferrari built for the street and their Dino descendants with Targa tops, V-6 and V-8 engines, more affordable prices, and higher production. You may well ask why these cars even belong in the same paragraph. The answer is both simple and complex. Beginning with the original racing versions of these cars, which in some cases literally raced against the Shelby Cobras in the early '60's, these are currently some of the costliest cars in this book, as are the Cobras. At the same time, their higher production little brothers have been some of the most successful models from their respective brands in the world marketplace, particularly in the USA. An obvious statement is that Volkswagen is the parent of Porsche, Fiat is the parent of Ferrari, and Carroll Shelby would not be nearly so famous without Ford. There has been market pressure since the middle '60's to build *affordable* exotic cars for Americans, and Americans more than anyone else have proven their love for convertibles. Except for a racetrack, Enzo Ferrari never cared whether he built any topless cars or not. When he did release a convertible model for the street, it was invariably added to the market years after the debut of its coupe equivalent, which generally was produced in a ratio of ten to one of the Spyder model. Combine America's obsession with convertibles with the very low production numbers and you can easily see why these were the first collector cars of our generation to blast way beyond the million dollar mark. The 427 Cobra, Ferrari NART Spyder, and Daytona Spyder have in recent years famously sold at auction for truly astronomical prices. The lesser models from these brands are the cars left for the rest of us. At this point in time, the former group should be discussed in terms of economics. The latter group at least are still *cars*.

Figure F13 - The 250 GT Series I Spyder was a bit sportier than its Cabriolet sister. Note the covered headlights, protruding bumper guards without actual bumpers, driving lights and the lack of vent windows on this Spyder. ©Luc106 (PD)

The Ferrari GTO coupe was released in 1962 as the ultimate street/race coupe, or Berlinetta in Ferrari lingo. The GTO was the ultimate low-production hotrod of the 250 Series. This is as good a place as any to describe the Ferrari nomenclature. The number refers to a rounded version of the metric displacement of one cylinder of the engine being described. Twelve times 250cc equals 3000cc, or three liters. When you examine the production chart of these V-12 Spyders, you can see the distinct pattern as the models employing the same basic engine design are enlarged over time. The 275 GTS was a 3.3 liter convertible, its later direct derivative was enlarged to nearly four liters, and the final versions were 4.4 liters. Just for a little slap-you-awake perspective, my 1990 Cavalier Z24 has a 3.1-liter Six, a bit larger than the legendary GTO V-12, and the 330 GTS has a V-12 that is only a gnat's butt larger than the 3.8 V-6 in my 2000 Mustang. The classic V-8 in the GTO's Pontiac namesake of 1964 was over twice the size of the V-12 in the current multi-million-dollar Ferrari.

Figure F14 - The Long Wheelbase 250 GT California began the trend of very sporty high performance road Ferraris that would eternally command stratospheric prices. As mentioned in the text, the trend is most famously associated with the racy 250 GTO Coupe. The Spyder was designed somewhat less for endurance racing and more for the weekend competitor. We might imagine that such a consumer would live in a castle. ©C C Bain (CC)

Enzo Ferrari was an engine man. He cared only about winning on the track and his opinion was that engine power and development was the surest way to win. This had been true at the beginning of The Sixties, but by the end of that decade Lotus had shown Mr. Ferrari a thing or two. The race cars were the first to benefit from more sophisticated chassis design, but few of these changes had reached the Ferrari road cars, even the vaunted Daytona Spyder. At least one famous auto journalist has said the Daytona drove like a truck. None of these hand-built V-12 Spyders had independent rear suspension. The earliest models, such as the 250 GT Cabriolet Series I still had drum brakes and the antiquated Houdaille lever-type shock absorbers. These two components would be updated during the production run of the Series II Cabriolets. Other mid-production updates for the Series II models would be overdrive, sixteen-inch wheels replaced by fifteens, disc brakes and twin distributors. The gross horsepower rating of the Series I SOHC V-12 was 240 and 260 for the Series II. The Colombo design of the Ferrari V-12, as well as the Dino V-6 and V-8 derivatives, replaced the Lampredi design utilized by the company in the Fifties. The 250 GT Cabriolet was not the very first Ferrari street convertible, but its production approximately fits the opening time frame of this book. The earliest V-12 Ferraris in the 250 Series still used the Lampredi engine, but those were cars built in very low numbers. The first V-12 Ferrari Spyder produced after 1955 was the Series I, which barely qualifies as a *production* model, but it used the Colombo V-12 and its Series II successor would be built in higher numbers. In today's marketplace, the Colombo engines are much more prevalent and parts are scarce for the Lampredi V-12.

Topless Italian Exotics

Figure F15 - Can you see the similarity between this light blue 275 GTS and its peasant cousin the Fiat 124 Sport Spider designed by the same man and built in the same factory? Base price of this loveliest of touring Ferraris in 1966 was $13,900. The current Hagerty's values are $1.8-2.2 million. ©Rex Gray, Southern California (CC)

As far as stratospherically priced Ferrari V-12 Spyders go, the Series II Cabriolet could be considered the bargain of the bunch. Its price is usually a little less than that of the later 275 GTS, the second highest production model among these rare cars. The Series II basically looks just like a LWB California Spyder with a larger windshield and without the fender vents. You could squint just a bit and say the Series II Cabriolet compares to its slightly racier pal the Spyder much as the Porsche 356 looks next to its Speedster variant. The comparison goes a little wacko when you talk modern pricing, though. Classic Speedsters are certainly collectible these days. Except for the rare Carrera models, their prices have never shot off like a Roman candle, as those for the California Spyders have done in recent decades. Blame ("Bueller?; Bueller?") Ferris Bueller and his plastic copycat for the insane prices! The Cabriolet V-12 is of a slightly lower tune and its interior trim and sound deadening is a little more complete.

Figure F16 - This deep red 330 GTS with its protruding nose and recessed headlights looks even more like a Fiat 124 Sport Spider. The front styling is also similar to that of the Alfa Romeo Duetto Spider. ©Motohide Miwa (CC)

The history of the Ferrari company takes us from a purely racing concern to the combined racing and production powerhouse of the modern era. Only two groups of Ferrari production road cars are covered in this book. The small number of V-12 Cabriolets and Spyders produced in anything approaching a series production pattern make up the first group. The Dino GTS V-6 and V-8 *targas* compose the second group. Ferrari produced a number of specialty-built or custom-ordered convertibles for road use in the years prior to the release of the 250 GT Cabriolet Series I, the oldest model discussed in this book. These models are not included simply because they could hardly be considered part of a series production. The numbers of each model were less than twenty of each one and even those were far from identical. Each car was practically a one-off, particularly with regards to styling and detail trim. All of these early cars had V-12 engines, generally of the Lampredi design. The V-12's in this book are from the later Colombo era. The convertibles covered in *Daydreams in the Wind* were all designed by Pininfarina. The lighter, racier Spyder designs were built by Scaglietti. The more luxurious Cabriolets with more detailed sound deadening and interior trim were built by Pininfarina. All of these models could be considered a series in production, even though running changes continued throughout the multi-year production periods. The Series II Cabriolet was the highest production model within this exclusive group and the NART Spyder was the rarest. Modern resale prices of these models easily reflect their relative exclusivity.

Topless Italian Exotics

Figure F17 - **From this rear view of the same 330 GTS, you can see the ubiquitous tan leather Ferrari interior with wood dash panel and steering wheel.** ©Motohide Miwa (CC)

One of the most outstanding reasons to buy a Fiat 124 Spider is that it was designed and built by Pininfarina and it is no coincidence that it looks a lot like a Ferrari 275 GTS. Introduced at the end of 1964, the 275 GTS would be the first of a series of four Spyders produced through 1969. The 124 Spider was, indeed, pretty much an affordable smaller copy of the 275 GTS with a four-cylinder engine, vinyl upholstery and other cost-cutting elements. The 275 GTS was the first Ferrari road convertible with a transaxle. The whole series would continue with a five-speed transaxle, four-wheel disc brakes, fourteen-inch wheels, tube shocks, and a live axle rear suspension. The 275 has a three-liter SOHC V-12 and a nose similar to that of the 124 Spider.

The leading difference between the 275 GTS and its 330 GTS descendant, aside from the obvious displacement increase, is its smoother, more modern nose, a face not that different from the Alfa Spider or Fiat 850 Spider of the same vintage. The 4-liter V-12 brought twenty more horsepower, now at 300 gross. This was the first in the series in which Campagnolo alloy wheels were standard and Borrani wires were optional. As with the others in the series, a SOHC V-12 drives the rear wheels through a full-synchromesh five-speed transaxle on a 94-inch wheelbase with four-wheel disc brakes.

Figure F18 - This interior shot of a black California Spyder shows off its tan leather interior. Note the wood steering wheel with polished solid spokes and the rearview mirror attached to the dash top. The long shift lever is not gated. The ignition switch is right of the steering wheel, on the dash between the large and small gauges. The four smaller gauges have an unusual design with black backgrounds in the lower halves and their red needles pointing onto black figures on white backgrounds. The solid white instrument on the far right is a clock. ©Herr Anders Svensson (CC)

The 365 GTS became sort of a low-production final footnote to the classic V-12 GTS Series. Only twenty would be built, mostly within 1969. The 4.4-liter V-12 design had already been introduced with the 365 Spyder California on the long 104-inch wheelbase. This model, too, would become a sort of footnote, with only fourteen of this Cabriolet-type produced. You can see from the chart that the main technical differences were the longer wheelbase combined with the older live axle rear suspension. The 365 GTS looks very similar to its 330 GTS immediate predecessor, except the vents behind the front wheels have been deleted. You can easily identify the 365 California by its long hood with covered headlights, side sculpting through the door handles like the 246 GTS, long overhang behind the rear wheels, and vertical stripes in its two-tone seat upholstery. Another unusual styling element was the combination of popup driving lights and covered headlights. This model was not actually in the same Ferrari sports racing lineage as its two older Spyder California namesakes. The 365 California could be considered even more of a boulevardier than the shorter wheelbase GTS models. The heavy cruiser's five-speed was in the center, not a transaxle, and power steering was standard, and probably necessary. About seven of the 365 Californias were shipped to the U.S. If a Ferrari wanted to imitate the look of a sleek Jaguar XK-E Roadster, this one would fit the bill.

Ferraris of the period covered in *Daydreams in the Wind* encompassed the application of three basic wheel designs, each from a different brand. Chrome Borrani wire wheels with knock-off hubs were far the most prevalent on the early cars. These were standard equipment on many models, more so on early ones than later ones. Early cars had sixteen-inch wheels with some models changing to fifteen inches in the early '60's. The 275 GTS brought fourteen-inch Borranis. Campagnolo alloy wheels were used in at least two styles on Ferraris, but there may have been only one type on the convertibles discussed in this book. These were silver alloy with a ring of small, square holes surrounding a chrome center knock-off hub. They were standard equipment on the 330 GTS, but were not particularly attractive or popular. Most 330 GTS models were sold with the same fourteen-inch Borrani wires that were standard on the 275 GTS, but were now optional. All nine of the NART Spyders had the less attractive fourteen-inch Campagnolos with the square holes, but this may have been the end of the utilization of this brand and type of wheel by Ferrari. Beginning with models first shown in 1968, Ferrari began using five-spoke Cromodora wheels. The 246 GTS would use a fourteen-inch Cromodora design with six small, rectangular holes surrounding a chrome bolt-on hub. If you compare this information to the chart below, you will surmise that, with one exception, all the Cabriolets and Spyders prior to the NART had Borrani wire wheels. The one exception was the small number of standard Campagnolo wheels shipped on some of the 330 GTS models with the same wheels as the NART. After the NART, some models such as the 365 California had the Borrani wires, but these heavy, high-maintenance wheels were being replaced by the stylish, lighter weight and lower maintenance Cromodora alloys. Did some of these later cars, including the 365 GTC/4, designed for the American market, have knock-off wheels? It seems that the knock-off spinners can be present as long as they do not protrude outside the rim of deep dish wheels. Every photo we have found of the 1971 GTC/4, whether with the standard Cromodora alloys or the optional Borrani wires, has the knock-off spinners.

The soul of the 250 GT Spyder California SWB was reborn as the 275 GTS/4 NART Spyder in 1967. We should all be aware by now that this model was built especially for the American market and Luigi Chinetti, the U.S. Ferrari distributor who ran the North American Racing Team. *Road & Track* called this the best sports car the magazine had ever tested. Personally, I have always been impressed by the concept of what I call *poured over the wheels styling* that seems to have inspired the 1968 Stingray Convertible. The smooth, long, low look was here to stay. If you can squint and see the 250 GT Cabriolet Series II in the 1965 Mustang Convertible, as I can, surely you can see the referenced Stingray resemblance, too. This styling design seemed to culminate in the 246 GTS introduced in '72 that so resembles the Stingray Coupe of similar vintage. As we all know now, it would be decades after the Daytona Spyder before Ferrari would produce another full convertible in full sports trim. The NART bridged the gap between the SWB California and the Daytona.

Figure F19 - This red NART Spyder has the standard Perspex covered headlights and optional chrome knock-off wire wheels. The NART was released as a USA-only model during the final year these items would be certified as legal in the U.S. market. Take note, too, of the lack of a side mirror on the driver's door.
©Marcusmv3 (GNU)

NART Spyder Chart

Serial	Factory	American	Interior	Changed	Notes
09437	Giallo Solare	Light Yellow	Black	Burgundy	Aluminum
09751	Giallo Fly	Cab Yellow	Black	NA	Aluminum
10139	Rosso Chiaro	Dark Red	Orange	Ferrari Red	Black Interior
10219	Giallo Fly	Cab Yellow	Black	Ferrari Red	1984 Repaint
10249	Rosso Chiaro	Dark Red	Black	NA	NA
10453	Blu Sera	Dark Blue	Black	NA	McQueen Car
10691	Blu Sera	Dark Blue	Black	NA	NA
10709	Silver Gray	Silver Grey	Red	Maroon/Tan	$27,500,000
10749	Argento Silver	Argento Silver	Red	NA	NA
11057	Grigio Scuro	Dark Grey	Black	Maroon	NA

NART Spyder Chart Notes:

The Light Yellow (Giallo Solare) #09437, the first car produced, was raced at Sebring 4/1/67 before it was repainted Burgundy and tested by *R&T* in 9/67. Then it appeared in *The Thomas Crown Affair*, released June 1968 in Burgundy. On the cover of *R&T*, this car had covered headlights, magnesium wheels, and no side mirror. In other photos, it has uncovered headlights, a driver's side mirror, and chrome wire wheels. In the movie, the burgundy car had magnesium wheels, covered headlights, mirror, and a radio antenna on the right front fender, just in front of the windshield.

The first two NARTS, numbers 9437 and 9751, had aluminum bodies. The Yellow #10219 was repainted Red in 1984. The Silver Grey with Red #10709 was repainted Maroon with Tan. This is the car that sold at an RM auction in Monterey for $27,500,000. The tenth NART, #11057, is the only one not imported into the USA. That car is currently in England.

Figure F20 - This bright yellow NART Spyder appears to have the optional wire wheels and a side mirror, but the headlamps are uncovered. I suspect that these changes were made to certify the car in California, or maybe even in some less restrictive state. ©Jon Kristian Bernhardsen (CC)

The company released its first road model with independent rear suspension in the 275 GTB of 1964. The Berlinetta would be updated with a four-cam head before the Spyder was introduced in 1967. Scaglietti developed the GTS directly from the GTB model with only minimal modification, other than the folding top. This would be the only Ferrari Spyder other than the Daytona equipped with six Weber carbs and of course its body style was unique to itself. According to *Road & Track*'s testers, the aluminum-bodied NART cost $14,400 and weighed 2455 pounds. Developing 300 gross horsepower from only 200 cubic inches, the NART did 0-60 in 6.7 and the quarter-mile in 14.7 seconds. Measured top speed was 155 mph. Note that *R&T* estimated the horsepower as 330. Both 275 GTB/4 models had a huge seventeen-quart dry sump! The front/rear weight distribution of the NART Spyder was 49/51, the same as the small-block Stingrays of 1968-72. Some sources, such as the *Illustrated Ferrari Buyer's Guide*, state that only nine Spyders have been accounted for, Wikipedia lists ten chassis numbers. However you slice it, the NART Spyder is surely one of the top-level sports car legends of all time.

There were 122 Daytona Spyders constructed in the early '70's that rival the NART for top banana position. With a new V-12 about one and a half times the displacement of the 275 GTS/4, the 352-hp 365 GTS/4 became the new king of the Ferrari hill at the end of 1969. The all-new sleek, envelope body covered a heavy sports car that still managed to rival the world's best for looks, performance and driving quality. The big issue at the time of its release was that Ferrari continued the front-engine design at a time when the new mid-engine type represented the vanguard. Regardless of its dated perspective or somewhat ponderous low-speed handling, the magazine testers of the day positively *loved* the Daytona. Along with its legendary GTO ancestor and its high-performance rival, the 427 Cobra, the Daytona Spyder was part of the original trio of exploding collectible car prices. Only the faithful may recognize a NART for the special rarity it is, but much of the car-staring public can ID a Ferrari Daytona. The stories and accolades were repeated for decades. It was the last of its kind. The front-engine V-12's were gone forever. It was the real man's Ferrari. It was the king of its kind. NartSmart! The Daytona Spyder is the Ferrari every ten-year-old aspiring race car driver wanted to own!

Figure F21 - Note the pop-up headlights on this 365 GTS/4. The European models had fixed lamps behind a Perspex panel. The Stingray look of the Daytona's nose allowed the car to be certified here without covered headlights. This shot of a chocolate brown Spyder with black top clearly shows the new style, five-spoke Cromodora alloy wheels that would become common on Ferraris from the Daytona forward. These were considerably more attractive than the magnesium wheels offered on the NART Spyder, the Daytona's direct predecessor. ©Mr. Choppers (GNU)

Figure F22 - This rear view of the same brown Daytona Spyder shows the shape of the black convertible top and the four chrome exhaust tips protruding below the rear bumper. Notice the unusual shape of the headrests. By the way, *Daytona* is only this model's nickname, named after the coupe model named for the legendary Florida racetrack. The car's parents officially named it 365 GTS/4. This translates into 365cc per each of twelve cylinders in a Gran Turismo chassis with a Spyder (two-seater convertible) body and a DOHC (4 cam) V-12 powerplant. How about that mouthful of car nomenclature? No wonder we Americans gave it a nickname! ©Mr. Choppers (GNU)

Ferrari V-12 Cabriolet & Spyder Comparison Chart

Model	Liters	Cams	Webers	HP	WB	Suspension
250 GT Cabriolet Series I	3.0	SOHC	3 2-bbl.	240	102	Live Axle
250 GT Cabriolet Series II	3.0	SOHC	3 2-bbl.	260	102	Live Axle
250 GT CA Spyder LWB	3.0	SOHC	3 2-bbl.	260	102	Live Axle
250 GT CA Spyder SWB	3.0	SOHC	3 2-bbl.	280	94	Live Axle
275 GTS	3.3	SOHC	3 2-bbl.	260	94	IRS
275 GTS/4 NART Spyder	3.3	DOHC	6 2-bbl.	300	94	IRS
330 GTS	4.0	SOHC	3 2-bbl.	300	94	IRS
365 GTS	4.4	SOHC	3 2-bbl.	320	94	IRS
365 California Spyder	4.4	SOHC	3 2-bbl.	320	104	Live Axle
365 GTS/4 Daytona Spyder	4.4	DOHC	6 2-bbl.	352	94	IRS

Figure F23 - This metallic brown Daytona Spyder shows off its sleek profile with its black top retracted underneath a relatively flat boot. ©Mr. Choppers (GNU)

Figure F24 - This is the little silver baby you have all been waiting to see, the Short Wheelbase 250 GT California. The SWB model was lighter and had a twenty-horsepower advantage over its predecessor, but its disc brakes instead of drums were its most significant improvement. Bueller? Bueller? ©Richebets (CC)

Ferrari V-12 Cabriolet & Spyder Production Chart

Model	Years	Built	Model	Years	Built
250 GT Series I	1957-59	36	Ferrari 365 GTS/4	1969-74	122
250 GT Series II	1959-62	212			
			1957-74 V-12 Spyders	Total	809
CA Spyder LWB	1959	45			

CA Spyder SWB	1960-63	50	Fiat Dino 2000 Spider	1966-69	1163
365 CA Spyder	1966-67	14	Fiat Dino 2400 Spider	1969-73	424
			Dino 246 GTS	1972-74	1180
Ferrari 275 GTS	1964-66	200			
Ferrari 330 GTS	1967-68	100	Ferrari 308 GTS	1977-80	3219
Ferrari 365 GTS	1968-69	20	Ferrari 308 GTSi	1981-82	1749
			Ferrari 308 GTS QV	1982-85	3042
275 NART Spyder	1967-68	10	1977-85 308 GTS	Total	8010

Ferrari Cabriolet & Spyder Production Chart Notes:

Many of the model years listed for Ferraris overlap a bit, since all models were not built in a linear sequence unto themselves and the chart has been overly simplified somewhat for general clarity of reading. Many of the fourteen 365 California Spyders were built in 1967, possibly after production of the NART began. Note that only about seven of the 365 Californias were sent to the U.S., whereas all ten of the NARTs were shipped here. Ninety-six of the 122 Daytona Spyders were exported to the USA. Notice that some sources, such as Wikipedia, state 246 GTS production as 1274 instead of 1180. The Dino *Collector's Guide* even lists both figures! The Dino *Collector's Guide* lists 1274 246 GTS models, including 235 right-hand-drive units sent to the UK. The same source lists 3219 308 GTS's, including 184 RHD models for England, plus 1743 308 GTSi models, including 67 for the UK. The 308 production figures in the chart were sourced from the Ferrari 308.com website.

Figure F25 - Note the silver body panel and headlight covers on this Ferrari Red 1972 365 GTS/4. Apparently some cars had this area in silver and some in the body color. Of course the original Italian design for the European market had clear Perspex over this area, Note also the chrome knock-off wire wheels on this museum display model. You can also see the low-profile vinyl boot that covers the black convertible top. ©Greg Gjerdingen, Willmar, USA (CC)

Classic Ferrari Tests Chart

Model & Details	HP	Weight	0-60	Quarter	TS
250 GTO 2953cc 3.55 axle (*250GTO*)	290	2450	5.9	NA	165
1967 275 GTS/4 NART Spyder (*R&T*)	330	2455	6.7	14.7	155
1967 330 GTS 3967cc 5SM 3.44 axle (*R&T*)	345	3105	6.9	14.9	146
1970 European 365 GTB/4 4390cc (*R&T*)	405	3600	5.9	13.8	173
1970 Ferrari Daytona Spyder	352	3700	5.0	13.6	174
1971 365 GTC4 (*R&T*)	320	3825	7.3	15.7	152
1972 Dino 246 GT (*R&T*)	175	2770	7.9	15.9	141
Ferrari 246GTS (*SCC*)	175	2820	8.2	16.0	NA
1974 246 GTS (*R&T*)	195	2910	8.0	16.2	141
1974 European 308 GT4 (*R&T*)	242	2930	6.4	14.6	152
1974 365 GTB/4 (*R&T*)	352	3615	7.2	15.7	NA
1976 European 308 GTB - Fiberglass (*R&T*)	243	2650	6.4	14.6	154
1977 Fiberglass 308 GTB (*R&T*)	240	3085	9.4	16.7	132
1978 308 GTS Spyder (*R&T*)	205	3305	7.3	15.8	145
1978 512 BB (*R&T*)	355	3340	5.5	13.7	180
1981 308 GTSi Spyder (*R&T*)	205	3250	7.9	16.1	147
1981 Mondial Coupe (*C/D*)	214	3108	9.3	16.0	138
Ferrari Mondial Coupe (*SCC*)	205	3460	8.2	16.3	140
308 Quattrovalvole (*C/D*)	230	3230	7.4	14.9	144
1982 512 BB (*R&T*)	360	3420	5.1	13.5	168
1984 Testarossa (*MT*)	390	3593	5.3	13.4	180
1984 288GTO (*R&T*)	400	2557	5.0	12.7	180
1986 328 (*C/D*)	255	2972	5.6	14.0	153
1987 Mondial 3.2 Cabriolet (*R&T*)	270	3086	7.0	NA	NA
1987 F40 (*R&T*)	478	2425	3.6	11.8	196
1990 Mondial t Cabriolet 3.4 (*C/D*)	300	3540	6.2	14.5	159
1992 512 TR Testarossa (*R&T*)	422	NA	4.7	12.9	192
1997 F50 (*R&T*)	514	2976	3.7	12.1	202

Classic Ferrari Tests Chart Notes:
A total of 40 GTO models were built, including 3 with 4-liter engines. The quarter-mile figure quoted for the 1978 512 BB is the factory claim. Several of the miscellaneous performance figures, particularly

those after 1975, are factory claims or represent European models. The 240 horsepower listed for the earliest 308 GTB's imported into the U.S. was actually the federalized 205 net horsepower. *250GTO = Ferrari 250GTO: 1962-64; Competition Berlinetta. C/D = Car and Driver. MT = Motor Trend. R&T = Road & Track. SCC = Sports Car Classics*, 1982.

Figure F26 - The rear view of this red '72 is nearly identical to that of the metallic brown Daytona Spider example pictured in this chapter. There are only a couple of small differences that do not show up in this small black and white photograph. The brown car has a tiny backup lamp between the split bumper halves and a small rectangular orange reflector set within the body groove beneath each pair of tail lamps. ©Greg Gjerdingen, Willmar, USA (CC)

Maserati Spyders

Figure F27 - **Maserati Mistral Spyder.** ©Brian Snelson, Hockley, Essex, England (CC)

This book would not be complete or correct without the inclusion of the Maserati Spyders of the 1955-75 period. To most Americans, Maserati has always been the #3 Italian exotic, the name that easily comes to mind, but there is no ready image to accompany it. The actual history of Maserati is that the company was involved in racing from as far back as The Roaring Twenties. There was a convertible model or two produced for road use prior to the ones discussed here, but they were not actual *production* cars. They were variants on a theme built by competing Italian coachbuilders. Few were totally alike and the total number of a model never surpassed twenty-five.

The third Italian exotic, of which all Americans are familiar, is Lamborghini. How could we miss the Countach, the single model of automobile that has graced more magazine covers than any in all of history? The company has been building cars for less years than either Ferrari or Maserati. The 350GT was released in 1964. Lamborghini has never been a convertible producer, and even the company's targa designs have been rare. The first one of these was the Silhouette, a beautiful design sandwiched between the troublesome Urraco and the more successful Jalpa. Only 52 Silhouettes were built and the model was never certified for sale in the U.S., hence the Silhouette is not included. But what of a few other uncertified cars that *have* been included? Why is that? Those models were inevitably closely linked to related models that were imported, such as the Fiat Dino Spider's connection with the Ferrari Dino 246 GTS. Likewise, a few models from a production period after 1975 have been included, such as the 308 GTS and the Alfa Spider. That is simply because these are direct continuations of particularly popular models. A few Lamborghinis have been listed in a performance chart purely for comparison purposes. None of these models have otherwise been discussed in *Daydreams in the Wind*.

Figure F28 - This Maserzti 3500 GT in metallic gunmetal gray shows off its standard chrome knock-off wire wheels, cream leather interior, and flat, snap-down top boot in black. ©Mr. Choppers (GNU)

Maserati as a producer of road cars can be defined quite easily. These are the Aston Martins of Italy. The Maserati convertibles are officially called spyders by the company, but if these models were built by Ferrari, they would be referred to as cabriolets. The models discussed here are some of both and a little of neither. They are two-seater Italian sports cars, but at the same time, these are not rip-roaring, persnickety race car derivatives. They are luxury two-seaters with more style and panache than the far more common Mercedes SL line. Their prices, specifications, performance capabilities, and tiny production numbers are much closer to the Aston Martin Volantes than most any competing brand you can name. All the Rolls-Royce Corniche Convertibles are four-seaters and even more lush and expensive. The sum total production of the 1960-72 models discussed here was just under 500 cars. As is the case with many brands included in this book, coupe production far exceeded the convertibles of most models, including these from Maserati. If you want to one-up the snobbery of a Mercedes SL while holding onto true sports car handling and driving quality, the Aston Martins and Maseratis offer the primo choices in an elevated price bracket.

Figure F29 - This interior shot of a Mistral shows its black leather seating and wood steering wheel. Unlike most Ferraris of the period, the shift lever is not gated. Most American drivers are not fond of those confounded chrome slot machines, anyway. The instrument layout would be more amenable to quick readings if the speedo and tach had been placed together in the center. Unfortunately, due to certain engineering obstructions within the dash or cowl design, some of our favorite Italian supercars have this same affliction.
©Craig Howell, San Carlos, CA (CC)

The first real production Maserati convertible was the 3500 GT of 1960. Most, but not all, of this model were practically identical versions designed and built by Vignale. The 3500 GT Spyder was personally designed by Giovanni Michelotti for Vignale. This is the same Michelotti who penned the Triumph TR-4 and Stag. The Mistral was designed by Michelotti for Frua and the bodies were built by Maggiora. The later Ghibli would be created by Giorgetto Giugiaro for Ghia. A handful of one-offs by competing design houses were built, too. If you squint, you will see comparisons between the 3500 GT and Ferrari's earliest convertibles produced within the timeframe of this book. The Maseratis are just a bit klunkier of style with a few more luxury features than the contemporary 250 GT Ferraris. Although exotic by American standards, Maserati powerplants are conservatively tuned. The 3500 GT had a 3485cc, DOHC, inline six-cylinder producing 220 horsepower through three Weber two-barrel carbs. It had the same 98-inch wheelbase as a 1963-82 Corvette and used a four-speed built by ZF. The earliest models had disc front and drum rear brakes. The model was distinguished by its sixteen-inch Borrani wire wheels. Even with a steel body, the weight did not exceed that of a contemporary Corvette.

As you would expect, the seats were high-quality leather and the steering wheel was a little too large and thin, at least compared to later models and standards.

Only a year after production began, a GTI model with a ZF 5-speed and Lucas fuel injection instead of Webers brought smooth drivability and fifteen more horsepower. Some American owners may have removed and discarded the injection system years ago, and they are likely regretting that impetuous choice. Although it requires an expert specialist, once the fuel injection is set up correctly, it will outperform the Weber carburetors and probably behave itself for years. An original injection setup obviously brings more at current extravagant auction prices. Only 242 combined 3500 GT and 3500 GTI Spyders by Vignale were produced for the worldwide market. There were two 3500 Spyders designed by Touring and one by Frua also built. (Some sources claim that Touring built five 3500 Spyders instead of only two.) The 3500 GT and GTI models comprise half the production of Maserati convertibles built between 1960 and 1972. It should then come as no surprise that the final twenty-five Ghibli SS models of the '70's are the most valuable of the series today.

The Maserati Spyder with the longest production run was the Mistral of 1964-70, although technically only one Mistral Spyder was constructed in 1970. Car styling was moving upwards in leaps and bounds in the Sixties, and the Mistral reaped these benefits as Maserati's representative convertible of the period. The Mistral began with the GTI's injected six-cylinder powerplant and ended production with a twice-enlarged version of the same engine. Its body lines were smoothed out a bit from the 3500 in a manner typical of the period. The biggest change was in the face. The 3500 GTI had displayed the upright, busy look of a late-Fifties design. The new Mistral introduced a smooth, rounded smile similar to that of the Ferrari 330 GTS or Alfa Duetto. The headlights were never covered, but they were tastefully recessed back from the bumper line. The interior design was updated to the style of the day with a smaller-diameter, wood steering wheel rim. The smaller steering wheel had four round holes in the spokes instead of long slots. The Mistral had a four-inch shorter wheelbase and one-inch smaller wheels, too. This was the first of the Maserati Spyders offered with air conditioning as an option. Many had electric windows, but some Mistrals were equipped with the roll-up type. Like the later 3500 Spyders, the Mistral had four-wheel disc brakes, and like all Maserati Spyders of the day, the bodies were steel. For some reason, Maserati built some coupes in aluminum or steel and aluminum combinations that brought rust to the areas where the two metals joined. The Mistral Spyder had a steel body with aluminum doors, hood, and trunk lid. The claimed weight of the Mistral was a little higher than that of the 3500 Spyder, probably attributable to more equipment and larger wheels and tires.

After constructing only twelve Mistrals in 1964 with the same engine as the previous 3500 GTI, the company increased the displacement to 3694cc with a slight lengthening of the stroke of its already undersquare design. Maserati produced 76 Mistrals in this 3.7-liter configuration. At some later (unknown) point in the production cycle, a 4014cc version was offered. The new 4.0-liter had both a larger bore and a longer stroke to produce ten more horsepower at lower revolutions, obviously with somewhat more torque. Thirty-seven of these 4.0 Mistral Spyders were produced in the latter part of the production cycle, 1967-70. I suspect that some 3.7's were still released after the first 4.0 was built. Considering the timeframe covering the new U.S. regulations of 1/1/68, I would expect all the later Mistrals sent to the U.S. to have the 4.0 engine and air conditioning.

Figure F30 - This deep blue-green Maserati Ghibli Spyder is a real looker! This example photographed in Berlin has chrome knock-off wires and a taut vinyl top that unfortunately has quite a three-quarter blind spot. ©HPS911 (CC)

Maserati had introduced its new V-8 Ghibli Spyder a little before the last 3500 GTI Spyder had been built. Keeping up with the muscle car mania of the period, Maserati updated its inline six-cylinder engine of many years to a new DOHC V-8 design that would power all Maseratis for years to come. The first topless Maserati V-8 was the Ghibli Spyder, a sleek, front-engine beauty destined to become probably the most collectible touring Maserati for all time. Obvious comparisons to Ferrari's Daytona Spyder of the same era are unavoidable. The two were each company's interpretation of what most fans felt would be the last of a breed, topless road runners with conventional drivetrains. Like the previously discussed Maserati Spyders, but not the Ferrari Daytona, the Ghibli had a solid axle out back. The Daytona utilized a five-speed transaxle with its V-12, while the Ghibli (in typical conservative Maserati fashion) attached its five-speed directly to the V-8 up front. The Ghibli even offered a three-speed automatic option, but it is unknown how many of these were produced or how many came to the USA. Like its predecessor the Mistral, the Ghibli had fifteen-inch wheels and four-wheel disc brakes, but the company rejected the Mistral's fuel injection for carburetors. The four two-barrel Webers may have seemed a step backward, but I bet the buyers of the time were pleased with this change.

The alloy V-8 of 4719cc put out 310 gross horsepower. If you want to visualize a comparison, the Corvette 283 produced 315 gross horsepower in an OHV format from the same displacement. (Some sources quote 330 gross horsepower for the 4.7-liter V-8.) The key difference is that the Corvette engine was pushed to its limit of drivability and reliability, whereas the DOHC Maserati V-8 is a model of civility. The SS model was introduced in 1970 with a 4930cc V-8 putting out an additional 25 horsepower, 335 total. Both engines were of an oversquare design, with a slightly lengthened stroke on the 4.9.

Figure F31 - This bright yellow Ghibli Spyder with black interior displays its top down underneath a sleek body-colored panel. Notice the bolt-on alloy wheels. ©The Car Spy (CC)

The top design of the fabric tops on the Maserati Spyders is of the usual Italian quality and ease of use. The tops on the GT, GTI, and Mistral models folded under a vinyl, snap-down boot. The Ghibli enjoyed the beauty and simplicity of a lift-up steel panel similar to a Corvette or Mercedes SL. Probably the weakest link in the top design is that all these models were practically hand built, with small variances in the fitting of the convertible tops, as well as various steel and aluminum body panels. Replacing a top could be a trying affair. None of these Spyders had power steering, either, not even the V-8 models. Contemporary testers sometimes noted the heaviness of the steering in the Ghibli, just as the Ferrari Daytona was often described as *truck-like*, particularly in low-speed traffic situations. Controls other than the steering were delightfully light. The later models benefited from four-wheel power disc brakes. Although the earlier models were about the same weight as a Corvette of the period, the Ghiblis were quite heavy. Current sources do not exactly agree on the weight figures, as shown in the chart below.

The brakes utilized were manufactured by Girling, the transmissions by ZF in Germany, and the solid rear axles by Salisbury. Not only are these components relatively sturdy, but parts and service are not difficult to locate. The conservatively tuned engines are famous for lasting about 50,000 miles. Engine rebuilds are by no means cheap, except by Ferrari standards, and those are the cars most often compared to Maseratis. Like the custom-fitted convertible top, one of the biggest issues with a Maserati Spyder is likely to be the custom-fitted body panels. The company often smoothed the final body fittings with a type of Bondo filler indigenous to Italian body constructors of the period. Expert body men especially experienced with this construction method may be needed to rebuild a Maserati Spyder to a perfect original look. This issue will most likely apply to a Mistral because it was built by Frua. The final common mechanical hurdle of restoration and maintenance probably lies with the Lucas mechanical fuel injection or Weber carburetor sets. Rubber seals easily deteriorate on the fuel injection and the Webers are not the easiest to tune. You should employ the help of an experienced expert with either one.

The best reason to purchase any of these Maserati Spyders is probably exclusivity without such a high maintenance demand on the owner. That latter demand is generally the weakest link of any of the Maserati's exotic Italian competitors. From the other side of the spectrum, you can approach the luxurious level of accommodations of an Aston Martin Volante without sacrificing much of the sound, fury and driving excitement of a Ferrari or Lamborghini. With only 500 of these exotic, endangered beasts in the world, you are not likely to ever see your reflection on any street in America.

Maserati Spyders Chart

3500 GT	*3500 GTI*	*Mistral*	*Ghibli*	*Ghibli SS*
1960 - 1963	1961 - 1963	1964 - 1970	1969 - 1970	1970 - 1972
242 (or 245)	242 (or 245)	120 (or 125)	100 built	25 built
Vignale	Vignale	Frua	Ghia	Ghia
Inline Six	Inline Six	Inline Six	DOHC V-8	DOHC V-8
3485cc DOHC	3485cc DOHC	DOHC *	4719cc	4930cc
3 2-bbl. Webers	Fuel Injection	Fuel Injection	4 2-bbl. Webers	4 2-bbl. Webers
ZF 4-speed	ZF 5-speed	ZF 5-speed	ZF 5-speed	ZF 5-speed
220 hp	235 hp	235 - 255 hp	310 hp	335 hp
98" WB	98" WB	94" WB	100" WB	100" WB
16" wheels	16" wheels	15" wheels	15" wheels	15" wheels
Borrani Wire	Borrani Wire	Borrani Wire	Campagnolo	Campagnolo
Disc / Drum	Disc / Disc	Disc / Disc	Disc / Disc	Disc / Disc
3042 pounds	3042 pounds	3153 pounds	3638 - 3902	3638 - 3902

Maserati Spyders Chart Notes:
*Three displacements of the Mistral Inline Six were used: 3500cc, 3700cc, and 4000cc. Production included twelve 3500's, 76 3700's, and 37 4000's. Twenty were RHD models sent to the UK. The three engine displacements claimed 235, 245, and 255 gross horsepower with 3485cc, 3694cc, and 4014cc, respectively. Most of the earlier Spyders had Borrani knock-off wire wheels, although Borrani steel disc wheels with aluminum rims and chrome hubcaps were available. Campagnolo magnesium alloy wheels were standard on the Ghibli and Borrani bolt-on wires were optional. The weights of the 3500 GT and GTI are probably not identical, but very close. The weight range for the Ghibli comes from Wikipedia. It is not specified which figure is for the Coupe and which for the Spyder, although convertible models are usually heavier.

Ferrari / Maserati Spyders Comparison Chart

Model	Type	C. I. / CC	HP	Wt.	Price
1959 Ferrari 250 GT Series 1	V-12	180 / 2953	240	2815	NA
1960-61 Ferrari SWB California	V-12	180 / 2953	280	2315	NA
1964-66 Ferrari 275 GTS	V-12	200 / 3286	260	2469	NA
1967 Ferrari 275 NART	V-12	200 / 3286	330	2455	$14,400
1967-68 Ferrari 330 GTS	V-12	242 / 3967	300	3415	$14,900
1970 Ferrari 365 GTS/4	V-12	268 / 4390	352	3600	NA
1972-74 Ferrari 246 GTS DOHC	V-6	145 / 2418	195	2380	$15,000
1975-80 Ferrari 308 GTS DOHC	V-8	179 / 2927	205	3305	$34,195
1981 Ferrari 308 GTSi	V-8	179 / 2927	205	3250	$52,640
Ferrari 308 GTS QV	V-8	179 / 2927	230	3230	NA
1959-61 Maserati 3500 GT	I-6	213 / 3485	220	3330	$12,300
1962-63 Maserati 3500 GTI	I-6	213 / 3485	235	3330	NA
1965 Maserati Mistral	I-6	225 / 3694	245	2600	NA
1966-70 Maserati Mistral	I-6	245 / 4014	255	2600	$14,720
1969 Maserati Ghibli Spyder	V-8	288 / 4719	340	3681	NA
1970 Maserati Ghibli SS Spyder	V-8	301 / 4930	355	3745	$20,000

Ferrari / Maserati Spiders Comparison Chart Notes:
The Ferrari 250 GT models, including the LWB California, had a 102-inch wheelbase. The SWB California, GTS models and NART had a 94-inch wheelbase. The 1966 365 California had a 104-inch wheelbase. The 330 hp listed for the NART comes from *R&T*; the *Illustrated Ferrari Buyer's Guide* states 300 hp for the NART. Considering engine displacement and design, the lower figure might be more accurate. The Maserati 3500 GT & GTI models had a 100-inch wheelbase. The Mistral had a 94-inch wheelbase. The Maserati Ghibli was built on a 100-inch wheelbase. Many of the weights quoted are dry figures (without fluids) claimed by the manufacturers. The original base retail prices quoted in some cases may not be exactly accurate for the model year or years listed.

Figure F32 - Just in case you forgot, this is what a Lamborghini Miura looks like. This 1968 model is metallic silver with medium gray vinyl interior. In this shot it is posed on a country road outside Austin, Texas, with my 1970 Stingray Coupe in the background. The Miura owner and I took the two cars out for an afternoon drive and photo shoot, a very pleasant memory of one fine day. ©1983 Floyd M. Orr Collection

Elegant Italian Sports Car Test Results Chart

Model & Details	HP	Weight	0-60	1/4	TS
1970 Lamborghini Miura S (*R&T*)	370	2905	5.5	13.9	168
1975 Lamborghini Countach (*Motor*)	375	2860	5.6	14.1	175
1976 Lamborghini Silhouette (*R&T*)	260	2750	6.8	15.2	147
1982 Lamborghini Countach LP 500S (*R&T*)	375	NA	5.7	14.1	150
1964-70 Mistral Spyder 4014cc Six (*IMBG*)	255	3153	6.5	14.9	152
1969-72 Ghibli Spyder 4719cc (*IMBG*)	330	3858	NA	17.7	160

Elegant Italian Sports Car Test Results Notes:
   Some of these figures are factory claims, not actual independent tests. Maserati produced only about 9100 cars from 1946 through 1978. Two-hundred and fifty Mexicos were built in 1966-68 and the company produced 1274 Ghiblis in 1967-72, including 125 Spyders. There were 1136 Indy 2+2 models produced in 1969-74. Maserati built 120 Mistral Spyders from 1964 to 1970. The company made 125 Ghibli Spyders in 1969-72, the last twenty-five of which were 4.9-liter SS models. Maserati produced 495 Boras in 1971-78 and at least 1635 Meraks in 1972-78. The Maserati Khamsin followed the Lamborghini Espada styling with its glass rear window in the tail; 352 were built in 1974-78. The Khamsin was the car I followed on Highway 6 in Houston with the ZZ Top license plate. Both models were designed by Marcello Gandini for Bertone. *C/D = Car and Driver. IMBG = Illustrated Maserati Buyer's Guide. R&T = Road & Track.*

Figure F33 - This very rare and valuable 1974 Ferrari Dino 246 GTS in black with tan interior was captured in Greenwich, CT. This Dino is loaded with factory options, including air conditioning ($770), power windows ($270), radio with power antenna ($415), wider wheels with fender flares ($680), and the vinyl racing seats designed for the Daytona ($115). Only sixty-three 246 Dinos were painted black by the factory and most of those were coupes. This is quite likely the very same Dino that sold at auction in California in 2013 for $473,000. ©Mr. Choppers (GNU)

Selected Exotic Italian Ratings Chart

Years	Model	Collect	Drive	Desire
1967 - 1973	Fiat Dino Spider	B	D	B
1972 - 1974	Ferrari Dino 246 GTS	A	D	A
1977 - 1982	Ferrari 308 GTS	C	B	A
1957 - 1962	Ferrari 250 Cabriolet	A	D	C
1959 - 1963	Ferrari California LWB & SWB	A	D	A
1966 - 1967	Ferrari 365 California	B	D	B
1964 - 1966	Ferrari 275 GTS	B	C	B
1967 - 1968	Ferrari 330 GTS	B	C	B
1967 - 1968	Ferrari NART Spyder	A	D	A

1969 - 1974	Ferrari Daytona Spyder	A	D	A
1964 - 1970	Maserati Mistral	B	D	B
1969 - 1972	Maserati Ghibli & Ghibli SS	A	D	A

Models Ratings Chart Definitions:

Years: In most cases, the years listed include the total production years for a particular model series. Some model years within a series may be considerably more desirable than other years.

Models: In some cases many variations are included in this category and in others the models included are very homogeneous. This is generally self explanatory.

Collectibility: This is what most of you want to know, the bottom line on how likely the model or series is likely to climb in value over the coming years.

Drivability: This is an indicator of how adaptable the machine can be to drive for transportation or pleasure in the modern world, considering collector value, parts availability, fuel quality, comfort, performance and miscellaneous other factors.

Desirability: This defines the nostalgic, emotional wow factor, without regard for collector values or everyday usage.

General: No machine is given a failing grade. If it made it into a rating chart, at least a few hobbyists find that model interesting.

Figure F34 - Here is a last look at that same red Ferrari LWB California Spyder pictured in front of a castle earlier in this chapter. When we look back at the era of great dollops of chrome punctuated by the extravagant tail fins of American cars of the same period, it is quite amazing to see a car of this sort of lasting beauty produced in 1959. ©C C Bain (CC)

Topless Italian Exotics

Chapter 7: *Flirtations with Comfort and Convenience*

Figure G1 - **The dash of this classic Sunbeam Alpine of unknown vintage is real wood veneer. Whatever the age, the wood-rimmed steering wheel has that old English look. This is not a garage queen brought out for a show. The odometer reads 62,837 miles and the wood on the dash needs restoration. Yes, the radio speaker is directing its sound to your knees.** ©Akela NDE (CC)

A car manufacturer occasionally tries to split the difference between a stark sports model and a comfortable touring car. This chapter includes four such examples of cars that although not true sports cars, belong in this book for somewhat obvious reasons. These cars were never racetrack inspired. They were designed for mass appeal on the streets of America and each succeeded. Each was intimately connected to a real sports model covered in this book. The Sunbeam Alpine was the calm sister of the Tiger. Datsun brought topless sports cars from the East to compete with the Brits back when we thought Honda was only interested in dominating the motorcycle market. The Corvair sports models competed successfully in the pony car marketplace, at least for a while. Two tons of convertible from *Thelma & Louise* were almost left on the silver screen, but we know that's not the whole story. Before Ford invented the *personal luxury car*, the Thunderbird was a sweet little two-seater and the Corvette's legendary nemesis in showroom sales. Come on and join the party, big girl, and just let the purists wail!

Sunbeam Alpine

Figure G2 - Wow, note the wild T-bird like fins on this early black Alpine! Would you believe the Sunbeam stylists had previously worked at Ford? If you look closely, you can see that this early car has a slick metal top boot. ©Rama (CC)

The Rootes Group in England built and sold 69,251 Sunbeam Alpines worldwide in 1959-68, but no figures are available for exactly how many cars were exported to the U.S., either collectively or by series. The worldwide production breakdown by series is shown in the chart. There is much to discuss about this affordable little sports convertible and opinions vary somewhat widely. First of all, this was not the first Alpine or the first Sunbeam sports convertible, but this is the version far the most common in the U.S. and it also falls solidly within the parameters of this book. Most of the discussion surrounds exactly what sort of car is the Alpine. Is it a baby Thunderbird? The styling and marketing of the two seemingly disparate models is very similar. The obvious resemblance to the early Thunderbird stemmed from the fact that one of the designers had previously worked for Ford. Is it a soft MG B for the chickadees? There would certainly be quite a consensus on that score. Is it nothing more than a declawed Tiger? For that matter, isn't the Tiger just a pipsqueak Cobra running on thirteen-inch wheels? However you categorize it, the Alpine was a conveniently comfortable little English sports car with just enough power and taut handling to make it fun to drive.

The Alpine was marketed in the USA among a distinctly competitive field. The base price strayed only a little from $2500 throughout its production. This pitted it squarely against the very popular MG B and Triumph Spitfire. You would pay more for an Alpine than a Sprite, Midget, or Spitfire, but most sports convertibles of the day were at least somewhat more expensive. However, none of these could rival the Alpine for convenience features for the money. The only one that could was the Fiat Spider/Cabriolet, the sales of which in the USA were somewhat minimal. Fiat's success in the U.S. market would improve exponentially with the introduction of the 850 and 124 Spiders, but these models reached our shores near the end of

Alpine production. In its heyday, the Alpine was a sort of one-of-a-kind, the only affordable, comfortable little English sports convertible.

The Alpine's convertible top was not a marvel of efficiency like that of the Italian cars of the day, but neither did it fire up a streaming cussing attack every time it required raising or lowering. Roll-up windows were present on all Alpines. All tops were permanently attached in true convertible fashion. The top may have required the detailed fiddling of other English cars, but when erected, it sealed out the wind and water better than most. The middle-period models even secured the top under a metal panel; the rest employed the common type of vinyl boot. A removable hardtop was also available. The hardtop version did not have a soft top because there was a small rear seat installed in its place. All Alpine Convertibles had rubber floor mats instead of carpet.

Figure G3 - This yellow Sunbeam Alpine from the early days has the fuel filler on the side of the right rear fender. Contrast this with the later model's filler located closer to the top of the fin. You can also see the single, large, horizontal bar in the grille design of the newer cars. The top is up on this example, but you can tell by the snaps that this car utilizes a vinyl boot. ©Dave 7, Lethbridge, Canada (CC)

The standard axle ratio was 3.89 with the base four-speed and 4.22 with the optional overdrive on Series I & II cars. The 4.22 axle was no longer available on the Series III cars. The 4.22 returned as an option, with or without overdrive, on the Series V. One of the best improvements to the Series III was the spare tire moved to an out of the way vertical position at the back of the trunk and twin gas tanks were added to the rear fenders. These two changes practically doubled the trunk space available for luggage.

First gear was not synchronized until a point into the 1964 model year. Series III cars got better seats, an improved top, a larger trunk, and a new steering wheel design. Series V cars had negative ground electrics with an alternator instead of a generator. Overdrive was an option on all Alpine models and about half of production had this desirable option for highway cruising speeds. There may be a corrosion problem with the aluminum head if the car has not been kept steadfastly supplied with antifreeze to hold back the problem.

Both the Alpine and Tiger had conventional steel bodies. Rust in interior sections of the bodywork is by far the biggest booger of old Alpines. With its superior undercoating from the factory, rust may be the most important damage to look for on a prospective Alpine purchase, but the issue is far less prevalent than on its lesser protected competition. Quite often the cars have not been repaired properly, usually the inexpensive way instead, at some point in their past history as cheap sports models. Most of the common areas such as wheel wells, doorsills, the floorpan, and at body joints are rust suspects. Watch out for patchwork repairs done with fiberglass and/or body filler. Not only was the gearbox updated to a synchronized first gear in the middle of Series IV production, but this newer box has proven to be more durable over time. Some replacement parts for the non-synchro gearbox have become nearly impossible to find, creating another big brownie point for the later models.

Figure G4 - Late model Sunbeam Alpine in British Racing Green with a tonneau cover and traditional silver-painted wire wheels. ©Allen Watkin, London, England (CC)

The way to identify the exterior of the early vs. late cars is by the tailfins, taillights, and gas filler cap. The fins on the early cars slope outward at the top, giving a distinct slant to the taillights. The fins on the later cars are still present, but subdued, stopping at the edge of the trunk line, in front of the rear bumper, leaving the taillights in a more directly vertical pose. The fuel filler is on the right rear fender of all models. On the early cars, it is distinctly within the side view of the right fin. On the later cars, it is located more toward the top of the wider, lower fin.

Figure G5 - A 1967 Venus Red Alpine is decked out with chrome knock-off wire wheels, whitewall tires, and twin mirrors. The top is underneath a conventional vinyl boot. ©Mick, Northamptonshire, England (CC)

The Alpine was improved a little with each series. The seats became more comfortable and adjustable. The trunk space was expanded. The gearbox was improved. The styling was modernized. The axle ratio and overdrive options fluctuated a bit over the production years with the displacement and horsepower changes. The acceleration times varied a bit, as shown in the chart, while the top speed remained relatively constant. Unlike many of its competitors, production ceased before federal regulations began to impact performance. The last two series had softer suspension that displeased hardcore drivers just a bit, but otherwise the Alpine remained consistently in a state of improvement during its production life. The final Series V models were loaded with standard equipment. Reclining bucket seats, a genuine convertible top, full-synchro four-speed, 12V electrical system, telescoping steering wheel, two-speed wipers, map light, full instrumentation, power front disc brakes, and Chrysler's exclusive 50,000-mile power train warranty were all included in the base price. Stuff that up your erector-set tops, MG and Triumph!

Although the Alpine was originally designed and produced by the Rootes Group in England, Chrysler bought chunks of the company over time. By the end of production, the American company owned the kit and kaboodle. As you probably already know, the company quietly axed the Tiger with its Ford 289 after the '67 model year. You would think the company's 273 Barracuda V-8 would fit in the engine bay, but it would not without overly extensive modification. Chrysler chose not to face the uphill battle of taming the Tiger into a cereal spokesman of all talk and no action with the coming regulations of 1968. The Alpine quietly walked off into the sunset with the Tiger.

Sunbeam Alpine Comparison Chart

Details	Series I	Series II	Series III	Series IV	Series V
Models	1959 - 1960	1961 - 1963	1963 - 1964	1964 - 1965	1965 - 1968
Production	11,904	19,956	5863	12,406	19,122
Engine	1494cc	1592cc	1592cc	1592cc	1725cc
Carburetor	2 Zenith 28	2 Zenith 30	1 Solex	1 Solex	2 Stromberg
Horsepower	83 hp	85 hp	88 hp	90 hp	100 hp
Four-speed	No Synchro	No Synchro	No Synchro	Synchro	Synchro
Shocks	Lever	Lever	Telescopic	Telescopic	Telescopic
Rear Fins	High	High	High	Low	Low
Suspension	Moderate	Moderate	Moderate	Softer	Softer
Weight	2200	NA	2185	NA	2220
0 - 60	15.2	14.0	18.1	15.5	14.0
Quarter-mile	20.6	19.3	22.2	20.0	19.3

Sunbeam Alpine Comparison Chart Notes:
Practically all Alpines had a top speed of approximately 100 mph, with only a little variation, mostly below this figure. All Alpines had an all-steel body and an 86-inch wheelbase.

The Land of the Rising Sun

Where was the bane of domestic U.S. car brands during the development of all this affordable sports car mania? Well, they were not actually asleep, but it did sort of appear that way from our distant Yankee tunnel vision. Although Datsun and Toyota had begun their assault on the small sedan market here, the real impact would not be felt nationwide until the later Sixties. Datsun and Toyota slowly invaded the American market throughout the Sixties with the Datsun 310 and 510 and the Toyota Corolla and Corona. There were many other sedan models, of course, but these were the big four sellers in the USA over a long period of time. Toyota built 351 Toyota 2000 GT's with Yamaha in 1967-70, but only about sixty of these were imported here. There were only two convertibles produced, as seen in the James Bond movie, *You Only Live Twice*, shot in Japan. Although the 2000 GT is certainly an interesting car, it lies outside the realm of this book of production sports convertibles.

Figure G6 - A 1967 white Datsun 2000 Sports on display. You cannot see it in this reproduction, but the front license plate says Fairlady, as these cars were called in Japan. You can clearly see the white parking lamps and right hand drive. ©160SX (CC)

Honda was building its position as the world dominator of motorcycle production. (Allow me to plug my previous release, *The Tiddler Invasion: Small Motorcycles of the Sixties*, for prodigious details on that subject.) Honda would not officially import a model into the nationwide USA until the Civic of the '70's. There is one little sports convertible that does deserve mention, however. In the mid-Sixties, Honda produced a tiny little convertible sports model for its own domestic market. The S-600 of 1965 was tested by *Road & Track*. The little

Flirtations with Comfort and Convenience

1640-pound topless squirt produced 57 horsepower from its motorcycle engine in both size and type. This was no thundering pavement pounder with its 17.8-second 0-60, 20.7 quarter-mile, and 90-mph top speed. Remember, this was shown to *R&T* at a time when the GTO was something other than a multi-million-dollar Ferrari. The S-600 was never officially imported and it would be several years before Honda established a dealer network for cars in the USA. *R&T* obtained the test vehicle from a motorcycle distributorship. Sports car fans in the U.S. were denied ownership of a little sweetheart. Honda technology was showing its wares in the four-wheel department, even at that early date. We older motorcycle nuts know that Honda was chasing Formula 1 fame from an early point in the firm's history.

Figure G7 - **This quaint little roly-poly convertible is a Datsun SPL-212, a very rare model in the USA, both then and now. The L stood for Left Hand Drive, so they built at least a few of them.** ©Ypy31 (PD)

Now we come to the only cars of the period from Japan that actually belong in this book, the Datsun Sports models produced by Nissan. Although these models began in 1960 and some small numbers of these early ones were imported into the USA, the numbers did not get serious here until the advent of the 1600/2000 series in 1965. Datsun had begun sending cars to the U.S. by the end of the Fifties, but the numbers were tiny. Even the sedan imports would not reach significant proportions here until 1965. You can see from the chart how the 1600 Sports outnumbered all the other models combined. The production numbered only 505 in total prior to the release of the 1500 Sports in 1963. It is clear in retrospect that the 1600 and 2000 built in 1965-70 were far the most significant of the series. If you squint at it, you can surmise that the

Fairlady SPL212 and SPL213 were the warm-up team for Nissan's new export plan. The 1600 and 2000 Sports were the main event, with the 1500 Sports as a sort of transitional group of models.

Datsun actually started with a fiberglass prototype of which only twenty were built and none were exported to the USA. The Fairlady series built from 1960 to 1962 were not particularly sporty models. They lacked sharp sports car handling characteristics and many mechanical advances such as disc brakes or a fully synchronized transmission. The top design was better than that of the English roadsters of the day. The styling did little to say *sports car*. Neither did the drum brakes and 1.2-liter engine, the stronger of two producing only 59 horsepower.

For purposes of simplicity, let's call the early, low-production models Fairlady and the later, high-production versions Sports. These were their names used for U.S. exports. Back in Japan and in other markets, the Fairlady moniker stayed with the series. The Fairlady models had an 87-inch wheelbase and the Sports models a 90-inch wheelbase. All bodies were steel. The two Fairlady models had a rounded, roly-poly sort of body look. The later Sports models were all very similar with more modern, angular lines. The total production of the two early Fairlady models was precisely 505. It is unknown how many of these came to the USA.

The 1500 Sports rapidly evolved during its short production period. A single-carb, 76-hp version of the SPL310 was offered in late 1963, but only 300 were produced. It is not known if any of these lower-powered versions made it to the USA. A second carburetor brought the power up to 85 hp in 1964. An improved interior and dash layout was introduced shortly before the 1500 was replaced by the 1600 early in 1965. The 1500 Sports included an AM radio, a clock, map lights, and a tonneau cover as standard. The 1500 Sports was the last model with thirteen-inch wheels.

Figure G8 - The red Datsun 1600 Sports is typical of the U.S. models, all of which had whitewall tires and disc wheels with chrome hubcaps. Unlike the many English cars of the period, none of the Datsuns had wire wheels. Base price in 1966 was $2546. You might have thought the fake hood scoop bulge was indigenous to the 2000 model, but all the 1600's and 2000's had it. ©Bill Abbott, photo modified by Mr. Choppers (CC)

The 1600 and 2000 would have fourteen-inch wheels, larger engines, and even more extensive equipment. The 1600 Sports would become the standard bearer until the introduction of the 240Z Coupe in 1970. The up-market 2000 with its overhead-cam engine would debut two years after the first 1600. The 1600 had a 3.89 axle and the 2000 had a 3.70. Both had stabilizer bars front and rear and in typical Japanese fashion, a strong 12V, negative-ground electrical system. Front disc brakes with rear drums were identical on both models. Fully synchronized transmissions were standard on both models. The 1600 had a four-speed and the 2000 a five-speed. Tops, seats and interior developments continued to improve slightly throughout the production period.

Just under one-thousand 2000 Sports models were produced in 1967 without certain U.S. safety accoutrements, and these cars are coveted by collectors. A 150-hp option with twin Mikuni carbs was offered on the U.S. 2000 in 1967 only. This Competition Package raised the top speed to 140 mph. Hagerty's currently rates the 1967 2000 at about $10,000 more than a 1968-70 model, even without the Competition Package. Federal regulations brought a taller windshield, padded dash, flatter switches, and other changes on the 1968 models. An additional visual cue for the 1968-70 models is the inside mirror mounted at the top of the windshield instead of on top of the dash, as in the 1965-67 models. Of all the Datsun Sports, the 1967 2000 is clearly the most coveted as a collectible, particularly if you find a model on which the Competition Package was installed at the factory. The second most desirable is a 1968-70 2000 and third is any 1600 Sports. The 1500 Sports and Fairlady models are worth less on the current U.S. market, even with their lower numbers currently in the USA.

The Datsun Sports brought Japanese reliability to the U.S. imported car market, particularly regarding electrical systems. They had soft tops that worked, too, but so did the Italians. I suspect the durability of the Datsuns' instruments and vinyl seats even surpassed that of the lower-priced Italian models. I would also expect the Datsuns to be ahead of the curve in areas such as oil leaks, transmission failures, and rust prevention. The Japanese have never been famous for Lost In Space electrical systems, dull paint formulas, or finicky carbs, at least not before the Fedral Guvmint started messing with Z Cars after the earliest production years.

Back in these heady days before Mazda decided to do a full autopsy on a Lotus Elan and copy it, sports car handling and driving quality still eluded the Japanese a bit. So did the finer points of styling that Lotus grasped so well. In the Sixties when the Datsun Sports models were built, the Japanese had not yet come to discern the complexities of suspension systems. They were still at the stage that *stiffer is better*. Although generally true, especially in relation to flatter cornering, the suspension must be properly *tuned* to the steering, chassis and tire design. Datsun was on top of things with anti-roll bars at both ends for flat cornering, but the ride was particularly harsh and jiggly, adding to a cacophony of small noises in the interior with the top up. The overall effect was of a very reliable, well-equipped touring car that rode like a small Datsun pickup truck. Remember those?

The Lotus Elan had beautifully clean styling appropriate for a small convertible sports car. Even the MG B had a low, wide stance with smooth lines. Some of us are attracted to the poured over the big wheels, bulldog-like stance of the Triumph TR-4A. Some of you, but not me, may be attracted to the Fifties tailfin look of the early T-bird or Alpine. The problem is that the Datsun Sports offers no such easily defined styling motif. Although not completely unpleasant, it clearly looks like it was styled by committee. The lines are too busy, never impressing with either smoothness nor sharpness. The windshield seems to be a little too upright. The flared wheel wells cover small, skinny tires. The slotted, silver-painted steel wheels with chrome hubcaps are boring and the standard whitewall tires scream anything but *sports car*. The necessary instruments are all on the dash and clearly, properly in front of the driver, but the overall effect of the interior seems uninspiring. I am usually an ass man, but the derriere of the Datsun Sports looks like it escaped from an old Buck Rogers serial!

So what have we got here? We have the first sports convertibles to be officially imported from Japan with nationwide distribution. We have great gobs of reliable systems that we so desperately needed in our imported sports cars. The electrical system stays on the job through the hard times. The instruments tell their tales religiously. The top goes up and down easily and seals out the weather. So the ride is rough, the noise level is high, and the styling is uninspiring. Why does the *Complete Book of Collectible Cars 1940-1980* not even include it, not even the special 1967 2000 Sports with the Competition Package? The answer is both direct and complex. America has always demanded that the Japanese earn respect from us for their products over a long period of time. The Datsun Sports were only the first of their breed. Look at the welcome mat we put out for the 1970 240Z. That model was beloved in the USA from the first one that arrived on our shores. Was it because we like coupes so much? Of course not. I think the earlier convertibles simply had to pave the way, in both styling and suspension development and emotional public acceptance of a sports car from the Land of the Rising Sun.

Figure G9 - This rear view of the same car as above displays its Buck Rogers tail light design. Does this remind you of the mufflers on the 1969 BSA Rocket Three motorcycle? Note the snaps for a conventionally attached top and vinyl boot design. ©Bill Abbott, photo modified by Mr. Choppers (CC)

Datsun Sports Chart

Details	Fairlady	Fairlady	1500 Sports	1600 Sports	2000 Sports
Model	SPL212	SPL213	SPL310	SPL311	SRL311
Years	1960 - 1961	1961 - 1962	1963 - 1965	1965 - 1970	1967 - 1970
Production	288	217	11,124	31,350	14,450
Engine	1189cc	1189cc	1497cc	1597cc	1982cc
Horsepower	47 hp	59 hp	85 hp	96 hp	135 hp
Carburetor	Single SU	Twin SU	Twin SU	Twin SU	Twin SU
Cam	OHV	OHV	OHV	OHV	SOHC
Shift	Four-speed	Four-speed	Four-speed	Four-speed	Five-speed
Gearshift	Non-synchro	Non-synchro	Non-synchro	Synchro	Synchro
Brakes	Drum	Drum	Drum	Disc / Drum	Disc / Drum
Weight	1984 pounds	1962 pounds	1900 pounds	1984 pounds	2006 pounds

Datsun Sports Chart Notes:
Most of the above production numbers were exported, many to the USA. *Wikipedia* states the SR311 weight as 2094. The 2006-pound weight of the 2000 Sports is from *Datsun 280ZX* and confirmed in a brochure for the 1969 model. This might be a factory quote of the dry weight.

Figure G10 - Nissan launched one of the sleekest convertibles ever with the 300ZX Convertible of 1993. This all-black model has its snug top up and shows off its stylish aluminum wheels. These elegant Nissan convertibles were produced in 1993-96 and relatively few were built. The DOHC 3-liter V-6 produced 222 net horsepower to propel the 3400-pound topless version of the much more common Z Coupe. ©Mr. Choppers (GNU)

Chevrolet Corvair Convertible

Convertible versions of the Corvair were produced within the 1962-69 period of the 1960-69 total Corvair model era. The Monza series was available as a convertible throughout, supplemented by the Spyder in 1962-64 and the Corsa in 1965-66. In all years, the Monza was the deluxe version of the Corvair with bucket seats, floor shift and a higher trim level. The Spyder was the sports package with a turbocharged engine in the early models and the Corsa was its fancier replacement with or without the turbo option. GM had realized by 1966 that the Corvair would never be the volume seller the company had originally planned. The straightforward Ford Falcon, Plymouth Valiant, Dodge Dart, and Rambler American, all with basic front engines and rear wheel drive, were far surpassing the Corvair's sales as an economy car. The Mustang was stampeding over the little Porsche wannabe with a long hood covering V-8 power. GM basically ceased further development of the Corvair after 1966.

Figure G11 - 1969 Corvair Monza Convertible in light blue. The interesting option packages were gone by this final production year, but the smooth body contours still looked good. ©Visitor 7 (CC)

You can see from the production chart that the 1962-66 Monza was by far the most common Corvair Convertible model. Positraction and Kelsey-Hayes knock-off wire wheels were added to the option list in 1962; however, it is unfortunate that the wire wheel option was not carried into the new 1965 styling era. Genuine factory wires were an option only with the original body style. By the way, all Corvair Convertibles had thirteen-inch wheels and there were no other

Flirtations with Comfort and Convenience

optional wheel styles, only a selection of hubcaps and wheel covers. Model year 1962 began with three 145-cubic-inch engine choices of 80, 84, and 102 horsepower. The 84-hp unit came only in Powerslide Monzas. Axle choices consisted of 3.27, 3.55, and 3.89 with very few restrictions. The hot turbo Spyder option package for the Monza Coupe and Convertible would appear later in the year. Base weights of the Corvair Convertibles ranged from 2625 for a '62 Monza to 2770 for a '69 Monza.

Four power ratings were listed for the Corvair in 1963: 80, 84, 102, and 150 horsepower. As with all years, all engines were of oversquare design. A 3.08 highway axle ratio was supposedly a new option in 1963, but it was available only with the 102-hp engine. A 3.27 axle was standard equipment on most models with 3.55 and 3.89 optional ratios. Spyders could have only the 3.55. All the manual transmissions were floor mounted and fully synchronized. The only automatic available in all years was the two-speed Powerglide, available with all normally aspirated powerplants. For some reason, the Monza alone had a 145-inch engine in 1963 with 9:1 instead of 8:1 compression, producing 84 horsepower and teamed only with the Powerslide. The 145 cubic inch Six produced 102 horsepower with a special camshaft. A fourteen-gallon fuel tank was mounted in the front compartment and the wheelbase was 108 inches. All Corvair Convertible interiors were vinyl and white was a new color for 1963.

Figure G12 - The red 1962 Monza shows the beginning of Corvair Convertible production. ©Joe Mabel (GNU)

The Spyder was originally an option package on the Monza that included a turbocharged engine, full instrumentation, and a few trim details. The Spyder was marketed as a model separate from the Monza in 1964. The Spyders had turbocharged engines with 150 horsepower. The Spyder option also included a gauge cluster, including a tachometer. Mandatory options with the Spyder included four-speed, 3.55 axle, heavy duty (sport) suspension, and sintered metallic drum brake linings.

Big changes to the drivetrain and chassis were instituted in 1964, while leaving the earlier body style alone. The 1964 car underneath the skin was already changed beyond the complaints lodged by Ralph Nader in his 1965 book, *Unsafe at Any Speed*. It was quite unfortunate that the tricky rear suspension layout had already been deleted prior to the book's release! The next year would bring a sexy new body that would be sold in high numbers for only two years. However, do not make the mistake of blaming Ralph Nader for the Corvair's demise. Chevrolet already knew by this time that the much bigger problems came from Ford's more accurate assessment of the American marketplace. Buyers wanted stylish cars with conventional drivetrains. Buyers who wanted to be chased by wheezy air-cooled engines would choose Beetles, Karmann-Ghias, and Porsches. Americans wanted either econoboxes with absolutely minimal service and maintenance or sporty cars that looked good and burbled with the sound of a V-8. The Camaro and Chevy II were rapidly pushing the Corvair out of the market. Here is a poignant little footnote on Corvair history. Chevrolet was experimenting with electric cars even back in the '60's. The Electrovair II was a 1966 Corvair Monza four-door hardtop with a 100-hp electric motor. The trunk was filled with silver-zinc batteries. The Marina Blue all-electric Monza is still kept as a museum piece by GM.

Figure G13 - The Corvair spare tire resided in the rear with the six-cylinder pancake engine. ©Michael Barera (CC)

Flirtations with Comfort and Convenience

All Corvair Convertibles used a flat six-cylinder, OHV engine with aluminum block and heads. There were only two displacements: 2.4-liter (145 c.i.) in 1962-63 and 2.7-liter (164 c.i.) in 1964-69. The 164 had a longer stroke, but both displacements were oversquare. Three carburetor arrangements were employed. Base engines had dual single-barrel carbs and the hotter variants had four one-barrels. The turbo models used a single sidedraft carburetor. All engines were air-cooled with wet sump lubrication. There was an array of base and optional engines with the dual carburetors over the production period that included gross horsepower ratings of 80, 84, 95, 102, and 110. The sports model engines included a 140-hp, four-carb model and two turbos of 150 and 180 horsepower. The base 145 c.i. aluminum flat six with 80 horsepower was increased to a 164 c.i. with a longer stroke in 1964, upping the base horsepower to 95. The optional 164 produced 110 horsepower. The previous 145 optional engine had made 95 horsepower. Although the Spyder option was now a 164, the turbo engine was still rated at 150 horsepower.

The improved rear suspension began with the 1964 model. The package included a front anti-roll bar, a CorvettE-Type transverse rear leaf spring, and softer springs all around. Engine displacement was upped to 164 in 1964. Monzas came with 95 horsepower with 110 horsepower optional. The 150-hp turbo Spyder was considered a separate model.

The new sleeker body was introduced in 1965. The new suspension and most of the powertrains remained the same. The base Corsa engine in 1965 was a 2683cc aluminum Six producing 140 horsepower from 164 cubic inches. The base Corsa 164 had four one-barrel carbs, dual exhausts, and a full instrument package. Powerglide was not available on Corsas-- yippeee! The base Corsa 164 engine was an option on the Monza. The Corsas had an optional 164-cubic-inch, 180-hp, turbocharged engine available with manual three or four speed transmissions. Air conditioning was not available with turbocharged engines due to a lack of under hood space. Notable options arriving with the 1965 model year included integrated AC, sport suspension with a quicker steering ratio, AM/FM stereo, and a telescoping adjustable steering column.

Sales dropped precipitously after 1966. Thinner, Astro bucket seats were made standard in Monzas in 1967 and a Delco 8-track was an option. Interiors in '67 offered a choice of only black, blue, or gold. The 140-hp Six, standard in the previous year's Corsa, was not listed as an option in the '67 brochure, but this engine could be special ordered by a dealer and a small unknown number, probably less than 300, were installed in 1967 Monzas. Surprisingly, the 140-hp option for Monzas reappeared in the '68 and '69 brochures. The seats would be widened and headrests added in 1969. Air conditioning was deleted from the 1968 and 1969 option lists due to a lack of engine compartment space taken up by the air pump necessary for emission control. FM stereo radios were no longer available in 1969, precipitated by a change in the radio pin connector design by the electronics manufacturer. These two deletions helped to depress sales right when such options were becoming popular in all cars. In 1969 only three engines and two axle ratios were offered. These included three 164-inch Sixes with 95, 110, and 140 horsepower. The base engine ran on regular and the optional ones on premium fuel. You could have any transmission and axle combo you wanted as long as it was the same old three choices with either a 3.27 or 3.55 axle, and even a few of those possible combinations were deleted for 1969.

Chevrolet built more than 1.7 million Corvair variants in the Sixties. Less than 150,000 of these were convertibles. A little more than 26,000 of these convertibles were the up-market sports trim level Spyder or Corsa models. A very significant percentage of the remaining Convertibles were Monzas that ranged from bland 1962 models with 84 horsepower and a two-speed automatic transmission controlled by a lever sprouting from the dash to 1969 models with a little more power, but no hope of even featuring either AC or a stereo radio! In between these two extremes were tens of thousands of Monza Convertibles with 95-110 gross horsepower, bucket seats, and a manual transmission on the floor. Although F41 Sport Suspension and a quick steering ratio of 16.1:1 were offered in most years, you might be shocked at how few buyers added these sporting essentials to the order blank. Other rare but interesting options were a plastic wood steering wheel, telescoping steering column, knock-off wire wheels, and an 8-track tape deck. Unfortunately, you cannot find all these goodies in one car. The wheels were discontinued years before the 8-track option became available. My best guess would be that if you include all the Spyders and Corsas, and all the Monzas with four-on-the-floor, the total number of interesting Corvair Convertibles originally produced by the factory might be about 50,000, maybe 60,000 at best. The single factor that constricts these numbers is that among Monzas in general, that stinking, dash-mounted Powerslide outsold the four-speeds by at least two or three to one! Gag me with a spoon! Barf out! How many four-speed Corvair Convertibles could still be rolling half a century later?

The good news is that none of these models, not even a 1964 Spyder Convertible, has reached the astronomical asking prices of many classic American heroes of the period. You will probably be able to find one you like for a fraction of the cost of a comparable Camaro or Mustang. The downside of course is that the Corvair will never be worth a whole lot in the future, either, probably not even as Ralph Nader's obituary is being read on *The Ten O'Clock News*.

Figure G14 - This is a nice example of a 1969 Monza with its top erect. The color is a pale greenish gold. The full wheel covers and whitewall tires were very common for this model. Wire wheel covers were a popular option. As you can guess, early examples had spinners, but the 1967-69 ones did not. ©Robert Spinello (GNU)

Corvair Convertible Production Chart

Model	Monza	Spyder	Corsa	Totals by Year
1962	13,995	2574		16,569
1963	36,693	7472		44,165
1964	31,045	4761		35,806
1965	26,466		8353	34,819
1966	10,345		3142	13,487
1967	2109			2109
1968	1386			1386
1969	521			521
Totals	122,560	14,807	11,495	148,862

Chevrolet Corvair Convertible Production Chart Notes:
All the above production figures were sourced from the *Complete Book of Collectible Cars 1940-1980*. Other sources have confirmed these same figures.

Corvair Convertible Engine Chart

Year	Model	Cu. In.	Liters / CC	HP	Carbs
1962-63	Monza (base)	145	2.4 - 2375cc	80 - 84 - 102	2 1-bbl.
1962-63	Spyder	145	2.4 - 2375cc	150 Turbo	Single
1964	Spyder	164	2.7 - 2683cc	150 Turbo	Single
1964-69	Monza (base)	164	2.7 - 2683cc	95 - 110	2 1-bbl.
1965-66	Corsa (base)	164	2.7 - 2683cc	140	4 1-bbl.
1965-66	Corsa (optional)	164	2.7 - 2683cc	180 Turbo	Single
1965-69	Monza (optional)	164	2.7 - 2683cc	140	4 1-bbl.

Corvair Convertible Engine Chart Notes;
The 84-hp, 145-inch engine was paired only with the Powerglide automatic in the Monza. The 140-hp, 164-inch engine with four single-barrel carburetors was available only with a manual transmission in the Corsa. The same engine was available in 1965-69 as an option in the Monza with either a manual or automatic transmission.

Alpine / Datsun Sports / Corvair Comparison Chart

Model	Type	CI / CC	HP	Weight	Price
1959-60 Sunbeam Alpine Series I	I-4	91 / 1494	84	2200	NA
1961-62 Sunbeam Alpine Series II	I-4	97 / 1592	84	2200	NA
1963 Sunbeam Alpine Series III	I-4	97 / 1592	88	2185	$2595
1964-65 Sunbeam Alpine Series IV	I-4	97 / 1592	90	2185	NA
1966 Sunbeam Alpine Series V	I-4	106 / 1725	100	2206	$2468
1967 Sunbeam Alpine Series V	I-4	106 / 1725	93	2220	$2567
1960 - 1961 Datsun SPL-212	I-4	73 / 1189	47	1984	NA
1962 Datsun SPL-213	I-4	73 / 1189	59	1962	NA
1963 - 1964 Datsun SPL-310	I-4	91 / 1497	85	1991	NA
1965 - 1970 Datsun SPL-311	I-4	97 / 1600	96	2094	$2766
1967 - 1970 Datsun 2000 Sports	I-4	121 / 1982	135	2116	$3095
1962 Corvair Monza	OP-6	145 / 2375	80	2625	$2846
1962 - 1963 Corvair Spyder Turbo	OP-6	145 / 2375	150	2675	NA
1963 Corvair Monza	OP-6	145 / 2375	84	2525	$2798
1964 Corvair Monza	OP-6	164 / 2683	95	2555	$2811
1964 Corvair Spyder Turbo	OP-6	164 / 2683	150	2580	NA
1965 - 1969 Corvair Monza	OP-6	164 / 2683	95	2695	$2682
1965 - 1969 Corvair Monza	OP-6	164 / 2683	140	2770	NA
1965 - 1966 Corvair Corsa Turbo	OP-6	164 / 2683	180	2720	NA
1967 - 1969 Corvair Monza	OP-6	164 / 2683	110	2725	NA

Alpine / Datsun Sports / Corvair Comparison Chart Notes:
All Alpines had an 86-inch wheelbase. The Datsun SPL-212 and SPL-213 had an 87-inch wheelbase. The Datsun SPL-310 and SPL-311 had a 90-inch wheelbase. All Corvairs had a 108-inch wheelbase. The original base retail prices quoted in some cases may not be exactly accurate for the model year or years listed.

The T-Bird Phenomenon

Figure G15 - **This shiny black 1956 Thunderbird is easily identified by its continental kit. Note the wide whitewalls, wire wheels and porthole hardtop, too.** ©Morven, Buena Park, CA (GNU)

I fought long and hard against including the classic Ford Thunderbird Convertibles in *Daydreams in the Wind*. Of course this silent battle was waged within my own sports car obsessed brain. As I once wrote somewhere on the Internet, I referred to myself as a *Legend Within His Own Mind*. I think that sums up what I am trying to communicate here. Sometimes you just have to say *What the...* and go where no self-respecting sports car has ever gone before. How can the star of this book be the Corvette without even mentioning its original nemesis, the T-bird? That pint-sized luxury boat of a convertible once outsold the Plastic Fantastic by a truly embarrassing ratio. My future favorite car was almost murdered by its own parents because of this travesty that occurred while it was still in its infancy. We all know the old story. I do not need to regurgitate it here. Americans could think of nothing to say other than *What the...?* when the Corvette was introduced with both side curtains and a Powerslide! What in the name of Ron and Rand Paul are you trying to sell here? You are either *pro* life and *pro* military spending or you are pro choice and want to rein in military spending. You either want to shift through four gears with the wind in your face or cruise to the beauty parlor with minimal fuss. Now which is it? The politician that knows his own constituency wins, and so does the car company that knows its own customers!

Figure G16 - Red 1955 Thunderbird parked next to a Porsche 930 Turbo. What a pair to be displayed side by side! ©Morven, Buena Park, CA (GNU)

All the first generation of Thunderbirds were convertibles with roll-up or power windows. There was no four-on-the-floor transmission option and most of the Birds had automatics, anyway. The two most unusual characteristics of the early Birds was that the removable fiberglass hardtop was considered standard equipment, with the soft convertible top as an option. Like most of the classic Corvettes, a buyer could order either or both tops. The second unusual component was the combination of a bench seat with a floor shift, as shared by all the 1955-57 T-Birds. Although we refer to these Birds as two-seaters, nothing ever stopped someone from squeezing in the middle for a short distance ride. Unlike the Corvette, the Bird blasted out of the gate with a standard four-barrel V-8 with dual exhausts. The '55-57 T-Bird was comparable to the equivalent Corvette in straight-line power and in power-to-weight ratio, but the Corvette was far sportier in cornering power and general handling. Once Chevrolet dumped the side curtains, the top design and overall comfort level approached that of the Birds.

However, the Birds flew out into the world of luxury, leaving any sporting pretense behind in 1958. The *Squarebirds*, as they would later be nicknamed, offered a fixed-roof coupe as the base model, but of course we only care about the Convertible. This second T-Bird series updated the powerplant with the 352 V-8 and the 430 would be added as an option in the second year of the new four-seat body style. As you can see in the chart, this new style added nearly a half ton

Flirtations with Comfort and Convenience

of all-new road-hugging weight, leaving the sports car pretense back at the ranch with the much lower production Corvette. From 1960 onward, the Thunderbird would just get fatter and fatter like the Las Vegas Elvis. At this point, you may well ask what the big fat T-Bird is doing in this book, anyway. The answer is that, like the Las Vegas Elvis, this car was certainly a major player in American history, disgusting though the ending of the story may be. The Corvette gets more ink than any other car in this book. I think the Corvette's original nemesis deserves at least a few pages. So let's just hold hands and follow Thelma and Louise off that cliff, shall we?

The third series of Thunderbirds kept marching deeper into the personal luxury car abyss. Ford settled on the 390 V-8 for the mass production of their new high-volume Bird. Oddly enough, the car kept its bucket seats, but the shifter moved to the column for all models. The last manual transmission was installed in a Bird in 1960. All models would now have Cruise-O-Matics. The 1962 and '63 models will forever carry the distinction of the rare and coveted Sports Roadster and M-code Birds. These two options, particularly together, will forever remain the most collectible of the four-seater Thunderbird Convertibles. The styling of the third generation looks a bit Buck Rogers today, but still more modern than the previous Squarebirds. For an American car of this era, the 1961-63 models were an example of good clean styling with minimal chrome doodads to muck it up. The big Bird would meet its long-term rivals beginning in this era. The late-season intro of the 1961 Oldsmobile Starfire would fire the first warning shot over its convertible bow from The General. The 1962 model would add a coupe with much larger sales numbers, but the coupe-only Pontiac Grand Prix introduced that same year would remain the Bird's most serious competition for decades to come. The General played its ace card with the cleanly styled Buick Riviera in 1963. Although the Riv was probably the Bird's most direct nemesis, it would never reach the Thunderbird's sales numbers.

The final series of T-Birds that included a convertible model was built in 1964-66. Clearly the biggest, heaviest, most ponderous models included in this book, these latest topless Birds did offer timeless styling that still looks good today. The clean lines with little chrome adornment surround an elegant cockpit with a bar-lounge-style wraparound rear bench seat. The Sports Roadster was gone but the styling was an elegant improvement.

The 1955 model was introduced with a 193-hp 292 with three-speed manual and an optional three-speed automatic with 198 horsepower as the result of a slightly higher compression ratio. The early version of the Ford-O-Matic was a three-speed that functioned like a two-speed automatic. The transmission started in second gear in all normal operation. The driver could move the lever into *Low* for a specific start in the transmission's first gear, and then upshift manually into *Drive*. All engines had floor shifters and six-volt electrical systems. Axle ratios in 1955 and 1956 were 3.73 with the three-speed manual, 3.92 with overdrive, and 3.31 with automatic. Dual exhausts exited through the rear bumper guards. The 1955 model had a bench seat and floor shift. All interiors were vinyl. Popular options in 1955 were power steering, brakes, and windows, radio, heater, whitewall tires, tachometer, clock, fender skirts, full wheel covers and wire wheel covers. A telescoping steering wheel was standard and a power seat was optional. The seat was a bench, not buckets. The top was manually operated and a power top was not an option. Production began in only three exterior and interior colors, offering several combinations of black, red or blue, all with white seat panels.

Figure G17 - A steel gray 1956 Thunderbird shows off its basic full wheel covers, widewalls, and contrasting white hardtop. The hood scoop on this and other early models was fake. ©Morven, Buena Park, CA (GNU)

The 1956 model brought the first portholes in the fiberglass hardtops and the continental kit that expanded available luggage space in the trunk. Soft tops were either black or white in 1956, but the optional hardtop was offered in many matching or contrasting colors. An optional color-keyed tonneau cover added a sporty flair. The drivetrains in 1956 included the standard 202-hp 292 with three-speed manual, optional 312 with 215 horsepower with overdrive, or 225 horsepower with automatic. All 1956 shifters were on the floor, all engines had dual exhausts, and the electrical system was 12-volt. All interiors were vinyl. The '56 model can be identified by its external spare tire, external side vents for interior ventilation, and exhaust tips moved out to the ends of the rear bumper. The spare tire added weight to the extreme rear of the car, precipitating a handling problem, so the continental kit look lasted only one model year. A Signal Seeking AM radio was a new option in '56. The seat was still a bench with white center panels and the shifter was in the floor, whether manual or Ford-O-Matic.

Flirtations with Comfort and Convenience

Figure G18 - Is it Coral? Is it Pepto Bismal Pink? Is it the Pink Panther? No, it's the most attractive of the two-seater Birds in a gag-me-with-a-spoon color! ©Morven, Buena Park, CA (GNU)

The 1957 Bird had a 270-hp 312 with dual four-barrels as the top option. A 285-hp version is mentioned in the brochure, but whatever produces the additional fifteen horsepower is not mentioned. *Wikipedia* mentions that two options were offered of the 312 with a Paxton supercharger rated at 300 and 340 horsepower. These are not mentioned in the brochure we have, but *Wikipedia* states that 211 were sold. A 245-hp, four-barrel 312 was optional with Ford-O-Matic or Overdrive. The 270-hp could be ordered with any transmission. The base powertrain was a 212-hp 292 with a two-barrel and Conventional Drive. The Conventional Drive was a standard three-speed. It is not stated whether it was on the column or floor. The optional overdrive kicked in and out automatically from third gear. The optional Ford-O-Matic was a three-speed automatic in the floor. Axle ratios in 1957 were 3.56 with the three-speed, 3.70 with overdrive, and 3.10 with automatic. The top availability in 1957 included a standard hardtop with or without portholes in the body color or a contrasting color. A soft top in black, blue, tan or white was optional with or without the hardtop. The '57 model is easily distinguished by its taller fins and spare tire mounted vertically in the trunk. The exterior paint was of a new, glossier formula and the exterior and interior color choices were expanded. The seat was still a bench with white inserts and the shift was still in the floor, however a redesigned dash panel was new for '57.

The 1958 Bird was nearly two feet longer and nearly a thousand pounds heavier. The '58 model was the first Ford with unibody construction. The 1958 engine was the 300-hp 352 with four-barrel and dual exhausts. The 1958 standard transmission was a manual three-speed with a 3.70 axle, with or without overdrive. The automatic was paired with a standard 3.10 axle with a 2.91 optional. The seat panels were still white, but buckets replaced the previous bench. A new dash layout in a dual-cowl motif looked a little sportier than that of the earlier models. Air conditioning was a new option and a power convertible top was new and standard equipment. A console was new and standard equipment for 1958, but surprisingly, when the Bird finally got bucket seats, the shift moved to the column! The 1958 model can be identified by the five pieces of filigree trim on the lower rear corner of each door.

Figure G19 - A Brandywine Red 1959 Square Bird poses for the camera. ©Morven, Buena Park, CA (GNU)

A choice of leather or cloth seats became standard in 1959, and a continental kit was optional. There is very little to visually distinguish the 1959 model other than the upholstery. Chrome trim was added to the *spear* on each door with the word *Thunderbird* spelled out in chrome script within and just behind the chrome spear. The big news for 1959 was the optional 430-cubic-inch V-8, the largest ever put in a Thunderbird.

The 1960 model can be identified by its triple tail lights, instead of the dual ones of the previous two years. The 1960 model received a new power-operated mechanism for the large, opening top boot / trunk lid panel. This meant the driver no longer had to get out of the car and step to the rear to manually lift the boot lid in order to raise or lower the convertible top. This new automated system would prevail through the production of the 1966 T-Bird Convertible, as well as the Lincoln Continental four-door convertible. The fiberglass rear seat cover of the upcoming Sports Roadster did not interfere with the top mechanism or the automatic operation of the boot panel, either. You could raise or lower the power top with the panel in place.

The '61 model had power drum brakes. The Swing-Away Wheel was a new option in 1961. The 1961 model had a new for Thunderbird 300-hp 390 V-8 with a 3.00 axle ratio. All T-birds through 1965 would have a 390. Power steering and power brakes were standard. Vinyl upholstery was standard with leather optional. There were no longer any manual transmissions available; all models utilized the new three-speed Cruise-O-Matic with a column shift. A console was still standard on all models. The 1961 can be identified by its clean side view styling with four horizontal chrome bars below the rear tail fins.

Flirtations with Comfort and Convenience

Figure G20 - This white '63 Sports Roadster is what every Bird collector wants. ©Morven, Buena Park, CA (GNU)

The 1962 Convertible weighed 4530; the '62 Sports Roadster weighed 4631. The wire-wheel knock-off spinners on the Sports Roadster were fake. The genuine bolt-on wire wheels on the SR were built by Kelsey-Hayes in a 48-spoke design. The axle ratio was 3.00:1. A new M-code optional 390 with three 2-barrel Holley carbs producing 340 horsepower was introduced in 1962. The option continued into 1963 with only 200 M-code cars produced in both model years collectively. Like the 48-spoke wires that broke apart when Sunbeam tried them on a Tiger, Elvis the King broke one on his Sports Roadster in hard cornering. The 1962 model can be identified by the pointless chrome trim pieces on the body sides behind the rear wheels.

The 1963 model was the first Bird with an alternator instead of a generator. The 1963 model can be identified in side view by its sculpted line over slanted chrome filigree trim on the doors. An AM radio was finally made standard with an AM/FM as an option for the first time on a Bird.

The 1964 model can be identified by the word *Thunderbird* spelled out in metal letters across the forward edge of the hood. The wire wheels and fiberglass tonneau combo from the previous Sports Roadster package were offered together as a dealer-installed option, but only about fifty were purchased. The 1964 wire wheels were fourteen-inch, like those of the previous Sports Roadster.

Power front disc brakes were standard in 1965. This was also the first year of the sequential turn signals, the same ones that would be applied to the later Shelby Mustangs.

The 1966 model could be identified by its egg crate grille with a large Thunderbird emblem in the center. The 428 option cost only $86, making it quite popular. An 8-track tape deck was a new option, although the AM/FM radio was still monaural.

Alpine, Datsun Sports, Corvair, Thunderbird

Figure G21 - You can see the top edge of the distinctively rounded, barroom style rear seatbacks on this black **1964 T-bird Convertible.** ©Morven, Buena Park, CA (GNU)

Thunderbird Convertible Specifications Chart

Model	Base V-8	Optional	Dry Weight	Front Brakes	Wheels
1955	193-hp 292	198-hp 292	2980 lbs.	Manual Drum	15-inch
1956	202-hp 292	215/225-hp 312	3088 lbs.	Manual Drum	15-inch
1957	212-hp 292	245/270-hp 312	3134 lbs.	Manual Drum	14-inch
1958	300-hp 352	None	3903 lbs.	Manual Drum	14-inch
1959	300-hp 352	350-hp 430	3903 lbs.	Manual Drum	14-inch
1960	300-hp 352	350-hp 430	3897 lbs.	Manual Drum	14-inch
1961	300-hp 390	None	4130 lbs.	Power Drum	14-inch
1962	300-hp 390	340-hp 390	4370 lbs.	Power Drum	14-inch
1963	300-hp 390	340-hp 390	4320 lbs.	Power Drum	14-inch
1964	300-hp 390	None	4441 lbs.	Power Drum	15-inch
1965	300-hp 390	None	4588 lbs.	Power Disc	15-inch
1966	315-hp 390	345-hp 428	4496 lbs.	Power Disc	15-inch

Thunderbird Convertible Specifications Chart Notes:

The first generation, two-seat Thunderbirds had a 102-inch wheelbase. All the four-seaters had a 113-inch wheelbase. The trunk was advertised as having twenty cubic feet in most model years. The quoted figure was for the hardtop models; the capacity of the convertibles was likely a little lower. The early three-speed automatics were Ford-O-Matics, or Fordomatic, as written in at least one brochure. This transmission utilized only second and third gear when operated in low stress conditions. First gear could be manually selected when starting or it would kick down under full throttle. The 1955-60 models had choices of a three-speed manual, with or without an overdrive on third gear, or a Ford-O-Matic in 1955-57 or a Cruise-O-Matic in 1958-60. All the shifters in these models were on the floor. All 1961-66 models had a three-speed Cruise-O-Matic on the column as the standard and only transmission choice. All weights listed are for base engine and transmission convertibles. Power drum brakes were optional throughout production of the first two Thunderbird series.

Figure G22 - This bright yellow '65 Bird shows off its aftermarket Sports Roadster package consisting of genuine wire wheels and a fiberglass panel covering the rear seats. The Thunderbird winged emblem replaced the Thunderbird letters across the nose of the 1964 model. ©Morven, Buena Park, CA (GNU)

Classic Ford Thunderbird Convertible Production Chart

Early Birds	Square Birds	Bullet Birds	Sports Roadsters	Flair Birds
1955: 16,155	1958: 2134	1961: 10,516	1962 SR: 1307	1964: 9198
1956: 15,631	1959: 10,261	1962: 8457	1962 SRM: 120	1965: 6846
1957: 21,380	1960: 11,860	1963: 5913	1963 SR: 455	1966: 5049
Total: 53,166	Total: 24,255	Total: 24,886	Total: 1882	Total: 21,093
			All Convertibles	125,282

Classic Ford Thunderbird Convertible Production Chart Notes:

The 1958 production number is particularly low because the new four-seat convertible model did not begin construction until June, 1958. Ford would resurrect the T-Bird Convertible as a two seater with removable hard and soft tops in 2002. Ford built 68,098 of the final T-Bird convertible in 2002-05. This model was powered by a 3.9-liter DOHC Jaguar V-8 of 252 horsepower with a five-speed automatic in 2002. Power was increased to 280 horsepower in the 2003-05 models. This last topless Bird was produced in a series of retro exterior and interior color patterns.

Selected Comfortable Sports Car Ratings Chart

Years	*Model*	*Collect*	*Drive*	*Desire*
1959 - 1968	Sunbeam Alpine	D	D	D
1965 - 1970	Datsun 1600 Sports	D	B	C
1967 - 1970	Datsun 2000 Sports	D	B	C
1962 - 1969	Corvair Monza Convertible	C	C	C
1962 - 1964	Corvair Spyder Convertible	B	C	B
1965 - 1966	Corvair Corsa Convertible	B	C	B
1955 - 1957	Ford Thunderbird	A	B	B
1958 - 1960	Ford Thunderbird Convertible	C	B	C
1961 - 1963	Ford Thunderbird Convertible	C	A	C
1962 - 1963	Ford Thunderbird Sports Roadster	B	B	B
1964 - 1966	Ford Thunderbird Convertible	C	A	C

Models Ratings Chart Definitions:

Years: In most cases, the years listed include the total production years for a particular model series. Some model years within a series may be considerably more desirable than other years.

Models: In some cases many variations are included in this category and in others the models included are very homogeneous. This is generally self explanatory.

Collectibility: This is what most of you want to know, the bottom line on how likely the model or series is likely to climb in value over the coming years.

Drivability: This is an indicator of how adaptable the machine can be to drive for transportation or pleasure in the modern world, considering collector value, parts availability, fuel quality, comfort, performance and miscellaneous other factors.

Desirability: This defines the nostalgic, emotional wow factor, without regard for collector values or everyday usage.

General: No machine is given a failing grade. If it made it into a rating chart, at least a few hobbyists find that model interesting.

Chapter 8: *Hybrid Hotrods - The Essence of Speed & Style*

Figure H1 - This interior design in a 1965 Shelby Cobra may or may not be perfectly original, but it certainly is a sight for nostalgic eyes. The seats are oatmeal colored and the dash and steering wheel are real wood. The top panel of the center console and the radio position may not be original. The radio itself is definitely of modern manufacture. The famous backward mounted shift lever is clearly displayed. ©Eli Christman, Richmond, VA (CC)

A name for this category of convertible sports car had to be created from scratch. There does not seem to be an adequate description commonly applied. Most, but not all of these are high-performance models. The one common thread is they all have drivetrains designed and constructed in the U.S. mated to bodies and interiors built by an entirely separate company. Most are sourced from Italy or England and most utilize a commonly produced American V-8. Examples range from the obscure to the legendary. Some have all the pizzaz of an antique and some flaunt their luxurious fittings. As nostalgic collectible cars, they are all *very* interesting.

Sunbeam Tiger, Shelby's Stepchild

Figure H2 - Red Sunbeam Tiger I with Minilite wheels in England. ©Brian Snelson, Hockley, Essex, England (CC)

A couple of years after the release of the legendary Shelby Cobra, a representative of the Rootes Group in England contacted Carroll Shelby about the possibility of a similar project. The Rootes Group had been producing its Sunbeam Alpine since 1959 as a comfortable alternative to the racing heritage of an MG or the bulldog image of a Triumph. The Alpine had been a steady seller as the alternative to the MG and Triumph for birds in England and chicks in the USA. The company had been impressed with what Shelby had done with the AC roadster and contracted him to design a Sunbeam equivalent. Carroll Shelby developed the Sunbeam Tiger, but thereafter the Rootes Group decided to have the car produced in England by Jensen. Rootes imported Ford 260 V-8's from Dearborn and paid Shelby a royalty for each car built. Shelby continued Cobra development and became famous also for Mustang modifications. The Rootes Group and Jensen quietly turned out 7083 Tigers in 1964-67.

The future of the Tiger would be cut short when Chrysler bought out the Rootes Group in early 1967. Chrysler continued production of the Alpine, but as you might guess, the company was not thrilled about selling a car with a Ford engine. Sources have stated that Chrysler did not have an engine that would easily fit within the Tiger's engine bay, so the Tiger was quietly dropped after 1967 production ended.

There were officially two Tiger models produced. The Tiger I or Series I was constructed from 1964-67 using the same basic 260 V-8 in all cars. The company produced 6450 Series I cars with most of production exported to America. Strangely, the 260 V-8 was used consistently in its original basic form with 164 gross horsepower. Sources state that this engine had dual exhausts of 1.75-inch diameter in all Tigers. Why was the horsepower rating not altered from that of the 260 Mustang? The Mustang had moved on to the 289 and discontinued the 260 in September '64. Rootes neither changed to the new 289 nor attempted power mods on the 260. All engines used the original single two-barrel carb, but with dual exhaust. (This kid was obviously not raised by Carroll Shelby!) Minimal changes were made to the suspension front and rear to accommodate the Ford V-8, including heavier springs to handle more than 400 pounds additional weight, mostly on the front wheels. The Tiger had rack and pinion steering instead of the recirculating ball type of the Alpine. All Tigers utilized the standard Ford four-speed and Girling power disc brakes in the front with drums in the rear. The Tiger had a walnut veneer dashboard not shared with the Alpine. Approximate performance included an 8.6-second 0-60 and a top speed of about 120. Initial base price was $3500.

Figure H3 - British Racing Green Tiger II 289. ©John Lloyd of Five Sunbeam Tigers, Concrete, WA (CC)

There was one key difference between a Tiger and a Cobra. Cobras were built in Los Angeles from bodies constructed in England and shipped over. Final assembly was always completed in the USA. All Tigers were constructed in England at the Jensen factory using Ford engines that were ordered and shipped to the car factory from the U.S. Ford engine plant. All

Tigers of any given period were built to identical specifications with no options or drivetrain modifications of any kind. These were shipped to the U.S. with all stock equipment installed. Both the distributor and individual dealers could, and did, install options from what was called the LAT (Los Angeles Tiger) Catalog. Looking at a copy of one such catalog, here is a list of those options: Edelbrock manifold with Holley four-barrel, Traction Masters, aluminum oil pan, aluminum valve covers, scatter shield, high-lift cam, limited-slip differential, heavy-duty clutch, aluminum wheels, headers and two-inch exhaust system, and numerous other items, large and small. Bone-stock Tigers from England are rare in the U.S. for ridiculously obvious reasons. The issue you as a current prospective buyer must face is whether or not certain performance equipment on the Tiger you want was installed at the original point of sale, does it affect the current or future value or not, and do you care or not?

Figure H4 - Sunbeam Tiger Dash. ©Motohide Miwa, USA (CC)

Most of the Series I Tigers were based on the Series IV Alpine of January 1964 until the Series V arrived in September 1965. These had positive ground electrical systems and metal boots over the folded soft tops. The later Series I Tigers, often referred to as Series 1A continued with the Ford 260 engine in the new Series V Alpine body. These cars featured the improvement of a negative ground electrical system, but the Mercedes-style metal top boot was exchanged for a conventional snap down vinyl boot. The final Tigers, produced only within the 1967 model year, were basically a Series V Alpine with the 200-hp Ford 289 installed instead of the final 1725cc Alpine four-cylinder.

A case of too little too late brought the 289 to the Series II model in 1967. Rootes had hardly had time to produce and market the Tiger II before Chrysler pulled the plug. Approximately 550 Tiger II models were built in 1967. The final U.S. sales were completed as 1968 models, even though actual production in England had ceased back in June of 1967. The larger V-8 brought the top speed up to 122 mph and the 0-60 time down to 7.5 seconds. You can spot a Tiger II by its different grille and GT stripes on the lower body sides.

Sunbeam Tiger Color Chart

Exterior	Interior	Exterior	Interior
Arctic White	Black	Mediterranean Blue	Black
Arctic White	Red	Midnight Blue	Azure Blue
Jet Black	Tan	Carnival Red	Black
Jet Black	Red	British Racing Green	Black

Sunbeam Tiger Color Chart Notes:
All color combinations may not have been available in all model years. Other colors or combinations may have been available in certain years. All soft tops were black, but optional hardtops could be ordered in the body color. These color combinations were sourced from a brochure printed in England for the U.S. and Canadian markets.

Sunbeam Tiger Production Chart

Model	USA	Shelby	Tigers United	Details
1964 Tiger I	1462	1649	7 prototypes	2565 (*R&T*) - $3499
1965 Tiger 1	1768	3020	3763 (4/64-8/65)	2653 wet
1966 Tiger 1A	1486	1826	2706 (8/65-2/66)	
Total Tiger I	4716	6495	6476	0-60 in 8.6 / 120 mph
1967 Tiger II	292	421	2 prototypes	2560 (*R&T*) - $3797
1968 Tiger II	101	151	73 (South Africa)	$3842
Total Tiger II	393	572	534 (12/66-6/67)	0-60 in 7.5 / 122 mph
Total Tigers	5109	7067	7085	

Sunbeam Tiger Production Chart Notes:
Exact Sunbeam Tiger production numbers are almost impossible to verify. Four companies (Shelby, Rootes, Jensen, and Chrysler) were involved and most of the original production records were lost long ago. The Shelby American Automobile Club has compiled the numbers by model year. The Tigers United and The International Registry of Sunbeam Tigers websites have compiled the numbers by series and production periods. All sources agree that there were gaps in the chassis numbers, complicating the enumeration process even further. The 73 cars sent to South Africa were built throughout the 1964-67

production period. These were not all 1968 models, as simplified in the chart. The *Shelby American Guide* and the *Complete Book of Collectible Cars 1940-1980* state exactly the same worldwide production numbers. *R&T = Road & Track*.

Snake Charmer

Figure H5 - This blue 1962 Cobra 260 was the first car produced. ©Jaydec (GNU)

The AC/Shelby Cobra picked up where the Tiger left off. Of course this is not chronologically correct: the Cobra was launched in 1962 and the Tiger followed it in 1964. What is true is that the Tiger was modified from its Alpine sister to a much lesser degree than the Cobra was from the AC Ace. Of course I am playing mind games with you because that statement is not exactly correct, either. Few Americans are aware of the degree to which the AC sports car was rapidly heading in the direction of the Cobra it would soon become, even before the first car was shipped to Shelby's operation in Venice, California.

The original Ford 260 V-8 replaced an English Ford Zephyr inline six-cylinder of similar displacement. AC had already been aware that the Bristol engine the company had been installing in its Ace was about to be dismissed from production. AC had already experimented with the installation of a 2.6-liter engine prior to the legendary contact initiated by Carroll Shelby. When Mr. Shelby contacted AC in 1962, he was expecting to install the Ford 221-inch V-8 into a body and chassis supplied by AC. However, this small V-8 was never installed, even in the first experimental Cobra, because Ford had already introduced its 260 by the end of 1962. Even the first Ford V-8 that Shelby had shipped to England was not a 221. AC personnel thought it was until years later when a measure of the bore proved it to be a Ford 260 V-8. The 221 had a 3.5-inch bore and the 260 had a 3.8; the two shared a 2.87-inch stroke. The Tiger comparison is mentioned because the V-8 was shipped to England, where it was installed in the car. With the exception of the dual exhausts, the 164-hp 260 and the 200-hp 289 were installed in the Tiger with a two-barrel carburetor and other basic specifications. Tigers could be modified after returning to the U.S. distributor if desired. Cobras were shipped from England to California without engines installed. Shelby then installed a highly modified 260 with four-barrel, dual exhausts, mechanical lifters, a hot cam and other performance modifications. At least some of the 289's and 427's were also highly modified, but many of the small blocks were standard 271-hp Mustang units and most of the 427's had the standard rated horsepower of 425. The 428's installed in some Cobras will be discussed later. It has not been verified if these were all standard 355-horsepower versions or not.

Figure H6 - This sky blue 428 Cobra may be a replica. ©Stahlkocher (GNU)

All Cobras shared certain characteristics and equipment. All models had a 90-inch wheelbase, tube frame, aluminum body, black leather upholstery, wood-rimmed steering wheel, black erector-set roadster top with side curtains, four-wheel manual disc brakes, limited slip differential, and independent rear suspension. A four-speed manual transmission was standard on all models (except for the last two automatic 427's built specifically for Carroll Shelby and Bill Cosby). An optional three-speed automatic was ordered on approximately thirty 289 Cobras. Although a wide range of rear axle ratios were offered on certain models, most of the production had a 3.31, 3.54, or 3.77. FM radio, air conditioning, power steering, and electric or roll-up windows were never offered as factory options. Either a single four-barrel or dual four-barrel carbs was standard or optional on all Cobras, depending on the model. A few small-blocks may have been produced with four two-barrel Webers, but the general opinion seems to be that these brought more cost and maintenance issues than they were worth.

Figure H7 - This 1966 427 Cobra in black at Bonhams in Paris is the real thing! ©2012 The Supermat (CC)

Figure H8 - The very rare black 1971 AC Frua 428 was sort of an Italian Cobra. The Italian coach builder created a smooth, modern body for an AC chassis powered by a Ford 428. ©Emmanuel D (PD)

A few late-model 289's with the chassis and body of the 427 were built and sold in England with right-hand-drive. Some of these may have had brown or shades other than black in the interior. The powertrains for these cars were installed in England by AC, not in the U.S. by Shelby. This English model is not included in any production figures charted in this book. The AC 289 Cobra was constructed alongside its replacement, AC Frua 428. These cars featured bodies designed and built by Frua in Italy and were powered by the same Ford 428 big-block as the later Cobras. Parts supplies for the AC 289 Cobra were used up by the end of 1968, but the Frua 428 would continue in production until 1973. There were only 29 Frua 428's built in total. Considering the necessary federal updates needed practically at the time production began, it is even doubtful if any of these made it to the USA. If so, they were most likely either the earliest models or gray-market cars brought here by individual owners.

As shown in the chart below, less than 1000 Cobras were constructed, helping to keep the prices ridiculously high in our modern auction market. Unlike many sports cars covered in this book, the more valuable and sought after Cobras tend to be from the middle of the production run. With most collectible cars, it usually seems to be either the beginning or the end of production that is most highly desirable. This is still true with the Cobras, of course, when you are talking about individual cars that may have been owned by famous celebrities or Shelby himself. However, as far as the general production run goes, enthusiasts are usually looking for 289's and 427's instead of 260's and 428's. As with all collectibles, condition and originality are everything. With Cobras, the first part is easy. It's a relatively crude and simple automobile. The second part is much tougher to ascertain: Cobras were assembled one at a time in several different facilities. Changes were made constantly according to parts availability and the whims of the boss. This is why it is still today difficult to enumerate exactly how many were built with 427's and how many with 428's and the same is true with many detail issues of the cars' construction. With such a huge fan base chasing astronomical prices for such low production, there is no shortage of printed material available. The leading accurate source for detailed information is generally considered to be the Shelby American Automobile Club. Consider this book a quick reference that places the Cobra into perspective in the world of classic sports convertibles.

The small-block Cobras were visually distinguished by their small radiator openings with egg crate grilles installed and minimal fender flares. All the big blocks had larger grille openings without inserts and wider bodywork featuring big, bulbous fenders to cover the 427 Cobra's wider tires.

Most Cobras were produced in standard colors of blue, red, white, black, green, or silver. A small, unspecified number were built in various optional colors. The standard wire wheels were painted silver and had knock-off hubs. Chrome wires were optional. All small-block Cobras came standard with 72-spoke, knock-off wire wheels. American Racing five-spoke alloys were optional, but few buyer's chose them because they preferred the classic wire look. The Halibrand wheels used on the big-blocks were true magnesium racing wheels and of two different designs, according to the availability at the time each car was built.

Cobras were built at three locations, as noted in the chart below. The first thirty cars were assembled at Dean Moon's Firestone tire shop in Santa Fe Springs, CA. All remaining small-block models were built at a new Shelby facility in Venice, CA, the same shop where Lance Reventlow had previously constructed his Scarab racers. All the big-block models were produced in a rented airplane hangar at the Los Angeles airport.

Hybrid Hotrods

Figure H9 - This updated interior belongs to a 1965 Cobra. Note the modern shoulder belts and white-faced gauges. This car is also possibly a fiberglass replica. ©Joe Mabel (GNU)

Shelby Cobra Specifications Chart

Mark I 260	Mark I 289	Mark II 289	Mark III 427	Mark III 428	427 S/C
1962	1963	1964 - 1965	1965 - 1967	1967 - 1968	1966 - 1968
260 V-8	289 V-8	289 V-8	427 V-8	428 V-8	427 / 428
4.3 liter	4.7 liter	4.7 liter	7 liter	7 liter	7 liter
4261cc	4736cc	4736cc	6965cc	7014cc	6965 / 7014
3.8 / 2.87	4.0 / 2.87	4.0 / 2.87	4.23 / 3.78	4.13 / 3.98	both types
260 hp	271 hp	271 hp	425 hp	355 hp	485 hp
Leaf Springs	Leaf Springs	Leaf Springs	Coil Springs	Coil Springs	Coil Springs
worm/sector	rack / pinion	rack / pinion	rack / pinion	rack / pinion	rack / pinion
flat wheel	dished wheel	dished wheel	dished wheel	dished wheel	dished wheel
Small Flares	Small Flares	Small Flares	Wide Body	Wide Body	Wide Body
Egg crate	Egg crate	Egg crate	Big Mouth	Big Mouth	Big Mouth
No Vents	No Vents	Side Vents	Side Vents	Side Vents	Side Vents
Wires	Wires	Wires	Halibrand	Halibrand	Halibrand

2100 pounds	NA	2170 pounds	2529 lbs.	NA	NA
75 built	51 built	499 built	300 inc. 428	300 inc. 427	< 51 built
SF / Venice	Venice	Venice	Los Angeles	Los Angeles	Los Angeles

Cobra Specifications Chart Notes:

The bore and stroke specifications in inches are shown below the displacements. The flat, non-dished steering wheel of the first Cobra series was distinguished by equidistant spokes and was used with all models built with worm-and-sector steering. All later models had dished steering wheels with a different spoke pattern. The two steering wheel designs were indigenous to the steering type and were not interchangeable. The numbers produced of each type include only production street cars. No competition models, coupes, or prototypes are included in these numbers. The exact number of S/C models is unknown: the 51 stated included a few full-race versions.

Figure H10 - This 1965 Cobra appears quite authentic, with the exception of the panel behind the seats. The panel seems to have been installed to house modern shoulder belts and a pair of stereo speakers. Take a closer look. Note the unusual hood pin design and the lack of a 427 emblem above the fender vent. Would you park a million-dollar, aluminum-bodied car within fifty feet of an ordinary modern sedan in a strip mall parking lot? Can you say fiberglass replica? ©Eli Christman, Richmond, VA (CC)

Shelby Mustang Convertible

Figure H11 - 1968 Shelby Mustang GT-350 Convertible in Candyapple Red. ©Rex Gray, Southern California (CC)

Although the 1966 is my favorite of all Mustang, and Shelby Mustang, model years, the last six cars originally produced, the legendary convertibles that Carroll Shelby built especially to give away to friends, were not actual production cars. These were simply never sold to the public. Many years later, an additional twelve cars would be produced as 1966 Shelby Mustang Convertibles. Some sources indicate a total of thirteen. Various sources disagree as to the details of the eighteen or nineteen cars, too. These details include which ones were originally painted which colors, which examples were equipped with automatic transmissions, and how many are still alive today. I have tried to sort out this conflicting information in the 1966 Shelby Convertible Chart shown later in this section. Some issues were simply not resolvable at the time of publication. What we do know is that most of the original six cars had standard black interiors, automatic transmissions, and air conditioning. The later cars were a little more diverse. Most were equipped with the Interior Decor Group and many had white interiors. Air conditioning and automatic transmission were included on many of this final baker's dozen.

One of the original six 1966 Shelby Convertibles is currently listed at Hagerty's for approximately $836,000. In contrast, the much more common 1968 Shelby Mustang GT-350 is only $103,000 and change. A 1968 GT 500 KR Convertible is currently $162,000 at Hagerty's. Other than the custom-built 1966, this will likely remain the most costly Shelby Mustang Convertible. The 1969-70 351-inch GT 350 will always be the cheapest Shelby Convertible, although this model was not the most numerous in its original production figure of 529, including both model years. In a general sense, each Shelby model year from 1965 to 1970 represented less and less actual influence from Carroll Shelby and his California manufacturing crew.

Figure H12 - The Candyapple Red 1969 GT-350 Convertible is adorned with gold striping and has a white interior and top. ©Sicnag (CC)

There is quite a bit of minor disagreement as to the exact number of 1969 and 1970 Shelby Mustangs produced and sold to the public, including the actual Convertible numbers. As stated in the Mustang Convertible Production Chart in the pony car chapter, 1124 were built in 1968 and this number is undisputed. The 529 total for 1969-70 Convertibles has not been conclusively proven. The total for 1969 and '70 Coupes and Convertibles produced according to Ford is 3350. According to the Shelby American Automobile Club, that number may be no more than 3150; however, SAAC has stated the number as 3294, according to some sources. Everyone agrees the total figure is somewhere between 3150 and 3350, but this leaves the 529 stated in this book for Convertibles open to interpretation. The totals have not been broken down between 1969 and 1970 Convertibles; however for both model years combined, there were 194 350's and 335 500's, assuming the accuracy of the total figure of 529 built in the period.

No one doubts that the serious sports car pedigree of the Shelby Convertibles diminished with each model year. Don't cough up a camshaft when I say this, but the difference between the 1961-66 T-bird Convertibles, particularly the M-code Sports Roadsters, and the 1970 Shelby Mustang Convertible was somewhat more subdued than many would like to admit. There is no doubt which one is sportier, particularly with regard to handling issues, and I would choose the Mustang over the Thunderbird's suspension any day, but the tonnage and styling similarities should be obvious by now. Of course the Birds were mass-produced in far higher numbers and none had so much as a floor-shift automatic to claim sports car status. No historian could deny that there is as much difference between a 1965 and 1970 Shelby Mustang as there is between a 1957 and 1966 T-bird Convertible. However, in the final analysis, they are all highly collectible Fords with a strong, relentless emphasis on the earlier models.

The Shelby Mustang Convertibles were differentiated from the standard Ford Mustang Convertibles of the period, mainly by their standard roll bars, additional fiberglass bodywork, window stickers full of standard equipment, and slightly massaged engines. Distinctive, yet minor, trim differences were also present to distinguish the Shelby models, but by the late Sixties, these accoutrements seemed more superfluous than functional. As both a sports car and convertible fan, I find this situation a little disheartening. Why could there not have been a production version of the 1966 Shelby Convertible? Of course this conundrum defines the whole book. What I continually fantasize about is an imaginary car that might exist within the triangle defined by the early Shelby Mustang, the Fiat Dino Spider, and the more modern Mazda Miata. We need the macho American muscle of the Shelby, the Italian panache of the Dino, and the modern comfort, convenience, and reliability of the Miata.

All Shelby Mustangs had dual exhaust systems, but their exit strategies varied considerably by year and model. All the early 1965 models had exhausts with glasspack mufflers that exited just in front of the rear wheels. In mid-65 production, cars shipped to California, Florida, and New Jersey changed to exhausts exiting conventionally at the rear. This design carried through all the 1966 models. Two exhaust tip configurations were used in 1967 and 1968. Some cars had the same quad arrangement as the standard Mustang GT with a pair of chrome tips on each side below the rear bumper. Other cars were produced instead with round, three-inch, double-walled, chrome tips. The 1969-70 cars had a pair of exhaust tips converged into a side-by-side pair of chrome rectangular openings centered below the rear bumper.

The 1968 Convertible was offered with a black or white top and a black or saddle interior. The 1969-70 models were offered in a different set of exterior finishes that included several new Grabber colors. Candyapple Red was the only color available in all three model years. White replaced saddle as an interior choice in 1969-70. The 1969-70 Convertibles are easily identified by their midlevel side stripes extending from behind the headlamps, through the side scoops, to the tail. The stripes on all earlier models were just above the rocker panels, like those on the much more common Mustang GT. The 1970 models were only modified '69's with hood stripes and front air dam added. A few 1970 Coupes were produced with red or saddle interiors, but all the 1969 and '70 Convertibles had black or white interiors with either black or white power tops. The rear windows were made of two pieces of glass, split horizontally, that folded with the top, a common design for Ford convertibles of the period. All the 1969-70 models had fiberglass front fenders, as well as hoods, to help offset the increased weight of the new Mustang body. The dual exhaust pipes were brought together at the center rear to exit through a pair of rectangular outlets set in a single frame underneath the bumper. This rectangular four-port exhaust outlet helped to distinguish the rear view of the 1969-70 models.

Figure H13 - You can clearly see the black hood stripes added to this Shelby GT-500 to designate it as a 1970 model. This example is a pretty metallic blue-green with gold stripes and black interior. ©Sicnag (CC)

The highest production year of all the Shelbys was 1968 with close to 4500 Coupes and Convertibles built. This was a unique year in several ways, not the least of which was the array of engines installed. The last year of the 306-hp, solid-lifter 289 had been 1967, so the 1968 GT350 used a 250-hp, hydraulic lifter 302 unique to the year for Shelby. The production year began with the same 360-hp 428 in the GT500 as in 1967, but there were two caveats. The first was that in some small number of cars, a 428 was not available at the time of assembly and a 390 was substituted. The second was that less than fifty cars were produced with the wilder, more racing oriented 427. It has never been verified exactly how many of each of these types were built or if any were installed in convertibles. It is known that all the 427's were paired with three-speed automatics.

The two listings in the chart below for a 427 engine have been included for completeness. The 427 was a racing engine that in rare cases Ford adapted to a street model. Its bore and stroke were a little more oversquare than those of the 428, a more street tractable engine. The 427 was never factory installed as an official option in either 1967 or 1968. The 1967 reference comes from the *Mustang Red Book* and the 1968 reference is noted in *The Shelby American Guide*. No engine code listing or any other details are included in the *Red Book* information for '67, but the *Red Book* verified the same *W* engine code for 1968 models. The *SAAC* states that no more than fifty 427's were installed in 1968. The *W* engine code is clearly valid for the '68 installations, but if a special engine code applied to the 1967 model, it is unknown at this time. All the '68 models had automatics. This may or may not also apply to the '67 models. Although the stated horsepower ratings are not the same for both years, the engine details may have been identical. The *Shelby Mustang Muscle Car Color History* makes no mention of a 427 installed in either production year. In any case, as it pertains to this book, it is somewhat unlikely that *any* 427's were installed in *any* Shelby Mustang Convertibles. Racing enthusiasts are always more interested in the lighter, more rigid chassis of the coupes.

The 1969 and 1970 Shelby Mustangs were designed and built with somewhat minimal input from Carroll Shelby. The Cobra name had been sold to Ford for use on the company's high-performance products and the actual production of the cars had been moved from California to Michigan. The 1969 model year had brought another size and weight increase to all Mustang models. Comfort and luxury were taking over the marketplace. The styling of the '69 and '70 Shelbys offered a new smoothness and coherence that earlier, but sportier, models had lacked. The new Shelby styling went beyond a few tacked on air scoops and stripes. The fenders and front and rear fascias were fiberglass parts unique to the Shelby models. The stripes and scoops were still present, but they had a more integrated look. The GT stripes were moved from just above the rocker panels up to midlevel on the body sides, stretching the full length of the car, from front to rear. The stripes retained their traditional GT stripe pattern, but were about twice as wide as those on '65-68 Mustangs.

The 1969-70 GT350 used a Windsor 351 with hydraulic lifters and a single four-barrel. This engine produced 290 gross horsepower while the GT500's 428 was still a conservatively rated 335-horsepower unit. The KR (King of the Road) designation was dropped, but the 1969 big-block was the continuation of this Cobra Jet 428. By this time, the Boss 302 and Boss 429, as well as the very high volume Mach 1 fastback, were overtaking the Shelby Mustang's performance image. Carroll Shelby was rapidly losing interest in his Mustang project. The base cars were growing larger and heavier with each generation and the performance equipment and distinctive Shelby image features were increasingly applied close to the Ford production line in Michigan. The fun, wild and crazy days were over, leaving performance builders surrounded by the insurance companies, the EPA and the NHTSA like Custer facing the cooperating Indian tribes. It was time for the ponies to stampede off into the sunset, leaving us all with fond memories.

Figure H14 - Here is another angle on that same 1968 GT-350. You can see the radio antenna on the left rear fender. This is the location Carroll Shelby intended for the installation on a car with fiberglass fenders. Some dealers installed radios in Shelby Mustangs and mistakenly placed the antenna on the front fender, as it was on production Mustangs with steel fenders. ©Rex Gray, Southern California (CC)

1966 Shelby Mustang Convertible Chart

Serial #	Exterior	Interior	Top	AC Option	Transmission
6S2375	Green	Black	White	Standard	Automatic
6S2376	Yellow	Black	White	Standard	Four-speed
6S2377	Red	Black	White	Standard	Four-speed
6S2378	Blue	Black	White	Standard	Automatic
6S2379	White	NA	NA	Standard	Automatic
6S2380	Pink	Black	NA	Standard	Automatic
6S2381	Red	Black	White	Optional	NA
6S2382	Blue	White	White	Optional	NA
6S2383	Blue	White	White	Optional	NA
6S2384	Blue	White	White	AC	Automatic
6S2385	White	White	Blue	Optional	NA
6S2386	Blue	White	Black	Optional	NA
6S2387	White	White	Blue	Optional	NA
6S2388	Blue	White	White	Optional	NA
6S2389	White	White	White	No AC	Automatic
6S2390	Black	Black	Black	Optional	NA
6S2391	White	White	Blue	AC	Automatic
6S2392	White	Black	Black	Optional	Automatic
6S2393	Red	Black	Black	Optional	Four-speed

1966 Shelby Mustang Convertible Chart Notes:

The official color names for the original six cars were Ivy Green, Springtime Yellow, Candyapple Red, Sapphire Blue, Wimbledon White, and Pink. All the original six cars produced in 1966 had standard black Mustang interiors. All the later twelve cars had Pony Interiors, possibly all of which were solid interior colors. The number 75 black car had a Paxton supercharger from the factory. The later #2389 white car also had the Paxton supercharger, claimed to be the only one of the last twelve so equipped. Sources state that eleven Shelbys were produced with the supercharger. This number includes coupes and it may include that final #2389 car, too. The official first six cars had the same 306-hp 289 as the 1965-66 coupes. It is not known exactly what engine each of the later twelve cars had. The final #2393 car had a standard black interior. The original owner of the Candyapple Red #77 car was Bob Shane, a member of The Kingston Trio. Bob Shane had earlier purchased a new 1963 260 Cobra and a 1965 289 Cobra from Shelby American.

One source states that only four original 1966 convertibles were built in green, yellow, blue and red. This statement disagrees with the chart shown above. The same source claims that the rear brake cooling scoops were not functional. I question this statement because why else would Shelby have reset them lower, below the convertible top when lowered, if not to make them functional for cooling the rear brakes?

Figure H15 - 1968 Shelby GT-500 in Blue with Black Interior and Top. ©Herr Anders Svensson (GNU)

Shelby Mustang Engine Chart

Model	Code	Cu. In.	HP	Induction	Trans.	Axle
1965	K	289	306	Single 4-bbl.	4-speed	3.89
1966	K	289	306	Single 4-bbl.	4SM / C4	3.89
1966	K	289	400	Paxton Supercharger	4SM / C4	3.89
1967	K	289	306	Single 4-bbl.	4SM / C4	3.89
1967	K	289	400	Paxton Supercharger	4SM / C4	3.89
1967	Q	428	355	Twin 4-bbl.	4SM / C6	3.50
1967	NA	427	425	Single 4-bbl.	4SM / C6	3.50
1968	J	302	250	Single 4-bbl.	4SM / C4	3.89
1968	J	302	NA	Ram Air w/4-bbl.	4SM / C4	3.89
1968	J	302	350	Paxton Supercharger	4SM / C4	3.89
1968	S	390	325	Single 4-bbl.	4SM / C6	3.50
1968	S	428	360	Single 4-bbl.	4SM / C6	3.50
1968	R	428	335	Single 4-bbl.	4SM / C6	3.50
1968	W	427	400	Single 4-bbl.	C-6 Auto.	3.50

| 1969 - 70 | M | 351 | 290 | Single 4-bbl. | 4SM / C4 | 3.25 |
| 1969 - 70 | R | 428 | 335 | Single 4-bbl. | 4SM / C6 | 3.50 |

Shelby Mustang Engine Chart Notes:

The standard axle ratios of the four-speed models are shown in the chart. Standard axle ratios on automatic cars were generally lower numerically: 3.50 on small-blocks and 3.25 on big-blocks. The 3.89 ratio may or may not have been standard on some 1966 GT-350H models with automatic transmissions. *Car and Driver* tested a Hertz model in May 1966, noting a 3.89 axle combined with a three-speed automatic. Optional axle ratios with Traction-Lok on the 1969-70 GT-350 were 3.00 and 3.50; on the GT-500 they were 3.91 and 4.30. The 1968 models with 390 engines could not be identified because the engine code for both types was *S* and the 390 was outwardly identical to the 428 Interceptor. NA = Not Available.

Figure H16 - Rear View of the same blue 1968 GT-500. ©Herr Anders Svensson (GNU)

The Confusing Street Shelby Mustang Production Chart

Model	Produced	Model	Produced
1965 GT-350 2+2	516	1968 Convertibles	1124
		All 1968 CP & CV	4450
1966 GT-350 2+2	2374		
Official 1966 Convertible	6	1969 GT-350	1279
Later 1966 Convertible	12	1969 GT-500	1871

		1969-70 (3150 or 3294)	3350
1967 GT-350 Coupe	1175		
1967 GT-500 Coupe	2050	1969-1970 GT-350 CV	194
1967 GT-500 Coupe with 427	47	1969-1970 GT-500 CV	335
		All 1969-70 Convertibles	529
1968 GT-350 Convertible	404		
1968 GT-500 Convertible	402	1970 (SAAC figure)	601
1968 GT-500 KR Convertible	318		
1968 GT-500 CV w/AC & 4-S	36	1970 (Ford figure)	786

The Confusing Street Shelby Mustang Production Chart Notes:

The total 1969-70 production number from Ford and/or Shelby records could be as few as 3150 or as many as 3350. The precise number 3294 has been stated by various sources. The 1970 models were conversions from leftover 1969 models and are included in the 1969 figures stated above. Total 1970 conversions numbered either 601 or 786 (plus three test prototypes), depending upon the stated source, either Shelby or Ford, respectively. All the stated Shelby Mustang production figures are close approximations compiled from Ford and Shelby records by the Shelby American Automobile Club and other sources. Forty-seven 1967 GT-500's were produced with 427's instead of 428's. These hotter big-blocks had solid lifters, dual four-barrel carbs, and 425 horsepower. They were visually indistinguishable from the milder, more common 428's. The cable TV show *What's My Car Worth?* stated in 2015 that only thirty-six Shelby Mustang GT500 Convertibles were built in 1968 with four-speed manual and air conditioning.

Figure H17 - Would you believe this little white racer with a roll bar, mag wheels and no windshield is the car Elvis drove in *Spinout*? Okay, then, don't believe it.... I have a few questions myself. Why are the headlights recessed? I do not recall seeing that look on a Cobra before. Nor have I seen side vents like these. The black side pipes are barely visible, but they are supported by a hanging bracket below the bodywork. This side pipe design and the subdued flares of the fenders indicate this is a 289, but most sources state that Elvis drove a 427 S/C model in the movie. The movie does, indeed, show a 427 model with side pipes, bulging fenders and normal headlights. Both cars are labeled as #11, but that could just be movie-making monkeybusiness. ©Thomas R Machnitzki (GNU)

Shelby Comparison Chart

Model	Type	CI / CC	HP	Wt.	Price
1964-66 Sunbeam Tiger	V-8	260 / 4262	164	2565	$3499
1967 Sunbeam Tiger II	V-8	289 / 4737	200	2560	$3797
1962-63 AC Shelby Cobra	V-8	260	164	2019	$5995
1964 AC Shelby Cobra	V-8	289 / 4727	271	2170	NA
1965 AC Shelby Cobra	V-8	289 / 4727	271	2315	NA
1966 AC Shelby Cobra	V-8	427 / 6998	425	2529	$7495
1967 AC Shelby Cobra	V-8	427 / 6998	425	2530	$9650
1968 Shelby Mustang GT-350	V-8	302	250	3000	$4238
1968 Shelby Mustang GT-500	V-8	428	360	NA	$4439
1968 Shelby Mustang GT-500 KR	V-8	428	400	NA	$4594
1969-70 Shelby Mustang GT-350	V-8	351	290	3100	$4753
1969-70 Shelby Mustang GT-500	V-8	428	360	NA	$5027

Shelby Comparison Chart Notes:
The Sunbeam Tiger had an 86-inch wheelbase. The Shelby Cobra had a 90-inch wheelbase. The 1968-70 Shelby Mustangs shared the same 108-inch wheelbase with their more common siblings. The original base retail prices quoted in some cases may not be exactly accurate for the model year or years listed. NA = Not Available.

Shelby's Snakes Performance Chart

Model & Details	HP	Weight	0-60	Quarter	TS
1962 Shelby Cobra 260 3:54 axle (*R&T*)	260	2100	4.2	13.8	153
1963 Shelby Cobra 289 (*Muscle*)	271	2350	5.8	13.8	NA
1964 Shelby Cobra 289 (*R&T*)	271	2170	6.6	14.1	139
1965 Shelby 289 Cobra (*Field*)	271	2550	4.5	12.2	NA
1965 427 Cobra - $7000 (*MT*)	425	2500	4.3	12.2	NA
1966 Shelby Cobra 427 (*R&T*, 1974)	425	2530	5.3	13.8	162
Shelby / Cosby Cobra 3SA 3.31 axle (*R&T*)	NA	NA	3.8	11.9	182
1965 Shelby GT-350 4S 3.89 axle (*C/D*)	306	3030	6.5	14.9	119
1965 Shelby GT-350 (*R&T*)	306	2790	6.8	14.7	124
1965 Shelby GT-350 3.89 axle (*Field*)	306	2515	6.5	14.9	127
1966 GT-350H 3SA 3.89 (*C/D*)	306	2884	6.6	15.2	117
1966 Shelby GT-350 4S 3.89 axle (*Life*)	306	3360	8.2	15.5	NA
1966 GT-350 Paxton 3SA 3.89 axle (*Life*)	390	3360	6.2	14.0	127
1967 GT-350 4SM 3.89 (*SCG*)	306	2723	7.1	15.3	129
1967 GT-500 4SM 3.25 (*SCG*)	355	3286	6.7	14.3	132
1968 GT-500KR 4S 3.50 axle (*Life*)	335	3780	6.9	14.6	130
1969 GT-500 428 3SA 3.50 (*SCG*)	335	3850	6.0	14.0	115
1967 Sunbeam Tiger II 289 (*R&T*)	200	2560	7.5	16.0	122

Shelby's Snakes Performance Chart Notes:

The 1965 Shelby GT-350 mileage was 7-14 mpg. There were 341 427 Cobras built in 1966-67. About 5000 Tigers were shipped to the U.S. There were 1011 Cobras and about 1500 1968 Shelby Convertibles, plus whatever number in '69 and about 200 more released as 1970 models.

C/D = Car and Driver. Field = Muscle Cars Field Guide by John Gunnell. *Life = Car Life. Muscle = Muscle Cars* by Phil Hall. NA = Not Available. *R&T = Road & Track. SCG = Sports Car Graphic*.

The Intermeccanica Connection

Figure H18 - Red 1965 Apollo 5000 GT. ©Rex Gray, Southern California (CC)

The Intermeccanica firm of Torino, Italy, founded by Frank Reisner in 1959 produced several noteworthy sports cars utilizing American V-8 drivetrains. The first of these was the Apollo GT, a coupe built in Oakland, CA, with the hotter version of the Buick aluminum V-8. Ninety Apollos were produced in the 1961-65 period. A convertible model was introduced late in the production period, but only eleven were constructed. The Apollo GT Coupe stands as the rarest car that the author of this book has ever ridden in or driven.

Let's begin with that drive. Somehow I made an acquaintance with the owner of an Apollo GT Coupe in 1971 in San Francisco. I lived in the San Jose area briefly during that year and while there, I met a guy who owned this very rare car built just across the bay in Oakland a few years earlier. My father had purchased a new 1962 Buick Special with the new at that time aluminum V-8. Of course this was the base two-barrel version hooked up to a three-speed automatic. Although that was a fun car to drive, especially for such an early American design, of course it was a toad compared to the Apollo.

The Apollo GT was a lightweight sports car with the hotter, four-barrel version of the Buick V-8 with a Corvette transmission and four-speed shifter. Yes, Maybelle, you could spot the origin of that familiar T-handle shifter from a mile away. I am not certain if the transmission was the wide or close ratio version (M20 or M21) and I do not know the axle ratio. The M20 was standard and the M21 optional. The driving quality of the car was nearly perfect. The engine was as smooth and responsive as a sports car nut could require. The overall effect was of that mystical smaller, lighter Corvette that I have always wanted but GM was too greedy for high production numbers to build. The sweetness of the Apollo's component list was delicious: dual exhausts, knock-off Borrani wires, English leather seats, wood-rim steering wheel, adjustable steering column, power front disc brakes, Jaeger instruments, limited-slip differential, and much more. One brochure claimed a 0-60 of 7.5 and a top speed of 140. The list price was $5987.

Figure H19 - 1962 Buick Special DeLuxe. Our Buick Special had the 155-hp aluminum V-8 with two-barrel carb and single exhaust. Other options on our car were automatic transmission, AM radio, and larger wheels. This example is displaying aftermarket wheels that appear to be the legendary Cragar S/S Mags, an unusual choice for a cheap little four-door sedan! ©Mr. Choppers (GNU)

Apollo GT production included 39 original coupes and one convertible. As many as twenty-four additional cars were later assembled in Dallas and Pasadena, Texas, as Vetta Venturas. Some sources quote as many as 88 total Apollos and Venturas produced. *Road & Track* and *Car and Driver* each tested a 1963 Apollo GT. Both test cars were 3500 GT models with the 200-hp Buick V-8. The *Car and Driver* car had the standard 3:36 axle, but the *R&T* car had a 3:90 axle. The 3:90 was never a standard Corvette ratio, so I am not sure if the stated ratio is correct or not. Assuming it is, was this a Buick ratio at the time? The weights listed were 2600 pounds for the *C and D* car and 2485 for the *R&T* model. The tested top speeds matched the axle ratios: 125 and 104. The acceleration times were very close with 8.2 and 16.2 with the 3:36 and 8.4 and 16.0 with the 3:90. Both cars were four-speeds, but it is possible one had an M20 and the other an M21.

The Apollo GT Coupe was built from 1962-65. The 1962 model is listed as having 190 horsepower and weighing in at 2270 pounds. The 1963 model is listed as having 200 horsepower and weighing 2484 pounds. The 1964-65 5000 GT is listed as having 250 horsepower and weighing 2650 pounds. The Apollo may have had drum rear brakes. The 5.0 liter version was built from mid-63 through 1965. The standard axle ratio was 3:36 with the 3:55 optional. The Spyder version was built from 1963-65. The 1963 Spyder had 200 horsepower and weighed 2540 pounds. The 1964 Spyder had 250 horsepower and weighed 2650 pounds. The dry weight was 2470 and the 0-60 time was 6.8 seconds. Note that the Coupe and Spyder 0-60 times and the weights listed are the same, so these are probably not exactly accurate. All Apollos had a 97-inch wheelbase, aluminum bodies, and fifteen-inch wheels. *Italian Sports Cars* states that only 88 Apollos were built between 1961 and 1966. The *Complete Book of Collectible Cars 1940-1980* states that only one convertible was actually built and sold as an Apollo GT. This source states that ten more convertibles were built and sold in Texas as Vetta Venturas. Prices listed are $6797 for the 3500 GT coupe and $7347 for the convertible. Prices for the 5000 GT are quoted as $7965 and $8950.

Figure H20 - A red Apollo GT is showing off its flat cornering prowess. ©Rex Gray, Southern California (CC)

Buick introduced the all-aluminum Buick Special V-8 of 215 cubic inches (3.5 liters) in 1961. The base engine with a two-barrel and single exhaust was rated at 150 gross horsepower, increased to 155 in 1962. This little jewel of a V-8 weighed only 318 pounds. The hotter version with a four-barrel and dual exhausts had 190 horsepower. A slight compression ratio increase brought this up to an even 200 in 1963. The aluminum engine proved too expensive for Buick and it was replaced in 1964 with a 5-liter, 300-cubic-inch version with a cast iron block and aluminum heads, weighing in at 405 pounds. This 250-hp V-8 was the one used in the 1964 Apollo GT models. The 1965 model had cast iron heads, adding yet another 62 pounds, but retaining the same 250 horsepower rating. All the Apollos of all model years utilized the high-performance versions of the Buick V-8.

Figure H21 - The upper view of a cab yellow 1967 Intermeccanica Italia Spyder clearly shows its top recessed into its black interior. Note the lack of headrests and vent windows. The electric antenna is recessed into the right front fender. The dual racing mirrors are chrome. Those styled steel five-lug wheels sure do look familiar. ©Rex Gray, Southern California (CC)

Figure H22 - Compare this silver 1972 Italia Spyder with the yellow car above. Although both have black interiors and tops, this later model has a wood steering wheel and of course headrests. The wheels are alloy instead of styled steel and the fenders have amber side marker lamps. The styling has been enhanced with the dark shading in the side vents and headlight trim. This is obviously the last production year that these pretty chrome, but generally useless, bumpers would be legal in the U.S. ©Mr. Choppers (GNU)

Intermeccanica released the Italia Spyder in 1967 for the 1968 model year. Examples have been identified as 1967 models. It is unclear whether or not some or all models sent to the U.S. had the 1968 detail requirements. Although the new Indra model would be introduced in 1971, apparently the last Italias were listed as 1972 models. The Italia was built on a 94-inch wheelbase powered by the Ford 271-hp 289 with a four-speed. The factory claimed a 0-60 time of 6.1 seconds with a 14.7 quarter-mile for the 2600-pound convertible. Top speed approached 140 mph with its standard 3.25:1 axle. The most significant change over the Italia's four-year production period was the engine. The 1969 model used the 250-hp 302, with hydraulic lifters and a four-barrel, of course. Acceleration slowed down to 6.9 and 15.3 seconds. The 1970 and '71 models regained much of the lost performance with the 310-hp, four-barrel 351 Cleveland producing claimed 6.5 and 14.0 second timings. These gross horsepower ratings were stated in SAE Gross and therefore not directly comparable with those of similar engines installed in Mustangs of the same period, but it is assumed these engines were more or less identical in both applications. The official Ford ratings for these engines with four-barrel carbs and hydraulic cams were 300-hp in 1970 and 285-hp in 1971 with the mandated lower compression ratios of the period. The number of Italia Spyders produced is unknown. Production of the total lineup, including coupes and 2+2 models, was about 500 cars. Hagerty's currently prices the 1967-72 Italia Spyder at $82,000-$178,000 for #4 to #1 condition examples.

Figure H23 - The beautiful blue 1972 Indra Spyder would not be legal in the U.S. with its chrome knock-off wires and minimalist bumpers. Note the pop up headlamps and vinyl boot that rather lumpily covers the recessed top. ©André Karwath aka Aka (CC)

The Italia Spyder was succeeded by the Indra Spyder in 1971. Only sixty Indra Spyders were built in the 1971-74 model years and there are only six verified as still surviving in the USA today. In consideration of the federal requirements of the day, the Indra was never officially exported to the U.S. This model was considerably more a luxury car than sports car, although it was still a sexy, topless two-seater. Weighing in at 2756 pounds dry on a 98-inch wheelbase, the Indra as it was introduced in 1971 was not a performance model like the Italia. The claimed acceleration figures were 7.1 and 16.5 with a top speed of 130 mph. The Indra utilized a European Opel 170-cubic-inch inline Six with Bosch fuel injection producing 177 horsepower. Since that weight quote was likely quite optimistic, I would question the claimed performance figures, too. Some sources state the weight and horsepower as remaining the same through 1974, but I doubt that is precisely the truth. As with most sports cars of the era, you can clearly see the nosedive in sportiness and ultimate performance as the Apollo is replaced by the Italia, which is then replaced by the Indra. Comfort and price went way up while driving excitement dribbled into the ditch.

Figure H24 - The white leather interior of the same car is quite modern and luxurious, a long way from the stark sports car simplicity of the original Apollo GT. Note the three-speed automatic, modern AM/FM/cassette stereo, elegant wood steering wheel and padded passenger grab bar. The two timekeeping instruments on the console have obviously been added for a retro rally. (Note the numbers on the exterior in the photo above.) That U-shape next to these instruments is a map reading lamp that is also obviously not standard equipment.
©Buch-t (GNU)

Monteverdi 375 Spyder

Figure H25 - The Monteverdi 375S Spyder is a true rarity among sports cars. Only a handful were imported here, if that many. This 1971 wine red example would have no trouble certifying its chrome bumpers that year, but the chrome knock-off wire wheels would have had to remain in Europe. This example also lacks side marker lamps and other U.S. requirements for 1972. The black vinyl top sports a fair-sized blind spot. ©Brian Snelson, Hockley, Essex, England (CC)

Monteverdi was a relatively short-lived specialty car brand based in Switzerland from 1967-76, with a small operation continuing until 1984. The company manufactured only one convertible model for a very short period of time. How short? Some sources say the convertible, officially named the High Speed 375/C, was built only in 1970. Other sources indicate the topless model may have been built as early as 1969 and as late as 1972. At least one source says that 375/C's were built from 1969 to 1974. Either way, only a handful of this specialty hybrid were produced. As you might guess, even less might actually have been exported to the U.S., particularly in relation to the same old bugaboo, the increasing regulations of the '68-72 period. The model is referred to here as a Spyder, which may or may not be correct. The topless model was designed in Italy by Frua, and like the AC 428, its similarity of styling to the Maserati Mistral is no coincidence. The bodies were constructed by Fissore in Italy and shipped to Switzerland, where Chrysler 440's were installed in the final assembly process. Again, we have a small discrepancy. Some sources indicate that the Monteverdi models used the basic 440 Magnum V-8 with a four-barrel and 375 gross horsepower. *Wikipedia* says that the 375/C Convertible had between 380 and 402 horsepower. Did any High Speed Convertibles have 440 Six Packs?

Monteverdi built a small number of exotic 375 Series models in 1966-77. Only a few of these were imported into the U.S. and most of those were probably early models before the stricter rules were enforced. The model line included a C (coupe), L (2+2), and S (spider). All were assembled in Switzerland with Chrysler 440 engines rated at 380 gross horsepower. The Monteverdis were in the 3500-pound, $50,000 weight and price class. The 1966-67 375 Spider was the most likely model imported into the U.S., considering the popularity of convertibles in the USA, combined with the advent of the new rules that went into effect on January 1, 1968.

This model had a 7210cc Chrysler 440 V-8 producing 380 horsepower and weighing in at 3630 pounds. The only price we have for this model is $50,000. Hagerty's currently rates this model at about $150,000 average and $240,000 for a perfect example.

The 1971 375 Convertible weighed 3748 pounds with the Chrysler automatic. Claimed performance figures were 0-60 in 5.5, quarter-mile in 14.5, and a top speed of 155 mph. The factory claimed 370 gross horsepower with a four-barrel carb. The few built in 1971 were sold only in Europe. This model had four-wheel disc brakes and fifteen-inch wheels. The company constructed a prototype in 1975 named the Palm Beach, a convertible successor to the High Speed, but it never went into production.

Excalibur Series I, II & III

Figure H26 - This early Excalibur Series I SS brings up a few questions. Apparently the hood is aluminum and the headers are solid steel instead of flexible tubes. The horns are set just in front of the door instead of in front of the grille, as on the later models. The nonfunctional doors are very low cut and the wheels are knock-off wires. A step pad mounted just above the side exhaust facilitates entry and exit. ©Nakhon 100 (CC)

The Excaliburs existed within their own Neverland of the sports car world. They were never exactly replicars nor production cars, but something in between. The company successfully fought off the derogatory *kit car* slander by consistently producing a high quality product. Although constructed from major components from other manufacturers, the Excalibur was never sold as a kit for home builders. Ex-Studebaker designer Brooks Stevens unleashed a bevy of copycat replicas that would never approach the strict quality control of his Excalibur line. The factory and production line were run by Brooks Stevens' two sons. The prototypes were constructed from aluminum, but all the production Excaliburs were fiberglass. The full lifetime of this series lasted from 1965 through 1993, but it is the earlier models we are concerned with here. The first three series were high-performance sports cars. The 1980-93 models not covered in this book were much heavier cars with long wheelbases and small, underpowered engines. Most of the Excalibur photos shown here are of 1982 and 1984 Series IV models simply because quality photos of the earlier models are very difficult to obtain.

Hybrid Hotrods

Figure H27 - This Excalibur Series III SS Roadster is parked on a street in Paris, France, not Texas. This beautifully polished retrospective of automobilia is in black with a tan leather interior. You cannot miss the side pipes and wide whitewalls. Take note of the way the side mirrors are attached to the tops of the covers over the dual spare tires. The chrome wire wheels are the bolt-on type. The windshield is of one piece and of a shallow height indigenous to the Roadster model. This car has triple windshield wipers like an early E-Type Jaguar. The hood ornament stands as proud as that of a Mercedes three-pointed star, a most apt comparison. ©LPLT (GNU)

According to the *Complete Book of Collectible Cars 1940-1980*, there were 168 of the original 1965-69 SSK Series I models built. This number may have only included the original Roadster and not the later Phaeton models in the series. It does not match the factory figure of 359 produced in that period. Most of the Excalibur series were produced in both two-seat and four-seat versions, with the four-seaters generally being more popular. The first 56 cars built in 1965 had the Studebaker Avanti's 290-horsepower, supercharged 289 V-8 powerplant, but access to this engine was denied by the demise of Studebaker. The 1966 Series I Roadsters were equipped with Corvette's 300-hp 327, producing a claimed top speed of 160 mph with a 0-60 acceleration time of 5.3 and the quarter in 14.1. The latter is believable for a 2100-pound SSK, but wind resistance might have held the top speed to a somewhat lower figure. The engine would be upgraded to the 350-hp 327 in 1967. The distinctive exterior tubular exhaust tubes were fake on the later Excaliburs, but they were supplied by the same German company that built the real thing for the original Mercedes SSK. Instruments were built by Stewart-Warner.

The retail price of the first production model was $7250. The base price was over $10,000 by the end of the '60's and with the legendary inflation of the '70's, had doubled again by 1976.

The Series I cars were built on a 109-inch wheelbase with front disc brakes. Standard equipment increased over the years to include by 1969 a tilt steering wheel, leather seats, air conditioning, Positraction, air horns, driving lights, and power steering and brakes. The Excalibur carried a spare wheel and tire on each side of the hood. When the car was equipped with standard chrome wires, even the two spares were of the same expensive wheel design. The weight of the 1969 Phaeton had climbed to 2600 pounds. The Roadster was still a hundred pounds lighter.

The Series II cars introduced in 1970 had a wheelbase increased to 111 inches and the engine was replaced by the optional Corvette 350 with 300 horsepower. Some few Series I cars were produced with the 350-hp 327. It is not known if any Series I or 1970 Series II cars were produced using the 350-horsepower 350. The Series II had the Corvette's independent rear suspension, four-wheel disc brakes, and four-speed transmission. The claimed top speed was a more honest 150 mph. A 1970 Roadster weighed 2900 pounds with a 300-hp 350. Standard axle was the 3:36 and the transmission was the Corvette M21 close-ratio four-speed.

Figure H28 - This big black 1982 Excalibur Roadster is on display next to a black Mercedes-Benz Limousine of classic vintage. This car is an unusual example. The emblem above the exhaust pipes says Mercedes-Benz and the hood ornament is a three-pointed star. The license plate states this is a Mercedes 500K Retro. Note that the spare tires are not encased. ©Pavel Sevela (CC)

The original Mercedes SSK of 1928 had a supercharged 7.1-liter SOHC inline six, which explains the six headers from the V-8 of the Excaliburs. Were all the doorless models the same as the SSK models or did both these types refer to the original stripper Roadsters? The chassis was changed from the Studebaker Lark derivative early on, but it is not known how many were built on the Lark frame. It is implied that the engine was changed to the Corvette 327 prior to the change in the chassis. I have never been able to accurately ascertain if this fact is true or not.

It would seem that the Studebaker engines would have coincided in the production schedule with all the Studebaker chassis. The Series II received four-wheel power disc brakes on a new frame not based on that of the Studebaker Lark. All the Studebaker derivatives were most likely SSK models with the Kompressor 289. Was the rear-mounted spare only on Roadsters, Series I, cycle-fendered, or SSK models? We really need a timeline of the changes from the factory!

The Series III of 1975 met the much more stringent federal requirements with the Corvette 454 and energy absorbing alloy bumpers. The Phaeton consistently outsold the Roadster throughout all three series. The last Series III Phaeton built in 1980 and powered by a 215-hp 454 had ballooned up to 4409 pounds. Even a 1975 Roadster with the same engine hit the scales at 4250. Its acceleration times had crept up to 8.7 and 16.7 seconds. Series III cars had leather buckets with headrests and fuller fenders.

Figure H29 - This light coral 1982 Phaeton with thin whitewalls is typical of the vintage. Compare this car to the next photo. It is obvious that this Series IV car is a very similar model to the white 1984 Series IV Phaeton shown below. It has the same two-piece windshield, two wipers instead of three, chrome trim on the spare tires, spotlights next to the windshield, center driving light, amber turn signals on the fenders, and elaborately styled, yet crude, front bumper. ©Selyobwoc (CC)

These were the last Excaliburs suitable to be included in this book. The Excalibur continued with the Series IV introduced in 1980, but that car was a larger touring car with an enormous 125-inch wheelbase powered by an anemic Chevrolet 305 V-8 coupled only with a four-speed automatic. The prince had turned into a toad! By 1985, the lackluster performance had dropped to a 14.5-second 0-60, a quarter-mile in 19.9, and a pitiful 93-mph top speed! In other words, it could keep up with a Fiat 850 Spider. Every accoutrement from a power top on down was now standard on this very heavy luxury boat. The final production total for all Excaliburs through 1993 was about 3200 cars. The official website says "less than 3500 automobiles in 40 years".

Figure H30 - This white 1984 Series IV Excalibur is a very attractive conglomeration of 1930's memories to cruise around in, and of course be seen in, but a sports car it is not. The all-white Phaeton has luxurious seating with contrasting piping on the leather seats. The dual spare tires are fully enclosed in stylish white with chrome trim. Although the construction and comfort of these later Excaliburs was exceptional, their sports car power and handling capabilities were a thing of the past. ©SV Lambo (CC)

The company built the first 97 cars without doors and 91 of these have been identified as still in the hands of collectors. All the SI-III models have true side pipes; these are just fakes on the 1980 cars onward. The 327/350 4-speed Phaeton listed under Series I may refer to either 350-inch displacement or 350-hp 327. This is not clear on the official website. Some cars had a Dual-Gate Shifter automatic. This option is more collectible now than the regular automatic. We do not know if that regular automatic is a Powerglide, Turbo-HydraMatic, or something else. The first cars had cycle fenders. The later, more common Roadster with long fenders and running boards was introduced in mid-1966, along with the new Phaeton model. The three most collectible characteristics of the Series II cars are the Corvette 454 on all models, the lesser number of four-speed cars, and the rare cycle-fendered models. Most of the Series II cars were Phaetons, but we do not know how many. All the Series III cars have the same 215-hp 454 engine, and most are probably automatics. Few Series III Roadsters were constructed. All the Series I-III cars had side curtains. The Series IV models were much slower luxury cars with a long, 125-inch wheelbase, Chevrolet 305 engine, automatic transmission, and power top, windows, and seats.

After completing almost 1000 of these Series IV luxury convertibles, the company began to slide into the oblivion of bankruptcy and sale of the company. This eventually led to the production in very small numbers of a long limousine model and a 1966 Cobra 427 copycat utilizing a Ford 302 with 215 net horsepower. This $52,000 embarrassment of a once proud name could easily be optioned up to about $60,000 in the 1990's, when approximately 175 Excalibur Cobras were sold.

Excalibur Production Chart

Series I Roadster	Series I Phaeton	Series II Roadster	Series II Phaeton	Series III Roadster	Series III Phaeton
1965 - 56	1965 - 0	1970 - 11	1970 - 26	1975 - 8	1975 - 82
1966 - 87	1966 - 3	1971 - 0	1971 - 0	1976 - 11	1976 - 173
1967 - 38	1967 - 33	1972 - 13	1972 - 52	1977 - 15	1977 - 222
1968 - 37	1968 - 20	1973 - 22	1973 - 100	1978 - 15	1978 - 248
1969 - 41	1969 - 44	1974 - 26	1974 - 92	1979 - 27	1979 - 340
Total - 259	Total - 100	Total - 72	Total - 270	Total - 76	Total - 1065
	S I - 359		S II - 342		S III - 1141
Roadsters	407	Phaetons	1435	Production	1842

Excalibur Production Chart Notes:

Locating accurate production figures for the Excalibur series is somewhat difficult. The documentation of the production of some models has clearly been more available than for other models in the series. Eleven of the earliest SSK Roadsters constructed had the Studebaker 290-hp 289 V-8 with four-speed. After the Studebaker engine ceased production, the Stevens Brothers contracted with GM to use the Corvette 300-hp 327, with the 350-hp 327 as an option. The details of this early production period are unknown as to exactly how many Excaliburs were built with the optional 350-hp 327 or an automatic transmission. Records are not available to show how many with each engine or transmission were Roadsters or Phaetons, either.

Tiger, Shelby, Intermeccanica, Monteverdi, Excalibur

Figure H31 - The rear of this cream 1984 Series IV Phaeton shows off the taut lines of its tan power top. Note the squared off trunk line and long, sweeping front and rear fenders. ©Slash Me (CC)

Excalibur Series I-II-III Chart

SSK	Series I	Early Series II	Late Series II	Series III
1965	1966 - 1970	1970 - 1971	1972 - 1974	1975 - 1980
109-inch WB	109-inch WB	111-inch WB	112-inch WB	112-inch WB
290-hp 289	300-hp 327	300-hp 350	270-hp 454	215-hp 454
Disc / Drum	Disc / Drum	Disc / Disc	Disc / Disc	Disc / Disc
6.70 x 15	7.00 x 15	G70/15	G70/15	GR70/15
2513 lbs. (R)	2645 lbs. (R)	2899 lbs. (R)	3801 lbs. (R)	4250 lbs. (R)
NA	2745 lbs. (P)	3000 lbs. (P)	3999 lbs. (P)	4409 lbs. (P)
5.3 seconds	5.4 seconds	6.5 seconds	6.3 seconds	8.7 seconds
14.1 seconds	14.1 seconds	15.0 seconds	15.0 seconds	16.7 seconds
TS: 116 mph	TS: 134 mph	TS: 121 mph	TS: 117 mph	TS: 108 mph
1965 - $7250	NA	NA	1975 - $18,900	1979 - $28,600

Excalibur Series I-II-III Chart Notes:

All Excaliburs had fifteen-inch wheels, although this has not been absolutely verified. The 1972-74 models all had Corvette 454 engines. If these followed the Corvette applications by year, all the horsepower ratings were net. The 1972 and 1973 models had 270 horsepower, but the 1974 model was rated at 275 horsepower. The 215-hp 454 used in the 1975-79 models was a truck big-block never available in the Corvette.

355

Hybrid Hotrods

The details listed for each series do not specify year or model, however, the weights are listed separately for the Roadster and Phaeton models. The engines listed for each series represent a simplification of actual production. In reality, engine choices and options overlapped each other within and through the series production. Most likely the later models are a little heavier than the earlier ones. The quoted performance figures are with a four-speed. Automatic times were generally a little slower, with top speeds remaining about the same as with the manual transmissions. Note that these top speeds are more realistic than those quoted elsewhere in the text. Some Series I cars had Powerglides and some Series II and III cars had Turbo-Hydramatics.

Figure H32 - Look at the vast difference between the rear of the Series IV Phaeton above and this special Lipstick Edition (whatever that means) 1982 Series IV Roadster. This swoopy rear view conceals a rumble seat that opens electrically. Note the built in step pads on the rear fender. The fancy name may refer to its red top, boot and interior. ©SV Lambo (CC)

Selected Hybrid Hotrods Ratings Chart

Years	Model	Collect	Drive	Desire
1964 - 1966	Sunbeam Tiger 260	B	C	C
1967	Sunbeam Tiger II 289	B	C	B
1962	Shelby Cobra 260	A	C	A
1963 - 1965	Shelby Cobra 289	A	C	A
1965 - 1968	Shelby Cobra 427	A	D	A
1966	Shelby Mustang GT-350 Convertible	A	D	A
1968	Shelby Mustang GT-350 Convertible	A	C	B
1968	Shelby Mustang GT-500 Convertible	A	C	B
1968	Shelby GT-500 KR Convertible	A	C	A
1969 - 1970	Shelby Mustang GT-350 Convertible	A	C	B
1969 - 1970	Shelby Mustang GT-500 Convertible	A	C	B
1961 - 1965	Intermeccanica Apollo GT Coupe	A	D	B
1965	Intermeccanica Apollo Convertible	A	D	A
1968 - 1971	Intermeccanica Italia Spyder	B	D	C
1971 - 1974	Intermeccanica Indra Spyder	B	C	C
1966 - 1967	Monteverdi 375 Spyder	B	D	C
1965 - 1970	Excalibur Series I	C	C	A
1970 - 1974	Excalibur Series II	C	C	B
1975 - 1980	Excalibur Series III	C	B	C

Models Ratings Chart Definitions:

Years: In most cases, the years listed include the total production years for a particular model series. Some model years within a series may be considerably more desirable than other years.

Models: In some cases many variations are included in this category and in others the models included are very homogeneous. This is generally self explanatory.

Collectibility: This is what most of you want to know, the bottom line on how likely the model or series is likely to climb in value over the coming years.

Drivability: This is an indicator of how adaptable the machine can be to drive for transportation or pleasure in the modern world, considering collector value, parts availability, fuel quality, comfort, performance and miscellaneous other factors.

Desirability: This defines the nostalgic, emotional wow factor, without regard for collector values or everyday usage.

General: No machine is given a failing grade. If it made it into a rating chart, at least a few hobbyists find that model interesting.

Figure H33 - A nice profile of a 1984 Series IV Phaeton in all white. ©Slash Me (CC)

Chapter 9: *The Early Pony Convertibles*

Figure I1 - As I have slobbered all over this 1965-66 Pony Interior design elsewhere in this book, you are surely aware that this is one of my favorite interior designs of all time. This example is even in my favorite color combination: silver blue and white. This example of a Mustang with the Interior Decor Group, as it was officially named, also has the optional console. When the console was ordered, it too had the matching plastic wood trim of the dash and steering wheel. Another angle of this same car's interior, shown in Chapter 1, displays the distinctive ponies embossed into the seat backs and the familiar wrinkly white vinyl boot. ©Herr Anders Svensson (GNU)

How does that famous opening line go? *It was the best of times, it was the worst of times, it was the age of wisdom, it was the age of foolishness.* The American pony cars were built in prodigious numbers, especially the coupes. Enormous numbers of them were never sports cars. They had klunky six-cylinder engines, automatic transmissions, loose steering, skinny tires and fancy hubcaps. They were too small to haul much, yet too ponderous to enjoy driving on tight, twisty roads. Many high performance models were developed and marketed to the max, but these were even more nose-heavy, particularly the top bananas of Woodward Avenue. However, what the new pony cars offered to the American sports car consumer was remarkable. They were more reliable and durable than most foreign sports cars of the day. The American manufacturers catered to the desires of the masses far beyond what had ever been done before. You could option out a pony for grocery runs, date night, the racetrack, circling the drive-in or a long distance vacation. With the right options, there was a pony for everybody.

Ride the Ponies

Figure I2 - This is Serial Number 00001, a Wimbledon White Mustang Convertible on display at the Henry Ford Museum. The interior and top boot are black. The car is equipped with the 260 V-8, Cruise-O-Matic, console, whitewall tires and the optional "knock-off" spinner wheel covers. ©Alvin Trusty (CC)

The inclusion of the early pony car convertible models is probably the most controversial element of this book. Why are these overweight four-seaters in a book with real sports cars? The reason is that they offered the only genuine alternatives from American manufacturers of the time. The Corvette and T-bird were generally more desirable and had only two seats, but their prices were out of range of so many young middle class buyers. The Corvette's power and the Bird's luxury shot above a horde of smaller, cheaper sports cars from Europe competing for American dollars. The pony cars easily expanded a lucrative price bracket within the market. The stripped convertibles cost about $3000 and $4000 would buy a nice one with many options. This put them between an MG B and an Austin-Healey 3000, between a TR-4 and a Stag, or between a 124 Spider and a Duetto.

Would you like to give up a little of that *wind in the hair, bugs in the teeth* for a little more *turn the key and go* American reliability or comfort in the heat or cold or the ability to freak out the church lady at the stoplight by burning rubber? A pony car may be right for you. Things have changed since these cars were fresh out of the dealership. Now many of them are sold at auctions for ridiculous prices. There are parts vendors and professional restorers of all sorts. Even with Plymouth and Pontiac dealers now extinct, certainly the availability in the U.S. of parts and service is far better than that for Austin-Healeys, MG's and Triumphs. Alfa Romeo fans better reside in a major city, dude. Think of these early pony cars as thinking outside the box. Maybe you do have Castrol in your veins, but you misplaced your stringback driving gloves in the back of the garage decades ago.

The basic list of models is very short. This book covers the 1955-75 period for many reasons. One is that the Postwar period in cars had morphed into the Baby Boomer era by 1955, but by 1975 the party was over, particularly for topless cars. The convertibles still standing on the 1976 display stands were few and far between, and I mean of *all* types of cars. The Mustang is, was, and will always be the most ubiquitous pony car. Ford built Mustang Convertibles consistently from 1964 through 1973. Carroll Shelby modified Mustang Convertibles only in 1968 and '69. (We know the last few 1970 models were just slightly altered '69's and the six 1966 versions built don't count as production cars.) Plymouth did not peel the top from a Barracuda until that model's second body style in 1967 and the last 'Cuda Convertible was in 1971. Camaro and Firebird Convertibles were produced throughout their initial body series in 1967-69. Dodge Challenger Convertibles were built only in 1970 and '71.

Figure I3 - One of the more unusual, and in my opinion, unfortunate, aspects of the original Mustang was that it did not have a respectable sports car set of instruments as standard equipment. To add to this insult, the Rally Pac option, as shown in this close-up of a 1966 dash, was the only way to get a tachometer in the original-bodied Mustang. The Rally Pac consisted of a tach on the left and a clock on the right, both attached to the steering column in the manner of an old hot rodder's purchase from the J. C. Whitney catalog. Note that the tach is overly *busy* in its face design and it does not even have a redline! This particular example is on a car with the Interior Decor Group. You can tell by the fake wood panel surrounding the in-dash instruments. My big question is why on earth would anyone cover up the lovely fake wood steering wheel of the IDG package with that cheap lace-on cover? ©PM Drive 1061 (GNU)

The big challenge today for a potential pony car buyer lies in the multitude of options piled onto *boring strippers*. All the base ponies had six-cylinder engines, three-speed manual transmissions, and darn few sporty accoutrements. No disc brakes, tachometers, quick steering, stiff suspension, wide tires, or aluminum wheels. Some even had bench front seats and/or three-on-the-tree! BOR-ing. At the other end of the scale were either the hulking big-block V-8's with their road-hugging weight over the front wheels or the high-stressed, high-maintenance top-line V-8's with solid lifters, multiple carburetors, and higher compression ratios than any modern gas pump can feed. A few general rules have always applied to pony car production: hardtops and fastbacks outnumber convertibles many-to-one; the great majority of production of all models are always six-cylinder strippers and base V-8's, with most of both having automatic transmissions; and most convertibles were built with base or mid-option V-8's. Four-speed transmissions were always produced in the minority and this was particularly true with convertibles. The pony car you and I most likely desire is relatively rare, production number wise. We want a mellow V-8 with a four-speed manual transmission, a combination not that difficult to find. The hard part is that in many cases, you had to buy the hot-rod special package to get the other stuff such as dual exhausts, disc brakes, a tachometer, quick steering, fancy wheels, quality tires, and that old standby, a taut suspension. There should be nothing wrong with that. Personally, I *love* the look of extra stripes, scoops, wings, and air dams. The problem is that there are so few *mellow* small-blocks sold with the sport packages. The Sport Package usually was a very good deal with a *mellow* big-block such as the Mustang 390 or the base 396 in an early Camaro, but you paid the price, although probably small, of the heavy front end. You could choose the racier small-block option, but the initial price and maintenance issues could be daunting; in today's market, particularly the high price. Chances are high that the company never offered their base V-8 engine with the better handling options. You may be in quite a quandary if you want to keep your baby stock and original.

A lot of car buyers and sellers don't respect originality nowadays. For the most part, I do not agree with this concept and I wish it would just go away. I particularly despise putting 17-20-inch wheels on cars that were built decades before such wheels were the latest fad. I am never fond of a car with an engine that was never intended to be in that model in the first place, either. I am not even sure I tolerate a car that has any engine that was not placed in it at the factory. But that's just me. Your attitude may differ.

There are a few items I am not against changing for modern street use, no matter how occasional. The first is tires. Boy, have we come a long way in tire technology! Modern tires are safer, stick better in the wet and in cornering, and last longer. Not only that, but they are available. You will have to pay a premium price from a specialty seller to put actual tires correct for the period on your drivable toy. If you are building or purchasing a trailer queen, fine, otherwise start your research at Tire Rack. Many of the pony cars discussed in this section are the ring-leading suspects for oversize tires. I would avoid that temptation like the plague. Nothing looks as right or resells for as much cash as the original sizes and types of wheels. An unusual choice you will have for this type of car is to put mags on it, aftermarket wheels from the car's own classic era, such as Cragar S/S. This idea is not that bad. Consider it like the little British roadster that has chrome wire wheels, never a factory option on that particular model, either, but very popular back in the day.

The two components of the interior you may be most tempted to update are the steering wheel and the sound system. There may have been a regular production option offered on your model that is available now as an upgrade. Although obviously not as pure a concept as keeping your car precisely as it rolled out of the factory, upgrading your model's interior components is the least sin you can commit against the purists. Some of the pony cars offered a choice of three steering wheels. There was the basic model that came with the base interior. There was an upgrade model, usually with more padding, that might have been a part of a luxury interior package. Then there was a sports car equivalent, usually with real or plastic woodgrain and three evenly spaced, unpadded spokes. This last model may or may not have originally been offered only within a particular optional sports package. If you are going to occasionally drive your baby on warm summer nights or sunny winter afternoons, the music emanating from the dash might be of primary importance to you. When your pony car was built there were AM stations providing The Beatles, Stones, and Steppenwolf as accompaniment to your teenaged cruising everywhere you went. Nowadays about all you will hear from that standard equipment AM radio are the sports scores and carefully crafted right-wing political rants.

Pony Car Convertible Production Chart

Model	*Production*	*Model*	*Production*
1964 Ford Mustang	28,833	1967 Pontiac Firebird	15,528
1965 Ford Mustang	73,112	1968 Pontiac Firebird	16,960
1966 Ford Mustang	72,119	1969 Pontiac Firebird	11,657
1967 Ford Mustang	44,808		
1968 Ford Mustang	25,376	1967 - 1969 Firebird	44,145
1969 Ford Mustang	14,746		
1970 Ford Mustang	7673	1967 Plymouth Barracuda	4003
1971 Ford Mustang	6121	1968 Plymouth Barracuda	2595
1972 Ford Mustang	6121	1969 Plymouth Barracuda	1273
1973 Ford Mustang	11,853	1970 Plymouth Barracuda	2494
		1971 Plymouth Barracuda	1146
1964 - 1973 Mustang	290,762		
		1967 - 1971 Barracuda	11,511
1967 Chevy Camaro	25,141		
1968 Chevy Camaro	20,440	1970 Dodge Challenger	3884
1969 Chevy Camaro	17,573	1971 Dodge Challenger	1857
1967 - 1969 Camaro	63,154	1970 - 1971 Challenger	5741

The Mustang received its first FM radio option at the same time as the GM ponies in 1967. The Mustang would not receive FM stereo until 1968. The Barracuda got FM mono as an option in '69 and the Barracuda and Challenger had optional FM stereo in 1970. The ubiquitous 8-track tape deck of the day was available in Mustangs from 1966 and in Camaros and Firebirds in 1967. The stereo tape format did not reach the Chrysler ponies until 1970. This pattern makes sense when you realize that Ford and GM were supporting the development of the 8-track system from the beginning. Few of you may be old enough to remember this, but phonograph record players were briefly tried in cars back in the day. They were an option on some 1956-58 Chrysler models. As you can imagine, the stylus could not be kept at a light enough weight to secure record life, while the bumps in the road caused rampant skipping. The first playable stereo car system was the Muntz four-track tape, a design that predated the much more familiar Lear eight-track system. Although never offered as a regular production option, you could still buy a four-track in the aftermarket in 1968. I put one from Western Auto in my Fiat 850 Spider. I am not sure if there were ever any in-dash four-track units. The optional 8-tracks in the pony cars were mounted near the radio in either the dash or console area.

Today we have already gone completely through the extensive era of in-dash cassette popularity and even production CD players may seem a little dated when they cannot handle MP3 discs. Radio receivers seem dated whenever they lack satellite radio capability. Visit the Crutchfield website to see the amazing array of Retrosound brand in-dash receiver units that not only will fit in the dash of your classic ponies, but include styling of the face and knobs that make them look as if they were born there! These latest retro designs allow you to plug MP3 players and USB thumb drives into them to release the music through your classic car's speaker systems. What more could you ask? Just remember to carefully remove, catalog and store any specific contemporary Sixties components for later resale of your classic ride. It's an opportunity to have your Sixties Time Machine attuned to your New Millennium Ears!

The problem you most likely will have to deal with concerns the low-quality gasoline we get at the pump today. On top of the low octane issue, we now have a big ethanol problem. Expect to diligently add StaBil to the tank if you want to keep decades old engine parts happy.

As a final modification choice, let's not forget the exterior paint. Some models offered special paint options for a little extra cost. If your car was originally equipped with any special paint option, a sane person would make certain it kept that special paint. If you do not care for the color, maybe you should look elsewhere. Paint codes can be found for practically any car, whether you are trying to identify how your car left the factory or seeking a suitable modern equivalent for a repaint.

1964 - 1973 Mustang Convertible

A number of years ago I wrote a story about the first Mustang I saw for the coffee table book entitled *Mustang: The Power, the Passion*. This story described in detail how I had an uncle who happened to be a Ford salesman at the time. He took my family and me down to the local dealership in the middle of the night just to show us the new Ford model he was so excited about. As a salesman, he was salivating over the many upcoming commissions. As a sixteen-year-old just becoming *really* excited over sports cars, the white, six-cylinder hardtop with a three-speed manual did not exactly make my engine roar, although I could see the possibilities coming in the near future. The Mustang on display had a red interior (not my favorite, to say the least) and a minimum array of options. There were basic hubcaps and no tachometer or top that folded down. The options of a sport suspension, fifteen-inch wheels, or a solid-lifter engine would not be available for a couple of months. By August I would have ridden in a dark blue Mustang Convertible with the base V-8 and automatic, but even that example was still not the sports model that could ring my bell.

Even though the convertible body style with bucket seats and a floor shift were standard Mustang fare from April, 1964, the early six-cylinder cars were anything but sporty. Unfortunately, the option list was of little help. The three-speed manual did not even have a synchronized first gear. The optional four-speed was a pedestrian design from England that offered nothing in the way of sporting ratios. Front brakes were drums only with power as an option. No sport suspension or quicker manual steering were available at any price. Standard wheels were thirteen inches but five fourteen inch wheels cost only an additional $7! There would be no way to elevate a Mustang Six above the dreaded *secretary special* label for decades to come. The Six would finally rival the 1965 base GT in net horsepower in 2000, and the later model's additional sports credentials would include a five-speed manual, aluminum wheels, four-wheel power disc brakes, and really quick steering. A 2015 Six will blow the doors off and out-handle even a K-motor GT of 1965. With the sole exception of the Firebird Sprint Six, no early pony car with a six-cylinder engine can even spell the word *spoats ca'*.

The ponies were born to run with American small-block V-8's. The big blocks would arrive in 1967, but that's a later story. Aside from the generators and standard thirteen-inch wheels, the main differences between the 1964 and 1965 Mustangs are the engines. (Yes, Maybelle, I know there are no *official* 1964 Mustangs.) The first year of production brought numerous changes to Mustang option availabilities, particularly the sports oriented components that brought the Mustang into the realm of this book. Note that some of the following have not been confirmed as absolute gospel in the timeframes listed.

Figure I4 - This rather plain looking light blue 1965 Mustang Convertible with black interior and top appears rather unassuming. Look at the front fender emblem. This is a very rare early K-code model with the 271-horsepower 289. ©Bull-Doser (PD)

According to the brochures, the 271-hp K engine, the Special Handling Package, and the 15-inch tire options became available in June 1964. The 225-hp 289 replaced the 210-hp 289 in September 1964. The 210-hp had a lower compression and ran on regular fuel. Both the 210-hp and the later 225-hp 289's had a single exhaust system. The four (count 'em, four) brochures published in the '65-'66 model years do not state that either engine had dual exhausts; however, dual exhausts would be a standard component of the GT package launched in April '65. This option package was available only with the 225-hp and 271-hp engines, including a dual exhaust system for the hydraulic lifter 289. Here is a little test: if the 225-hp engine did not already come equipped with dual exhausts, why was the GT package the same option price with either engine? Numerous small changes were necessary in the undercarriage to accommodate the dual exhausts and small price changes were reflected in similar changes. The five-gauge instrument cluster made standard on the '66 model dropped the option price of the Interior Decor Group and the trim rings on the 1966 Styled Steel Wheels dropped that option price a little, too. The answer is that the K-engine package was about fifty bucks cheaper *with* the GT package than it was *without* the GT package. The GT package price already included the cost of dual exhausts and the Special Handling Package and that fifty dollars was deducted if you added the 271-hp engine.

An interesting question arises concerning the Special Handling Package from this same period. The *Mustang Red Book* states that the Special Handling Package was available only on the 200-hp and 225-hp 289's. What about the 210-hp D-code engine? I do not have an easy answer to this question. Maybe the release schedule of these options changed after the brochures were printed. The 1964 brochure indicates that this package would be available in June, along with a fifteen-inch wheel option and the 271-horsepower K engine. The question is whether or not any Mustangs were built in June-August of 1964 with the 210-hp 289 and the Special Handling Package, with or without fifteen-inch wheels?

Figure I5 - The 1965 Mustang GT Convertible is a rare color combination in Prairie Bronze with a white top and all-white Pony Interior. This GT also has styled steel wheels and whitewall tires. Its powerplant is the standard GT version of the A-code 225-hp unit with dual exhausts. ©Sicnag (CC)

By April 1965 the dust bunnies had settled on the Mustang's sports car aspirations. The GT option package took the pony closer to the sports car ideal. It still may have been too big and heavy to ever be a *real* sports car, but it was a very sporty car from this point onward. Whatever the overly styled dash layout, long wheelbase and rear seat took away was easily offset by the comfort, convenience, and reliability of an American car with a big engine, effective top design, and dependable electrical system.

Before we continue to the 1967-73 Mustangs, let's pause for a few comments concerning current collector values. Many Mustang fans are like me in that they truly love the original, clean, svelte body before Ford began its Arnold Schwarzenegger plan for the car. You know, the one that Lee Iacocca called a *fat pig*. Although in previous years, the first-body Mustang was one of the earliest Sixties cars to catch the attention of the Baby Boomer Collectible class, in recent years there seems to be a relentless obsession with exceptionally rare and/or large V-8 engines in all the early pony cars. Since the initial reason for the enlargement of the Mustang was to accommodate big block engines, this plan obviously began with the 390 option in 1967. The current result has been that now a 1967 model with an original 390 can cost considerably more than a 1965 or '66 with any engine except the rare 271-hp K! This pattern in various forms followed the Mustang through its last first-generation convertible of 1973. One caveat of course is that very few convertibles were ever produced with the largest, or more specifically the raciest, engines. This means that the tiny production numbers of high performance, muscle car sort of convertibles keeps these values in the stratosphere. Needless to say, many models of slightly less rarity and performance are consistently available as nice, *drivable* pony cars.

Figure I6 - This yellow 1966 Convertible displays the grille, hood trim and fake side scoop design of 1966, but the grille pony and wheel covers are from a 1965 model. This example is very typically equipped for the era with 289 V-8 and whitewall tires. The standard interior is black and so is the top. Note the AM radio antenna on the right fender. ©Bull-Doser (PD)

Mustang Convertible Production Chart

Model	Production	Model	Production
1964 1/2	28,833	1968 Shelby	1124
1965	67,774	1969	14,746
1965 Pony	5338	1969-70 Shelby	529
1966	59,599	1970	7673
1966 Pony	12,520	1971	6121
1967	44,808	1972	6121
1968	25,376	1973	11,853
	Total 1964 - 1973	Convertibles	292,415

Mustang Convertible Production Chart Notes:
As a point of reference, Mustang Convertible production would return in 1983, when 23,438 were built. The annual production climbed up to 42,244 in 1989. Another high point would be hit in 1994 with 53,714 produced, including 10,000 Cobras. Figures remained high at 48,264 in 1995. Surprisingly there were only 37,053 1999 Convertibles with the new 35th Anniversary styling. Convertible production peaked in 2000 at 61,592 (plus, controversially, 100 Cobras). The Cobras were technically 1999 models.

Figure I7 - Look closely at this 1966 Convertible with styled steel wheels and whitewall tires, just like the car above. This example has a Pony Interior matching the exterior and a white convertible top and boot. I believe the color is called Tahoe Turquoise with Aqua interior. What is unusual about this car is that the AM radio antenna is on the left side. That is because this is a right hand drive Mustang. ©Sicnag (CC)

The 1967 model brought bulkier styling to squeeze the 390 into the engine bay. This first big block produced 320 horsepower, quickly diminishing the appeal of the more expensive 289 K, the last year of its production. Although the styling bulk was a negative component of the new second generation, 1967 did bring a number of improvements. The 390 was a low-priced, low-maintenance alternative to the 289 K. The optional tachometer was larger and in the instrument panel where it belonged. The optional AC was now properly integrated into the dash. Cruise control was a new option if you could stomach the required automatic transmission. Power front disc brakes replaced the old manual variety and a glass rear window was a new option for convertibles. This was the only year you could still get a K motor and the original styled steel wheel design with a better tach and power disc brakes.

The Early Pony Convertibles

Figure I8 - A 1967 Mustang in Candy Apple Red with black interior and top, styled steel wheels and whitewall tires. ©Sicnag (CC)

The Mustang delved deeper into the big block madness in 1968. This drove the Mustang toward the muscle car concept as it drifted away from the pleasure of a convertible. The higher emphasis on the larger high-performance engines naturally lessened the interest in convertibles. Note in the production chart at the end of this article the steep drops in convertible production every year from 1966 through 1971. The 428 joined the engine lineup and the term *Cobra Jet* entered the Mustang lexicon. For the first three months of the '68 model year, you could even special order a racing 427 with 390 horsepower as an expensive $622 option. The '68 model otherwise continued much like the '67, with only minor trim differences. If you like vent windows, note that the Mustang kept them through 1968 when the GM ponies dumped them. Shelby brought out his version of the Convertible to be built in small numbers through the miniscule changes of early 1970. Although all the Mustang Convertibles through 1973 are included in this book to complete the first Mustang series, the models following 1968 dropped further and further into the *longer, lower, wider, heavier* abyss. *Fat pigs*, indeed!

Figure I9 - This 1968 Mustang Convertible shows the standard hood indentations and wheel covers. The whitewall tires were still a popular option that year. ©Bull-Doser (PD)

The Grande Hardtop was introduced in 1969 and that alone should tell you something! The Bosses were introduced at the opposite end of the fun scale. All these models were built as coupes only and convertible production continued to drop. Luxury interiors and convenience features faced off against the top-line Bosses, the high volume Mach 1's, and the Cobra Jet options. SelectShift Cruise-O-Matics began to *really* outnumber four-speed transmissions. The days of the Mustang as a nimble convertible were basically over. The 1970 model continued with only minimal changes, but the '71 brought new body lines, an extremely horizontal and impractical rear window on the fastback coupes, and the last body redesign before the rather embarrassing Mustang II of 1974. Thank goodness there were no Mustang II convertibles, so I could readily stop this story at this point. The 1971-73 Convertibles that were produced were for the most part either minimally optioned cruisers or luxury boats. Either way, these cars were boring! A small number of Convertibles were produced with Dual Ram Air Induction 351's and four-speed transmissions, but I bet these are rare beyond belief.

The Early Pony Convertibles

Figure I10 - Compare the subtle differences in the shape of this red '69 Convertible with the 1968 model above. The vent windows and hood indentations are gone, and so are the F-O-R-D letters from the nose. This example has a white vinyl interior and optional styled steel wheels. Compare these wheels to those on the Italia Spyder in Figure H21. Notice how the fake comb-shaped vent appears tacked on and backward on the 1969 model. The 1970 model will be little changed from the 1969, with the most obvious clue being a pair of horizontal slots outside the headlamps on the '70 model. ©Detect and Preserve (CC)

Figure I11 - This rare white on white 1971 Mustang Convertible has the 351 Ram Air option package. Note the round chrome hood pins, blacked out hood, and black *hockey stick* side stripes. ©Bull-Doser (PD)

The summation of the first generation Mustang Convertible story is quite simple and it would appear that most of the relative prices of these machines will remain within the same framework for the foreseeable future. The '64-'66 models will always be special as collector models. The GT package and Interior Decor Group options will always be popular and original K engines will always be vehemently sought. The 1967-68 models will offer the aforementioned performance and convenience features lacking in the earlier models, while still holding on to that elusive first-pony look and nimble feel. The 1969-70 years will remain the transition period to the less popular, and less valuable, final body style in the series. The obsession with muscle cars and rare high-performance engines will continue to dominate the auction blocks, leaving many lower-optioned Convertibles available as nice collectible drivers. Of course even at the lower price levels, condition and originality are everything. Rust will always be a potential problem and so will the low-octane gasoline with ethanol that we buy at the pump today. If you happen to be a fan of that final Mustang Convertible body style, look at the bright side. Your issues with rust and fuel are likely to be less and so is the price you will pay for your new collector car.

Figure I12 - A red 1973 Mustang Convertible with white interior, optional chrome hubcaps and trim rings. Strangely enough, this option was part of the standard equipment for the Mach 1 for that year. ©Mr. Choppers (GNU)

Sixties Mustang Base Convertible Chart

Inline Sixes	HP	Wt.	Price	V-8 Models	HP	Wt.	Price
1964 I-6 170	101	2740	$2671 *	1964 260	164	NA	NA
1965 I-6 200	120	2740	$2671 *	1964 289	210	NA	$2900 *
1966 I-6 200	120	NA	$2766 *	1965 289	200	NA	$2847 *
				1966 289	200	2904	$2943 *
1967 I-6 200	120	2892	$2699				
1968 I-6 200	115	2924	$2815	1967 289	200	3080	$2988 *
				1968 289	195	3112	$3104 *
1969 I-6 200	115	2942	$2832				
1970 I-6 200	120	3190	$3025	1969 302	220	3210	$3142 *
				1970 302	220	3240	$3331 *
1971 I-6 250	145	3209	$3227				
1972 I-6 250	98	NA	$3158	1971 302	210	3261	$3227
1973 I-6 250	99	3299	$3295	1972 302	140	3147	$3244
				1973 302	141	3216	$3382

Sixties Mustang Base Convertible Chart Notes:

* Price includes optional four-speed manual transmission. Any prices listed without an asterisk are stated with the standard three-speed, as no four-speed was offered with the base engine on these particular models and years. The prices listed for the 64-66 Mustang Sixes include the $114 four-speed option. A four-speed was available on the '64-'66 Mustang Sixes, but the four-speed was available only with the V-8's in all later Mustangs of this period. Note that in the 1964 models, the 260 V-8 was not available with a four-speed, so that quoted price includes both the 210-hp, four-barrel 289 and four-speed options. The 64-66 Mustangs were offered with a $31 Special Handling Package on all V-8 models, but this option disappeared after 1966.

Here is the big pony car dilemma summarized. With the exception of the Firebird Sprint Six or a carefully optioned Camaro Six, no base six-cylinder Mustang or otherwise was ever available with stiff suspension, tight steering, and a sporty four-speed. The four-speed option for the 1964-66 Mustang was an English Ford design with a very wide ratio and the Special Handling Package was offered on V-8's only. As stated in the *Car Life Mustang* book, the V-8 essentially adds 300 pounds to the front end. The engine is just the beginning: the heavier car needs larger suspension bits, power steering and brakes, etc.

Figure I13 - Compare this blue 1973 Convertible with NACA ducts on the hood to the 1971 Ram Air pictured above. Both models have styled steel wheels, hockey stripes, white interiors and vented hoods on basically the same body, but there are several subtle differences. ©Bull-Doser (PD)

Sixties Mustang Sports Convertible Chart

Model	HP	Price	Model	HP	Price
1965 GT A Code 289	225	$3065	1969 GT Q Code 428	335	$3691
1965 GT K Code 289	271	$3183	1969 GT R Code 428	335	$3824
1966 GT A Code 289	225	$3148	1970 H Code 351	250	$3441
1966 GT K Code 289	271	$3265	1970 M Code 351	300	$3489
			1970 Q Code 428	335	$3752
1967 GT C Code 289	200	$3193	1970 R Code 428	335	$3817
1967 GT A Code 289	225	$3246			
1967 GT K Code 289	271	$3365	1971 H Code 351	240	$3488
1967 GT S Code 390	320	$3400	1971 M Code 351	285	$3536
			1971 C Code 429	370	$3815
1968 GT J Code 302	230	$3317	1971 J Code 429	375	$3879
1968 GT S Code 390	325	$3523			
1968 GT R Code 428	335	$3628	1972 H Code 351	177	$3285
			1972 Q Code 351 CJ	266	$3359
1969 GT H Code 351	250	$3347	1972 R Code 351 HO	275	$4056

1969 GT M Code 351	290	$3373			
1969 GT S Code 390	320	$3561	1973 H Code 351 CJ	177	$3423
			1973 Q Code 351 CJ	266	$3489

Sixties Mustang Sports Convertible Chart Notes:

All prices include the optional four-speed manual transmission. The 1965-69 models include the GT sports package not offered on the 1970-73 models. The GT package was discontinued after slow sales in the 1969 model year. The 1968 S Code 390 GT price includes mandatory front power disc brakes. The 1968 R Code 428 Cobra Jet price included staggered rear shocks, Ram Air hood, four-speed and front power disc brakes. This package actually produced about 400 gross horsepower. The price quoted above for this model may be a little low. Only a few 428CJ Convertibles were built and it is possible that none had the four-speed manual transmission. A few '68 Mustangs were produced with the W Code 390-hp 427 and three-speed automatic, but it is doubtful if any of these were convertibles. The 1969 428 engines came with close ratio four-speeds. The Cobra Jet R Code version included the Shaker Hood Scoop, but the official power rating remained at 335.

Figure I14 - This blue 1968 Mustang Convertible is the way I like to remember the Mustangs of the period. This is a GT with the 390 and aftermarket Cragar S/S mag wheels, the original chrome five-spoke design that started the trend and made it famous. ©P-O Olsson (PD)

1967 - 1969 Camaro Convertible

Figure I15 - This rich, dark red 1967 Camaro SS shows a boot that could fit a little better. Notice the fake vents on the raised hood and the rear mounted radio antenna. ©Rex Gray, Southern California (CC)

Chevrolet finally responded to the pony car stampede in September, 1966. The big-block 396 was not immediately available at that time, but Chevy had wisely developed the Camaro with an engine bay large enough for it. All three original Camaro Convertible models were available with hamsters peddling six cylinders up through the famous porcupine 396, at least since November. Aside from the big-block capability, the new Camaro matched the 1967 Mustang with its integrated AC, AM/FM radio, power disc brakes, cruise control, and in-dash tachometer. Note that some of the lesser gauges were mounted down low, in front of the shift lever. This was not exactly a true sports car selling point. The Camaro (and Firebird) offered optional power windows from the beginning. These offered the obvious advantage of lowering or raising, with a power top, without the driver getting out of his seat. Note that although the Mustang had an optional power top from the beginning, it did not have power windows available until 1970. Weird, man, just weird!

Figure I16 - A close-up of the same 1967 SS shows its matching dark red vinyl interior with automatic transmission shifter in the console displaying three auxiliary gauges at the driver's knee level. Note the deep dish steering wheel and very red interior, including all interior panels and bright red carpet, too. ©Rex Gray, Southern California (CC)

The Camaro and Firebird offered convertibles only in their initial three-year design. Unlike the Barracuda and Mustang, neither offered a fastback body style in these years, either. With the exception of the Z/28, all engines and option packages were offered on convertibles alongside the hardtops. Due to the 1967 release occurring three years after the GTO unleashed the musclecar phenomenon, the engine bays were all designed to handle large V-8's from the beginning. Although a disgusting three-on-the-tree shifter was standard with all engines, all Camaros, even the 140-hp Six offered fully synchronized four-speed manual transmissions with a choice of axle ratios as options. Chevrolet's F-41 sport suspension, quick steering ratios, disc brakes, power brakes, power steering, tachometer, and air conditioning options were available across the board. Probably the biggest negative with the equipment of the original Camaro was the two-speed Powerslide automatic. The three-speed Turbo Hydra-Matic was optional only with the 396. The same pattern was true of the Firebird, too, with the three-speed automatic available only with the big-block 400.

With 20/20 hindsight we can all clearly see the *redneck yahoo* image that has stubbornly stuck to all Camaros for decades now. There is little we can do about this. It is much like the *silk shirt with gold chains and a cowboy hat* that Burt Reynolds so adeptly attached to the Trans Am in 1977. If you are a fan of classic Camaros, you just have to look the other way and ignore it. Mustang fans have their own cross to bear with the *Fix Or Repair Daily* meme. You are not alone in suffering derogatory comments. Fiats face the *tinworm* while the British try to keep their chins raised above the *Prince of Darkness*. Camaros will always offer the advantages of high production numbers, general reliability and longevity, affordability, and American driving quality. There were three basic categories of Camaro Convertibles produced in the 1967-69 period.

The first and far most common category was the six-cylinder and two-barrel, small-block variety. Engines in all three model years included the 140-hp base six, a 155-hp larger six, and the 210-hp 327 V-8. All Camaros had three-speed column shifts as standard, but most likely the majority of this group had two-speed Powerglides, either on the column or the floor with the optional console. Thankfully, the Turbo Hydra-Matic was offered as an option with *all* engines in both Camaros and Firebirds in 1969. You will not likely find many sporting options such as proper instruments, handling suspension, or four-speeds in this group, although these things were certainly available. As with the Firebird, you could even add dual exhausts to the two-barrel 327, although no increase in horsepower was advertised.

Figure I17 - **A gold 1968 SS-350 with the Rally Sport package, too, usually referred to as an SS/RS Camaro. Note the standard SS features of white stripes around the nose and chrome hubcaps with trim rings. The fake hood vents are a bit more elaborate than those on the '67 SS. The antenna on this car is on the front fender. You can spot its model year by the lack of headrests and vent windows. Surprise! This is a right hand drive car.** ©Sicnag (CC)

The middle category is the one most celebrated within the sports car realm of this book. Engine options included the 275-hp 327 with single exhaust and four-barrel carb and the 295-hp 350 offered only with the Super Sport package. Strangely, the 275-hp 327 was replaced with a 350 making only 255 horsepower in 1969. There are several good sports car choices among this group, since you could add most of the sporting options to a V-8 running on regular gasoline. Of course, too, such an engine is a little easier to adapt to the *cat pee with ethanol* we buy at the pump today. You are actually much more likely to locate an SS 350 today than you are one of the lesser V-8's with the sporting accoutrements added a la carte. With the SS package you get all the cutesy stripes and emblems, as well as better handling components. The higher compression ratios will not be happy drinking common unleaded, however. You will obviously find a much higher percentage of four-speeds, floor shifts, and tachometers among the Super Sports.

Figure I18 - A 1969 Azure Turquoise Camaro 350 typical for its type with a black vinyl interior and top and styled steel wheels. ©Sicnag (CC)

The big-block 396 Camaros are of course the auctioneers' darlings of inflated prices for the street racers of then that have evolved into the trailer queens of today. The queen bee of this group is obviously the Indy Pace Car Convertible of 1969. If you can stomach orange houndstooth seats, then this is obviously the cat's meow of early topless Camaros. These were all white with orange Z-28 look alike stripes and orange interiors. The soft tops were all white. Engine options included all those for the other SS models: 300-hp 350 and the legendary porcupine 396 in 325, 350, or 375 gross horsepower ratings. Two things to keep in mind about the Indy Pace Car are (a) it was nothing more than a loaded SS with Z-28 hood and deck stripes and (b) was produced for public sale *only* in 1969. You may find '67 or '68 Pace Car Convertibles out there, even at the fancy auctions-- maybe even *particularly* at the fancy auctions -- but these are all fakes. Hang onto your wallet! If you are gagged with a spoon by orange, there were plenty of SS 396 Convertibles built in many nice colors. Their current prices vary with the porcupine's horsepower ratings. You can be assured that the higher the rating, the more likely the car will be happier strutting its stuff quietly at shows than taking you for a sunny Sunday afternoon drive on cat pee with ethanol.

More than with any car in this book, with the possible exception of the Mustang, you can find an infinite variety of engine and other replacement parts for a Camaro. A multitude of these, particularly for the common 327 and 350 V-8's, will not be original type equipment.

Remember that redneck yahoo mentioned earlier? Countless Camaros have had their engines modified by backwater mechanics over the years, and this may be the leading Achilles' heel of the Camaro as a collectible classic. Watch out for the aftermarket, oversized wheels and tires, too. They are almost as common as a small-block Chevy with headers and a hotter cam. Body parts should be pleasantly available compared to those for imports. Many panels were the same for both Camaros and Firebirds. The main thing to be wary of is accident damage or rust. Cars that have lived their whole lives in the Southwest usually bring premium prices for a good reason.

Figure I19 - An orange-red 1969 Camaro RS Convertible with white top, 350 engine and chrome aftermarket wheels. Note the distinctive three slots on each side of the grille. Compare this to the gold 1968 SS/RS shown above. ©Bull-Doser (PD)

You would think that the much lower production numbers of Firebirds would raise their prices considerably above that of the classic Camaros, but that rarely seems to be the case. The glaring exception is the tiny number of Trans Am Convertibles produced. With all others you can shop among the Camaros and Firebirds with a reasonable expectation of commonality in the prices asked. Even the '69 Pace Cars are not that rare today. The most poignant concept you might want to take away from this discussion of Firebirds and Camaros is that they were better cars than their Mustang and Chrysler competitors in certain key ways. GM styling of that period was truly magical: smooth, flowing lines with just the right amount of silly adornment. GM offered electric windows, big-block engines, extremely reliable automatic transmissions, tilt steering wheels, carefully styled steel wheels, effective air conditioning, low, sports-car-like seating and handling, and in general the best engineering for mass-produced cars of the day. Ford was always the first with a better idea. Chrysler always followed behind in the tracks of the leaders with much larger engineering and styling budgets. General Motors took its time and baked its cars to perfection... at least within a price point in the market.

Camaro Convertible Production Chart

Model / Option / Option Package	1967	1968	1969	Totals
Power Convertible Top	11,783	9580	9631	30,994
M20/21 4-speed (including coupes)	47,539	46,295	64,317	158,151
F-41 (including coupes)	5968	7117	5929	19,014
Dual Exhausts (including coupes)	6722	4462	5545	16,729
Tachometer (including coupes)	27,078	20,263	30,934	78,275
Power Windows (including coupes)	4957	3304	3058	11,319
Air Conditioning (including coupes)	28,226	35,866	44,737	108,829
Cold Air Hood (all SS / Z-28)	NA	NA	10,026	10,026
Rally Sport (including coupes)	64,842	40,977	37,773	143,592
Indy Pace Car Convertibles (Z-11)	NA	NA	3675	3675
SS 350 (including coupes)	29,270	12,496	22,339	64,105
SS 396 325-hp (including coupes)	4003	10,773	6752	21,528
SS 396 350-hp (including coupes)	NA	2579	2018	4597
SS 396 375-hp (including coupes)	1138	4303	4578	10,019
SS 396 375-hp L-89 (inc. coupes)	NA	272	311	583
All Camaro SS Models	34,411	30,423	35,998	100,832
All Six-cylinder Convertibles	5285	3513	1707	10,505
All V-8 Convertibles	19,856	16,927	15,866	52.649
Total Convertible Production	25,141	20,440	17,573	63,154
Total Camaro Production	220,906	235,147	243,085	699,138

Camaro Convertible Production Chart Notes:
   In addition to the standard wide and close ratio four-speeds, 3394 Camaros were equipped with the M22 "rock crusher" transmission in 1968-69, but I seriously doubt if any were installed in convertibles. The Cold Air Hood production numbers included all the Indy Pace Cars. The L-89 option was aluminum heads for the 375-hp 396. A 1969 Pace Car with the 375-hp 396, four-speed and only 20,000 miles on it sold for $187,000 in 2010.

Figure I20 - The 1969 Pace Car Convertible is certainly one of the most collectible of early Camaros. Its main competition in the desirability department would be the Z28 Coupes. In addition to the standard orange stripes and interior, this car has the Pace Car decals installed on the doors. The Pace Car consisted of a bevy of mandatory options on an SS/RS Convertible. The door decals were delivered in the car's trunk. Most buyers probably left them there. Although the official Pace Car option price was minimal, the mandatory options and single color combination unique to the model made it a very distinctive and desirable Camaro. This example is an SS-396, but the Pace Car was also offered as an SS-350. ©Bull-Doser (PD)

Sixties Camaro Base Convertible Chart

Model	HP	Price	Model	HP	Price
1967 Base 230 Six	140	$2888	1969 Base 230 Six	140	$3030
1967 Optional 250 Six	155	$2915	1969 Optional 250 Six	155	$3056
1967 Base 327 V-8	210	$2993	1969 Base 327 V-8	210	$3135
1967 327 Dual Exhausts	210	$3014	1969 327 Dual Exhausts	210	$3166
1967 Opt. 327 4-bbl. V-8	275	$3086	1969 Opt. 350 4-bbl. V-8	255	$3188
1968 Base 230 Six	140	$2986	*Mid-Year Entries*		
1968 Optional 250 Six	155	$3013			
1968 Base 327 V-8	210	$3092	1969 Base 307 V-8	200	$3135
1968 327 Dual Exhausts	210	$3118	1969 Opt. 2-bbl. 350 V-8	250	$3156
1968 Opt. 327 4-bbl. V-8	275	$3185			

Sixties Camaro Base Convertible Chart Notes:

The 1967-69 Camaro Six was available with a four-speed, and the prices stated include the four-speed option. All of these came standard with a three-speed transmission. The optional four-speed generally cost about $200 more, from $180-235 depending on the brand, model, and year. The Base 327 V-8 was changed to a 307 and the Optional 4-bbl. 350 was changed to a 2-bbl. 350 in the middle of the production year. These changes are represented in the last two chart entries. Dual exhaust was an option for the 1967 and 1968 Camaro 327's, but the option price is not available. The 210-hp 327 and the 255-hp 350 of the 1969 Camaro are priced with the standard single exhaust, but both were offered with a dual exhaust option.

Sixties Camaro Super Sports Convertible Chart

Model	HP	Price	Model	HP	Price
1967 SS 350 L-48	295	$3204	1968 SS 396 L78	375	$3592
1967 SS 396 L-35	325	$3257	1968 SS 396 L89	375	$3960
1967 SS 396 L-34	350	NA			
1967 SS 396 L-78	375	$3494	1969 SS 350 L-48	300	$3431
			1969 SS 396 L-35	325	$3451
1968 SS 350 L-48	295	$3303	1969 SS 396 L34	350	$3732
1968 SS 396 L-35	325	$3355	1969 SS 396 L78	375	$3778
1968 SS 396 L34	350	$3461	1969 SS 396 L89	375	$4173

Sixties Camaro Super Sports Convertible Chart Notes:

All prices include an optional four-speed manual transmission. All engines were OHV V-8's with single four-barrel carburetors and dual exhausts. Camaro brochures show only the 325-hp 396 in 1968 and '69. No 350 or 375 horsepower 396 is shown in any Camaro brochure we have, but other sources say these engines were installed, at least in small quantities. The Camaro.com website states that 1138 SS models were produced with the 375-hp 396 in 1967. A 1967 SS 396 convertible with the 325-hp engine weighed 4003 pounds. The base SS 350 package had two price increases in 1969: $296 - $312 - $328.

1967 - 1969 Firebird Convertible

The first generation Firebird Convertible has always been one of my favorites and here is why. It was the only pony car offered with a *sporty* six-cylinder engine package and all the optional V-8's were very desirable. The Sprint Six put out 215 horsepower. The base V-8 326 two-barrel could even be ordered with dual exhausts and it ran on regular fuel. The 326 H.O. was almost as fast as the 400 and its price was exceptionally affordable. The 400 brought the big-block cache, Ram Air options, and today, tons of collectibility. The styling was similar to that of the Camaro, but the body was lowered down on its suspension a little more. Its Rally II styled steel wheels were the most attractive in the pony car universe at the time. The Firebird had dual headlights, whereas the Camaro had single lamps. One interesting statistic is that Camaro production outnumbered Firebird production in these first three years by more than two to one. However, only about 9% of the Camaros were convertibles; about 16% of Firebirds were convertibles. A proper set of gauges was optional on both cars, but these were placed down low on the optional console in the Camaro. Even the fuel gauge was taken out of the driver's face in this arrangement. The Pontiac hood tach may have been a silly idea, but at least it was in the driver's proper line of sight.

Figure I21 - A typical 1967 Firebird Convertible in blue-green with white interior and top. The vent windows easily identify it as a '67 model. ©Jeremy, Sydney, Australia (CC)

John DeLorean became famous for accomplishing three little things as an executive at Pontiac, and later at Chevrolet. As head of Pontiac in 1964, he allowed Jim Wangers to develop the GTO, hence establishing the official *musclecar*, as *Road & Track* named it. Long before he built his own sports car and found himself trapped in an infamous cocaine sting, DeLorean was a true sports car fan. He wanted Pontiac to develop and mass produce a true sports car called the Firebird, named after a 1954 Pontiac experimental model. Upper GM management insisted that a two-seater would never have volume production potential and forced DeLorean to accept the Camaro as his basis for a Pontiac sports model. The best he could do would be to increase the *sportiness* level of the Pontiac variant and he did just that. The Firebird was introduced with a body lowered on its suspension and its standard inline six-cylinder engine was even an overhead cam design. Several iterations of the big-block 400 were available as options from the beginning of production in '67 and the legendary Trans Am would be launched before the first series was superceded. Oh, yeah, three years later, the Corvette would *finally* have a four-speed, Positraction and tinted glass as standard on all models. That was DeLorean's idea. Coincidentally, or maybe not, all three of his good ideas were released after the start of the normal production year for GM cars. The GTO was released in the Spring of 1964, the Firebird in February of 1967, and the 1970 Stingray in January of 1970.

Figure I22 - This gold 1967 Firebird Convertible with matching interior has the 400 V-8 and Rally II wheels.
©Dave 7, Lethbridge, Canada (CC)

The Camaro and Firebird were produced simultaneously in 1967-69 with minor differences, both technical and cosmetic. In my personal opinion, the Firebird wins in the first two years and the Camaro is preferable in 1969. This is all very subjective of course, but I love poured over the wheels styling. I am a big fan of smooth, curved lines with minimal false adornment. The 1967 and '68 Firebirds and Camaros have the smooth, round, naturally flared wheel wells I adore. The '69's have an odd straight line over the wheel wells that I think detracts from the overall look. The 1967-68 models have that natural curve shared with the early Oldsmobile Toronado and all the Mako Stingrays. I think GM changed this fender line for no particular reason, just to be changing it. Elsewhere in this book, you will read how the Austin-Healey Sprite and MG Midget also had straight lines over the fenders, but these were structural. When the lines were later curved, the factory discovered that the curved fender wells weakened the structure and they were subsequently changed back to straight lines. To the best of my knowledge, this issue does not apply to Firebirds or Camaros. The fender flares of the earlier models are simply more attractive. The 1969 Camaros received a different treatment on their side trim and front grille and headlamp areas. I think the 1969 styling favors the Camaro in these areas. Lastly, I am not a fan of the bulbous split grille on the 1969 Firebirds. I like the original, wider, flatter look of the Firebird face. As always, your opinion may differ. The '69 model did, however, receive a few small improvements. The face design of the hood tachometer was updated with a more professional, less cartoonish look. The seats were a little softer and headrests were now standard on all models.

Figure I23 - This rear view of the same gold 1967 Firebird displays its fake wood steering wheel, gold top boot that matches the interior, and the discreet red 400 emblem on the trunk lid. ©Dave 7, Lethbridge, Canada (CC)

Figure I24 - One of the stranger ideas Pontiac built in the Sixties was the optional tachometer mounted on the hood of the car. Although this supposedly clever idea was to place the **RPM** reading squarely within the driver's line of sight, the designers ignored the obvious intrusion of rain and bug splats on the windshield! The hood tach option is distinctly visible on this **1968 400 Convertible.** ©Alf van Beem (PD)

Within this classic 1967-69 time period, we had the Corvette, the Mustang, and the first generation Barracuda Convertible as competition. All the other choices were imported. The Corvair was sort of on its last tire, so to speak. Ford had already established the beachhead with the long hood and short deck styling of a front-engine, rear wheel drive car as the standard bearer of American sporty car success. It had become obvious that no American car company was seriously interested in producing a two-seater convertible sports car outside the Stingray reign. What we got in early 1967 was the next best thing. General Motors would not produce anything closer to a genuine sports car until the Fiero GT of the mid-Eighties.

GM did consistently do something that has always severely irritated me. The company belligerently refused to equip standard models, no matter how high the sporting pretensions, with four-on-the-floor shifters. All the early Camaros and Firebirds had three speed manuals as standard transmissions. Only the Firebird 400 big-block and the Sprint 6 package included a floor shift. All the rest were threes on the trees! The second most irritating issue concerned the many overly styled dash designs that offered precious little helpful information to the serious driver. Although Ford and Chrysler were somewhat guilty of this nonsense, GM was the worst, from Pontiac's Hood Tach to Chevy's fuel gauge on the optional console!

What about the positive attributes? Fortunately there were plenty to applaud. All Camaros and all Firebirds, from 1967 to the present day, are some of the best driving cars for Americans on U.S. roads. They may be faddishly styled and ponderous on tight English country lanes, but they are the cat's meow for adaptation to American driving conditions. Most of the big V-8's run and run with minimal maintenance. The small rear seats provide more than adequate space to haul any items the driver needs to have immediately handy. There is no substitute for air conditioning in The South. FM stereos and tape decks can minimize the mind numbing of endless freeways or backed up traffic. If you can stand an automatic transmission, even these earliest Firebirds and Camaros offered a cruise control option, although few were so equipped back when premium fuel was forty-cents and radar was something only the U. S. Navy used. Color choices, particularly of interiors and convertible tops, were much more extensive than those of imported cars, which in many cases offered only black and black. The conveniences of power windows and top allowed the roof to be raised or lowered from the driver's seat. The big news of the 1969 models was of course the midyear introduction of the Trans Am, of which the eight convertibles produced will always be the *ne plus ultra* of GM pony car collectibility. The four with four-speeds will most likely always remain a little more coveted than the four built with Turbo Hydra-Matics.

When looking for a classic Firebird Convertible, your biggest problem will probably be locating one in good condition with the equipment you desire. You can see from the chart that only about 2/3 as many Firebird Convertibles were produced as 1967-69 Camaros. Although heavily promoted in ads of the day, Sprint and H.O. Convertibles comprised only a sliver of Firebird production. Contemporary *Consumer Reports* articles consistently bad-mouthed the Firebirds, especially the OHC Six engines. Particularly compared to most of the imported sports cars of the day, I would take the *CR* criticisms as a poot of exhaust fumes. The early Firebird Convertible was one of the best ideas spawned by John Zachary DeLorean, and it still is a very desirable classic *sports car*.

Figure I25 - This shot of a 1969 Firebird white interior shows off its stylish thin-backed vinyl seats. Unfortunately, though, the steering wheel looks like it escaped from a Buick family sedan. ©SV Lambo (CC)

The Early Pony Convertibles

Figure I26 - The face of the 1969 Firebird changed considerably from that of the 1967-68 models. Sporting the latest in body-colored Endura plastic around the headlights, the distinctive new Pontiac split grille look was emphasized. Notice the new creased fender lines and fake side vents, too. This orange with white interior Firebird 350 has the hood tach, too, but it is barely discernable from this photo angle. ©SV Lambo (CC)

Firebird Options Production Chart

Model / Option / Option Package	1967	1968	1969	Totals
Sprint 6 Manual Convertible			213	213
Sprint 6 Automatic Convertible			54	54
Sprint 6 Manual (including coupes)	2963	1216		4179
326 / 350 Manual (including coupes)	8224	16,632		24,856
Manual Transmissions (inc. coupes)	27,971	32,910	20,840	81,721
326 H. O. (including coupes)	6078			6078
350 H. O. Manual (including coupes)		3784		3784
350 H. O. Auto (including coupes)		2638		2638
400 H. O. (including coupes)	18,635	18,714	11,522	48,871
400 H. O. Convertible	3660			3660
All Six-cylinder Models	17,664	18,494		36,158

All V-8 Models		64,896	88,618		153,514
Total Convertible Production		15,528	16,960	11,657	44,145
Total Firebird Production		82,560	107,112	87,708	277,380

Firebird Options Production Chart Notes:

The 1967 model had a 15.4-gallon fuel tank, enlarged to 18.5 gallons in 1968 and '69. Power windows were ordered on 2283 Coupes and Convertibles in 1967. Two of the 3660 400 H. O. Convertibles had the Ram Air option; both were automatics. The actual availability with restrictions of some options in some model years has not been confirmed. There may have been no Sprint 6's, and only limited Ram Air 400's, built with AC; the *Firebird Red Book* and the official Firebird brochures of 1967-69 do not agree on this issue. Cruise control may have been available only on V-8's. Convertible tops could be ordered in Cream, Blue, or Turquoise in 1967 and Teal or Gold in 1968. Tops in 1969 were Parchment, Dark Green, or Dark Blue. Of course white or black convertible tops were available in all years.

Sixties Firebird Base Convertible Chart

Model	*Engine*	*C. I.*	*HP*	*Wt.*	*Price*
1967 Firebird Base	SOHC I-6	230	165	3247	$2903
1967 Firebird Base V-8	OHV V-8	326	250	3399	$3182 *
1967 Base V-8 Dual Exhaust	OHV V-8	326	250	3399	$3213 *
1968 Firebird Base	SOHC I-6	250	175	3303	$3180 *
1968 Firebird Base V-8	OHV V-8	350	265	3466	$3286 *
1968 Base V-8 Dual Exhaust	OHV V-8	350	265	3466	$3317 *
1969 Firebird Base	SOHC I-6	250	175	3376	$3230 *
1969 Firebird Base V-8	OHV V-8	350	265	3528	$3341 *
1969 Base V-8 Dual Exhaust	OHV V-8	350	265	3528	$3372 *

Sixties Firebird Base Convertible Chart Notes:

* These prices include the cost of the four-speed manual transmission. All of these came standard with a three-speed transmission. The optional four-speed generally cost about $200 more, from $180-235 depending on the brand, model, and year. The Base Firebird Six was not offered with a four-speed in 1967. Dual exhaust on the Firebird Base V-8 was a $31 option in each year.

Sixties Firebird Sports Convertible Chart

Model	Engine	C. I.	HP	Wt.	Price
1967 Firebird Sprint Six	OHC I-6	230	215	3289	$3214 *
1967 Firebird H. O. 350	OHV V-8	326	285	3423	$3257 *
1967 H. O. 400	OHV V-8	400	325	3434	$3357 *
1967 H. O. 400 Ram Air	OHV V-8	400	325	3434	$3857 *
1968 Firebird Sprint Six	OHC I-6	250	215	3355	$3307 *
1968 Firebird H. O. 350	OHV V-8	350	320	3504	$3372 *
1968 Firebird 400	OHV V-8	400	330	3562	$3542 *
1968 Firebird 400 H. O.	OHV V-8	400	335	3562	$3542 *
1968 H. O. 400 Ram Air	OHV V-8	400	335	3575	$3626 *
1969 Firebird Sprint Six	OHC I-6	250	215	3429	$3361 *
1969 Firebird H. O. 350	OHV V-8	350	325	3569	$3426 *
1969 Firebird 400	OHV V-8	400	330	3589	$3591 *
1969 Firebird 400 H. O.	OHV V-8	400	335	3589	$3575 *
1969 H. O. 400 Ram Air IV	OHV V-8	400	345	3589	$4072 *
1969 Firebird T/A (HO w/RA III)	OHV V-8	400	335	3589	$4404 *

Sixties Firebird Sports Convertible Chart Notes:
   * All prices include four-speed transmissions. Although the Firebird Sprint Six was available with a four-speed in all years, the '67 Base Six came only with a three-speed; however, a four-speed was available with all Firebird engines in '68 and '69. Surprisingly, Pontiac claims 230 hp for the Sprint Six with manual transmission in '69, but only the regular 215 hp in 67-68. Note that the 1968 Firebird brochure states the weight of the HO 400 models as two-hundred pounds *less* than stated in the chart, but those figures make no sense, so I have adjusted the figures as if the brochure includes a one-digit typo, which I strongly suspect is the case. Unless some reason can be uncovered that these particular models are lighter than the HO 350 or the '69 HO 400, they are being left as stated in the chart. There were eight Trans Am Convertibles with 335 hp built in 1969, four with four-speeds and four with automatics. The Ram Air IV option is not listed in the chart because no Trans Am Convertibles had it, although a number of Trans Am Coupes did. The 1969 Trans Am price may not be precisely accurate due to the specific wording of the option price listings we have available and different sources do not exactly agree. The $4404 includes $195 for the four-speed option, a figure that may have been included twice.

1967 - 1971 Barracuda Convertible

Figure I27 - A red 1967 Barracuda Convertible is a typical example of an early topless Barracuda. The 1968 and '69 models appeared much the same. The later models did not have P-L-Y-M-O-U-T-H lettering on the forward edge. The fake vents in the center of the hood are clearly visible in this shot. So are the silver-painted steel wheels with exposed lugs and optional whitewalls. ©Bull-Doser (PD)

The Barracuda edition of the Plymouth Valiant was launched at practically the same time as the Mustang in the Spring of 1964, but the Barracuda lacked a couple of key advantages. The first is that although the new Plymouth was based on the compact Valiant sedan, just as the new Ford was based on the compact Falcon sedan, the Mustang received a classic sports car look with a long hood and a short trunk lid. The Barracuda was new from its Valiant heritage only in its distinctive fastback roof with huge wraparound rear window. The engine compartment was the exact same size as that of the Valiant, leaving most of the Barracuda with the sedan's boring styling. The second issue is that the Barracuda was released without the fanfare and media blitz enjoyed by Ford dealers all over America when the Mustang was released.

The Early Pony Convertibles

Figure I28 - This 1967 Barracuda S Convertible in white with black top and interior shows off its taut-fitting top, black side stripes, polished steel wheels and redline tires. ©Jeremy G 3030 (CC)

Figure I29 - A 'Cuda 340 Convertible in an optional color called TorRed with white interior and top. Note the large hood scoop, hood pins, and chrome steel Rallye wheels. This is a right hand drive car. ©Sicnag (CC)

The most power you could order for a '64 Barracuda was a 180-horsepower, two-barrel 273. No convertible or sports package was available. The 1965 model year brought a four-barrel, 235-horsepower 273 and the Formula S sports package. A convertible and hardtop were added in 1967 with a new body restyle that could *barely* squeeze in a 280-hp 383 without power steering, power brakes, or AC! Since the 383 was available only with the Formula S package, which could be ordered only on the fastback, there were no 1967 383 Convertibles, anyway. The engine lineup improved considerably in 1968. The 273 V-8 was replaced by a two-barrel 318 with 230 gross horsepower. You could now order a Formula S Convertible with a 275-horsepower 340 or a 300-horsepower 383. The latter was still a stupid idea without the power options necessary to control the front-end weight. Buyers purchased 1270 383's anyway. Only 683 Barracudas, including all three body styles in 1969, were pushed out the dealership doors with the 383. The 'Cuda performance package and the 440 four-barrel with 375 horsepower were also introduced in 1969, but none of these were available on the Convertible.

Figure I30 - This is the 1971 'Cuda with the Shaker Hood option in Sassy Grass Green with white vinyl interior and top. This is one of only nineteen 1971 'Cuda Convertibles with the Shaker Hood. The easily identified differences between this model and the 1970 are the dual headlights and grille design of staggered panels. ©Bull-Doser (PD)

Figure I31 - A 1971 'Cuda Convertible in Curious Yellow with white interior and top and the 440 Six Pack engine combined with the Shaker Hood, a rare combination in a Barracuda Convertible. Only seventeen 'Cuda Six Pack Convertibles were constructed in 1971. This picture shows the size of the hole cut into the hood. The cutesy name for the optional paint color derives from a 1967 Swedish X-rated movie entitled *I Am Curious (Yellow)*. The plotline of this controversial underground film was similar to that of the comical references to the fictional title *Rochelle, Rochelle* in several episodes of *Seinfeld* decades later. ©Brett Weinstein (GNU)

The final Barracuda body of 1970 and '71 was larger than all previous Barracudas. Its 108-inch wheelbase was the same as that of the Mustangs, Camaros, and Firebirds of the '60's, but two inches shorter than that of its new companion, the Challenger. Both models finally had the nice long hood, short deck look of the other ponies. Both models also received the full array of Chrysler performance engines that now fit into a much larger engine bay. You could now have the prerequisite power steering and brakes with all engines. Air conditioning was still restricted from some of the high performance models. All these engines and the 'Cuda sport packages could be ordered on convertibles in 1970 and this choice continued into 1971 for the Barracuda, but not the Challenger, which lost its R/T Convertible option, and the big engines with it, in 1971. The top 383 in 1970 offered 335 horsepower and the 440 Six pack with 390 horsepower was added. As with most cars from all brands in 1971, some of the ultimate power ratings of 1970 would be lost to the enforcement of lower compression ratios. With the demise of the fun performance packages, it is just as well that the Barracuda and Challenger Convertibles were dropped after 1971, leaving only the Mustang Convertible to soldier on embarrassingly in 1972-73.

Figure I32 - Here is the rear view of that same Curious Yellow 'Cuda 440 Six Pack. ©Brett Weinstein (GNU)

The 1970 and '71 'Cudas brought several additional performance-related options. These included hoods with flat-black paint, hood scoops and hood pins. The most sought after option today is the Shaker Hood produced in very small numbers. Rear spoilers, tape stripes, and styled steel wheels were also available. Most of these options were available in either 'Cuda packages or individually. Chrysler was particularly enamored of high-performance rear axle packages, offering several choices with the more powerful engines of both Barracudas and Challengers. Like the Challengers, the Barracudas had their own special selection of $14 paint options with wild and crazy names. These included Vitamin C, Lemon Twist, In-Violet, Curious Yellow, and Sassy Grass Green. This silly option is valued today, so finding a Barracuda in one of these original paint colors is a plus. The 1971 'Cuda model had a large new black or white panel on its rear flanks that I personally do not find attractive. Your tastes may vary.

At this point in time, you will probably pay a higher price for a 'Cuda than a Challenger. You can see from the chart below that considerably more Challengers were produced in 1970-71. There were more R/T's than 'Cudas, even with the latter production continuing into 1971. Of course the Hemi 'Cuda Convertible is one of those stratospherically priced collectibles, but if you are reading this book, you are likely more interested in collectible cars that the 99% can afford. Regardless of whatever we might prefer, even a 440 Magnum pretty much makes any

The Early Pony Convertibles

Barracuda or Challenger into a trailer queen these days. As with the other pony convertibles, the small-block with a fitment of options that enhance handling and driving enjoyment is probably the most satisfying car for most of this book's potential readership. In the case of the Barracuda, that means the 275-horsepower 340 with a four-speed. The four-barrel 383 is another good choice in the later models with power steering and brakes. If you can purchase a nice convertible with the 'Cuda package without mortgaging your house, that's even better!

Barracuda Base Convertible Chart

Model	HP	Price	Model	HP	Price
1967 Base Six 225	145	$2779	1970 Base Six 225	145	$3034
1967 Base V-8 273	180	$3039 *	1970 Base V-8 318	230	$3330 *
1967 Opt. 4-bbl. 273	235	$3136 *	1970 Opt. 383 2-bbl. 383	290	$3421
			1970 Opt. 383 4-bbl. 383	330	$3468 *
1968 Base Six 225	145	$2907			
1968 Base V-8 318	230	$3192 *	1971 Base Six 225	145	$3002
			1971 Base V-8 318	230	$3103
1969 Base Six 225	145	$2976	1971 Opt. 383 2-bbl. 383	275	$3383
1969 Base V-8 318	230	$3270 *	1971 Opt. 383 4-bbl. 383	300	$3441 *
1969 Opt. 4-bbl. 340	275	$3387 *			

Barracuda Base Convertible Chart Notes:
 * Four-speed floor shift option is included in these prices. All of these came standard with a three-speed transmission. The optional four-speed generally cost about $200 more, from $180-235 depending on the brand, model, and year. None of the Chrysler six-cylinders were offered with a four-speed. The 1970 and 1971 Barracuda and Challenger 383 two-barrel engines were not available with a four-speed and the 383 required the optional three-speed automatic, included in the prices quoted. The 1971 Barracuda and Challenger 318 was not offered with a four-speed. The 1970 Challenger 340 price includes styled steel Rallye wheels. Note that the 1971 Challenger brochure states that the 318 was available with a four-speed. The chart reflects the information stated in the *Dodge & Plymouth Muscle Car Red Book*.

1970 - 1971 Challenger Convertible

Figure I33 - This 1970 Dodge Challenger Convertible in gold has the six-cylinder engine and optional chrome luggage rack. The plastic woodgrain steering wheel was standard equipment with the base vinyl interior, this one in black. ©Christopher Ziemnowicz (PD)

The Dodge Challenger was like the guy who showed up at the party with all the good drugs, quality booze, and high-class call girls in tow... but too late. The party was already winding down. The Challenger was an all-new design by the same guy who penned the original 1966 Charger. A full array of big-block engines fit into the wide engine bay with ease. Buyers could choose from the Hemi, 440 Six pack, 440 Magnum, or 383 Magnum in the R/T sports package. An unusual plethora of rear axle packages were offered with the high performance engines. The interior designs were mature and luxurious and the exteriors abounded with wild colors with cutesy names. All sorts of stripes and decals decorated the paint. There were only two years a Challenger Convertible was available, 1970 and 1971. The R/T option was available on convertibles only in 1970, which meant the 440 and 426 big-blocks were also available on convertibles only in '70. The differences between the '70 and '71 models were otherwise small, however the engine lineup sacrificed a little power to lower compression ratios, as in much of the 1971 auto industry. Challenger production would struggle forward through 1974 with fixed-roof models of lesser power and interest each succeeding year.

For the topless sports car enthusiast, the Challenger is included in this book as the official representative of the last, and largest, gasp of the initial pony car phenomenon. It shares its distinctly un-sporty bulk with the final Mustangs of the era 1971-1973. All these models offer road-hugging weight, luxurious interior furnishings, and relatively low production numbers, particularly if you are seeking a model with the right options for a properly equipped sports car. The Shelby Mustangs, Plymouth 'Cudas, and Challenger R/T's could be considered appropriate competitors, both then and now. Take a look at the charts. Shelby Mustang Convertibles are only *slightly* less common than 'Cuda and R/T Convertibles combined! On a lesser price scale, the moderate V-8 powered later Mustangs, Barracudas and Challengers could also be considered equals. General Motors threw in the towel on pony convertibles when the company released its 1970 Camaros and Firebirds late in the '70 production year.

Figure I34 - This is a black 1970 Challenger with the 275-hp four-barrel 340 option package, not to be confused with the R/T model, which came only with the 383, 440, and 426 engines in 1970. There is no such car as a Challenger R/T 340 Convertible. The factory applied some of the R/T equipment to a small number of what were listed as base V-8 models at the top of the window stickers. This car has the 340 Engine Package, which included the R/T hood, Rallye wheels and larger tires, and a stiffer suspension. No special stripes or labels were included. The white interior was produced only in vinyl. The outside mirror is chrome, not color keyed to the exterior. This example also has the separate hood pin option. The wheel lip moldings were supposedly deleted with the application of the special 340 engine package. This may or may not have been true of all the cars produced. ©Sam Krieg (GNU)

Challengers were always a little larger, heavier, more luxurious than their Barracuda sisters. With the inclusion of the earlier, Valiant-based Barracuda designs, the rarity of the Dodge Challenger models becomes apparent, although there were somewhat more 1970-71 Challenger Convertibles built than Barracuda Convertibles of the same period. From a topless perspective, you can also surmise that a high percentage of these convertibles from both brands had automatic transmissions. The luxury options took some examples even further away from the sports car ideal.

Let's get down to the details. Although the R/T option was removed from the 1971 catalog, you could still order a topless Challenger with a roaring 340 four-barrel or the equivalent 383. R/T hoods, hood pins, stripes and wheels could also be added. Compared to a base V-8/automatic model, this would indeed be a rare beastie, but it well might dodge some of the auction hysteria experienced by a buyer of a genuine R/T. As shown in photos in this book, watch out for fake R/T's at inflated prices. The special parts can easily be purchased even today to tart up a base V-8 Challenger. The leading visual differences between a 1970 and 1971 Challenger are the divided grille and divided tail lamp panels. Fake brake-cooling scoops in front of the rear wheels were added to true (i.e., hardtop) R/T's in '71, but these can be added to a convertible, too. Of course the sixth digit in the VIN will be a *1* or a *0*. No matter which engine the car has, the Shaker Hood option is rare and desirable. The 340 engine is probably the most satisfying ever put into a Challenger to complement the comprehensive driving experience. Although not quite as antsy from the launch pad as its slightly smaller little brother 'Cuda, a big-block Challenger still carries much of its prodigious weight over the front axle. Fans of sports car handling will prefer the 340 over the monster motors in both these Mopars.

Figure I35 - A 1970 Challenger R/T with the base 383 Magnum engine. This example is red with black interior and top. These are aftermarket chrome steel wheels. Note that the hood scoops have gloss black trim. The R/T labels are within the side stripes beneath the front fender *Challenger* emblem. ©Nakhon 100 (CC)

Several collectibility issues are associated with the Challengers. First of all, the modern obsession with the top big-block engines takes a little heat off the more average convertible editions. This is both good and bad. Pricing of the nice convertibles is held down, but a nice 340 or 383 convertible, particularly without the R/T package or a four-speed manual, will not automatically bring you a profit at resale time years down the road. Of course if you choose to pay a premium for one of the very rare 1970 R/T Hemi or 440 Convertibles, the price will likely remain stratospheric as long as the car remains intact. Just be absolutely certain that you are not buying a counterfeit edition. There are many of those out there. Secondly, the Challengers were built in a large selection of acrylic metallic colors, but the High Impact Paint Colors, a $14 option at the time, are especially valued today. These are the ones with the silly names such as Plum Crazy (probably the most popular), Green Go, Tor-Red, Citron Yella, and Sublime.

Barracuda & Challenger Convertible Production Chart

Model	PB 6	DC 6	PB V-8	DC V-8	'Cuda	R/T	Totals
1967	859	NA	3144	NA	NA	NA	4003
1968	551	NA	2044	NA	NA	NA	2595
1969	300	NA	973	NA	NA	NA	1273
1970	257	378	1687	2543	550	963	6378
1971	132	83	721	1774	293	NA	3003
Totals	2099	461	8569	4317	843	963	17,252

Barracuda & Challenger Convertible Production Chart Notes:
PB 6 = Plymouth Barracuda Six Cylinder. DC 6 = Dodge Challenger Six Cylinder. PB V-8 = Plymouth Barracuda V-8. DC V-8 = Dodge Challenger V-8. The V-8's referenced in this group represent base V-8 models and V-8 option choices without the special 'Cuda or R/T sport packages. The original Barracuda fastback coupe debuted in midyear 1964. Plymouth sold 23,443 Barracudas in 1964 and 64,596 in 1965. The S package debuted in 1965. There were 38,029 sold in 1966. The 1965 figure may be incorrect.

Figure I36 - This Banana with black interior and top R/T Convertible from 1970 has a different hood configuration than the car in the previous photo. This example has the $25 Hood Performance Paint option. This paint is flat black and the hood scoops are body color instead of gloss black. ©Bull-Doser (PD)

Challenger Base Convertible Chart

Model	HP	Price	Model	HP	Price
1970 Base 225 Six	145	$3120	1971 Base 225 Six	145	$3105
1970 Base 318 V-8	230	$3417 *	1971 Base 318 V-8	230	$3207
1970 Opt. 2-bbl. 383 V-8	290	$3508	1971 Opt. 383 2-bbl. 383	275	$3487
1970 Opt. 4-bbl. 383 V-8	330	$3555 *	1971 Opt. 383 4-bbl. 383	300	$3545 *
1970 Opt. 4-bbl. 340 V-8	275	$3732 *	1971 Opt. 4-bbl. V-8 340	275	$3658 *

Challenger Base Convertible Chart Notes:
 * These prices include the four-on-the-floor shifter and transmission. All of these came standard with a three-speed transmission. The optional four-speed generally cost about $200 more, from $180-235 depending on the brand, model, and year. Models without an asterisk were not available with a four-speed manual.

Figure I37 - A 1971 Challenger Convertible optioned out with factory chrome styled steel wheels, scoop hood, tape stripes, and hood pins. The hood scoops are body color. The engine is the 383 Magnum four-barrel, the top engine offered in the Convertible in 1971. The side mirror is chrome and the interior and top are white vinyl. This example is painted the very popular option called Plum Crazy, a bright metallic purple, of course.
©Bull-Doser (PD)

The Early Pony Convertibles

Sixties Chrysler Pony Car Sports Convertible Chart

Model	HP	Price	Model	HP	Price
1968 Formula S 340	275	$3379	1971 'Cuda 383	300	$3589
1968 Formula S 383	300	$3414	1971 'Cuda 340	275	$3634
1969 Formula S 340	275	$3432	'71 'Cuda 440 Six Pack	390	$3842
1969 Formula S 383	330	$3468	1971 Hemi 'Cuda 426	425	$4486
1970 'Cuda 383	330	$3628	1970 R/T 383	335	$3730
1970 'Cuda 440	375	$3759	1970 R/T 440	375	$3861
1970 'Cuda 440 Six Pack	390	$3878	1970 440 Six Pack R/T	390	$3980
1970 Hemi 'Cuda 426	425	$4513	1970 Hemi R/T 426	425	$4652

Sixties Chrysler Pony Car Sports Convertible Chart Notes:
All engines are OHV V-8's. All prices include four-speed transmissions. There were no Challenger R/T Convertibles built in 1971. The sportiest '71 Challenger Convertibles were the 340 and 383 four-barrel engines with dual exhausts. Since there were no R/T Convertibles offered in 1971, the final chart entries in the Challenger Base Convertible Chart above for the 383 and 340 models with four-barrel carbs represent the most exciting Challengers available in 1971, the last year of Challenger Convertibles.

Figure I38 - A red Challenger Convertible with black top and interior sits innocently on display at an outdoor car show. What's wrong with this picture? The answer is both simple and complex. The simple part is that this is a counterfeit Chrysler muscle car. You can call it what you will, but this is the truth. There were no R/T Convertibles produced in the 1971 model year. The split grille is from 1971. The R/T hood, flat black hood paint, hood pins and body side tape stripes had been available as separate options on Challenger Convertibles, some in 1970 and some in 1971. The 440 Six Pack engine, as noted on the hood emblems, was available only on R/T models. This could be a 1970 R/T with a 1971 grille, but then how would the 1971 R/T hood paint and body side tape stripe design, both containing the 1971 R/T logo, be explained? Finally, there are no fake rear brake cooling vents that were part of the 1971 R/T package. ©Herr Anders Svensson (GNU)

Figure I39 - Here is the classic counterfeit Challenger, a 1971 Hemi R/T Convertible in Tor-Red with white interior. Everything on this car is as fake as the brake cooling vents in front of the rear wheels. This particular counterfeiter chose to include them, whereas the creator of the previously pictured 440 Six Pack model did not bother. This photo at least shows what the optional Shaker Hood should look like on a proper 1970 big-block R/T. When you analyze the production figures in the charts, you will see why these Challenger Convertibles are some of the most commonly counterfeited American models on the market today. These include their sister 'Cuda models, too. ©Bull-Doser (PD)

Pony Car Features Introduction Year Chart

Feature	Mustang	Camaro	Firebird	Barracuda	Challenger
Under-dash AC	1964	NA	NA	NA	NA
Integrated AC	1967	1967	1967	1970	1970
Cruise Control	1967	1967	1967	NA	NA
Radial Tires	1968	NA	NA	1974	1974
Big Block Engine	1967	1967	1967	1967	1970
Power Top	1964	1967	1967	1970	1970
Power Windows	1970	1967	1967	1970	1970
Disc Brakes	1965	1967	1967	1966	1970

Pony Car Features Introduction Year Chart Notes:
The 1967 Barracuda received a 383 big-block option, but it was not available on the convertible until the 1968 model year.

Pony Car Performance Coupe & Convertible Production Chart

Model	Production	Model	Production
1965 Ford Mustang GT	15,079	1967-69 Camaro SS 350	64,105
1966 Ford Mustang GT	25,517	1967-69 Camaro SS 396	36,727
1967 Ford Mustang GT	24,079		
1968 Ford Mustang GT	17,458	1967 Camaro Z-28 Coupe	730
1969 Ford Mustang GT	5396	1968 Camaro Z-28 Coupe	7199
		1969 Camaro Z-28 Coupe	20,302
1965-69 Mustang GT	87,529		
		1967-69 Z-28 Coupe	28,231
1965 Mustang K Code	7273		
1966 Mustang K Code	5469	1969 Camaro 427 ZL-1	69
1967 Mustang K Code	472		
		1970 'Cuda 383 Convertible	550
1965-67 K Code	13,214	1970 'Cuda Shaker Hood CV	8
		1970 'Cuda Six Pack CV	29
1967 Ford Mustang 390	28,800	1970 Hemi 'Cuda CV	14
1968 Ford Mustang 390	11,475	1970 AAR 'Cuda Coupe	2724
1969 Ford Mustang 390	10,494		
		1971 'Cuda Shaker Hood CV	19
1967-69 Mustang 390	50,769	1971 'Cuda Six Pack CV	17
		1971 Hemi 'Cuda CV	7
1969 Mustang 428 CJ	13,193	1971 'Cuda Convertible	293
1969 Mustang Boss 302	1628	1970 R/T Convertible	963
1970 Mustang Boss 302	7013	1970 440/426 4S CV	249
1969 Mustang Boss 429	857	1970 Hemi Challenger CV	5
1970 Mustang Boss 429	499	1970 T/A Coupe	2399
1971 Mustang Boss 351	1800		
		1971 Challenger 340 CV	176
1969-71 Boss Mustang	11,797	1971 Shaker Hood CV	11
		1971 440 Six Pack R/T	250
1969 - 73 Mach I	213,000	1971 Challenger Hemi R/T	71

		1971 RT Hardtop		3814

Pony Car Performance Coupe & Convertible Production Chart Notes:

Except where noted, all these figures include both coupes and convertibles. The stated Boss 351 and Mach I numbers are approximations. Only five 1970 and two 1971 Hemi 'Cuda Convertibles had four-speeds. The Shaker Hood Scoop was an option on 1970 Barracudas with the 340, 383, or 440 engine. It was standard with the Hemi. The Shaker Hood was optional on all 1970 Challengers with four-barrel V-8's. *Camaro and Firebird: GM's Power Twins* quotes only 602 Z-28's in 1967. Plymouth built 652 Hemi 'Cudas in 1970, but only fourteen were Convertibles. The total number of 1970 'Cudas was 19,515.

Mustang Test Results Chart

Model & Details	HP	Weight	0-60	1/4	TS
1965 HT 200 Six 3SA 3.00 (*Guide*)	120	2670	15.1	19.5	90
1965 CV 260 3SA 3.00 axle (*Guide*)	164	2950	11.2	18.8	101
1965 HT 289 4SM WR 3.00 (*Guide*)	200	2930	9.0	17.0	109
1965 HT 289 3SA 3.00 axle (*Guide*)	225	2890	8.5	16.8	110
1965 2+2 289 4SM CR 3.89 (*Guide*)	271	3050	8.3	15.9	120
1965 2+2 4SM CR 3.89 axle (*Muscle*)	271	2840	7.6	15.9	NA
1965 2+2 289 4SM CR 3.89 (*Field*)	271	2840	7.5	15.7	NA
1965 4SM 4.11 axle (*SCG*)	271	3280	7.5	15.7	117
1966 289 3-S Automatic	200	NA	10.9	17.9	NA
1967 2+2 390 (*Muscle*)	335	3255	7.4	15.6	NA
1967 GT 390 3SA 3.00 axle (*C/D*)	320	3897	7.3	15.2	124
1968 390 2+2 GT 3.25 axle (*C/D*)	325	3546	6.3	14.8	127
1969 Grande HT 351W 3SA 2.75 (*Life*)	290	3420	8.0	15.6	119
1969 Mach 1 428CJ 3SA 3.91 (*Life*)	335	3715	5.5	13.9	121
1969 Boss 302 4SM 3.91 axle (*Life*)	290	3610	6.9	14.9	118
1969 Boss 429 4SM 3.91 (*Life*)	375	3870	7.1	14.1	118
1970 Mach 1 351C 3SA 3.00 (*MT*)	300	NA	8.2	16.0	120
1971 Boss 351 4SM 3.91 axle (*C/D*)	330	3560	5.8	14.1	117
1971 Mach 1 429 (*Muscle*)	370	3805	6.5	14.6	NA
1972 351C HO 4SM 3.91 axle (*C/D*)	275	3604	6.6	15.1	120
1973 Mach 1 351CJ 3SA 3.25 (*RT*)	266	3680	8.5	16.2	120
1999 3.8 V-6 Convertible	190	NA	8.6	16.5	NA
2000 3.8 V-6 5SM CP	190	3115	7.0	15.5	120
2001 Bullitt Coupe 4.6 V-8 (*Field*)	265	3273	5.7	14.1	NA

Mustang Test Results Chart Notes:
Convertibles with Pony Interiors numbered 17,858 in 1965-66. The 390 lost favor quickly after the introduction of the 428 in 1968, when production dropped to well under 12,000 each year in 1968-69. The 1999 Cobra Convertible had 320 horsepower and weighed 3429 pounds. All 1964-1970 Mustangs, Camaros, Firebirds, and Barracudas had a 108-inch wheelbase. The Mustang would stretch to 109 in 1971. The Challenger had a 110-inch wheelbase.

3SA = 3-Speed Automatic. 4SM = 4-Speed Manual. 5SM = 5-Speed Manual. CR = Close Ratio Transmission. WR = Wide Ratio Transmission. *Field* = *Muscle Cars Field Guide*. *Guide* = *Mustang: A Complete Guide*. *Life* = *Car Life*. *Muscle* = *Muscle Cars* by Phil Hall. *SCG* = *Sports Car Graphic*.

Other Pony Car Test Results Chart

Model & Details	HP	Weight	0-60	Quarter	TS
1968 AMC AMX 390 (*Field*)	315	3205	6.6	14.8	122
1970 AMC Javelin SST 390 (*Muscle*)	325	3375	7.6	15.1	NA
1967 Camaro SS 350 (*C/D*)	295	2920	7.8	16.1	NA
1967 Camaro SS 396 4SM (*MT*)	325	3180	6.0	14.5	NA
1967 Camaro Z-28 302 4S 3.70 (*C/D*)	290	3250	6.7	14.9	124
1968 Camaro Z-28 302 4S 4.10 axle (*Life*)	290	3355	7.4	14.9	133
1968 Camaro SS 396 3.07 axle (*C/D*)	325	3670	6.6	15.0	134
1969 Camaro SS-396 HT (*Muscle*)	375	3490	6.8	14.8	NA
1970 Z-28 Camaro 350 4S 4.10 axle (*Life*)	360	3580	6.5	14.5	119
2014 Camaro 427 Z28 (*MT*)	505	3800	4.0	12.3	172
2014 Camaro 427 Z28 (*C/D*)	505	3800	4.4	12.7	172
1970 Challenger R/T Six Pack CV (*Life*)	390	3900	7.1	14.6	NA
1970 Challenger R/T 3SA 3.23 axle (*C/D*)	425	3890	5.8	14.1	146
1970 Challenger T/A (*Field*)	290	3585	6.0	14.5	NA
1965 Barracuda Formula S (*R&T*)	235	3200	8.2	15.9	118
1968 Barracuda 340 Formula S 3.55 (*C/D*)	275	3330	5.9	14.3	125
1969 Barracuda 340 S 4S 3.91 axle (*Life*)	275	3470	7.1	14.9	120
1970 AAR 'Cuda 340 4S 3.55 axle (*Life*)	290	3630	7.0	14.5	125
1970 AAR 'Cuda 340 4S 3.55 axle (*C/D*)	290	3585	5.8	14.3	128
1967 Firebird Sprint 230 HT (*Muscle*)	215	3470	10.0	17.5	NA
1967 Sprint 230 4SM 3.55 axle (*R&T*)	215	NA	10.1	17.2	NA
1967 Firebird 400 4SM 3.90 axle CV (*C/D*)	325	3598	5.8	14.4	114

1968 Firebird 400 HO 3.55 axle (*C/D*)	335	3550	5.5	14.2	110
1970 Trans Am 400 4S 3.91 axle (*Life*)	345	3690	6.3	14.5	NA
1970 Trans Am 400 Ram Air IV (*Field*)	370	3550	5.7	14.1	NA
1971 Trans Am 455 (*Field*)	335	3578	5.9	13.9	NA
1973 Trans-Am SD 455 (*Muscle*)	310	3775	7.3	15.0	NA
1975 Trans Am 400 (*Muscle*)	185	3860	9.8	16.8	NA
1976 Pontiac Trans Am 455 4SM (*R&T*)	200	3750	8.4	15.9	110
1976 Trans Am 455 (*C/D*)	200	NA	7.0	15.6	118
1977 Trans Am W72 400 4SM (*C/D*)	200	3830	9.3	16.9	110
1980 Trans Am Turbo 4.9 THM (*C/D*)	210	NA	8.2	16.7	116
1984 Trans Am 5.0 HO (*R&T*)	190	NA	7.9	16.1	124
1985 Trans Am 5.0 HO 5SM (*C/D*)	190	NA	7.6	15.6	135
1987 Firebird GTA 350 4SA 2.77 axle (*R/T*)	210	3274	7.1	15.5	145

Other Pony Car Test Results Notes:

Many of the stated weights from the *Muscle Car Field Guide* may be dry weights for the same models with lighter drive trains. The 172 mph top speed listed for the 2014 Z28 is a claimed top speed by Chevrolet. The two Z28's were tested in the April or May 2014 issues of both magazines. *MT* reported 15 mpg and *C/D* displayed the mileage range of 13-19 EPA mpg. The Z28 weighed 402 pounds more than the 2013 Stingray with the same engine.

There were 2116 1971 Trans Ams built. The 1987 and 1988 Trans Am and GTA had a slightly detuned Corvette engine as an option. This version of the 240-hp L98 made 210 horsepower in 1987 and 225 in 1988.

C/D = *Car and Driver*. *Field* = *Muscle Car Field Guide* by John Gunnell / *Life* = *Car Life* / *Muscle* = *Muscle Cars* by Phil Hall. *R&T* = *Road & Track*.

Selected Early Pony Convertibles Ratings Chart

Years	Model	Collect	Drive	Desire
1964 - 1966	Ford Mustang Base Convertible	C	C	C
1965 - 1966	Ford Mustang GT Convertible	B	C	A
1967 - 1970	Ford Mustang Base Convertible	D	C	C
1967 - 1969	Ford Mustang GT Convertible	C	C	B
1971 - 1973	Ford Mustang Base Convertible	D	C	D
1971	Ford Mustang HO Convertible	C	C	C
1967 - 1969	Chevrolet Camaro Base Convertible	D	C	D
1967 - 1969	Chevrolet Camaro SS 350	C	C	C
1967 - 1969	Chevrolet Camaro SS 396	B	C	B

Years	Model	Collectibility	Drivability	Desirability
1967 - 1969	Chevrolet Camaro SS 396 L-89	A	D	A
1969	Chevrolet Camaro Pace Car	B	C	A
1967 - 1969	Pontiac Firebird Base Convertible	D	C	D
1967 - 1969	Firebird Sprint	C	C	C
1967 - 1969	Firebird 350 HO	C	C	C
1967 - 1969	Firebird 400 & 400 HO	B	D	B
1969	Trans Am Convertible	A	D	A
1967 - 1969	Plymouth Barracuda Base Convertible	D	B	D
1968 - 1969	Barracuda Formula S Convertible	C	B	C
1970 - 1971	Plymouth Barracuda Convertible	C	C	C
1970 - 1971	Plymouth 'Cuda 340 Convertible	A	B	A
1970 - 1971	Plymouth 'Cuda 383 Convertible	B	B	B
1970 - 1971	Plymouth 'Cuda 440 & Six Pack	A	C	A
1970 - 1971	Plymouth Hemi 'Cuda Convertible	A	D	A
1970 - 1971	Dodge Challenger Base Convertible	C	C	C
1970	Dodge Challenger R/T 340 / 383	B	D	B
1970	Dodge Challenger R/T 440 & Six Pack	A	C	A
1970	Dodge Challenger Hemi R/T	A	D	A

Models Ratings Chart Definitions:

Years: In most cases, the years listed include the total production years for a particular model series. Some model years within a series may be considerably more desirable than other years.

Models: In some cases many variations are included in this category and in others the models included are very homogeneous. This is generally self explanatory.

Collectibility: This is what most of you want to know, the bottom line on how likely the model or series is likely to climb in value over the coming years.

Drivability: This is an indicator of how adaptable the machine can be to drive for transportation or pleasure in the modern world, considering collector value, parts availability, fuel quality, comfort, performance and miscellaneous other factors.

Desirability: This defines the nostalgic, emotional wow factor, without regard for collector values or everyday usage.

General: No machine is given a failing grade. If it made it into a rating chart, at least a few hobbyists find that model interesting.

Chapter 10: *Corvettes Take Us to 1990*

Figure J1 - A red interior in this shiny Tuxedo Black 1960 Corvette shows off its classic style. The mirror is attached to the dash like that of the 1958 Ferrari California pictured on the title page of Chapter 6. The white plastic shift knob is correct for the year. Note the almost vertical angle of the large-diameter, red plastic steering wheel. That's the speaker for the optional AM radio directly behind the mirror, We heard Elvis in glorious monaural sound back in those good old days! ©Elmschrat (GNU)

The Corvette has always been the uncouth brute that somebody brought to the party. They squeak and they rattle and everybody has one, or knows somebody who does. Only certain models are rare in the USA and most live closer to nostalgia than the auction house. Aside from the ponies, the Corvettes are the most accessible, reliable, and cost effective of all the classic sports cars in this book. Unlike the tons of Corvette reading material available elsewhere, this book tries a different approach. Of course all the Corvette Convertibles of 1953-75 are covered, but the story envelops all the common models with removable tops up through 1990. All these are legally considered antiques and they cover the broad spectrum from nostalgic drivers to trailer queens. The Corvette is a true sports car for Americans.

Rose Colored Goggles from the Mists of Time

Figure J2 - A Panama Yellow Corvette on display one foggy morning captures the nostalgia perfectly for me. Some enthusiasts consider the '58 to be the ugliest of all Corvettes, but as you will learn from the story below, my personal fascination with Corvettes began with the style of the 1958 model. The fake vents on the hood are indigenous only to the '58. The chrome trim strips over the trunk lid, also indigenous to the '58, are not visible from this angle. ©Sicnag (CC)

Like any other car, a Corvette to me has always been a car in which to *go somewhere*. When I was eyeball to taillight with a 1953 Buick, I lived in a very small town, even smaller than Mayberry, which I recently learned from a rerun was a fictional burg of 2000 residents. Where did my family always go? It was twenty-five miles down Valley Hill into the Mississippi Delta of Greenwood. It was about a hundred miles over to the old Elvisland and the home of my mom's family, Tupelo. It was about 120 miles north to the current Elvisland and the city I most often visited in my formative years, Memphis. I was a bit young, isolated, and naive to be aware of the Corvette's birth at that innocent time. I was a big fan of full-sized fins on full-size Cadillacs, just like Elvis drove. I am not exactly sure when the Corvette entered my lexicon, but it was just after 1957. In spite of what the Corvette purists think, and in spite of many stories about clean styling you will read in this book, it was the 1958 or later model that caught my jaundiced eye. At that time I didn't give a rat's nest of EPA wiring about fuel injection, but I did notice the smooth styling of the car Todd and Buzz drove through the family's black-and-white living room box once a week.

There has never been a shadow of doubt that I like every Corvette model better than the previous one up until 1971, when the EPA made GM drop the compression ratios. I like the 1980 model for its lower weight, Darth Vader integrated air dam and spoiler look, and its respectable performance. Whoever did it can shove that 85-mph speedometer up his tailpipe, and I hope it hurts! My favorite C4 is the 1989 Convertible with six-speed. I like the transmission and styling of the wheels, but I am not a fan of the altered dashboard of the 1990 or the rounded exterior ends of the 1991. I love the 1998 C5 Convertible, as well as the later C5 Convertibles. I have little interest in any C6 models except the 2013 427 Convertible. I am such a sucker for those bulges behind the headrests! Remember the T-bird Sports Roadster? I also like the stripes that remind me of the Shelby Mustang GT-350 of 1965 and the engine displacement of 1966-69.

There were three specific times in my life when I purchased a new car, but the Corvette of those model years was not under consideration. The 1968 Fiat 850 Spider was a very cheap sports car at under $2500 and I was a naive college kid painting houses for my contractor uncle in the summer season. There is no doubt that if I could have afforded a $4000 car, it would have been a British Racing Green Triumph TR-250 with black interior and top and wire wheels. Remember, I said I was naive. In the long run I would have been much happier with a Firebird Convertible in blue with a white interior and four-speed. The only tough decision would have been the engine options. In my favorite year of the Firebird, the Sprint 6 had 215 horsepower, the two-barrel 350 came in at 250, and the four-barrel version brought 320 gross horsepower. What would have made this decision so tough is that the Sprint 6 offered the lighter front end and the 350 H.O. offered tons of power for the money, but the base 350 could have optional dual exhausts and it ran on regular! In case you are wondering, I was mad at Ford for changing the body of the 1967-68 Mustang and making it heavier. I was not crazy about the engine, transmission, and suspension availabilities of those years, either. I *loved* the '68 Corvette from the first moment I saw it, but five grand was just too far out of my price range. Of course I would have struggled to keep the tank filled with premium with a 400-hp L68, too. I know that sounds stupid now when gasoline costs ten times what it did then. To add insult to injury, a family tragedy would cost me that lucrative painting job before the summer was even over. Delivering barbeque sandwiches on the night shift to college dorm rooms didn't pay nearly as well, although the 52-horsepower of my Fiat Spider preconditioned me for the high performance of the Simca and Beetle delivery cars!

My 1969 Impala sedan with 350 four-barrel and Turbo Hydra-Matic was a boring machine to look at and drive in 1977. It was a two-tone brown with a tan interior. I called it The Inconspicuous Mobile. I finally had a job that paid better than barbeque delivery and I wanted something sportier. Unfortunately 1977 was one of the *worst* years in automotive history to choose a new car. Every engine in America was strangled down to its last gasping breath. This time the Corvette was not even on my radar screen. The '77 model had lots of standard luxury features, but the rear window was no longer removable, the interior was claustrophobic, the luggage space was minimal, and the fuel economy was pathetic. Whatever car I selected would be used for several long distance runs annually, but the big problem was the price. Adding air conditioning, L-82, and stereo would drive it over the $10,000 mark. Once again the Firebird was a contender, this time a white Trans-Am with white interior and the correct 6.6 Pontiac 400 engine. Accept no substitutes! Although this baby could be had for about $7000, its hauling capacity and fuel mileage were hardly outside the Corvette realm. It was not a particularly fast car, no matter what *Smokey and the Bandit* led you to believe. Mr. Naïveté rides again. I bought a Toyota Corolla SR-5 Liftback (sportwagon) for about $4500. Its price was excellent for the time, its dash and interior layout were commendable and its standard specification list was more so. Its handling with stiff suspension and minimal weight over the rear driving wheels was passable. The weakness was the 75-horsepower engine. Not only was the car slow, but you had to run the stink out of it to keep up with traffic. I would sell it three years later for almost as much as I paid so it could be replaced with a 1970 LS-5 Coupe. Why did I do that? Seventeen miles per gallon. That's how much consumption I could drain out of the SR-5 around town and also the mileage I got on highway excursions in the LS-5 with its Positraction 3.08. The numbers *5* and *17* were the only things these two vehicles had in common.

I have always loved the 1965-66 Mustang Convertible as much as any other collectible car. Ford recreated the original Mustang's style and charisma in 1999 and by then I knew that my eighteen-year affair with the LS-5 Stingray was growing stale. Before you get your *Corvette*-embroidered panties in a knot, allow me to mention that there were *many* extenuating circumstances brewing. My wife was slowly losing athleticism due to loss of a hip and arthritis. The low seating, small doors, and stiff suspension were no longer appropriate. There were several factors concerning the nature of the beast, too. The 1970 big block was becoming a car more appropriate for a trailer ride than the crummy pump Exxon available in the late Nineties. It was reaching that point in every old Corvette's life when it is time to retire from traffic into a world of restorations and car shows. By the time I had fully made up my mind about this momentous change, I could order a 2000 Mustang, so I did. I had to wait a couple of months for a new 16-inch wheel to be available and then a couple more months for delivery. It is the color I had so lusted after in the 1965-67 Sting Ray: bright blue with white top and interior. There were 4979 Bright Atlantic Blue Mustangs built in 2000, and of course the majority of these were coupes. The rarest interior color was white, partially because it was available only with the leather option, and the rarest convertible top color was also white. This remains a very rare color combination for Mustangs today and my new baby has yet to show 7000 miles on her odometer. Psychologically, it is a 1966 Nassau Blue Sting Ray Convertible.

Figure J3 - 2000 Bright Atlantic Blue Mustang Convertible. Yes, I know it is heresy, but my own current convertible is a Mustang Six with a four-speed automatic. Although never to become a collectible with those two disgusting components, this car is a very rare color combination for the year and body style. I had to wait a few months into the model year to order the car with these 16-inch wheels. Only 4979 Mustangs, out of 215,393 Coupes and Convertibles, were painted this bright metallic blue in 2000. The white leather was the least common interior color and black and tan convertible tops far outnumbered white ones. The white stripes were optional only on Sixes. ©2000 Floyd M. Orr Collection

The important thing to keep in mind when reading this book is that cars are meant to drive, to go somewhere. Of course I enjoy the occasional car show and I have certainly known many restoration experts, but my focus has always been on nice, original, unrestored cars you can drive! You will find an emphasis on older, affordable Corvettes here. The fascination with the detailed history of the marque and its many special high performance racing options has been covered elsewhere, repeatedly, and repeatedly. Yes, I know the legendary L-88 was marketed as having only 430 horsepower while the real figure was about 560. I have never seen one. The closest I have ever come was a 1969 L-89. Let's talk about Corvettes you as a fan or potential buyer might actually encounter in the real world and at an affordable price. Let's talk about the later, slower C3's and the multitude of high-tech C4's that are out there waiting for you to discover and take home. There are C1's with basic powerplants and option packages that you might be able to afford. You probably want to know how you can afford a C2 Sting Ray. That could be a difficult but not impossible task. Consider a 1964 with the base 327. You might even try to choke down one with a Powerslide, three-speed, or a non-original engine. How badly do you want to drive a classic Sting Ray with that luscious body covering a mechanical faux pas?

Everybody knows the most denigrated Corvette year is the 1976. Personally, I think past enthusiasts have made too much of that model's Vega steering wheel, although it is true that the '76 has little to distinguish it, sandwiched between the last convertible of 1975 and the last flying buttresses of 1977. The latter model usually receives a little more approval for its higher standard equipment content. The '75 Coupe has the dubious distinction of the lower horsepower rating and the first single exhaust with a catalytic converter. It is difficult to say at this point if the '75 Convertible will retain much cache long after the topless model has returned in 1986. We might sum up the bottom feeder pack by saying the 1974-77 base engine coupes may always remain the cheapest available Corvettes. If all options, colors, and condition are held static within the prospective buyer's mind, you might consider each of these model years to be more desirable than the previous group. Obviously a 454 four-speed 1974 Convertible rates far above other choices within this narrow model range.

This brings us to a challenging concept for this book. What will be the future of the many C4's available as drivers or collectible cars? Although less C4's were produced than C3's, practically all the C4's look extremely alike. The 1991-96 models are a little more rounded off at the ends and the power ratings slowly inched upward over the production span. The dash was redesigned in 1990. There were several special editions, but even the vaunted ZR1 looked little different from a base coupe. There may have been more than half a million Makos built, but a '68 is very different from a 1982 in many facets, both visual and mechanical. Will at least some of the C4 models race to the bottom of the collectibility chart, boosting nice old tunnelback '74-'77 coupes up a notch? That is the question.

The next obvious set of questions concern models from the remaining series. From the point of publication of this book, the C6's and C7's have a ways to go before entering the classic car hobbyist market. The C1's, C2's, and early C3's have already been there for a long time. The first dilemma to be faced with driving any of these on the streets today concerns the low quality of modern gasoline and the high density of traffic most everywhere, all the time. The fuel problem can be dealt with in several ways. You can use expensive fuel additives, modify your car's classic engine, or try a delicate blend of both procedures. As far as the traffic goes, only you know exactly what the conditions are in your area. Are the C5's already classic cars? Have they almost, but not quite, reached that point? You can certainly guess that the less common Convertibles and Z06 Coupes are more likely to be the popular hobbyist collector machines of the future.

Figure J4 - My 1970 LS-5 Coupe had the 390-hp 454, wide-ratio four-speed, and optional wheel covers. Black was not a factory color in 1970, but I just did not want it to be all green. I left the green interior as is, but had it painted in the correct acrylic lacquer in a color standard in 1969. Note the identifying white parking light lenses. The proper way to identify a 1970 model is by its combination of these lights, headlamp washers, and fiber optics. A console emblem also displays the original high-compression gross horsepower ratings of the 1970 models. ©1983 Floyd M. Orr Collection

Corvette Generation Quick Chart

Wheelbase	Displacement	Horsepower	Base Price	Notes
C1 - 102	235 - 265 - 283 - 327	150 - 360	$2774-4038	Solid axle - Trunk
C2 - 98	327 - 396 - 427	250 - 435	$4252-4388	IRS - FB Coupe
C3 - 98	327 - 350 - 427 - 454	300 - 435	$4320-18,290	T-top - Stereo - 3SA
C4 - 96	350	205 - 405	$21800-37225	16" wheels - HB

Corvette Generation Quick Chart Notes:

The horsepower ratings are gross from 1953 through 1971 and net thereafter. Convertible base prices were slightly lower than Coupes through 1975 and considerably higher from 1986-onward. IRS = Independent Rear Suspension. FB = Fixed-roof fastback. 3SA = Turbo Hydra-Matic three-speed automatic transmission. HB = Opening Hatchback.

Impressions of America's Sports Car

Figure J5 - 1953 Corvette in its only color combination for the year: white body, black top, red interior, and wide whitewall tires. ©Kowtoonese (CC)

The complete Corvette experience includes the selection, purchase, and ownership of a classic Corvette. Neither a history nor a buyer's guide, this book offers the most depth in the least words to describe particular segments of life with a Corvette and its place in Americana. No one piece of man-made hardware has ever had more significance in this arena than the Corvette. This is the Corvette's story told without rules. The more successful of the stories should bring All-American emotions to the surface like an apple pie thrown in the face. Let's begin with a set of capsule impressions of the antique Corvettes with removable tops year by year from 1953 through 1990. So much printed material is currently available on these models that little further detail should be necessary to be repeated here.

The 1953 model is so rare, scarce and valuable as a collectible that it hardly needs mention. The company built only 300 for this first model year. All were white with red interior and black top and all had 150-hp inline six-cylinder engines with two-speed automatic transmissions. The shifters were in the floor and the bucket seats were relatively wide and flat. All options were mandatory and there were not many of those. The instruments were spread across the dash in a not very sporting manner. Brakes were drum and there were no power options of any sort. The cars were true roadsters with side curtains and no exterior door handles. Many detail changes for the next model year have ensured the extreme rarity of true first-year models.

Corvettes Take Us to 1990

Figure J6 - 1954 Corvette in a museum display. ©LSDSL (CC)

Production volume increased tenfold for the 1954 model year and a few colors other than white were offered. The Blue Flame Six continued plodding along with its two-speed slushbox and the side curtains still insulted the sensibilities of most potential American buyers. Chevrolet still struggled throughout the year to shove them out the door. If you locate an early Corvette with a six-cylinder and automatic, chances are sky high that it is a '54, no matter what the seller tries to claim. Buyer beware since the '54's are the market toads of the original Corvette body style.

The new Chevy V-8 saved the Corvette's butt in 1955, but due to the overstock of the 1954 road toads, only 700 were produced. Although the new V-8 engine was lighter and a lot more powerful, the old body still suffered from its side curtains, Powerglide and drum brakes. A few six-cylinder '55's were constructed, but do not be deceived into thinking these rarities are extra valuable. As we are all fully aware today, the Corvette is synonymous with the small-block V-8. Colors and options continued to slowly expand.

Figure J7 - Light Beige interior of a Gypsy Red 1955 Corvette. ©Dave 7, Lethbridge, Canada (CC)

Duntov entered the picture with the 1956 model and his influence shows. The new body was a bit heavier, but the styling was improved, the side curtains were banished back to England where they belong, and new performance options were added. Most importantly, the Corvette finally got a three-speed manual transmission.

Most enthusiasts particularly love the 1957 model. I am not one of them, but you can make up your own mind. I prefer the better dash layout, quad headlights, and wider body of the later models, even if they are heavier. What most Corvette fans love so much is that the 1957 was the first year of both a four-speed transmission and fuel injection. They also like the trim body, clean styling, and lineup of 283-cubic-inch V-8's. There is little doubt that the four-speed adds quite a bit of current monetary value to any '57 model today, but it is the injection that drives the modern auction values through the roof. If you love the styling and just want the four-speed, you can save a bundle by selecting a base-engine carbureted model. Almost twice as many '57's were built as 1956 models with the same body and most have the four-speed manual option.

Enthusiasts usually consider the 1958 model as the ugliest classic Corvette due to its chrome-adorned body. You can look at it that way or the same way you drool over a '59 Cadillac Convertible, as one of the ultimate statements of the Fifties. The biggest improvement of the '58 model is its new dash layout with instruments clustered where they belong in front of the driver. Yes, the wider body did gain a little weight over the svelte '57, but engine power increased along with the weight.

Figure J8 - Aztec Copper 1957 Corvette with Hardtop and Beige Interior. ©Sicnag (CC)

Figure J9 - Ermine White Fuel Injected 1960 Corvette with red interior and contrasting silver cove. ©Rex Gray, Southern California (CC)

The 1959 model lost a bit of chrome trim and gained even more power; however, its body style would continue practically unchanged through the following year. This would serve to make the body seem a bit ubiquitous before the new Sting Ray rear clip was introduced in 1961. By the way, all these models up through 1962 are convertibles with conventional trunks, an accoutrement the Corvette Convertible would lose until 1998! Beginning with the '56 models, power tops and windows would become increasingly more popular options.

If there is any Corvette that is difficult to tell apart from its predecessor, it is the 1960 model. It was nearly identical visually to the '59. Its claim to fame was new higher compression for the two fuel-injected engines, increasing each by twenty-five horsepower. The earliest versions of the top-banana 315-hp fuelie even had aluminum heads, the first for a Corvette, but a problem caused them to be deleted from the specs of this engine option early in the production year.

As we now know, the Sting Ray concept for the Corvette had begun several years before 1963. The first production hint of what was to come was the new rear styling of the 1961 model when the vertical strip taillights buried in smooth fins were replaced with round dials below a sharply creased rear deck. Unlike the later Sting Ray Convertibles, this rear deck still enclosed a functioning trunk lid. Strangely enough, the remainder of the body stayed the same and the overall styling effect worked better than you might have expected. Like its brothers going back to 1956, most of the Corvettes of the period had an optional second color painted in their side coves. One reason the '56-'57 models are considered so *clean* is that various sorts of chrome trim was added to the coves on all the '58-'61 models.

Figure J10 - Note the trunk lid outline on this 1961 Corvette with the new Sting Ray tail section. The trunk would be sacrificed to the space needs of the independent rear suspension and larger wheels and tires of the Sting Rays and Stingrays. This car is black with silver painted coves. ©Berthold Werner (GNU)

The 1962 model has the cleanest styling of all the wide-body, real-convertible early Corvettes. The side coves were still cut into the body, but the chrome trim was minimized and the optional contrasting color was dropped. More chrome was deleted from the headlight trim, too. The engine displacement was increased to 327 cubic inches and even the base engine had 250 gross horsepower. There still was no power steering, independent rear suspension, or disc brakes, so the handling was still distinctively truck-like in nature. The wide-ratio four-speed was introduced with the 250 and 300 horsepower 327. All previous four-speeds had been the close-ratio type with a 2.20:1 low gear. From '62-'65 the lower performance engines were paired with the wide ratio four-speed, while the close ratio version was reserved for the high-performance models only. A choice of wide or close-ratio four-speed would be offered on certain engine options from 1966-onward.

Figure J11 - The 1962 model had smoother contours on the body sides and the first narrow whitewalls on a Corvette. The lack of trim in the cove area brought the deletion of the popular separate cove color option of the 1956-61 models. ©Greg Gjerdingen, Willmar, USA (CC)

The 1963 Sting Ray Coupe introduced what has continued for decades the only fixed-roof Corvette that has remained consistently more valuable than its convertible sister. Of course this is the exception to the rule of one of the key tenets of this book. Another one would be the Mercedes Gullwing that shares the Split Window Coupe's legendary status. You could also make the case that the Sting Ray Coupe presents a more stunning appearance, with the Convertible having the same general shape as all previous Corvettes. The model year brought a new ladder frame and independent rear suspension with the sexy body, but the Corvette was still the same large, some would say *bulky*, sports car with quick handling and lots of conventional V-8 power delivered to the rear wheels. Power windows were still an option, but the power top was gone for decades to come. Power steering and power drum brakes were finally added to the option list. The convertible top still stowed neatly underneath a flip-up panel. The body style was destined to be considered the Marilyn Monroe of American cars, forever sealing the envelope of its high prices. If you are purchasing a potential '63 Convertible, be aware that this model had many detail components unique to the year, and some that were changed by the factory even before the model year production ended. If you are looking for a genuine Split

Window Coupe, watch out for an altered rear window on a '64 model. Counterfeiters are out there.

Figure J12 - **White 1963 Convertible with hardtop on display at Bonhams in France.** ©The Supermat (CC)

The 1964 model had its styling cleaned up a bit. This will always be the most affordable classic Sting Ray. The fake hood louvers were deleted, leaving the indentations in the plain hood indigenous only to the '64 model. It also had wheel covers unique to the year and offered the first white interior in a Corvette.

Most enthusiasts consider the '65 model one of the most desirable of all Corvettes, and it is easy to see why. Disc brakes were finally standard equipment. A few drum brake models were built, but who wants them? Look for discount prices on these. This would be the last year for fuel injection until 1985 and the first year for a big-block option. The 425-hp 396 was introduced in the spring and built for only a few months. It is your choice whichever makes you break out in a sweat, the last fuelie or the first big-block; either will require a premium price today. The majority of the '65's were built with carbureted 327's, just as you might expect. The model year also brought cleaner styling and mag-style chrome wheel covers.

Figure J13 - The hood indentations without fake vents are clearly visible in this shot of a black 1964 Sting Ray Convertible. ©Allen Watkin, London, England (CC)

The '66 was a continuation in most respects, and as I have probably mentioned, my personal favorite of all Corvette years. It's too bad that the seating is too low for me and the air conditioning inadequate for my Deep South environment. AC had become a Corvette option in 1963, but very few were ordered. The air conditioning system lacked the sophisticated design we take for granted today, and overheating was still a problem, particularly with big-blocks. Displacement was increased to 427 cubic inches and a lower-compression big-block with hydraulic lifters was now a very affordable, and highly practical, engine choice. The hot-rod big-block was still offered, interestingly rated at 450 horsepower early in production, but stated as only 425 horsepower in the later versions. The actual engine specs supposedly were identical and even the 390-horsepower model with the milder cam had the neat big-block hood design indigenous to both '65 and '66 models. You can discern the '66 from its near-twin '65 small-block cousin by trim details in the seat upholstery, wheel covers and other chrome bits. All 1965-66 models have three-slot functional side air vents for brake cooling. Identical factory side pipes are a very valuable option on any '65-'67 Sting Ray with any engine.

Figure J14 - This clean yellow 1967 Sting Ray Convertible has several popular options: removable hardtop with black vinyl covering, AM/FM radio, and whitewall tires. The engine is the 327 and the standard chrome hubcaps and trim rings of 1967 are present. ©Greg Gjerdingen, Willmar, USA (CC)

Most enthusiasts claim the 1967 Sting Ray as the ultimate collectible Corvette, and although the '66 is my personal favorite, I certainly can see their point. There are a number of styling detail differences between the 1965-1966 and 1967 Sting Rays. Although the '67 is a cleaner design to most eyes, I happen to prefer the side vent design and mag-style wheel covers of the earlier type. The 1967 has a *busier* side vent and I am not a fan of conventional steel silver wheels with chrome hubcaps and trim rings. Your opinion may differ, of course. The one big issue I cannot deny is that the big-block hood scoop with black, white, or red hood stripe is the best stinking hood design of all stinking time! Burt Reynolds can stuff his *screaming chicken* wherever he wants and I realize the cold-air hood of a 1973 Corvette or my own 1990 Cavalier Z-24 is more efficient, but damn, that '67 Sting Ray big-block hood looks *perfect*! Gimme some side pipes, earplugs, and an Exxon card and I'm in Corvette heaven, baby!

The 1968 neo-Stingray was a difficult animal to classify. The first time I saw an ad, or brochure (I don't remember which), I was *hooked*! Hey, man, it's a coupe that has a removable roof and rear window like the earlier Porsche Targa without the German price and air-cooled wheeze. What's not to like? The is the most significant *coupe* to be fully featured in this book. In this particular case, I think the coupe is more attractive than the convertible. In reference to the 1977 Trans Am mentioned above, the T-tops invented for the Corvette offered a slim center bar and a removable rear window, two things never offered on the Pontiac Trans Am. The new body did offer several advantages. For those who wonder why the wonderful Sting Ray body style had to be changed, keep in mind that the wretched two-speed Powerslide was the only automatic that could fit within the earlier style. Note also the lack of room for a proper central air conditioning system and a cooling system with the earlier bodies that was relentlessly inadequate for the big-block engines. Lastly, note that a conventional, horizontally mounted stereo radio could fit into the '68's wider console design, offering an FM Stereo option for the first time. The '68 model was one of the most notoriously poorly assembled by the St. Louis factory and many detail changes were made after the model year.

Figure J15 - Note several distinctive new features of the 1968 Convertible. The standard hubcap design is altered slightly from that of the 1967. The big-block hood is entirely different and the vent windows are gone forever. As a 1968 model, there is a door lock button separate from the door handle and there is no optional side vent trim available. There was no Stingray name on the '68 model. This Polar White car belonged to Alan Shepard. Several famous U.S. astronauts have owned Corvettes and having owned ten models over time, Shepard was a leading proponent of the marque. ©350z33 (GNU)

The official Stingray name returned in 1969, the highest production year between 1953 and 1976. Keep in mind that the '69's were produced for an extraordinarily long production year and the rapid pace kept the assembly boogers coming until John DeLorean stepped in and slowed things down in 1970. The very popular '69 model year included the longest, most exciting option list in Corvette history, although in truth the '67 and '68 lists were almost as extensive. These were the only three years the three-two-barrel carbs and the super-high-performance big-blocks were simultaneously available.

The 1970 model brought a satisfyingly sober type of Corvette. Sandwiched directly between the unbridled power and production of the '69 and the slide into the EPA and NHTSA stranglehold, the low-production 1970 model could be considered either the last great classic Corvette muscle car or the beginning of the end. The '70 model was the best built Corvette in years, while also being the last model with unrestricted fuel requirements. The planned mechanical lifter LS-7 never entered production, leaving the 390-hp LS-5 as one of the last great big-blocks. The last gasp of a high-compression, solid-lifter small-block was introduced with 370 horsepower not available with air conditioning. These two models are still the hot ticket today. Look for an LT-1 Convertible with close-ratio transmission and 3.70 rear end for ultimate collectibility or an LS-5 Coupe with wide-ratio four speed, 3.08 axle, AC and power options for the ultimate touring cruiser. All Corvettes were built with four-speeds, Positraction and tinted glass as standard equipment for the first time.

Nineteen-seventy-one brought minimal changes with the most obvious being drops in compression ratios to run on unleaded fuel. The 1971 looks practically identical to the '70 and '72 models. Being neither the first nor the last in the series has always banished the '71 to a level of slightly less interest to collectors, so asking prices could be just a bit lower. The exception to this rule is the 425-hp LS-6 that was somehow slipped past the censors that year. Only 188 were built so expect the price to be ridiculous if you even can locate such a beastly 454. The LT-1 was toned down in power and offered with air conditioning. Special ZR-1 and ZR-2 racing packages were installed on a tiny number of highly collectible specials.

The last Stingray with chrome bumpers and a removable rear window on the coupe has made the 1972 model somewhat special. Don't be frightened off by the low *net* power ratings: actual horsepower was much the same as in 1971. Somewhat surprisingly, collectors are drawn to this *last of the breed*.

Many fans like the 1973 and later models with their body-colored safety bumpers and lack of *gimmicks*, as they would call them, such as the windshield wiper door, headlamp washers, and fiber-optic system of the previous models. Count me out of that group. I think those rather silly accoutrements add little to the enjoyment of the car; however, the removable rear window adds convertible feel, the chrome bumpers add style, and everybody loves the additional power of the earlier models. On the plus side, the new style aluminum wheels, radial tires, and cowl induction graced the Corvette for the first time. The emasculated 454 would be gone after one more year, leaving the ubiquitous L-48 and L-82 350's that began in '73 to power Corvettes for years to come.

Figure J16 - A red 1974 Stingray Coupe is quite typical of a very large herd. The modern cost effectiveness of this series in today's market is covered later in this chapter. The 1974-77 Coupes with the 350 small-block V-8 were, relatively speaking, identical. This example even has the most common replacement tire for these cars, the BFG Radial T/A. Note the standard hubcaps and trim rings, rear antenna, Stingray fender emblem, cold-air hood, and of course, the open T-tops. ©Robert Spinello (GNU)

The 1974 model is the only Stingray with a split rear body-colored bumper. It is the last with not only the big-block, but the final true dual exhaust system for many years. This was the result of a single catalytic converter that began in 1975. Although a distant vision of its former self, a 454 four-speed Convertible is still a desirable collectible Corvette. As far as the later, slower Mako Convertibles go, even I find the sloped tail attractive. It may have lost the down force and legendary racing charisma of the Kamm tail, but its smooth lines complement the 1974 model's new nose.

The last Corvette Convertible for a decade was produced in 1975. This was also the lowest rated horsepower for a Corvette since the Blue Flame Six of '54, although the L-48's 165 net horsepower was in reality considerably more power than the 155 gross rating of the 1954 six-cylinder. The 1975 model was also about 700 pounds heavier than the 1954 roadster.

Somebody has to be the denigrated stepchild of the family and most Corvette fans have selected the 1976 model. The horsepower, big engines, pretty bumpers, dual exhausts, removable windows, and convertibles were gone, leaving a high-production boulevardier with a Vega steering wheel. At least the power ratings were up a bit from the pit of 1975.

The final luxury model with the original Coupe roofline featured power steering and brakes, leather upholstery and other additions as standard. The power continued to crawl upward while the interior space remained claustrophobic with limited luggage capacity. White interior became a choice in a Stingray body for the first time.

Figure J17 - The 1978 Pace Car is still the jewel of that Corvette year for collectors. ©Greg Gjerdingen, Willmar, USA (CC)

The Pace Car and Silver Anniversary dominated the 1978 news. The new fastback rear window significantly increased the luggage space while adding weight. Access was still from only behind the seatbacks, but the roofline made loading and unloading much easier than before. A pull-out screen shielded your stuff from the afternoon sun or the prying eyes of the city. The acoustics were improved for decent stereo sound. The dash and console design was updated and 60-Series tires were a new option. The Silver Anniversary offered a stylish new look for an affordable price, however, the Pace Car hogged all the publicity of the day. Dealers went bananas with padding the showroom prices, much as they had previously done with the 1970 Datsun 240Z and they would repeat again twenty years later with the Mazda Miata. After the initial hoopla, prices fell back to earth for the Pace Car. If you want one now, it may cost you twice the price of a regular '78, but in today's dollars, that is still not a lot of money. The current Hagerty's number is about $30,000. Now if you happen upon a Pace Car similar to the one an old Corvette Club friend of mine bought new, then that is another story. He selected an L-82, close-ratio four-speed model with leather seats and all the rest of the desirable options. This car has spent its entire life with very low mileage and secure in an all but temperature controlled garage in a dry environment. I even distinctly copied his car and garage scenario with my current Mustang. A Pace Car like that one is currently about $75,000 at Hagerty's.

The heaviest Corvette is the 1979 model. It also represents the largest number produced at 53,807 for the model year. This was the last year for a manual transmission with the optional L-82 or a close-ratio option for the same engine. The 1979 option list was also one of the longest and juiciest. Don't count out this interim model between the 25th Anniversary excitement and the Darth Vader at the fat farm of the future.

Chevy sent the 1980 model to the fat farm, making many detailed weight-saving improvements. Aerodynamic pieces were better integrated into the body and the lighter overall weight brought new performance and efficiency. There were only two negative issues with the '80 model: the lack of an L-82 with four-speed option and that stinking 85-mph speedometer in a 140-mph car! Both the L-48 with four-speed and the L-82 with automatic were surprisingly quick. California buyers got stuck with a putt-putt 305.

Two-tone Corvettes were sold for the first time since 1961. In this case, the two colors were separated horizontally at the beltline. This was also the year production moved to Bowling Green and the previous lacquer paint was changed to enamel. This was the last Mako with a four-speed manual, although there was a new computer involved.

The 1982 model finished the Mako's long production run with a pseudo-fuel-injection induction system and a new four-speed automatic. Unfortunately, all 1982 models were equipped only with the Cross-Fire Injected 350 and automatic transmission. The production volume was way down from previous Stingrays and the '82's were some of the best constructed of all the Makos. The shining star of 1982 was clearly the Collector Edition, the first hatchback Corvette. This model sports one of the classiest, most stylish of Corvette interiors. The matching exterior isn't bad, either. The Collector is the only Mako with a multi-toned, luxurious leather interior. The Collector Edition is currently showing a Hagerty's average of $15,000, just a little more than a regular '82 model. Hagerty prices of all the 1982 models have been as flat as a pancake now for more than three years. As far as future bargains go, it is my opinion that the Collector Edition is one of the best in this book.

The *all-new* 1984 Corvette utilized exactly the same drivetrain as the 1982 Mako in a new chassis and body. The single removable roof panel offered an unobstructed view at the price of torsional rigidity when removed. All but 6443 of the prodigious '84 output had the four-speed automatic transmission. This minority had a new 4+3 overdrive manual that you could consider either a seven-speed manual, or a pain in the posterior, depending upon your attitude. This transmission dropped into overdrive gears at low speeds or low-load conditions without driver input, leaving the 1981 model as the last with a *regular* four-speed manual transmission. With the extended production year that began in early 1983, more 1984 Corvettes were built than any other model year except 1979. Many were equipped with the optional Z51 suspension that became a derogatory legend for its sheer stiffness. It looked good on the road test data sheets, though.

Genuine fuel injection finally returned in 1985, this time an electronic type, as opposed to the mechanical 1957-65 version. The two systems share practically nothing in common. The 1985 model was a greatly improved car with many detail changes from its introductory 1984 brother.

Figure J18 - A 1986 Pace Car Convertible in white with the decals affixed to the doors, something you are unlikely to encounter on the street. The decals on the windshield state that this example is an NCRS winner with only 6706 miles on it. Note the white convertible top and standard issue wheels. ©Bull-Doser (PD)

A true convertible Corvette returned in 1986, albeit at a $5000 price premium over the coupe. Introduced later in the '86 model year, the Convertible also brought aluminum heads for both models. There were 732 yellow Indy Pace Car Convertibles built, but their only claim to fame was the yellow paint that matched the official pace car.

Nineteen-eighty-seven was one of those somewhat boring model years of detailed improvements. Five horsepower was added to the 350 with new roller lifters and the Twin-Turbo built by Callaway was introduced as a non-factory option. The best news of '87 was the new Z-52 handling package. This suspension offered an improvement over the base model while forgoing the extreme harshness that had made the Z-51 a legend on bumpy roads. The Z-51 would continue in various guises for the autocrossers and their kidney belts for many model years to come.

Nineteen-eighty-eight was another year of detail improvements, the most noticeable being the new six or twelve-slot wheel design. The standard sixteen-inch wheel with six slots is actually somewhat rare, since 17,326 of the 22,789 Corvettes of the year had the optional 17-inch wheels with twelve slots standard with the Z-51 and Z-52 handling packages.

The cumbersome 4+3 manual was finally replaced by a slick six-speed manual in 1989. The removable hardtop option returned for convertible models at an ice-breaking $1995 price. According to Hagerty's, the hardtop is worth half that on a '90 model today. A luggage rack option returned to convertibles, too, last available on Convertibles in 1975 and Coupes in '77.

This book concludes with the 1990 Corvette for two distinct reasons: (1) this was the most recent official antique at the time of writing; and (2) I like the styling of the 1990 trim and wheels better than that of the 1991-1996 C4. The approximate first half of the C4 era had ended with an increase of only twenty horsepower since the advent of electronic fuel injection back in '85. This was an era of steady detail improvements in the Corvette. At this point in time, each forward year in the C4 generation will cost you a little more, but you will obtain a slightly updated car. Convertibles always cost more than Coupes, no matter how the roof is removable, but I don't have to explain that again, do I?

Figure J19 - Venetian Red 1956 Corvette with red interior, beige top, white coves and widewall tires. Note the fender vents. The 1956 and '57 models were practically identical visually. Black tops were rare in 1956, but very common in 1957. White convertible tops were the most popular color in both years. No four-speed or fuel-injected cars were built in 1956. ©Bull-Doser (PD)

Production by Model Year, Body Style and Series Chart

C1 - C2	C3	C4 - C5	C6 - C7
1953 - 300	1968 - 28,566	1984 - 51,547	2005 - 37,372
1954 - 3640	1969 - 38,762	1985 - 39,729	2006 - 34,021
1955 - 700	*Gills - 67,328*	1986 - 35,109	2007 - 40,561
Fins - 4640		1987 - 30,632	2008 - 35,310
	1970 - 17,316	1988 - 22,789	2009 - 16,956
1956 - 3467	1971 - 21,801	1989 - 26,412	*Exposes - 164,220*
1957 - 6339	1972 - 27,004	1990 - 23,646	
Singles - 9806	*Egg crates - 66,121*	*Kammtails - 229,864*	2010 - 12,194
			2011 - 13,596
1958 - 9168	1973 - 30,464	1991 - 20,639	2012 - 11,647
1959 - 9670	*Transitions - 30,464*	1992 - 20,479	2013 - 13,466
1960 - 10,261		1993 - 21,590	*GS Gills - 50,903*
Duals - 29,099	1974 - 37,502	1994 - 23,330	
	1975 - 38,465	1995 - 20,742	**C6 - 215,123**
1961 - 10,939	1976 - 46,558	1996 - 21,536	
1962 - 14,531	1977 - 49,213	*Rounders - 128,316*	2014 - 37,288
Ducktails - 25,470	*Buttresses - 171,738*		2015 - 34,240
		C4 - 358,180	
C1 - 69,015	1978 - 46,776		**C7 - 71,528**
	1979 - 53,807	1997 - 9752	
1963 - 21,513	*Fastbacks - 100,583*	1998 - 31,084	Total Production
1964 - 22,229		1999 - 33,270	Through 2015:
Drums - 43,742	1980 - 40,614	2000 - 33,682	
	1981 - 40,606	2001 - 35,627	**1,623,386**
1965 - 23, 562	1982 - 25,407	2002 - 35,767	
1966 - 27,720	*Vaders - 106,627*	2003 - 35,469	Average Annual
1967 - 22,940		2004 - 34,064	Production:
Discs - 74,222	**C3 - 542,861**		
		C5 - 248,715	**26,184**
C2 - 117,964			

Production by Model Year, Body Style and Series Chart Notes:
 Fins = Roadsters / *Singles* = Single Headlight Models / *Duals* = Dual Headlight Models / *Ducktails* = Sting Ray Rears / *Drums* = Drum Brakes / *Discs* = Disc Brakes / *Gills* = Vertical Slot Side Vents / *Egg*

crates = Crosshatch Style Side Vents / *Transitions* = Bumper Changes / *Buttresses* = Fixed Small Rear Windows / *Fastbacks* = Fixed Fastback Rear Windows / *Vaders* = Integrated Front Air Dams / *Kammtails* = Original C4 Body Style / *Rounders* = Rounded Off C4 Body / *Exposes* = Exposed Headlights / *GS Gills* = Open Side Vents.

Figure J20 - 1961 Corvette on display in Paris. This car is Fawn Beige with matching interior and white top and side coves. Notice the crease over the rear wheel wells, indicating the new Sting Ray type rear styling of the '61 model. ©The Supermat (CC)

Corvette Convertible Production Chart

C1 All	*C1 4-Speeds*	*C2 CV*	*C3 CV*	*C4 CV*
1953 - 300		1963 - 10,919	1968 - 18,630	1986 - 7315
1954 - 3640		1964 - 13,925	1969 - 16,633	1987 - 10,625
1955 - 700		1965 - 15,378	1970 - 6648	1988 - 7407
1956 - 3467		1966 - 17,762	1971 - 7121	1989 - 9749
1957 - 6339	1957 4S - 664	1967 - 14,436	1972 - 6508	1990 - 7630
1958 - 9168	1958 4S - 3764		1973 - 4943	
1959 - 9670	1959 4S - 4175	72,420	1974 - 5474	Total C4
1960 - 10,261	1960 4S - 5328		1975 - 4629	42,726
1961 - 10,939	1961 4S - 7013			
1962 - 14,531	'62 4S - 11,318		70,586	1953 - 1990
				Convertibles

69,015	32,262			254,747

Corvette Convertible Production Chart Notes:
 A small, unknown number of 1955 V-8 models were equipped with a three-speed manual; all other '55 models had Powerglide. Approximately half the '56 models had three-speeds and half had Powerglides. The 1963-69 numbers represent convertibles only, but the automatic transmission models are included in these figures, too. Most of the 1963-67 models had four-speeds. These were all M20 wide-ratios in 1963-64 until the close-ratio M22 was introduced in '65. Only thirty of these were built that year. The M21 close-ratio was released in 1966 and this transmission slightly outnumbered the production of the wide-ratio M20 in both '66 and '67. The 1970-75 numbers include only Convertibles; the four-speed was *finally* made standard in 1970. The 1986-90 figures include only Convertibles, both manuals and automatics. Note that only 14-34%, depending on the year, of 1986-90 models had manual transmissions. Chances are that these figures for Convertibles only are even lower.

Figure J21 - The side pipes have been added after production to this beautiful black 1964 Convertible. The pipes were not available as an option until 1965. This car also has the knock-off aluminum wheels that were available in 1964, but few '64 models left the factory with them. Only 806 cars out of more than 22,000 Coupes and Convertibles left the factory with these in 1964. It is highly likely these were added later, as were the side pipes. Note the correct indented hood for 1964. ©Sicnag (CC)

First Standards & Options

1953: Fiberglass roadster body - Blue Flame Six - Powerglide - Headlight stone guards
1954: Color choices - Tubeless tires - Directional signals - Windshield washers
1955: 265 V-8 engine - Three-speed manual transmission - Soft top color choices
1956: Roll-up/electric windows - Hardtop - Power top - 2-4 bbl. - transistor radio
1957: Four-speed transmission - 283 engine - Fuel injection - Positraction - Inca Silver
1958: Quad headlights - Better dash layout - Pebble-grain vinyl interior - 9-tooth grille
1959: Optional sun visors - T-handle shifter - Black interior
1960: Rear stabilizer bar - Thermostatic radiator fan - Aluminum radiator - 24-gal. tank
1961: Quad tail lamps - Sting Ray rear shape with trunk - Fawn interior
1962: 327 engine - Body-color headlight rims - Narrow whitewall tires - Rocker panels
1963: AC - IRS - FM - PS - PB - Z06 - Alpha option codes - Tinted glass - Leather
1964: White interior & top - Transistor ignition - F40 suspension
1965: Side vents - Disc brakes - M22 4-speed - 396 engine - Side pipes - Big block hood
1966: 427 engine - Optional headrests & shoulder belts - M21 CR - F41 - Gold line tires
1967: 3-2 bbl. - L88 - L89 - Redline tires - Six-inch wheels - Vinyl-covered hardtop
1968: Turbo Hydra-Matic - Integrated AC - T-top/removable rear window - 7" wheels
1969: Tilt wheel - Stingray name - 350 engine - Headrests - 8-inch wheels - RWL tires
1970: LT-1 & 454 engines - Metal side vents - Integrated shoulder belts
1971: Lowered compression for lower octane requirement - LS6 - ZR1 - ZR2
1972: Net hp ratings - LT-1 with AC - Standard alarm system
1973: Body-color front bumper - L82 - LS4 - Door Guard Beams - Cowl Induction
1974: Two-piece body-color rear bumper - Silver leather - FE7 Gymkhana - Dual horns
1975: Rubber bumper guards - HEI ignition - Catalytic converter - Blue or red leather
1976: Vega steering wheel - First year of coupes only and white interior in a C3
1977: PS, PB & Leather standard - Cruise control - Roof panels on luggage rack - 8-track
1978: PC / SA - 60 Series - Glass roof panels - Rear speakers - CB - Power door locks
1979: Standard sport seats - Optional air dam & spoiler - Cassette - Halogen high beams
1980: Integrated air dam & spoiler - 3:07 only - CA 305 - cornering lamps
1981: CCC - ETR - Two-tone paint - fiberglass monoleaf - Enamel paint - Clearcoat
1982: Crossfire Injection - Hatchback - Four-speed automatic
1984: Single roof panel - Digital instruments - Clamshell hood - 16-inch wheels - 4+3
1985: Modern electronic fuel injection - Overdrive switch on manual shifter
1986: ABS - VATS - Electronic AC
1987: Z52 - Illuminated driver's visor mirror - Callaway Twin Turbo Coupe
1988: 17-inch wheels - Nippondenso AC compressor
1989: 6-speed manual - FX3 selectable suspension - Low tire pressure warning system
1990: CD player - Oil life monitor - Hybrid instrument panel - ZR-1

Figure J22 - 1953 Blue Flame Six. ©Kowtoonese (CC)

C1 Corvette Engine Chart

O. C.	Years	C. I.	Bore	Stroke	HP	Induction	C. R.	Lifters
B. F. 6	1953	235	3.56	3.94	150	3 1-bbl.	8.0	Solid
B. F. 6	1954-55	235	3.56	3.94	155	3 1-bbl.	8.0	Solid
V-8	1955	265	3.75	3.00	195	4-bbl.	8.0	Hydraulic
Base	1956	265	3.75	3.00	210	4-bbl.	8.0	Hydraulic
469	1956	265	3.75	3.00	225	2 4-bbl.	9.25	Hydraulic
449	1956	265	3.75	3.00	240	2 4-bbl.	9.25	Solid
Base	1957	283	3.88	3.00	220	4-bbl.	9.5	Hydraulic
469(A)	1957-61	283	3.88	3.00	245	2 4-bbl.	9.5	Hydraulic
579(A)	1957-59	283	3.88	3.00	250	RFI	9.5	Hydraulic
469(B/C)	1957-61	283	3.88	3.00	270	2 4-bbl.	9.5	Solid
579 B/E	1957	283	3.88	3.00	283	RFI	10.5	Solid

Base	1958-61	283	3.88	3.00	230	4-bbl.	9.5	Hydraulic
579D	1958-59	283	3.88	3.00	290	RFI	10.5	Solid
579	1960-61	283	3.88	3.00	275	RFI	11.0	Hydraulic
579D	1960-61	283	3.88	3.00	315	RFI	11.0	Solid
Base	1962	327	4.00	3.25	250	4-bbl.	10.5	Hydraulic
583	1962	327	4.00	3.25	300	4-bbl.	10.5	Hydraulic
396	1962	327	4.00	3.25	340	4-bbl.	11.25	Solid
582	1962	327	4.00	3.25	360	RFI	11.25	Solid

C1 Corvette Engine Chart Notes:
Sources disagree as to the compression ratio of the 1956 engines. Some sources say that all had an 8.0:1 ratio and some say that all had 9.25. The '56 brochure does not mention the 210 or the 240, but lists the 225 as 9.25:1. Until further evidence proves otherwise, the 1956 listings above have been split. The 270-hp option code was listed as 468 in 1961. The 275-hp option code was 353 in 1961. The 315-hp option code was 354 in 1961. All C1 engines had iron blocks. NA = Not Applicable. O. C. = Option Code. C. I. = Cubic Inches. HP = Horsepower. C. R. = Compression Ratio. RFI = Ramjet Fuel Injection.

Figure J23 - The instruments are properly clustered behind the steering wheel in this red 1961 interior. Notice the Wonder Bar AM Radio, white plastic gear shift knob, T-handle reverse lock-out shifter, and single radio speaker behind the dash-mounted rearview mirror. ©Berthold Werner (GNU)

C1 Corvette Performance Chart

Model	Details	Source	0-60	1/4	TS	MPG
1953	235 150-hp Powerglide 3.55 axle	R&T	11.0	17.9	108	16-20
1954	235 150-hp Powerglide 3.55 axle	R&T	11.0	18.0	107	16-20
1955	265 195-hp Powerglide 3.55 axle	R&T	8.7	16.5	119	18-22
1956	265 225-hp Powerglide 3.55 axle	R&T	8.9	16.5	121	NA
1956	265 225-hp 3SM 3.55 axle	MT	7.4	15.9	129	NA
1956	265 3-speed manual 3.55 axle	ASC	7.5	16.0	120	NA
1956	265 225-hp 3SM CR 3.27 axle	SCI	7.5	15.9	120	NA
1956	265 225-hp 3SM CR 3.55 axle	R&T	7.3	15.8	130	13-16
1956	265 240-hp 3SM CR 3.55 axle	SSSC	6.3	14.9	148	NA
1956	265 240-hp 3SM CR 4.10 axle	SSSC	6.3	15.0	130	NA
1957	283 250-hp fuel injection	1953	7.6	15.6	115	NA
1957	283 250-hp fuel injection	MT	7.2	NA	NA	NA
1957	283 270-hp 3S manual 3.55 axle	SSSC	6.8	15.0	122	NA
1957	283 283-hp FI 4SM CR 4.11 Posi	MT	5.8	14.3	133	NA
1957	283 283-hp FI 4S CR 3.70 axle	CBC	5.9	14.5	135	10-15
1957	283 283-hp FI 3S manual 3.70	SCI	6.6	14.2	125	NA
1957	283 283-hp FI 4-speed 4.11 Posi	R&T	5.7	14.3	132	11-16
1958	283 230-hp 3SM 4.11 Posi	MT	9.2	17.4	103	13
1958	283 245-hp 3SM 4.11 Posi	MT	7.6	15.9	112	13
1958	283 250-hp FI 4S CR 4.11 axle	MT	7.6	15.6	114	15
1958	283 250-hp FI 3.70 axle	CBC	7.6	15.7	120	NA
1958	283 250-hp FI 4S CR 3.70 axle	SCI	7.6	15.7	125	15-18
1958	283 290-hp FI 4S CR 4.11 Posi	MT	6.9	15.6	119	14
1959	283	Corvette	8.0	15.0	NA	NA
1959	283	MT	7.8	15.0	NA	14
1959	283 250-hp FI 4S CR 4.11 axle	Tests	7.6	15.6	NA	17-22
1959	283 250-hp FI 4S 3.70 axle	CBC	7.8	15.7	120	NA
1959	283 290-hp FI 4S CR 4.11 Posi	R&T	6.6	14.5	128	11-17
1959	283 290-hp FI 4S CR 4.11 Posi	MT	6.7	14.6	130	NA

Year	Specs	Source	0-60	1/4 mi	TS	MPG
1959	283 290-hp FI 4.11 axle $5127.80	*SCI*	6.6	14.9	130	NA
1960	283 270-hp 4S CR 3.70 axle	*MT*	8.4	16.1	124	NA
1961	283 230-hp 4S 3.70 axle	*CBC*	8.3	NA	NA	NA
1961	283 230-hp	*1953*	7.9	NA	NA	NA
1961	283 230-hp Powerglide 3.55 axle	*SSSC*	7.7	16.5	109	NA
1961	283 270-hp four-speed 3.70 axle	*SSSC*	5.9	14.6	131	NA
1961	283 315-hp FI 4S CR 3.70 Posi	*MT*	7.4	15.4	130	NA
1961	283 315-hp fuel injection	*1953*	5.9	NA	NA	NA
1961	283 315-hp FI 4S 3.70 axle	*CBC*	6.0	15.5	140	NA
1961	283 315-hp FI 4S 4.11 axle	*SSSC*	5.5	14.2	128	NA
1961	283 315-hp FI 4S CR 4.11 Posi	*R&T*	6.6	14.2	128	11-17
1962	327 3.70 axle	*C/D*	NA	15.0	NA	NA
1962	327	*1953*	NA	14.2	NA	NA
1962	327 360-hp FI 4S 3.70 axle	*SCG*	5.9	14.5	150	NA
1962	327 360-hp FI 4.11 axle	*Car Life*	5.9	14.0	NA	NA
1962	327 360-hp FI 4S CR 4.11 Posi	*C/D*	6.1	14.4	121	10
1962	327 360-hp FI 4S CR 3.70 Posi	*MT*	5.9	14.9	132	13-16

C1 Corvette Performance Chart Notes:

The Corvette got its first optional axle ratio of 3.27 in 1956. The close ratio (CR) 4-speed was available on some C1 models, but you could not select a close ratio as a choice. The mellower engines were wide ratio (WR) only and the wilder engines were close ratio only. Quarter-mile and 0-60 mph times are in seconds. TS = top speed in MPH. MPG = miles per gallon, rounded to a whole number.

1953 = Richard Nichols' *1953 to the Present & The Classic Corvette*. AAC = *Corvette: An American Classic*. ASC = Jay Koblenz' *Corvette: America's Sports Car*. CBC = Richard M. Langworth's *The Complete Book of Corvette*. C/D = *Car and Driver*. Corvette = Barry Coleman's *Corvette*. MT = *Motor Trend*. R&T = *Road & Track*. SCG = *Sports Car Graphic*. SCI = *Sports Cars Illustrated*. SSSC = *America's Star-Spangled Sports Car*. Tests = *Corvette Road Tests*.

Figure J24 - Here is a front view of the white fuel-injected 1960 Corvette shown earlier in this chapter. ©Rex Gray, Southern California (CC)

C2 Corvette Engine Chart

O. C.	Years	C. I.	Bore	Stroke	HP	Induction	C. R.	Lifters
Base	1963-65	327	4.00	3.25	250	4-bbl.	10.5	Hydraulic
L75	1963-66	327	4.00	3.25	300	4-bbl.	10.5	Hydraulic
L76	1963	327	4.00	3.25	340	4-bbl.	11.25	Solid
L84	1963	327	4.00	3.25	360	RFI	11.25	Solid
L76	1964-65	327	4.00	3.25	365	4-bbl.	11.0	Solid
L84	1964-65	327	4.00	3.25	375	RFI	11.0	Solid
L79	1965-67	327	4.00	3.25	350	4-bbl.	11.0	Hydraulic
L78	1965	396	4.10	3.76	425	4-bbl.	NA	Solid
L36	1966-67	427	4.25	3.76	390	4-bbl.	10.25	Hydraulic
L72	1966	427	4.25	3.76	425	4-bbl.	11.0	Solid
Base	1967	327	4.00	3.25	300	4-bbl.	10.0	Hydraulic
L68	1967	427	4.25	3.76	400	3 2-bbl.	10.25	Hydraulic
L71	1967	427	4.25	3.76	435	3 2-bbl.	11.0	Solid
L89	1967	427	4.25	3.76	435	3 2-bbl.	11.0	Solid
L88	1967	427	4.25	3.76	430	4-bbl.	12.0	Solid

C2 Corvette Engine Chart Notes:

All C2 engines had cast iron blocks. The 427 L88 rated at 430 gross horsepower actually produced 560 gross horsepower. NA = Not Available. *O. C.* = Option Code. *C. I.* = Cubic Inches. *HP* = Horsepower. *C. R.* = Compression Ratio. RFI = Ramjet Fuel injection.

Figure J25 - This shot I took at an NCRS event in New Braunfels, TX, back in The Eighties is a very precious photo to me. This is a 1965 Nassau Blue 396 Convertible. The car to the right of it is a 1965 396 Convertible in Rally Red. The red car's aluminum wheels and side pipes are pictured on the back cover of this book. The blue car has the wheel covers with spinners standard for 1965 and the quieter exhaust system. Both cars have been fully restored to NCRS specifications. ©1986 Floyd M. Orr Collection

C2 Corvette Performance Chart

Model	*Details*	*Source*	*0-60*	*1/4*	*TS*	*MPG*
1963	327 300-hp Powerglide 3.36 axle	*Car Life*	7.2	15.5	130	NA
1963	327 300-hp 4S 3.36 axle	*CBC*	6.1	14.5	118	NA
1963	327 300-hp 4S 3.36 axle	*C/D*	6.2	14.5	118	NA
1963	327 360-hp FI 4S CR 3.70 Posi	*MT*	5.8	14.5	135	14-18
1963	327 360-hp FI 4S 3.70 axle	*SCG*	5.6	14.2	151	NA
1963	327 360-hp FI 4S 3.70 axle	*Autocar*	6.5	14.6	146	NA
1963	327 360-hp FI 4S CR 3.70 axle	*R&T*	5.9	14.9	142	11-14

Year	Engine	Source	0-60	1/4 mi	TS	MPG
1964	327 300-hp Powerglide 3.36 Posi	R&T	8.0	15.2	130	12-16
1964	327 300-hp 4S 3.36 axle CV	R&T	6.5	14.5	127	16
1964	327 375-hp FI 4S CR 4.11 Posi CP	MT	5.6	14.2	134	12-21
1965	327 300-hp 4S WR 3.36 Posi	MT	7.5	15.8	124	NA
1965	327 375-hp FI 4S CR 3.70 Posi	R&T	6.3	14.4	138	11-15
1965	327 375-hp FI 4S CR 4.11 Posi	MT	5.6	14.2	134	NA
1965	396 425-hp 396 4S CR	ASC	NA	14.0	140	NA
1965	396 425-hp 4S CR 3.70 Posi	R&T	5.7	14.1	136	9-12
1966	NA	1953	NA	14.0	150	NA
1966	427 425-hp 3.36 axle CV	Car Life	5.7	14.0	130	12
1966	427 425-hp 4S CR 4.11 axle CV	MT	5.6	13.4	135	NA
1966	427 425-hp 4.11 axle Coupe	SCG	4.8	NA	140	NA
1966	427 425-hp 3.36 axle Hardtop	C/D	5.4	12.8	152	NA
1967	327 300-hp 4S 3.36 Posi Hardtop	R&T	7.8	16.0	121	14-18
1967	L-71 427 435-hp 4S CR 3.55 Posi	MT	5.5	13.8	143	NA
1967	L-88 427 430-hp 4S CR	MT	4.9	13.1	150	NA
1967	L-88 427 430-hp 4S CR	1953	4.9	12.9	183	NA

C2 Corvette Performance Chart Notes:

The close ratio (CR) 4-speed was available on the 1963-65 models, but you could not select a close ratio as a choice. The mellower engines were wide ratio (WR) only and the wilder engines were close ratio only. The first time the M21 was an optional choice on any particular engine was 1966. Beginning in 1966, you could get the 350-hp 327 or the 390-hp 427 with either WR or CR. The bottom and top engines still offered little choice: WR with the base engine and CR with the solid lifter bunch. Quarter-mile and 0-60 mph times are in seconds. CV = Convertible. TS = top speed in mph. MPG = miles per gallon, rounded to a whole number. Luci Baines Johnson owned a C2 convertible while Dad was in the White House.

Sources: 1953 = 1953 to the Present & The Classic Corvette. AAC = Corvette: An American Classic. ASC = Jay Koblenz' Corvette: America's Sports Car. Autocar = Autocar. Car Life = Car Life. CBC = The Complete Book of Corvette. C/D = Car and Driver. MT = Motor Trend. R&T = Road & Track. SCG = Sports Car Graphic.

The Coveted Sting Rays and Exciting Stingrays

Figure J26 - A beautifully restored 1965 Fuelie. In addition to the presence of fuel injection in its last year of production, this Milano Maroon small-block Sting Ray has knock-off aluminum wheels. It is a bit unusual to see one with a white top and blackwall tires. ©Shane Mattaway (GNU)

The primitive solid axle, heavy steering, and traditional styling gave way to independent rear suspension, power steering, FM radio and stunning styling. The horsepower continued to build until it was poured over the wheels of psychedelic styling. Then the power slowly faded as Convertible production was continually diminished by FM Stereo, power windows and air conditioning. The 98-inch wheelbase, ladder chassis lasted from 1963 to 1982. It began with the first Corvette Coupe and ended with the first hatchback Corvette. The base horsepower to weight ratio ended about where it began, but the joy ride in the middle was excitement personified.

Let's analyze this often repeated story of excitement. We all know it began in late 1962 with the Split Window Coupe and slowly dissolved into a morass of boulevardier stories of stylish cruisers grown too old to rock and roll. For our purposes in this book, we are dividing the Makos at the line between the '75 and '76 models, at which point there were no longer any Convertibles or big-blocks. We were looking at a future of only T-tops and a single optional engine at best for a decade. Each model year the Corvette generally became more comfortable, civilized, house-broken and boring. Considering that this had been dictated by the new laws of the land, there was little we could do about it. During the next phase, GM would slowly accept the new reality of higher technology requiring higher prices and Corvette performance would gradually begin to improve. The 1975 model year would forever represent the trough of Corvette power and performance. The '75 model was the first with a catalytic converter, but it earned a special place in history (and this book) as the last Stingray Convertible.

Figure J27 - The 1963 interior had a number of detail differences from the later model Sting Rays. A few of these are shown here. The shiny silver centers of the instrument faces are indigenous to 1963. So is the signal seeking AM radio. Late 1963 models and all later Sting Rays had the optional AM/FM mono unit or no radio at all. Note the vertical radio face. One of the reasons for the interior restyle for 1968 was to allow the installation of normal horizontal radio dials and stereo speakers. The steering wheel matches the Saddle interior color. A fake woodgrain plastic steering wheel was standard in 1964. The white plastic shift knob is not correct: the '63 models had black plastic shift knobs. ©Tino Rossini (CC)

The '63 and '64 models introduced the flabbergasting look of the new Sting Ray. The Corvette could now have power steering, power brakes, air conditioning, and an FM radio. Unfortunately, the steering turned narrow six-inch wheels, the brakes were drums, the air conditioning was minimally integrated and effective, and the AM/FM radio was still mono. The side vents were fake, as were those on the hood of the '63 models. The 1964 model was distinguished by its lack of fake vents, leaving unnecessary indentations in the hood. As with its first-bodied little brother the '68, there were many details of the 1963 unique to the year. Educate yourself fully on these before seeking and purchasing either model. Nineteen-sixty-four is the only Corvette model year in which white is offered as an interior color in either vinyl or leather and in all models with all exterior colors. The 1964 and 1968 models have plastic walnut-grain steering wheels.

Figure J28 - This Ermine White fuel-injected 1964 Corvette has incorrect hubcaps and trim rings similar to those of the later Stingray bodies. Wheel covers unique to 1964 were the standard offer and nearly all the 1964 models left the factory with them. This is a nice looking car, but obviously not an NCRS level restoration to originality. ©Sicnag (CC)

The Sting Ray excitement began in earnest in 1965 with the introduction of disc brakes, big-block engines, big-block hoods, functional side vents, mag wheel covers, and loud side pipes. Optional off-road pipes exiting out back remained on the option list from 1963 to 1967. One of the most coveted options has always been the rare knock-off aluminum wheels of 1963-66. A bolt-on version of these were indigenous to 1967 only and aluminum wheels would not reappear on the option list until 1976. Whether you particularly like their looks or not, any aluminum wheels that were factory optioned on a specific Corvette always add to the car's value. Hope you have the original window sticker or build sheet from atop the gas tank to conclusively prove this. Many fans want the last model with mechanical fuel injection and many want the first big-block. These will always be the most valuable '65 models, whichever you choose. Right now at Hagerty's, the 396 is averaging about $95,000 and the fuelie $90,000 and both, as you would expect, are trending upward. These are Convertible quotes with Coupes coming in about $12-15,000 less with a similar upward trend.

Figure J29 - The 1966 Sting Ray identifies its year by the Corvette script emblem on the driver's side hood panel. This Rally Red 327 with black interior has aluminum wheels and side pipes. Isn't it amazing how many more Sting Rays have these originally rare options now than they did back then? ©Bull-Doser (PD)

The 1966 model brought two 427 engines replacing the short-lived 425-hp 396. The new solid-lifter 427 was originally listed as having 450 horsepower, but this was *mysteriously* dropped back to 425 before the end of the model year. Actually, I don't think there was much of a mystery. Although the larger version of the same engine should produce increased power, I think Chevy was becoming a little paranoid of the meddling insurance companies. The next year's 435-horsepower rating would forever be considered *conservative*, so I suspect the 425 rating of the earlier 427 was, too. Although it has never gotten the enthusiastic press of the solid-lifter 427, the newly released 390-horsepower model with hydraulic lifters has always been one of my favorite Corvette engines. This is the low-stress, low-maintenance, high-torque powerhouse that has always been available with air conditioning, power steering, automatic transmission, and any other comfort additives. In the hot climate in which I live, there is no substitute for AC! Nineteen-sixty-six would be the next year after 1955 that all Corvettes had single four-barrel carbs only, and this trend would return in 1970 and continue through 1981. This was also the first year that all had disc brakes, too. Except for the seat panels and a few other very minor details, the '66 looks just like the '65. When seeking out one of these, be wary of counterfeits with big-block hoods and/or side pipes, and of course matching numbers are very important in this price range. The '65 and '66 big-block models are usually cheaper than the '67's because enthusiasts tend to love the bolder hood and multiple carbs of the later model. Small-blocks of these years tend to be more equal in value.

Figure J30 - The 427 emblem is missing from the side of the big-block hood scoop on this 1967 Convertible. This example is Silver Pearl with red interior and matching red hood stripe. The wheels are the standard type for '67 and so are the side pipes. The only suspicious note from this photo is that missing emblem. ©Sicnag (CC)

Somebody has to be at the top of the food chain and the solid-lifter 427's hold that honor. Don't bother looking for one of these unless you are ready to cough up six figures. The price drops downward, in some cases precipitously, as you sort through the lower-powered big-blocks, then down to the 327's. A good old Powerslide can knock a hole in the price, too, but are you sure you want the car that badly? A general rule of thumb is that a four-barrel 427 starts at a base line and the tri-power version increases the price only a little, but the L-71 solid-lifter doubles the price and the L-89, with the only difference being the rare aluminum heads, doubles it again! The current price for one of the twenty L-88's built in '67, the only year with the Sting Ray body, is approximately $2-3.5 million for either body style. The two factory options that everyone wants are the side pipes and aluminum wheels. The convertibles are distinctly more expensive than the coupes in all the lesser, more common drivetrain combinations. As of the time of publication, the 327 models were showing little if any price growth. Peak prices for these occurred back in 2006, so you might consider them a bargain. Will this relentless excitement over big-blocks continue into the future? Probably, but I certainly think we are currently open any time now for a big economic correction that could easily knock them down a notch.

Among the respected older brothers of the Stingray clan, the '68 model has become known somewhat as the problem child. The powertrain excitement carried forth unabated from the '67 model, but the new body and its assembly quality were controversial from the beginning. The company took on a lot of detail changes while upping the production rate, so you can surmise the result. Some Corvette fans mourned the demise of the earlier model's vent windows, and of course many more missed the vast elbow, head and shoulder room of the Sting Ray. There were numerous changes to cheer about for the 1968 design, however. The engineers could never seem to get enough cooling to what we now call the mid-year big-blocks, but by 1970 that problem would be vanquished. Wider wheels and tires, fully integrated central air conditioning, and stereo sound systems were just three items that could never fit within the confines of the Sting Ray design. Let's see, am I forgetting something? Oh yeah, that stupid, stoopid, disgusting, two-speed Powerslide was *finally* deleted from the Corvette option list, replaced by a proper Turbo-Hydramatic that could now be fitted underneath the wide console of the new Stingray body. Now that's real progress!

Figure J31 - The rear clip could appear a little massive from this angle on the 1968-72 Stingray Convertibles. This pretty 1969 example in Burgundy with black interior has the optional chrome luggage rack and vent trim.
©Greg Gjerdingen, Willmar, USA (CC)

Many would consider 1969 the pinnacle of the Sixties Muscle Car Phenomenon. Of course this point could be argued all day long. Many call 1967 the pinnacle because it precedes significant emission controls. Some would say 1970 because the largest engine appeared and some pony and muscle cars, such as the Chevelle SS454, the Plymouth 'Cuda and Superbird, and the Dodge Challenger hit their strides in that year. Of course some will claim it was 1968 just to be ornery. With the Stingray, 1969 was a carryover year from '68 in both body and drivetrain. The production of both the L-89 and L-88 were way up from the meager numbers of 1967; hence the really high values of the those few with the Sting Ray body. The '68 model did out-muscle the '69 on one point: 624 L-89's were built compared to 1969's 390.

Figure J32 - The 1969 Stingray in black with black top with the 427 hood and side pipes of a design used only in 1969 makes an ominous presence on the street. This example amplifies the effect with its chrome wheel trim rings removed. This car has a red interior, optional chrome trim on the side vents offered only in '69, and the ubiquitous aftermarket BF Goodrich Radial T/A tires. This was the first year tires with raised white letters were offered. They were Firestone Wide Ovals and less than 2400 sets were sold as an original equipment option. ©Mr. Choppers (GNU)

Okay, I'm a little biased about this one. Back in 1980 I thought it was about time I sought out a '65-'72 Corvette. As much as I lusted after the 1965-67 body, one sit-down in a Coupe of one of these years, I do not remember which, cured me of that lust. I am a scrawny little guy with a short torso and long legs and I just do not fit well in the Sting Ray body. One of its claims to fame is that it is so appropriate for American football players, but that's just not me. Although one of the leading complaints of the Stingray body style is its cramped interior, being a little guy that issue never bothered me much. Soon after this I realized, too, that I needed the tilt wheel option to bring the steering wheel down to my low seating position. This option was not available until 1969. I have always been quite individualistic in my outlook, so I care little what others think of me. The one thing I won't do is to blow smoke up your ass, as the saying goes. The perfect Corvette engine for me is the L-68 400-hp 427 with three two-barrels and that delicious triangular air filter. Remember that I am not a drag racer or a keeper of trailer queens. I don't much care that this model is worth less on the current market than the solid-lifter version. I also don't much care that the three carburetors add little to the performance of the L36 four-barrel. The result of all this is that it led me to seek out a 1969 L-68. The short version is that I did not find one.

What I did find was a 1970 LS-5 Coupe with all the options that were important to me: wide-ratio four-speed, AC, optional wheel covers (I am not a fan of hubcaps with trim rings), power steering, power brakes, 3:08 rear axle, and a few options I cared less about. What I had not fully realized until I did more research is that the 1970 model had several new positive attributes over the '69 model. The flared wheel wells made it look even lower, wider and sexier. The improvements in the cooling system made even the 454 run decently cool in the very hot environment in which I live. The seat belts routed through the seatbacks was cool. Most of all, the 17,316 built in 1970 brought the assembly quality back to a level distinctly above that of 1968 and '69. To add the icing to the cake, the 1970 model I found on a used car lot was an early production model with the open element air filter.

Figure J33 - This pretty Mulsanne Blue 1971 Convertible sits next to a red 1961 Corvette. Note the right side mirror. This second chrome mirror was not a factory option. The Dual Sport Mirror option began in 1977. ©Sicnag (CC)

Nineteen-seventy also brought the LT-1, one of the more interesting Corvettes of all time. If you can find an LT-1 Convertible in the right color with the right options, stash it in your garage. I think this is one of the Corvettes that will always have significant value in the future. This is the last year for unfettered compression ratios, leaving the LS-5 and LT-1 as hot tickets for collectors, although these will not do well with our current fuel availability. The LT-1 is the only small-block Corvette to come standard with a big-block hood. Note that the stripes on this hood are very specific to the model and year, too. The LT-1 would be the final solid-lifter small-block Corvette and none of the '70 models were air conditioned. A special ZR-1 racing package was available with the LT-1 engine in 1970-72, but the '70 model had the highest horsepower, of course. The total ZR-1 production included 25 in 1970, only 8 in '71, and 20 in '72. Thanks to John DeLorean, no Corvette ever again would be cursed with a three-speed manual transmission. The low production of 17,316, the improved quality control, and the last high-compression engines ensure the future desirability of the 1970 models.

The next year was an interim of minor changes. It takes a sharp eye to identify a 1971 model from either a '70 or '72. Lower compression brought lower horsepower ratings all around. The only exception was the claim to fame for the '71 year, the 425-horsepower, 454-inch LS-6. The current Hagerty's ratings show a sharp increase in the value of the LS-6 in recent years, but in my opinion this model is still undervalued for the future. Hagerty's is currently showing a $105,000 average for the Coupe and $160,000 for the Convertible. The top price for the top condition Convertible is still listed as about $250,000 in 2015. With only 188 constructed, including both body styles, I expect the 1971-only LS-6 to keep climbing the price chart. Keep in mind that the previous year's 460-hp LS-7 was pulled from the market before production began, making the LS-6 the top banana 454. Of course the most valuable LS-6 today would be one of the twelve produced with the ZR-2 racing package.

Figure J34 - Mille Miglia Red 1972 LT-1 Sting Ray Convertible. ©Sicnag (CC)

Many Stingray fans really like the 1972 model, the last with classic chrome bumpers and removable rear windows on the coupes. The fiber optics and headlamp washers of the previous models were replaced with a standard alarm system. Power continued to decline, but by not nearly as much as it appeared from the new net horsepower ratings. Air conditioning was available with the LT-1 engine, but little joy could be derived from its emasculated power. The final year of the LS-5 fared little better. Prices of the '72 models seem to have flat-lined since about 2012. Will these prove to be sleepers in the future, or just good buys as occasional cruisers? If you want the classic look in a model that will not choke, cough and spit quite so disgustedly on modern gasoline, a '72 model could be a fine choice.

You could say that the '73 model truly began the transformation of the hot-blooded Stingray into a comfortable boulevardier. The LS-4 was a new 275-hp 454 and it would last only one more model year. The venerable L-48 and a new, hydraulic-lifter L-82 would carry the engine lineup for many years to come. The Corvette got its first cowl-induction hood with the demise of the troublesome, vacuum-actuated windshield wiper cover. Radial tires and guard beams in the doors were welcome new features. Convertible fans lamented the fixed rear window in the Coupe. Opinions have always been split over the front safety bumper combined with the traditional Kamm tail and delicate chrome rear bumper. Like their older brothers, prices of the '73's have flat-lined somewhat, and the high production number of the Coupes has kept them in the bargain basement. Less than 5,000 Convertibles were built in '73, making them a model to watch, especially with the LS-4 and close-ratio four-speed.

Figure J35 - 1974 Convertible in Medium Red. ©Stoskett (GNU)

Nineteen-seventy-four brought the final demise of the Stingray's delicate chrome bumpers. The Kamm tail was gone, diminishing downforce at high speeds. The final year of the big-block Stingray made the LS-4 the obvious collectible of the year, and Convertibles were once again in low production, making them desirable today. Is the hot ticket not obvious? You want to find a 454 Convertible with the close-ratio four-speed and air conditioning! Although we lost the downforce of the Kamm tail, in my opinion the sloped rear of the 1974-75 models looks particularly attractive with the Convertible body. Only 47 of the Z07 racing packages were installed on Corvettes this year, including both LS-4 and L-82 engines, making these a hot collector ticket today. All 1974 Stingrays would be the last without catalytic converters and with true, separate dual exhausts.

Somebody has to come in last, right? The 1975 base L-48 produced only 165 net horsepower. The L-82 option would add forty more horses, but surprisingly, only 7% of new-car buyers chose it! Less than half that many, just over a thousand, added the close-ratio four-speed that year. Boulevardier, my ass... wait a minute, maybe there was some truth to the application of that derogatory term. The '75 model, with its abominable exhaust and pitiful power ratings, did have one horn to toot: it was the last true Corvette Convertible for a decade. There is little doubt that the 1975 hot item is an L-82 Convertible with close-ratio four-speed and air conditioning, although the latter was on nearly all the '75 models produced. Take note that the vinyl covered hardtop option for the Convertible introduced back in 1967 bottomed out at only 279 ordered in its final year, so this may be a collectible item to consider, too. The huge majority of '75 models were very boring L-48 Coupes with Turbo Hydra-Matic transmissions and common luxury options of the day such as tilt steering wheel, FM stereo, and power brakes, steering, and windows. One final bright spot for collectors was the Z07 racing package offered for the last time. It is unknown how many, if any, of the 144 Z07's built were Convertibles.

Figure J36 - 1975 Convertible in Classic White with Black Interior and Top. ©Wallerdog (CC)

C3 Corvette Engine Chart

O. C.	Years	C. I.	Bore	Stroke	HP	Induction	Lifters
Base	1968	327	4.00	3.25	300	4-bbl.	Hydraulic
L79	1968	327	4.00	3.25	350	4-bbl.	Hydraulic
L36	1968-69	427	4.25	3.76	390	4-bbl.	Hydraulic
L68	1968-69	427	4.25	3.76	400	3 2-bbl.	Hydraulic
L71	1968-69	427	4.25	3.76	435	3 2-bbl.	Solid
L89	1968-69	427	4.25	3.76	435	3 2-bbl.	Solid
L88	1968-69	427	4.25	3.76	430	4-bbl.	Solid
L48	1969-70	350	4.00	3.48	300	4-bbl.	Hydraulic
L46	1969-70	350	4.00	3.48	350	4-bbl.	Hydraulic
ZL1	1969	427	4.25	3.76	560	4-bbl.	Solid
LT1	1970	350	4.00	3.48	370	4-bbl.	Solid
LS5	1970	454	4.25	4.00	390	4-bbl.	Hydraulic
L48	1971	350	4.00	3.48	270	4-bbl.	Hydraulic
LT1	1971	350	4.00	3.48	330	4-bbl.	Solid
ZR1	1971	350	4.00	3.48	330	4-bbl.	Solid
LS5	1971	454	4.25	4.00	365	4-bbl.	Hydraulic
LS6	1971	454	4.25	4.00	425	4-bbl.	Solid
ZR2	1971	454	4.25	4.00	425	4-bbl.	Solid
L48	1972	350	4.00	3.48	200	4-bbl.	Hydraulic

LT1	1972	350	4.00	3.48	255	4-bbl.	Solid
ZR1	1972	350	4.00	3.48	255	4-bbl.	Solid
LS5	1972	454	4.25	4.00	270	4-bbl.	Hydraulic
Base	1973	350	4.00	3.48	190	4-bbl.	Hydraulic
L82	1973-74	350	4.00	3.48	250	4-bbl.	Hydraulic
LS4	1973	454	4.25	4.00	275	4-bbl.	Hydraulic
Base	1974	350	4.00	3.48	195	4-bbl.	Hydraulic
LS4	1974	454	4.25	4.00	270	4-bbl.	Hydraulic
L-48	1975	350	4.00	3.48	165	4-bbl.	Hydraulic
L82	1975	350	4.00	3.48	205	4-bbl.	Hydraulic
L-48	1976-77	350	4.00	3.48	180	4-bbl.	Hydraulic
L82	1976-77	350	4.00	3.48	210	4-bbl.	Hydraulic
L48	1978	350	4.00	3.48	185	4-bbl.	Hydraulic
L82	1978	350	4.00	3.48	220	4-bbl.	Hydraulic
L48	1979	350	4.00	3.48	195	4-bbl.	Hydraulic
L82	1979	350	4.00	3.48	225	4-bbl.	Hydraulic
LG4	1980	305	3.74	3.48	180	4-bbl.	Hydraulic
L48	1980	350	4.00	3.48	190	4-bbl.	Hydraulic
L82	1980	350	4.00	3.48	230	4-bbl.	Hydraulic
L81	1981	350	4.00	3.48	190	4-bbl.	Hydraulic
L83	1982	350	4.00	3.48	200	C-F I	Hydraulic

C3 Corvette Engine Chart Notes:

All C3 engines had carburetors except the 1982 models, which had Cross-Fire Injection, a sort of hybrid fuel injection system. The 427 L88 rated at 430 gross horsepower actually produced 560 gross horsepower. The 180-hp 305 engine with three-speed Turbo Hydra-Matic was the only powertrain available in California in 1980. Horsepower ratings from 1968-71 are gross; 1972-82 ratings are net. NA = Not Available.

RIDE OF THE VAMPIRES

This parody of two of my favorite types of movies, vampires and police procedurals, was previously published in a slightly different presentation mode in my first book, *Plastic Ozone Daydream* in 2000. As presented here, this is a composite edit of two stories, first released in serial form in 1989 and 1992. The original release dates are important because Jerry Seinfeld, an avid Porsche fan and collector, premiered a very similar concept on the television series *Seinfeld*. The episode entitled *The Bottle Deposit* first aired on May 2, 1996. Not only was this my favorite *Seinfeld* episode of all time, but the plotline was partially a parody of a police procedural involving the personification of cars. Jerry's car is stolen by the Saab mechanic. When Jerry is called down to the police warehouse to identify his stolen Saab Convertible, he discovers the car in question is not his, but that of a woman who closes the scene when she identifies her Saab Turbo. I want to make it clear that to the best of my knowledge, Mr. Seinfeld did not get this idea from me, nor I from him.

This story was inspired by the work of Anne Rice and many movies and TV shows. The locations in and around Austin, TX, are real. I lived in Buda, TX, a small suburb on the south side of Austin at the time this was originally written. My 1970 big-block Stingray was locked in its garage most of the time, but like any caged animal, it was dying to escape. This is a story dedicated to all the high-performance 1965-72 Corvettes squirreled away in dark garages everywhere across the USA.

Wednesday morning 3 a.m.:

"What have we got here, Sergeant?"

"Another one, Captain. This one's an Austin-Healey Sprite. Poor little thing's eyes are bugged out even more than usual. Looks kinda like a big bug on its back, with its little wheels spinnin' like that…"

"Like the last one? Any gas in its tank?"

"Not a drop. Darnedest thing. How did it get here with its tank empty?"

"Dead on its back. Any evidence at all this time?"

"Just those tiny bits of fiberglass the special team found…"

"You mean like that found at the scene with that old derelict MGB down on South Lamar last week?"

"Yeah. Except that one was at least right side up. We just figured the rusty old piece of English tin had a hole in its gas tank. Wouldn't be the first, would it? Until now we weren't even sure the fiberglass should be considered evidence."

The following Monday about 2:15 a.m., the Homicide Squad of the A.P.D. found itself swarming throughout a normally quiet residential neighborhood out on Bee Caves Road. They had been called to the scene of the messiest sports car homicide the team had ever to investigate. Blocking the middle of the street in this otherwise highly tasteful and Yuppified district was the shiniest black Ruf Porsche 930 you can imagine, and its present condition caused the first officers on the scene to barf in the bushes before they began their investigation. This machine had been one of real beauty: a highly modified 930 Targa with the full Ruf treatment and whaletails everywhere! What the team witnessed now was an upside down Porsche with its turbo stuffed into its own tailpipe! The plastic Targa roof panel was splattered all over a neighboring yard, the ultra-wide tires were shredded, and long, claw-like scratches marred the shiny black finish all the way down each side. This time the squad was expecting the empty fuel tank and the tiny shards of fiberglass, but their delicate tummies were not prepared for a pale, off-white leather interior desecrated in gooey black gear lube with the message, "Eat this, Krautsnot!"

Back in the safety of his A.P.D. office, the lieutenant relaxed and carefully considered the gruesome evidence his team had amassed in the last two weeks. The mayor was having a duck over the lack of his team's progress. The pressure was on, but he had to examine every shred of what they had. This was no time to panic. The old B on South Lamar was the first they had found. Since the nicest looking baby blue E-Jag convertible he had ever seen was parked unharmed just down the street from the B, his team had not even been called in until after the Sprite incident. Surely the mayor could understand how they had assumed the old B had just had a rust attack! Good grief! Now they had a serial killer on their hands. First a derelict, then something some nuts call a classic, and then that rich brat has to go and call the mayor personally about the loss of his $100,000 toy. See what we get when we have Halloween and a full moon in the same month? Why did the nut leave that beautemous Jag untouched? What's the connection? How did the victims reach their destinies with death with no gas in their tanks? And most of all, who-or-whatever did it has to be really big and strong. Whenever we catch up to him, I sure hope we have the swat team along!

The legend begins in the very early Fifties, when Jaguars were brought into the New World by servicemen returning from duty in Europe. They brought back their XK's, 120's and 140's, sleek and sexy beasts with adequate power and exciting looks, and hidden within their British souls were the souls of those not yet born, those with more power and lightweight plastic bodies. The original descendants had the Sixes and skinny tires of their forefathers, and their docile natures were also similar. Then came from a foreign land a strange old warlock named Zora. At first the magic he conjured was mild enough to escape the attention of the authorities, but by '63 the cat was out of the bag. His newest magic was even more intense and lasting than that of the Jaguars. There was no looking back. These new critters were immortal. Their magic would never die. They would be beautiful in any age. Their power would never be surpassed. They would never forget from whence they came. The Jaguars may growl with an accent, but they still spoke some sort of English, at least throughout the E-Type years. They would be bosom-buddies forever. Like the Jaguars, their thirst would never be slaked. It would become legendary. So would their immortality to all the lesser mortals, at least until 1982, when their numbers seemed to stop growing and oil stocks dipped a bit. The creatures tired of fighting progress. They added no new recruits to their army of gas guzzlers. They altered their clothing so that not only did they all look pretty much alike, but they looked more like the herd of mortals from the Orient. They developed new electronic means to quench the ravaging thirst and exercised their paws so that their size was increased dramatically. Now they could run faster while being less dangerous to mortals at the same time! Throughout The Eighties the numbers of the dangerous ones have been decreasing, while the new breed manages to run with the Asian herd. The vampire killers don't seem to notice the front row of the stampede. It's the lone wolves with the bulging muscles and heavy appetites that are limited to the dark hours.

Chief Carbunkle tried to tell the mayor why he thought the attacks had begun lately in his town. The last straw had come back in July when the mayor's plan for a new convention center had passed in the election. He knew something was coming when the election was over. The town just cannot handle another reason for a traffic jam in that particular area. He knew that if the drivers did not revolt, the cars would… and it seemed now that they did, in a manner not even a seasoned old detective like himself could imagine. This sort of gas-thirsty savagery would torque anyone's mind! It was Halloween and every dressed-up werewolf and goblin in three counties was down parading on Sixth Street. The Chief and the mayor had had about all they could take.

"Just what do you intend to do to protect all the Porsches and Ferraris parked near Sixth Street tonight, Carfunkle?"

"The name is Car<u>b</u>unkle, and we have the entire VK Squad down on Sixth right now."

"If just one of those overpaid brats complains to me, you're not going to hear the end of it! Do you read me?"

"Like you know what, Mr....."

The lieutenant broke in suddenly. "Chief! It's happened again. A red Testarossa up in Wells Branch, near Round Rock. I guess he thought we would all be on Sixth, so he hit the place we would least expect!"

"See, mayor. I told you it was the overcrowding on I-35 that caused this whole mess! Now the problem has spread to a humongous North Austin neighborhood with only one little old entrance. Now are you ready to listen to a little reason?"

Within the hour Chief Carbunkle had the complete report on his desk. The mayor didn't listen to reason... politicians never do. The chief had much more important matters on his mind now anyway: like why, once again, what seemed to be an obvious potential victim sat unharmed and healthy as any Ferrari in that devastated Wells Branch garage. The report was conclusive: a black, *fiberglass* 1977 GTB snorted like any healthy horse right there beside the irreparably ripped and drained red Testarossa! The fiberglass bits of ubiquitous evidence present at the scene had a coating of blue, not black. The puzzle continues.... The Testarossa had missed the nauseating violent attack suffered by the earlier, Germanic victim, but the fuel cell drainage was a complete job as usual. Fortunately there was a new bit of evidence: at the time of the attack, nosy neighbors had heard unusual growling noises coming from the garage. They described the sounds as being very deep and gutteral, very unlike the shrieks-of-ripping-silk sounds usually originating from that garage.

By the time the police and their hot-snot VK Squad had arrived at the scene in Wells Branch, an ancient beast of blue was zapping through the radar traps on South I-35, its tank full of hot Italian juice and its howl breaking the hot Austin night. The side pipes on the plastic monster roared as they never had before. The brute's relatively small paws gripped at the hot pavement while the heart of the beast breathed through its shiny delta-shaped mouth as if Halloween would never end. The revenge was complete. Out of the cluster of monsters haunting the nights in this hot-blooded town, he was the king and he knew it. The sweet night-justice was complete when the red TR lay whining like a wounded colt at his feet. The GTB had remained cowered in its corner, the look of understanding fading across its face. The best moment had come when all the Testarossa's blood had been drained and that silly-looking mirror just curled up and fell off. With sweet thoughts flowing through its three carbs and its forever stylish plastic cloak slipping through the wind, the king vampire breezed quickly down its home street toward the safety of a dark and windowless garage. Timeless clothes and fathomless power had not altered its need for the dark. Leave the light of day to those insecure mortals who must strut for their Yuppie keepers, lest they go out of style, forever.

Years ago there were many more of our kind. The Fearless Vampire Killers have taken care of many of us and the hordes of incompetent highway rollers have done away with the remainder of the missing, those gone forever. Those who go on, go on indefinitely. Fire can destroy us, and so can the rollers if our very skeletons are crushed severely by their steel frameworks, but otherwise we are the immortals. No clothes have ever been more stylish than ours. No hearts have ever been larger or stronger. Our only weaknesses are our insatiable thirst and our flagrant style that is so obvious that we live in darkness only and rest throughout the daylight hours. Our descendants have adapted to the daylight somewhat, but we the vampires of our kind, must remain in the dark. The ancient ones, especially the males with their additional body structure, are the wisest of our kind. A strange twist of fate caused the warlock himself to remove the structure from the males born in 1964-on. Now in 1989 even the Kings born in '67 like me look to those wise ones of '63 for our glimpses of the future. All our younger brothers continued to drink the blood through 1982. The mortals who keep us were even brazen enough to call the last of us "Collectors". We are the immortal drinkers of the universe. The less of us there are the more powerful we become. We are immortal. We are beautiful. We are the kings of our kind. We are *vampires*....

Figure J37 - A dusky photo of one of the most desirable *vampires* shows a Sunfire Yellow 1967 big-block Sting Ray Convertible. This old vampire has a black interior and hood stripe and whitewall tires on aluminum wheels. This is an NCRS restoration. Is that an appropriate name for a vampire color or what! ©Bull-Doser (PD)

Friday, April 27, 1990, has arrived. It is just past 8 p.m. and the bugs in the back yard have begun their lovely buzzing. The full moon outside is so bright that some critters can see just like in daylight. The breeze is quite stiff and from the south, carrying the faintest scent from swarming engines howling toward San Marcos. The delicate aroma is being sucked through the open garage door. The Hunger is building like a Whitley Streiber novel. Slow and persistent as a spilled jar of homemade molasses, the feeling is coming over me. Wild beasts are not built to be caged like green monsters from Mars. We are the descendants of a warlike race. It is a full moon and a magical date. We must hunt-- later, when we can run at speeds suitable for vampires. We have an organized run to San Marcos tonight. Code name: LS-5. That's where five of us honor the pentagram by riding lickety-split down the freeway in a special 4-27-90 configuration: LT-5 in front (the hare); back a ways the L71, L68, and L89; and the LS-5 (Max) at the rear. Remember the vampire hunters tend to nest down there on the east side of the freeway, just north of our designated exit ramp, so back down off the howling side pipes before that point. Max has always sought the gentleman Dracula image. His mellow bellow is somewhat less likely to excite the Mustangs.

Meanwhile at Austin Police Headquarters, the night had begun to heat up just after sunset, only a couple of short hours after an exhausted Chief Carbunkle arrived at his north Austin abode....

"A.P.D.; Lieutenant Morris Minor speaking. *What* just arrived D.O.A. at Breckenridge Garage? A Prelude and an Integra? You got a couple of snotty twinkies on your agenda-- so what? Twinkies kick the bucket every day. What else is new?"

The caroner on the other end of the line was slowly losing his patience. "You better send someone over here right away to take the statements of the witnesses who found 'em or the chief's gonna dry-clean your suit with you in it!"

"Chief C.'ll have my hide if I disturb him now...."

"Get your differential in gear now, exhaust breath! The victims have all the same telltale signs as those sports cars attacked on Halloween two years ago. Call Carbunkle so he can get his investigation underway at once."

Sergeant Tuesday (no relation to Ms. Weld) arrived at Breckenridge to find one 1988 Prelude and one 1989 Integra Coupe, both white with red interiors, devoid of a drop of gas in their tanks, scrapes and scratches all over 90% of their frail little bodies, and both dead as doornails. There were two witnesses, both of whom missed getting a good look at the perpetrator or perpetrators just by moments. Both mentioned a strong smell of burning rubber at the scene, and immediately prior to their arrival, they had heard growling noises and desperate, high-pitched screams. The lady of the duo was too nauseated to move in very close to the victims, but the male witness reported a puzzling new clue when he peered at the internals. Placed on each red driver's seat were two small flags in a cross pattern! Could the attacker have done this to mark his territory? Sergeant Tuesday would certainly detail this bit of information to Chief Carbunkle as soon as he arrived at headquarters.

The black beast of the night waited at the I-35 entrance ramp at FM 2001. He could see their bright eyes approaching from the north. The four of them were running in a tight little pack. True to plan the ZR-1's bright eyes led the patrol. The dimmer eyes of his followers were close behind and he could hear their uproarious howls. As their approach closed in, the mellow bellow of the big beast rose in intensity and the big paws began clawing the ground. He fell into the pace in his appointed position at the rear of the pack. Bringing up the rear, he got a real snootful of their bloodthirsty aromas: special blends of high-octane, high-flying bat juice, the remaining vestiges of burning rubber, and the putrid stench of a zillion tiny, melted radio buttons. The pack raced on toward their juicy destination, a Perrier Tasting Convention in San Marcos. Thoughts of what sort of tasty Yuppie wheels they expected to find caused their big air filters to moan in anticipation.

A disgruntled Chief Carbunkle stomped into police headquarters. The whole place was a'buzz about the attack. An old and unsolved crime was back on the agenda.

"What makes you think the same maniac has returned to the scene, Tuesday?"

"The clues are all the same, Chief, and now we have a new element. If this really is the vampire returned to the scene, how could he have handled those crosses we found this time? Do the flags attached protect him somehow?"

"We don't even know if it is the same monster. It could be a copycat killing. The only intriguing thing is why did he wait so long? Usually copycats want that celebrity while the story is hot. All we need is more of those critters. One is bad enough. Any clues as to which direction he headed after the attack?"

"The witnesses place the attack at about 8:45 p.m., about a block west of Guadalupe, just north of The Drag. The beast probably headed toward I-35 for a quick escape. Officers have been called into the area from all directions."

The night was as still as a Studebaker with a dead battery when they saw the bright, luminous eyes approaching from the distance. Their bodies were still warm from the presence of their overindulged masters who were now stuffing their faces and swilling Perrier within the building standing next to this semi-desolate parking lot. The eyes grew brighter and the howls began to cut the still San Marcos air. A cat shrieked in the distance and the neighborhood mutts began to send the message of danger across the noisy dog network. Suddenly the once quiet parking lot was filled with the deep growls and hypnotic eyes of the vampire pack. Each one quickly selected a victim freshly filled with Exxon or Texaco and began the silent, deadly attack. A big black-as-night ZR-1 made the first strike, leaving a haughty and uppity BMW 750iL drained and shivering in its Pirellis. The same blue howler that Carbunkle had been tracking for years jumped upon the shiny silver Acura while snarling under his 24-year-old breath, "I'll show you who's a Legend!" The rest of the pack enjoyed morsels almost as tasty. A big white beast, just a year younger than the big blue howler, had a Lexus for dinner. Little brother L-89 munched the lean cuisine of a Q45, and the big bubba with 454 inches of appetite had a 320i appetizer and an in-Vigor-ating Acura entrée. The Audi V-8 quivering nearby was left alone. He had enough problems....

"Chief Carbunkle, the Georgetown and San Marcos police have been notified of the urgency of the situation and The Vampire Killer Squad is waiting for your orders."

"Where are they now, Tuesday?"

"In the briefing room, sir."

"I know where the VK squad is, you blockhead. Sometimes I think your radiator is only half full. Where are the perpetrators?"

"How did you know there are more than one of them, sir?"

"The last time we had one of these critters loose, there was only one victim at a time, but this time we already have two. Have we got a lab report yet?"

"We have a report that a couple of Hyundais were swatted off the southbound entrance ramp of I-35. That's got to be them, sir. The lab people unearthed, if you'll pardon the pun, a bit of unusual looking dirt from the Prelude's rear seat and...."

"I hate puns, and who cares if the Prelude owner was a slob?"

"But this particular dirt, sir, is not common in Central Texas, or anywhere else in this state. The lab guys report that this particular type of dirt had to have come from the St. Louis area!"

"Has the victim's family been contacted concerning this bit of evidence?"

"She has owned the Prelude since new, she's never been north of Texarkana, and she doesn't even know anybody in St. Louis."

"Let's mobilize the VK Squad."

"Men, we have a nasty job to do here and let's get on with it. There are already two victims and we expect many more before sunrise. You all know that we are dealing with beasts of the night. They especially like the full moon, too. The lab has discovered a new clue for us, a bit of dirt indigenous to the St. Louis area. We also found a pair of crossed flags within the interior of one of the victims, along with the usual shards of fiberglass and paint chips. On this particular night they seem to prefer victims of the Oriental persuasion, especially the high-bred variety. We're putting an alert through to all the local TV stations for all such potential victims to return to their garages at once and lock the doors down tight. If the beasts are headed for San Marcos, which my gut feelings tell me they are, we have alerted the Mustangs to chase them back up here, where we shall set a trap for them. I want all you men to surround the area of I-35 at Onion Creek. That's an area of light traffic and very few escape exits. My gut tells me there's some of that St. Louis dirt secreted away in a number of garages in Austin, and we're going to keep those terrorists from returning to it."

Chief Carbunkle was right about a few things, but his knowledge of the vampires and their motives is distinctly limited. It is an unpublished fact that they rarely become active without a reason. The howling blue legend was awakened a few years ago when the plan for a new Austin Convention Center was passed. This center will be at exactly the spot where Austin does not need it: a location that will surely make a horrible traffic situation even worse. Carbunkle tried to tell the mayor this, but the mayor failed to heed the call of safety and common sense over the voice of big money. Although Austin has a new mayor now, the same old political mistakes are still being made for profit. If there is a location for an airport that will surely make traffic worse, then that's the spot where it will certainly be. No matter how much unemployment Austin has, we still always seem to have more and more cars choking the streets. At a more prosperous time in Austin, Porsches multiplied in the streets. Now we have The Nineties and Japanese snotmobiles are proliferating. The vampires are being kept in a dormant state within their dark garages for longer and longer periods of time. In recent months some have been venturing into Round Rock on dark Saturday nights to be with other creatures of the night. These others are not vampires and the thirst must be contained carefully in order not to alert the police of these escapades. The Nineties have brought confusion and frustration for many of the older vampires, but many of the younger members of the pack have adapted to these Saturday night escapes.

A new development of which Carbunkle is unaware is that the vampires have a new member in their pack, a true child of The Nineties. He is the first new vampire since 1982. We call him ZR-1, named for one of his great ancestors. As far as we know the original ZR-1 is no longer alive, but his legend is well known among our kind. To bring him to life, we had to use the expertise of some Okie mariners. The special dirt on which he sleeps has to be brought secretly from Stillwater, Oklahoma, and carefully blended with soil from Kentucky. Although this newcomer will never replace our legends from The Sixties, we now at least have fresh blood to carry on the tradition after all the legends have been sealed within garages permanently.

Hearing the howls of victory over The Hunger, the overstuffed Yuppies scrambled out into the dark parking lot to a scene of carnage beyond their limited imaginations. The 750iL's tires were completely flat and its graphite-toned exterior was covered in deep scratches. The 320i and the Vigor were both upside down. The Legend looked as if its engine bay had been attacked by a jaws of life and its leather interior had been completely ripped apart by sharp claws. Not only was the Q45 as trashed as the others, but its interior and trunk were full of trash, as in tree stumps, dead leaves, softball-sized rocks and other debris! The Lexus showed the least obvious damage, with the exception of the American flag blowing in the breeze with its flagpole jammed right through the steel roof of the Lexus!

We blasted out of that parking lot with our air filters moaning and our tires squalling! The fresh taste of high octane lubed my Rochester with its sweet aroma. Above the bass rumblings of my twin voices the swirling orchestrations of the *Dracula* soundtrack cut the night air. We went rushing by the waiting herd of Mustangs without a shred of fear. We are vampires, the kings of our kind! They're just Fords. The chase began immediately, and although we could not hear it, the voice of Chief Carbunkle, now known as the best vampire hunter in Texas, was crackling on police radios all around us. We came swarming up I-35 like bats headed for the safety of the Congress Avenue Bridge. Six Mustangs were sniffing our tails while an anxious VK Squad positioned itself on I-35 just north of Buda, effectively blocking the freeway northbound lanes and both exit roads. Carbunkle and his men were toting enough crosses to make the KKK proud and enough garlic to stink up the entire Adams Extract plant.

Chief Carbunkle never counted on the black-magic cunning of the vampires. Over the odors of burning rubber and petrol, the brief scent of garlic blew downwind. Expecting a whiff of cinnamon and vanilla, my big air filter was wide open for the scent when a snort of the dreaded garlic suddenly choked my pores. Overcoming a sudden allergic reaction, I popped open the Rochester's big secondaries and leapt into the lead, ahead of a puzzled and fearless black ZR-1. Once I blocked his hasty path, I immediately signaled for a quick exit onto my home turf at the North Loop exit of Buda. The startled ZR-1 and the rest of the pack quickly followed. By the time we had completely left the freeway, all had smelled the dreaded garlic and were no longer in awe of my sudden leadership. This was my territory and I led them carefully westward on North Loop to FM 967, where a maze of narrow two-lanes would lead to Dripping Springs, Wimberley, or elsewhere. The two closest Mustangs slid out of control and rolled when we made the sudden change of direction. Unfortunately the remaining four were still with us. Leading them carefully on a pursuit into the boondocks was not at all difficult. Getting rid of them was blood simple, if distasteful: as you might imagine, Fords taste awful!

After the disgusting Ford bodies were disposed of, I parted company with the rest of the pack. We needed to hide the carcasses this time so we just shoved them behind the big pile of gravel out on RR 967 where the road construction is going on in the daylight hours. The road crew will find them in the morning, but we shall be safely garaged by then. The older members of the pack understood the plan by this time. We had friends in Dripping Springs who would shelter us until the sun goes down tomorrow. ZR-1 had had sense enough to bring a little of his special Oklahoma dirt along for emergencies and the friends could certainly supply the right stuff for the legends of the night since they harbored fugitives of The Sixties of their own. Our quiet parting belied the sadness we all felt due to the long time that might transpire before another such glorious hunt is organized. At least we added to our magnificent memories of the wonderful experiences of vampires. In my black magic imagination I can clearly picture a frustrated Chief Carbunkle pulling out what little is left of his hair....

"Sergeant Tuesday, why do you think Bruce Wayne has so much hair? He must be 43 now and half the time he looks like a damn hippie!"

"I don't know for sure, Chief, but I've heard that vampires don't age...."

Figure J38 - This Marina Blue 1967 big-block Sting Ray has a black top and hood stripe. Unlike the earlier *vampire* pictured, this one has standard exhaust and redline tires instead of whitewalls. Both cars feature the correct bolt-on aluminum wheel design available only in 1967. ©Stoskett (GNU)

C3 Corvette Performance Chart

Model	Details	Source	0-60	1/4	TS	MPG
1968	327 300-hp 4-speed	60th An	6.5	NA	NA	NA
1968	327 350-hp 4S CR 3.70 axle	CBC	7.5	15.5	130	11-15
1968	327 350-hp 4S Coupe	R&T	7.7	15.6	NA	13
1968	327 350-hp 4S CR 3.70 Posi CV	R&T	7.7	15.6	128	11-15
1968	427 400-hp Coupe	C/D	5.7	14.1	NA	NA
1968	427 435-hp 4S CR 3.55 Posi	MT	6.3	14.1	150	NA
1968	427 435-hp L89 4S CR Posi	CR	6.5	13.4	142	NA
1968	427 435-hp 4S CR 3.55 axle	1953	6.0	14.0	150	NA
1968	L-88 - 1968 body 100 lbs. more	1953	NA	NA	185	NA
1968	L-88 427 430-hp THM 3.36 Posi	R&T	6.8	14.1	151	11
1969	350 300-hp THM Coupe	R&T	8.4	16.0	NA	14
1969	427 435-hp 4S CR 4.11 Posi	MT	6.0	14.3	123	NA
1969	L-71 427 435-hp	C/D	5.3	13.8	NA	NA
1969	427 435-hp 4S CR 4.11 Posi CV	R&T	6.1	14.3	122	10

Year	Description	Source	0-60	1/4 mi	Top	MPG
1969	427 435-hp 4S CR 4.11 Posi CP	R&T	7.0	13.9	119	10
1969	L-88 427 430-hp	R&T	6.8	14.1	151	9
1969	L-88 427 430-hp THM 3.36 Posi	MT	5.6	13.6	150	NA
1969	427 ZL-1 585-hp 2900 pounds	ASC	NA	12.9	170	NA
1969	ZL-1 585-hp 3.70 axle 2908 lbs.	SSSC	NA	12.1	NA	NA
1970	LS-5 454 390-hp THM 3.08 Posi	R&T	7.0	15.0	144	9
1970	LT-1 370-hp 4S CR 4.11 Posi	AAC	5.7	14.2	122	11
1970	LT-1 370-hp 4S CR 4.11 Posi	R&T	7.2	14.4	135	13
1970	LS-7 460-hp M22 4S HD CR	SCG	NA	13.9	NA	NA
1971	L-48 270-hp THM 3.08 Posi	C/D	7.1	15.6	132	NA
1971	LT-1 330-hp 4S CR 3.70 Posi	C/D	6.0	14.6	137	NA
1971	LT-1 330-hp 4S WR 3.55 Posi	MT	5.9	14.3	135	NA
1971	LS-5 365-hp THM 3.08 3675 lbs.	C/D	5.7	14.2	141	NA
1971	LS-6 425-hp 4S CR 3.36 3478	C/D	5.3	13.8	152	NA
1971	LS-6 454 425-hp	ASC	5.5	13.9	150	NA
1972	350 200-hp 4-speed Posi	60th An	8.5	15.2	NA	NA
1972	LT-1 350 255-hp 4S CR 3.70 Posi	MT	6.9	14.3	140	NA
1972	LT-1 350 255-hp 4-speed Posi	60th An	6.8	14.1	NA	NA
1972	LS-5 454 270-hp 4-speed Posi	MT	6.9	14.3	140	NA
1972	LS-5 454 270-hp Coupe	Great	6.8	14.1	NA	NA
1973	L-48 350 190-hp THM Posi	Cars	6.8	NA	NA	14
1973	L-82 350 250-hp 4S CR 3.70 Posi	C/D	6.7	15.1	117	NA
1973	L-82 350 250-hp 4S CR 3.70 CP	R&T	7.2	15.5	124	15
1973	LS-4 454 275-hp 4S CR 3.55 Posi	C/D	6.4	14.6	NA	NA
1973	LS-4 454 275-hp THM 3.08 Posi	C/D	6.4	14.7	NA	NA
1973	LS-4 454 275-hp THM 3.08 Posi	MT	6.8	14.1	132	NA
1974	L-82 350 250-hp 4SM 3.70 Posi	MT	7.5	15.8	125	14-15
1974	L-82 350 250-hp 4S 3.70 Posi	CBC	7.5	16.0	124	12-15
1974	L-82 350 250-hp 4S 3.70 Posi	R&T	7.4	15.8	124	14
1975	L-48 350 165-hp THM 2.73 Posi	MT	9.6	16.4	123	NA
1975	L-48 350 165-hp THM 2.73 CP	C/D	7.7	16.1	129	12-15
1975	L-82 350 205-hp 4-speed manual	C/D	7.7	16.1	NA	NA

1976	L-82 350 210-hp 4SM 3.55 Posi	R&T	8.1	16.5	132	14
1976	L-48 350 180-hp 4-speed manual	60th An	6.8	15.4	NA	NA
1976	L-48 350 180-hp 4SM CR 3.36	C/D	6.8	15.4	121	NA
1976	L-82 350 210-hp 4-speed manual	60th An	6.8	15.3	NA	NA
1976	L-82 350 210-hp THM 3.70 axle	C/D	6.8	15.3	121	NA
1976	L-82 350 210-hp THM 3.36 axle	C/D	7.1	15.3	124	NA
1977	L-82 350 210-hp THM 3.55 Posi	MT	8.8	16.6	132	17
1977	L-82 350 210-hp 4S 3.70 axle	CBC	7.0	15.5	NA	13-16
1977	350 210-hp 4S WR 3.70 Posi	R&T	6.8	15.5	132	15
1978	L-48 350 185-hp THM 3.08 Posi	C/D	7.8	16.1	123	15
1978	L-82 350 220-hp 4S WR 3.70 Posi	R&T	6.5	15.2	132	15
1979	L-82 350 220-hp 4S CR 3.70 Posi	MT	7.3	15.7	120	16
1979	L-82 350 220-hp THM 3.55 Posi.	R&T	6.6	15.6	130	12
1979	L-82 350 220-hp 4-speed manual	60th An	6.6	15.6	NA	NA
1979	L-82 350 220-hp 3.55 Positraction	R&T	6.6	15.3	127	NA
1980	350 190-hp THM	Muscle	8.1	16.2	NA	NA
1980	350 190-hp 4S manual 3.07 Posi	C/D	7.6	15.9	123	14
1980	L-82 350 230-hp THM	NA*	7.4	15.4	NA	NA
1981	L-81 350 190-hp 4-speed manual	60th An	8.1	NA	NA	NA
1981	L-81 350 190-hp four-speed	R&T	9.2	17.0	NA	NA
1981	L-81 350 190-hp 4SM 2.72 Posi	MT	7.3	15.5	NA	15-21
1982	L-83 200-hp 4S auto 2.87 axle	C/D	8.1	15.9	125	14
1982	L-83 200-hp 4S auto. 2.87 axle	R&T	7.9	16.1	125	21

C3 Corvette Performance Chart Notes:

Quarter-mile and 0-60 mph times are in seconds. CV = Convertible. THM = Turbo Hydra-Matic. TS = top speed in mph. MPG = miles per gallon, rounded to a whole number. The March 1969 issue of *R&T* contained the test of an L-71 Convertible that has been verified by other sources. The performance listings of the L-71 Coupe and L-88 by *R&T* have not been verified as legitimate. These were either quoted in *R&T* as being from *Car Life* or the quoted source is incorrect.

1953 = 1953 to the Present & The Classic Corvette. 60th An = Corvette: 60th Anniversary. AAC = Corvette: An American Classic. ASC = Corvette: America's Sports Car. Great = Corvette: The Great

American Sports Car. MT = *Motor Trend.* Muscle = *Muscle Cars* by Phil Hall. *NA** = My Quarter Mile.com website (magazine unspecified). *R&T* = *Road & Track.* SSSC = *America's Star-Spangled Sports Car.*

Bargains of the Current Era

There are two particular series of Corvettes that could be considered the top collector car bargains of this entire book. I am talking about two model groups that will provide endless classic satisfaction for an exceptionally low price. This is pointedly true when you factor in the easy availability of parts and service for these models anywhere in the USA. The selections I am speaking of are the 1976-82 Corvette T-top Coupes and the 1986-90 Corvette Convertibles. Even more common, and cheaper than both, are the 1984-90 targa coupes. These models are condemned to always remain the stepchildren of the collectible Corvette market. The rare, expensive Z07 racing package was discontinued after 1975. The later Makos were all coupes with removable T-tops. The main body consideration was the increased rear glass area of the later version. The enormous total of 302,981 of these were constructed in St. Louis and Bowling Green. In contrast, they built only 42,726 of the early C4 Convertibles. So why are their values so close? The answer is excruciatingly simple: the older models offer the classic Mako style in much less complex machinery. Neither type offers the level of performance or style of their older brothers or younger sisters, yet they are still Corvettes. They will always be examples of America's Sports Car.

Figure J39 - Here is a final look at the same 1978 Pace Car pictured earlier. This example has the desirable L-82 optional engine. Indiscernible in this photo are the special red-lined wheels indigenous to the Pace Car model. ©Greg Gjerdingen, Willmar, USA (CC)

Right now in 2016 a nice example of most any little classic foreign topless sports car will cost you at least as much as these two types of Corvette. As I am sure you are aware, the parts scavenger hunt will be much more extensive for the foreign models. Even your small-town Chevy dealer knows what to do with an OHV V-8 and there are Corvette specialty shops and suppliers literally out the wazoo! When you have completed your restoration to your personal satisfaction level, you have a vehicle with most of the modern amenities. Overheating big-blocks and high-compression engines that ping themselves to death on modern fuel have already joined the Trailer Queen Parade. Except for its sheer rarity on the street, you can drive one of these anywhere you want. The AC and cruise control work effectively. The tops seal out wind and water as they should. You can drive as fast as you dare on the freeway and sail around corners with impunity. Yes, all of these models are particularly simpatico with smooth roads. That's usually what happens when you add stiff suspension and wide tires. These models all have the 350 V-8 producing between 180 and 245 net horsepower. The most distinctive variance in these engines is the induction system. The 1976-80 models are the last Corvettes produced with a single, regular four-barrel carburetor. The 1981 model added primitive computer control to the carb. The 1982 and '84 models had the pseudo-fuel-injection Chevy called Cross-Fire Injection. The 1985-90 models have what we now consider normal, digital fuel injection. All models will run on low-lead fuel, but the latest ethanol additives may present a few maintenance problems. All have expensive catalytic converters that may need to be replaced to pass state inspections in some areas. (The 1990 limitation of this book gives these cars the *antique* denotation. Otherwise, they would all have to pass emission inspections in most states.) Since there are no trunks in this group, luggage capacity and access leaves a bit to be desired. The exception will be the 1982 Collector Edition with its hatchback, and of course the 1984-90 Coupes offer the same convenience.

Figure J40 - This 1982 Corvette in white is practically identical in appearance to its 1980-81 brothers. The elongated *Crossfire Injection* fender emblem gives it away. For the first time since 1955, every stinking one of this model year's Corvettes had an automatic transmission. At least it was a new four-speed automatic! ©Bull-Doser (PD)

One of the central considerations for these two bargain types should be the removable roof style. The separate T-tops of the earlier models offer easy security with their internal clamps. You can even add aftermarket T-top locks that will stop any potential thief of either the car or the tops themselves. The hardtop option of the later convertibles will offer the same level of security, except it requires two people to lift off or replace the top in the garage. The later soft top is of course totally convenient to use at the expense of some theft security and wind noise at speed. Of course it does not hold in air conditioned air in 100-degree temperatures very well, either. The original owner paid a $5000 price for the topless model over the Coupe and the removable hardtop cost an additional $2000. Eventually these choices will bring a premium price. Will that ever top the value of a late-model Mako, that is the question. There are soft top variants available in the aftermarket to replace the heavy, bulky standard T-tops, and of course you can have optional see-through tops on the fastback Makos. The twin soft tops offer no security protection, but they are incredibly handy for a rain emergency when the situation allows you to leave the standard tops back at the house. The glass tops are elegant and certainly interesting, but they may be a bit troublesome. For starters, these are heavy and a bit cumbersome to handle when removing or placing within the rear compartment. Remember that only the '82 Collector Edition has an opening hatchback. Of course the glass can crack in a handling mishap, too.

Let's face it, the 1976 model is probably the most boring Corvette ever produced. The hot ticket, if we can use that phrase without laughing, would be an L-82 with the M21 close-ratio four-speed, FE7 Gymkhana suspension, and air conditioning. The white interior, offered with many exterior colors in '76, is probably somewhat rare. The '77 model had slightly more power and several previous options were made standard. Four new options were offered for the first time in 1977: an 8-track tape player, cruise control with Turbo Hydra-Matic only, Sport Mirrors, and a luggage rack designed to carry the T-tops.

Figure J41 - The front view of the 1982 Collector Edition shows the dark bronze to metallic beige decals on the hood and sides. ©Greg Gjerdingen, Willmar, USA (CC)

Aside from the Pace Car and Silver Anniversary, the 1978 model offered a number of changes and improvements in comfort, convenience and drivability. The aforementioned specials will always command higher prices than several year models on either side, especially the Pace Car. This is the only exception, current price-wise, to the rest of the cars in this 1976-90 group. The Corvette bargains included in this group, and in this article, can usually be purchased for $30,000 or less, even the really nice ones. A nice Pace Car with L-82 and four-speed currently will cost you about $30,000 minimum, and in some cases much more. The '78 model offered the now kitschy CB radio option and aluminum wheels became very popular. Glass roof panels were first offered in 1978, but their popularity had not caught on yet, making one of the less than 1000 cars built with this option in 1978 desirable. A glove box and larger gas tank brought more cruising convenience. The biggest advantage of the '78's is probably the increased luggage space underneath the fastback rear window. The '79 model has the distinction of being the last dead-conventional model with a long option sheet containing no computerized carburetors or transmissions or restrictions on engine and transmission combos. The '78 Pace Car's modern seat design was made standard on all models in '79 and the Pace Car's front air dam and rear spoiler were made optional. The Corvette finally got a cassette deck option and glass roof panels became very popular.

The 1980 model with its standard AC and better aerodynamics was an improved car, and one of my personal favorites, but with its 85-mph speedo and engine/transmission restrictions, most fans do not consider it a star. I have always liked the fact that it lost about 250 pounds and its ground effects were much better integrated than those of the '79. The new factory and painting process began in 1981, offering a bit of distinction, and it would be the last manual four-speed Corvette. The new Computer Command Control (CCC) unit took responsibility for the engine's ignition timing and fuel mixture. New digital ETR radios with easy, precise tuning, were a new option in 1981. The Collector Edition of 1982 was a special beauty for sure. It was the first factory Corvette to bust the $20,000 base retail price barrier, yet an average condition example still comes in well under $30,000 today to be included within this bargain group. Its more mundane pals gave you the four-speed automatic and Cross-Fire Injection without the hatchback luggage compartment, and you can buy the best one of these in town today for far less than $30,000. The standard car could be ordered with the unusual interior colors of Silver Gray or Silver Green. Although the former was available in '81 and '82 with numerous exterior choices, the Silver Green was unique to the 1982 model, and only with the matching Silver Green exterior color. The beauty of the bunch, of course, is the Collector Edition's multi-toned exterior with matching leather interior in Silver Beige.

Figure J42 - The rear view shows the large hatchback rear window, smooth Kamm tail, and bronze-tinted acrylic T-top panels of the same 1982 Collector Edition. Note the special wheels in both photos. ©Greg Gjerdingen, Willmar, USA (CC)

After a decade lost in the wilderness, the true convertible returned in 1986, bringing aluminum heads and a new anti-lock braking system with it. Only manual soft tops were offered initially on the Convertible's return. The carryover year of 1987 offered the new popular Z52 suspension and otherwise minimal change. Better looking wheels and other accoutrements arrived in 1988. A footnote hardly worth mentioning is the 35th Anniversary Coupe offered in 1988. There were 2050 of these built at an option price of $4795. That exorbitant price added a tinted roof and a white leather interior, both of which were attractive additions, but the other details included worthless doodads and ugly white wheels. You will pay $4-5000 more for a 35th Anniversary today, a total price even higher than that of a nice '88 Convertible. This reflects a recent spike in the auction price of the 35th Anniversary, an interesting footnote if you are looking for future value accumulation, or if like me, you're just a sucker for a white interior. In contrast, all 1989 models had the same beautiful twelve-slot wheels that had been optional in '88, without the white paint. The previously popular Z52 suspension option was dropped in 1989. and a removable hardtop returned to the option list. This $267 option in 1975 returned at $1995 in 1989! The recalcitrant 4+3 manual transmission was finally replaced with a nice six-speed. This is probably the best reason to buy an '89. The 1990 model received an improved dash layout with a digital speedometer and new analog gauges. Some may like the new swoopy look of the driver's side dash, but others may find it less coherent with the overall style of the original C4 body. The Corvette would lose some of its crisp front and rear styling, and a new, less attractive wheel design would be introduced in 1991. This final statement is only my opinion, of course. You may actually prefer the rounded styling, fake side vents, and new wheel design.

Yuppies in the Wind Tunnel

Figure J43 - This 1986 Corvette Convertible is painted the same yellow as the official Pace Car and the dealer has affixed the decals to the doors. This car has a black top and interior. The polished aluminum wheels are aftermarket. ©Sicnag (CC)

This section covers the 1984-90 Coupes and Convertibles. After the fourteen-year history of the Stingray, the 1984 C4 Corvette enjoyed a long-awaited and much ballyhooed introduction early in 1983. There has never been a new car introduction quite like it. The new model, in classic Corvette tradition, would be introduced with exactly the same drivetrain as the 1982 Stingray, a 205-hp 350 with Cross-Fire Injection and a four-speed automatic transmission. A manual four-speed with three computer-controlled overdrive gears would become available toward the end of the very long production year. The total for that long period would become the second-largest Corvette production year, probably for all time, bested only by 1979. The C4 brought countless changes, large and small, to the venerable Corvette, but we are not going to regurgitate them all here, one more time. The dash was electronic, the seats were improved, the chassis was tighter, the wheels wider and the suspension stiffer, at least on the popular Z-51 sport suspension model. The engine would receive genuine fuel injection with an upgrade to 230 net horsepower in '85 and manual transmissions would be available throughout the production year, making them much more common on 1985 cars than 84's.

The story relevant to this book concerning these models is the new top design. The Convertible would return in 1986, leaving the '84 and '85 models in a special position as Coupes only. The new removable roof design was a copy of the legendary Porsche Targa, with a single, wide, lightweight panel that could be stored in the luggage area behind the seats. The standard panel was body colored, as standard on previous Corvette Coupes. A transparent plastic panel could be substituted for the opaque one for about $600. From the 1987 model onward, the transparent roof panel option could be either blue or bronze, and the buyer could order both a body-colored and a see-through panel for about $900.

There are several key differences between the removable coupe panels of the older Stingray and the newer C4. The optional transparent T-top panels were made of glass, scratch resistant and heavy, yet breakable if you accidentally dropped one. The plastic single panels of the C4 Coupes were large and cumbersome, but they would certainly have been much less practical if made of the heavier glass material of the earlier twin models. I have never understood precisely why, but all the single top panels of all the C4 Coupes require a special wrench to fasten and unfasten the top to the windshield header. Perhaps it is a well thought out anti-theft concept, since the earlier Stingray T-tops were somewhat at risk, particularly when the car was parked with the windows down. If you are considering the purchase of one of these 1984-85 Corvette *bargains of the century,* be aware that unlike the engineering of the previous Stingray T-top Coupes, the removal of the single roof panel of a C4 Corvette affects its structural rigidity. The removal of the T-tops of a '68-'82 Coupe will influence the chassis rigidity to a small degree, but this effect is much increased with the removal of the top panel of a C4 Coupe. Yes, it is true that the removal of the rear window of a 1968-72 Coupe will decrease the rigidity and increase the squeaks and rattles of the chassis and body, but who cares? The wind rush and drivetrain roar of a pseudo-convertible with large tires and a big engine quickly overpower the annoying noises at speed! If you are considering the purchase of the 1984 or 1985 C4 Coupe due to the incredible bargain prices of today, you may wish to keep this discussion in mind.

Let's recap one of my favorite subjects of this book. The 1976-81 T-tops are a pain in the butt to remove and secure in the rear luggage compartment, not to mention retrieving them out for a sudden rain shower. The single top panel of the 1984-85 Coupe, or the 1986-90 Coupe, aside from the special tool required, commonly stored in the glove compartment, is more convenient to store behind the seats. This is particularly true when comparing the 1978-81 Stingray models with the optional, very heavy, and somewhat delicate, glass roof panels to the lighter single panel of see-through tinted plastic on the C4 Coupes. Keep in mind two things. The transparent T-top panels are the heaviest and transparent single panels are the lightest. The removable opaque tops of all models lie between these two extremes in weight and handling ease.

Corvettes Take Us to 1990

Figure J44 - Notice that the wheel design on this black 1987 Convertible is the same as that of the 1984-86 models. The more stylish design would premier in 1988. ©Greg Gjerdingen, Willmar, USA (CC)

One of the biggest advantages to selecting an early C4 is the modernity of the design. These models were carefully created from wind tunnel tests to maximize fuel mileage even with a large engine and huge tires. Not only will these cars still run just fine on today's pump gas, but their efficiency at cruising speeds is quite phenomenal. Of course you will never reach the test mileage claims of some sources because the cars were tested with roof panels attached. You will pay a mileage penalty with the roof removed from either the Coupe or Convertible, but the resulting fuel cost will be modest compared to that of any C2 or C3. The one adjustment you make for any car in this book, even the 1984-90 C4, is to periodically add a little Sta-Bil fuel stabilizer to the tank for protection from our modern fuel with ethanol content. That stuff tends to rot certain rubber components and draws moisture to places it does not belong. You can buy the latest high-priced Sta-Bil product designed specifically for this purpose, but the original formula we have been putting in our boats and lawn mowers for winter storage will work just fine.

Which model among the early C4's should you choose? Let's begin by repeating the mantra of this book: the Convertible is practically always more desirable as a collectible and so is the manual transmission. This eliminates the majority of the 1984 models and raises the bar for the 1986-onward group. Since the '89 model is the first with the manual six-speed instead of the annoying 4+3, the 1989-90 models are automatically pushed up the chart. Although it was the first C4, the high-production 1984 Coupe with four-speed automatic will probably remain the very cheapest way to enter the Corvette universe for many years to come. The '85 model offers a little softer Z51 suspension and more horsepower from its electronic fuel injection. More 4+3's were built in 1985, too.

Figure J45 - **White 1988 Corvette Convertible.** ©Greg Gjerdingen, Willmar, USA (CC)

The 1986 model brought the Convertible back into production, although later in the production year so there are not that many of these out there. Do not be seduced by any sort of *Pace Car Replica* BS. All the '86 Convertibles came with the door decals in the trunk, even those not painted yellow. All the 1986 Convertibles were considered Pace Cars. Speaking of colors, many 84-87 Coupes had two-tone paint. In general, a solid red, black, white, or blue Corvette is nearly always more desirable, even in these two-tone model years. The only exception in the early C4's is the 1988 35th Anniversary Coupe in white and black with its special white leather interior. It is the only Corvette for many years either before or after 1988 to offer a white interior. The 1987 models are somewhat undistinguished: go for the 4+3 Convertible. More attractive wheels arrived in '88 and the six-speed graced the '89 model with a smile from the owners. The '90 model would be the last with the original sharp-lined styling of the early C4 and the first with the new curved dash layout with more analog instruments.

At the time of this publication, these cars generally cost more as the model years progress. With the relentless obsession most of us have for topless cars with manual transmissions and increasingly more power, I do not foresee this situation changing. If I was in the market to purchase a new toy, I would probably choose an early C4 Convertible over any other car in this entire book. Make mine a white 1989 Convertible with black top and interior and six-speed. I prefer the earlier interior and exterior styling and I have a thing for the twelve-slot wheels. The surprising part is that I would have ordered this very car new from a dealer with the most minimal options of any model in Corvette history. All the extra-cost equipment this model needs to be perfect are the Bose stereo and luggage rack. Varrrrroooom!!

Figure J46 - 1989 Corvette Convertible in Triple Black, as the young whippersnappers like to say. This has always been my favorite C4 due to the combination of this wheel design with the original angular C4 dashboard style and Kamm tail. ©Sicnag (CC)

C4 Corvette Engine Chart

O. C.	Years	Models	C. I..	Bore/Stroke	HP	Induction	Shift
L83	1984	Coupe	350	4.00 x 3.48	205	C-F I	4SA
L98	1985-86	CP / CV	350	4.00 x 3.48	230	TPI	4SA/4+3
L98	1986	CP / CV	350	4.00 x 3.48	235	TPI	4SA/4+3
L98	1987-88	CP / CV	350	4.00 x 3.48	240	TPI	4SA/4+3
L98	1988	Coupe	350	4.00 x 3.48	245	TPI	4SA/4+3
L98	1989-91	CP / CV	350	4.00 x 3.48	240	TPI	4SA/6SM
L98	1989-91	Coupe	350	4.00 x 3.48	245	TPI	4SA/6SM
L98	1990-91	Coupe	350	4.00 x 3.48	250	TPI	4SA/6SM
LT1	1992-95	CP / CV	350	4.00 x 3.48	300	TPI	4SA/6SM
LT1	1996	CP / CV	350	4.00 x 3.48	300	TPI	4SA
LT5	1990-92	ZR1	350	4.00 x 3.48	375	TPI	6SM
LT5	1993-95	ZR1	350	4.00 x 3.48	405	TPI	6SM
LT4	1996	CP / CV	350	4.00 x 3.48	330	TPI	6SM

C4 Corvette Engine Chart Notes:
The 1984 model had Cross-Fire Injection. All other years had electronic fuel injection. The 235-hp L98 of 1986 had aluminum heads and was not actually an option, but standard equipment in late-production coupes and all convertibles. The 245-hp L98 of 1988-89 had louder exhaust and 3.07 differential and was available only on coupes. The same situation applies to the 1990-91 models with five additional horsepower. Some 250-hp coupes had 3.33 axles instead of 3.07. All ZR-1 LT5 engines had 32 valves and were built by Mercury Marine in Stillwater, OK. C-F I = Cross-Fire Injection. TPI = Tuned Port Injection.

C4 Corvette Performance Chart

Model	Details	Source	0-60	1/4	TS	MPG
1984	L-83 350 205-hp 4SA Z51 3.31	MT	7.0	15.4	144	16-28
1984	L-83 350 205-hp 4SA Z51 3.31	CBC	7.0	15.5	140	16-20
1984	L-83 350 205-hp 4SA 3.07 Posi	C/D	6.7	15.1	142	14
1984	350 205-hp 4S auto 3.31 Posi Z51	C/D	6.7	15.2	138	16
1984	L-83 350 205-hp 4SA 3.31 Z51	R&T	7.1	15.5	137	18
1984	L-83 350 205-hp 4+3 3.07 Z51	R&T	7.1	15.6	136	15
1984	L-83 350 205-hp THM 2.87 Posi	R&T	7.0	15.3	139	16
1985	L98 350 230-hp 4S Automatic	1953	6.0	14.0	150	NA
1985	L98 350 230-hp 4SA 3.07 Posi	C/D	5.7	14.1	150	16
1985	L98 350 230-hp 4+3 Z51 3.07 Posi	C/D	6.0	14.4	150	16
1986	350 230-hp 4+3 3.07 Posi CV	C/D	6.0	14.5	144	14
1986	350 230-hp 4+3 3.07 Posi Coupe	R&T	5.8	14.4	154	16-19
1986	350 230-hp 4+3 Z51 3.07 Posi CP	R&T	5.8	14.4	154	19
1987	350 240-hp 4+3 manual 3.07 axle	CBC	6.5	15.0	150	16-18
1987	350 240-hp 4+3 Convertible	MT	6.3	15.1	NA	NA
1987	350 240-hp Convertible	R&T	6.3	14.8	133	17
1988	350 240-hp 4-speed automatic	C/D	5.6	14.3	NA	NA
1988	350 245-hp 4+3 3.07 Z51 Coupe	C/D	6.0	14.2	152	17
1988	350 245-hp 4+3 3.07 Z51 Coupe	R&T	6.0	14.6	158	18
1988	350 245-hp 4+3 Z52 3.07 Posi CV	R&T	6.0	14.6	158	19
1989	L98 350 245-hp 6-speed manual	60th An	5.4	NA	NA	NA
1989	L98 350 245-hp 6SM 3.33 CV	R&T	6.6	14.8	155	20

Year	Model	Source	0-60	1/4 mi	Top	MPG
1990	L98 350 245-hp 6S manual CV	R&T	6.3	14.8	NA	NA
1990	L98 350 245-hp 4S THM Coupe	R&T	6.2	14.7	NA	NA
1990	L98 350 250-hp 6-speed manual	MT	5.7	14.3	NA	NA
1990	LT5 375-hp 6SM 3.54 axle ZR-1	R&T	4.9	13.4	172	19
1990	LT5 375-hp 6SM ZR-1	C/D	4.9	13.4	171	16
1990	LT5 375-hp 6SM ZR-1	C/D	4.6	12.9	176	14
1990	LT5 375-hp 6SM 3.45 axle ZR-1	World	4.3	12.8	NA	NA
1991	L98 245-hp 3.45 axle Coupe	R&T	6.2	14.8	NA	18
1991	L98 245-hp Convertible	NA*	5.6	14.1	NA	NA
1991	L98 245-hp Coupe	NA*	5.3	13.9	NA	NA
1992	LT-1 350 300-hp 4SA	Great	5.3	13.9	NA	NA
1992	LT-1 350 300-hp 6-speed manual	Great	4.9	13.7	NA	NA
1992	LT-1 350 300-hp 6-speed manual	MT	5.7	14.1	NA	NA
1992	LT-1 350 300-hp	C/D	5.1	NA	161	NA
1992	LT5 350 375-hp ZR-1	C/D	4.7	NA	179	NA
1992	LT5 350 375-hp ZR-1	NA*	5.6	13.9	NA	NA
1992	LT5 350 375-hp ZR-1	Great	4.3	12.9	NA	NA
1993	LT1 350 300-hp 6-speed	MT	5.6	14.0	NA	NA
1993	LT1 350 300-hp	NA*	5.3	13.9	NA	17-25
1993	LT5 350 405-hp 6SM ZR-1	MT	4.9	13.1	NA	NA
1993	LT5 350 405-hp 6SM ZR-1	NA*	5.2	13.6	NA	NA
1994	LT1 350 300-hp 6-speed manual	R&T	5.7	14.1	NA	NA
1994	LT1 350 300-hp automatic	NA*	5.5	14.1	NA	NA
1994	LT5 405-hp 6-speed manual ZR-1	MT	5.2	13.6	NA	NA
1994	LT5 405-hp 6-speed manual ZR-1	NA*	4.7	13.1	NA	NA
1995	LT1 350 300-hp	NA*	5.2	13.7	NA	NA
1995	LT5 405-hp 6-speed manual ZR-1	NA*	4.9	13.1	NA	NA
1996	LT1 350 300-hp 6-speed manual	C/D	5.1	13.7	NA	NA
1996	LT1 Grand Sport	NA*	4.7	13.3	NA	NA
1996	LT1 Collector Edition	NA*	4.9	13.3	NA	NA

C4 Corvette Performance Chart Notes:

All C4 ZR-1's were hatchbacks with removable roof panels. Quarter-mile and 0-60 mph times are in seconds. TS = top speed in mph. MPG = miles per gallon, rounded to a whole number. Numerous magazines tested the 1990 ZR-1 pre-production model, which used a 3.54 axle ratio. Production models changed to a 3.45 axle. The *R&T* test was of a pre-production 3.54. I am uncertain which axle the *Car and Driver* test cars had, but I suspect the earlier car had the 3.54 and the later one the 3.45. The DOHC LT5 was designed by Lotus and built by Mercury Marine.

1953 = 1953 to the Present & The Classic Corvette. *60th Ann* = Corvette: 60th Anniversary. *CBC* = The Complete Book of Corvette. *C/D* = Car and Driver. *Great* = Corvette: The Great American Sports Car. *MT* = Motor Trend. *NA** = My Quarter Mile.com website (magazine unspecified). *R&T* = Road & Track. *World* = Corvette World.

Figure J47 - How about a last look at a Silver Pearl 1966 Sting Ray 427 Convertible with side pipes, aluminum wheels and the gold line tires available as an option only in 1966? ©Nakhon 100 (CC)

Selected 1953-90 Corvette Ratings Chart

Years	Model	Collect	Drive	Desire
1953	Corvette Roadster	A	D	A
1954 - 55	Corvette Blue Flame Six Roadster	A	D	B
1955	Corvette V-8 Roadster	A	D	A
1956 - 62	Corvette Convertible	B	C	B
1963-64	Sting Ray Convertible	B	B	B
1965-67	Sting Ray Convertible 327	A	B	A
1965-67	Sting Ray Convertible 396 & 427	A	C	A
1968 - 69	Stingray Coupe & Convertible	A	C	B
1970 - 72	Stingray Coupe & Convertible	A	C	B
1973 - 1977	Stingray Coupe 350	C	B	C
1973 - 75	Stingray Convertible 350	B	B	B
1973 - 74	Stingray Convertible 454	A	B	B
1978 - 79	Stingray Coupe	C	A	C
1980 - 82	Stingray Coupe	C	A	C
1982	Stingray Collector Edition	A	B	A
1984 - 1990	Corvette Coupe	D	A	C
1986 - 90	Corvette Convertible	B	A	B

Models Ratings Chart Definitions:

Years: In most cases, the years listed include the total production years for a particular model series. Some model years within a series may be considerably more desirable than other years.

Models: In some cases many variations are included in this category and in others the models included are very homogeneous. This is generally self explanatory.

Collectibility: This is what most of you want to know, the bottom line on how likely the model or series is likely to climb in value over the coming years.

Drivability: This is an indicator of how adaptable the machine can be to drive for transportation or pleasure in the modern world, considering collector value, parts availability, fuel quality, comfort, performance and miscellaneous other factors.

Desirability: This defines the nostalgic, emotional wow factor, without regard for collector values or everyday usage.

General: No machine is given a failing grade. If it made it into a rating chart, at least a few hobbyists find that model interesting.

The Future May be Ludicrous and Ridiculous.. but It Still Might be Fun!

Figure J48 - 2013 Stingray 427 Convertible ($76,900) with special 60th Anniversary ($1075) and graphics ($850) packages. It also has the 4LT/1SC Equipment Group ($9500), the Carbon Fiber Package ($2995), and obviously not shown from this angle, Cyber Gray Metallic Headlamp Surrounds ($590), required with the 60th Anniversary Package. Of course there could be even more options not apparent from this Chevrolet Media photo. We know this car cost at least $91,910. The paint is Arctic White, the interior is Blue Diamond leather, the power convertible top is blue, and the stripes are Pearl Silver Blue. Chevrolet produced a total of 2552 427 Convertibles in their single year of availability. Only 1181 were painted Arctic White. Certainly less than 1000 looked precisely like this. ©2013 Chevrolet Corvette Media Pages

"What a day for a daydream, What a day for a daydreamin' boy
And I'm lost in a daydream, Dreamin' 'bout my bundle of joy
It's starrin' me and my sweet dream. 'Cause she's the one that makes me feel this way...."

Excerpts from the lyrics to *Daydream* by The Lovin' Spoonful (John Sebastian, 1966)

Corvettes Take Us to 1990

Appendix

Glossary

Bertone - The Italian design and construction firm that has designed and built the bodies of the Fiat 850 Spider featured in this book and most of the Lamborghinis, practically all of which have been closed models.

Bosch - A German producer of spark plugs and other automotive components that is relevant to the cars featured in this book for its fuel injection systems. Many European car makers eventually adopted Bosch Jetronic fuel injection to pass U.S. emissions regulations.

Cabriolet - This is the name utilized by several German brands to denote what Americans call a convertible. A Cabriolet has a more highly developed convertible top design, beyond that of a simple roadster.

Convertible - To some extent or another, all the cars covered in this book could be loosely referred to as *convertibles*, at least in an open car sense of the word. More specifically, all American cars with soft tops that fold down, but are permanently attached to the body, are absolutely referred to as convertibles.

DOHC - Double Overhead Cam is the most exotic and highest performing of the engine designs covered in this book. This system involves the opening and closing of the valves on each cylinder bank with separate cams. An inline DOHC engine has two cams and a DOHC V-design has four cams.

Drop Head Coupe - This is the term used by English companies to define a convertible or cabriolet model, a more luxurious, convenient top design than that of a roadster.

Erector Set Top - Most English cars of the 1955-65 period employed a convertible top design in which the top frame (bows) were carried in the trunk along with the vinyl top fabric as a separate item. The frame had to be manually erected and then the fabric fastened to the frame. In some cases, the frame, but not the fabric, was permanently attached to the car body. The slang term derives from the toy Erector Sets we played with as young boys.

Flat Four - This engine design has four cylinders laid 180 degrees apart with a pair on each side. This opposed four-cylinder engine design was an OHV type used in only four German models covered in this book: VW Karmann Ghia and Porsche's 356, 912, and 914.

Flat Six - This opposed engine design was applied to only three models in this book: the Porsche 911, Porsche 914/6, and the Chevrolet Corvair. The Porsche models were normally aspirated SOHC designs. Most of the Corvair models utilized a basic OHV design of the flat six, but the hottest models were turbocharged.

Inline-4 - This is far the most common engine design among the small, affordable sports cars in this book. These include OHV, SOHC, and DOHC types.

Inline-6 - This is the engine design commonly used in all the early Jaguars, Austin-Healey 3000, MG C, later Triumph TR's, Mercedes SL's, and many others. Jaguar employed a DOHC design, Mercedes used an SOHC type, and the more primitive English models utilized straightforward OHV applications.

Intermeccanica - This is probably the Italian car manufacturer least known to Americans. The company's products have always featured Italian coach building expertise with reliable, cost-effective V-8 powertrains.

Motorbooks International - The original U.S. publisher and/or distributor of practically all the enthusiast car books that have been available in the USA during recent decades. Titles have either been published in Osceola, Wisconsin, directly or elsewhere (mostly England) and distributed in the USA. MBI was sold to The Quarto Group (founded in London in 1976) in 2004. The majority of the books on this author's shelves have been out of print for decades, providing the impetus for the creation of *Daydreams in the Wind*. The details of these many enthusiast automobiles need to be available for generations to come.

NCRS - National Corvette Restorers Society. The cars that can meet the high NCRS standards for Corvette originality are some of the most desirable of all Corvettes.

Pininfarina - The Italian body constructor that has built many of the legendary touring Ferraris, as well as the Fiat 124 Spider, Fiat Dino Spider, several Alfa Spiders, and even the Cadillac Allante of 1986-93.

Phaeton - This term is usually applied to a large four-seat convertible of particularly elegant trim and specifications. The phaeton model may not be as sporty as the roadster of the same series, but it is usually quite rare and collectible. The term *convertible* is applied loosely here, as most phaetons have more in common with roadsters than true convertibles. The tops are attached, but there are usually no side windows in the doors.

Powerglide - The General Motors two-speed automatic transmission that this author considers woefully inadequate as an application in any sporting vehicle. Two gear speeds are simply not enough. This automatic is referred to as a *Powerslide* due to the manner in which the engine must spin up to a high rpm level and then suddenly sacrifice engine speed and vehicle momentum when the transmission shifts into the distant high gear.

Prince of Darkness - This is a derogatory label that was long ago placed on the Lucas electrical systems of Sixties British roadsters. The author did not coin this phrase. In their defense, the English companies had been bombed nearly out of existence by Germany during World War II. They were doing good to be resurrected as well as they were in the postwar period.

Roadster - This is probably the most contentious descriptive word in this book. The term originally referred to an open sports car with a completely removable soft top and completely removable side curtains made of clear vinyl or rigid plexiglass in a frame that was also removable. In more recent years, the term has been loosely applied to all sorts of sports cars with removable tops. For example, all the Jaguar E-Type Roadsters are actually genuine convertibles.

Scaglietti - The Italian auto body construction firm that has built many legendary Ferrari models, particularly the racy Berlinettas. These bodies have usually been more delicate and susceptible to rust and corrosion than those built as touring models by Pininfarina.

SOHC - The Single Overhead Cam is the simplest and cheapest step up from an overhead valve engine design, allowing a little more horsepower to be extracted at slightly higher engine revolutions. An inline engine has one cam and a V-type engine has two. Each cam both opens and closes the valves.

Solex Carburetor - This French brand of carburetor was used on some models built by Alfa Romeo, Porsche, and Volkswagen. Mikuni in Japan licensed the Solex design for use on both cars and motorcycles.

Spider - This is the common term applied to any Italian, two-seater convertible.

Spyder - Strangely enough, there is no letter "y" in the Italian alphabet, but this spelling has been officially applied to many models of Italian open sports cars.

Stromberg Carburetor - Stromberg is the brand name often applied to carburetors produced by Zenith. Many English cars used carbs labeled as Zenith-Stromberg in the early years the companies were struggling to meet U.S. emissions rules.

SU Carburetor - This was an early British carburetor designed by the Skinners Union company founded in 1905. The Hitachi carbs used on the Datsun Sports models were based on the SU design. Most of the English cars in this book used SU carbs prior to 1968, when many models were switched to Zenith-Strombergs for the U.S. market.

Targa - Porsche coined the term, named after the Targo Florio race event in Italy, to refer to a model with a removable top panel, of either a rigid or folding type, attached to a rear roll bar sort of structural hoop. The bar can have actual rollover safety attributes or not and its contribution to structural stiffness varies with the model. Since that time, any sports car with a similar top design has been referred to as a targa.

T-top - This roof type consists of a pair of rigid removable panels over the passenger compartment. When the panels are removed, a T-shaped structural bar is visible. As opposed to the Targa top design, T-tops are formed from the same elaborate, but heavy, structure as the rest of the roof. Some are formed of glass, also very heavy, or plexiglass.

Turbo Hydra-Matic or THM - The three-speed automatic transmission built by General Motors and applied to many cars in this book as either standard or optional equipment.

V-6 - Although extremely common today in all sorts of models, the V-6 engine type has been applied to only a few rare, low-production models covered in this book. These include the Fiat Dino and Ferrari Dino 246.

V-8 - This is the engine design applied to most American sports cars, including Corvettes and all high-performance pony cars. In tiny production numbers at lofty prices, the V-8 design was also used by Maserati, Aston Martin, and Ferrari. Practically all the American V-8's are of an overhead valve design and practically all the imported designs are overhead cam.

V-12 - Twelve-cylinder engines are the most exotic of all, used in the Series III XK-E Jaguar and several early Ferrari Spiders. Within the parameters of this book, these include the NART Spyder and the production touring Ferrari models.

Weber Carburetor - This is the legendary Italian brand utilized by Fiat, Ferrari, and other Italian companies. Weber carbs have even been offered as the hot ticket in the aftermarket for early Mustangs and other V-8 models.

Zenith - This is the parent company name that built the Stromberg carburetors of the Sixties and Seventies. The carburetors on many MG's, Jaguars, and Triumphs exported to the USA of this period were often referred to as Zenith, Stromberg, or Zenith-Stromberg. The distinguishing characteristic of these carburetors was that they were factory set to meet certain emission standards. They could not easily be tuned or modified by car owners to produce more power with increased emission levels.

Figure K1 - A final image of an E-Type, a 1970 XK-E Series II 4.2 Roadster in Pale Primrose with black interior and top. Happy trails! ©Dave 7 from Lethbridge, Canada (CC)

Bibliography

AC (Shelby) Cobra: 1962-67; Marks I, II, III; 260, 289, 427, F. Wilson McComb, Tim Parker, Editor, Osprey AutoHistory, Osprey Publishing Limited, London, England, Distributed by Motorbooks International, Printed in Spain, 1984.

Art of the Automobile, The,: The 100 Greatest Cars, Dennis Adler with Forward by Jay Leno, Harper Resource, an imprint of HarperCollins Publishers, New York, NY, Printed in China, 2000.

Automobile Quarterly, Vol. 21 No. 4, Automobile Quarterly, Inc., Fourth Quarter, 1983, "A Sporting Elegance: The Third Generation Thunderbirds, 1961-66" by Peter Frey and "P Stands for Possibilities: Pontiac's 1984 Fiero" by Lowell Paddock.

A-Z British Cars 1945-1980, Graham Robson, Herridge & Sons, Ltd., 2005.

A-Z of Cars 1945-1970, Michael Sedgwick, Bay View Books, Devon, UK, 1986.

Book of the Porsche 356, The, Brian Long, Veloce Publishing, Ltd., England, Distributed in the USA by MBI, 1996, 2008.

Camaro and Firebird: GM's Power Twins, John Gunnell, Edited by Brian Earnest, Krause Publications, a division of F+W Media, Inc., Printed in the USA, 2010.

Car and Driver, September 1963, "Road Test: Apollo 3500-GT".

Car and Driver, May 1966, "Road Test: Shelby Mustang GT-350 H".

Car and Driver, August 1966, "Road Test: Lotus Elan S2: A Purist's Potpourri of Sophisticated Engineering Features, the Lotus Elan Coupe Deserves Its Pedigree".

Car and Driver, September 1966, "Ken Miles and the Editors of Car and Driver Road Test Six Sports Roadsters".

Car and Driver, March 1967, "Road Tests: Chevrolet Camaro Z-28 & Pontiac Firebird 400: Another Candidate for the Mustang's Sporty-car Crown Hits the Pavement. Will It Succeed? Only the Youth Market Knows for Sure".

Car and Driver, July 1967, "Fiat-Abarth OT-1000 Spider".

Car and Driver, September 1967, "Road Test: Triumph Spitfire Mk. III: The Very Best Reason to Buy a Spitfire is Because the Thing is a Ball to Drive".

Car and Driver, March 1968, "Six-Car Comparison: The Sporty Cars".

Car and Driver, April 1968, "Road Test: Toyota 2000 GT" & Triumph TR-250 Ad.

Car and Driver, September 1969, Corvette Stingray L-71 427 Road Test.

Car and Driver, November 1969, "Road Tests: De Tomaso Mangusta & Dodge Challenger R/T Hemi" and "1970 Imported Cars & 1970 American Cars" Charts.

Car and Driver, February 1970, Chevrolet Chevelle SS-454 LS-6 450-hp Road Test (5.4 seconds 0-60 / 13.8-second quarter-mile).

Car and Driver, July 1970, "Road Tests: AAR Cuda & Fiat 850 Racer".

Car and Driver, February 1971, "Road Test: Fiat 124 Spider: A Small Package of Mental Health and Spiritual Well Being".

Car and Driver, June 1971, Road Test Comparison of 1971 Corvettes.

Car and Driver, December 1972, Road Test of Two Corvettes, L-82 350 & LS-5 454.

Car and Driver, January 1973, "Road Test: Lotus Elan Sprint: Lotus Worshippers are Addicted to Cornering - Each Turn a Challenge of Man and Machine".

Car and Driver, March 1973, "Road Test: Porsche 914 2.0, There are Several 914s, but Only One Feels Like a Real Porsche".

Car and Driver, May 1973, "Road Test: Firebird Trans Am SD-455".

Car and Driver, September 1974, "Shelby GT-350: Everyman's Real Racer" by William Jeanes.

Car and Driver, January 1975, "Pontiac GTO: The Original Muscle Phenomenon" by David E. Davis, Jr.

Car and Driver, May 1975, "America's Best Sports Car: Bricklin or Corvette?" by Don Sherman.

Car and Driver, March 1976, Road Test of the L-48 4-Speed and L-82 Automatic.

Car and Driver, April 1976, Road Test of the Corvette with L-82 Automatic (3.36 axle).

Car and Driver, August 1976, "Topless Cars: The Convertible is Dead? Baloney! CD's Tongue-Out, Wind-in-the-Hair, Bugs-in-the-Teeth Comparison Test" by Don Sherman.

Car and Driver, January 1977, "Road Test: Toyota Corolla Liftback" and "Eight Years Later, Because of One Man's Singular Obsession… The Morgan is Back!" and "Inside the New Morgan Plus 8: A Different Kind of Replicar, Because It's a Replica of Itself" by Charles Fox.

Car and Driver, March 1977, "Road Test: Ferrari 308 GTB".

Car and Driver, April 1977, "Road Test: Firebird Trans-Am".

Car and Driver, May 1977, "Road Test: TVR 2500M".

Car and Driver, October 1977, "Road Test: Corvette" by Brock Yates.

Car and Driver, January 1979, "This Little Lamborghini Went to Dinner" by Patrick Bedard and "Firebird Face-Off" by Don Sherman.

Car and Driver, March 1979, "TVR 3000S" by Rich Ceppos.

Car and Driver, August 1979, "Road Test: MG Midget" by Mike Knepper.

Car and Driver, May 1980, "Road Test: Chevrolet Corvette" by Patrick Bedard.

Car and Driver, August 1980, "Road Test: Triumph TR-8 Convertible".

Car and Driver, March 1982, "Comparison Test: Last-of-Their-Kind Corvettes" by Don Sherman.

Car and Driver, March 1983, "Road Test: Corvette!" (1984 model).

Car and Driver, October, 1983, "Road Test: Chevrolet Corvette" (A base car and a Z51 were tested together and the Z51 offered practically no measurable performance advantage.).

Car and Driver, March 1984, "Road Test: Chevrolet Celebrity Eurosport" by David E. Davis, Jr.

Car and Driver, December 1984, "Road Test: Chevrolet Corvette" by Rich Ceppos.

Car and Driver, February 1986, "Road Test: Chevrolet Corvette Convertible" by Patrick Bedard & "Road Test: Pontiac Fiero GT" by Rich Ceppos.

Car and Driver, March 1986, "Road Test: Mercedes-Benz 190E 2.3-16" by Larry Griffin.

Car and Driver, April 1986, "Short Take: Chevrolet Cavalier Z24" by Larry Griffin.

Car and Driver, April 1988, Cavalier Z24 Test (8.3 / 16.3 / 119 mph / 20 mpg).

Car and Driver, September 1988, Corvette Z51 Test.

Car and Driver, December 1988, "Road Test: 1969 Dodge Charger Daytona" by Patrick Bedard.

Car and Driver, June 1989, "Road Test: 1989 Chevrolet Corvette ZR-1".

Car and Driver, August 1989, "Road Test: Chevrolet Lumina Euro" by Rich Ceppos & "Road Test: Nissan 300ZX" by Arthur St. Antoine.

Car and Driver, September 1989, "Road Test: Mazda MX-5 Miata" by Arthur St. Antoine.

Car and Driver, April 1990, "Road Test: Chevrolet Corvette ZR-1" by Rich Ceppos.

Car and Driver, June 1990, "Road Test: Jaguar's Glorious E-Type" by Pete Lyons.

Car and Driver, July 1990, "Road Test: Ferrari Mondial t Cabriolet" by Csaba Csere.

Car and Driver, September 1990, "The Eroticars" by Patrick Bedard.

Car and Driver, September 2010, "Road Test: 2011 Corvette Grand Sport Convertible".

Car and Driver, October 2012, "Road Test: 2013 427 Stingray Convertible".

Car and Driver, May 2014, Camaro 427 Z28 & 2014 Corvette Stingray Tests.

Car Collector and Car Classics, October 1979, "Winged Warriors" by David Plias.

Car Exchange, May 1980, "Tiger Tiger Burning Bright" by Jack Vines and "Superbird!" by Gerry Burger.

Car Exchange, May 1981, "Trans Am Run-off: Three Cars and the Open Road" by Gerry Burger (1969, 1970, & 1973 Trans Ams).

Car Exchange, December 1983, "Challenger T/A" by Bill Coulter, "'70 Cuda" by Tony Hossain, "The Jet-Smoother '66 Chevrolet" by Tony Hossain, and "60's Stickers and Stripes" by Phil Hall.

Cars of the Sizzling '60s: A Decade of Great Rides and Good Vibrations, The Auto Editors of *Consumer Guide*, Publications International, Ltd., Printed in China, 2001.

Chevrolet Corvette: 1968-82; 305, 327, 350, 427, & 454 V8s, Thomas Falconer, Tim Parker, Editor, Osprey AutoHistory, Osprey Publishing Limited, London, England, Distributed by Motorbooks International, Printed in Spain, 1983.

Classic Corvette, The, Richard Nichols, Bison Books Corporation, Printed in Hong Kong, 1983.

Classic Ferrari, The, Godfrey Eaton, Bison Books Corporation, Greenwich, CT, Printed in Hong Kong, 1983.

Complete Book of Collectible Cars, 1940-1980, The, Richard M. Langworth, Graham Robson and the Editors of Consumer Guide, Beekman House, Publications International, Ltd., Printed in the USA, 1982.

Complete Book of Corvette, The, Richard M. Langworth and the Auto Editors of Consumer Guide, Beekman House, Publications International, Ltd., Printed in Yugoslavia, 1987.

Convertible, The: An Illustrated History of a Dream Machine, Ken Vose, Chronicle Books, San Francisco, Printed in Hong Kong, 1999.

Convertibles: History and Evolution of Dream Cars, Giuseppe Guzzardi and Enzo Rizzo, White Star S.p.A., JG Press, World Publications Group, Inc., East Bridgewater, MA, Printed in China, 1998.

Corvette, Barry Coleman, Gallery Press, New York, Designed in England, Printed in Spain, 1983.

Corvette: 1953 to the Present, Richard Nichols, Bison Books Corporation, Published by Gallery Books, Printed in Belgium, 1985.

Corvette: 60th Anniversary, by The Editors of *Consumer Guide*, Publications International, Ltd., Printed in China, 2005, 2013.

Corvette: America's Star-Spangled Sports Car, The Complete History, Karl Ludvigsen, Automobile Quarterly Publications, Princeton Publishing, Inc., Second Edition, Fourth Printing, Printed in the U.S.A., 1973, 1974, 1975, 1977.

Corvette: An American Classic, Edited by Spence Murray and the staff of Specialty Publications Division, Petersen Publishing Company, 1978. Contains several poignant articles written by little known GM employees from the contemporary period.

Corvette: America's Sports Car, Jay Koblenz and the Auto Editors of *Consumer Guide*, Beekman House, NYC, Publications International, Ltd., Skokie, IL, 1984.

Corvette Black Book Super Deluxe Edition 1953-1986, The, Michael Antonick, Michael Bruce Associates, Inc., Motorbooks International Publishers & Wholesalers, Inc., 1983.

Corvette Black Book 1953-1993, The, Michael Antonick, Michael Bruce Associates, Inc., Motorbooks International Publishers, 1992.

Corvette Black Book 1953-2000, The, Michael Antonick, Michael Bruce Associates, Inc., 1999.

Corvette Black Book 1953-2014, The, Michael Antonick, Michael Bruce Associates, Inc., 2014.

"Corvette Fever", Peter Egan, *Road & Track* website, February 28, 2012.

Corvette Fever, August 1981, Vol. 3, No. 4, "Great Corvette Engines: 427's" by Roger Huntington.

Corvette Fever, December 1981, Vol. 3, No. 6, "The Corvette 350 Engine" by Roger Huntington.

Corvette Fever, February 1982, Vol. 4, No. 1, "The ZR-1 Story" by Pat Schlutow (Cortez Silver 1970 Coupe built 2/12/70).

Corvette Fever, April 1982, Vol. 4, No. 2, "Wayne Walker's ZL-1" by Pat Stivers & "Iso and Bizzarini: Corvette Powered GTs" by Theodore Alexander.

Corvette Fever, June 1982, Vol. 4, No. 3, "The Early Corvette V-8's" by Roger Huntington.

Corvette Fever, April 1983, Vol. 5, No. 2, "The 1984 Corvette" by Pat Stivers & "Elusive Prey: A Look at Corvette's American Predators" by Theodore C. Alexander, Jr.

Corvette Fever, April 1984, Vol. 6, No. 2, "Zip's Z06" by Pat Stivers.

Corvette Fever, June 1985, Vol. 7, No. 3, "High Compression Engine and Low Octane Gasoline" by William D. Siuru, Jr., PE.

Appendix

Corvette Fever, August 1985, Vol. 7 No. 4, "The Inside Story: Skin-Deep Interiors" by Steven Sterling (how to install interior door panel skins from Corvette America).

Corvette Fever, October 1985, Vol. 7. No. 5, "The '86 Corvette".

Corvette News, February/March 1977, Vol. 20, No. 3, "1962: That Was the Year That Was".

Corvette News, October/November 1977, Vol. 21, No. 1, "1978: Corvette Silver Anniversary".

Corvette News, October/November 1978, Vol. 22, No. 1, "Corvette '79: The First Step in Corvette's Second Quarter-Century".

Corvette News, April/May 1979, Vol. 22, No. 4, "1978 - The Year That Was".

Corvette News, October/November 1979, Vol. 23, No. 1, "1980 Corvette: Leading the Way to a New Decade of Excitement for the Sports Car Enthusiast".

Corvette News, December/January 1980, Vol. 23, No. 2, "1968: The Year That Was".

Corvette: Past - Present - Future, Consumer Guide Magazine Classic Car Bimonthly, April 1982, Volume 335.

Corvette Road Tests, Published by Surrey, England Book Distributors, Marketed in the USA by J & M Publishing Group, Lynchburg, VA, Sold through Motorbooks International. (No publication date listed, but the latest model covered is 1978.).

Corvette: The Great American Sports Car, John Gunnell, Edited by Brian Earnest, Krause Publications, a division of F+W Media, Inc., Printed in the USA, 2010.

Corvette World, July 1989, Premier Issue, Harris Publications, Inc., "Special Section: Muscle Vettes" (articles by Nick Brunt and Jerry Heasley), "Special Report: ZR-1" by Gliff Gromer & "Corvette Value Guide".

Cycle World Magazine, Joseph C. Parkhurst, Editor & Publisher, Parkhurst Publishing Company, Inc., Long Beach, CA, 1964-1969.

Datsun 280ZX, Nissan Motor Company, Ltd., Printed in Japan, 1978.

De Lorean: Stainless Steel Illusion, John Lamm, Senior Editor, *Road & Track*, with Commentary by Former DMC Executive Mike Knepper, The Newport Press, Santa Ana, CA, Printed in Singapore, 1983.

Dino: The Little Ferrari: V6 and V8 Racing and Road Cars - 1957 to 1979, Doug Nye, John W. Barnes, Jr. Publishing, Inc., Scarsdale, NY, First Published by Osprey Publishing, Ltd., Printed in Great Britain, 1979.

Dodge & Plymouth Muscle Car Red Book, Peter C. Sessler, MBI Publishing Company, 1991.

Enthusiast's Guide to Corvette Facts 1953-1978, The, J & M Publishing Group, 1977.

Essential Fiat 124 Spider and Coupe: The Cars and Their Story 1966-85, Martin Buckley, Motorbooks International, 1998.

Ferrari, Godfrey Eaton, Exeter Books, Colour Library International Ltd., Printed in Spain, 1983.

Ferrari 250GTO: 1962-64; Competition Berlinetta, David Clarke, Tim Parker, Editor, Osprey AutoHistory, Osprey Publishing Limited, London, England, Distributed by Motorbooks International, Printed in Spain, 1983.

Ferrari Dino 246, 308 and 328: A Collector's Guide, Alan Henry, Motor Racing Publications, Ltd., Croydon, England, 1988, 1996, 1998.

Ferrari: The Sports/Racing and Road Cars, Godfrey Eaton and the editors of *Consumer Guide*, Beekman House, NY, Publications International, Ltd., Skokie, IL, Printed in the USA, 1982.

Ferraris for the Road, Henry Rasmussen, Fifth Book in The Survivors Series, Motorbooks International, Printed in Hong Kong, 1980.

Firebird and Trans Am: Enthusiast Color Series, Bill Holder and Phil Kunz, Edited by Chad Caruthers, Motorbooks, an imprint of MBI Publishing Company, Printed in China, 2002.

Ford Muscle Cars: Enthusiast Color Series, Mike Mueller, Motorbooks International Publishers & Wholesalers, Inc., Printed in Hong Kong, 1993.

Ford Mustang: Enthusiast Color Series, Mike Mueller, Motorbooks International Publishers & Wholesalers, Inc., Printed in Hong Kong, 1995.

Great Cars of the 20th Century, Arch Brown, Richard M. Langworth and the Auto Editors of Consumer Guide, Publications International, Ltd., Printed in the USA, 1998.

Great Marques: Ferrari, Godfrey Eaton, Edited by John Blunsden, Octopus Books Limited, London, Printed in Hong Kong, 1980.

Hot Rod, May 1963, "Chevrolet's 427 Mystery V8" by Ray Brock (the origins of what would come to be known as the Mark IV "porcupine" 396-427-454 big block).

Hot Rod, January 1965, "Tiger Tiger Burning Bright" by Dick Wells (Sunbeam Tiger 260).

Hot Rod's Corvette No. 2, Petersen Publishing Company, 1978.

Hot Rod's Corvette No. 4, Petersen Publishing Company, 1980.

Illustrated Aston Martin Buyer's Guide, Paul R. Woudenberg, Motorbooks International Publishers & Wholesalers, Inc., 1986.

Illustrated Austin-Healey Buyer's Guide, Richard Newton, Motorbooks International Publishers & Wholesalers, Inc., 1984.

Illustrated Corvette Buyer's Guide, Michael Antonick, Motorbooks International Publishers & Wholesalers, Inc., 1983.

Illustrated Ferrari Buyer's Guide, Dean Batchelor, Motorbooks International Publishers & Wholesalers, Inc., 1981.

Illustrated Firebird Buyer's Guide, Second Edition, John Gunnell, Motorbooks International Publishers & Wholesalers, Inc., 1992.

Illustrated High-Performance Mustang Buyer's Guide, Peter C. Sessler, Motorbooks International Publishers & Wholesalers, Inc., 1983.

Illustrated Jaguar Buyer's Guide, James Hoehn, Second Edition, Motorbooks International Publishers & Wholesalers, Inc., 1984, 1987.

Illustrated Lamborghini Buyer's Guide, Rob de la Rive Box, Published by Motorbooks International Publishers & Wholesalers, Inc., 1983.

Illustrated Lotus Buyer's Guide, Graham Arnold, Published by Motorbooks International Publishers & Wholesalers, Inc., 1986.

Illustrated Maserati Buyer's Guide, Richard Crump and Rob de la Rive Box, Motorbooks International Publishers & Wholesalers, Inc., 1984.

Illustrated M.G. Buyer's Guide, Richard Knudson, Motorbooks International Publishers & Wholesalers, Inc., 1983.

Illustrated Porsche Buyer's Guide, Dean Batchelor, Motorbooks International Publishers & Wholesalers, Inc., 1983.

Illustrated Triumph Buyer's Guide, Richard Newton, Motorbooks International Publishers & Wholesalers, Inc., 1984.

Isorivolta: The Men, The Machines, Winston Scott Goodfellow, Giorgio Nada, Editor, Giorgio Nada Editore Publications, Printed in Italy, 1995, 2001.

Italian Sports Cars, Winston Goodfellow, MBI Publishing Company, Printed in Hong Kong, 2000.

Jaguar E-Type, The: A Collector's Guide, Paul Skilleter, Motor Racing Publications, Ltd., London, England, 1979, 1980, 1981, 1983.

Jaguar XKE Collection No. 1, 1961-1974, Compiled by R. M. Clarke, Brooklands Books, Surrey, England, no date listed, but the most recent reprinted test report is October 1974.

Lamborghini, by the Auto Editors of Consumer Guide, Publications International, Ltd., Printed in Yugoslavia, 1991.

Lamborghini Miura: The Definitive Analysis of Lamborghini's First Sensational V12 Supercar, Peter Coltrin and Jean-Francois Marchet, Edited by Tim Parker, Osprey Publishing Ltd., London, England, 1982.

Lamborghinis, From 350 GT to Jalpa, The: A Collector's Guide, Chris Harvey, Motor Racing Publications, Ltd., London, England, 1982.

Lamborghini Urraco & the V8s: Urraco, Bravo, Silhouette, Athon, Jalpa, Jean-Francois Marchet, Tim Parker, Editor, Osprey AutoHistory, Osprey Publishing Limited, London, England, Distributed by Motorbooks International, Printed in Spain, 1983.

Lotus Elan and Europa, The: A Collector's Guide, John Bolster, Motor Racing Publications, Ltd., London, England, 1980.

Lotus Elan Collection No. 1, 1962-1974, Compiled by R. M. Clarke, Brooklands Books, Surrey, England, no date listed, but the most recent reprinted test report is June 1974.

Lotus Elan Collection No. 2, 1963-1972, Compiled by R. M. Clarke, Brooklands Books, Surrey, England, no date listed, but the most recent reprinted test report is February 1979.

Lotus Europa Collection 1966-1975, Compiled by R. M. Clarke, Brooklands Books, Surrey, England, no date listed, but the most recent reprinted test report is September 1975.

Maserati Bora & Merak: V8 & V6 Giugiaro Designed, Mid-engined GT, Jan P. Norbye, Tim Parker, Editor, Osprey AutoHistory, Osprey Publishing Limited, London, England, Distributed by Motorbooks International, Printed in England, 1982.

Daydreams in the Wind

Maserati Road Cars: The Postwar Production Cars 1946 to 1979, Richard Crump and Rob de la Rive Box, John W. Barnes, Jr., Publishing, Inc., Scarsdale, NY, Osprey Publishing Limited, London, Printed in Great Britain, 1979.

Motor Trend, March 1958, "Sam Hanks Tests (Four 1958 Corvettes)".

Motor Trend, November 1965, "New Avanti II Road Test" by Bob McVay and 1966 Shelby Cobra & Mustang GT-350 introduction.

Motor Trend, December 1967, "Buying a Used Supercar" by Michael Lamm and "Supercars" (an extensive comparison test of eight intermediate muscle cars with three-speed automatics).

Motor Trend, August 1971, "The Three Positions of Lotus: Europa, Elan S4 and Elan +2: Antidotes for the Blahs and for a Succession of Shining Moments - Camelot on Wheels" by John Christy.

Motor Trend, November 1971, "Triumph's Transcendent Three: TR6, GT6, Spitfire: Quite Possibly the Answers to Those Who Contend That the British Have Lost the Knack of Building Cars with Guts and Soul" by John Christy.

Motor Trend, June 1972, Road Test of the Corvette LT-1.

Motor Trend, April 1974, "The Middies (Handling is a Mid-Engined Sports Car)" by John Lamm.

Motor Trend, December 1975, "Performance Returns: Driving Impressions: 1976 Pontiac Firebird Trans Am 455", by Gary Witzenburg.

Motor Trend, May 1976, "The Affordable Sports Cars: Comparison: The List of Sports Cars for Less Than $5000 is Smaller Now, But There are Still Four You Can Have Without Destroying Your Annual Budget".

Motor Trend, September 1977, "The Alfa Romeo Trio" by John Christy.

Motor Trend, June 1978, "You Can Afford a Ferrari" (308 GTS) by William Jeanes.

Motor Trend, November 1978, "TVR Roadster" by Fred Stafford.

Motor Trend, July 1979, "Corvette vs. Diablo" (1979 L-82) & "Driving Impression: Aston Martin Volante: Only 80 Americans Will Own This $70,000 Convertible" by William Jeanes,.

Motor Trend, December 1979, "Fantasy Flagships" (1979 L-82).

Motor Trend, June 1980, "TR8 V-8: A Mighty Triumph" by Fred M. H. Gregory.

Motor Trend, January 1983, "Cobra Cornucopia: History's No. 1 Thrill Ride Revived - In Assorted Flavors" by Kevin Smith (ERA Cobra, Aurora Mk. II, Butler Cobra, & Contemporary Classic Cobra).

Motor Trend, March 1983, "Road Test: The New Corvette" by Kevin Smith, "Plasticars on Parade" by Jim McCraw, and "Retrospect: 1953 Chevrolet Corvette" by Len Frank.

Motor Trend, April 1984, "Road Test: Pontiac 6000 STE vs. Chevrolet Celebrity Eurosport" by Don Fuller.

Motor Trend, March 1988, "Road Test: Pontiac Fiero GT" by Daniel Charles Ross.

Motor Trend, January 1990, "Road Test: Porsche 911 Speedster" by Jeff Karr (Leaky top that is difficult to erect and leaks onto optional power leather seats costing $3316, although the manual top folds down under a fiberglass panel like the Corvette.).

Motor Trend, October 2005, Corvette C6 Z06 Road Test.

Motor Trend, October 2007, Corvette C6 Z06 Road Test.

Motor Trend, May 2014, Camaro 427 Z28 Test.

Muscle Cars, Phil Hall and the Editors of Consumer Guide, Castle Books, Publications International, Ltd., Printed in the USA, 1981.

Muscle Cars Field Guide: American Supercars 1960-2000, John Gunnell, Edited by Brian Earnest, Krause Publications, Inc., 2004.

Mustang, 35th Anniversary Collector's Edition, Publications International, Ltd., Printed in China, 1999.

Mustang: A Complete Guide, A *Car Life* Special Edition, Dennis Shattuck, Editor, Bond Publishing Company, Newport Beach, CA, Printed by Kalmbach Publishing Company, Milwaukee, WI, 1965.

Mustang Legends: The Power. The Performance. The Passion. Various Contributors, Edited by Michael Dregni, Voyageur Press, Stillwater, MN, Printed in China, 2004.

Mustang Red Book Early 1965-1995 Second Edition, Peter C. Sessler, MBI Publishing Company, 1990, 1995.

Mustang Red Book 1964½-2000 Third Edition, Peter C. Sessler, MBI Publishing Company, 1990, 1995, 2000.

Original Austin-Healey 100, 100-Six and 3000, Anders Ditlev Clausager, MBI, 2002.

Original MGB with MGC and MGB GT V8: The Restorer's Guide to All Roadster and GT Models 1962-80, Anders Ditlev Clausager, Bay View Books, Ltd., Devon, England, 1994, Published by MBI in the USA, 1995, Herridge & Sons, Ltd., Reprint Edition, 2011.

Panteras for the Road, Henry Rasmussen, Seventh Book in The Survivors Series, Motorbooks International, Printed in Hong Kong, 1982.

Porsche 911 Red Book 1965-1999, Patrick C. Paternie, MBI Publishing Company, 2000. Printed in the USA.

Porsche 914 & 914/6: The Definitive History of the Road & Competition Cars, Brian Long, Veloce Publishing, Ltd., England, distributed in the USA by MBI, 1998, 2001, 2006.

Porsche Family Tree, The: A Guide for Porsche Models from 1948 to 1981, Porsche Audi Division, Volkswagen of America, Inc., 1980.

Road & Track Corvette Portfolio 1997-2002, Brooklands Books, Ltd., 2002, Printed in China.

Road & Track On Corvette 1953-1967, Brooklands Books, Copyright CBS, Inc. (No publication date is listed, but the most recent reprinted article from *Road & Track* is from the February 1975 issue.).

Road & Track On Ferrari 1968-1974, Brooklands Books, Copyright CBS, Inc. (No publication date is listed, but the most recent reprinted article from *Road & Track* is from the November 1974 issue.).

Road & Track Presents Exotic Cars, 1983, CBS Publications, "Road Test: Chevrolet Corvette" (1984).

Road & Track's Buyer's Guide for 1974, "Road Tests: Corvette L82 Coupe, Ford Pantera L, Jensen-Healey, Lotus Europa Special 5-Speed, Maserati Bora, Triumph Spitfire Mark IV: A Larger Engine Restores Performance & Imparts Flexibility to a Good Small Sports Car, and TVR 2500M".

Road & Track's Buyer's Guide for 1996, Descriptions & Specifications for all 1996 Models, Including the Corvette.

Road & Track's Exotic Cars 5, 1987, CBS Magazines, "Ferrari Daytona Spyder: A Legend from Day One" by John Lamm.

Road & Track's Guide to Sports & GT Cars for 1976, Road Tests of the 1976 Corvette, Fiat X1/9, Fiat Sport Spider, Maserati Merak, MGB, MG Midget, Toyota Celica GT, and Triumph Spitfire.

Road & Track's Guide to Sports & GT Cars, 1980, "Road Test: Chevrolet Corvette".

Road & Track's Guide to Sports & GT Cars, 1982, "Road Test: Chevrolet Corvette".

Road & Track's Guide to the All New Corvette, by John Gibson, Jonathan Thompson, and Paul Van Valkenburgh, 1983, CBS Publications, New York.

Road & Track's Road Test Annual for 1966, Dean Batchelor, Editor, John & Elaine Bond, Publishers, Bond Publishing Company, Newport Beach, CA, 1965, Tests Conducted During 1965 and Reprinted from *Road & Track*, "Road Tests: Alfa Giulia Spider Veloce, Austin-Healey 3000 Mk. III, Corvette (396), Fiat 1500 Spider, Ford Mustang GT-350, Honda S-600, Lamborghini 350 GT, Plymouth Barracuda S, Porsche 911, and Triumph Spitfire Mk. 2 & TR-4A".

Road & Track's Road Test Annual for 1973, Tests Conducted During 1972 and Reprinted from *Road & Track*, "Road Tests: Dino 246 GT, Ferrari 365 GTC/4, Jaguar E-Type V-12: A Magnificent Engine in an Outclassed Body, Jensen-Healey, Lamborghini Jarama, Lotus Elan Sprint: The Best Elan Yet, and Still One of the Best Cars in the World for the Enthusiast, Lotus Europa Twin Cam, Porsche 911E, and Porsche 914".

Road & Track, June 1954, "Road Testing the Corvette".

Road & Track, July 1955, "Road Test: The Corvette V8".

Road & Track, July 1956, "Road Test: Two Corvettes".

Road & Track, August 1957, "Road Test: 4-Speed Corvette".

Road & Track, August 1958, "Road Test: Austin-Healey Sprite".

Road & Track, January 1959, "Road Test: 1959 Corvette".

Road & Track, January 1961, "Road Test: 1961 Corvette".

Road & Track, August 1961, "Road Test: Austin-Healey Sprite Mark II".

Road & Track, September 1961, "Road Test: MG A 1600 Mk. II".

Road & Track, October 1962, "Road Test: 1963 Corvette".

Road & Track, November 1963, "Road Test: Apollo GT".

Road & Track, March 1964, "Road Test: Sting Ray Automatic".

Road & Track, June 1964, Test of the Shelby 289 Cobra.

Road & Track, December 1964, "Road Test: 1965 Corvette Sting Ray".

Road & Track, February 1965, "Road Test: Austin-Healey 3000 Mk. III".

Road & Track, May 1965, "Road Test: Mustang GT-350" & "Road Test: Triumph TR-4A".

Road & Track, July 1965, "Road Test: Lamborghini 350 GT" and "The Musclecars" by James T. Crow & "Porsche 912" by Gunther Molter.

Road & Track, August 1965, "Road Test: 425 BHP Corvette".

Road & Track, February 1966, "Road Test: Porsche 912".

Road & Track, February 1967, "Road Test: 1967 Corvette" and "After the New Wears Off: Corvette Sting Ray, 36,000 Miles Later" by Ron Wakefield.

Road & Track, April 1967, "Road Test: Porsche 911S Coupe".

Road & Track, June 1967, "Road Test: Toyota 2000GT".

Road & Track, July 1967, "Fiat-Abarth OT 1000 Spider".

Road & Track, September 1967, "Road Tests: Ferrari 275 GTS/4 NART: The Most Satisfying Sports Car in the World, MG Midget III & Triumph Spitfire Mk. 3: Basic Sports Cars That Continue a Proud Tradition, & Sunbeam Tiger II: Latest Version Offers the 289-cu-in, Ford V-8 Engine", "Driving Impressions: Three New Fiats: Our Henry Tries the Fiat Dino Spider, the Fiat 124 Sport and the Fiat 125 Sedan" by Henry N. Manney, and "Sprite: The Enchanted Frog" by Jack P. Maloney.

Road & Track, December 1967, "Road Test: Triumph TR-250: The Big TR Gets a 6-cyl. Engine and Undergoes a Personality Change".

Road & Track, January 1968, "Road Test: 350-hp Corvette".

Road & Track, February 1968, "Carroll Shelby's Personal Cobra is the Cobra to End All Cobras".

Road & Track, April 1968, "Road Test: Fiat 850 Spider: As Soundly Built as it is Beautiful" & "Driving Impression: Maserati Mistral: A Delightful Car with a Personality All Its Own" by Tony Hogg.

Road & Track, May 1968, "Road Test: Lamborghini Miura".

Road & Track, March 1969, "Road Test: 435-hp Corvette".

Road & Track, June 1969, "Comparison Test: Four Luxury GTs" - Stingray with 300-hp 350 and Turbo Hydra-Matic against a Mercedes 280SL, Porsche 911T, and an XK-E. The Porsche came in first with the Mercedes and Jaguar in the middle. The Corvette finished last based on its flashiness and lack of refinement.

Road & Track, March 1970, "Owner Survey: Chevrolet Corvette Stingray" & "Road Test: 2.2 Porsche 911S: Performance on the Order of an American Supercar but Without the Stigma of Low Cost".

Road & Track, April 1970, "Road Tests: Datsun 240Z, Fiat 850 Racer, Lamborghini Miura S, & Porsche 914: The New Mid-engine Roadster is Fun, But It's Leisurely Performance and High Price Make It Less Than a Bargain", and "Owner Survey: Fiat 850 Coupe & Spider" & "After the New Wears Off: One Owner's Experience with an 850 Spider" by Jonathan Thompson.

Road & Track, June, 1970, "Road & Track Comparison Test: Four Sports Cars: How Did the Fiat 124 Spider, MGB Mk. II, Porsche 914 & Triumph TR-6 Measure Up on a 1250-mile Run?".

Road & Track, July 1970, "Road Tests: Porsche 914/6: This One's a True Porsche, but at $6000-plus It's Hardly for the Masses" & "TVR Vixen & Tuscan" and "Owner Survey: Fiat 124 Spider & Coupe".

Road & Track, September 1970, "Road Test: 454 Corvette".

Road & Track, June 1972, "TC to GTB: Evolution of the Sports Car 1947-72: First of Two Parts - Clamshell Fenders to E-Type" by Ron Wakefield & "Owner Survey: Datsun 240Z".

Road & Track, January 1973, "Road Test: TVR Vixen 2500 M".

Daydreams in the Wind

Road & Track, February 1973, "Road Tests: Porsche 914 2-Liter: Bigger 4-cylinder Engine Gives the Popular 914 a Boost" & "TVR Vixen 2500 M".

Road & Track, March 1973, "Road Test: Jensen-Healey".

Road & Track, April, 1973, Track Test: "Back to Basics: Track Testing Nine Showroom Stock Sports Cars, the Entire Field in SCCA's Newest Class. Not a Fair Group, Exactly, but Certainly Sporting".

Road & Track, June 1973, "Road Test: Corvette LT-1 Coupe" (This is the original printing of the same test listed as L82 Coupe in the *1974 Buyer's Guide*.).

Road & Track, September 1973, "Development and Evolution of the Mustang, 1960-1973: What Began at the Fairlane Inn in 1960 Became One of Motoring's Great Success Stories. Can Ford Repeat It?" (plus "The Shelby Mustangs: Ol' Shel Worked His Magic for a While"), by Mike Knepper and "The Shelby Mustangs".

Road & Track, November 1973, "Road Test: 5-Speed Lotus Europa Special".

Road & Track, February 1974, "Comparison Road Test: Five Exotic Opens: Premium Machinery & Open-Air Motoring in $64,012 Worth of Cars".

Road & Track, July 1974, "Classic Road Test: Cobra 427: Carroll Shelby's 7-liter Weapon", by Tony Hogg.

Road & Track, September 1974, "Used Car Classic: Series 1 Jaguar E-Type: Beginning a New Series on Attractive, Nearly Modern Cars Everyone Can Afford" by Michael V. Gregory and "Driving Impression: 1965 E-Type Roadster" by Ron Wakefield.

Road & Track, November 1974, "Owner Survey: Porsche 914: How reliable is the VW-Porsche Hybrid Sports Car?" & "Used Car Classic: Alfa Romeo 1600 & 1750, 1964-1971: These Italian Sports Cars Offer Driving Pleasure and Good Value for Money" and "Driving Impression: 1967 Duetto Spider" by Peter Bohr.

Road & Track, February 1975: "Used Car Classic: Corvette Sting Ray, 1963-67: Fast, Reliable Sports Cars for the Budget-Minded Enthusiast" and "Classic Road Test: 1965 Fuel-Injection Corvette: High Point for the American Sports Car" by Joe Rusz.

Road & Track, September 1975, "Used Car Classic: MGB, 1962-1967: A Lot of Fun for Very Little Money" (plus Driving Impression: 1967 MGB Roadster) by Thos L. Bryant".

Road & Track, December 1975, "Used Car Classic: Porsche 901 Series: How to Enjoy Porsche Performance, Styling and Economy at Less Than Half the Cost of a New One (plus Driving Impression: 1967 Porsche 911)," by Joe Rusz.

Road & Track, March 1976, "Road Test: Corvette & Super Corvette" & "Tested in Europe: Ferrari 308 GTB" by Paul Frere.

Road & Track, May 1976, "Road Test: MG Midget Mark IV: It's Showing Its Age, But the Basic Elements of Driving Pleasure are Still There" & "Used Car Classic: Austin-Healey Sprite / MG Midget 1958-1970: Good Handling and Simplified Design Characterize These Inexpensive Sports Cars" by Thos L. Bryant (plus Owner Impressions by John Lamm).

Road & Track, June 1976, "Comparison Test: The Affordables: A Head-to-Tail Confrontation Between Six Moderately Priced Sports Cars: Fiat 124 Spider, Fiat X1/9, MGB, MG Midget, Triumph Spitfire, and Triumph TR7", "Eastward Ho! What It Was Really Like Out There" by Henry N. Manney III, "Used Car Classic: Austin-Healeys, 1953-1967: Marvelous Cars That Changed the Sports Car World" by Thos L.

Bryant & Dave Ramstad, "Driving Impressions: Three Austin-Healeys" by Thos L. Bryant, and "Road Test: Pontiac Firebird Trans-Am: Gadzooks But This One's a Wurlitzer".

Road & Track, August 1976, "Road Test: Toyota Corolla SR-5 Liftback" & "Tested in Europe: Lamborghini Silhouette" by Ron Wakefield.

Road & Track, October 1976, "Used Car Classic: 1953-1967 Triumph Sports Cars: Reviving the TR2, 3 and 4 - Ample Driving Fun for Not Very Much Money", by Thos L. Bryant.

Road & Track, February 1977, "Road Test: Ferrari 308 GTB".

Road & Track, March 1977, "Used Car Classic: Trans-Am Pony cars" by Allan Girdler.

Road & Track, May 1977, "Road Test: Alfa Romeo Spider" & "Owner Survey: Fiat X1/9".

Road & Track, June 1977, "A Brief History: All the Corvettes" by John Lamm & "Road Test: Corvette Stingray".

Road & Track, September 1977, "Used Car Classic: Triumph Spitfire and GT6, 1962-1970: Incomparable Cars in Their Price Classes" by Thos L. Bryant (and Owner Impressions by John Dinkel).

Road & Track, November 1977, "Road Test: Volkswagen Beetle Convertible".

Road & Track, March 1978, "Road Test: Maserati Merak SS".

Road & Track, April 1978, "Road Test: Chevrolet Corvette".

Road & Track, July 1978, "Road Test: Ferrari 308 GTS" & "Used Car Classic: Sunbeam Alpine & Tiger: Comfort and Sportiness Combined" (and Driving Impressions) by Thos L. Bryant and "The Tiger: A Marvelous Automotive Fantasy Come True" by William Carroll.

Road & Track, September 1978, "Toyota 2000GT" by James T. Crow (approximately 70 brought to the U.S. in 1967-68).

Road & Track, November 1978, "Used Car Classic: Fiat 124 Sport Coupe & Spider, 1968-1972" by Thos L. Bryant.

Road & Track, December 1978, "Road Test: TVR Taimar Roadster".

Road & Track, April 1979, "Comparison Road Test: Four Automatic Sports & GT Cars".

Road & Track, September 1979, "Road Test: Triumph TR7 Convertible".

Road & Track, February 1980, "Used Car Classic: Fiat 850 Spider: Lovely to Look at, Fun to Drive, But Be Prepared to Maintain It" by Thos L. Bryant (plus Owner Impressions by Jonathan Thompson).

Road & Track, March 1981, "Road Test: Ferrari 308 GTSi".

Road & Track, February 1982, "Avanti" by Joe Rusz.

Road & Track, November 1982, "Road Test: Chevrolet Corvette" (Collector Edition).

Road & Track, March 1983, "Road Test: (1984) Chevrolet Corvette", "Creating the Corvette" by Jonathan Thompson, "Corvette Family Tree, 1953-1983", and "The Corvette Racer: A Sprite Driver's View from a Safe Distance" by Peter Egan.

Road & Track, June 1983, "Owner Survey: Ferrari 308".

Road & Track, August 1983, "Corvette vs. Ferrari 308GTBi Quattrovalvole vs. Porsche 928S vs Porsche 944".

Road & Track, January 1984, "A Performance Pair: Chevrolet Corvette vs. Nissan 300-ZX Turbo" & "A Gearbox Smarter Than Your Average Driver" (4+3) by Dennis Simanaitis.

Road & Track, March 1984, "Six 2-Seaters: Morgan 4/4 2000, Alfa Romeo Spider Veloce, Mazda RX-7 GSL-SE, Nissan 300ZX, Pontiac Fiero S/E, Honda Civic CRX 1.5. What's Your Pleasure?", "Used Car Classic: 1955-1962 MGA: Little Treasure" by Peter Bohr.

Road & Track, October, 1984, "The Enthusiast's Bargain Bests: The 10 Best Used Car Buys Between $5000 and $10,000", by Peter Bohr.

Road & Track, December 1984, "Road Test: 1985 Chevrolet Corvette".

Road & Track, September 1985, "Fastest Cars in America" by Thos. L. Bryant.

Road & Track, February 1986, "Corvette Comparison: 1986 Z51 vs. 1968 L88" & "Corvette Convertible" by Steve Kimball.

Road & Track, April 1986, "Used Car Classic: Chevrolet Corvette 1968-1977" by Peter Bohr & "Tracking the Mille Miglia" (a comparison test including the Corvette Coupe).

Road & Track, May 1986, "Road Test: Chevrolet Cavalier Z24".

Road & Track, August 1986, "Driving Impression: Pontiac Fiero GT".

Road & Track, November, 1986, "Collectible, Fun and Cheap: Twelve Ways to Find Happiness Below $2500" by Peter Bohr.

Road & Track, March 1987, "Used Car Classic: Triumph TR6: Sturdy and Stylish, with Just Enough Privation to Remind You It's a British Roadster" by Peter Bohr.

Road & Track, June 1987, "Road Test: Corvette Convertible".

Road & Track, October 1987, "Extended Use Report: Chevrolet Corvette at 35,000 Miles".

Road & Track, June 1988, "Affordable Collector Cars: Triple Your Money in 10 Years? Appreciating Collectibles: What's Worth Saving Till the Year 2000? Real Estate Deeds? CDs? Cars!?" by Peter Bohr.

Road & Track, August 1988, "Update: Long-Term Tests: Chevrolet Cavalier Z24, Acura Legend Coupe L, and Pontiac Fiero GT.

Road & Track, October 1988, "Used Car Classic: Fiat X1/9 1974-1982" by Peter Bohr.

Road & Track, November 1988, "Long-Term Affordable Classics: MGB Wrap Up" by Peter Egan.

Road & Track, December 1988, "1989 Corvette 6-Speed" by Douglas Kott.

Road & Track, May 1989, "Used Car Classic: Jaguar E-Types: Sexy, Sumptuous, Swift… and You Wanna Talk Price? (with Buying an E-Type)" by Peter Bohr & "Road Test: Nissan 300ZX".

Road & Track, June 1989, "Owner Survey: Chevrolet Corvette 1984-1988" by Peter Bohr & "Road Test: Corvette ZR-1".

Road & Track, July 1989, "Road Test: Mazda MX-5 Miata".

Road & Track, March 1990, "Used Car Classic: 1971-1985 Alfa Romeo Spiders: A Ragtop Charmer from a Grand Marque - and the Price is Right (including On the Road)" by Peter Bohr.

Road & Track, June 1991, "How to Buy Classic Sports Cars" by Peter Bohr.

Road & Track, January 1992, "Road Test: Chevrolet Corvette LT1" by Andrew Bornhop.

Road & Track, January 1997, Road Test of the Ferrari F50.

Road & Track, August 2002, 50th Anniversary Corvette Six-Speed Test.

Road Test, 1966, "Fiat 1500 Spider: The Wind-in-the-Face Two-Seat Sports Car Has Evolved into a Cabriolet with Creature Comforts. Here's a Shining Example".

Road Test, August, 1967, "The Alfa Duetto: A Revealing Report".

Road Test, October, 1967, "Fiat 850: Another Beauty Queen from Italy".

Road Test, February, 1969, "TR Spitfire: $2345 West Coast P.O.E.".

Road Test, December 1975, "Jensen-Healy J-H5".

Road Test, February, 1977, "Pontiac Firebird TransAm 400 T/A".

Shelby American Guide, Richard J. Kopec, Shelby American Automobile Club, West Redding, CT, 1978, 1979, 1980, 1981.

Shelby Mustang: Muscle Car Color History, Tom Corcoran, Motorbooks International, 1992, 1993, Printed in Singapore.

Sports Car Classics, Petersen Publishing Company, Los Angeles, CA, 1982, "Road Test: Dino" by T. C. Browne, "Ferrari Mondial" by Tony Swan, "The Great Cars of Lamborghini" by T. C. Browne, and "Lamborghini Miura: Twelve Cylinders, Sideways...".

Sports Car Graphic, September 1967, "Road Test: Lotus Elan S/E: It's a Unique and Admirable Car for the Skilled Enthusiast!"

Sports Car Graphic No. 4, Petersen Publishing Company, Winter 1980, "Ferrari 308 GT4" by Ro McGonegal, "Checking in with Frank Reisner" by Burge Hulett, and "The Excalibur" by Burge Hulett.

Sports Car Graphic No. 6, Petersen Publishing Company, June/July 1980, "Triumph TR8 (Convertible)" by Jim MacQueen and "The Sun Finally Shines on Apollo" by Leon Mandel.

Sports Car Graphic, Petersen Publishing Company, Summer 1981, "L81 Corvette" by Peter Frey.

Sprites and Midgets, The: A Collector's Guide, Eric Dymock, Motor Racing Publications, Ltd., London, England, 1981.

Standard Guide to British Sports Cars, John Gunnell, Krause Publications, Iola, WI, 2004.

Supercars: The World's Finest Performance Automobiles, Jeremy Sinek, Edited from *Motor* magazine test reports, Domus Books, Northbrook, IL, Originally Published in Great Britain (1979), Printed in Hong Kong, 1979.

This Old Corvette: The Ultimate Tribute to America's Sports Car, Various Contributors, Edited by Michael Dregni, Voyageur Press, Stillwater, MN, Printed in China, 2003.

Triumph TRs, The: A Collector's Guide, Graham Robson, Motor Racing Publications Ltd., London, England, 1977.

Daydreams in the Wind

TVR 1960-1980, Compiled by R. M. Clarke, 1981, Brooklands Books, England (There is no copyright date on the book. The most recent article reprinted is a test of the Tasmin Coupe from August 1980, and ads for the Tasmin Convertible are also reprinted.).

TVRs, Grantura to Tasmin, The: A Collector's Guide, Graham Robson, Motor Racing Publications, Ltd., London, England, 1981.

Ultimate Automobiles, Alberto Martinez (photography) & Jose Rosinski (text), Motorbooks International, Printed in France, 1985.

Ultimate Mustang, Patrick Covert, with William Bozgan, DK Publishing, Inc., New York, NY, Printed in Taunton, MA, 2001.

Vette, September 1983, Vol. 7, No. 5, "396: The Ultimate Street Corvette" by Martyn L. Schorr, "1966: Year of the 427" by Martyn L. Schorr, "The LT-1 Story" by Roger Huntington, and "1967: The Year of Tripower" by Nick Brunt.

Vette Vues Fact Book of the 1968-1972 Stingray, M. F. Dobbins, Second Edition, Published by Dr. Murrell F. Dobbins, PhD., Glenside, PA, 1983.

Internet Bibliography

AC Frua 428 - supercars.net/cars/4754.html
AC 428 Frua Spider - pietro-frua.de/1965_ac.htm
Alfa Romeo Spider Production Figures - carsfromitaly.net
Alfa Romeo Spider Production Figures - duettoregister.com
Aston Martin DB6 - supercars.net/cars/68.html
Aston Martin Heritage - astonmartin.com/heritage/past-models
Austin-Healey Colors - smithsclassics.com/austin-healey/35-austin-healey-original-colors
Austin Healey Experience, The - ahexp.com
Austin-Healey Paint Codes - ahexp.com/article/bmc-paint.html
Automobile Specifications for an extensive list of brands - automobile-catalog.com
Big Healeys - austinhealey.com/big.html
Bonham's Auctions - bonhams.com/auctions
Camaro Production Option Codes - thecamaro.com
Camaro Research Group - camaros.org/pdf/options.pdf
Car and Driver - blog.caranddriver.com
Car Brochures - lov2xlr8.no/brochures
Car Magazine Master Index - brianschreurs.org/www.coltranet.com/zines/index.html
Classic Thunderbird Club International - ctci.org/tbirdhist.php
Corvette 427 Stingray (2013) - chevrolet.com/culture/article/2013-chevy-corvette-427.html
Corvette World Brochures - corvette-world.com
Datsun Sports - datsunsports.com
Dodge Challenger Detailed History - challengerspecs.com/challengerhistory_b3.htm
Dodge Challenger History - edmunds.com/dodge/challenger/history
Excalibur Automobile Corporation - excaliburclassics.com/excals.html
Ferrari 250GT - auto.ferrari.com/en_US/sports-cars-models/past-models/250-gt-cabriolet
Ferrari NART Spyder - supercars.net/cars/532.html
Ferrari NART Spyder at Sotheby's - rmsothebys.com/lots/lot.cfm?lot_id=1060853
Ferrari Production Figures - Ferrari308.com
Fiat 1500 - fiat1500.com
Fiat Club America - fiatclubamerica.com
Firebird Gallery - firebirdgallery.com
Ford Thunderbird History - edmunds.com/ford/thunderbird/history
Hagerty Valuations - hagerty.com/apps/valuationtools/search/auto
Healy Data - healeydata.com
Hemmings Motor News - hemmings.com
Intermeccanica History - intermeccanica.com/athird.net/about/history
International Registry of Sunbeam Tigers - rootes1.com
International Triumph TR Registry - trregistry.com
Jag Lovers Web - jag-lovers.org
Jaguar E-Type Colors - hubpages.com/autos/Jaguar-E-Type-Original-Colors
Jaguar E-Type Exterior Colors - xkedata.com/catalog/colors
Jaguar Experience, The - jagexp.com
Jaguar XK-120 History - suffolksportscars.com/suffolk-ss100/jaguar-history/XK120-jaguar
Jaguar XK-140 Specifications - uniquecarsandparts.com.au/car_info_jaguar_xk140.php
Jaguar XK-150 History - gbclassiccars.co.uk/jaguar_xk150.html
Jaguar XK-150 Production - jagxk.com/xk-150-info.html
Jensen Healey - jensenhealey.com/market/marketplace.html
Jensen Healey (How Stuff Works) - auto.howstuffworks.com/jensen-healey.htm

Jensen Healey Preservation Society - jensenhealey.com
Karmann-Ghia - karmannghia.com/home.asp
Lotus Elan - lotuselan.net
Lotus Elan Central - lotuselancentral.com
Lotus Elan Sprint - lotuselansprint.com
Maserati - maseratiusa.com
Maserati Ghibli Spyder - classicdriver.com/en/car/maserati/ghibli/1969/202768
Maserati Ghibli Spyder (Supercars) - supercars.net/cars/1114.html
Maserati Mistral - rmsothebys.com/lf15/london/lots/1964-maserati-mistral-37-spyder/1076626
Maserati Mistral (Supercars) - supercars.net/cars/1129.html
Mercedes-Benz SL History - edmunds.com/mercedes-benz/sl-class/history
Mercedes SL History by Model - oursl.com/news/SLhistory/SL-History.htm
MG B Color Charts - mgb-stuff.org.uk/paint.htm
MG Color Charts - teglerizer.com/mgcolors
MG C Paint Colors - http://www.them-g-c.com/index_files/Page977.htm
MG Specifications and Colors - mg-cars.org.uk
Monteverdi 375 Series - auto.howstuffworks.com/monteverdi-375-series.htm
Monteverdi Museum - madle.org/emontemus.htm
Morgan Motor Company - morgan-motor.co.uk
Morgan Motor Company History - morgan-motor.co.uk/history
Morgan Sports Car Club - mscc.uk.com/modelhistory.html
Motorbase, The Encyclopedia of Motoring - motorbase.com
Muscle Car Performance Test Results - MyQuarterMile.com
Old Car Manual Project - oldcarbrochures.com
Old Car Manuals Project - tocmp.com
Plymouth Barracuda History - cudabrothers.com/history.php
Plymouth Barracuda History (Early Models) - allpar.com/model/cuda.html
Plymouth Barracuda History (Late Models) - allpar.com/model/cuda-E-body.html
Plymouth Barracuda Second Generation - challengerspecs.com/challengerhistory_b2.htm
Pontiac Firebird History - transamworld.com/fbird-history-php.php
Pontiac Firebird Specifications - oldride.com/library/pontiac_firebird.html
Porsche 356 History - autoeclub.com/porsche-356-manufactured-stats.htm
Porsche 356 Spotter's Guide - mejor.com/356/356picar.htm
Porsche 911E Registry - 911e.org/specs.php
Porsche 912 Registry - 912registry.org/history.htm
Porsche 914 History - classicmotorsports.com/articles/porsche-914
Porsche Speedsters - speedsters.com/history.htm
Rocky Mountain Healey Club Factory Colors Codes - rmahc.com/colorcodes.html
Shelby Cobras - hemmings.com/magazine/hmn/2012/05/1962-1967-Shelby-Cobra/3711811.html
Shelby Timeline - luukb.home.xs4all.nl/history.html
Spridget Guru - spridgetguru.com
Sprite Spot Color Codes - spritespot.com/ditzler.htm
Square (T-) Birds - squarebirds.org/vbulletin/showthread.php?t=1721
Sunbeam Alpine History - sunbeamalpine.org/index.php?categoryid=16
Sunbeam Alpine Specifications - gbclassiccars.co.uk/sunbeam_alpine.html
Sunbeam Specialties, Inc. - rootes.com
MG Experience, The - mgexp.com
Shelby Cobras (link index), The - thecarsource.com/shelby/cobra/cobra_contents.shtml
Sunbeam Tigers United - tigersunited.com/history/prodfigures.asp
Triumph Experience, The - triumphexp.com

Triumph TR6 Master Catalogue - trf.zeni.net/TR6bluebook/6.php
Triumph TR6 Painting Guide - bowtie6.com/repairs/paint.htm
TVR - tvr.co.uk
TVR Car Club - tvr-car-club.co.uk
TVR Tuscan - sportscardigest.com/cars-for-sale/king-of-the-tvrs-1967-tvr-tuscan
Vintage Cars America - vintagecarsamerica.com
Wikipedia - en.wikipedia.org

Internet Bibliography Notes:
All *http* and other prefixes have been deleted for brevity. Specific web pages are referenced in some cases and home pages in others, depending upon the URL length and the appropriateness of the specific reference. Obviously many of the whole websites will be quite useful to particular enthusiasts. The final entry here, *Wikipedia*, has been used extensively as a readily available secondary source for comparison to other sources. The special niche of *Wiki* allows contributions from widely divergent sources. In many cases *Wiki* quotes online and print sources that have in themselves been researched to verify information contained in this book.

Daydreams in the Wind

Photo Credits

Front Cover: 1961 Jaguar XK-E Roadster in Opalescent Silver Blue with Dark Blue Interior and Top - Greg Gjerdingen from Willmar, USA - (CC)
Back Cover (top): 1961 Mercedes-Benz 190 SL - ProfReader - (CC)
Back Cover (bottom): 1965 Corvette Sting Ray 396 at NCRS event in New Braunfels, TX, 1986 - Floyd M. Orr Collection

Front Matter

1. 1961 Jaguar XK-E Roadster in Red - Alf van Beem - (PD)
2. 1966 Shelby 427 Cobra Black - The Supermat, Bonhams Auction, Paris, 2012 - (CC)
3. Ferrari 275 GTS Rear View in Silver Blue - Rex Gray - (CC)
4. 1962 Sateen Silver Corvette at the 2012 NCRS Show, San Diego - Kowtoonese - (CC)

Chapter 1 - Introduction

A1. 1963 Jaguar XK-E S1 Interior - Emmanuel Didier - (PD)
A2. 1950 Chevrolet Deluxe 2-Door Sedan - Floyd M. Orr Collection - (1974)
A3. 1957 Oldsmobile Super 88 Sedan - John Lloyd, Concrete, WA - (CC)
A4. 1965 Pontiac Bonneville Convertible in White - Sicnag - (CC)
A5. Morris Minor Red Interior - Brian Snelson, Hockley, Essex, England - (CC)
A6. 1959 Corvette Roman Red Rear View - Lebubu93 - (CC)
A7. Jaguar XK-E S2 4.2 Dash - Dawid783 - (GNU)
A8. Mustang Interior Decor Group Seats - Herranderssvensson - (GNU)
A9. 1968 Austin-Healey Sprite Mk. IV - MiataSprite - (GNU)
A10. 1968 Triumph TR-250 in BRG Front View - Mr. Choppers - (GNU)
A11. 1977 Toyota Corolla SR-5 Liftback - Floyd M. Orr Collection - (1977)
A12. Austin-Healey Sprite Mk. IV & Miata - MiataSprite - (GNU)
A13. 1978 Corvette Pace Car Left Side View - Greg Gjerdingen, Willmar, USA - (CC)
A14. 1967 Chevrolet Camaro Six-Cylinder Convertible - Mr. Choppers - (GNU)
A15. 1965 Apollo 5000 GT Red Left Side View - Rex Gray, Southern California - (CC)
A16. Jaguar XK-120 Drop Head Coupe in White - Nightflyer - (GNU)
A17. Austin-Healey 3000 Mk. III in BRG - Allen Watkin, London, England - (CC)
A18. Triumph Spitfire Mk. 2 in Red with Top Up - Akela NDE - (CC)
A19. Green Karmann-Ghia Cabriolet Top Up in New Orleans - Infrogmation - (GNU)
A20. Green Porsche 911T Targa - Nakhon 100 - (CC)
A21. Chevrolet Corvair Convertible Red Rear Top Up - Christopher Ziemnowicz - (CC)
A22. Black 1970 Corvette Coupe Rear - Floyd M. Orr Collection - (1983)
A23. Black 1970 Corvette Coupe Open - Floyd M. Orr Collection - (1983)
A24. 1972 MG Midget Engine - Dave_7, Lethbridge, Canada - (CC)
A25. 1965 Shelby Cobra 427 Engine - Joe Mabel - (GNU)
A26. Knock-off wire wheels on 1969 Corvette 427 - Floyd M. Orr Collection - (1980)
A27. 1962 Austin-Healey 3000 Mk. II Interior - Valder137 - (CC)
A28. Jaguar XK-140 DHC Interior in Norway - Frodo Inge, Holland - (GNU)

Chapter 2 - English Commons

B1. Triumph TR-4A Dash in France - Arnaud 25 - (PD)
B2. Triumph Spitfire Mk. I in Red with Top Up - Sicnag - (CC)

Appendix

B3. Black MG B - Bull-Doser - (PD)
B4. Austin-Healey 100 Red Folded Windshield - Floyd M. Orr Collection - (1985)
B5. 1961 Austin-Healey 3000 Mk. II - Mick, Northamptonshire, England - (CC)
B6. 1963 MG Midget in Red - Hugh Llewelyn, Bristol, UK - (CC)
B7. 1959 BRG Austin-Healey Bugeye Sprite with Top Up - TTTNIS - (CC)
B8. Triumph Spitfire Mk. 2 in Red with Wire Wheels - Akela NDE - (CC)
B9. 1960 Red Austin-Healey Bugeye Sprite with Wire Wheels - Hajotthu - (GNU)
B10. 1963 Austin-Healey Sprite Mk. II, Rockville, MD, 2008 - Carolyn Williams - (CC)
B11. MG Midget in Blue with Tonneau Cover - Nightflyer - (GNU)
B12. Austin-Healey Bugeye Sprite - Supermac 1961, Chafford Hundred, England - (CC)
B13. 1965 Austin-Healey Sprite Mk. III in Red - Sicnag - (CC)
B14. Austin-Healey 100S of Daniel Schlatter - Rama - (CC)
B15. 1958 Austin-Healey 100/6 in Gloucestershire, England - Adrian Pingstone - (PD)
B16. 1955 Austin-Healey 100M BN2 in Black - Sicnag - (CC)
B17. Light Green Austin-Healey 100M - Dave_7, Lethbridge, Canada - (CC)
B18. 1964 Austin-Healey 3000 in Maroon - Bull-Doser - (PD)
B19. 1967 Austin-Healey 3000 Mk. III Black - Mick, Northamptonshire, England - (CC)
B20. Austin-Healey 3000 Mk. III Silver - Allen Watkin, London, England - (CC)
B21. 1955 British Racing Green Austin-Healey 100M - Chris 73 - (GNU)
B22. MG A Rear View in Black with Luggage Rack - Robotriot - (GNU)
B23. Cream MG A with Top Up - Charles01 - (GNU)
B24. Red 1975 MG B with Top Up - Mr. Choppers - (GNU)
B25. MG C in White - Alf van Beem - (CC)
B26. 1979 MG Midget in Gold - ChiemseeMan - (PD)
B27. British Racing Green MG B with Top Up in the Wet - Oxfordian Kissuth - (CC)
B28. 1965 MG Midget in White - Sicnag - (CC)
B29. Red MG Midget in Italy - Luc106 - (PD)
B30. Late Model MG Midget Dash Layout - Klugschnacker - (CC)
B31. Triumph TR-4 in Red at the Hudson British Car Show - Bull-Doser - (PD)
B31. MG 1966 Accessory Order Form - Floyd M. Orr Collection - (2015)
B32. MG 1966 Radio & AC Accessory Descriptions - Floyd M. Orr Collection - (2015)
B33. 1960 BRG MG A Twin Cam Rear View - Mr. Choppers - (GNU)
B34. Gold MG B with Wire Wheels - Spanish Coches - (CC)
B35. MG C in Pale Primrose - Allen Watkin, London, UK - (CC)
B36. Red MG A with Tonneau Cover - Tvabutzku1234 - (CC)
B37. British Racing Green Triumph TR-6 - Sicnag - (CC)
B38. Triumph TR-4 Front View - TR001 (author) - (CC)
B39. 1962 Red Triumph TR-3B - Taymoss - (GNU)
B40. 1965 Triumph Spitfire Mk. II in Black - Bull-Doser - (PD)
B41. 1974 Triumph Spitfire Mk. IV in Blue - Hunttriumph1500 - (PD)
B42. Triumph TR-3A, British Car Show, Ottawa, Canada, 2010 - Bull-Doser - (PD)
B43. Yellow 1955 Triumph TR-2 at the Knebworth Classic Car Show - Charles01 - (CC)
B44. Red Triumph TR-4A with Wire Wheels - Martini-IansV - (GNU)
B45. Triumph TR-250 in Valencia Blue with Surrey Top - Simon Clay - (GNU)
B46. Austin-Healey 3000 Mk. III, Martini Legends, Circuit of Montjuic - Mutari - (PD)
B47. MG C in British Racing Green in Montreal, Canada - Bull-Doser - (PD)
B48. Triumph Spitfire Mk. IV Interior - Akela NDE - (CC)
B49. 1980 Triumph Spitfire 1500 in British Racing Green - Bull-Doser - (PD)
B50. 1973 MG B in Black with Top Up - Paste - (GNU)

Chapter 3 - Elegant English Eccentrics

C1. 1968 Jaguar XK-E Interior - Jaguar Media Pages
C2. 1974 Triumph Stag in Blue - The Car Spy - (CC)
C3. 1973 Triumph Stag in Yellow - Dave_7 from Lethbridge, Canada - (CC)
C4. 1972 Triumph Stag in Red with Top Up - TR001 - (CC)
C5. 1957 Morgan 4/4 Series II in White - Sicnag - (CC)
C6. Green Morgan Plus 4 in the Netherlands - Alf van Beem - (CC)
C7. Red Morgan Plus 8 with Top Up, Rear View - Amaud 25 - (CC)
C8. 1968 Morgan Plus 4 in Two-Tone Beige - Bull-Doser (PD)
C9. Jensen-Healey in Yellow - Dave_7 from Lethbridge, Canada - (CC)
C10. Tan 1973 Jensen-Healey with Top Up - Dave_7 from Lethbridge, Canada - (CC)
C11. Jensen-Healey Lotus Engine - ColinMB - (CC)
C12. Jensen-Healey White Interior - Akela NDE - (CC)
C13. 1975 Jensen-Healey JH 5 in Red - Ozzadavies - (CC)
C14. Blue 1979 TVR 3000S with Chrome Bumpers - ColinMB - (CC)
C15. Green 1969 TVR Tuscan at Mallala Motor Sport Park, Australia - GTHO - (CC)
C16. White 1978 TVR 3000S - Dave_7, Lethbridge, Canada - (CC)
C17. 1979 Blue TVR 3000S U.S. Model with Standard Wheels - ColinMB - (PD)
C18. 1964 Lotus Elan in Red with Top Up - TTTNIS - (CC)
C19. Red 1963 Lotus Elan 1600 S1 with Hardtop - Dave_7, Lethbridge, Canada - (CC)
C20. 1969 White Lotus Elan S4 SE - Floyd M. Orr Collection - (1977)
C21. Lotus Elan Sprint in Blue - Brian Snelson, Hockley, Essex, England - (CC)
C22. 1970 Lotus Elan S4 SE - Akela NDE - (CC)
C23. Lotus Elan Sprint in Yellow - Tony Hisgett, Birmingham, England - (CC)
C24. 1969 White Lotus Elan S4 SE Interior - Floyd M. Orr Collection - (1977)
C25. Red & Cream Lotus Elan Sprint with Windows Up - Alf van Beem - (CC)
C26. British Racing Green Jaguar XK-120 with Whitewalls - PLawrence99cx - (CC)
C27. Red 1953 Jaguar XK-120 DHC in Germany - Lothar Spurzem - (CC)
C28. 1954 Jaguar XK-140 in Black - Ekki01 - (GNU)
C29. Jaguar XK-150S Roadster in Black - Herranderssvensson - (GNU)
C30. Red 1961 Jaguar XK-E Rear View at Bonhams - Thesupermat - (CC)
C31. Red 1963 Jaguar XK-E S1 Roadster - Dan Smith in Indianapolis - (CC)
C32. 1968 Jaguar XK-E in Bronze - Bull-Doser - (PD)
C33. 1969-70 Jaguar XK-E in British Racing Green - Stahlkocher - (GNU)
C34. 1968 Jaguar XK-E S1.5 Rear View in Silver Blue - Rudolf Stricker - (PD)
C35. 1968 Jaguar XK-E S1.5 Engine - TTNIS - (CC)
C36. 1972 Jaguar XK-E S3 in All Black at Bonhams - Thesupermat - (CC)
C37. 1965-67 Jaguar XK-E 4.2 Series I Interior - Nightflyer - (GNU)
C38. Jaguar XK-140 Roadster in Silver Blue - Spartan7W - (CC)
C39. 1955 Maroon Jaguar XK-140 Drop Head Coupe - LA2 - (GNU)
C40. Black 1972 Jaguar XK-E S3 at Bonhams - Thesupermat - (CC)
C41. 1974 Blue-Green Jaguar XK-E Series III V-12 - Bull-Doser - (PD)
C42. 1965-67 Red Jaguar XK-E S1 4.2 at Pebble Beach - (JMP)
C43. 1959 Aston Martin DB2-4 Mark III DHC - Mr. Choppers - (GNU)
C44. 1965 Aston Martin DB5 Vantage - Shane D. Mattaway - (GNU)
C45. 1967 Aston Martin DB6 Volante Vantage - Mr. Choppers - (GNU)
C46. 1979 Aston Martin V-8 Volante S1 with Tan Top Up - Mr. Choppers - (GNU)
C47. 1981 Aston Martin V-8 Volante - Martin Pettitt, Bury St. Edmonds, UK - (CC)
C48. 1986-89 Aston Martin V-8 Volante in Dark Blue - Mr. Choppers - (GNU)

Appendix

C49. White 1986 A M Volante U.S. at Lime Rock Concours - Mr. Choppers - (GNU)
C50. Red 1989 A M Vantage Volante U.S., Bonhams, Greenwich - Mr. Choppers (GNU)

Chapter 4 - Germans

D1. 1968 Green Porsche 912 Targa Interior with Zip-Out Window - Valder137 - (CC)
D2. 1961 Karmann-Ghia Cabriolet in Cream - Martin V. - (GNU)
D3. Karmann-Ghia Cabriolet in Light Blue - Rudolf Stricker - (GNU)
D4. Green 1968-70 Karmann-Ghia Cabriolet Rear View - Masur - (PD)
D5. Yellow 1960+ Karmann-Ghia Cabriolet - Michael Spiller, Bradford, UK - (CC)
D6. 1968-70 Karmann-Ghia Cabriolet in Green - Masur - (PD)
D7. 1957 Porsche 356A Speedster - Mr. Choppers - (GNU)
D8. Early Model Porsche 356 Cabriolet in Steel Blue - Nakhon100 - (CC)
D9. Red Porsche Speedster in Monterey, CA - Motohide Miwa - (CC)
D10. 1959 Silver Porsche 356A Cabriolet in Palm Springs, CA - Rex Gray - (CC)
D11. 1966 Porsche Targa Prerelease Brochure - Floyd M. Orr Collection - (2015)
D12. 1968 Green Porsche 912 Targa with Zip-Out Rear Window - Valder137 - (CC)
D13. Porsche 911T Targa 2.4 in Silver - Thesupermat - (CC)
D14. Porsche 912 Targa in Dark Red - Cjp24 - (GNU)
D15. Porsche 911 Targa in Gold - Toni V - (CC)
D16. Orange Porsche 914 with Black GT Stripes - Pujanak - (PD)
D17. 1970 Porsche 914/6 - Michael Barera - (GNU)
D18. Yellow Porsche 914 - N914 - (PD)
D19. Porsche 911 Targa in Red with Top Up - nakhon 100 - (CC)
D20. Black 1960 Porsche Super 90 & 1965 SC - Greg Gjerdingen, Willmar, USA - (CC)
D21. 1964 Porsche 356C 1600 Cabriolet in The Hamptons - Mr. Choppers - (GNU)
D22. Silver 1958 Mercedes-Benz 300 SL Roadster - Sicnag - (CC)
D23. Red 1957 Mercedes-Benz 300 SL - Christopher Ziemnowicz - (PD)
D24. 1963 Mercedes-Benz 300SL Hardtop in Palm Springs - Rex Gray - (CC)
D25. Mercedes-Benz 230SL in Red - AlfvanBeem - (PD)
D26. 1967 Mercedes-Benz 250SL in White - Mr. Choppers - (GNU)
D27. White 1968 Mercedes-Benz 230SL Pagoda Top at Bonhams - Thesupermat - (CC)
D28. 1971 Mercedes-Benz 280 SL in Dark Green - Bull-Doser - (PD)
D29. Black Mercedes-Benz 280 SL with Top Up - Spanish Coches - (CC)
D30. Mercedes-Benz 280 SL Hardtop - M 93 - (PD)
D31. M-B 450 SL Gray RHD Front in New South Wales, Australia - jeremyg3030 - (CC)
D32. M-B 450 SL Gray RHD Rear in New South Wales, Australia - jeremyg3030 - (CC)
D33. HG Motorsports Mercedes-Benz 300SL Gullwing, Pebble Beach - Axion23 - (CC)
D34. Mercedes-Benz 280 SL with Top Up in East Hampton, NY - Vetatur Fumare - (CC)
D35. Brown Mercedes-Benz 190 SL Rear View - Rudolf Stricker - (PD)

Chapter 5 - Fiats & Alfas

E1. Fiat 850 Spider Interior - Alexxsandro - (CC)
E2. 1968 Red Fiat 850 Spider with Top Down - Lothar Spurzem - (CC)
E3. Fiat 1500S Spider in Black - Berthold Werner - (GNU)
E4. Fiat 850 Spider in Yellow - Robotriot - (GNU)
E5. Red Fiat 850 Sport Spider with Top Up - Tvabutzku1234 - (PD)
E6. White 1968 Fiat 850 Spider Front View - Floyd M. Orr Collection - (1968)
E7. 1967 Fiat-Abarth 1000 Spider - Floyd M. Orr Collection - (1967)

E8. Fiat 124 Spider in Green - Pujanak - (PD)
E9. Fiat 124 Spider - Bidinson (owner & photographer) - (CC)
E10. Red Alfa Romeo Giulia Spider - Marvin Raaijmakers - (CC)
E11. Red Alfa Romeo Giulietta Spider - Brian Snelson - (CC)
E12. White Alfa Romeo 2000 Touring Spider - CHK46 - (GNU)
E13. 1961 Alfa Romeo 2600 Touring Spider - Genossegerd - (GNU)
E14. Alfa Romeo Duetto Spider in Red - E. Peiffer - (GNU)
E15. White 1969 Alfa Romeo Duetto Spider - Pat Durkin, Tustin, CA - (CC)
E16. Alfa Romeo Spider Series 2 Front View - Rudolf Stricker - (CC)
E17. Alfa Romeo 2600 Touring Spider in Italy - Luc106 - (PD)
E18. Alfa Romeo Spider Series 2 - Rudolf Stricker - (CC)

Chapter 6 - Exotics

F1. 1958 Ferrari Spyder CA LWB Red Interior - Rex Gray - (CC)
F2. Red Fiat Dino Spider Front View - Allen Watkin, London, England - (CC)
F3. Green Fiat Dino 2000 Spider Rear View in Italy - Luc106 - (PD)
F4. Red Fiat Dino Spider 2400 Top Up in Germany - Hubert Berberich - (PD)
F5. Red Fiat Dino Spider 2400 Rear View in Germany - Hubert Berberich - (PD)
F6. Red 1973 Dino 246 GTS Chairs & Flares in Springs, NY - Mr. Choppers - (GNU)
F7. Dino 246 GTS in Metallic Baby Blue - Allen Watkin, London, England - (CC)
F8. 1972 Dino 246 GTS in Black - Rex Gray, Southern California - (CC)
F9. Red Dino 246 GTS with Bumpers and Top Panel Removed - Dan Smith - (CC)
F10. Gunmetal Gray Ferrari 308 GTS - Floyd M. Orr Collection - (1985)
F11. Red 1979 Ferrari 308 GTS - TTTNIS - (PD)
F12. Red Ferrari 250 GT Series II Pininfarina Cabriolet - Mr. Choppers - (GNU)
F13. Brown 1958 Ferrari 250 GT Series 1 Spyder - Luc 106 - (PD)
F14. 1959 Ferrari 250 LWB California Spyder Front View - CCBain - (CC)
F15. Blue Ferrari 275 GTS - Rex Gray - (CC)
F16. Red Ferrari 330 GTS Front View - Motohide Miwa - (CC)
F17. Red Ferrari 330 GTS Rear View - Motohide Miwa - (CC)
F18. Ferrari Spyder California Interior - Herranderssvensson - (CC)
F19. Red 1967 Ferrari 275 GTB/4 NART Spyder - Marcusmv3 - (GNU)
F20. Ferrari NART Spyder in Yellow - Jon Kristian Bernhardsen - (CC)
F21. Brown 1973 Ferrari Daytona Spyder Front View - Mr. Choppers - (GNU)
F22. Brown 1973 Ferrari Daytona Spyder Rear View - Mr. Choppers - (GNU)
F23. Brown 1973 Ferrari Daytona Spyder with Top Down - Mr. Choppers - (GNU)
F24. Silver Ferrari 250 GT California Short Wheelbase - richebets - (CC)
F25. 1972 Ferrari Daytona Spyder Front - Greg Gjerdingen from Willmar, USA - (CC)
F26. 1972 Ferrari Daytona Spyder Rear - Greg Gjerdingen from Willmar, USA - (CC)
F27. 1967 Maserati Mistral Spyder - Brian Snelson, Hockley, Essex, England - (CC)
F28. Maserati 3500 GT Spyder in Gunmetal - Mr. Choppers - (GNU)
F29. Maserati Mistral Interior - Craig Howell, San Carlos, California - (CC)
F30. Green Maserati Ghibli Spyder in Berlin - HPS911 - (CC)
F31. Maserati Ghibli Spyder at the Chelsea Auto Legends, England - The Car Spy - (CC)
F32. 1968 Lamborghini Miura and 1970 Corvette - Floyd M. Orr Collection - (1983)
F33. 1974 Dino 246 GTS Chairs & Flares, Greenwich, CT - Mr. Choppers - (GNU)
F34. 1959 Ferrari 250 LWB California Spyder, Close Front View - CCBain - (CC)

Chapter 7 - Conveniences

Appendix

G1. Sunbeam Alpine Dash (Early Steering Wheel Design) - Akela NDE - (CC)
G2. Sunbeam Alpine Series I in Black - Rama - (CC)
G3. Sunbeam Alpine in Yellow - Dave_7, Lethbridge, Canada - (CC)
G4. Sunbeam Alpine in British Racing Green - Allen Watkin, London - (CC)
G5. Sunbeam Alpine in Red with Knock-off Wire Wheels - Mick, England - (CC)
G6. 1967 Datsun 2000 - 160SX - (CC)
G7. Datsun SPL212 in Red & White - Ypy31 - (PD)
G8. Red 1966-67 Datsun 1600 Sports Rear View - Bill Abbott - (CC)
G9. 1967 Datsun 1600 Sports - Photo by Bill Abbott, Modified by Mr. Choppers - (CC)
G10. 1993-94 Black Nissan 300ZX Convertible - Mr. Choppers - (GNU)
G11. Blue 1969 Chevrolet Corvair Convertible in Palm Springs, CA - Visitor 7 - (CC)
G12. 1962 Red Chevrolet Corvair Monza Convertible - Joe Mabel - (GNU)
G13. 1966 Chevrolet Corvair Engine in Ann Arbor, MI - Michael Barera - (CC)
G14. 1969 Chevrolet Corvair Monza Convertible with Top Up - Robert Spinello - (GNU)
G15. Black 1956 Ford Thunderbird Continental Kit - Morven, Buena Park, CA - (GNU)
G16. Red 1955 Ford Thunderbird - Morven, Buena Park, CA - (GNU)
G17. 1956 Ford Thunderbird - Morven, Buena Park, CA - (GNU)
G18. Coral 1957 Ford Thunderbird Hardtop - Morven, Buena Park, CA - (GNU)
G19. 1959 Ford Thunderbird in Brandywine Red - Morven, Buena Park, CA - (GNU)
G20. 1963 Ford Thunderbird Sports Roadster - Morven, Buena Park, CA - (GNU)
G21. Black 1964 Ford Thunderbird Convertible - Morven, Buena Park, CA - (GNU)
G22. 1965 Ford Thunderbird SR Aftermarket - Morven, Buena Park, CA - (GNU)

Chapter 8 - Hybrids

H1. 1965 Shelby Cobra Interior - Eli Christman, Richmond, VA - (CC)
H2. Red Sunbeam Tiger - Brian Snelson of Hockley, Essex, England - (CC)
H3. BRG Sunbeam Tiger - John Lloyd of Five Sunbeam Tigers, Concrete, WA - (CC)
H4. Sunbeam Tiger Dash - Motohide Miwa, USA - (CC)
H5. 1962 Shelby Cobra #1, Shelby American Museum, Las Vegas, NV - Jaydec - (GNU)
H6. Shelby Cobra 428 - Stahlkocher - (GNU)
H7. Black 1966 Shelby 427 Cobra at Bonhams, Paris, 2012 - The Supermat - (CC)
H8. 1971 AC Frua 428 in Black - EmmanuelD - (PD)
H9. 1965 Shelby Cobra Interior with White Gauge Faces - Joe Mabel - (GNU)
H10. 1965 Shelby Cobra Top View - Eli Christman, Richmond, VA - (CC)
H11. 1968 Shelby GT-350 Convertible - Rex Gray in Southern California - (CC)
H12. Red 1969 Shelby GT350, Charlotte Motor Speedway, April 2014 - Sicnag - (CC)
H13. Blue 1970 Shelby GT350, Charlotte Motor Speedway, April 2014 - Sicnag - (CC)
H14. 1968 Shelby GT-350 Convertible - Rex Gray, Southern California - (CC)
H15. Blue 1968 Shelby GT-500 Front View - Herranderssvensson - (GNU)
H16. Blue 1968 Shelby GT-500 Rear View - Herranderssvensson - (GNU)
H17. *Spinout* Shelby 427 Cobra in Tunica, MS - Thomas R Machnitzki - (GNU)
H18. 1965 Apollo 5000 GT Top View - Rex Gray, Southern California - (CC)
H19. 1962 Buick Special DeLuxe - Mr. Choppers - (GNU)
H20. 1965 Apollo 5000 GT Front View - Rex Gray, Southern California - (CC)
H21. Yellow 1967 Intermeccanica Italia - Rex Gray, Southern California - (CC)
H22. Silver 1972 Intermeccanica Italia - Mr. Choppers - (GNU)
H23. Blue 1972 Intermeccanica Indra Wire Wheels - André Karwath aka Aka - (CC)
H24. 1972 Intermeccanica Indra White Interior - Buch-t - (GNU)

Daydreams in the Wind

H25. 1971 Monteverdi 375C Palm Beach w/375-hp Chrysler 440 - Brian Snelson - (CC)
H26. Excalibur Series I SS in Black - Nakhon100 - (CC)
H27. Black 1977 Excalibur Series III Roadster SS in Paris - LPLT - (GNU)
H28. 1982 Black Excalibur Roadster - Pavel Sevela - (CC)
H29. 1982 Coral Excalibur Phaeton with Top Up - Selyobwoc - (CC)
H30. White 1984 Excalibur Phaeton - Slashme - (CC)
H31. 1984 Cream Excalibur Series IV Rear Swoop - svlambo - (CC)
H32. White 1982 Excalibur Series IV Lipstick Edition Rear View - svlambo - (CC)
H33. White 1984 Excalibur Phaeton Side View in Bavaria - Slashme - (CC)

Chapter 9 - Ponies

I1. Ford Mustang Pony Interior Decor Group - Herranderssvensson - (GNU)
I2. 1965 Mustang CV #1, Henry Ford Museum, Dearborn, MI - Alvin Trusty - (CC)
I3. 1966 Ford Mustang Rally Pac - PMDrive 1061 - (GNU)
I4. 1965 Ford Mustang with K-Code Engine - Bull-Doser - (PD)
I5. 1965 Ford Mustang GT in Prairie Bronze - Sicnag - (CC)
I6. 1966 Ford Mustang in Yellow - Bull-Doser - (PD)
I7. 1966 Ford Mustang with Styled Steel Wheels - Sicnag - (CC)
I8. 1967 Ford Mustang in Candy Apple with Styled Steel Wheels - Sicnag - (CC)
I9. 1968 Ford Mustang Convertible in Red - Bull-Doser - (PD)
I10. 1969 Ford Mustang Convertible in Red - Detectandpreserve - (CC)
I11. White 1971 Ford Mustang Ram Air, Montreal, Quebec, Canada - Bull-Doser - (PD)
I12. Red 1973 Ford Mustang - Mr. Choppers - (GNU)
I13. 1973 Blue Ford Mustang with NACA Duct Hood - Bull-Doser - (PD)
I14. 1968 Ford Mustang 390 Convertible in Blue - P-O Olsson - (PD)
I15. Red 1967 Chevrolet Camaro SS Convertible - Rex Gray, Southern California - (CC)
I16. 1967 Chevrolet Camaro SS Red Interior - Rex Gray, Southern California - (CC)
I17. 1968 Gold SS RS Chevrolet Camaro - Sicnag - (CC)
I18. 1969 Chevrolet Camaro 350 in Azure Turquoise - Sicnag - (CC)
I19. 1969 Chevrolet Camaro RS Convertible in Orange - Bull-Doser - (PD)
I20. Chevrolet Camaro 1969 SS Pace Car in Ontario, Canada - Bull-Doser - (PD)
I21. Green 1967 Pontiac Firebird Convertible - Jeremy, Sydney, Australia - (CC)
I22. Gold 1967 Pontiac Firebird 400 Front View - Dave_7, Lethbridge, Canada - (CC)
I23. Gold 1967 Pontiac Firebird 400 Rear View - Dave_7, Lethbridge, Canada - (CC)
I24. Red 1968 Pontiac Firebird 400 with Hood Tach - AlfvanBeem - (PD)
I25. 1969 Pontiac Firebird White Interior - svlambo - (CC)
I26. Orange 1969 Pontiac Firebird with Hood Tach - svlambo - (CC)
I27. 1967 Plymouth Barracuda in Red - Bull-Doser - (PD)
I28. White 1967 Plymouth Barracuda Formula S with Top Up - jeremyg3030 - (CC)
I29. 1970 TorRed Plymouth 'Cuda 340 Convertible - Sicnag - (CC)
I30. 1971 Plymouth Shaker 'Cuda in Sassy Grass Green - Bull-Doser - (PD)
I31. Plymouth 1971 Cuda 440 Six Pack (one of 17 SP's) - Brett Weinstein - (GNU)
I32. Plymouth 1971 Cuda 440 Six Pack in Curious Yellow - Brett Weinstein - (GNU)
I33. Gold 1970 Dodge Challenger Six - Christopher Ziemnowicz - (PD)
I34. Black Dodge Challenger R/T with White Interior - Sam Krieg - (GNU)
I35. Red 1970 Dodge Challenger R/T - Nakhon100 - (CC)
I36. 1970 Dodge Challenger R/T in Banana - Bull-Doser, Quebec, Canada - (PD)
I37. Plum Crazy 1971 Challenger 383 - Bull-Doser, St. Lambert, Quebec, Canada - (PD)
I38. Red 1971 Dodge Challenger Fake R/T 440 Six Pack - Herranderssvensson - (GNU)

Appendix

I39. 1971 Challenger Fake Hemi R/T in Tor-Red - Bull-Doser, Quebec, Canada - (PD)

Chapter 10 - Corvettes

J1. 1960 Tuxedo Black Corvette with Red Interior - Elmschrat - (GNU)
J2. 1958 Panama Yellow Corvette - Sicnag - (CC)
J3. Bright Atlantic Blue 2000 Ford Mustang - Floyd M. Orr Collection - (2000)
J4. Black 1970 Corvette 454 Coupe - Floyd M. Orr Collection - (1983)
J5. 1953 Corvette at the 2012 NCRS Show in San Diego - Kowtoonese - (CC)
J6. White 1954 Corvette - LSDSL - (CC)
J7. 1955 Gypsy Red Corvette Light Beige Interior - Dave_7, Lethbridge, Canada - (CC)
J8. 1957 Aztec Copper Corvette with Hardtop & Beige Interior - Sicnag - (CC)
J9. 1960 Ermine White Fuelie Corvette Rear - Rex Gray, Southern California - (CC)
J10. 1961 Tuxedo Black Corvette with Wire Wheels - Berthold Werner - (GNU)
J11. 1962 Tuxedo Black Corvette Side View - Greg Gjerdingen, Willmar, MN - (CC)
J12. Ermine White 1963 Sting Ray at Bonhams in France 2014 - The Supermat - (CC)
J13. 1964 Sting Ray in Tuxedo Black with Knock-off Wheels - Allen Watkin - (CC)
J14. 1967 Sting Ray in Sunfire Yellow - Greg Gjerdingen, Willmar, MN - (CC)
J15. 1968 Corvette 427 in Polar White (Alan Shepard's car) - 350z33 - (GNU)
J16. 1974 Red Corvette Coupe - Robert Spinello - (GNU)
J17. 1978 Corvette Pace Car Left Rear - Greg Gjerdingen, Willmar, MN, USA - (CC)
J18. 1986 Corvette C4 Pace Car in White - Bull-Doser - (PD)
J19. 1956 Corvette in Venetian Red - Bull-Doser - (PD)
J20. 1961 Fawn Beige Corvette in Paris - Thesupermat - (CC)
J21. 1964 Tuxedo Black Sting Ray Aluminum Wheels and Side Pipes - Sicnag - (CC)
J22. 1953 Corvette Engine at the 2012 NCRS Show in San Diego - Kowtoonese - (CC)
J23. 1961 Tuxedo Black Corvette Dash - Berthold Werner - (GNU)
J24. 1960 Ermine White Fuelie Corvette Front - Rex Gray, Southern California - (CC)
J25. 1965 Nassau Blue Corvette Sting Ray 396 - Floyd M. Orr Collection - (1986)
J26. 1965 Corvette Sting Ray Milano Maroon Fuelie - Shane Mattaway - (GNU)
J27. 1963 Corvette Sting Ray Dash in Saddle Interior - Tino Rossini - (CC)
J28. Ermine White 1964 Corvette Sting Ray Fuelie with Wrong Wheels - Sicnag - (CC)
J29. Rally Red 1966 Corvette Sting Ray Convertible with Side pipes - Bull-Doser - (PD)
J30. 1967 Corvette Sting Ray Convertible in Silver Pearl - Sicnag - (CC)
J31. Burgundy 1969 Stingray 350 - Greg Gjerdingen, Willmar, MN, USA - (CC)
J32. 1969 Tuxedo Black Corvette 427 with Side Pipes - Mr. Choppers - (GNU)
J33. 1971 Stingray Convertible in Mulsanne Blue - Sicnag - (CC)
J34. 1972 Mille Miglia Red Stingray LT-1 Convertible - Sicnag - (CC)
J35. 1974 Stingray Convertible in Medium Red - Stoskett - (GNU)
J36. 1975 Stingray Convertible in Classic White - Wallerdog - (CC)
J37. Sunfire Yellow 1967 Corvette Sting Ray Convertible NCRS - Bull-Doser - (PD)
J38. 1967 Corvette Sting Ray Marina Blue 427 Convertible - Stoskett - (GNU)
J39. 1978 Corvette Pace Car Right Side - Greg Gjerdingen, Willmar, MN, USA - (CC)
J40. White 1982 Corvette Coupe - Bull-Doser - (PD)
J41. 1982 Corvette Collector Edition Front - Greg Gjerdingen, Willmar, USA - (CC)
J42. 1982 Corvette Collector Edition Rear - Greg Gjerdingen, Willmar, USA - (CC)
J43. 1986 Corvette C4 Pace Car Yellow with Wrong Wheels - Sicnag - (CC)
J44. 1987 Black Corvette Convertible - Greg Gjerdingen, Willmar, MN, USA - (CC)
J45. 1988 White Corvette Convertible - Greg Gjerdingen, Willmar, MN, USA - (CC)
J46. Black 1989 Corvette C4 Convertible with Top Up - Sicnag - (CC)

Daydreams in the Wind

J47. 1966 Corvette Sting Ray 427 in Silver Pearl - Nakhon 100 - (CC)
J48. 2013 Corvette Stingray 427 Collector Edition 60th Anniversary - (MP)

Appendix

K1. Yellow 1970 Jaguar XK-E Series 2 - Dave_7 from Lethbridge, Canada - (CC)
K2. 1966-67 White Austin-Healey Sprite with Top Up - Floyd M. Orr Collection - (1967)
K3. Bridgehampton Blue 1971 Corvette Stingray Convertible in UK - Charlie, UK - (CC)

Source Codes: CC = Creative Commons License / GNU = GNU's Not Unix License / MP = Corporate Media Pages / PD = Public Domain

Appendix

Photo Index

Alfa Romeo 2000 Spider　238
Alfa Romeo 2600 Spider　239, 246
Alfa Romeo Duetto Spider　240, 241
Alfa Romeo Giulia Spider　237
Alfa Romeo Giulietta Spider　236
Alfa Romeo Spider Veloce　242, 247
Aston Martin DB2-4 Mark III　163
Aston Martin DB5 Convertible　165
Aston Martin DB6 Volante　166
Aston Martin V8 Volante　168-169, 171-172, 175
Austin-Healey 100　46
Austin-Healey 100/6　59
Austin-Healey 100M　60-61, 65
Austin-Healey 100S　58
Austin-Healy 3000　24, 39, 47 ,62-64, 101
Austin-Healey Bugeye Sprite　49, 51, 54
Austin-Healey Sprite Mk. II, III, IV　10, 15, 52, 55, 519
Buick Special DeLuxe　342
Chevrolet 150 DeLuxe　2
Chevrolet Camaro　18, 377- 381, 383
Chevrolet Corvair　30, 301-303, 305
Chevrolet Corvette 427 (2013)　481
Chevrolet Corvette C1　vii, 7, 411-412, 417-422, 431, 433, 436-437, 440
Chevrolet Corvette C2　423-425, 434, 441, 443-447, 458, 463, 479
Chevrolet Corvette C3　16, 31-32, 36, 416, 426-428, 448-453, 467-469, 471, 520
Chevrolet Corvette C4　430, 472, 474-476
Datsun 1600 Sports　297, 299
Datsun 2000 Sports　295
Datsun SPL-212　296
Dodge Challenger　399-405
Excalibur　349-353, 355-356, 358
Ferrari 250GT Cabriolet　261, 262
Ferrari 275 GTS　v, 264
Ferrari 330 GTS　265-266
Ferrari Daytona Spyder　271-274, 276
Ferrari Dino 246 GTS　254, 255, 257, 286
Ferrari Dino 308 GTS　258, 260
Ferrari NART Spyder　269, 270
Ferrari Spyder California　249, 263, 267, 273, 287
Fiat 124 Sport Spider　232 ,234
Fiat 850 Spider　223, 226-228 ,230
Fiat 1500S Cabriolet　224
Fiat-Abarth 1000 Spider　231
Fiat Dino Spider　250-253
Ford Mustang　9, 359, 361, 366-373, 375-376, 414
Ford Thunderbird　308-309, 311-316
Frua 428　326
Intermeccanica Apollo GT　19, 341, 343
Intermeccanica Indra　345-346

Intermeccanica Italia　344
Jaguar E-Type 1968　149, 151-152
Jaguar E-Type Interior　1, 8, 109, 154
Jaguar E-Type Series 1　iii, 147-148, 159
Jaguar E-Type Series 2　150, 486
Jaguar E-Type Series 3　153, 157, 158
Jaguar XK-120　144-145
Jaguar XK-140　20, 40, 145, 155-156
Jaguar XK-150　146
Jensen-Healey　119-120, 122-124
Lamborghini Miura　285
Lotus Elan　133-135, 138, 142
Lotus Elan Sprint　137, 139, 143
Maserati 3500GT Spyder　278
Maserati Ghibli Spyder　281-282
Maserati Mistral Spyder　277, 279
Mazda Miata　15
Mercedes-Benz 190 SL　209, 221
Mercedes-Benz 230 SL　211
Mercedes-Benz 250 SL　212-213
Mercedes-Benz 280 SL　214-215, 218
Mercedes-Benz 300 SL　210-211
Mercedes-Benz 300 SL Gullwing　218
Mercedes-Benz 450 SL　216-217
MG Accessories Order Form　80-81
MG A　67-68, 87
MG A Twin Cam　82
MG B　45, 69, 72, 84, 107
MG C　70, 86, 102
MG Midget　34, 49, 53, 71, 74, 77, 79
Monteverdi 375S　347
Morgan 4/4　114
Morgan Plus 4　115, 117
Morgan Plus 8　116
Morris Minor　6
Nissan 300ZX　300
Oldsmobile Super 88 Holiday Sedan　3
Plymouth Barracuda　393-397
Pontiac Bonneville Convertible　5
Pontiac Firebird　385-390
Porsche 356 1965 SC　206
Porsche 356 Cabriolet　186, 189, 207
Porsche 356 Speedster　185, 187
Porsche 911 Targa　28, 190, 192, 195, 205
Porsche 912 Targa　179, 191, 193
Porsche 914　199, 202
Porsche 914/6　200
Porsche Super 90　206
Shelby Cobra　iv, 35, 319, 324-326, 328-329, 338
Shelby Mustang GT-350　330-331, 334
Shelby Mustang GT-500　333, 336-337
Sunbeam Alpine　289-293
Sunbeam Tiger　320-322

Toyota Corolla SR-5 Liftback   13
Triumph Spitfire   25, 44, 50, 91, 93, 103
Triumph Stag   110-112
Triumph TR-2   96
Triumph TR-3A   95
Triumph TR-3B   90
Triumph TR-4   89
Triumph TR-4A   43, 98
Triumph TR-250   11, 100
Triumph TR-6   88
TVR 3000S   125, 129, 131
TVR Tuscan V-8   127
Volkswagen Karmann-Ghia   27, 180-184

Appendix

Chart Index

Affordable English Antiques Ratings   106
Affordable Italian Ratings   248
Affordable Italian Test Results   247
Alfa Romeo Spider   243
Alfa Romeo Spider Production   244
Alpine/Datsun/Corvair Comparison   307
Aston Martin Comparison   174
Aston Martin Engines   170
Aston Martin Production   172
Austin-Healey (Big) Colors   64
Austin-Healey (Big) Comparison   63
Austin-Healey (Big) Production   66
Austin-Healey Sprite Colors   56
Austin-Healey Sprite Production   54
Chevrolet Camaro Base Convertible   383
Chevrolet Camaro Production   382
Chevrolet Camaro SS Convertible   384
Chevrolet Corvair Engines   306
Chevrolet Corvair Production   306
Chevrolet Corvette C1 Engines   436
Chevrolet Corvette C1 Performance   438
Chevrolet Corvette C2 Engines   440
Chevrolet Corvette C2 Performance   441
Chevrolet Corvette C3 Engines   453
Chevrolet Corvette C3 Performance   463
Chevrolet Corvette C4 Engines   476
Chevrolet Corvette C4 Performance   477
Chevrolet Corvette Convertible Production   433
Chevrolet Corvette Generations   416
Chevrolet Corvette Production   432
Chevrolet Corvette Ratings   480
Chrysler Pony Car Production   402
Chrysler Pony Sports Convertibles   404
Classic English Test Results   105
Classic Ferrari Test Results   275
Collectible Open Sports Cars   21
Comfortable Sports Car Ratings   317
Conveniences Added to A-H, MG, Triumph   100
Datsun Sports   300
Dodge Challenger Base Convertibles   403
Early Pony Convertibles Ratings   410
English Six-Cylinder Comparison   104
Eccentric English Comparison   132
Elegant English Ratings   177
Elegant English Test Results   176
Elegant Italian Test Results   285
English Six-Cylinder Comparison   104
Excalibur Production   354
Excalibur Series Comparison   355
Exotic Italian Ratings   286
Ferrari / Maserati Spyders Comparison   284
Ferrari NART Spyder   269

Ferrari V-12 Convertibles Comparison   272
Ferrari V-12 Convertibles Production   273
Fiat 850 Spider   232
Fiat / Alfa Spider Comparison   245
Fiat Cabriolets   225
Fiat Dino Spider Colors   254
Fiat Spider Production   235
Ford Mustang Base Convertible   374
Ford Mustang Convertible Production   368
Ford Mustang Sports Convertible   375
Ford Mustang Test Results   407
Ford Thunderbird Production   316
Ford Thunderbird Specifications   315
German Sports Car Ratings   220
Hybrid Hotrod Ratings   357
Jaguar Comparison   162
Jaguar E-Type Colors   160
Jaguar E-Type Roadsters   161
Jaguar XK Production   158
Jaguar XK Series   157
Jensen-Healey Colors   124
Karmann-Ghia Cabriolets   184
Karmann-Ghia Production   182
Lotus Elan Colors   140
Lotus Elan Comparison   142
Maserati Spyders   283
Mercedes-Benz SL Comparison   216
Mercedes-Benz SL Production   219
MG A / B / C   86
MG A / B / C Production   82
MG B Mark I Colors   83
MG B Mark II Colors   84
MG B Mark III Colors   85
MG B Production   73
MG C Colors   85
MG Midget Mark I-III Colors   74
MG Midget Mark IV & 1500 Colors   75
MG Midget Production   77
Morgan Production   117
Other Pony Car Test Results   408
Plymouth Barracuda Base Convertible   398
Pontiac Firebird Base Convertible   391
Pontiac Firebird Options   390
Pontiac Firebird Sports Convertible   392
Pony Car Convertible Production   363
Pony Car Features Introduction   405
Pony Car Performance Production   406
Porsche 356 Production   188
Porsche 914 Model Year Production   203
Porsche 914 Calendar Year Production   204
Porsche Performance   204
Porsche Targa Comparison   207

517

Porsche Targa Engines   196
Porsche Targa Production   197
Shelby Cobra Specifications   328
Shelby Comparison   339
Shelby Mustang 1966 Convertible   335
Shelby Mustang Engines   336
Shelby Performance   340
Shelby Street Mustang Production   337
Spridget & Spitfire Comparison   78
Sprite/850/Elan/Miata Comparison   143
Sunbeam Alpine Comparison   294

Sunbeam Tiger Colors   323
Sunbeam Tiger Production   323
Triumph Spitfire Colors   94
Triumph Spitfire Production   94
Triumph TR-3A Colors   95
Triumph TR-4A & TR-250 Colors   97
Triumph TR-6 Colors   97
Triumph TR-Series Comparison   99
Triumph TR-Series Production   98
TVR Tuscan & 3000S Production   130

About The Author

Floyd M. Orr is a retiree from the financial services industry who enjoys writing nostalgic books about subjects from his favorite American era, The Sixties. Each of his books is based upon years of participation in and observation of popular culture. This eighth book in his Nonfiction in a Fictional Style Series is the culmination of four years of compilation of data and intensive research on his favorite type of classic cars. The author has a true obsession about cars, but it is not one easily pigeonholed. He is not a mechanic or an engineer. His leading interests and education are in psychology and sociology. Cars are our Number One toys. They are a reflection of our culture with a depth unparalleled. The overwhelming influences on *Daydreams in the Wind* have been *Road & Track*, the writings of Peter Egan, classic road tests and brochures, the *Illustrated Buyer's Guide Series* in the USA and the *Collector's Guide Series* from the UK.

Figure K2 - White Austin-Healey Sprite with Black Top and Interior. This photo taken of a new Sprite at the dealership in Columbus, Mississippi, represents my genuine humble beginnings. I had yet to actually drive a genuine sports car at the time I took this shot with my trusty Kodak Instamatic. Of course I would have preferred a Sprite in British Racing Green with wire wheels and blackwall tires, but as a poor college student at the time, I could not afford a down payment, even on a Sprite! ©1967 Floyd M. Orr Collection

Daydreams in the Wind

The author's driving experience began in 1959 with a 1957 Oldsmobile Super 88 on an abandoned airport runway in Greenwood, Mississippi. His first convertible experience was in a 1962 Bonneville that same year. Another close friend got a new 1965 Mustang Convertible with a 260 V-8. A significant pattern was emerging. The author resided on the campus of Mississippi State University for most of the period between 1964 and 1976. Much of his driving experiences from the actual era featured in this book emanated from that location. However, the author's broad interests took him to Memphis first and later to Dallas countless times in his young adult driving years. He has never desired to live anywhere other than in the midst of the car culture in California or Texas. He lived in Silicon Valley for much of 1971, but the nights there were too chilly for top-down motoring. He returned to MSU for five more years until finally choosing the warmer, drier climate of Texas. His everyday driving environment shifted to freeways when he permanently moved to Dallas in late 1976. He has lived in the Austin, Texas, area with his wife and five cats since 1980. The newest car he owns is a 2000 model, and of course the top stays down perennially. This author values few experiences more than a nighttime cruise with the top down.

Figure K3 - 1971 Stingray Convertible in Bridgehampton Blue. When a 246 GTS, NART Spyder, or even a 308 GTS lies far beyond your pay grade, this is the best view available. Hmmm, is it any wonder I have always been a *butt man*? ©Charlie, UK (CC)

Appendix

www.ingramcontent.com/pod-product-compliance
Lightning Source LLC
Chambersburg PA
CBHW082032230426
43670CB00016B/2632